ADMINISTERING EXCHANGE SERVER

Administering Exchange Server

Mitch Tulloch

McGraw-Hill
New York • San Francisco • Washington, D.C.
Auckland • Bogotá • Caracas • Lisbon • London
Madrid • Mexico City • Milan • Montreal • New Delhi
San Juan • Singapore • Sydney • Tokyo • Toronto

McGraw-Hill

A Division of The ***McGraw-Hill*** *Companies*

Copyright © 2000 by The McGraw-Hill Companies, Inc. All rights reserved. Printed in the United States of America. Except as permitted under the United States Copyright Act of 1976, no part of this publication may be reproduced or distributed in any form or by any means, or stored in a data base or retrieval system, without the prior written permission of the publisher.

1 2 3 4 5 6 7 8 9 0 AGM/AGM 9 0 4 3 2 1 0 9

ISBN 0-07-135386-0

The sponsoring editor for this book was Michael Sprague and the production supervisor was Clare Stanley. It was set in Century Schoolbook by D&G Limited, LLC.

Printed and bound by Quebecor/Martinsburg.

Throughout this book, trademarked names are used. Rather than put a trademark symbol after every occurrence of a trademarked name, we use names in an editorial fashion only, and to the benefit of the trademark owner, with no intention of infringement of the trademark. Where such designations appear in this book, they have been printed with initial caps.

Information contained in this work has been obtained by The McGraw-Hill Companies, Inc. ("McGraw-Hill") from sources believed to be reliable. However, neither McGraw-Hill nor its authors guarantees the accuracy or completeness of any information published herein and neither McGraw-Hill nor its authors shall be responsible for any errors, omissions, or damages arising out of use of this information. This work is published with the understanding that McGraw-Hill and its authors are supplying information but are not attempting to render engineering or other professional services. If such services are required, the assistance of an appropriate professional should be sought.

This book is printed on recycled, acid-free paper containing a minimum of 50 percent recycled de-inked fiber.

ACKNOWLEDGMENTS

Thanks first and foremost to my wife and editorial associate, *Ingrid Tulloch*, for her research, proofreading, and other technical help in making this book and our company MTIT Enterprises a success. Thanks, Schatz!

Thanks to *Escape Communications Corp* (`www.escape.ca`) both for hosting my Web site (`www.mtit.com`) and for allowing me to come in and fool around with their SMTP mail server so I could create the walkthrough for Chapter 16 of this book.

Thanks also to *Jill Lampi*, a DNS/systems administrator at Escape who assisted me with the walkthrough in Chapter 16.

Thanks to my agent *David L. Rogelberg* of Studio B Productions Ltd. (`www.studiob.com`) who has helped me achieve my modest degree of success as a writer.

Thanks to *Michael Sprague*, my editor at McGraw-Hill, who has provided me with invaluable editorial assistance that has helped shape this book into its present form.

Thanks to *Orlando* of Ciao's Cafe, who makes the best Expresso in the city and whose coffee kept me going while I was writing this book.

Finally, thank you to *my readers* who have enjoyed and profited from my previous books and have emailed me many helpful comments concerning them. I hope that this present book will be both useful and enjoyable to you as well. Feel free to contact me via email at `info@mtit.com` if you should wish to comment about anything in this book or if you find any errors or omissions.

CONTENTS

INTRODUCTION

Exchange Server is one of the most successful products in Microsoft's history. In a few short years, it has grown in market stature until it has eclipsed all other messaging server products in quarterly sales of seats, including the popular Lotus Notes. The majority of Fortune 500 companies now use Exchange as their primary messaging system, and others are looking to adopt it.

Exchange is a huge success story for Microsoft, and this book is designed to help busy network administrators get up and running with it quickly.

Features of This Book

As a *Microsoft Certified Trainer* (MCT) and a consulting *Microsoft Certified Systems Engineer* (MCSE), I've tried to create a book that is both useful for self-study and also practical in nature, with real-life hands-on content wherever possible. Many of this book's features will be useful for busy network administrators who need to plan, implement, configure, maintain, and troubleshoot Exchange:

- *An up-to-date focus.* This book covers Exchange Server 5.5 to the point of having applied Service Pack 2 for the product, which is the latest version and service pack for Exchange at the time of writing.
- *Task-based titles.* Titles of chapters and walkthroughs indicate a specific administrative task that is covered by the section, such as "Administering Recipients," "Monitoring Exchange," "Planning an Exchange Organization," and so on.
- *Walkthroughs.* Most of this book's chapters include at least one step-by-step walkthrough, taking the reader through the process of putting into practice what the chapter teaches. Readers are encouraged to follow along and perform these walkthroughs on their own systems, if they have the necessary hardware and software available.
- *Screen shots.* Numerous screen shots are used to maintain reader focus and complement the text of each chapter, making the book suitable for learning both while sitting at an administrative workstation or riding the bus to work.
- *For more information.* At the end of each chapter is a section outlining further reference materials the reader can peruse in order to dig deeper into some of the issues discussed in the chapter.

Who Should Read This Book?

This book is primarily intended for you **busy network administrators** who need to implement Exchange in your company or organization. It is designed to be easy to follow, covers the main aspects of Exchange, and gives advice or tips wherever possible to make life easier for you. After all, I know how hard life is for you. With the mantra of 24 x 7 x 365 availability with cell phones and pagers and laptops, running a corporate network today is an all-consuming job. If you're not already familiar with Exchange Server, this book will get you up and running quickly and painlessly. If you are already familiar with some aspects of Exchange but not with others, simply turn to the chapters you are interested in and you will quickly learn the features of the aspects that interest you.

As well, this book is indirectly targeted towards you **individuals pursuing MCSE certification** who need to prepare for the Microsoft exam on Exchange. Although this book is not a typical study guide with sample test questions and review lists, nevertheless individuals preparing for the Exchange exam should find the book extremely helpful as a way of getting familiar with the product and how to configure and use Exchange Server. After all, even Microsoft tells users that the real key to exam success is familiarity with the product, not cramming exam questions or memorizing definitions and lists. Readers of my earlier book *Administering IIS4* (McGraw-Hill Professional Publishing, 1998) have often told me that the book, although similarly designed for network administrators, nevertheless was of immense use to them in preparing for their IIS4 exam. This present book is modeled after the same style as the earlier one and should be equally useful for both types of readers.

Overview of Chapters

Chapter 1, "Overview of Exchange Server 5.5," provides a brief introduction to Exchange Server 5.5 and covers the capabilities and features of Exchange, the history of Microsoft mail server products, different editions of Exchange, and a comparison with other mail systems.

Chapter 2, "Planning an Exchange Organization," covers how Exchange fits into the corporate messaging environment, the steps involved in planning and implementing an Exchange organization, different messaging topologies for an Exchange organization, and factors to consider when planning the number of sites to use.

Chapter 3, "Installing Exchange," covers system requirements for installing Exchange, installation issues for Exchange, installing Exchange on a fresh system, upgrading from previous versions of Exchange, unattended installations of Exchange, other configuration issues, and troubleshooting installation problems.

Chapter 4, "Under the Hood," provides an introduction to the architecture and operation of Exchange Server. It covers the Exchange core components, optional components, directory structure and share points, database files, message flow, and different address types.

Chapter 5, "Tools for Administration," looks at the tools for administering an Exchange organization with its sites and servers. It covers the GUI-based tools for administering Exchange (primarily focusing on the Exchange Administrator program), the command-line utilities for Exchange troubleshooting and maintenance, Windows NT tools and utilities for administering Exchange, the BackOffice Resource Kit (BORK) utilities, and the topic of Exchange permissions and roles.

Chapter 6, "Administering Recipients," focuses on the task of creating Exchange recipients and covers the different types of Exchange recipients. It also examines creating and configuring mailboxes, distribution lists, and Custom Recipients.

Chapter 7, "Administering Clients," looks at the various types of mail clients that can be used together with Exchange. It covers the different types of Exchange clients, installing Microsoft Outlook, and configuring Outlook Profiles.

Chapter 8, "Administering Sites," looks at how to configure a new Exchange site and focuses on configuring directory objects that are site-wide in scope such as site configuration, DS site configuration, Information Store site configuration, MTA site configuration, and site addressing directory objects.

Chapter 9, "Administering Servers," looks at the various directory objects that can be used to configure server-level Exchange settings, such as the Server and Servers containers, Directory Service, the Message Transfer Agent, the Private Information Store, the Public Information Store, and System Attendant directory objects.

Chapter 10, "Administering Site Connectors," considers how to establish messaging connectivity between two Exchange sites using the Site Connector and covers the different types of Exchange connectors, the Connections Container, and the Site Connector.

Chapter 11, "Administering Directory Replication," looks at how to establish directory replication between two connected sites. It also covers the Directory Replication process, the Directory Replication Connector, and using the Exchange Performance optimizer.

Chapter 12, "Administering Public Folders," looks at how to create, manage, access, and replicate public folders in a multi-site Exchange organization. It also examines creating and configuring Public Folders, configuring Public Folder Client permissions, and implementing Public Folder replication and affinity.

Chapter 13, "Administering Address Book Views," looks at how to create customized address lists called Address Book Views and covers the Global Address List (GAL) and Address Book Views.

Chapter 14, "Administering X.400 Connectors," covers the X.400 messaging standards, X.400 addressing, MTA Transport Stacks, and X.400 Connectors.

Chapter 15, "Administering MS Mail Connectors," looks at how to establish messaging connectivity between an Exchange organization and a legacy Microsoft Mail 3.x messaging system. It also covers Microsoft Mail, the Microsoft Mail Connector, and directory synchronization.

Chapter 16, "Administering Internet Services," covers Internet protocols supported by Exchange, configuring Internet Protocols, the Internet Mail Service, and the Internet News Service.

Chapter 17, "Administering Dynamic RAS Connectors," covers installing and configuring the Dynamic RAS connector.

Chapter 18, "Administering Message Routing," considers how messages are routed through an Exchange organization and to foreign mail systems. It also covers message routing, the GWART, connected sites, and address spaces.

Chapter 19, "Monitoring Exchange," examines how to monitor the health and status of servers and connectors in an Exchange organization, and covers Server Monitors, Link Monitors, and Performance Monitors.

Chapter 20, "Maintaining Exchange," looks at how to maintain an Exchange organization, focusing on how to maintain the various Exchange database files. Backing up Exchange, command-line maintenance utilities, and disaster recovery tips are also covered.

Chapter 21, "Migrating to Exchange," looks at how to migrate users on legacy and third-party mail systems to Exchange Server and covers the Exchange Migration Wizard and migrating from MS Mail to Exchange.

Chapter 22, "Administering Outlook Web Access," looks at the optional Outlook Web Access component of Exchange Server, which allows users to access their mailbox and public folders using a standard Web browser like Internet Explorer or Netscape Communicator.

Table of Walkthroughs

The following table lists the step-by-step walkthroughs that are included in various chapter of this book. Some walkthroughs include subsections and these are signified as bulleted items in the table.

Chapter	Walkthroughs Included
1	None
2	Planning an Exchange organization
3	Installing Exchange Server Enabling Message Journalling
4	None
5	Using the Exchange Administrator ■ Assigning the Permissions Admin Role ■ Specifying Auto Naming Conventions ■ Miscellaneous Tasks (Creating recipients containers, etc.)
6	Creating and Configuring Mailboxes ■ Creating a Mailbox using Exchange Administrator ■ Creating a Mailbox Using User Manger for Domains ■ Using Mailbox Templates ■ Modifying Mailbox Settings Creating and Configuring Distribution Lists Creating and Configuring Custom Recipients
7	Installing Microsoft Outlook 98 Configuring and Testing Outlook Profiles
8	Configuring a Site ■ Creating and Downloading Offline Address Books ■ Defining Custom Attributes ■ Public Folder Creation Settings
9	Configuring a Server ■ Disable Circular Logging ■ Configuring Deleted Item Recovery and Mailbox Storage Limits ■ Testing Message Limit Settings

Chapter	Walkthroughs Included
10	Creating and Configuring a Site Connector ■ Creating a Site Connector ■ Testing the Site Connector ■ Cleaning Mailboxes
11	Creating and Configuring a Directory Replication Connector ■ Testing Directory Replication ■ Running Performance Optimizer ■ Message Tracking ■ Advanced Message Tracking
12	Creating and Testing Public Folders ■ Creating a Public Folder ■ Configuring Public Folder Affinity ■ Replicating Public Folders
13	Creating an Address Book View ■ Testing the Address Book View ■ Adding a Recipient ■ Moving a Recipient ■ Creating an Empty Container ■ Modifying an Address Book View ■ Restricting Access to Address Book View Containers ■ Finding Recipients in Exchange Administrator
14	Creating and Resting an X.400 Connector ■ Removing Existing Connectors ■ Installing an MTA Transport Stack ■ Creating an X.400 Connector ■ Testing the X.400 Connector
15	Configuring a Microsoft Mail Connector ■ Testing the Connector
16	Installing and Testing the Internet Mail Service ■ The Scenario ■ Installing the Internet Mail Service ■ Testing the Internet Mail Service
17	Creating and Testing a Dynamic RAS Connector ■ The Scenario ■ Installing and Configuring the Remote Access Service ■ Testing RAS ■ Creating a RAS Override Account ■ Installing a RAS MTA Transport Stack

Chapter	Walkthroughs Included
	■ Creating and Configuring a Dynamic RAS Connector ■ Testing the Dynamic RAS Connector
18	Understanding Message Routing ■ The Scenario ■ Test One ■ Test Two ■ Test Three
19	Installing and Testing a Server Monitor ■ Testing the Server Monitor Installing and Testing a Link Monitor ■ Testing the Link Monitor
20	Using Eseutil Using Isinteg Using Mtacheck
21	Migrating an MS Mail 3.5 Postoffice
22	Installing and Testing Outlook Web Access

Disclaimer

Although I have tried hard in good faith to make this work as accurate and reliable as possible, neither myself (the author) or my publisher (McGraw-Hill) assumes any liability or responsibility whatsoever for any loss or damage arising from the information presented in this book. In other words, the information provided in this book is presented on an "as is" basis. The author recommends strongly that you test all procedures and suggestions outlined in this book on test machines before implementing them on production machines and that you refer to Microsoft's official documentation for Exchange as the authoritative guide to configuring and using the product.

Mitch Tulloch, B.Sc., Dip.Ed., MCT, MCSE
http://www.mtit.com
info@mtit.com

Winnipeg, Canada 1999

CHAPTER 1

Overview of Exchange Server 5.5

Introduction

Electronic mail or email is the lifeblood of the corporate world. This chapter provides a brief introduction to Exchange Server 5.5, Microsoft's latest offering in the arena of mail servers. After reading this chapter, you will have a basic understanding of

- Capabilities and features of Microsoft Exchange
- The history of Microsoft mail server products
- Different editions of Exchange
- Comparison with other mail systems

What Is Microsoft Exchange?

Microsoft Exchange Server is Microsoft's flagship mail server and may arguably be the most successful product that Microsoft has developed to date. Not that Exchange has sold more copies than Windows, but instead because of its increasingly important role in sustaining the flow of information throughout today's business environment. Here are some facts Microsoft likes to boast about:

- Exchange has sold almost 30 million seats in its mere three years of existence, with almost five million seats being sold in the first quarter of 1999 alone.
- On a quarterly per-seat basis, Exchange is now outselling Lotus Notes and Lotus cc:Mail, and has almost wiped Novell's GroupWise, Netscape's Collabra, and most other LAN-based messaging platforms out of the market.
- It is now the leading messaging platform among Fortune 500 companies, with companies like General Electric and Boeing having deployed over 130,000 seats (clients) each. As of January 1999, eight corporate customers have implemented Exchange using over 100,000 seats. Among Fortune 1000 companies, 62 percent of those recently surveyed said they either used Exchange or planned to migrate to Exchange.
- Exchange is used by the U.S. Department of Defense as the basis of their Defense Messaging System (DMS), which replaces their older Automatic Digital Network (AUTODIN) communications system.

Exchange DMS includes special features such as support for clients that use MISSI/Fortezza hardware encryption devices and is available only from Lockheed Martin Federal Systems.

After considering the above facts, one might wonder what exactly makes Exchange so popular? After all, isn't it just a program for forwarding email from place to place like the popular UNIX Sendmail program? The truth is Exchange is much more than just a mail forwarder.

What Exchange Can Be

Exchange can be many things to different companies, depending on how they want to use it. Some of the ways that Exchange can function in your company include the following:

- *A comprehensive messaging and collaboration solution.* Exchange Server is only half of a client/server messaging system, the other half being Outlook, Microsoft's full-featured messaging client and *Personal Information Manager* (PIM) that is both included with Exchange and is offered as a component of Microsoft Office. By combining Outlook with Exchange, companies can provide users with a full-featured system for managing their messages, calendars, contacts, tasks, and shared documents, providing full groupware functionality for users to collaborate effectively in the achievement of business goals.
- *A platform for developing collaborative workflow applications.* By using Outlook's capability to create custom forms for presenting and organizing information, and by using Exchange's server-side scripting capabilities, developers can create workflow applications to enable users to collaborate on their business goals. Examples of such applications include customer tracking, product libraries, bulletin boards, and so on.
- *An extensible, integrated business solution.* Because of its close relationship with other Microsoft BackOffice products like SQL Server and Internet Information Server, Exchange can be extended to support database and Web functionality. For example, SQL Server can automatically send email messages through Exchange when certain conditions arise in the database. Outlook Web Access, included with Exchange and supported by Internet Information Server, enables remote users to access their mail remotely using only a standard Web browser.

- *A cost-effective choice for a business to make.* A number of studies have indicated that migrating from legacy host- and LAN-based mail systems to Exchange can increase user productivity, decrease support and administration costs, and lower the *total cost of ownership* (TCO). Migrating to an all-Exchange solution might involve some large direct costs up front in the form of hardware capital expenditures, software and licensing fees, and technical and end-user training costs, but in the long run, businesses will save money. And for CEOs who care for the bottom line, that's important!

History of Microsoft Exchange

To put the most recent version of Exchange in perspective, let's review the history of Microsoft's messaging server products and how they've grown to where they are today. This will provide us with a perspective on where Exchange has come from and where it is going. It will also help us understand some of the differences between Exchange and other popular LAN-based messaging systems.

Goodbye MS Mail

The first offering of a mail server product from Microsoft was called *Microsoft Mail for PC Networks*, or simply *MS Mail*. Actually, Microsoft didn't create it; like many large corporations, Microsoft sometimes grows by buying other companies and their products. MS Mail was really created by a company called Consumer Software in the late 1980s, and it was originally called Network Courier. Microsoft purchased version 2.0 of Network Courier in order to get into the mail server game just after Lotus Corporation themselves acquired cc:Mail from another company (two can play that game!). Microsoft renamed the product MS Mail 2.1 (no sense calling it MS Mail 1.0) and then improved it in later versions 3.0, 3.2, and 3.5. From the start, MS Mail was intended to run on DOS-based network servers like Microsoft LAN Manager and Novell NetWare, but MS Mail 3.5 could run on Microsoft Windows NT 3.51 as well.

MS Mail was designed to operate as a *store-and-forward* mail server. The mail server is simply a file server with a specific shared directory structure created on it. This shared directory structure is commonly called the Postoffice, since it forms a temporary holding area where mail is delivered while waiting to be picked up. The details are as follows: when a client program or User Agent running on a user's workstation wants to send email to someone else on the network (and this could include an attachment), the client program copies the message to the appropriate directory on the mail server. There it sits until the user to whom the mail was sent checks their inbox on the server and retrieves the message. In this type of system, the mail clients do all of the processing, while the server just sits there and stores messages and other control information. Messages are moved in the same way users copy files from one folder to another.

Of course, it's a bit more extensive than that. MS Mail also included an administration program called Admin.exe that enabled the network administrator to create and delete mailboxes for users, create distribution lists, manage address lists, and perform other administrative housekeeping tasks. And your mail network could be quite complex, with multiple post offices positioned on multiple MS Mail servers throughout your company network. In order for a user whose mailbox was on one server to send mail to a user on another server, some means of routing (delivering) the message from one server to the other was required. The component that enabled MS Mail to do this was called the *Message Transfer Agent* (MTA).

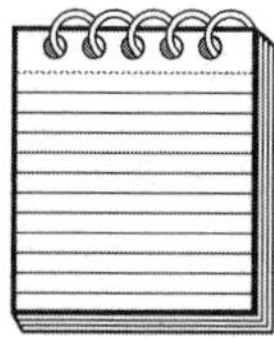

NOTE: *You may wonder where terms like User Agent and Message Transfer Agent come from. They are part of the X.400 specifications developed by the International Telecommunications Union or ITU. X.400 is a series of standards for implementing a global messaging system, similar in capabilities to the SMTP mail system used on the Internet but different in architecture and design. For more information on X.400 concepts and terminology, refer to Chapter 14, "Administering X.400 Connectors."*

The client program that was used to send and receive email using MS Mail was simply called Mail. Later versions of MS Mail included support for additional features such as

- A calendaring client program called Schedule+, which was separate from the Mail client program and could be used for scheduling appointments and booking meetings between users.
- A directory synchronization capability for harmonizing addressing information on all MS Mail servers in an organization to create a single *Global Address List* (GAL).
- Support for remote users to access their mail using Microsoft Remote Mail software.

- A programming interface called *Messaging Application Programming Interface* (MAPI) that enables developers to write C/C++ or Visual Basic programs that are mail-enabled, such as a word processing program that can mail its documents to users.
- Gateways for exchanging MS Mail messages with users on other mail systems. This included gateways for X.400, SMTP, PROFS, and SNADS mail systems (PROFS and SNADS were host-based mail systems that ran on IBM mainframe computers that used IBM's System Network Architecture (SNA)).

The main difficulties with MS Mail were that it was DOS-based and not very scalable. When you tried to deploy it in an enterprise with thousands of users distributed over many servers, it became quite awkward to manage. Another disadvantage was that the shared directory structure (Postoffice) on a MS Mail server had to be shared with everyone having Full Control permission—not very secure, to say the least! Enter Exchange Server . . .

Hello Exchange Server

Having wet their appetite for the messaging server market, Microsoft developed a new messaging server from scratch and called it Exchange Server or simply Exchange. This new product was released in 1996 as Exchange 4.0. Where was Exchange 1.0, 2.0, and 3.0? It didn't make sense to go from MS Mail 3.5 to Exchange 1.0, as users might interpret this as a step backwards.

Anyway, Exchange 4.0 was the first truly *client/server* mail server, in which both the client (also called Exchange) and the server shared in the processing of messages. This was possible through a technology developed by Sun Microsystems for its Unix platform servers that was adapted by Microsoft to Windows platforms: the *Remote Procedure Call* (RPC). RPCs are a mechanism by which a piece of software on one computer can invoke function calls on a piece of software on another computer. In essence, RPCs enable developers to distribute the various parts of an application (called a distributed application) over different machines on the network and have them work together and run as if the entire application resided on a single machine. In the case of Exchange Server/Exchange Client, the two pieces of software form a client/server application.

Why all the fuss? The main advantage of this system over the passive store-and-forward system used by MS Mail was that once the client delivered a message to the server, the server could then notify the message recipient directly that something was waiting in their mailbox to be picked up. No polling was necessary as in MS Mail, where a client periodically checked with the Postoffice to ask "Is there any mail for me yet?" This reduced network traffic and made more efficient use of resources on both the client and the server computers.

Another improvement was that Exchange 4.0 was designed to run specifically on the Windows NT operating system platform, and all Exchange server functions were integrated into the server as Windows NT services (the equivalent of Unix daemons—server processes that run continually in the background and wait for something to do).

Another advantage of using a client/server architecture was security. Instead of the shared folder system used in MS Mail that was not secure, Exchange 4.0 stored user messages in a database structure based on Microsoft's *Joint Technology Engine* (JET) database technology. No system of shared folders was needed, making for a more secure messaging environment.

Since Exchange 4.0 ran on Windows NT 3.51, it could make use of the *graphical user interface* (GUI) of Windows to provide a much more accessible and easy-to-use administration program (still called Admin.exe just like in MS Mail). The Exchange Administrator program could display all the necessary information about the various mail servers, users, and other manageable objects in an Exchange organization. It presented this information in a hierarchical view similar to Windows Explorer. Administrators could use this program to easily administer an entire Exchange organization from a single workstation.

Exchange 4.0 included similar connectivity options to foreign mail systems like MS Mail and came with connectors (gateways) for X.400, SMTP, PROFS, SNADS, and even MS Mail itself. In fact, Exchange managed an MS Mail network even better than it could manage itself. Exchange public folders replaced the simple shared folders used in MS Mail and enabled developers to create workflow and tracking applications using forms. Exchange 4.0 even included a Web Connector that allowed users to access their mail using a standard Web browser like Microsoft Internet Explorer or Netscape Navigator (albeit clunkily).

And since the release of Exchange 4.0, Microsoft has continued to improve the product, first with Exchange 5.0, which included integrated support for important Internet protocols like POP3, NNTP, and LDAP, better Web access to mail, and an improved MAPI client called Microsoft Outlook. Exchange 5.5, the most recent version, also includes support for the Internet protocols IMAP4 and LDAPrev3, secure messaging through SSL,

S/MIME and X.509 digital certificates, optional IRC chat services, integrated support for Microsoft NetMeeting, and other features that are described below. Suffice it to say that we've come a long way since MS Mail—oops, Network Courier!

Features of Exchange 5.5

First before we look at the features of Exchange 5.5, we need to consider the editions or ways in which this product has been packaged by Microsoft. Each of these four different packages is targeted to a specific level of business needs.

Exchange Packages

Presently, Exchange 5.5 can be obtained in four ways:

- *Exchange 5.5 Standard Edition.* This version runs on Windows NT 4.0 and is targeted for small- to medium-sized companies that plan on either implementing email for the first time or want to upgrade their legacy mail systems for something state-of-the-art. The Standard Edition of Exchange includes the following components:
- Exchange 5.5 Server itself
- Outlook 97 client
- Internet mail service for connecting to SMTP hosts on the Internet
- cc:Mail connector for connecting to Lotus cc:Mail systems
- Lotus Notes connector for connecting to Lotus Notes systems
- MS Mail connector for connecting to legacy MS Mail networks
- Internet news service for connecting to USENET
- Chat service for hosting IRC chat rooms
- Various developer tools (not discussed in this book)
- *Exchange 5.5 Enterprise Edition.* This version is targeted for the large enterprise environment that has greater scalability, availability, and interoperability needs for their messaging solution. Enterprise Edition includes everything in the Standard Edition plus the following:
- X.400 connector for connecting to X.400-based messaging systems (popular in Europe).

- IBM OfficeVision/VM/SNADS/PROFS connectors for connecting to host-based mainframe mail systems common in older enterprise environments.
- Support for Microsoft Cluster Server. Exchange 5.5 Enterprise Edition can be installed on Windows NT Server 4.0 Enterprise Edition, which includes two-node failover clustering support for minimizing server downtime and increasing availability by using the Microsoft Cluster Server, which is included in the Enterprise Edition of Windows NT Server 4.0.
- Unlimited data store. The maximum size of each of the two Information Store databases in previous versions of Exchange was only 16 gigabytes or 16 GB (1 GB = 1,024 MB), which meant that if your company had a lot of users, you had to install a lot of Exchange servers—a management headache! The size of the Information Store database on the Enterprise Edition, however, is limited only by the storage capacity of your hardware (and your budget, and how long it takes to perform your backup, and . . .). Actually, the size limit on the Information Store for the Enterprise Edition is 16 terabytes or 16 TB (1 TB = 1,024 GB), which for all practical purposes is more than enough for any purpose—at least for now!
- A new algorithm for dynamically allocating physical system memory called *Dynamic Buffer Allocation* (DBA), which allows Exchange to effectively use a full complement of 4 GB of installed RAM and distribute its use effectively in four-way *Symmetric Multiprocessing* (SMP) systems.

- *BackOffice Server 4.5.* BackOffice Server is an integrated suite containing the whole line of Microsoft's server products, including Windows NT Server, Exchange Server, SQL Server, Proxy Server, and so on. The most recent version of BackOffice Server (version 4.5) includes Exchange Server 5.5 (Standard Edition) along with Service Pack 2 for Exchange 5.5.

  BackOffice Server includes an integrated setup program that walks you through installing the various components of BackOffice, including a set of built-in scenarios for typical business needs. After installation is complete, a series of to-do lists guides you through the process of integrating your new server into your corporate environment, such as installing connectors to join your Exchange Server to your existing Exchange organization (if you have one).

  BackOffice Server also includes a new integrated administration tool called *Microsoft Management Console* (MMC), which provides a single console for managing BackOffice Server and each of its components. Four starter consoles are provided with different levels of administrative functionality to help you get started, but you can also customize them to suite your needs.

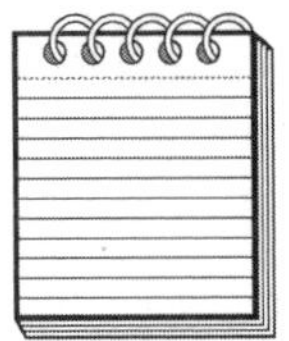

NOTE: *Using the MMC to administer Exchange is definitely something to take note of, since Microsoft is planning to migrate all administrative tools for the next version of BackOffice products that will be designed to run on the upcoming Windows 2000 Server operating system. Microsoft will eventually create a snap-in for the MMC that will provide the full functionality of the Exchange Administrator program currently used to administering the stand-alone version of Exchange Server. Although this book deals primarily with the Enterprise Edition of Microsoft Exchange Server 5.5, administration of other editions is essentially the same.*

The MMC actually first appeared in the Microsoft Windows NT 4.0 option pack, which contained version 4.0 of Microsoft's popular Web server platform, Internet Information Server 4.0 (IIS4). For an introduction to IIS4 and how to manage it using the MMC, see my book Administering IIS4 *from McGraw-Hill.*

- *BackOffice Small Business Server 4.5.* The Small Business Server or SBS is an integrated suite of Microsoft server products targeted at small businesses, providing them with easy-to-use networking, messaging, and Internet services. SBS includes Exchange Server 5.5 together with Outlook 2000 as part of its offerings, but before you run out and buy it, you need to be aware that there are what Microsoft calls "subtle differences" between the SBS version of Exchange and the "commercial off-the-shelf" or COTS version you buy separately. The most significant limitation from a mail administrator's point of view is that the SBS version of Exchange only includes one connector, the Internet Mail Connector. You can't install any other connectors on SBS, such as the X.400 Connector or Site Connector, so SBS is really designed as part of a stand-alone messaging solution and is not intended to be integrated into an enterprise-level Exchange organization.

NOTE: *Just in case you were wondering, you can't hack into the registry of SBS to enable it to support other connectivity options. People have tried (and failed). Besides, you shouldn't even try since that violates the licensing agreement of SBS.*

Don't despair, though, if you bought SBS and planned on using it as your messaging solution for your enterprise. You can always upgrade it to the full version of Exchange Server and buy more Client Access Licenses *(CALs).*

Another limitation on SBS is that it supports a maximum of 50 licensed client computers, which means it really is limited to small businesses. There's no way around this limit unless you upgrade SBS to the full version of Windows NT Server 4.0.

Finally, SBS is completely administered by a single, simple, and intuitive wizard-based taskpad interface. You don't even see the Exchange Administrator program at all, since SBS was designed to be set up and run by novices, rather than geeks like us. Because of these limitations on SBS as a corporate messaging solution, we won't discuss it any further in this book.

Exchange Features

In this book, we're working specifically with Exchange Server 5.5 Enterprise Edition, since this version has the widest range of supported features and can be used at all levels of business enterprise. This section briefly discusses most of the significant features of Exchange 5.5, but many of them are also explained in much more detail in later chapters of this book. The features here are grouped together into various categories and some are omitted that were mentioned previously:

System Architecture and Operation

- Tight integration with the Windows NT architecture model. Exchange components like the Information Store, Message Transfer Agent, and System Attendant are implemented as Windows NT services that can be started, stopped, and paused without needing to reboot the operating system.
- Support for least-cost message routing, including failover support for remote links that go down in a mesh topology messaging system.
- Integrated monitoring tools: Server monitors for monitoring Exchange services on any server in an organization and link monitors for monitoring the status of messaging links between your Exchange organization and foreign mail systems.

- An X.500-based LDAP distributed directory service for managing all objects in an Exchange organization including sites, servers, connectors, message stores, recipients, address lists, and public folders. Directory replication between Exchange sites can be scheduled.
- Support for the *Active Directory Service Interface* (ADSI) that synchronizes the Exchange directory with foreign LDAP directory services and takes advantage of the active directory of the upcoming Windows 2000 server platform.
- A fault-tolerant message store, consisting of two Information Store databases with their associated transaction logs.
- Mailbox disk quotas and message size limits to maximize the efficient use of disk and network resources.
- Deleted Item Recovery functionality to enable accidentally deleted messages to be quickly recovered.
- Message tracking, a troubleshooting utility for tracing the path of a message as it is routed through your Exchange organization.

Administration

- A unified Administration tool (the Exchange Administrator program), which presents a hierarchical view of all objects in an Exchange organization and allows you to easily add, delete, and configure objects using property sheets.
- Full integration with Windows NT administrative tools, including Event Viewer and Performance Monitor for monitoring and troubleshooting purposes. Mailboxes can be created for users when user accounts are created with User Manager for Domains. An enhanced form of Windows NT Backup is also installed with Exchange in order to simplify the backup of key Exchange components. Online (hot) backup of key Exchange components is supported.
- A Performer Optimizer is included to ensure that Exchange is installed and configured optimally for your current hardware configuration.
- A Migration Wizard migrates users mail accounts and messages from legacy mail systems like Microsoft Mail and third-party mail systems like Lotus Notes, Lotus cc:Mail, Novell GroupWise, Netscape Collabra, and IBM PROFS and SNADS host-based mail systems.
- Support for virtual organizations, so that more than one company can use a single Exchange server as their joint messaging solution without interfering with each other's address books.

Connectivity

- Site Connector, for easily linking sites together in an Exchange organization.
- X.400 Connector, which provides support for X.400 messaging, the ITU standard for global messaging systems that is widely implemented in Europe and other parts of the world. Support for X.25 networking is included also.
- Internet Mail Service, which provides support for SMTP messaging, the Internet standard for global messaging that is the predominant messaging system in the world today.
- Internet News Service, which enables connectivity between Exchange and the USENET news system on the Internet.
- Dynamic Remote Access Service (RAS) connector, which enables sites to be linked by low-bandwidth dialup WAN links using Windows NT's RAS.
- Microsoft Mail Connector, which enables coexistence between Exchange and legacy MS Mail messaging systems. Additional components are included to support directory synchronization between these two systems as well.
- Additional connectors for Lotus Notes, Lotus cc:Mail, DEC All-In-One, and IBM OfficeVision PROFS and SNADS.

Internet Support

- Support for *Simple Mail Transfer Protocol* (SMTP) mail forwarding using the Internet Mail Service connector.
- Support for *Post Office Protocol version 3* (POP3) and *Internet Mail Access Protocol version 4* (IMAP4) mail access protocols.
- Support for *Hypertext Transfer Protocol* (HTTP), so that when used in conjunction with Microsoft Internet Information Server (IIS), users can access their mail anywhere using a standard Web browser. This is made possible by Outlook Web Access, an Active Server Pages-based application that runs on the IIS server.
- Support for *Network News Transport Protocol* (NNTP), which makes it possible to have an Exchange server function as a USENET news host to download newsgroups and messages for clients to read using the Microsoft Outlook Express newsreader. Local NNTP newsgroups can also be created using Newsgroup Public Folders.
- Support for *Lightweight Directory Access Protocol version 3* (LDAPv3) access to the Exchange directory service.

Security

- Tight integration with the Windows NT security model. Users only need to log on their domain in order to access their mail and only one password is required.
- Support for message encryption and X.509v3 digital signatures using the integrated Key Manager Server, which can function within a *Public-Key Infrastructure* (PKI) based either on the Microsoft Certificate Server or some third-party organization like Verisign, Inc. Both *Secure Sockets Layer version 3.0* (SSL 3.0) for Web access and *Secure MIME* (S/MIME) for Outlook are supported.

Clients

- Includes Win32, Win16, and Macintosh versions of Microsoft Outlook.
- Supports all standard Internet POP3/IMAP4 mail clients like Microsoft Outlook Express, Qualcomm's Eudora, Netscape's Messenger, and so on.

Collaboration and Development Tools

- Public folders enable users to post messages and documents, create discussion groups, and create form-based workflow applications to support collaboration between users on business projects.
- Exchange Scripting Agent, which creates event-driven server-side workflow applications with public folders.
- IRC-compliant chat service and *Internet Locator Service* (ILS) for real-time collaboration between users using Microsoft NetMeeting.
- Full integration capability with other BackOffice products like Microsoft SQL Server for building enterprise-level collaboration and workflow applications.
- Comes with Outlook 97 (or Outlook 98 if Service Pack 2 for Exchange 5.5 is installed), a powerful *Personal Information Management* (PIM) system for messaging, scheduling, contact and task management, and designing custom collaboration and workflow tools based on forms.
- Includes a single-user copy of Microsoft Visual InterDev, a powerful development platform for building advanced workflow applications.

Exchange Goes Platinum

This is probably as good a place as any to mention the upcoming version of Exchange, code-named Platinum and clandestinely referred to by Microsoft support specialists as Exchange 6.0. Platinum will be the fourth release of Exchange, and according to Microsoft its features will include the following:

- Tight integration with the upcoming Windows 2000 family of operating system platforms (Windows 2000 Standard Server, Windows 2000 Advanced Server, and Windows 2000 Datacenter Server). In particular, the Exchange directory service will be closely tied to the Active Directory of Windows 2000. Administration of all Exchange functions will also be done using Windows 2000's MMC administrative interface.
- An integrated Web store for storing both Web documents and Office 2000 documents for a truly "all-in-one" business experience.
- Support for unified messaging (mail/calendar/voice/fax/video) accessed through hand-held wireless devices, T.120-based data conferencing for real-time collaboration using Microsoft NetMeeting, four-way clustering for high-availability in mission-critical business environments, and a whole host of new techno-goodies.

Well, at least that's what they promise! And they'll probably deliver.

Comparison with Other Mail Systems

If you've bought this book, you've probably already decided on Exchange as a messaging solution for your company, but let's take a minute more to compare Exchange with other messaging solutions that are currently available. Remember, marketing comparisons should always be taken with a grain of salt.

Exchange vs. Lotus

The Microsoft-Lotus war has been raging since Microsoft first acquired Network Courier from Consumer Software and renamed it Microsoft Mail. It shows no sign of slowing down now that Lotus is in the IBM camp. With the latest release by Lotus of its R5 Notes/Domino groupware system, Lotus has narrowed the features gap with Exchange, but there are still some significant differences.

According to Microsoft:

- R5 now includes a database of unlimited size. Microsoft points out that Lotus is just playing catch-up with Exchange Server in this regard and that the Notes database is only "certified" up to 64 GB of storage capacity.
- The R5 database is now transaction-based for greater fault-tolerance and recoverability, which Exchange has been since the beginning.
- The R5 directory infrastructure actually consists of a number of different databases, while Microsoft's Exchange directory database is a single database (together with associated transaction logs, checkpoint files, and temporary files).
- R5 now supports X.509 v3 digital certificates for secure messaging using S/MIME, which the Exchange 5.5/Outlook 98 combination already supports.
- The R5 client lacks some of the messaging, scheduling, and collaboration features that are supported by Outlook 98. At least, Microsoft thinks R5 clients fall down on a feature-by-feature basis.
- The Exchange/Outlook combination is an easier platform than R5 for developing custom workflow and collaboration applications. Notes/Domino developers would probably disagree, though.

Things are different according to Lotus, however:

- The Exchange/Outlook combination isn't true "groupware" at all; it is merely email with basic public folder discussion groups added on. That's an oversimplification, but you do need other products like IIS4 and SQL server 7.0 if you really want to use Exchange as the basis of a powerful, enterprise-level workflow and collaboration system. But Microsoft does, in fact, integrate all the necessary products and tools into a single server solution: Microsoft BackOffice Server.
- Notes/Domino compares favorably with Exchange/Outlook in a feature-for-feature basis and even exceeds it in some areas. This is probably true.
- Notes/Domino runs on both Unix and NT, while Exchange is limited to running on NT alone. They may have a point there, since high-end Unix systems definitely outclass present NT systems in power and scalability, though Windows 2000 will considerably narrow the gap.
- Lotus disputes many of Microsoft's marketing claims about how well Exchange Server is doing compared to Notes/Domino. For example, Lotus claims that they are still number one in the messaging/

collaboration department by a wide margin with record-breaking sales each quarter, despite Microsoft's statistics to the contrary. Lotus also claims that studies show Notes/Domino entails a lower TCO than Exchange/Outlook does, while Microsoft says studies show the opposite. And while Microsoft claims that 30 of the Fortune 500 companies have chosen to standardize their messaging platform on Exchange Server, Lotus claims that Notes is deployed for both messaging and groupware in 42 of those companies. Interpret that how you will; statistics can be quite misleading, as anyone who has ever read the classic book *How to Lie with Statistics* by Darrell Huff can testify (a good read).

Both sides are probably stretching the truth in the Microsoft-Lotus war. The reality is that both are widely-implemented, powerful messaging/collaboration solutions, and who will eventually win is anyone's guess. One ace-in-the-hole that Microsoft has, however, is that it has virtually sewn up the office tools market with its Microsoft Office suite of products. The more Microsoft can leverage this to their advantage with regard to Exchange, the more Lotus has to worry about. But don't expect everybody to rush out and upgrade to Office 2000 as soon as it is released!

Exchange vs. GroupWise

Just as the Microsoft-Novell server war has picked up as late with the recent release of Novell NetWare version 5 and the delays in releasing Microsoft Windows 2000, similarly Microsoft Exchange continues to fight it out with Novell's GroupWise messaging platform. Here Microsoft seems to have a clear advantage, however. According to Microsoft, GroupWise 5.5 falls down in several key areas:

- Poor integration with Novell's own *Novell Directory Services* (NDS), while Exchange will shortly be effectively integrated into the Active directory of the upcoming Windows 2000 platform.
- Still playing catchup in the area of Internet protocol support. GroupWise has no support for the NNTP, iCalendar, or vCalendar protocols.
- Still playing catchup in the area of security, with support for S/MIME only being included in the most recent version, 5.5.
- Poor integration with Windows NT Server, since GroupWise runs as an application on NT instead of as a service. As a result, GroupWise needs its own logging and performance monitoring tools, which means

administrators need to learn new things, which means more training costs, and so on.

- No disk quota limits for individual users. Exchange does stand out in this area over GroupWise.
- No use of transaction logs for the message store database, which means that online incremental backups cannot be done, only online full backups.

And what does Novell say?

- GroupWise compares favorably with Exchange feature-by-feature and exceeds it in some areas.
- GroupWise is a cross-platform messaging/collaboration solution, with clients and server agent support for NetWare, Windows NT, and UNIX.
- The GroupWise Administrator program is integrated into the NetWare Administrator program NWAdmin, which means that GroupWise is tightly integrated with the NDS directory.

Exchange vs. Suitespot

Finally, a distant third competitor for Exchange is Netscape's Suitespot communications and Web server platform. Suitespot provides messaging, collaboration, Web publishing, and content management functionality and includes as one of its components the Netscape Collabra 3.5 mail server (which can be migrated to Exchange using the Exchange Migration yool, should you so desire). Suitespot itself more properly compares with Microsoft BackOffice Server, since it includes a directory server, certificate server, proxy server, and is usually bundled together with a third-party database program like Oracle or Informix. According to Microsoft, however:

- Suitespot must be administered using an HTML interface, while Exchange uses a single, unified administration program. Of course, an HTML interface is a plus if you have to do remote administration.
- Suitespot's security infrastructure is poorly integrated with Windows NT's security subsystem (but Suitespot is available for the UNIX platform as well).
- Exchange uses single-instance message storage while Suitspot does not—a minus if you use a lot of distribution lists for mass mailings.
- Suitespot does not support online backups but must be "taken down" in order to back up the message store.

- Suitespot only supports SMTP messaging, while Exchange also supports X.400 and connectivity with other third-party messaging solutions like Lotus Notes and cc:Mail. On the other hand, *Simple Mail Transfer Protocol* (SMTP) messaging is the standard for the Internet and is the most widely-implemented messaging protocol around. Microsoft even says that its Platinum version of Exchange (see below) will make SMTP a peer of X.400 in terms of how deeply these protocols are implemented within the Exchange architecture. Exchange currently must convert SMTP messages to its own proprietary format when storing them in its Information Store databases. Platinum will enable the MIME content of SMTP messages to be stored directly in the Information Store without needing conversion.

And what does Netscape say by way of comparing the two products? Not much. Netscape doesn't say much these days anyway. They appear to be suffering an identity crisis due to various corporate mergers and takeovers.

Where Do We Go from Here?

In the next chapter, we will look at planning an enterprise-level implementation of Exchange Server. It is important to plan your implementation before you start installing Exchange on different servers. Otherwise, you might have extra work to do or may even have to start all over again from the beginning. Included will be a discussion of the architecture of Exchange Server and the topology of an Exchange organization.

For More Information

This is probably the best time to point you towards some of the more useful Exchange resources that are available on the Internet. In later chapters, I'll try to point you to specific documents and URLs where possible, but for now we'll just list a few general ones.

Web Sites

Still one of the best places to look for information on Exchange is Microsoft's own Web site. There you will find feature sheets, licensing information, white papers, case studies, deployment tips, migration advice, extra tools, information about conferences, and a free evaluation copy of Exchange Server. It's well worth the time browsing this site, despite the marketing hoopla. Check it out at

```
www.microsoft.com/exchange
```

And if you're implementing a combined Exchange/Outlook setup, be sure to also check it out at

```
www.microsoft.com/outlook
```

If you don't have a subscription to Microsoft TechNet or if you absolutely must have up-to-the-minute technical support materials for Exchange, go to the following URL, select "Support Products by Highlight", and search for "Microsoft Exchange:"

```
support.microsoft.com/support
```

You can also access TechNet online if you don't have a subscription to the monthly CDs. This site also hosts live chats with other professionals and Webcasts of technical seminars. You need to subscribe. Check it out at

```
www.microsoft.com/technet
```

Sue Mosher's terrific Exchange site can be found at

```
www.slipstick.com
```

Other great sites for information on Exchange are

```
www.swinc.com
www.exchangestuff.com
www.msexchange.org
www.amrein.com/EWORLD
www.mail-resources.com
```

Newsgroups

A number of newsgroups are available on Microsoft Exchange/Outlook on Microsoft's public USfENET server:

```
msnews.microsoft.com
```

The newsgroups of interest fall into two general categories:

```
microsoft.public.exchange.*
microsoft.public.outlook.*
```

If you have a question, try posting to one of the more active groups like

```
microsoft.public.exchange.admin
```

Magazines

About the only one worth looking at is the one run by the editors of *Windows NT Magazine*:

```
www.winntmag.com/newsletter/exchange
```

CHAPTER 2

Planning an Exchange Organization

Introduction

In Chapter 1, "Overview of Exchange Server 5.5," we mentioned that reliable email is the lifeblood of the business world. If this is so, then proper planning is the first step in implementing Exchange in an organization. After reading this chapter, you will have a basic understanding of

- How Exchange fits into the corporate messaging environment
- 10 steps involved in planning and implementing an Exchange organization
- Different messaging topologies for an Exchange organization
- Factors to consider when planning the number of sites to use

Why Planning Is Important

Microsoft designed Exchange Server so it can be used as an "out-of-the-box" messaging solution for companies of all types. Exchange is simple to install, easy to get up and running, and provides full functionality to clients like Outlook 98 and Outlook 2000 with little configuration and tuning needed. If you are an experienced system administrator working for a fairly small company (less than 100 users), you can probably get Exchange up and running and your users connecting to it for messaging and collaboration without anything more than the Readme file included on the Exchange compact disc and the *Getting Started* manual available from Microsoft (it's also available in Books Online once you've got Exchange installed.)

On the other hand, you could easily get yourself into trouble following this approach, especially if

- Your company has hundreds or thousands of users or it is expanding fast enough that it will shortly have this many users.
- Your company has more than one physical location and the network is spread out over a *Wide Area Network* (WAN).
- You already have an existing mail system that you want to either combine with or upgrade to Exchange.

If any of these factors apply to your situation, and you're an "I-can-figure-this-out-for-myself" kind of person, you may find yourself reinstalling Exchange after a few weeks or months and wishing you had taken the time to get familiar with the product first and do a little planning before you jumped right in.

And that's what this chapter is all about. If you don't carefully plan an Exchange implementation for a large or growing company with coexistence and migration issues, you will easily find yourself in hot water and wishing you had taken the time to do things properly. Exchange is a powerful, scalable messaging solution that can supply the needs of companies ranging from a few dozen users located in one building to over a hundred thousand spread out all over the world. The larger and more complex the scenario, the better to spend time carefully evaluating your needs and planning your design before actually starting the implementation process.

Steps for Implementing Exchange

Exchange has been around long enough and has a large enough installation base that clear strategies have evolved in how to implement it in large or growing business environments. Many of these steps are just common sense, while others require a deep understanding of the technical architecture and operation of Exchange Server. Some steps are more of an art than a science, such as trying to estimate the total rate of message flow within your company and how this might evolve with time. Other steps might seem too time-intensive for the busy administrator to pursue, such as running simulation messaging trials on a testbed server to see how it performs under a load. And sometimes there is just no best way of doing things, since a trade-off is involved, such as the tradeoff between

- Using many servers, each hosting a small number of mailboxes, or using only a few servers, each hosting a large number of mailboxes.
- Using multiple sites with cheaper low-end hardware and multiple onsite administrators, or using one site with expensive high-end hardware and only a few administrators located centrally.
- Configuring, tuning, and maintaining complex messaging links like the X.400 Connector and Dynamic Remote Access Server (RAS) connector between locations linked with cheap, low-bandwidth 56- or 128-kbps WAN links, or upgrading the WAN links to expensive, high-bandwidth 1.544-Mbps T-1 lines and establishing a single easy-to-administer Exchange site.

- Configuring, tuning, and maintaining connectivity with legacy mail systems in your company like Microsoft Mail or PROFS, or migrating users and their messages to Exchange without disrupting the daily flow of users' mail.

In the following subsections, we'll be examining the various steps that can be involved in a large-scale implementation of Microsoft Exchange in your company. Not every step will apply to your situation, and some issues can be deferred until later, but it is a good idea to use this broad framework as a guide for developing your own written plan for implementing an Exchange-based messaging solution for your organization. Even if you need to bring in outside consultants at some point, this chapter will help you understand the process so you can ask intelligent questions and keep them on their toes.

In fact, that's really the secret to any effective planning process: asking lots and lots of questions. If you are doing all the planning yourself, you must answer many of your questions yourself, but you may also need to hold discussions with management concerning their needs and expectations, survey users about their present systems and how they feel about an upgrade, talk with colleagues and peers in the information technology (IT) community about their own experiences with implementing Exchange, and so on. So let's begin.

Step 1: Determine Your Users' Needs

The whole point of network applications like Exchange is to provide services for users so they will be able to do their job efficiently and easily (and so they will be able to make money for the company, so the company's shareholders will be happy, so the stock value of the company will increase its market capitalization, so that the company will have more money to hire more users, so that . . .). Therefore, any attempt at coming up with a plan to implement Exchange in an enterprise should begin and end with the users. It's no use spending a lot of time and money implementing a new messaging system in a company only to find out later that users are complaining about slow response times, cumbersome client software, inadequate mailbox quotas, or poor technical support.

These are some of the issues related to users that you should consider when planning an Exchange implementation:

- *What kind of messaging and collaboration tools do users need to get their work done? And what will they need a year or two years from now?* When doing any sort of planning for network upgrades or new applications, you should always consider three things:

- *What are we using right now?* Begin by performing an inventory of your present messaging and groupware applications (if any), looking at both the server and client side of the equation. Pay careful attention to departments that are using the same software but different versions. You may need this information when you plan your upgrades.
- *What are our current needs?* Since you're reading this book, you've determined that you need to upgrade the back end of your messaging system to Exchange, but what version of Exchange do you need? Will the standard version provide enough raw power and connectivity options to satisfy your users' needs? Or do you need the Enterprise Edition with its better memory management, greater symmetric multiprocessing support, and unlimited message store features to support your users? And from the perspective of your users, do you need to upgrade their client messaging software to Microsoft Outlook, or can you stay with your present mail client for a while? If you plan to upgrade to Outlook, which version will you be using? If you have Microsoft Office 97 installed, will you remain with Outlook 97 or will you upgrade to Outlook 98? Have you considered Outlook 2000 as an option? On the other hand, if SMTP email functionality is all your users require, will Microsoft Outlook Express be sufficient? Or are your users already used to some third-party SMTP messaging client solution like Qualcomm's Eudora Pro or Netscape Messenger?

  If Internet mail is all your users require, then any third-party SMTP messaging client will probably be sufficient. But if they need the added functionality of scheduling, contact management, task management, public folder discussion groups, and so on, then you will probably want to move them to Outlook, unless you plan to have Exchange coexist with some other groupware system that you already have installed like Lotus Notes. If that's the case, then maybe you should be asking yourself why you plan to install Exchange in the first place, as administering a single messaging/groupware system is usually easier than administering two of them, despite the connectivity options included with Exchange that allow an Exchange organization and a Lotus Notes system to interoperate. Exchange includes useful tools for migrating from existing systems like Lotus Notes, so unless there are real reasons for staying with the other system (like compatibility with partner companies' systems or the company's large investment in legacy mainframe-based systems), you are probably better off either migrating everything to Exchange or finding a different solution within the context of your existing systems framework.

Training

Have you also talked with management about factoring in costs for training users in how to effectively use any new client software you plan to install? Administrators need to be concerned about such non-technical or "soft" issues when they are planning upgrades. Management also needs to be told in no uncertain terms that just providing users with powerful tools does not usually make them experts in using them. Or does management expect you, the busy administrator, to do a quick one-hour seminar to train users on how to use the software? Is this part of your job description and do you feel qualified to train users? Chances are, you are an administrator because you're a "back-room" technically minded sort of person, and training people is not really your thing. Having spent years as a trainer and educator myself, I have seen the payoff that comes from training people properly when new systems are installed or old ones are upgraded. If you want to save yourself and your system support staff endless time and frustration, I suggest you lobby strongly with management at the very start of your Exchange project that funding for training be built-in to the whole process from the beginning and not left as a possible add-on at the end if money permits. I would even argue that you simply won't upgrade users' client messaging software unless they will be getting a minimum of a day's training on it from a professional training company like Productivity Point International. Don't back down on this as long as you feel you have the leverage to push it through. If you have been a network and systems administrator for your company for more than three years or so, you're probably indispensable to them and can have your own way if you push hard enough.

Another related issue is your own training needs as an administrator and those of your staff. Do you feel you have the necessary technical training to comfortably plan and implement the system you need? If your contract does not already provide you with several paid weeks of technical training per year at an accredited training institution, then lobby strongly for it at your next salary review. Microsoft Certified Technical Education Centers *(CTECs) are qualified to offer* Microsoft Official Curriculum *(MOC) classroom training on any Microsoft product, with most courses designed specifically for IT professionals who plan, implement, maintain, and troubleshoot Microsoft products like Exchange Server. Taking one or two weeks of MOC training on Exchange at an accredited CTEC not only provides you with reference materials, hands-on product experience, and a chance to ask your instructor questions, but it also gives you the opportunity to interact with other IT professionals taking the course, swap ideas and stories, and build a network of colleagues who can help you out with advice when you get stuck during the implementation process. See the section, "For More Information," at the end of this chapter for information about training solutions that can meet your own and your users' needs.*

- *Where will we be a year or two from now?* Always, always plan for tomorrow and not for today. If you plan your Exchange implementation on the basis of your company's current needs, then by the time you have finished implementing your new system, the needs may have escalated to the point that your original plan is underpowered and inadequate. Talk to management about future plans for the company, expected growth (or decline) in total number of employees, impending new directions and initiatives, and consider what hardware and software will be needed to support your company well into the future—at least for the next two years anyway.
- *How can the users in your company be classified as far as their messaging and collaboration needs are concerned?* Most companies contain users who have different kinds of messaging needs. Microsoft suggests that users might be classified into three different categories on the basis of their average daily use of messaging and scheduling client software. The numbers are fairly arbitrary and were devised when Exchange 4.0 was in its heyday. The corporate use of email continues to rise sharply, but the divisions they suggest are useful nevertheless:
- *Heavy users*, who typically read up to 20 messages per day, send up to eight messages per day, and make 20 schedule changes per day.
- *Moderate users*, who read 15 messages per day, send six, and make five schedule changes.
- *Light users*, who read five messages per day, send three, and make one schedule change.

  You will need to come up with numbers for each category (heavy, moderate, light) for your own company. You might do this by surveying users in different departments and analyzing the results. Or if your present mail system supports the collection of messaging statistics, collect at least a week's worth of statistics during a period of normal business activity. The main reason for doing all this work is that once you have statistics about the messaging characteristics of each type of user in your company and the number and location of those different types of users, you can then make some estimates regarding the total message storage disk space required by your users and the total network bandwidth needed to carry messaging traffic over your LAN, and especially over any WAN links you have. We'll talk about these things next.

- *What are the message storage (disk space) requirements for your users? And how will you control them?* This is one of the most important considerations to plan for in implementing Exchange. Although message storage in Exchange can be implemented in two different ways, if you are using a Microsoft Exchange/Outlook combination messaging solution, consider the following:
  - *Client-side storage*, where users' messages are stored in their personal storage folder (*.pst) files on their own machines. Although this greatly reduces the disk space (and cost) of your Exchange Server machines, it usually makes it impractical to back up users' messages. Backup agents could be installed on each user's machine to perform a network backup, but in a company that works around the clock, this would leave no available backup window and could saturate network traffic for hours each night. Most companies do not opt for this solution.
  - *Server-side storage*, where users' messages are stored in the information store on their home Exchange Server. The *information store* is a set of databases located on an Exchange Server that is used for storing messages, attachments, and other documents. Server-side storage is the solution most often chosen, since it greatly simplifies the process of backing up users' message folders. Unfortunately, this may create great demands on the amount of disk storage space needed for each Exchange Server. In addition, if maintaining a complete messaging history is important for users or is part of company policy, then high reliability for the message storage is essential. Because of this, fault-tolerant, hardware-based RAID-5 disk systems are often used for mission-critical message storage in corporate environments, and these are not cheap. Therefore, determining at the outset of your plan how much message storage space is needed (and will be needed) is an important consideration so that you don't underspend or overspend on your disk storage solution.

Network *.pst files

*A third option used by some companies is to locate users' *.pst files on a network share on a generic file server machine. RAID-5 can be used with this machine to provide fault-tolerant message storage and scalability. Using this setup simplifies backup of users' messages and can unload some* *of the work from your Exchange Server machines, although the Information store on the Exchange machines is still used for receiving messages and for processing any inbox rules users have created. But it does introduce another factor into the equation (the file server) and can have an impact on network traffic. Most administrators implement message storage on the Exchange Servers themselves.*

To determine the amount of disk space needed for each user to store their messages (both messages they receive from other users and copies of messages they themselves have sent, assuming they have configured their clients to keep copies of all sent messages), you again need to classify your users according to type. Again, the numbers for each category may not be typical for users in your company. You need to determine what storage ranges you should use for classifying your users by either analyzing the usage of your current mail servers or by sampling users' desktop machines if local *.pst files are currently being used.

- *Heavy storage requirements*, where the user's disk space needs are about 50 MB in size. Managers and executives often fall into this category, as maintaining an electronic paper trail may be essential for them in pursuing old leads, justifying their decisions, or covering their butts. I know some managers who have never deleted a single email message since they started using email and are using over 300 MB of storage space to hold their old messages. They won't consider archiving these messages since "you never know" when you might need to dig up some old message in order to get some business going. Other types of users who might fall into this category are CAD/CAM workers, graphic artists who work with large image files, and so on. The unfortunate fact is that with the advent of integrated messaging solutions for Exchange that allow users to store email, schedule information, facsimiles, voice, and multimedia content in a single Information store, it is likely that in the near future *all* users will have such heavy storage requirements.
- *Moderate storage requirements*, where users disk space needs are about 15 MB in size. This probably typifies the storage requirements of an average user in a relatively "technologically-savvy" business environment.
- *Light storage requirements*, where users disk space needs are about 5 MB in size. This probably only characterizes users to whom email is a relative newcomer in their corporate environment or simply those users who are too busy doing "real work" to bother sending a lot of email to others. It would also include those users who are functionally

tidy people and who delete old messages they no longer want (or delete old messages to cover their butts).

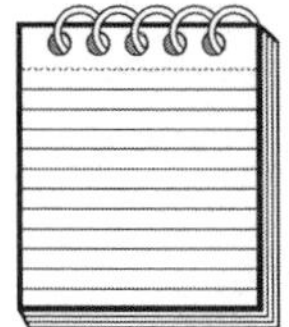

Message Journalling

Deleting an old message doesn't always cover your butt! Service Pack 1 (or higher) for Exchange 5.5 includes an additional feature called Message Journalling, which enables Exchange to save an extra copy of every message sent or received by a user in your Exchange Server organization. Some companies may want to do this in order to keep tabs on how employees are using their corporate email. Other companies may be required to maintain copies of all messages for legal reasons; even if this is not a legal requirement for your business sector or in your country, your corporate lawyers may advise you to implement this regardless. A walkthrough of how to implement Message Journalling is included in Chapter 3, "Installing Exchange," in case you need to know how to do this.

Once you have profiled the total message storage requirements for users in each location or department of your company, and once you have determined how many Exchange Servers will support each location or department in your company, you will have an idea of the total disk storage requirements for the information store on each Exchange Server in your company (we'll talk more about how many users a single Exchange Server should support in Step 8). The formula is simple. For each Exchange Server, calculate

Info Store (MB) = Number of Heavy Users * 50 MB
+ Number of Moderate Users * 15 MB
+ Number of Light Users * 5 MB

You could abbreviate this formula as

IS (MB) = 50H + 15M + 5L

However, you're not finished yet; some additional factors need to be considered when calculating the disk space needed to host the information store on an Exchange Server:

- Exchange uses a method called *single-instance storage* for storing messages that are addressed to multiple recipients, such as those addressed to recipients on a distribution list. Exchange stores only one copy of the message in the information store, along with a set of pointers (which take up very little disk space) that point to the various intended recipients. This is done to minimize the storage space used when distribution lists are heavily used. For example, if a message of size 15 kB is sent to 10 different recipients, you might expect that each recipient stores a copy of the received message in their own mailbox folders within the information store, resulting in a total of 150 kB (10 * 15) of storage space being used to store the received copies of the message. This is not the case however; only a little more than 15 kB of space is needed, since only one copy of the received message is stored along with pointers within each user's mailbox folders to where the message is located within the information store. (Note that if a message is sent to recipients on more than one Exchange Server, each server will need to store a copy of the received message within its information store.) Because of single-instance storage, the disk space requirements of the information store are reduced by a factor called the Single Instance Storage Ratio (we'll call it the SI), whose value typically ranges from one to two, depending on how heavily distribution lists are used within the company. Our formula now becomes

IS (MB) = (50H + 15M + 5L) / SI

- Exchange also includes a feature called *deleted item recovery*, which allows messages deleted by users to be temporarily saved within the information store in case the user needs to "undelete" them. Instead of permanently deleting messages, Exchange merely marks them "hidden" as far as users are concerned. If a user has unintentionally or mistakenly deleted a message and not too much time has passed, they can use the Recover Deleted Items menu in Microsoft Outlook (version 8.03 or later) to locate a deleted message and undelete it. Delete item recovery periods can be configured at the information store level (for all users) and at the mailbox level (for individual users), as will be discussed later in this book.

  The point is, if deleted item recovery is enabled for all users, this will typically add about another 10 percent or so to the storage space requirements of the information store on your Exchange Servers, and possibly even more if a long deleted item retention time is selected. Our (rather approximate) formula now becomes

  IS (MB) = 1.1 * (50H + 15M + 5L) / SI

- Next, utilities that may be used to *defragment or repair the information store,* should it become fragmented or corrupted, require a rather large working space in order to operate, typically about 100 percent of the size of the information store! So we really need to double our current disk space for the information store:

  IS (MB) = 2.2 * (50H + 15M + 5L) / SI

- Finally, we need to accommodate the *potential growth in the size of the information store* due to new employees being added to the company and existing employees becoming more "email-savvy." We should make sure we have room to grow by at least a factor of two:

  IS (MB) = 4.4 * (50H + 15M + 5L) / SI

  If, once you plug some reasonable numbers into this formula, you get some number like 37,823.09511 MB, you should *always round up*, in this case to something like 40 GB or 50 GB of storage space.

Backups

At this point, you also need to look at your disk storage requirements from the point of view of performing backups. Although the information store for Exchange Server, Enterprise Edition, is theoretically as high as 16 TB, you have to ask yourself how large an information store you can effectively backup, given your backup window time interval (typically 1 A.M. to 3 A.M. at night). If your tape backup system only supports 15 GB per hour, an information store of 50 GB might be technically unfeasible from the point of view of performing backups. Your possible solutions are to upgrade to a more powerful tape backup system or to use two or more Exchange Servers instead of one for this particular department or location within your company. How many users you should realistically host on a single Exchange Server is discussed in more detail in Step 8.

A related issue to determining message storage space requirements for users is deciding *how you will control the size of users' mailboxes*. Although a few individuals can reasonably demand unlimited message storage capabilities (the Boss is probably one of them), in most cases it makes sense to apply storage limits to users' mailboxes so that they don't get completely out of hand. Otherwise, there will be those who decide that they've just got to keep that message from a colleague who sent them the entire copy of the Encyclopaedia Britannica as an attachment to a message! Exchange allows you to configure mailbox size limits at both the information store level (for all users) and at the mailbox level (for individual users), as will be discussed later in this book.

Another thing to note is that thus far we have only talked about the disk storage requirements for users to store mailbox folders (message and attachments) within the information store. These items are stored within the *private information store*, so the formula we derived above is only applicable for the private information store on an Exchange Server. There's also a *public information store* that is used to store the messages and documents that are posted to *public folders* hosted on Exchange Servers. If your company makes (or plans to make) collaboration between users using public folders a high-workflow priority, then you also need to estimate the total amount of disk space that will be needed to store public folders and their contents. Since you can implement Exchange with separate servers hosting mailboxes and public folders, this typically is a separate estimate that needs to be done. We will leave it for you as an exercise to come up with a formula for how to estimate the total disk storage space for the public information store on Exchange public folder servers in your enterprise.

- *What are the message traffic (network bandwidth) requirements for your users? And how will you control them?* This is also an important consideration when you plan an implementation of Exchange in your company. Unfortunately, calculating network traffic due to message traffic is not a trivial task, even though it is so obviously important. After all, if you are implementing a powerful messaging solution like Exchange, you have to make sure your network can accommodate the added traffic that might result. If you don't plan for this ahead of time, you may find yourself coming cap-in-hand to your boss after setting up your Exchange servers and asking for "more gruel" so that you can buy some new 100-Mbps Ethernet switches. It would have been much better to anticipate this need in advance!

  In Step 3, we'll talk more about profiling your company network, but for now let's try to ask a simple question: if you have N users each sending about M messages per day, with the average size of a message being S kilobytes, how much network bandwidth can Exchange and its clients be expected to use? The answer to this question can depend on a lot of different factors:

  - Is the traffic fairly uniform during the day or does it *peak significantly at certain times of the day?* Available network bandwidth for Exchange (that is, total bandwidth minus bandwidth used by all other network applications) must be able to accommodate traffic bursts significantly above the average; otherwise, bottlenecks occur that may cause unacceptable delays in message delivery. Bursts in network traffic can result from more frequent messages than average and larger messages than average, or both.
  - What is the *messaging topology of your Exchange organization*? Do you have many sites or just one large site? Are you using a lot of low-

powered servers or just a few high-powered ones? Are you using dedicated servers that each function in a particular role, such as mailbox servers, public folder servers, and connector (gateway) servers? Or do most of your servers function in multiple roles? All of these factors are important in determining the actual possible paths that messages may flow about your network, and hence can have a significant impact from point to point on how much bandwidth Exchange will utilize.

- How many Exchange Servers have a *public information store* on them? Even if they are not being used to host public folder replicas, twice each day (12:15 A.M. and 12:15 P.M. GMT) a process runs on each Exchange Server to check if a status message regarding the public folder hierarchy has been sent within the last 24 hours. If no such message has been sent, the server having a public information store creates and sends one to all other servers having public information stores. A good tip for minimizing this traffic is to remove the public information store from any Exchange Servers in your organization that will *not* be used to host public folder replicas (you can always create a new public information store on them later if you change your mind.) If your users tend to create a lot of public folders, note that each time a public folder is created (or deleted) a similar status message is created and sent by the server hosting the new public folder to all other servers having a public information store.
- Public folder replication traffic itself can be a significant source of Exchange-related background traffic on the network. Where possible, try to use *public folder affinity,* instead of replicating folders between sites.
- In addition to email and public folder traffic, Exchange generates a lot of *special Exchange-related network traffic* for its own internal operation, especially in a multi-site environment. Each of these system functions generates traffic of a particular size and frequency, some of which can be tailored and scheduled, while others can't. (Messages created and sent by users cannot be scheduled and are sent as soon as possible by Exchange). Typical sources of such additional traffic (sometimes called "background traffic") include the following:
    - Directory replication between Exchange Servers within a site and between servers in different sites. This in turn depends on the messaging topology of your organization, the frequency with which directory information is updated in the Exchange directory, how directory replication traffic is scheduled, and so on. If you delete objects from the Exchange directory, this also causes network

traffic as *tombstones* are replicated between all Exchange servers in your organization. Most directory replication traffic is related to the transmission of updates themselves; very little is needed for the overhead of the directory replication process.

- Another factor affecting directory replication traffic is the number of attributes you have specified for your mailbox objects. For example, when you create a new mailbox, you only specify the user's last and first names, alias, and directory name and leave everything else blank. It will take about 3.5 kB of traffic to replicate this information to another server in that site. However, if you populate all the fields on the Mailbox property sheet, including Address, City, State, Phone numbers, and so on, the traffic needed to replicate the updated information increases to about 5.8 kB.
- Another factor related to directory replication is whether you are replicating information between servers in the same site or between servers in different sites. Intra-site (within a site) replication traffic is always sent in uncompressed form using RPCs, while inter-site (between sites) replication traffic may be compressed up to five times by directory replication bridgehead servers if sufficient directory updates warrant doing so (if more than 50 kB of replication traffic needs to be compressed, Exchange automatically compresses the traffic to utilize bandwidth more efficiently.)
- Adding a new Exchange server to a site results in the entire directory database being replicated to the new server. This should obviously be done during low-usage periods like late at night or on weekends in order to avoid maxing out the network and preventing people from accessing their mail. If you have to add an Exchange Server to an existing site at a new location, which is at the end of a slow WAN link, you may want to actually build the machine and install Exchange on it at the existing location where the other Exchange Servers are located. Once its directory has been updated, physically move it to the other location at the end of the WAN link.
- The type of connector used to join sites together can affect the amount of network traffic generated when these connectors are used for forwarding messages. The X.400 Connector is more efficient byte-wise for forwarding messages between sites and generally makes better use of available bandwidth than either the Site connector or the *Internet Mail Service* (IMS). The X.400 Connector suffers in one obvious area, however: security. Message headers and body part names are transmitted in clear text

(unencrypted) by the X.400 Connector and anyone using a packet sniffer on the network link would be able to read this information directly. The Site connector, although it may result in perhaps 10 to 50 percent more network traffic than the X.400 Connector (the smaller the average message, the more efficient the X.400 Connector is with regard to bandwidth usage), is generally preferred when possible due to its greater resiliency and its encryption of session traffic.

- The *Knowledge Consistency Checker* (KCC) runs every three hours on each Exchange Server, which causes traffic between Exchange sites. This is discussed later in the book.
- If RPC connectivity between two servers in the same site cannot be established within 30 seconds (perhaps due to network congestion), RPC error messages are generated (causing additional network congestion).
- If Exchange servers are deployed on Windows NT member servers, network traffic will occur when Exchange servers need to authenticate users trying to log on to their mailboxes with domain controllers on the network (this traffic occurs even though the users are already logged on to their workstations.)
- Are link and server monitors running to monitor the status of services on your Exchange Servers and the status of your messaging links? If so, this will cause additional Exchange-related traffic.
- Network backup traffic, as far as it is related to your Exchange Servers, must also be considered Exchange-related traffic and can consume significant bandwidth at certain times of the day. It's always a good idea to use a separate subnet connecting your servers to your tape drive units to avoid using general network bandwidth for doing backups.

As a result of the above considerations, you can see that our simple question involving the variables N, M, and S has no easy answer. The best that can usually be done is to monitor the messaging-related traffic for your existing mail system, perform some intelligent "guesstimates," and try to implement Exchange in your company using the various guidelines and tips that you find throughout this book. A time-consuming but worthwhile exercise if you are going to install dozens of Exchange Servers in an enterprise is to perform a testbed installation and simulate the message traffic load against your target hardware platform. See Step 8 for more.

Homing Mailboxes

Of all the issues relating to optimizing messaging traffic, organizational structure and network topology are probably the most significant. A few important methods can minimize the contribution due to message traffic in terms of the total amount of Exchange-related traffic that can occur on your network:

- *First, try to determine patterns in message flow within your company. If users in the accounting department send 80 percent of their messages to users in the same department and only 20 percent of their messages to users in other departments, try to locate all mailboxes of accounting department users on the same Exchange Server. In this way, a message sent from one accounting user to another doesn't have to be handled by the Exchange* Message Transfer Agent *(MTA) service (the component of Exchange responsible for routing messages from one mail server to another) and is instead handled locally by the information store service. In other words, no network traffic is generated, other than the clients connecting to the server to send and retrieve messages. An Exchange Server on which a user's mailbox is located is considered in Exchange terminology to be the user's* home server, *and the user's mailbox is said to be* homed *on that server.*
- *Second, wherever possible, group users who frequently need to send messages to each other on the same network segment. A* network segment *is a portion of a LAN or WAN that is separated from other segments by devices such as bridges or routers. By locating similar users and their mailboxes on the same network segment, congestion at bridges and routers can be relieved and network traffic can be localized instead of being added to that of other segments.*

Similar arguments can be made for where to locate public folder servers as well.

- *What are the specific connectivity needs of your different types of users?* In a large organization, different users may have different special connectivity needs. Here are some examples:
  - Mobile users need to be able to access their email remotely. You might implement this using the Dynamic RAS Connector together with the Remote Access Service (RAS) of Windows NT server. On the other hand, you may decide to use a public Web server and implement the *Outlook Web Access* (OWA) feature of Exchange to allow users to access their mail using only a standard Web browser like Internet Explorer or Netscape Navigator.

- Special groups might need access to public messaging systems like the Internet's SMTP mail system or a public X.400 messaging network like those used in Europe. You need to determine where these users are located in your company and on which Exchange servers you will install the necessary connectors.
- For security and confidentiality reasons, management may require that all communications by certain groups of users make use of public-key encryption mechanisms. You will need to install the *Key Management* (KM) Server component on one of your Exchange Servers in order to use of this feature.

The best thing to do here is to profile the different groups of users in your company and list the specific needs they may have.

Step 2: Identify Your Company's Organization and Locations

You've probably already done this in order to access the needs of your users, but, if not, profile the organizational structure and geographical locations for your company. The organizational structure will be helpful for identifying groups of users who could have their mailboxes homed on the same server (see the previous note "Homing Mailboxes"), and the geographical information will help you later on in determining the locations of your Exchange sites and the boundaries between them.

It can be helpful if you make some sort of block diagram showing the various locations, with the size of the blocks roughly representing the number of users at each location. An alternative is to use a copy of a real map (of your city, state, country, continent, or the whole world, depending on the size and scope of your enterprise) and mark the locations of your business centers using dots of different sizes. I prefer the block diagram since it is more conceptual and abstracts away unnecessary information.

Step 3: Profile Your Company's Network

The next thing to do is to add details of your network connectivity to your block diagram or map of your enterprise, showing the types of LANs used at each location and the type of WAN connection between different locations. This is an important step in the planning process, because your messaging system will run on top of your network and will be subject to the limitations and characteristics of the network itself. In fact, it is not uncommon during this stage of the planning process to discover that you may need to upgrade your LAN speeds in order to support the anticipated extra network traffic due to the increased use of messaging services. Typically, you may also upgrade your WAN links or add additional ones in order to provide redundancy for fault-tolerance purposes.

Some of the issues you need to consider here are:

- *How large is your entire network?* If your network is very large with multiple WAN links, then you may want to create a number of Exchange sites and use various connectors to connect these sites together, especially if the WAN links are slow links such as dedicated 56- or 64-kbps DDS leased lines, dedicated 56- or 64-kbps Frame Relay links, dial-up 64- or 128-kbps ISDN connections, or dedicated or dial-up X.25 packet-switching services. On the other hand, if you have faster WAN links such as dedicated 1.544-Mbps T-1 lines or super fast 44.736-Mbps T-3 lines, you are probably better off using only a single site, instead of multiple sites. This issue of when to use one site and when to deploy multiple sites is discussed further in Step 5.
- *Which type of LAN architecture and WAN links are you using?* The most popular LAN architecture being deployed today is *Switched Ethernet*, which uses high-speed, 100-Mbps switches to connect stations together, instead of hubs. This is because hubs provide a form of connectivity called a collision domain. All stations that are part of the same collision domain must contend for access to the network and share its total available bandwidth. And because of collisions that occur when two or more stations simultaneously try to gain access to the network, hubs don't even deliver the total bandwidth that they promise. The more stations you have connected to a hub (or a series of hubs if they are cascaded or stacked together), the more collisions occur and the greater the bandwidth losses. For example, a 100-Mbps hub will typically sustain a maximum network bandwidth of only 60 percent, or about 60 Mbps. If 10 stations (servers or workstations) are connected to this hub, each station typically only receives one-tenth of this network bandwidth, or a *total available bandwidth* per station of only 6 Mbps (1/10 * 60). Now for normal email messaging, this might seem like more than enough, but if your users regularly attach large files, like medical imaging files, to their messages and send them, then a fair chunk of bandwidth may be eaten up. In addition, you need to consider the bandwidth used by all the other applications running on the network: domain controllers synchronizing, users logging on and off, database programs, intranet HTTP traffic, Duke Nukem (oops!), and whatever else might be in use at your company.

Pretty soon those 100 Mbps hubs start to look pretty anemic, and the *net available bandwidth* for each station may just barely be enough to support text-based messaging and Exchange replication traffic.

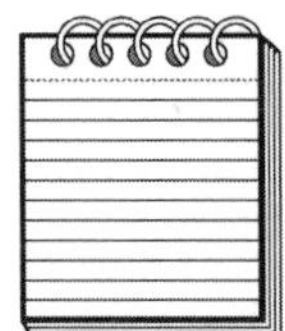

Available Bandwidth

The formula is simply:

Net Available Bandwidth for Exchange	=	*Total Available Bandwidth*	–	*Bandwidth Used by Other Applications*

The total available bandwidth of a LAN or WAN connection is determined by the hardware used or the level of service provided by the telecommunications carrier. The net available bandwidth can be determined using a network sniffer like Microsoft Network Monitor, which is included with Microsoft Systems Management Server *(SMS). You can use Network Monitor to view instantaneous information about the percent of network utilization (which indicates the net available bandwidth) and frames per second (which lets you know how busy your routers and bridges are).*

When collecting information about network traffic patterns, especially over slow WAN links, you also determine the traffic patterns of your link. This includes measuring bandwidth utilization during different times of the day over a period of at least a week and looking for peak bursts in traffic when the network is most heavily used. These bursts need to be characterized both in terms of their size and duration to see whether they will have a significant impact on the flow of messaging and other Exchange-related traffic when it is introduced. A good tool for characterizing network link usage with time is Performance Monitor, one of the administrative tools included with Windows NT Server. You should collect statistics on bytes total / second for the network link under consideration and analyze its variation with time.

The solution is to upgrade your hubs to 100-Mbps Ethernet switches. An Ethernet switch forms a momentarily dedicated connection between the transmitting and receiving stations that are connected to its ports. The result is that each station on the LAN receives a full 100-Mbps of total available bandwidth, which is enough for all but the most bandwidth-hungry applications. If your LANs are still running 100-Mbps hubs (or even slower media like 10BaseT or thinnet, 4- or 16-Mbps Token Ring, or 2.5 Mbps ArcNet), you may need to seriously consider whether your underlying network architecture will be able to support the enhanced messaging services that Exchange will be providing to your users.

You need to even more carefully consider the capacities of your *WAN links* and whether they should be upgraded. Having all your Exchange Servers deployed in a single site simplifies the job of administering your Exchange messaging system, but minimum net available bandwidth that needs to exist between two Exchange Servers in order for them to be deployed in the same site is 64 kbps. Note that this is net available bandwidth, not total available bandwidth. A 128-kbps Frame Relay link has a total available bandwidth of 128 kbps, but if it is being used for other purposes, such as remote database access, synchronizing remote BDCs, and so on, the net available bandwidth left for Exchange-related purposes may be only 30 or 40 kbps. This isn't enough to allow you to establish acceptable intra-site connectivity and forces you to deploy your two locations as two different sites.

- *What network operating systems and protocols are you currently running?* If you already use Windows NT Server 4.0 as your in-house network operating system and TCP/IP as your network protocol, upgrading to Exchange Server should be simple. Just make sure you upgrade your servers to Service Pack 3 or higher for Windows NT before you install Exchange on any of them.

  If you are running a mixed NetWare/NT environment, or you need to bring Windows NT into your NetWare-based network in order to use Exchange as your messaging solution, there are some things you need to consider:

  - If you have already deployed *TCP/IP* as your network protocol in your NetWare environment, implementing Exchange will be easy. Just install Windows NT Server 4.0 on your new machines (along with Service Pack 3 or higher) along with Exchange Server, and create a Windows NT account on a PDC and a mailbox on your Exchange Server for testing purposes. Then install a Microsoft network client on your NetWare workstations, and install the appropriate messaging client like Outlook on the workstations. Now log on to the PDC with the Windows NT account as well as to the Exchange mailbox using Outlook. If everything works fine, you're ready to either set up your NT/Exchange accounts/mailboxes and have your Exchange-based messaging system begin to coexist with your existing messaging system, or more likely you are ready to begin migrating the account and mailbox information from your existing system to NT/Exchange.
  - If you are using a NetWare-based network that supports only *IPX/SPX* as the LAN protocol, you'll need to also install Microsoft's NWLink IPX/SPX-compatible transport protocol and possibly *Gateway Services for*

NetWare (GSNW) on the Windows NT Server before installing Exchange on that machine. NWLink supports the RPC mechanism needed for MAPI-based Exchange clients like Outlook to communicate with Exchange Server and for Exchange Servers within a site to communicate with each other. Installing GSNW enables your Exchange Server to have direct access to file and print services running on a NetWare server, which could be important if you want to migrate your NetWare user accounts and Novell GroupWise mailboxes to Windows NT and Exchange, for example. Additionally, if the network segment on which the Exchange Server is running has no NetWare server running on it, you need to install the SAP Agent service on the Exchange Server so that it can advertise its networking services to NetWare clients on the segment. If your client machines are running Windows 98, you should install both Client for Microsoft Networks and Client for NetWare Networks on your user workstations to enable them to connect with both the NT Server running Exchange and the NetWare File and Print servers on the network. If your client machines are running NT Workstation, you should install *Client Services for NetWare* (CSNW) on these machines to allow them to access both server operating systems on the network.

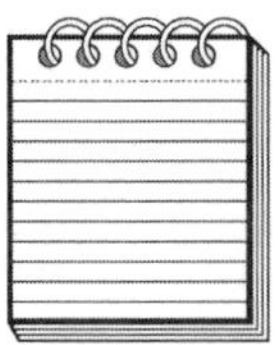

NetWare and TCP/IP

Better yet, if you are still running Novell NetWare 3.x or 4.x with IPX/SPX, and if you don't want to upgrade your file and print services to Windows NT Server, consider upgrading your servers to NetWare 5 with its native support for TCP/IP. Using TCP/IP greatly simplifies running Exchange as your messaging system in a Novell networking environment. After all, if you are planning to do one upgrade (to Exchange), why not do two at the same time? Spend the money while you got it! Opportunities (and money) for major upgrades are often few and far between.

If you are running some other legacy network protocol such as NetBEUI or AppleTalk, you probably want to upgrade your network to TCP/IP before you go any further. TCP/IP is the network protocol of choice nowadays, because of its power and flexibility and because it is required for connectivity with the Internet.

- *How much do your WAN links cost to use?* Most bandwidth-on-demand WAN links like dial-up ISDN and Frame Relay have a flat monthly fee together with a per-packet or per-minute usage charge. You need to check out what you are currently using and how much it costs, since upgrading to dedicated, high-speed, fixed-cost links like T-1 lines may seem overly expensive but could, in fact, turn out to be highly cost-effective.

Costs have another dimension as well. You will probably want to set up redundant WAN links between different locations to ensure that messaging services are maintained by the backup link, should the primary link go down. A primary WAN link might typically be a T-1 or fractional T-1 link, while a backup link could be Frame Relay, ISDN, or even a 56-kbps V.90 modem connection. When you configure the message-routing table, *Gateway Address Routing Table* (GWART), for your Exchange Servers, which govern the flow of messages throughout your organization and beyond, the faster primary link can be given a lower routing cost value to ensure it is instead of the slower secondary link, unless the primary link goes down, in which case the GWART automatically routes messages over the secondary link to ensure they are delivered to their destination.

WAN Link Costs and the Number of Sites

As a general rule, if two company locations are linked by a WAN link whose cost is based on the amount of data sent over the link, you probably want to make each location a separate site. This will allow you to have finer control over the amount of Exchange-related traffic between the two locations.

- *Will your LAN devices and WAN links support the necessary transport protocols for your messaging solution?* This is probably only a concern if you are planning to implement the X.400 Connector for connecting to a public X.400-based messaging system, such as the ATLAS system in France. X.400 is a commonly used messaging protocol in Europe and in certain parts of Asia, and the X.400 Connector for Exchange supports three different types of network transport for connecting to these systems: TP0/X.25 (public packet-switching service), TP4/CLNP (Ethernet), and TCP/IP (Internet). If you are using anything other than TCP/IP, you may need to make sure that your access routers support the transport protocol you are using.

Remember, once you have gathered information to answer all these questions, add information about your network to the block diagram or map you made in the previous step. This will give you a concise and intuitive look at your needs and capabilities and will greatly assist you in the rest of the planning process.

Step 4: Establish Naming Conventions

Before you plan your sites (one of the main steps in planning an Exchange implementation), you need to consider how to name them and other elements of your Exchange messaging system. Before we can discuss this, we need to discuss the hierarchical nature of an Exchange messaging system, and this is as good a time as any to do so. The Exchange hierarchy has three main levels:

- The *Organization*, which represents the topmost entity in the Exchange hierarchy and comprises all the Exchange sites and their servers within your enterprise. The name of your organization should be unique, representative of the name of the largest business unit characterizing your enterprise and should represent something that does not change with time, as changing the name of your organization involves reinstalling Exchange on all Exchange Server machines within your enterprise. You can use up to 64 characters to name your organization. As an example (which we shall use in this book), a suitable name for a company's Exchange organization whose main business identifier is MTIT Enterprises might be simply MTIT. You must specify the name of the organization you are joining (or creating) when you install Exchange on a machine.
- *Sites*, which represent groupings of Exchange Servers, typically are the result of geographical reasons. The name of a site should be unique, representative of the name of the business unit at that location (or the location itself), and should not change with time, as changing the name of a site involves reinstalling Exchange on all Exchange Server machines within that site. (However, Service Pack 1 includes the Move Server Wizard which makes reinstalling Exchange unnecessary) A company with offices in Atlanta, Seattle, and Miami might have an Exchange organization with three sites named Atlanta, Seattle, and Miami respectively. Site names can be up to 64 characters in length. You must specify the name of the site you are joining (or creating) when you install Exchange on a machine.
- *Servers*, which are groupings of Exchange Servers within a specific site. The name of a server should be unique, easy to remember, and should not change with time, as changing the name of a server involves reinstalling both Windows NT and Exchange on the machine. Server names can be up to 15 characters in length. You specify the name of a server when you install Windows NT Server on a machine. Note that in Windows NT parlance, the server name is called the NetBIOS name of the machine.

Naming Servers

If you plan to use DNS for host name resolution on your network, don't use underscore characters ("_") in your server names. Use dashes ("–") instead, as name servers can handle these. If you plan to use logon scripts, do not include any spaces in the names of your domain controllers.

The only other decision you should make at this point regarding naming conventions is how you will name *mailboxes* for your users. Probably the simplest solution is to name users' mailboxes after their Windows NT user account names. For a user like Mary Smith, a typical Windows NT username might be MSmith or MaryS. If this is the case, then your mailbox naming will be simple. Occasionally, two users might merit the same username; for example, Mary Smith and Martin Smith might both logically be assigned the username MSmith. The resolution in this case is to name one account MSmith1 and the other MSmith2 or something similar. Such username assigments can get sticky, especially in government agencies where Mary Smith's username becomes MSmith-MKT for Mary Smith in the marketing department.

The same situation exists for Exchange mailboxes, but the only difference is that when you create a new Windows NT user account, you must manually specify the username, while with Exchange the mailbox name or alias name can be automatically generated from the user's given name, initials, and surname. For more information on how to consider Auto Naming options, see Chapter 5, "Tools for Administration."

Step 5: Determine Site Boundaries

We are now ready for some major decisions, namely, how many Exchange sites we will install in our organization, where the boundaries of these sites will be, and how messaging connectivity will be established between them. These are all crucial decisions that can affect the efficiency, reliability, and even the viability of our Exchange implementation. This process is generally called determining the *messaging topology* of your Exchange organization.

First, we need to look a little deeper into this idea of an Exchange site. We said before that a site is a grouping of Exchange Servers, usually based on geographical considerations. This is a bit of a simplification. The following paragraph is a more technical and abstract-sounding definition of an Exchange site.

> An Exchange site is a grouping of Exchange Servers that are connected by network links that can support high-speed synchronous *remote procedure call* (RPC) connections.

This sounds like a bit of a mouthful, but let's take a look of it one part at a time so it becomes more understandable. What it really says is that underlying network transports between all Exchange Servers in a site must

- *Support RPC connections.* Exchange Servers within a site use RPCs to exchange directory information with each other. This is different from servers in different sites that communicate with each other by using system-generated email messages (using whatever mail transport has been established between the sites by the installed connector).
- *Be a permanent network connection.* In order to have synchronous communications, the link between each pair of servers must be permanent, that is, not a dialup connection. By contrast, the Dynamic RAS Connector together with the RAS of Windows NT Server can be used to establish messaging connectivity between Exchange Servers located in different sites.
- *Have sufficient net available bandwidth.* We mentioned before that a good rule of thumb is that Exchange Servers can only be in the same site if they have at least 64 kbps of net available bandwidth on the network link joining them together. In practice, it is probably safer to increase this to a minimum of 128 kbps. What this means in practice is that Exchange Servers within a specific site are connected by either a
  - LAN connection through a switch or hub
  - T-1 or fractional T-1 line
  - Dedicated Frame Relay connection
  - Some other high-speed WAN connection

Now that we have a better idea of what a site is, we can look at how to determine the number of sites we need to implement and the boundaries or extent of these sites. We will consider three rules of thumb in discussing how to establish site boundaries in an organization:

- The first rule of thumb is *define sites on the basis of geographical location.* In other words, if a company called MTIT Enterprises has three different offices in Atlanta, Seattle, and Miami, then you should probably create three sites for your MTIT organization. At least, there's no real reason for creating more than three sites. In the early days of implementing Exchange, some administrators tried to create sites on the basis of organization functions also. Thus, at the head office there would be one site for management, one for marketing, one for technical support, and so on. This idea was quickly abandoned because it became an administrative nightmare. Geography is really the only valid basis for creating Exchange sites, since offices in different locations are generally connected by slow, expensive WAN links, instead of the fast, cheap network connectivity that exists in even a simple 10BaseT LAN.

- The second rule of thumb may seem to contradict the first: *use as few sites as possible (and only one if feasible.)* The main reason for this is simplicity of administration. The essential ingredient for using a single, large site instead of multiple, different sites is to have lots of available network bandwidth, and WAN bandwidth has been steadily dropping in price in the last few years as new connectivity options have been offered by telecommunications service carriers. Furthermore, the importance of email and workflow applications has been steadily increasing, justifying the cost of investing in more expensive, dedicated, high-speed WAN links to replace existing slow ones.

  Another reason for using as few sites as possible is to *keep the size of the message routing tables (GWART) down in size.* The larger and more complex the messaging topology (number and interconnectivity of sites) of your Exchange organization, the heavier the load on the MTA components of your Exchange Servers as they process messages to determine which route they should be sent over. This is especially true of *mesh topology* networks (see Figure 2-1), where there are numerous redundant interconnections between different locations or sites.

  As a simple example, if there are N sites in an Exchange organization, all fully connected to every other site in a complete mesh topology configuration, then each site will be connected to N-1 other sites and the total number of network paths will be N*(N-1), which increases approximately as the square of the number of sites. But the GWART can contain entries for all possible routes to all possible sites in the organization. A little fiddling with the math suggests that the maximum number of entries for the GWART grows roughly at the rate of N^N or exponentially with the number of sites N. So it pays to keep the number of sites low in your organization, at least for a mesh topology. Why use a mesh topology then, even with only a few sites? The answer is simple: redundancy. In a messaging system based on a mesh topology, a WAN link between two sites could go down and there's always another route by which messages can travel between the two sites. So some degree of redundancy is always recommended.

On the other hand, most really large Exchange implementations these days are based on a *hub-and-spoke topology*, in which one site is chosen as the central site to which all other sites are connected. The hub site is typically located at corporate headquarters, while branch offices in different locations form their own sites and are connected directly to the hub site and not to each other. All message routing therefore takes place through the hub, which needs to have servers that are powered accordingly. Servers in the hub site are basically dedicated to functions like messaging routing and inter-site connectivity, while most users' mailboxes are located at the spoke sites. Unlike the mesh topology described above, however, this system does not have routing tables that grow as quickly when the number of sites increases. In fact, there is only one path between any two spoke sites, through the hub. So with N spoke sites each connected to N other sites (namely N-1 spoke sites plus the hub site), the number of GWART entries is of the order of N^2. To compare the two systems, the number of GWART entries in a five-site spoke-and-hub network would be about 5^2 or 25, while the same number of sites in a mesh topology network could generate a GWART with somewhere around 5^5 or over 3,000 different entries.

Unfortunately, using a hub-and-spoke messaging topology also introduces a single point of failure for your message system: the hub. If the hub site at the headquarters goes down, all messaging between different branches immediately ceases. And if a WAN link between a spoke site and the hub goes down, that spoke site is effectively isolated from the rest of the organization. Of course, there are ways around these problems. For example, you can install connectors on several Exchange Servers at the hub for maintaining connectivity with the spoke sites, instead of just on one connector server. That way, if one connector server goes down, others can take its place. You can also have a backup dialup modem or ISDN links set up between the spoke sites and the hub so that if the primary WAN link goes down between a spoke site and the hub, the backup link can kick in to maintain some degree of messaging traffic.

Locating the hub site at company headquarters only works if you have a clearly defined central location in its organizational structure. But what if it doesn't? If administrative functions of your company are distributed across multiple locations, and provided you have high-speed permanent network connectivity between these locations, they can all constitute a single hub site to which the spoke sites can attach. And if even the spoke sites have high-speed permanent network connectivity

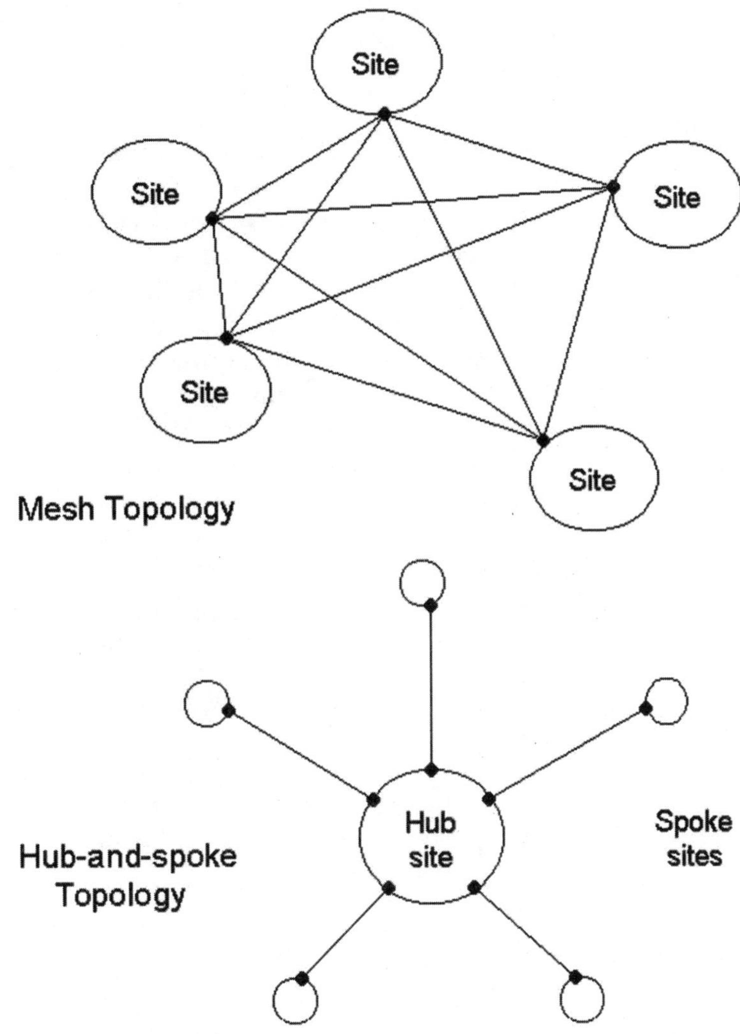

Figure 2-1 Two different Exchange messaging topologies for an enterprise.

installed, you may as well just use one large Exchange site and keep things as simple as possible.

Limits of Sites

At what point does the number of sites start to become a problem? Experience shows that if you have about 30 or more sites, you've got to start paying careful attention to how you tune the various replication processes that Exchange Server uses: directory replication, public folder replication, and address book view replication.

- The third rule of thumb is *Exchange Servers can only be in the same site if they are either in the same Windows NT domain or in domains that trust each other*. They key point here is that you must consider your existing Windows NT domain structure when defining your site boundaries. Two Exchange Servers located in different domains that have no trust between them cannot be in the same site, as authenticated RPC connections cannot be established between them. So generally speaking, one Exchange site can span several domains, provided trusts exist between the domains. These trusts do not need to be in both directions, as long as you use the trusted domain as the one in which to locate all user accounts, including the Exchange Service Account. This enables both users and Exchange services to be authenticated anywhere within the site. And just as one site can span several domains, one domain can contain several sites, as in a Windows NT network with WAN connections to remote locations that uses a single domain model. There is no hard-and-fast rule about how to match domains to sites—just keep it simple!

At this point in the planning process, you should be able to indicate on your block diagram or network map where your site boundaries are located.

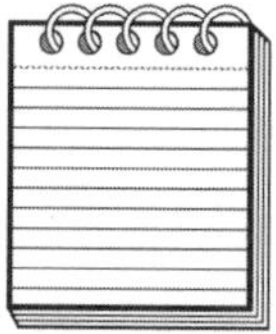

Domain Models

Implementers of Windows NT at the enterprise level (meaning when thousands or tens of thousands of users are distributed over multiple locations) generally base the domain structure of their networks on one of four different models (see Figure 2-2):

- *The* Single Domain Model, *which is good for about 25,000 user accounts and the simplest to implement and administer.*
- *The* Single Master Domain Model, *consisting of one master (accounts) domain trusted by multiple resource domains. This allows user administration to be separated from resource administration. Many large companies that have a central headquarters and a number of branch offices use this model.*
- *The* Multiple Master Domain Model, *consisting of several master (accounts) domains trusted by multiple resource domains. This model is scalable to perhaps 100,000 user accounts or more, but it suffers from having a lot of trust relationships to administer (and a lot of global and local groups to create). This complex model is not widely implemented and is one of the reasons why Windows NT does not scale so well in the enterprise. Windows 2000 with its Active Directory will overcome these limitations.*

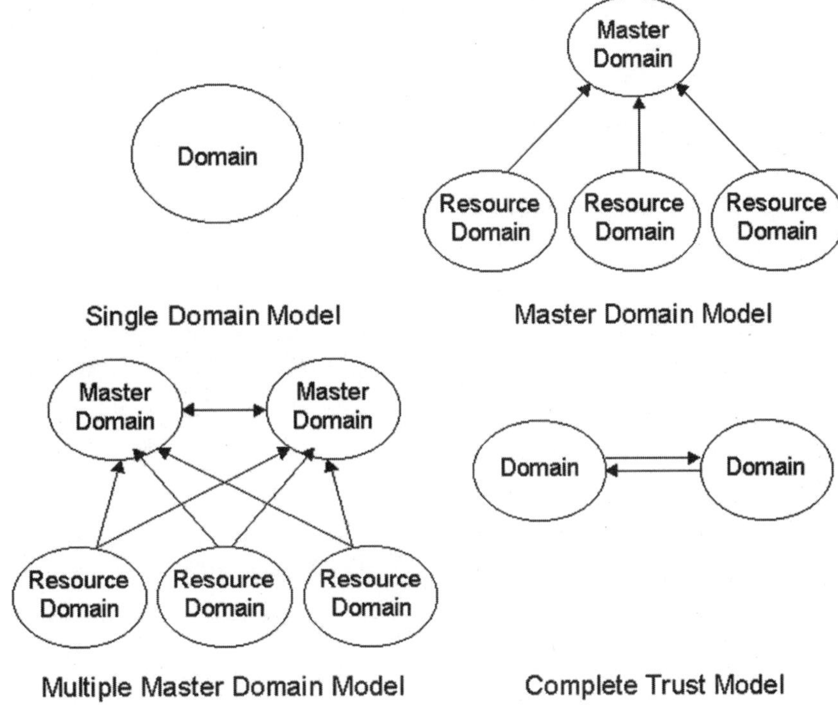

Figure 2-2
The four different domain models for Windows NT.

- *The* Complete Trust Model*, in which every domain trusts every other domain with two-way trusts. This model is more widely implemented than it should be and is usually implemented by administrators who don't know what they're doing (but make it work anyway).*

Step 6: Establish Messaging Connectivity

Now that you have decided on the locations and boundaries of your sites, you need to select connectors for establishing messaging connectivity and directory replication between your sites. You also need to consider how to establish connectivity with foreign mail systems your users may need access to, like the Internet's SMTP mail system or a public X.400-based messaging system, or even connecting to some other Exchange organization. The different connectivity tasks are listed here:

- *Connecting sites together within your organization.* Sites must be linked together for a number of reasons, such as exchanging email messages and replicating directory information or public folder contents. Four different choices can be made regarding which connector to use for joining two sites together. These four choices are

- Site Connector
- X.400 Connector
- Dynamic RAS (DRAS) Connector
- Internet Mail Service (IMS)

Each of these connectors has its own advantages and disadvantages as far as joining sites together is concerned, as summarized in Table 2-1.

- *Connecting your organization to other mail systems.* The X.400 Connector and Internet Mail Service described above can be used to

Table 2-1

Connectors for Joining Sites Together.

Connector	Advantages	Disadvantages
Site	▪ Easy to configure ▪ No message translation is performed	▪ Needs a permanent network connection (LAN or dedicated WAN link) ▪ Message size cannot be controlled ▪ Connection cannot be scheduled
X.400	▪ Message size can be controlled ▪ Connection can be scheduled ▪ Routing of messages can be controlled ▪ Most efficient use of network bandwidth ▪ Can connect sites together over a public or private X.400 backbone messaging system	▪ More complex to configure ▪ Must configure network transport which routers/bridges must also support
DRAS	▪ Connection can be scheduled and controlled ▪ Works over non-permanent (dial-up) network connections	▪ More complex to configure (requires an understanding of Windows NT RAS) ▪ Slow—usually used with modems or dial-up ISDN connections ▪ Is said to be unreliable—breaks easily
IMS	▪ Message size can be controlled ▪ Can be configured to send, receive, or send and receive ▪ Can connect sites together over the SMTP mail system of the Internet	▪ More complex to configure ▪ Connection cannot be scheduled ▪ Message translation must be performed

connect your Exchange sites together and to establish messaging connectivity between your Exchange organization and a foreign (external) messaging such as the Internet. In addition, Exchange includes several other connectors that can be similarly used:

- MS Mail Connector, for connecting your Exchange organization to a legacy Microsoft Mail messaging system
- Lotus Notes Connector, for interoperating with third-party Lotus Notes systems
- cc:Mail Connector, for connecting to Lotus cc:Mail systems
- PROFS and SNADS connectors, used in conjunction with Microsoft SNA Server for providing messaging connectivity between your Exchange organization and an IBM mainframe-based messaging system like PROFS or SNADS

Using the characteristics of these four connectors, choose suitable connectors for joining your sites together and mark them on your block diagram or network map. Indicate also which sites will implement connectivity with legacy, third-party, and foreign mail systems.

Step 7: Plan for Coexistence and Migration

You may want to establish messaging connectivity (coexistence) with legacy messaging systems like MS Mail or third-party for several reasons. You may choose to maintain these mail systems running side by side with Exchange for a period of time. Possible reasons for doing this include:

- The *complexity* of moving everything over to Exchange all at once. Most migrations are done in stages and must be carefully planned and tested before they are implemented.
- Users may feel attached to the *old way* they are sending mail and may take some time to be suitably trained and coaxed before they venture forth into the software jungle anew to wrestle with the tiger called Upgrade (I waxed poetic there, but not very well).
- Third-party systems may provide you with *functionality* that Exchange doesn't have, and you may want to continue running these two systems side by side indefinitely or until one outdoes the other in the upgrade cycle.

Exchange includes connectors for establishing a coexistence between an Exchange organization and the following messaging systems (not all versions of each product are supported):

- Lotus Notes
- Lotus cc:Mail
- MS Mail (PC and AppleTalk versions)
- PROFS and SNADS

In addition, Exchange includes a Migration Wizard that simplifies the process of migrating from the following mail systems to Exchange systems (not all versions of each product are supported):

- MS Mail for PC Networks
- Lotus cc:Mail
- Lotus Notes (included in Service Pack 1)
- Novell GroupWise
- Netscape Collabra

Migration and MS Mail connectivity are considered in separate chapters in this book.

Step 8: Select Hardware Platforms

At this point, it is time to consider questions like how many Exchange servers will you use in each site, and what hardware will these servers run on? The main question to consider here is, will you use a few high-powered machines or many low-power ones in each site? A related question is, what are the hardware characteristics of an Exchange server, given its user requirements and server roles? Let's consider the issues involved:

- Exchange Servers can function in a variety of different *roles*. As mentioned previously, a server can be dedicated to a specific role, such as
- Hosting user mailboxes (Home Server)
- Hosting public folder replicas (Public Folder Server)
- Expanding distribution lists (Expansion Server)
- Establishing connectivity with legacy, third-party, or foreign mail systems for messaging or directory replication (Connectivity Server)
- Managing public-key security for the organization (Key Management Server)

and so on. Any particular Exchange Server may be functioning in one, two, or many different roles within your organization. In addition, Exchange Servers may have other functions in a Windows NT-based network such as acting as domain controllers, RAS servers, gateways to NetWare servers, client installation points, and so on. A general rule of thumb is, *the more roles a server has to play, the greater are its hardware requirements*. This is pretty obvious. Another rule of thumb is, *the larger the enterprise, the more you should make use of Exchange Servers having only one dedicated role*. This is simply an economy of scale at work.

Connectivity Servers

If you plan to dedicate certain Exchange servers to the sole function of providing messaging connectivity with other sites or mail systems, you can delete either the private information store (used for hosting mailboxes) or the public information store (used for hosting public folder contents) from the machine. Which one should you delete? It's best to delete the public information store to avoid unnecessary public folder hierarchy status messages from being generated, as discussed earlier in this chapter. Leave the private information store intact (Exchange won't allow you to delete both stores on a machine), but don't create any mailboxes on the machine.

Domain Controllers

Should you install Microsoft Exchange on a Windows NT domain controller?

- *Most administrators will tell you to install Exchange only on member servers. The main reason is simply that when a machine is a domain controller, it needs a lot of RAM for storing its SAM database in memory in order to speed up logons and pass-through authentication of users and processes. The Microsoft Exchange Optimizer, a wizard included with Microsoft Exchange that can be used to optimize the configuration of an Exchange system after its hardware or role has been modified, includes a feature for limiting the amount of memory that Exchange will use. This is important on domain controllers, as Exchange will typically try to use all available memory on a server for its own purposes, swapping unneeded processes to disk in the process. If you are installing Exchange on a domain controller, make sure that you add* lots *of RAM and use the Optimizer to limit the use of available memory by Exchange so that the server can still function optimally in its role as a domain controller.*
- *On the other hand, if you install Exchange on a domain controller, it can reduce network traffic since the server can authenticate users and other servers itself, instead of redirecting the authentication traffic over the network.*
- *You can install Exchange on a BDC, but it is not recommended that you install Exchange on a PDC, because if the PDC should die, you may have trouble keeping your other Exchange Servers up and running properly.*

- *Should you use a few high-powered servers or many low-powered ones for implementing Exchange?* There is really no answer to this question; it's all give and take. Table 2-2 lists some of the advantages and disadvantages of using a few high-powered servers, while Table 2-3 does the same regarding using many low-powered ones.
- *What are the most important hardware components as far as Exchange performance is concerned?* In order of decreasing importance, these factors are
- *I/O subsystem.* This includes the speed and number of disk controllers, the number and types of disks installed, use of hardware-implemented RAID technologies, and so on. Some general tips are
  - Use the fastest drives with the best performing controllers you can get.

Table 2-2

Using a Few High-Powered Exchange Servers.

Advantages	Disadvantages
More users per server mean more *local delivery* of messages and therefore less network messaging traffic	More users per server mean larger information stores, which take longer to back up
Less directory replication traffic occurs	More users per server means more users are affected when the server goes down
The system is specifically designed to be upgraded and repaired easily	High-powered hardware scales upwards in cost

Table 2-3

Using Many Low-Powered Exchange Servers.

Advantages	Disadvantages
Few users per server means fewer users are affected when the server goes down	More servers means more hardware to maintain and more things that can go wrong
Few users per server means smaller information stores that can be backed up more quickly	More servers means more directory replication
Low-powered hardware is cheap and allows existing hardware resources to have their usage lifetime extended	Fewer users per server means less local delivery of messages and therefore more network-messaging traffic
More servers allow more options with regard to dedicated server roles and customization	Older hardware is more likely to break down than newer high-powered stuff

    - Use disk striping (RAID 1) or disk striping with parity (RAID 5) formatted with NTFS for most of your Exchange components, including the information stores, since this combination provides the best random I/O access.
    - Place your transaction logs on a volume formatted with FAT, since FAT provides better sequential I/O access.

- *Memory.* Microsoft recommends a minimum of 32 MB of RAM for Exchange (although it can be coaxed to run on only 24 MB). That's the minimum RAM, but the recommended value is twice that (64 MB). You will probably want to go much higher than that, depending on how much load your server experiences.
- *Network subsystem.* Use the best 100-Mbps network cards you can get. Use several cards for each server to increase bandwidth still further if needed.
- *Processor.* Having a fast processor on a Connectivity Server is especially important, as the MTA is a CPU-intensive process on such a server. Faster is generally better, and on systems with *symmetric multiprocessing* (SMP) support, Exchange can take advantage of up to four processors to distribute its server threads between them.

- *How many users can have their mailboxes on a single Exchange Server?* This seemingly innocent question has an interesting answer. Tests show that a typical high-performance SMP server with four 200-MHz or faster processors, 2 GB RAM, SCSI hardware RAID, and a Fast Ethernet network card can support up to 10,000 users effectively. The fact of the matter is, most administrators seldom host more than 2,000 users on a single Exchange Server, no matter how powerful the hardware. The main reason has to do with disaster recovery. A server hosting 10,000 users might need an information store as large as 400 or 500 GB in size, depending on how heavily users use the server. It's hard enough to consider efficiently backing up such a store, let alone trying to recover a system that lost its RAID subsystem through massive failure. And consider how long it would take to run Exchange command-line utilities for compacting or repairing the information store database! Furthermore, if the server went down for even an hour, 10,000 users in your company would be without their email. That's a scary thought to consider! One possible solution is to use *Microsoft Cluster Server* (MSCS) to provide two-node failover support for your Exchange Server machines. However, this is an expensive solution to implement, since Exchange can only run on one node of a cluster at a time, so the other high-powered node is just sitting there unused until the first one fails (if it ever does). MSCS is also quite complex to administer in its current form, so using it may not be justifiable from a *return-on-investment* (ROI) perspective.

- *How can you determine which hardware you need to be able to meet the requirements of your Exchange implementation plan?* One solution would be to set up a testbed Exchange server and see how it performs under a simulated message load. Compare its measured performance to your estimated messaging needs and determine whether it will do the job or should be further beefed-up. This procedure is called capacity planning and is typically used when you will need to purchase a number of similar machines and you need to test one in order to see if they will perform according to your expectations. Some of the tools you can use to simulate a messaging load on an Exchange Server include
  - Microsoft Exchange Server *Load Simulator* (LoadSim), a tool from Microsoft that runs on Windows NT machines. LoadSim can be used together with an Exchange client like Outlook to simulate a heavy load from MAPI-based clients. You must use the correct version of LoadSim for your particular version of Exchange (4.0, 5.0, or 5.5). LoadSim used to be included on the CD in previous versions on Exchange, but it is not included on the Exchange 5.5 CD. Instead, you can download the tool and find further instructions on how to use it at `www.microsoft.com/exchange`.
  - *Internet Load Simulator* (InetLoad) for simulating a heavy load from POP3 or IMAP4 clients. Inetload can also be downloaded from Microsoft's Web site.

  An alternative to running your own load simulation is to talk with some experienced Exchange administrators to see what they think of your choice for a hardware platform that meets your messaging needs.

Step 9: Develop a Staged Implementation Plan

Well, you're almost done. It's time to commit everything to writing, make PowerPoint slides, and go see your boss to try to sell him your plan.

Step 10: Begin Implementing Your Plan

That's what the rest of this book is about!

Walkthrough: Planning an Exchange Organization

To finish this chapter, we'll take the first of many walkthroughs you will find in this book to help you implement various aspects of Exchange in your enterprise. This first walkthrough is a simple planning exercise to help you assimilate the material you learned in this chapter.

Scenario:

- Your company has 3,200 users distributed at three locations: Chicago, Boston, and Cincinnati. Your users can be profiled as follows:
- Chicago: 2,500 users consisting of:
  - 200 heavy users
  - 1,500 moderate users
  - 800 light users
- Boston: 500 users consisting of:
  - 300 heavy users
  - 200 moderate users
- Cincinnati: 200 users consisting of:
  - 200 light users
- The company is growing and its messaging needs are expected to double over the next two years.
- Distribution lists are used on a fairly regular basis for distributing product updates, support bulletins, and other timely information.
- Users want to keep all their messages indefinitely, and regular backups need to be performed.
- Users in Chicago mostly send messages among themselves, while users in Boston and Cincinnati tend to send messages throughout the whole organization.
- Chicago and Boston have been making light use of a Lotus Notes system for collaboration between users, but this will be migrated to Exchange and developers will create workflow and collaboration applications based on Exchange public folders. Approximately 50 GB of public folder storage space will be needed by each of these locations, and they will need to be able to access information in each others' public folder hierarchies. However, Exchange will immediately be used for email after it is implemented, although it may take an additional

six months before the developers have finished their public folder applications and users are migrated away from their Lotus Notes databases.

- Users in Boston also need fast access to the Internet's SMTP mail system for mailing out marketing information to prospective clients. The other two locations have lesser need for Internet mail.
- Both Chicago and Boston have implemented 100-Mbps Switched Ethernet networks, while Cincinnati is still using a 10BaseT LAN.
- All three locations are pure NT shops, no NetWare or Unix anywhere.
- Chicago and Boston want to administer their own network hardware and software, while Cincinnati has an administrator come over from Boston whenever work needs to be done.
- The WAN link between Chicago and Boston is a full T-1 line and is approximately 30 percent utilized on the average, with brief bursts due to file transfers up to 80 percent utilization for intervals as short as a minute or two. A dialup 128-kbps ISDN line is used as a backup link between these two locations.
- The WAN link between Boston and Cincinnati is a 128-Kbps dialup ISDN link that is 60 percent utilized. No backup link is provided.
- Management has authorized expenditures for redundant hardware, if required, but is reluctant to upgrade the existing WAN connections, other than a fractional T-1 line running at 386 kbps to support SMTP connectivity with the Internet for Boston. Reliable messaging is a priority and management is willing to make capital expenditures for good hardware as far as computers are concerned.
- The directory database of Exchange information will be fairly static; not much directory replication traffic will occur once the system is completely configured and running, other than creating and deleting mailboxes for employees that come and go.
- Users have no special connectivity needs, as management has not yet allocated funds to buy users laptops. That will come about a year later and doesn't need to be considered at this time.

What will you do?

Step 1

- The private information store disk requirements are
  - Chicago = 4.4 * (50*200 + 15*1500 + 5*800) / 1.5 = 107,677 MB = 104 GB

- Boston = 4.4 * (50*300 + 15*200) / 1.5 = 52,800 MB = 52 GB
- Cincinnati = 4.4 * (5 * 200) / 1.5 = 2,933 MB = 2.9 GB

- The public information store requirements are 100 GB for both Chicago and Boston if public folder replication is configured and 50 GB each if public folder affinities are used. However, installation of a dedicated public folder server in each site will be deferred until developers have completed the workflow applications that will run on them.
- The Boston private information could probably be backed up using a two-hour backup window, but the Chicago private information store is too big to back up. Chicago will have two Exchange Servers, each hosting a private information store of approximately 52 GB in size.
- Mailbox size limits will be implemented along with deleted item recovery, but no attempt will be made to configure users' messages to expire after a given period of time.

Steps 2 and 3

Figure 2-3 shows a block diagram with the various locations and the network connections between them.

Steps 4, 5, and 6

- Sites will be named after the cities they are in, while Exchange Servers will be named after Shakespearean characters.
- Three sites will be used: Chicago, Boston, and Cincinnati (see Figure 2-4). Why three? Chicago and Boston each want to manage their own servers, so it makes sense to make them separate sites that use separate Exchange Service accounts. Cincinnati is connected to Boston by a slow WAN link that has insufficient net available bandwidth to

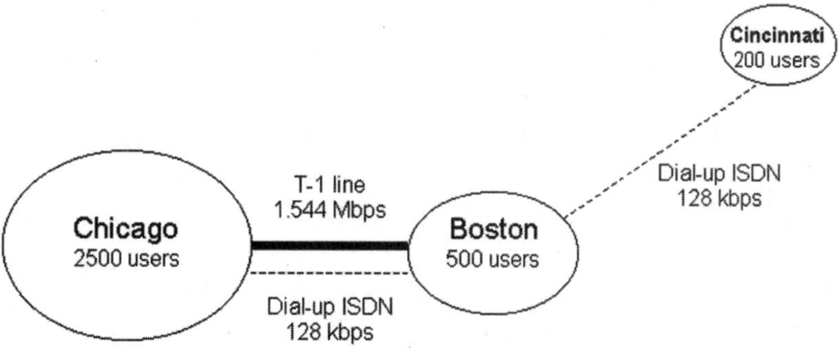

Figure 2-3 A block diagram showing locations and network connections.

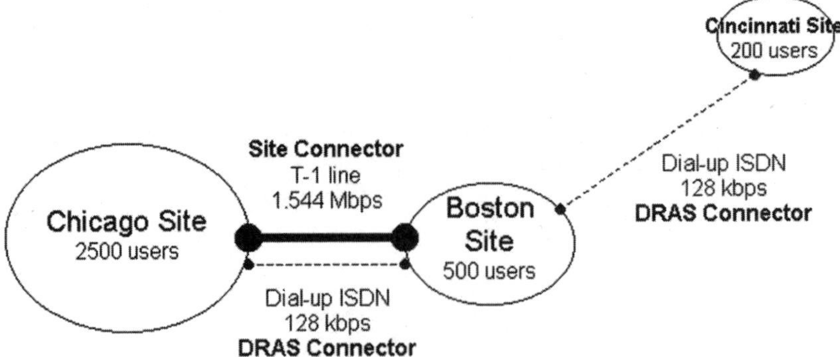

Figure 2-4 Revised block diagram showing sites and connectors.

allow it to be part of the Boston site. In addition, the link is dialup and not permanent, so the lack of RPC connectivity between them precludes these two locations being in the same site.

- In terms of connectivity, Chicago and Boston will be connected with the Site Connector, since the T-1 link is fast and has plenty of available bandwidth for messaging services. In addition, a Dynamic RAS (DRAS) Connector will be configured to make use of the backup ISDN line, if necessary, as an alternate messaging route. Boston and Cincinnati will be connected with a DRAS Connector, since the link is dialup and the messaging needs of Cincinnati are light.

Steps 7 Through 10

- A Lotus Notes Connector will be installed in Chicago to support the coexistence of the Lotus Notes software for both Chicago and Boston users. The connector is located in Chicago because of the preponderance of users there.
- The Internet Mail Service (IMS) will be installed in Boston since that site especially requires connectivity with the Internet SMTP mail system. Other sites can access the Internet through Boston.
- Hardware is standardized as being 400-MHz Pentium II machines with 100BaseTX network cards and between 256 and 1 GB of RAM, depending on the site.
- Two Exchange Servers will be deployed for the Chicago site because of the large number of users being supported. One server will be deployed in Boston and one in Cincinnati.
- All Exchange Servers will have their public information store deleted.

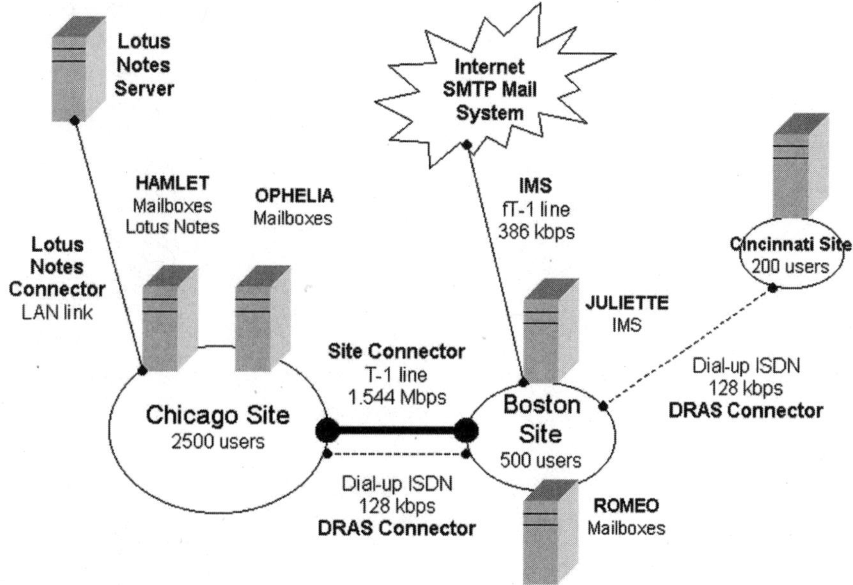

Figure 2-5 Final block diagram for Exchange implementation plan.

- A second Exchange Server will be deployed at Boston and dedicated to fast SMTP connectivity with the Internet.
- The plan is written down.
- The plan is approved.
- The implementation is begun! (See Figure 2-5.)

Where Do We Go From Here?

In the next chapter, we will jump right in and look at the process of installing our first Exchange Server for our organization. A walkthrough will lead you through the process and also show you how to implement message journalling for your organization.

For More Information

Additional information on planning an Exchange implementation can be found in the manual called *Concepts and Planning*, which can be obtained from Microsoft. This book is also available once you install Exchange Server on a machine as part of the online documentation called Books Online. It may be more useful to purchase the printed version from Microsoft, however, so you can read it on the subway and make notes in the margins.

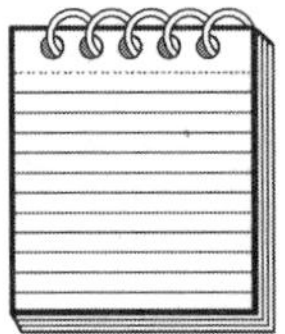

Printed Manuals

One of my pet peeves with Microsoft is that a representative recently told me by phone that printed manuals will not be available for future versions of Exchange, as they are being phased out in 1999. All future manuals will be either locally-installed, local, browser-based versions or online versions. I think this idea stinks, at least until the cost and ease-of-use of hand-held "electronic book" hardware drops significantly to make them as useful and convenient as printed books. Until then, if you feel like I do about it, phone Microsoft and give them an earful, especially since they have supposedly just reorganized their entire company to make it more "customer-focused." Let's hope that by the time this book is out Microsoft has changed their policy on "printed manuals" and has decided to continue publishing them.

TechNet

Microsoft TechNet is a valuable resource and well worth the annual fee of $300. It provides you with a wealth of information on products like Exchange including manuals, resource kits, technical notes, and software.

The following are the titles of some technical notes on Exchange found in TechNet that relate to the issues discussed in this chapter. You should also be able to find these notes online at the Exchange home site at

```
www.microsoft.com/exchange
```

or at Microsoft's Personal Support Center Web site at

```
support.microsoft.com/support
```

Here are the relevant titles:

- MS Exchange Architectural Planning and Design
- MS Exchange Server 5.5 Advanced Backbone Design and Optimization
- Setting up MS Exchange Server 5.5 in a Novell NetWare Environment
- MS Exchange Management Requirements: Best Practices at a Large Company

- MS Exchange Server 5.5: Calculating Users per Server
- Real-World MS Exchange Server Deployment Issues—A Compaq Perspective
- MS Exchange Server Planning and Design Optimization Guide

Training

Productivity Point is one of North America's largest computer training companies and offers a full line of training options from *Microsoft Official Curriculum* (MOC) training on Exchange Server for IT professionals to one-day end-user training in Microsoft Outlook. Check out their Web site at

```
www.propoint.com
```

and look for an office near you.

Utilities

Another tool you can use for capacity planning of your hardware platform for Exchange Server is Dell's PowerMatch tool available from Dell's Web site at

```
http://support.dell.com/filelib/download/index.asp?fileid=1637
```

Of course, this tool only applies if you are going to use Dell hardware for your Exchange servers.

CHAPTER 3

Installing Exchange

In Chapter 2, we examined the process of planning an Exchange implementation in an enterprise. Once you've done your homework and planned everything out, it's time to take the plunge and start installing Exchange. After reading this chapter, you will have a basic understanding of

- System requirements for installing Exchange
- Installation issues for Exchange
- Installing Exchange on a fresh system
- Upgrading from previous versions of Exchange
- Unattended installations of Exchange
- Other configuration issues
- Troubleshooting installation problems

System Requirements for Installing Exchange

Prior to installing Exchange, make sure you have the necessary hardware and software installed on your system. Ensure that your system meets the minimum requirements and preferably meets or exceeds the recommended requirements.

Hardware Requirements

Table 3-1 shows the minimum and recommended hardware requirements for installing Exchange on Intel-based systems (see the Release Notes on the compact disc for information regarding installing Exchange on RISC-based systems.) If you are installing the Standard Edition of Exchange

Table 3-1

Exchange Server Hardware Requirements.

Subsystem	Minimum	Recommended
Processor	Pentium 60	Pentium 133 or higher
Memory	24 MB	32 MB or higher
Disk	250 MB free	500 MB free or higher

Server, you can probably successfully complete an installation using only the minimum hardware requirements, but if you are installing Enterprise Edition make sure that you use at least the recommended requirements, unless your installation is only for testing or exam preparation purposes. A real-life production system should be installed on hardware sufficiently powerful to support it in its role within the enterprise.

Here are some further notes regarding system requirements:

- Exchange can make use of symmetric multiprocessing (SMP) systems.
- Use as much RAM as possible, up to 2 GB if necessary on heavily used production systems.
- Performance is limited by the efficiency of the disk subsystem you are using. A good recommendation for Exchange is to use
  - One physical disk for the operating system, applications, and the pagefile. The pagefile on an Exchange Server should have a minimum size equal to the amount of RAM installed in the machine, plus 100 MB. Format this disk using the Windows NT File System (NTFS) for security reasons.
  - One physical disk for the transaction logs. Since these logs are written sequentially to disk, using a separate disk for them will improve their performance. You may also want to mirror this disk with an additional physical disk using the disk mirroring (RAID 0) capability of the Windows NT administrative tool Disk Administrator. Format this disk using the File Allocation System (FAT) as this file system gives better sequential I/O performance than NTFS.
  - A stripe set (RAID 1) for installing the remaining components of Exchange Server such as the private and public information store databases, the directory service database, and the message transfer agent directories and files. Since these components use random access disk I/O, using a stripe set will improve their performance. Format this disk using NTFS for security reasons. If you like, you can also move the pagefile to the striped volume for better performance.
- There are no “requirements” for the network subsystem on an Exchange Server, but obviously you need a network card if you want to send mail. Generic 10BaseT cards like NE2000 should be avoided, as they may cause a bottleneck in server performance. Use the best 10-Mbps cards you can get, or preferably use 100-Mbps cards in a Switched Ethernet environment for the best performance in enterprise-level installations. For even higher throughput, install several cards in the server instead of only one.

- An SVGA monitor and supporting video card are best if you plan to install Exchange Administrator on the server for local administration purposes.

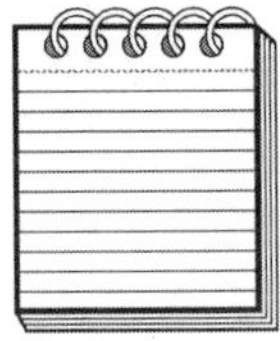

RAID 1 or RAID 5?
Although Microsoft recommends using RAID 1 (stripe set) for installing the various components of Exchange on a Windows NT Server, most Exchange administrators prefer RAID 5 (stripe set with parity) instead. Although RAID 1 gives the better I/O performance than RAID 5, they prefer RAID 5 because of its fault-tolerance nature. In any case, using an external hardware-based RAID 5 unit is preferred over the Windows NT tool Disk Administrator for creating a software-based RAID 5 disk system. You get what you pay for, and hardware RAID will give you much better performance than software RAID.

Software Requirements

The following software must be installed on your machine prior to installing Exchange:

- Windows NT 4.0 Server
- Windows NT 4.0 Service Pack 3 or later

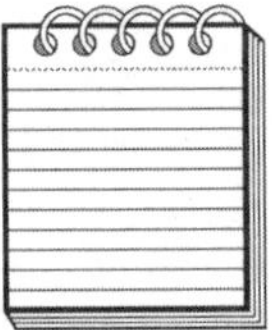

Service Pack 3 (SP3)
If you are unsure of whether Service Pack 3 has been installed on your Windows NT Server or not, start the administrative tool called Windows NT Diagnostics on your server and select the Version tab. If a service pack has been installed on the machine, it will be displayed here.

Here are some further notes regarding software requirements:

- If you plan on using Exchange for Internet SMTP mail, you must have the TCP/IP protocol installed. Since most Exchange implementations are done in TCP/IP networking environments though, this is usually a moot issue.
- If you are going to install the Outlook Web Access component of Exchange on your server, make sure that you have Service Pack 4 (or later) for Windows NT 4.0 installed.
- If you plan to use the server for messaging connectivity with a legacy MS Mail for AppleTalk Networks machine (a Macintosh machine), you

must install Windows NT Services for Macintosh and configure it properly. This subject is beyond the scope of this book. Refer to any good book on Windows NT administration for information on how to install and configure Services for Macintosh on Windows NT Server.

- If you want to install Internet Explorer 4.0 or higher on your Exchange Server, make sure you install IE 4.0 first. If you install IE 4.0 after installing Exchange, it causes problems with the registry. If you have already done this, however, you have an out; see the Release Notes on the Exchange CD.
- If you are going to install Exchange in a clustering configuration using Microsoft Cluster Server, you must use Windows NT Server 4.0 Enterprise Edition and upgrade it to Windows NT 4.0 Service Pack 4. Installing Exchange in a clustering environment is beyond the scope of this book. For more information on installing Exchange using Microsoft Cluster Server, see the documentation on the Exchange CD that is displayed during the installation process.

Installation Issues for Exchange

You may need to be aware of a few other issues before you install Exchange on your system:

- You can install Exchange either on a member server (stand-alone server) or a domain controller (PDC or BDC). Installing Exchange on a PDC is not recommended (but it can be done.) If you install Exchange on a BDC, make sure you beef up your hardware requirements accordingly to support authentication and replication traffic.
- You cannot locate the Exchange database files on a partition that uses the Windows NT Distributed File System (DFS). The database files must be located on a local file system.
- If the Microsoft Chat service is already installed on the system, stop it using Services in the Control Panel before you install Exchange.

Installing Exchange on a Fresh System

We're ready to begin installing our first Exchange Server for our Exchange organization. This section looks at doing a *fresh* install, that is, installing Exchange on a machine on which no earlier version of Exchange exists. For information about *upgrading* earlier versions of Exchange to version 5.5, see the next section.

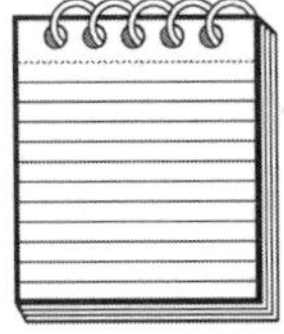

First Server

The first Exchange Server you install in an organization is kind of special, especially if you plan to use Microsoft Outlook as your client. The calendaring feature of Microsoft Outlook makes use of a special hidden public folder or System Folder on Exchange called the Schedule+ Free / Busy folder. This folder is created by default on the first Exchange Server you install in your organization. If the folder is corrupt or deleted, Outlook users will not be able to see each others' schedules for booking meetings and events. It is therefore a good idea to replicate this folder to one or more additional Exchange Servers in your site and to servers in other sites if you want to be able to schedule meetings across site boundaries.

To create a replica of the Schedule+ Free / Busy Folder on another Exchange Server in your site, open the property sheet for the Public Information Store of that server in the Exchange Administrator program, select the Instances tab, and add the folder by moving it from the left-hand listbox to the right. See Chapter 5, "Tools For Administration," for information on how to use the Exchange Administrator program.

Preparing for Installation

A few things must be done before you insert the Exchange CD into the CD-ROM drive of your machine. We'll assume you've already done all the planning, including determining the name of the site you will create or join, the role to be played by the server in your messaging infrastructure, and so on. We'll also assume you've looked at the Readme file, which can be found in the root directory of the Exchange CD. The Readme file contains the Release Notes for the product and may have last-minute information about hardware and software compatibility and other issues that may be of importance to you. It's always a good idea to look at the Readme file (if there is one) before you install any new software. Make sure you also

- Log on with a user account that will be used for administering Exchange later, as the account you are logged on to during installation is granted special privileges on Exchange called the Permissions Admin role. Initially, this will be the only user account that can be used to administer Exchange until you assign other accounts this role. The account you log on with to install Exchange must be a valid domain account and a member of the Administrators group.

- Create a special user account called the Exchange Service Account (also called the Site Service Account) using the administrative tool User Manager For Domains. This user account will be used by Exchange Servers to authenticate each other for forwarding messages and directory replication and has full permission on all objects within the Exchange directory. The service account is also needed whenever you want to add a new server to a site or a new site to an organization. The service account can be named whatever you wish (typically ExchangeService or something similar is used, but you can also use Bob or Judy as the name of the service account) and should be given a complex password, since it has the highest level of privileges on an Exchange machine. Don't use the account for logging on to a Windows NT machine; leave it strictly for Exchange to use. Make sure when you create the account that you deselect the option User Must Change Password at Next Logon and select the option Password Never Expires.

Service Account

You can change the password of the service account if you feel it has become compromised, but you cannot change the account itself. In other words, if you delete the service account using User Manager For Domains, you're in big trouble! None of your Exchange services will be able to start. And it's no use trying to create a new Windows NT account with the same name as the old service account, since accounts are known internally to NT by their Security Identifiers *(SIDs), not by their names. Your new account will not have the same SID as the old account and Exchange therefore will not recognize it. Call Microsoft tech support for this one!*

If you forget afterwards which of your domain user accounts is the one you assigned the role of being the Exchange service account, you can find out which one it is by opening the property sheet of the Configuration container in the Exchange Administrator program and selecting the Service Account Password tab to view its name. Of course, if the Exchange services are down on the machine, you won't be able to start the Exchange Administrator program, but you can still find out the name of the service account by using the Registry Editor (regedt32.exe) and looking up the value of ObjectName in the following registry key:

```
HKEY_LOCAL_MACHINE
  SYSTEM
    CurrentControlSet
      Services
        MSExchangeSA
```

Walkthrough: Installing Exchange Server

We'll now look at installing Exchange step by step. Begin by inserting the Exchange Server CD into your CD-ROM drive. We'll be using the Enterprise Edition of Exchange, since we want to take full advantage of its additional capabilities. If Autorun is enabled on your machine, the initial splash screen for Exchange will appear (see Figure 3-1). If it does not, click Start, Run, and enter the following path and press OK (we'll assume that D: is your CD-ROM drive letter):

```
D:\Launch.exe
```

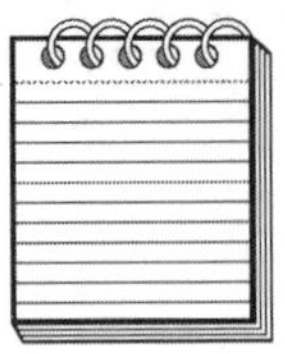

Launching Setup

If you only want to install Exchange and its components from the Exchange CD, you could click Start, Run, and enter the following path and click OK:

```
D:\Server\Setup\I386\Setup.exe
```

The five options on this screen and the sub-options beneath them are as follows:

Figure 3-1 The initial Exchange Server setup splash screen.

Version 5.5

Enterprise Edition
for the English Language

- Setup Server and Components
- Release Notes
- Documentation
- Online Resources
- Exit

Goto Server Setup Menu

(c) 1986 - 1997 Microsoft Corporation. All rights reserved.

- *Setup Server and Components:* Installs Exchange Server and allows you to specify which optional components to include:
  - *Microsoft Exchange Server 5.5:* Starts the Setup program for installing Exchange.
  - *Chat Services:* Installs the Microsoft Chat Service to support IRC-based chat clients (requires Internet Information Server 2.0 or higher).
  - *Applications & Authoring Tools:* Installs tools like the Frameset Design Time Control, Discussion Wizard for FrontPage, and Application Farm Sampler.
  - *Internet Location Services:* Installs ILS service to support Microsoft NetMeeting (requires that you change the port number for LDAP access to the Exchange Directory from its well-known value 389 to some other value).
  - *Resource Kit:* Installs the sampler of tools and documents from the Exchange Server Resource Kit.
  - *Connector for Lotus Notes:* Provides messaging and directory connectivity with Lotus Notes servers.
  - *Connector for IBM OfficeVision / VM:* Provides messaging connectivity with OfficeVision/VM mainframe-based messaging systems (requires Microsoft SNA Server).
  - *Connector for SNADS:* Provides messaging connectivity with SNADS mainframe-based messaging systems from IBM (requires Microsoft SNA Server).
- *Release Notes:* Allows you to read an HTML-based version of the Readme file located in the root directory of the Exchange CD and requires a frames-enabled browser like Internet Explorer 3.01 or higher.
- *Documentation:* Allows you to read HTML-based versions of various Exchange Server manuals located in the \Docs folder on the Exchange CD.
  - *Exchange Server:* Provides pre-installation access to Books Online, HTML-based versions of five different Exchange manuals, which can also be obtained from Microsoft in print form. These manuals are entitled Getting Started; Concepts and Planning; Operations, Maintenance, and Troubleshooting; and Migration. Requires Internet Explorer 3.01 or higher.
  - *Chat Service:* Online manual for the Microsoft chat service.
  - *Connectivity:* Online manuals for the Lotus Notes, OfficeVision/VM, and SNADS connectors.

- *Quick Setup:* A document leading you through the basic steps of setting up an Exchange organization and installing Exchange Server.
- *Clustering with Exchange Server:* A document guiding you through deploying Exchange on a Microsoft Cluster Server machine.
- *Online Resources:* A list of URLs to portions of Microsoft's Web site dealing with Exchange issues (the links are subject to change).
- *Exit:* Terminate the installation process.

We'll select Setup Server and its components, then Microsoft Exchange Server 5.5, and the install process begins. Setup looks for a previously installed version of Exchange, displays the EULA (End-User License Agreement), and displays a screen asking you to select the type of installation you want to perform:

- *Typical* installs Exchange Server, the Exchange Administrator program, and Books Online on the machine.
- *Custom* allows you to install any or all of Exchange Server, Exchange Administrator, Books Online, and Outlook Web Access.
- *Minimum* installs Exchange Server only, minus the frills.

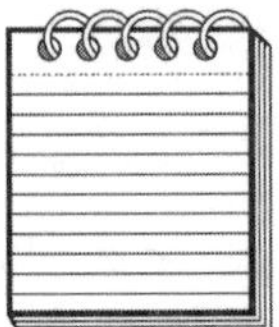

Custom Install

Why might you choose not to install any component on a machine except Exchange Server itself? If you already have the Exchange Administrator installed on a different machine, you don't need to install it on your current machine, although you should always have a several machines in your organization with Exchange Administrator installed on it, at least two in each site for fault-tolerance and redundancy.

On the other hand, note that you can install only *the Exchange Administrator program if you like. In fact, Exchange Setup can be run on a Windows NT 4.0 Workstation machine in order to do just that: install the Exchange Administrator on the workstation so that Exchange Servers can be remotely administered from an administrator's workstation console. This is a very common practice in an enterprise: run the services on the servers and manage them using tools installed on workstations.*

Let's select the Custom option to gain the most flexibility and control of the installation process (see Figure 3-2). We'll deselect Outlook Web Access and select the other three options.

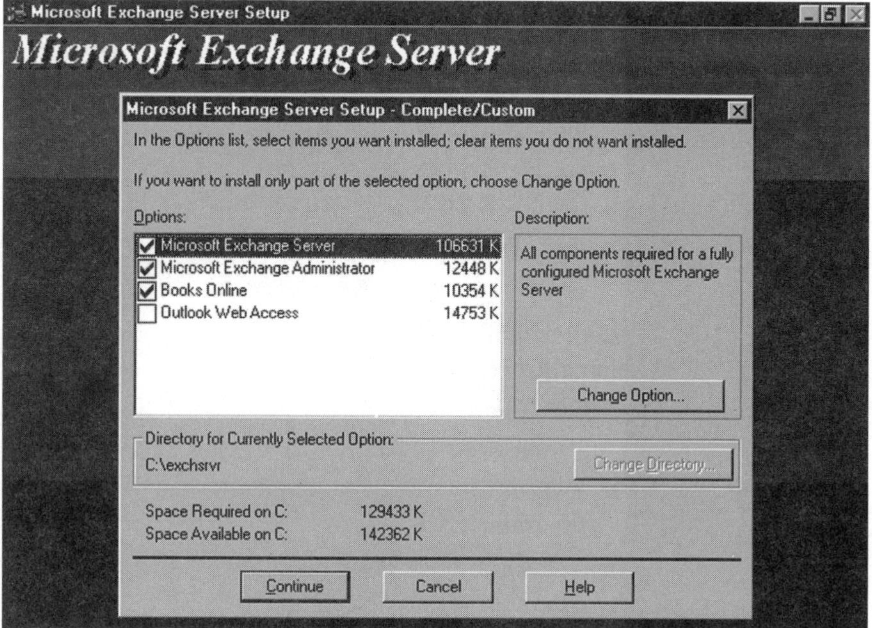

Figure 3-2 Custom installation of Exchange.

Of the four options listed in the Complete/Custom dialog box of Figure 3-2, only the first one, Microsoft Exchange Server, has sub-options that can be selected or omitted. Select Microsoft Exchange Server and click the Change Option button. A new dialog box appears, allowing you to select or omit the following Exchange components:

- *MS Mail Connector* provides messaging connectivity with legacy Microsoft Mail systems.
- *cc:Mail Connector* provides messaging connectivity with third-party cc:Mail systems from Lotus.
- *X.400 Connector* is used both for connecting Exchange sites together and for messaging connectivity with private or public messaging systems based on the X.400 specifications of the *International Telecommunications Union* (ITU).
- *Event Service* enables developers to create custom workflow applications using Exchange public folders with server-side scripting.
- *Key Management Server* is used to implement secure messaging using X.509v3 digital certificates and public-key cryptography.

We'll select only the MS Mail and X.400 connectors and deselect the rest.

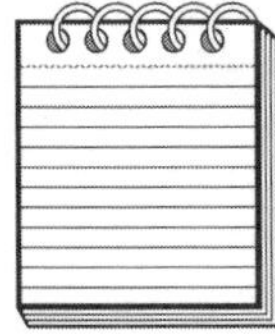

Maintenance Mode Setup

If we decide later that we want to install one of the Exchange components we skipped over, just rerun Setup in what is called maintenance mode *and select one of the following options:*

- Add/Remove: *Adds or removes Exchange components*
- Reinstall: *Repeats the last installation to restore missing files and settings*
- Remove All: *Removes Exchange from the machine (some files may remain)*

At this point, you'll be prompted to enter the 10-digit key for your Exchange CD, after which a Product ID number is presented to you in case you should ever need to call Microsoft for technical support with Exchange on this machine. Then you'll be prompted to specify the number of *Client Access Licenses* (CALs) you have purchased for your clients to be able to legally access Exchange.

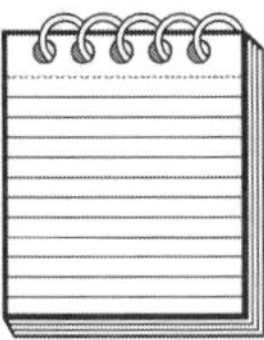

CALs

CALs are what makes enterprise-level software so expensive to implement. It's one thing to purchase a copy of Exchange and a server license to allow you to legally install it; it's another thing entirely to purchase the 5,000 CALs you need for those 5,000 client machines that will be connecting to your Exchange Server in order to send and receive messages. Licensing is a complex issue, but some simple points include the following:

- *Exchange requires one CAL for each client computer that will connect to it and use its services.*
- *Client machines need a CAL to connect to Exchange no matter what operating system or mail client (Microsoft or not) they're running.*
- *CALs are based on the number of client machines, not the number of people who use them.*
- *CALs for Exchange software may be per seat only (not per server) and may be either Exchange Server CALs or BackOffice CALs.*
- *CALs are required even for users connecting to Exchange over the Internet, except for anonymous connections (such as an Internet user accessing a public folder).*

For more information on licensing, try the following URLs from Microsoft's Web site:

`www.microsoft.com/licensing`

`www.microsoft.com/exchange`

At this point, you will be presented with the dialog box shown in Figure 3-3. You must choose whether to

- *Create a new Exchange site:* If this is the first Exchange Server you are installing, you must also specify the name of your new Exchange organization at this point. If you are joining an existing organization, enter the name of that organization and specify your new site name.
- *Join an existing site:* If you have already installed at least one other Exchange Server in your enterprise, you can join the site to which it belongs by specifying the name of the Exchange Server already on the network. To determine the name of an Exchange Server, log on interactively to the server console, open the Network utility in the Control Panel, and view the server's name (called its NetBIOS name) displayed on the Identification tab.

Join an Existing Site

If you incorrectly specify the name of an Exchange Server in an existing site, you want to join this new server too, or if the target server doesn't exist, Setup will respond with the error DS_E_COMMUNICATIONS_PROBLEM, meaning that RPC connectivity could not be established between the Exchange directory services on the new server and on the existing one.

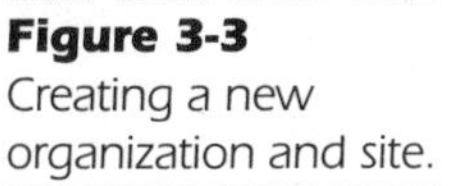

Figure 3-3
Creating a new organization and site.

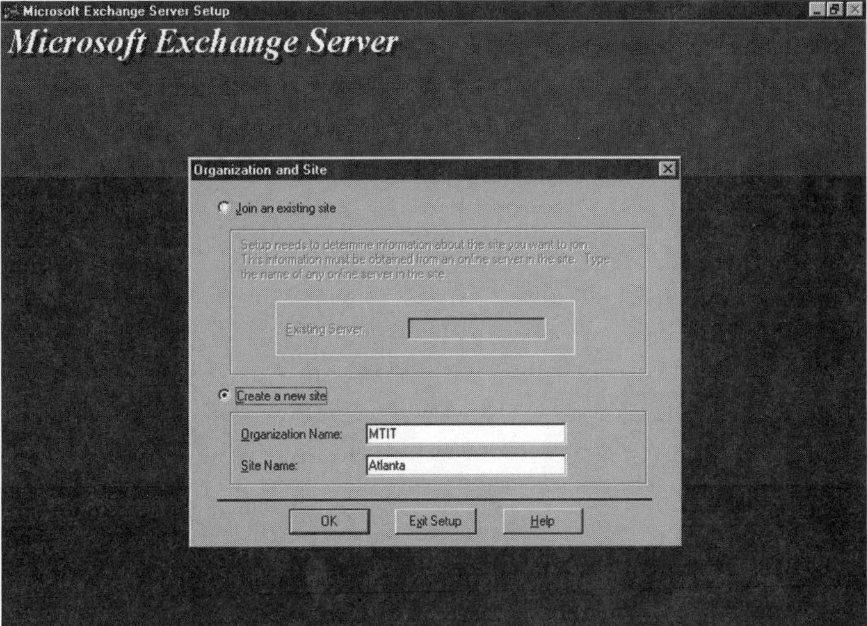

We'll select the option to create a new organization called MTIT and a new site called Atlanta. Exchange asks you to confirm this action.At this point, you'll be presented with a dialog box for specifying the name and password of the Exchange Service Account (see Figure 3-4.) The easiest thing to do is to click the Browse button and select the appropriate account from the list of domain accounts and groups displayed. If the service account is in another domain (it must be in a trusted domain), you can select List Names From and specify the name of the trusted name.

At this point, since this is the first Exchange Server we are installing in our organization, a dialog box appears with a message indicating that the Exchange service account has been granted three special system rights that it requires in order to enable Exchange to function properly. These three rights are

- Log on as a service
- Restore files and directories
- Act as part of the operating system

Click OK and Exchange verifies that the service account exists and is configured properly, after which Setup begins to copy files. This process will

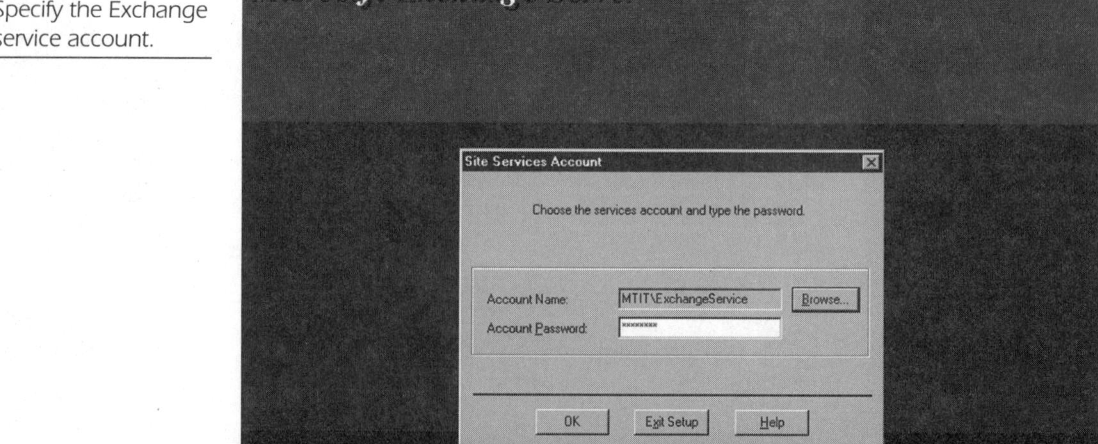

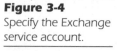

Figure 3-4
Specify the Exchange service account.

take a minute or two. After files are copied, Setup installs the various Exchange services, updates the registry, creates the Exchange directory database, and starts each of the Exchange services in their proper order. If everything goes well, you'll soon be presented with the dialog box saying:

> Microsoft Exchange Server Setup has completed successfully. You can now optimize your Exchange Server installation for this specific machine by running the Exchange Server Optimizer. The Optimizer can also be run at a later time.

Choose the Run Optimizer button to run the Optimizer now rather than later. This starts the Exchange Optimizer program, which tunes Exchange's use of the memory and disk subsystems to ensure the server performs. After reading the Welcome screen, click Next and Exchange will stop its various services from running so that you can tune the server. The next screen provides you with a number of options to select (see Figure 3-5). We'll

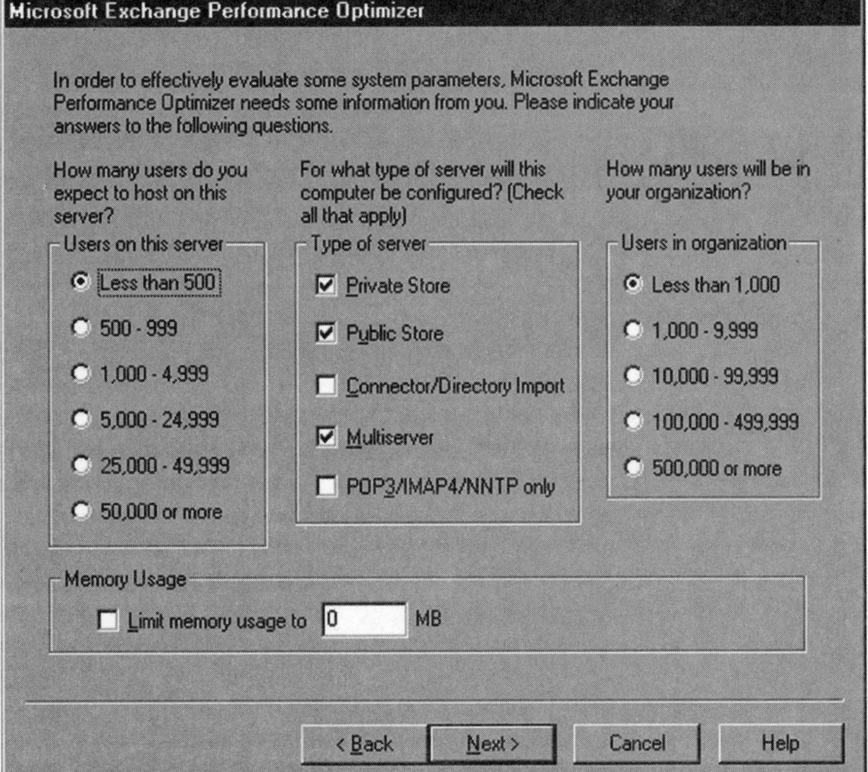

Figure 3-5 Running the Exchange Optimizer.

explain these various options in Chapter 11, since the Optimizer is a tool you will probably have to run again before long, and we'll just accept the defaults for now and click Next.

Optimizer now examines the configuration of your disk subsystem, looking for disks, partitions, and RAID volumes over which to distribute the various Exchange directories and files. After a short interval, a screen is displayed in which Optimizer suggests which partitions or volumes the Exchange database files and transaction logs should be moved to in order to provide optimal performance of the server (see Figure 3-6). In our configuration, Optimizer suggests moving

- Database and MTA files to the NTFS-formatted RAID 1 stripe set E.
- Transaction log files to the FAT-formatted RAID 0 mirror set F.

Click Next and Optimizer suggests we make a backup of the database files before proceeding even though there's nothing in them yet, since this

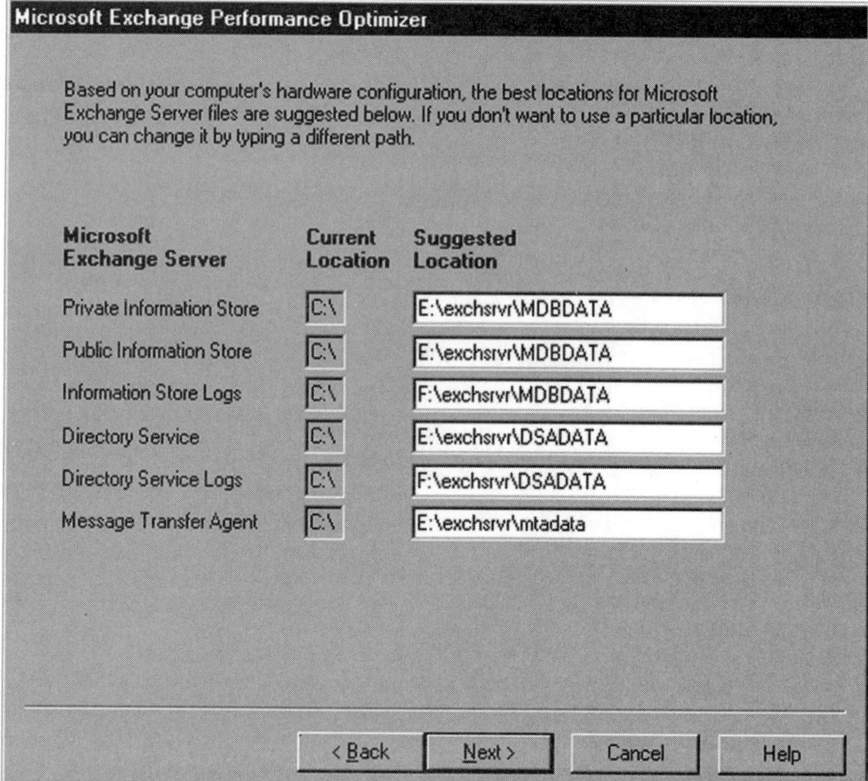

Figure 3-6 Optimizer's suggested locations for database and transaction files.

is a fresh install. Select to move the files automatically and click Next, and Optimizer relocates the files from their default installation location of C: to their new locations. Finally, Optimizer asks whether you want to restart the Exchange services, which you do by just clicking Finish.

Once the Exchange services are restarted, you will be returned to the initial setup splash screen. Click Exit at the top-right corner to quit Setup.

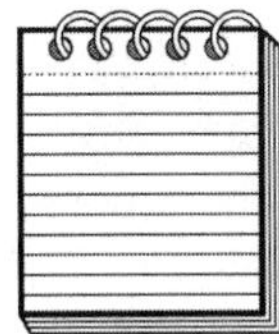

Setup Log

Exchange Setup creates a log in the root of your C: partition called Exchange Server Setup.log, which can be used by advanced administrators to troubleshoot Exchange installations that go wrong. You might use this in conjunction with Microsoft support specialists in a pinch.

Once Installation Is Complete

A few quick post-installation tasks are in order now:

- Verify that the core services of Exchange Server are started and running properly. Use the Services utility in the Control Panel and verify that the following services have started as their status entry:
  - Microsoft Exchange Directory
  - Microsoft Exchange Information Store
  - Microsoft Exchange Message Transfer Agent
  - Microsoft Exchange System Attendant

  Ignore any other Exchange services listed for now. We'll look at Exchange services in more detail in the next chapter.
- Check the application log using the administrative tool Event Viewer to see if any error or warning events are related to Exchange.
- Try starting the Exchange Administrator program and connecting to your server to see if it will function. Using the Exchange Administrator program is covered in Chapter 5, "Tools for Administration."
- Be sure to assign the Permissions Admin role to any other users who will have the job of administering your new Exchange server. Also assign this role to your backdoor administrator account in case your own account becomes inaccessible. Exchange permissions are covered in Chapter 5.

Upgrading from Previous Versions of Exchange

Exchange Server 5.5 can coexist with earlier versions of Exchange (the minimum requirement being that the older version be Exchange Server 4.0 with SP2 or higher installed), but it is a good idea to upgrade your older Exchange Servers so that you can take full advantage of the new features and functionality of version 5.5. Three key rules will help protect you during any kind of system or application upgrade:

- *First Rule:* Plan the upgrade process for your machines carefully and in such a way that machines with older versions of the software can maintain full interoperability with machines having newer versions until the upgrade process has been completed on all machines.
- *Second Rule:* Do a trial upgrade of a non-critical test machine to make sure you fully understand the upgrade process before upgrading any mission-critical production machines.
- *Third Rule:* Perform a full backup before upgrading production machines, just in case.

Some other issues to consider when performing an upgrade from earlier versions of Exchange include

- Stop all monitoring programs before starting the upgrade. Specifically, you should
  - Make sure Windows NT Performance Monitor is not running.
  - Make sure Windows NT Event Viewer is not running.
  - Disable any Server Monitors you have running under Exchange or put them into maintenance mode.
  - Disable any Link Monitors you have running under Exchange or put them into maintenance mode.
- Upgrade Standard Edition to Standard Edition, and Enterprise Edition to Enterprise Edition.
- Use the proper localized version of upgrade software. In other words, don't try to upgrade a U.S. English version of Exchange with a Japanese one.
- Set aside enough time to fully complete the upgrade, usually a weekend. Exchange Servers can take a long time to upgrade, particularly if they have a large number of big mailboxes or a large directory database. Figure on one or more hours per gigabyte of

information store size. In other words, an information store with 50 GB of information can take two days or more to upgrade. Connector (bridgehead) servers, whose only function is to provide connectivity with other sites and mail systems, and which are not used to host user mailboxes or public folders, can be upgraded much more quickly. Of course, upgrade times also vary a lot with the type of machine being used. Machines with fast processors, tons of memory, and fast hardware RAID will upgrade more quickly than 486s with 24 MB of RAM and IDE hard drives (yes Virginia, you *can* install Exchange on a 486!).

Upgrading Exchange 4.0 to 5.5

Exchange Server 4.0 machines must be first upgraded to Exchange Server 4.0 Service Pack 2 or higher (if this has not already been done) before you can upgrade them to version 5.5. The only exception to this is if you have only one Exchange Server in your entire organization and plan on keeping it that way. Before you commence the upgrade, you should also make sure that Windows NT 4.0 Service Pack 3 or higher is also installed on the machine, as this is a prerequisite for installing Exchange 5.5. Otherwise, the upgrade process is fairly simple:

- Start the Exchange 5.5 setup program by inserting the CD.
- When you are asked whether you want to remove the old version or upgrade to the new version, select Upgrade.
- Setup informs you that the database files will be converted into a newer format, so make sure you have a full backup of the server!
- Enter the CD key and record the product ID number.
- Setup now stops the Exchange services on the previous version of Exchange.
- When informed that if you later want to install additional Exchange 4.0 servers on your network and must follow some special steps to do so, just ignore this and click OK (once you start the upgrade process for your network, don't install any new copies of the old version or it can cause directory problems).
- Under Database Upgrade Options, select Standard (this is the only one you can choose in this case).
- The upgrade process now continues with the database files being upgraded first (this is the part that can take a long time) and then the remaining components of Exchange..

- Exchange services then restart and you are prompted to run the Exchange Optimizer program (do it) and then you're done. If other Exchange Servers are part your organization, your upgraded server will now update its directory information from these servers through directory replication, which takes place in the background.

Upgrading Databases

When you upgrade Exchange 4.0 to 5.5, the databases are upgraded in a series of steps as follows:

- *The private information store is upgraded from version 4.0 to 5.0.*
- *The public information store is upgraded from version 4.0 to 5.0.*
- *The directory is upgraded from version 5.0 to 5.5.*
- *The private information store is upgraded from version 5.0 to 5.5.*
- *The public information store is upgraded from version 5.0 to 5.5.*

This helps to explain why the process takes so much time, and why upgrading from 4.0 to 5.5 takes almost twice the time that upgrading a similar server from 5.0 to 5.5 takes.

Upgrading Exchange 5.0 to 5.5

Exchange 5.0 can always be upgraded directly to 5.5, regardless of whether any Exchange 5.0 service packs have been installed on the server. The process is almost identical to the one described above for upgrading 4.0 to 5.5 with one notable exception: when the Database Upgrade options dialog box is displayed, there are two active choices you can choose from:

- *Standard Upgrade:* This option leaves your Exchange database files in their current locations and upgrades them where they are. If this is the only option available, it's because you don't have enough disk space to perform a fault-tolerant upgrade.
- *Fault-Tolerant Upgrade:* This option is selected by default. It first backs up Exchange databases to temporary locations, upgrades the backup copies to the new version, and then replaces the original databases with the upgraded backup copies. This process makes it easier to recover should Setup fail to complete.

Unattended Installations of Exchange

You can perform an unattended or batch-mode version of Setup to install Exchange if you have a number of identical machines that need to be installed at the same time. To do this, you make use of a Setup configuration file called Setup.ini. This is a text file that answers the various prompts that Setup normally requests you to respond to when Setup is run. Three sample Setup.ini files are located in \Server\Support\Batsetup\Setup on the Exchange CD named Setup1.txt, Setup2.txt, and Setup3.txt. To use any of these files, copy one to your hard drive, edit it as desired to reflect the details of your own Exchange organization, rename it Setup2.ini, and run Setup from the Run box of the Start menu with the following options:

```
D:\Server\Setup\I386\Setup.exe /qD:\Setup2.ini
```

For information on how to create and modify Setup.ini files, see the comments embedded in the three sample files on the CD.

Other Post-Installation Issues

Let's now consider three more issues that may need to be dealt with after completing an Exchange installation:

- Installing Exchange service packs
- Tuning system performance
- Enabling messaging journalling

Installing Exchange Service Packs

Microsoft provides periodic service packs for its various products to correct problems that have been discovered, to update tools and utilities, and otherwise improve and extend the functionality of the product so it can perform better. In between releases of service packs, when a problem is discovered with a product, a hot fix is posted on Microsoft's Web site so that those who need the fix can immediately obtain and apply it. Most users though are content to wait until the next service pack comes out so they can apply the fixes all in one shot. In other words, "If it ain't broke, don't fix it!"

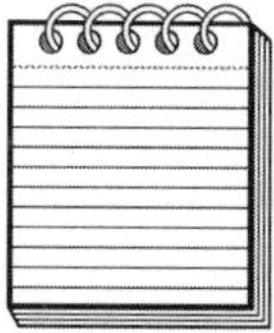

Service Packs

You might want to check with other Exchange administrators on the Exchange USENET newsgroups prior to installing a brand new service pack, since service packs from Microsoft occasionally break more things than they fix!

The current service pack for Exchange 5.5, as of this writing, is Service Pack 2 and includes a number of updated and new features (some of these features were first included in Service Pack 1; service packs are cumulative, and you only need to install the last in a series.) We'll look at some of these new features elsewhere in the book, but for now here's a partial list (full documentation is provided on the Readme file on each service pack CD, which contains the release notes for the service pack and is a must read):

- An updated Exchange client: Outlook 98
- Improvements to Outlook Web Access (OWA)
- Move Server Wizard for moving Exchange servers between sites (something that could not be done before)
- Improvements to the Key Management (KM) server
- Message Journalling capability
- Clean Mailbox tool
- Additional migration tools
- Other goodies

Installing an Exchange service pack is easy to do. Just put the service pack CD in the CD-ROM drive on the server, click Start and Run, enter the following path, and click OK (if drive D: is the CD-ROM):

```
D:\Server\Eng\Server\Setup\I386\Update.exe
```

Then follow the prompts.

Tuning System Performance

A few basic steps can be taken to configure the Windows NT Server that Exchange is installed on in order to optimize Exchange's performance. These tasks include optimizing three basic system resources: processor, memory, and disk subsystems. Let's look at these steps now:

- You can boost the CPU performance for Exchange so that it receives a larger share of processor resources on the machine. To do so, open the

System utility in the Control Panel, select the Performance tab, and make sure the Boost slider is set to None. This gives lower processor preference to foreground applications and more to background services like the Exchange Server services.

- You can optimize the way Windows NT Server uses memory in order to provide Exchange with a bit more, which can be helpful on systems with insufficient memory. Open the Network utility in the Control Panel, select the Server service, and click Properties to display the dialog box shown in Figure 3-7. Make sure the option Maximize Throughput for Network Applications is selected.
- Another option is to configure the Windows NT pagefile to be sufficiently large enough to meet Exchange's demands. A rule of thumb suggested by many administrators is to configure the initial size of the pagefile to be equal to the total amount of physical RAM plus 100 MB, although you can't go wrong making it even a bit larger. You can also move the pagefile to a stripe set (RAID 1) drive to improve performance even further. To configure the pagefile, go back to the System utility in the Control Panel, select the Performance tab, click the Change button, and specify a new initial size (and possibly location) for the pagefile, making the maximum size about 50 MB larger than the initial size.

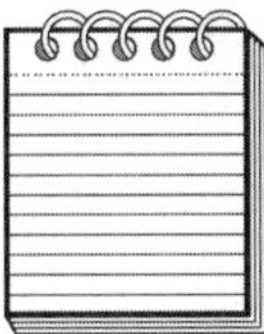

Pagefile

Note that removing the pagefile entirely from the C: drive and placing it on a stripe set means that if a STOP error (the "blue screen of death") occurs, your system will be unable to dump debugging information to a memory.dmp file. Thus, you will have lost an important tool for troubleshooting serious system

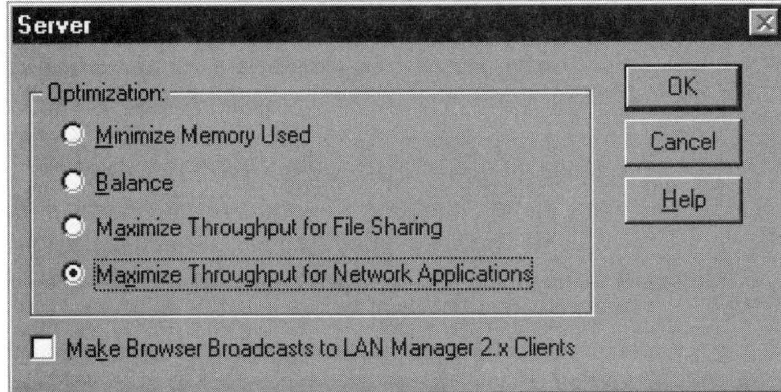

Figure 3-7
Optimizing memory for Exchange.

problems. You could split the pagefile between C: and the stripe set, with the size of the portion on C: equal to the amount of physical memory in the machine. This would allow you to still be able to generate a dumpfile when a STOP error occurs.

Message Journalling

Enabling message journalling is another post-installation issue that many Exchange administrators have to consider, particularly those who work in government-owned networks where Big Brother wants to keep an eye on everything his employees are doing. Message Journalling was first introduced in Service Pack 1 for Exchange 5.5. It enables Exchange to save copies of every email message sent or received by users. Messages can be saved for all users in a server, site, or entire organization, while saved messages can be stored in a mailbox or public folder or be forwarded to a custom recipient. Message Journalling saves

- Messages sent or received by Exchange users
- Messages posted to public folders
- Messages relayed by the Internet Mail Service (IMS)
- Read receipts for messages that have been received and read
- Delivery reports for SMTP messages that are sent

Walkthrough: Enabling Message Journalling

Message Journalling is configured by editing the registry (*Caution! Don't make a mistake!*). If message journalling is to be used in a site or organization, every Exchange server in that site or organization must have the save Exchange service pack installed (either SP1 or SP2) and each server in the site or organization must also be configured for message journalling. Since this is really a post-installation issue, let's walk through the steps of configuring Message Journalling for our SampleCorp organization. This extensive procedure assumes some familiarity with creating recipients using Exchange Administrator and running Exchange Administrator in *raw mode*. These concepts are discussed in later chapters, so you might want to skip this now and come back to it later on. If you want even more detail than is shown here, read the Readme file on the service pack.

Begin by installing Service Pack 1 or 2 for Exchange 5.5 (we chose SP2). Start the Exchange Administrator and connect to the local server (called MICKEY in our setup). From the menu, select File, New Mailbox, then click OK in the dialog box that says you must switch to the Recipients container, and the property sheet for your new mailbox appears (see Figure 3-8). We will now create a mailbox for storing the message copies created by the Message Journalling feature. Let's give our new mailbox the following values for its fields:

- First Name: Message
- Last Name: Journalling

This automatically generates a display name of "Message Journalling" and an alias of "MessageJ". Leave the rest of the fields blank, click OK, select Create a New Windows NT Account, and click OK several times until you return to the Exchange Administrator screen. Now close Exchange Administrator.

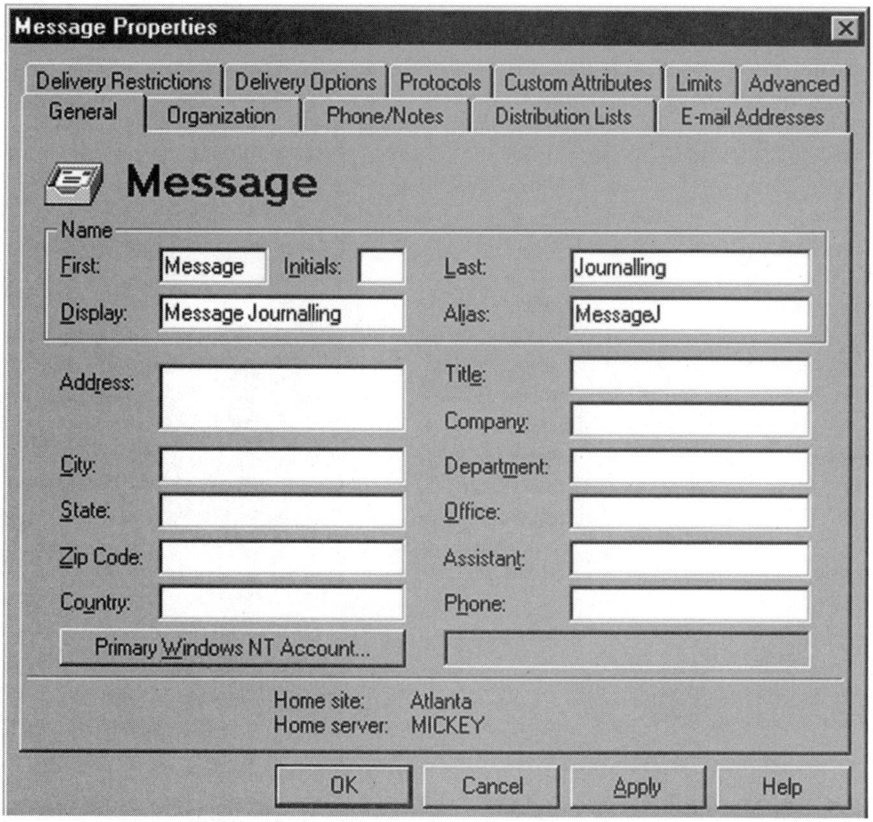

Figure 3-8
Creating a recipient to receive copies of messages created by Message Journalling.

Next, open Registry Editor (regedt32.exe) and follow these steps:

1. Add a registry value to specify that messages copied by Message Journalling will be forwarded to the mailbox whose alias is MessageJ. First, you have to find the *distinguished name (DN)* of recipient MessageJ. You do this by starting Exchange Administrator in *raw mode* by using Start, Run, and typing

   ```
   C:\Exchsrvr\Bin\Admin.exe /r
   ```

   Raw mode exposes all of the nuts and bolts of the Exchange directory. Select the Recipients container, select the user whose display name is Message Journalling, and then go to the File menu and select Raw Properties. This opens the raw properties sheet for MessageJ (see Figure 3-9). Select Obj-Dist-Name in the listbox and write down the string shown in the Edit Value textbox. This string is

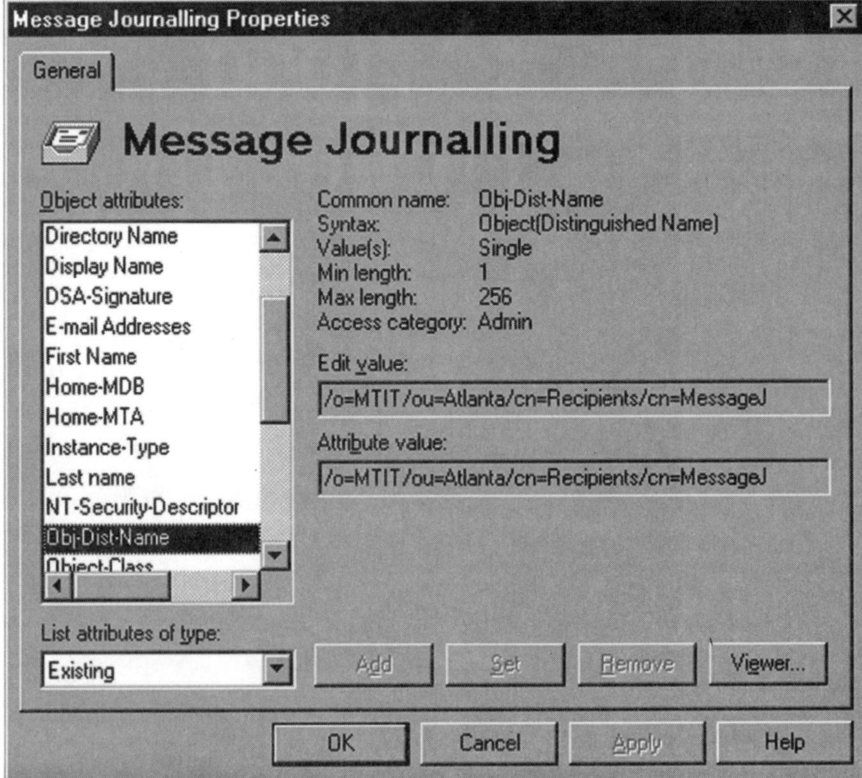

Figure 3-9 Raw properties of mailbox "MessageJ".

the distinguished name of the mailbox MessageJ. In our case, this string is

```
/o=MTIT/ou=Atlanta/cn=Recipients/cn=MessageJ
```

2. Close the raw properties sheet and switch back to Registry Editor and open the key:

```
HKEY_LOCAL_MACHINE
  SYSTEM
    CurrentControlSet
      Services
        MSExchangeMTA
          Parameters
```

Add a new Value using the Edit menu as follows (see Figure 3-10):

```
Value Name = Journal Recipient Name
Data Type = REG_SZ
Value = /o=MTIT/ou=Atlanta/cn=Recipients/cn=MessageJ
```

(Substitute the above value with your own if you are following along.)

3. Add a registry value to specify which level Message Journalling is to be configured at: server, site, or organization level (we'll choose organization-wide message journalling.) Add a new Value as follows:

```
Value Name = Per-Site Journal Required
Data Type = DWORD
Value = 0
```

(Using Value 1 enables Message Journalling at the site level, and 2 enables it at the server level.)

4. Add a registry value to route all SMTP messages through the information store. This is only relevant if the Internet Mail Service is installed, so we will have to do this later. Open a new registry key:

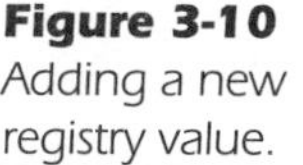

Figure 3-10 Adding a new registry value.

```
HKEY_LOCAL_MACHINE
  SYSTEM
    CurrentControlSet
      Services
        MSExchangeIMC
          Parameters
```

Add a new Value as follows:

```
Value Name = RerouteViaStore
Data type = DWORD
Value = 1
```

5. Add a registry value to route all local messages through the *message transfer agent* (MTA). Open a new registry key:

```
HKEY_LOCAL_MACHINE
  SYSTEM
    CurrentControlSet
      Services
        MSExchangeIS
          ParametersSystem
```

Add a new value as follows:

```
Value Name = No Local Delivery
Data type = DWORD
Value = 1
```

Now restart the server for these changes to take effect. We'll test this feature of Message Journalling later on in the book.

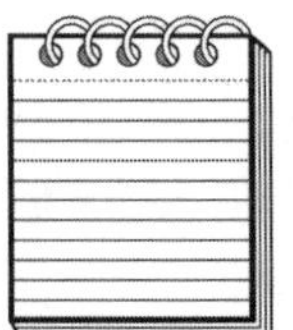

Message Journalling

Message Journalling produces an additional hit on the MTA, so you may need to beef up your hardware to handle it. The mailbox that will receive copies of all messages may even need to be placed on a dedicated server with a lot of disk storage space.

Troubleshooting Installation Problems

Here are a few tips regarding installation problems and how to resolve them:

- If for some reason Setup fails to complete properly, you may end up with a partial install of Exchange. You can often resolve this by simply running Setup again. Use the Services utility in the Control Panel to make sure all Exchange services are stopped and configure their Startup value as Disabled. Then reboot the server and rerun Exchange Setup.

- If Setup continues to fail, you may have a network problem. Verify that the primary domain controller (PDC) can be accessed from your machine. Check the configuration of networking hardware, protocols, and services on your machine.
- If Setup fails while you are adding a new Exchange Server to an existing site, the failed machine may nevertheless have had time to replicate partial information concerning the directory of the other Exchange Server in the site that you specified during Setup (when you were asked if you wanted to join an existing site, you had to specify the name of an existing Exchange Server in the target site you want to join.) You should use Exchange Administrator to connect to that server and delete any reference to your failed server in the directory hierarchy. Then rerun Setup on the failed machine, selecting Remove All components of Exchange. Run Setup once again to attempt another install.

For More Information

Additional information on installing Exchange can be found in the *Getting Started* manual, which can be obtained in print form from Microsoft. This book is also available once you install Exchange Server on a machine as part of the online documentation called Books Online. It can also be accessed by simply inserting the Exchange CD into the CD-ROM drive on any Windows NT or Windows 98 machine, and when the Exchange splash screen appears, select Documentation and then Exchange Server. Another good source of information are the Readme.doc files on the Exchange CD and on the Exchange Service Pack CDs (they are also available on TechNet).

TechNet

Here are some of the titles from the Technical Notes section of the Exchange section on the TechNet CD that relate to installing Exchange:

- MS Exchange Server 5.5 Upgrade Procedures
- Strategies for MS Exchange Service Packs and Version Upgrades

- MS Exchange Server 5.5 Service Pack 1 Release Notes
- MS Exchange Server 5.5 Service Pack 2 Release Notes

Exchange Server 5.5 Resource Guide

This is also available on TechNet or sold separately by Microsoft, and contains some good material in the following chapters:

- Chapter 2: Planning and Steup
- Chapter 11: Troubleshooting

CHAPTER 4

Under the Hood

In Chapter 3, we looked at installing Exchange Server, but before we start learning how to administer Exchange, we need to spend some time looking under the hood to see how it works. Although this chapter provides a basic introduction of the architecture and operation of Exchange Server, some additional topics will be left until later chapters as appropriate. After reading this chapter, you will have an understanding of

- Exchange core components
- Exchange optional components
- Exchange directory structure and share points
- Exchange database files
- Exchange message flow
- Exchange address types

Exchange Core Components

Exchange Server is based on a component architecture that includes four core components and a number of optional components that can be added to provide extra functionality. All components of Exchange are implemented as *Windows NT services*, which allows them to be tightly integrated into the architecture of Windows NT Server and take advantage of its security model and multithreaded operation. In addition, services can be stopped, started, and paused independently using the Services utility in the Control Panel without the need of rebooting the server. This minimizes the amount of downtime for configuring Exchange.

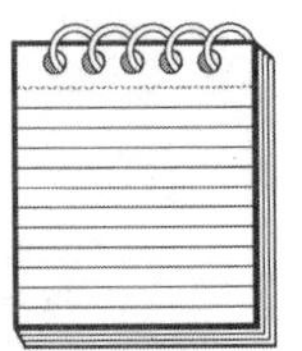

Restarting Services

Normally, when you make configuration changes to a component of Exchange Server using the Exchange Administrator program, you do not need to stop and restart the associated Exchange service in order for that change to take effect. The only exception seems to be the Internet Mail Service *(IMS), which may need to be stopped and restarted after making certain configuration changes.*

If, for some reason, you make a configuration change to Exchange and it doesn't take effect, you can always try stopping and restarting the associated service. If you don't know which service you may need to restart, you can stop all Exchange services by stopping the Microsoft Exchange

System Attendant service first (see Figure 4-1). You will be informed that stopping this service will also stop the other Exchange services as well. This is due to dependencies between the different Exchange services (all other Exchange services are dependent upon the System Agent being started). However, if you stop all your Exchange services, you will have to restart each Exchange service individually (but starting either the directory, Information Store, or Message Transfer Agent will automatically start the System Attendant).

The four core components (services) of Exchange are the

- Microsoft Exchange Directory (or Directory Service (DS))
- Microsoft Exchange Information Store (IS)
- Microsoft Exchange Message Transfer Agent (MTA)
- Microsoft Exchange System Attendant (SA)

These four services are automatically installed when Exchange Setup is run, and all four of them must be running in order for Exchange to work. Let's now look at each one of these services and how they work together.

Directory Service (DS)

The Exchange Directory Service, together with the Directory Database, maintains all information about the configuration of Exchange sites,

Figure 4-1
Exchange services.

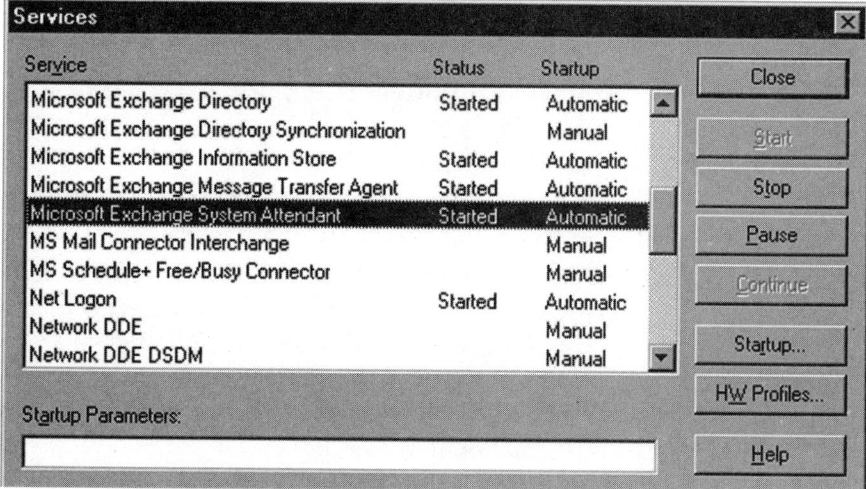

servers, components, recipients, and address lists. The Directory Database for Exchange is based upon the *Lightweight Directory Access Protocol* (LDAP) standards, which in turn are derived from the X.500 directory recommendations of the *International Telecommunications Union* (ITU). The roles of the Directory Service and Directory Database are complementary (the Directory Service together with the Directory Database is usually referred to simply as the directory). Let's examine these two components separately:

- *Directory Database*: This is a hierarchical database that stores information about all aspects of an Exchange organization. A complete copy of this database is stored on every Exchange Server in the organization, and these copies are kept up to date using directory replication. If an object in the database is modified, such as the Address attribute of a Mailbox object, that modification is made within the database residing on a single Exchange Server using the Exchange Administrator program, and then the modification is replicated to all other Exchange Servers using directory replication. We'll look at the Directory Database further later in this chapter.
- *Directory Service*: This is a Windows NT Service that maintains the contents of the Directory Database on that server. Directory replication is performed by this service, and Exchange Administrator uses this service when it connects to an Exchange Server to administer it.

The Directory Service also creates and maintains the *Global Address List* (GAL) of all recipients in the organization. This GAL can be accessed by client programs in order to look up information about Exchange recipients. For example, a client could query the Directory Service to look up the address attribute for a user named Joan Smith. Exchange supports directory lookups by three different types of clients:

- *LDAP clients* using TCP/IP network protocol. For example, if an Exchange organization is connected to the Internet using the IMS, a user on the Internet with an LDAP client like Microsoft Outlook Express can connect to the Directory Service on an Exchange Server in order to view information in the GAL.
- *Hypertext Transfer Protocol (HTTP) clients* using TCP/IP network protocol. In the same scenario as above, if *Outlook Web Access* (OWA) is installed in the Exchange organization, then a user on the Internet with a standard Web browser like Microsoft Internet Explorer or Netscape Navigator can connect to the Directory Service and view information in the GAL.

- *MAPI clients* using any network protocol that supports RPCs (usually TCP/IP or IPX/SPX). MAPI stands for Messaging Application Programming Interface, a Microsoft technology for low-level programming calls to the messaging subsystem on a Windows operating system platform. The primary MAPI client is Microsoft Outlook (not to be confused with Microsoft Outlook Express), a full-featured *Personal Information Management* (PIM) client that can connect to the Directory Service and view information in the GAL.

A good analogy for the directory is to think of it as a kind of address book. If a message needs to be delivered to a recipient, the recipient is looked up in the directory to determine its address. For example, in Microsoft Outlook, if you want to send Joan Smith a message, you can just type "Joan Smith" in the To: box of your message window. When you send the message, Exchange will look up "Joan Smith" in the directory to find her address so that the message can be routed to its destination, the mailbox of Joan Smith on her home server.

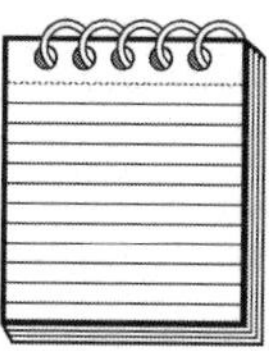

Recipient

We've bandied the word "recipient" around a lot without really defining it. A recipient is something that can receive a message. Five types of recipients exist in Exchange:

- Mailboxes, *which are associated with Windows NT user accounts within your Exchange organization*
- Custom Recipients, *which represent users located outside your organization*
- Distribution Lists, *which are mailing lists for mass mailings*
- Public Folders, *which are used for sharing messages and collaboration*
- Mailbox Agents, *which are programs that can receive message and respond to them in some way*

We'll look more at recipients and how to create and configure them in a later chapter.

Information Store (IS)

Like the directory, the Information Store also consists of both a database (two, actually) and a service that maintains and allows access to that database (and like the directory, the Information Store service together with the two Information Store databases are usually referred to simply as the Information Store). Although the Directory is responsible for storing and maintaining the attributes of recipients and other objects in an Exchange organization, the Information Store is responsible for storing the actual messages received by those recipients. Specifically, there are two Information Store databases, each of which stores messages for a different kind of recipient:

- *Private Information Store*: This database stores messages and their attachments that are received by mailbox recipients, the type of recipient associated with Windows NT user accounts in an Exchange organization. Each user in the organization typically has one mailbox, which contains their Inbox, Outbox, Sent Items, Deleted Items, and other personal folders. Typically, only one user is associated with each mailbox, although you can associate multiple users with a single mailbox (in case someone will be leaving the company soon and you want to give their replacement joint access to the mailbox).
- *Public Information Store*: This database stores messages and documents that have been posted to Public Folders on this server. Public Folders are a type of recipient that is shared by a group of users, enabling them to collaborate on projects by sharing information with each other.

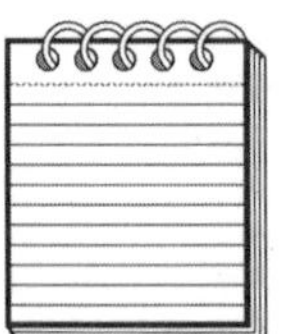

Mailbox Locations

Make sure you understand the fact that mailbox information is stored in two different locations in Exchange.

The attributes *of a mailbox are stored in the Directory Database on all Exchange Servers in an organization. Attributes include things like the last name, first name, address, phone number, title, department, and other information specifically related to the user who owns the mailbox. For example, if a mailbox is created for Sean Jones, there will be a mailbox object called SeanJ (if Exchange naming conventions are configured accordingly) in the Directory Database of every Exchange Server in the organization (once directory replication has distributed this information to all of them).*

The contents *of a mailbox are stored in the Private Information Store on the associated user's* home server, *that is, the Exchange Server on which the mailbox object was created. Contents include messages and their attachments received from other recipients, and copies of sent messages created by the user (if the mail client is configured to save these).*

Public Folders are a little different. Their attributes are stored in the Directory Database of all Exchange Servers (just like mailboxes), but their contents may be stored on several Exchange Servers if Public Folder replication is configured accordingly. We'll look at this in more detail in a later chapter.

A good analogy for the function of the Information Store is to think of it as a kind of post office. Any message that is created (for example, by a mail client program like Microsoft Outlook) must first be delivered to the post office (the Information Store), which then looks up the address of the destination recipient in the address book (the directory) and then usually hands it off to a mail delivery person MTA to send it on its way.

The Information Store supports a special feature known as *single-instance storage*. What this means is that if a message is addressed to several recipients, it is only stored once within the Information Store. An example would be a message sent to a Distribution List consisting of 10 target recipients. Only one copy of the message is stored in the Information Store, along with pointers to the 10 recipients to whom it is intended. Once the message is passed to the MTA for delivery, the MTA expands the list and creates 10 copies of the message, one for each intended recipient. The point of single-instance storage is that it reduces the amount of disk storage space needed for the Information Store databases. This can be a significant saving when companies make heavy use of distribution lists, for example, for mass mailing of sales information to clients.

These two Information Store databases are maintained by the single Information Store service; stopping the Microsoft Exchange Information Store service on an Exchange Server prevents both users from accessing their mail on that server and prevents users from accessing Public Folders hosted on that server. The Information Store can be accessed by several types of clients:

- *MAPI clients* like Microsoft Outlook can directly access the contents of the Information Store databases. For example, Joan Smith can directly access both the messages stored in her mailbox in the Private Information Store on her home server and can access any messages posted to Public Folders in the Public Information Store (provided she has suitable access permissions for that folder).
- *Post Office Protocol version 3 (POP3) clients* like Microsoft Outlook Express or Eudora can similarly access the contents of their mailbox in the Private Information Store database on that server.
- *Network News Transport Protocol (NNTP) clients* like Outlook Express or FreeAgent can similarly access the contents of Newsgroup Public Folders in the Public Information Store database on that server.

One or Two?

An Exchange Server must have at least one Information Store database, even if you aren't using it for hosting users' mail messages or hosting Public Folder replicas. Specifically, an Exchange Server can have either

- *A Private Information Store and a Public Information Store*
- *A Private Information Store only*
- *A Public Information Store only*

If a server has only a Private store, it is usually called a Mailbox Server. If a server has only a Public Store, it is usually called a Public Folder Server. By default, when you install Exchange, it creates both a Private and a Public Store on the server. You can then delete one of them if you don't need it using the Exchange Administrator program (you can recreate the deleted store later if you change your mind). Having only one store on a server can significantly improve the server's performance by freeing up additional system resources and reducing the load on the CPU and disk subsystems.

Which store should you delete if your server doesn't need either stores (for example, if it will be used as a Connectivity Server or Messaging Bridgehead Server for routing messages to other sites or mail systems)? Delete the Public Store and leave the Private Store unused in this case. The reason is that a Public Store, even if unused, will still generate an overhead of system messages relating to Public Folder replication, and hence use up some available network bandwidth. Private stores do not generate this type of traffic.

Message Transfer Agent (MTA)

The MTA is the component that is responsible for routing messages to other Exchange Servers, other sites, and other mail systems. In other words, if a message needs to be sent to a recipient different than the one the originator's Mailbox is homed on, the MTA handles the job. A good analogy is to think of the MTA as a kind of mail delivery person; if someone drops off a message at the post office (the Information Store), the post office give the message to the deliver person (the MTA) who makes sure it is delivered properly. Actually, what really happens is that the message gets passed from MTA to MTA until it arrives at its final destination, the remote post office (the Information Store of the destination recipient's home server), which then notifies the recipient (the mail client program) to collect its mail. We'll look more at the mechanics of message delivery later.

Another responsibility of the MTA is that it expands distribution lists so that copies of the original message stored in the Information Store are sent to each recipient on the list (refer to information on *single-instance storage* above).

System Attendant (SA)

The final core component of Exchange is called the System Attendant, which quite properly attends to the general functions of the system. In other words, the System Attendant is a kind of umbrella service that helps everything else work together and performs specific functions that other services don't perform. In our analogy, we could think of the System Attendant as a combination of administrative, clerical, and janitorial staff that keeps the whole postal system humming and flowing. Specifically, the System Attendant is responsible for

- Managing the operation of Server Monitors for monitoring the status of Exchange services on a machine
- Managing the operation of Link Monitors for monitoring the status of a messaging link between Exchange and a foreign mail system
- Generating the internal routing tables (GWART) in order for messages to be routed effectively to remote sites and foreign mail systems
- Generating a recipient's email addresses when a new recipient is created
- Maintaining the consistency of the directory replication process between all Exchange servers in a given site
- Managing advanced security features for a Mailbox such as digital signatures

Exchange Optional Components

We'll look more closely in a moment at how the four core components of Exchange work together to deliver messages, but for now let's continue our look at Exchange components by looking at the various *optional* components that can be installed. Many of these will be discussed more fully later, so here they will be listed along with a brief description of what they do.

Each of these optional components is implemented as a Windows NT Service, just like the core components. Note that some of them are only available with the Enterprise Edition of Exchange (marked with an asterisk). Here are the various optional components:

- *Microsoft Mail Connector*: This component enables messages to be sent to and received from a *Microsoft Mail* (MS Mail) messaging system. MS Mail is a legacy Microsoft messaging system that was the precursor to Exchange. There are actually two versions of MS Mail, one for PC networks and one for AppleTalk networks, so there are two versions of the connector as well.
- *Directory Synchronization*: This component complements the MS Mail Connector by enabling directory information (specifically, address lists and recipient attributes) to be exchanged between the Exchange Directory and an MS Mail system.
- *Microsoft Schedule+ Free/Busy Connector*: This component also complements the MS Mail Connector and enables scheduling information to be exchanged between Exchange and an MS Mail system.
- *Key Management Server*: This component can be installed to provide support for advanced security features like digital signatures and sending encrypted messages.
- *Outlook Web Access*: This component can be installed to enable users to access their messages using a Web browser instead of a traditional mail client program.
- *Internet Mail Service*: This component enables messages to be sent to and received from an SMTP mail system, such as that found on the Internet.
- *Internet News Service*: This component can be installed to enable Exchange to function as a Usenet host in order to participate in the Internet's Usenet news system. It can also create Usenet-style newsgroups hosted internally on Exchange Public Folders, and allow clients to access these newsgroups for reading and posting messages.
- *Event Services*: This component enables you to write server-side scripts that can process messages posted to Public Folders for creating workflow and collaboration programs.
- *Connector for cc:Mail*: This component enables messages and directory information to be exchanged with Lotus cc:Mail systems.
- **Connector for Lotus Notes*: This component enables messages and directory information to be exchanged with Lotus Notes systems.

- **Connector for SNADS*: This component enables messages to be exchanged with IBM *SNA Distribution System* (SNADS) mainframe-based mail systems.
- **Connector for IBM OfficeVision / VM (PROFS)*: This component enables messages to be exchanged with IBM OfficeVision/VM (PROFS) mainframe-based mail systems.

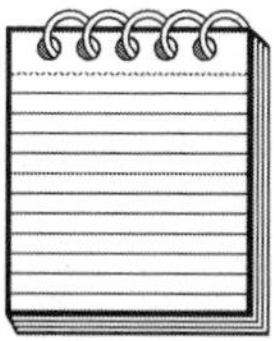

Connectors

If you're already a bit familiar with Exchange, you'll notice that the above list includes some but not all of the various Exchange connectors. A connector is an Exchange component that allows messages to be delivered outside a site to a remote site or a foreign mail system. Exchange includes a number of different connectors including the Site Connector, X.400 Connector, Dynamic RAS Connector, IMS, MS Mail Connector, and so on. Some of these connectors are implemented within the core Exchange services, while others like the MS Mail Connector must be installed during setup and run as separate services under Windows NT. We'll look more at connectors in later chapters.

Exchange Directory Structure and Share Points

Let's take a look at the changes to the directory structure made on a Windows NT Server by installing Exchange on it. Figure 4-2 shows a simplified directory structure if all Exchange files are created on a single partition C: drive. Note that all Exchange directories are subdirectories of the master directory `\exchsrvr`. If you install Exchange on a system with multiple drives or partitions, the Exchange Performance Optimizer that runs at the end of setup will distribute some of these files onto other partitions. Each partition that has Exchange files will have a master directory `\exchsrvr` along with various subdirectories under it.

Table 4-1 briefly summarizes the various subdirectories of `\exchsrvr` and what they are used for. If you have additional components installed on your Exchange Server like the Connector for Lotus Notes, you may have additional subdirectories not listed in this table.

In addition to creating the directory structure shown in Table 4-1 and populating it with files, installing Exchange also creates several new share points. Some of these shares are visible in Figure 4-2. The Exchange shares are listed in Table 4-2, along with a brief description of what they are used for.

You should generally not modify the permissions set for these shares.

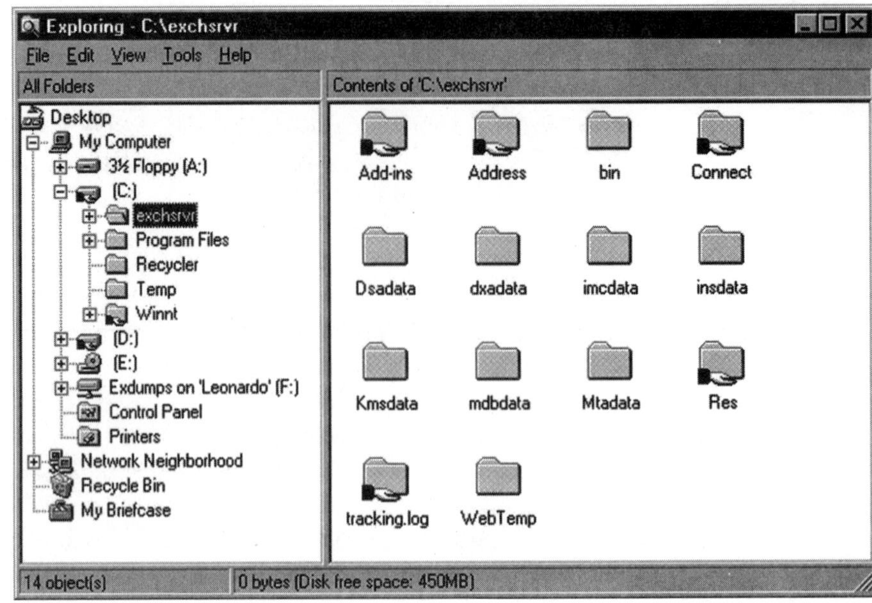

Figure 4-2 Exchange directory structure.

Table 4-1 Exchange Server Directory Structure.

Subdirectory	Description
`\Add-ins`	Contains miscellaneous extension DLLs for various connectors.
`\Address`	Contains proxy generator DLLs for generating email addresses for new recipients.
`\Bin`	Contains binaries (executable programs) such as the GUI tools Admin.exe (Exchange Administrator) and Perfwiz.exe (Performance Optimizer) and command-line tools like Edbutil.exe (Exchange Database Maintenance Utility) and Mtacheck.exe (Message Transfer Agent Maintenance Utility). Also various supporting files.
`\Connect`	Contains miscellaneous DLLs to support various connectors.
`\Dsadata`	Contains the Directory Database files.
`\Dxadata`	Used for directory synchronization with an MS Mail messaging system.
`\Imcdata`	Contains various working directories on the IMS for all messages to be queued and delivered.
`\Incdata`	Used by the Internet News Service.
`\Kmsdata`	Used by the *Key Management* (KM) Server (if installed).
`\Mdbdata`	Contains the Information Store database files (for both stores).

Subdirectory	Description
\Mtadata	Contains various working directories and files for the MTA to be able to queue and deliver messages.
\Res	Contains miscellaneous DLLs that are used by Event Viewer and the Performance Monitor.
\Tracking.log	Contains log files for message tracking (if enabled).
\Webdata	Contains the components of Outlook Web Access (if installed).

Table 4-2

Exchange Share Points.

Share	Description
Add-ins	Enables access to Exchange SDK objects
Address	Enables access to address objects
Connect$	Enables access to connectors (hidden share)
Maildat$	Enables access to shadow Postoffice when MS Mail Connector is used (hidden share)
Resources	Enables access to event logging files
Tracking.log	Enables access to message tracking log files

Exchange Database Files

Let's now take a look at the database files for the Directory and Information Store. These are critical files that need to be backed up regularly, as they contain the configuration information that defines your Exchange organization and the messages that users send and receive.

Directory Database Files

The Directory Database files are located in the `\exchsrvr\dsadata` directory and comprise the following files:

- `Dir.edb`, which stores the actual database records. The format of this database is based upon a Microsoft database technology called *Joint Engine Technology* (JET), which is the same technology used in other Windows NT Services that use database structures, such as DHCP and WINS.

- `Edb.log`, which is the current *transaction log file* and is used to track any changes (transactions) made to the Directory Database.
- `Edb.chk`, which functions as a *checkpoint file* and is used to keep track of which transactions in the `Edb.log` file have been committed (written to the `Dir.edb` file).
- `Temp.edb`, a temporary work file used for storing transactions that are still in progress.
- `Res1.log` and `Res2.log`, which function as *reserved log files* and are used only when disk space is low to ensure the integrity of the Directory Database.

The file structure of the Directory Database looks a little complicated, but it has its purpose; transaction log files and the associated database files are intended to improve the performance of writing changes to the database, ensure the integrity of the database in case of system failure, and enable the database to recover from certain kinds of failure.

How the Directory Database Is Updated

Updates are written to the Directory Database something like this: the Exchange database engine writes data in 4-kB blocks called pages. Database records are swapped as needed between the disk and a cache in RAM (Exchange 5.5 is tuned to use all available RAM for caching database files, so you can always improve the performance of Exchange by adding more RAM). Modifications are then made to the pages in RAM (since it is faster than writing to disk) and then these "dirty" pages (pages that have changes made to them) are flushed to the database file on disk (after enough of them have been accumulated to do an efficient write operation to the database file). The result is that the actual database file (Dir.edb) on disk is never completely up to date, since some changes may exist as dirty pages in the RAM cache that have not yet been flushed. In fact, the normal state of the database file is to be inconsistent at all times, unless of course you perform an orderly shut-down of the server, which flushes all dirty pages from RAM and thus brings the database file completely up to date. But in this arrangement, if the server suddenly crashes and memory is lost, valuable database updates will also be lost.

How does Exchange protect against such a loss? The answer is that Exchange uses a transactional database technology. A *transaction* is a group of operations performed on a database (such as a record being inserted, modified, or deleted) that follows a specific pattern called *ACID*, which stands for *Atomic, Consistent, Isolated,* and *Durable:*

- *Atomic*, meaning that it's either all or none when it comes to the operations in a transaction. If any one of them fails, the transaction fails; if they all succeed, the transaction succeeds.
- *Consistent*, which means that the database moves from one correct state to another and is never inconsistent or incomplete.
- *Isolated*, which means that changes made to a database are not visible until they have been committed.
- *Durable*, which means that transactions that have been committed are preserved in some form in the database files so if the system crashes, the database can be recovered and no information is lost.

To make this system work, the Exchange databases use the transaction log files, checkpoint files, and other files described above. For example, when the administrator makes a modification to the properties of an Exchange component using the Exchange Administrator program, that change must be updated within the Directory Database, which stores all configuration information concerning an Exchange organization. The Exchange Administrator program uses MAPI to send the update to the Directory Service, which contacts the Exchange database engine and begins a new transaction. The database engine writes the transaction in the RAM cache (thus "dirtying" one of the pages in RAM) and synchronously (simultaneously) records the transaction in the transaction log (`Edb.log`). Updates are written to these transaction logs sequentially, recording database transactions one after another by appending each new transaction to the existing ones (this also helps to improve Exchange performance, since writing transactions to a sequential file is much faster than trying to write them to the database file itself, which has a complex hierarchical structure, involves updating indexes, uses random I/O access, and so on). The transaction is thus completed in memory and recorded in the transaction log.

When enough transactions have been written to memory to perform an efficient write operation on the database file, the dirty pages are flushed and their contents are written to the database file (`Dir.edb`), at which time the checkpoint file (`Edb.chk`) is also updated to reflect that the transactions have been committed to disk (actually this "bunching up" of transactions only happens if the server is extremely busy; if the server load is light, the transaction logs are committed almost instantaneously to the database file). The transaction logs themselves are not reread; they are written sequentially and are only read if a recovery has to be performed.

As a result, the database file (`Dir.edb`) together with the transaction log file (`Edb.chk`) (or the uncommitted transactions in memory) comprise a complete and consistent database. Actually, there may be several transaction log files, depending on the number of updates that have been made to the database. These log files are named `Edb00001.log`, `Edb00002.log`, and so on. The current transaction log is always called `Edb.log`; once it is full, its name is changed to `Edbnnnnn.log`, where `nnnnn` is the generation number of the log file, starting with hexadecimal 1 and increasing incrementally by one. By default, transaction log files are always 5 MB in size, even when few transactions are written to them (see Figure 4-3).

The point is that if the system crashes and memory is lost, no information has been lost and the database can be completely and accurately recovered. The transaction logs together with the database file form a completely consistent database at all times. If the server crashes, the Directory Service, once restarted, will replay the transaction logs to ensure that all uncommitted transactions in the transaction logs are committed to the database file. The Directory Service uses the checkpoint file (`Edb.chk`) for recovery purposes, since the checkpoint file indicates which transactions in the transaction log have already been committed (the "inactive" portion of the transaction file) and which are still uncommitted (the "active" portion of the file). The checkpoint file uses a pointer to indicate the point in the sequence of transactions where this dividing point (checkpoint marker) occurs, and thus greatly

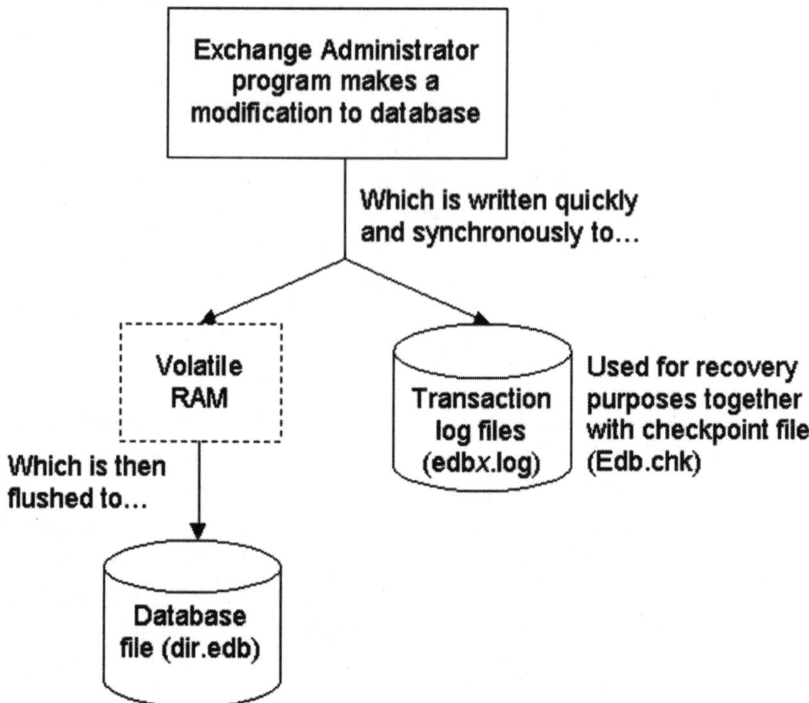

Figure 4-3 The process by which modifications are made to the Directory Database.

speeds up the recovery process when Exchange is restarted after an improper shutdown. Otherwise, all the transactions in the transaction logs would need to be reviewed to determine whether they have been committed or not.

Location of Transaction Logs

Now it's obvious why it is a good idea to locate the transaction logs on a separate physical disk from the database file—they're important! Place the transaction logs on a dedicated physical disk if possible (that is, a disk on which only *the transaction logs are located and nothing else) and mirror the disk for greater fault tolerance. Don't use a stripe set with parity for the transaction logs. Since they are written sequentially instead of randomly, better performance is achieved by using a single physical disk instead. And by having only transaction logs on the disk, the disk drive heads will move a minimum amount during disk writes, enabling transactions to be written to disk as quickly as possible. If you must place the transaction logs on a disk with other files (such as operating system files), make sure your server has lots of RAM so paging will be minimal.*

Also, always make sure you backup both your database files and their associated transaction log files!

Circular Logging

One strange feature of Exchange is the possibility of using circular logging for the transaction log files. Circular logging is basically a method of economizing on disk space. When circular logging is enabled, what happens is that once a transaction log file becomes full, its remaining transactions are committed and it is then deleted and a new (empty) transaction log file is created in its place (actually Exchange will generally maintain up to four transaction log files when circular logging is enabled; if a fifth one needs to be created, the oldest one is deleted). This is fine for protection against a sudden system failure, but it means that you have to always perform full backups every day. If you perform a full backup on Monday and then incremental (or differential) backups on other days, then your backup set may be missing some transaction logs if they were deleted at some point during the week. If your system experiences a catastrophic disk failure, you will be unable to completely restore your database from your backup set. So if circular logging is enabled, then you must perform a full backup every day to ensure you have an up-to-date database file (`Dir.edb`) from each day, along with the day's transaction log (`Edb.log`), which contains any uncommitted transactions from the day.

Circular logging was a great idea when disk drives were expensive items, but it is a lousy idea today in the era of cheap mass storage. And believe it or not, circular logging is enabled by default on Exchange Server. So one of the first things you will want to do after installing Exchange is to *turn circular logging off!* You can do this using the Advanced tab on the Server property sheet in Exchange Administrator (explained later in this book). Otherwise, buy lots and lots of tape cassettes for your tape backup device.

One more thing: if you perform *online* backups (backups while the Exchange services are still running), unneeded transaction log files (files that have only committed transactions in them) will automatically be deleted from your hard drive, thus keeping them from building up and eating away at your disk space. Online backups cause old transaction logs to be deleted and the "inactive" portion of the current transaction log (`Edb.log`) to be erased as well.

Information Store Database Files

Everything we've said above is also true for the Information Store database files, with one small exception: there's two of them. The Information Store database files are located in the `\exchsrvr\mdbdata` directory and consist of the following:

- `Priv.edb`, which is the database file for the Private Information Store (contains messages and attachments for users homed on the server)
- `Pub.edb`, which is the database file for the Public Information Store (contains the contents of Public Folder replicas hosted on the server)
- The additional transactional database files `Edb.log`, `Edb.chk`, `Temp.edb`, `Res1.log`, and `Res2.log`

Of course, if the server is a mailbox server and has only a Private Information Store, there will be a `Priv.edb` file, but not a `Pub.edb` one. If the server is a Public Folder Server and has only a Public Information Store, there will only be a `Pub.edb` file in this directory.

Exchange Message Flow

Now that we have had a close look at the architecture of Exchange Server, let's consider its operation in the area that is most important, namely, message delivery. To do this, we will look at what is known as *message flow*, the path or route which an email message follows as it is passed from component to component (from service to service) on an Exchange Server, from server to server in an Exchange site, and on to other sites or mail systems. We'll actually look at the first case in detail (called *single-server message flow*), then extrapolate to messages sent within a site (called *single-site message flow*), and finally extrapolate the case of messages sent outside a site. We'll look at how messages are routed beyond a site later once we have talked about connectors.

Single-Server Message Flow

Let's consider an Exchange Server with two mailboxes created in its Private Information Store:

- Mailbox *JoanS* for user Joan Smith
- Mailbox *SeanJ* for user Sean Jones

What happens when Joan Smith tries to send a message to Sean Jones? We'll assume that each user is using the standard MAPI client that comes with Exchange, namely Microsoft Outlook. The sequence of steps looks something like this (see Figure 4-4):

1. Joan creates a message addressed to Sean using her copy of Outlook and clicks Send.
2. Joan's copy of Outlook then connects using RPCs with the IS service and submits her message to the service.
3. The IS service looks at the address of the target recipient (Sean), which is contained in the message header, and checks with the Directory Service (DS) to find out which server Sean's Mailbox is homed on.
4. The result of querying the Directory Service is that Sean's mailbox is homed on the same server as Joan's.
5. Now that the Information Store knows where to deliver the message, it moves the message from Joan's Outbox to Sean's Inbox, both of which are located within the Private Information Store on the server.
6. The Information Store then tries to contact Sean's copy of Outlook using RPCs to inform it of the presence of a new message in his Inbox. If Sean's copy of Outlook is not running, the Information Store will wait for Sean's Outlook to contact it later.

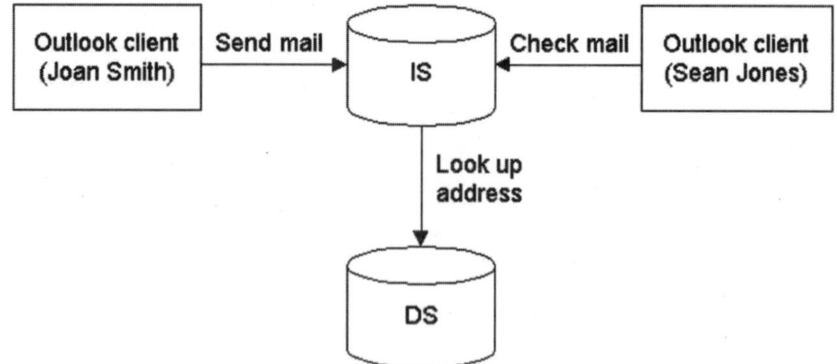

Figure 4-4 Single-server message flow on Exchange.

Single-Site Message Flow

Now let's make it a little more interesting. What if Joan and Sean's mailboxes are on two different Exchange Servers, yet both of which, however, are in the same site? The main difference here is that another core component of Exchange, the MTA, is responsible for actually getting the message moved from one server to the other. The steps are a little more complicated but should be easy to follow (see Figure 4-5):

1. Joan creates a message addressed to Sean using her copy of Outlook and clicks Send.
2. Joan's copy of Outlook then connects using RPCs with the IS service and submits her message to the service.
3. The Information Store service checks the address of the target recipient (Sean) with the Directory Service (DS) to find out which server Sean's Mailbox is homed on.
4. The result of querying the Directory Service is that Sean's Mailbox is homed on a different server as Joan's, so the Information Store passes the message to the MTA for delivery.
5. The MTA on Joan's server checks with the Directory Service to determine whether the target recipient (Sean) is located in the local site or a remote one.
6. The Directory Service tells the MTA that the target recipient is in the local site, whereupon the MTA on Joan's server uses RPCs to locate and connect to the MTA on Sean's server. This connection is known as an *association*.

7. The MTA on Joan's server now forwards the message to the MTA on Sean's server.
8. The MTA on Sean's server checks the address of the target recipient (Sean) with the Directory Service to find out whether the message needs to be forwarded further.
9. The Directory Service tells the MTA that the target recipient (Sean) has his mailbox on that server, so the MTA delivers the message directly to Sean's Inbox within the Private Information Store on that server.
10. The Information Store then tries to contact Sean's copy of Outlook using RPCs to inform it of the presence of a new message in his Inbox.

Message Flow Beyond the Local Site

Finally, we'll mention briefly what happens when Joan and Sean are in different sites, or when Joan belongs to the Exchange organization and Sean is on a foreign mail system like the Internet's SMTP mail system. The only change is that when the MTA on Joan's server checks with the Directory Service to determine whether the target recipient is in the local site or a remote site (or foreign mail system), it determines that the target recipient is outside the local site. So instead of trying to contact another server in the

Figure 4-5
Single-site message flow.

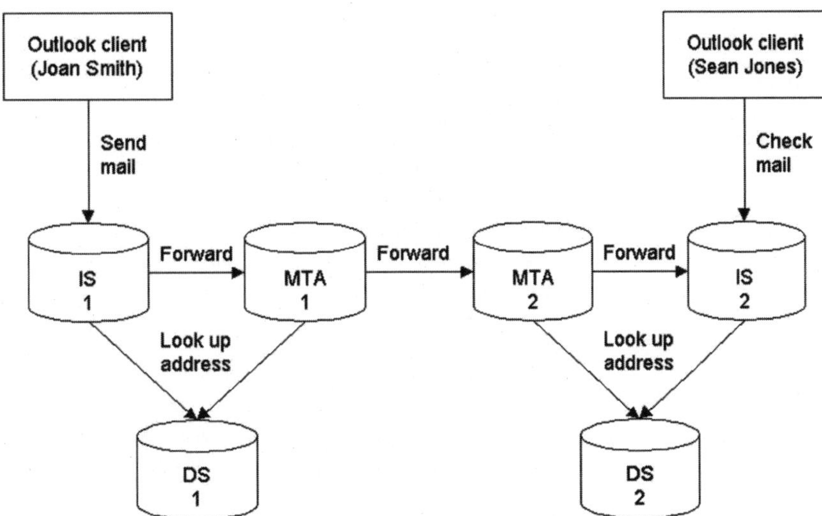

local site, the MTA consults the GWART to determine which installed connector to forward the message to (messages get forwarded to remote sites and foreign mail systems using connectors).

Once the message arrives at the remote site (or foreign mail system), the MTA on the appropriate connector server in the remote site contacts the MTA on the target recipient's server and forwards the message to it. This second MTA gives the message to the information store (alternatively, if the message is delivered to a foreign mail system, then the MTA or its equivalent in the foreign mail system handles it from there). We'll look more at message routing and the GWART in a later chapter.

Exchange Address Types

We'll complete this chapter (it's long and technical and has no walk-throughs) with one more topic: the different types of addresses that Exchange uses for delivering messages.

Distinguished Name (DN)

The most basic type of address used by Exchange for delivering messages is the *distinguished name (DN)*. The DN is the native addressing format used by Exchange. When a message needs to be routed to another site or mail system by the MTA, the MTA first looks at the target recipient's DN and tries to see if it can route the message using this address before it tries any other type of address.

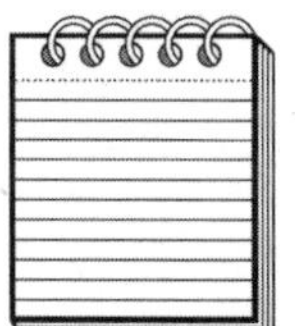

Multiple Address Types

Exchange recipients typically have several addresses, each of a different type. These different addresses are created using proxy generators *when the recipient itself is created. For example, Mailboxes typically have four different addresses, one of each of the following types:*

- *EX, the native address type for Exchange (the DN)*
- *X400, an X.400 Originator/Recipient address*
- *MS, an MS Mail address*
- *SMTP, a standard Internet email address*

There are two reasons for recipients to have multiple addresses:

- *When sending mail to a foreign mail system, the message must have a destination address that the foreign mail system can understand. Thus, multiple address types are generated to support interoperability with other mail systems.*
- *If routing by one type of address fails for some reason, the MTA can try the other addresses to see if one will work. This provides a measure of fault-tolerance for message routing and delivery purposes.*

Note that if other connectors have been installed, such as the Connector for Lotus Notes, recipients may have additional addresses beyond the four listed above.

Every object in the Exchange Directory Database is uniquely identified by its distinguished name. The distinguished name for an object contains the name of the Exchange organization, the name of the site the object is in, and specific information about the object to identify it within the site. For example, the distinguished name for Joan Smith's mailbox (which has the alias JoanS), which is located within the Atlanta site of the MTIT organization, would be

```
o=MTIT/ou=Atlanta/cn=Recipients/cn=JoanS
```

Distinguished names are read from right to left. Mailbox JoanS is located within the Recipients container of site Atlanta, which is part of organization MTIT. The general form of the distinguished name for a Exchange recipient is

```
o=<organization>/ou=<site>/cn=Recipients/cn=<mailbox_alias>
```

assuming that there is only one Recipients container and that the Mailbox is located within it in the Exchange directory hierarchy. Here we have the following variables:

- `o` stands for organization (organization name).
- `ou` stands for organizational unit (site name).
- `cn` stands for common name (used for any other parts of the distinguished name).

Originator/Recipient (O/R) Address

O/R addresses are based on the X.400 messaging standard. Exchange uses O/R addresses for the two following reasons.

- To provide messaging interoperability with foreign X.400 mail systems. Such systems are popular in Europe and some other parts of the world, but are less common in this hemisphere.
- To provide a backup address type, should the MTA be unable to route a message using the distinguished name of the target recipient.

O/R addresses are fairly complicated and consist of a series of hierarchical attributes. The idea is that X.400 provides a standard for a global messaging system and enables O/R addresses to be defined so that every recipient in the world has a unique O/R address. A typical O/R address for Joan Smith's Mailbox might be

```
c=US;a= ;p=MTIT;o=Atlanta;s=Smith;g=Joan;
```

Here the various attributes represent the following:

- `c` stands for country (United States)
- `a` stands for *Administrative Management Domain* (ADMD), which represents the third-party carrier service that provides the X.400 messaging backbone to the company. A typical example might be `a=Sprint` or `a=MCI` if either of these companies provide an X.400 messaging backbone service, but if connectivity with a foreign X.400 mail system is not being used, then the ADMD field is typically represented by a single space character, as shown in the sample address above.
- `p` stands for *Private Management Domain* (PRMD), which represents the company using the service provided by the ADMD. In Exchange, this is the name of the Exchange organization (MTIT).
- `o` stands for organization, and funnily enough, here this means the Exchange site (Atlanta), not the Exchange organization.
- `s` stands for surname (Smith).
- `g` stands for given name (Joan).

Aren't you glad you don't have to memorize O/R addresses?

MS Mail

Exchange automatically generates MS Mail addresses for each mailbox, just in case you plan to implement messaging connectivity between your Exchange organization and a legacy MS Mail network. MS Mail addresses have a simple format:

```
<Network_Name>/<Postoffice_Name>/<Mailbox_Name>
```

This breaks down into the following:

- Network Name, which corresponds to the name of the Exchange organization
- Postoffice Name, which corresponds to the name of the Exchange site
- Mailbox Name, which corresponds to the name of the Mailbox (alias name)

Thus, for example, the MS Mail address for Joan Smith's mailbox would be

```
MTIT/ATLANTA/JOANS
```

SMTP Mail

Finally, Exchange also generates an SMTP email address for each mailbox, just in case you plan to implement messaging connectivity with the Internet (a rather common occurrence). The general format for an SMTP address is

```
<user>@<domain>
```

For example, the SMTP address for Joan Smith by default would be

```
joans@atlanta.MTIT.com
```

Where Do We Go From Here?

Now that we have examined the architecture and operation of Exchange, it's time we had a look at the various tools we can use to administer an Exchange organization, primarily the Exchange Administrator program. This is the topic of our next chapter.

For More Information

Additional information on Exchange architecture and operations can be found in the Exchange Server manuals or in their online version, Books Online. In particular, the books *Getting Started* and *Concepts and Planning* deal with Exchange address types in various contexts, while the book *Maintenance and Troubleshooting* deals with the issue of circular logging.

Microsoft TechNet

Here are some of the titles from the Technical Notes section of the Exchange section on the TechNet CD that deal directly or indirectly with the architecture and operation of Exchange:

- Best Practices for Exchange Database Management
- X.400 Concepts and Terminology
- Internet Email Basics
- MS Exchange 5.5 Backup and Restore Basics
- MS Exchange Disaster Recovery Parts 1 and 2
- MS Exchange Server Planning and Design Optimization Guide

Exchange Server 5.5 Resource Guide

The Exchange Server 5.5 Resource Guide is also available on TechNet or sold separately by Microsoft. Chapter 4, "Maintaining MS Exchange Server," and Chapter 5, "Addressing and Routing," also are a good source of information on this this topic.

CHAPTER 5

Tools for Administration

In Chapter 4, we considered the architecture and operation of Exchange Server, looking "under the hood" so to speak at features like Exchange Services, database files, address types, and message flow. Now it's time to take a look at the tools for administering an Exchange organization with its sites and servers. A core component of any messaging system is the administrative tools used to manage its services, resources, and performance. Exchange Server 5.5 comes with a complete set of administrative tools, both GUI and command-line based, for administration, maintenance, and troubleshooting of Exchange-based messaging systems. After reading this chapter, you will have an understanding of

- The GUI-based tools for administering Exchange, primarily focusing on the Exchange Administrator program
- The command-line utilities for Exchange troubleshooting and maintenance
- Other Windows NT tools and utilities for administering Exchange
- *BackOffice Resource Kit* (BORK) utilities
- Exchange Permissions and Roles

There is also one walkthrough exercise in this chapter, which deals with using Exchange Administrator.

GUI-Based Tools

Exchange Server includes powerful GUI-based tools for administering Exchange sites, servers, services, and recipients. These tools include the following:

- *Exchange Administrator*, the primary tool for administering sites, servers, services, and recipients in an Exchange organization. As approximately 95 percent of all Exchange administration is done using this tool, we will be spending most of this chapter getting familiar with how to use it.
- *Performance Optimizer*, a wizard-based tool we saw already in Chapter 3, which can analyze the hardware configuration of your machine to determine how best to allocate memory, locate database and transaction files, and otherwise tune your system for optimal performance. We will examine this tool in detail when we introduce Exchange connectors in a later chapter.

- *Migration Wizard*, a wizard-based tool that is used to migrate mailboxes and their messages from legacy mail systems like Microsoft Mail 3.x and from third-party mail systems like Novell GroupWise, Collabra Share, and Lotus Notes/cc:Mail. We will study this tool in a later chapter.
- *Microsoft Outlook*, which essentially is a mail client program and not an administrator's tool, yet nevertheless is needed by administrators for performing one important administrative function that no other Exchange tool can perform: creating new public folders. We will defer examining this tool until Chapter 12, "Administering Public Folders."

Exchange Administrator

By far, the primary tool you will be using to administer your Exchange organization is the Exchange Administrator program. As we mentioned in the last chapter, all configuration information concerning the sites, servers, services, recipients, and other elements of an Exchange organization are stored in an LDAP-style database called the directory. Exchange Administrator is the primary tool for viewing and modifying information in the Exchange Directory database. You can also use the Exchange Administrator menu to connect to Exchange Server and perform common administrative tasks like

- Creating and configuring new mailboxes, distribution lists, and custom recipients
- Moving mailboxes to other servers in a site
- Cleaning mailboxes by deleting unessential messages
- Creating and configuring connectors, transport stacks, monitors, information stores, newsfeeds, address book views, and other Exchange components and services
- Configuring directory and Public Folder replication
- Exporting and importing information about recipients
- Extracting lists of user accounts from Windows NT and NetWare servers
- Starting and stopping Server and Link Monitors
- Opening the Message Tracking Center to troubleshoot message delivery problems

- Viewing newsgroup hierarchies
- Configuring permissions, export file formats, and auto naming conventions

We won't look at how to perform all of these actions in this chapter, but instead will defer most of them to later chapters where we can perform them in context.

Figure 5-1 shows the Exchange Administrator program after it has connected to our server MICKEY, which we installed in Chapter 3 as the first Exchange Server in the site Atlanta of the Exchange organization MTIT. Note that the main window of Exchange Administrator is divided into two window panes, similar to the standard Windows file management utility, Windows Explorer. These two panes are

- *The Container pane*. This left-hand pane shows all objects in the Directory that are *containers*; that is, they are directory objects that can contain other directory objects.
- *The Contents pane*. This right-hand pane shows all the directory objects that are contained within the container selected in the left-hand pane. These objects may be either containers (containing additional objects) or *leaf objects* (representing the end of a branch in the directory tree).

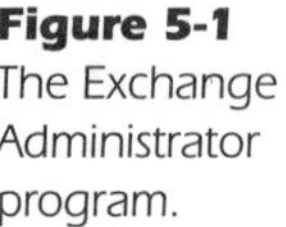

Figure 5-1 The Exchange Administrator program.

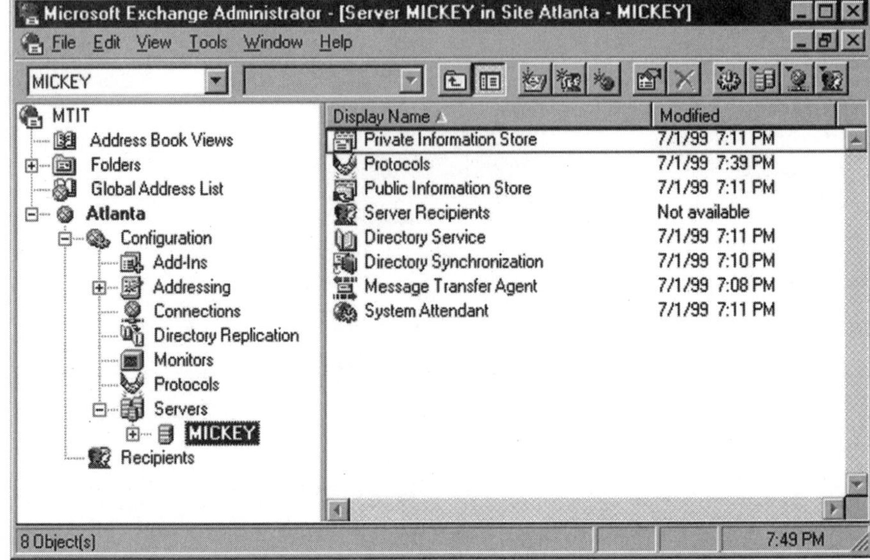

For example, in Figure 5-1, the Server container MICKEY is selected in the container pane and the contents pane shows the various directory objects in that container. Some of these objects in the contents pane are leaf objects and therefore only appear in the contents pane, while others are containers and therefore appear in both panes.

The hierarchical set of directory objects displayed in the Exchange Administrator program is referred to as the *directory hierarchy*. Taking a closer look at the directory hierarchy as displayed in the container pane of Figure 5-1, we see that the root object in the directory hierarchy is the organization container, which in this example has the name MTIT. Directly beneath this root object, the second-level objects in the directory hierarchy are fairly standard and include the following:

- *Address Book Views*. This container holds any address book views you have created for your organization. *Address book views* are subsets of the *Global Address List* (GAL) and are used to create customized address books for users.
- *Folders*. This includes containers for both Public Folders (for users to share information with each other) and System Folders (which support features like the calendaring function of Microsoft Outlook).
- *GAL*. This leaf object is a master list of all recipients in the organization.
- *Sites*. These containers define the sites in the organization and contain the recipients and configuration information for the site.

In our figure, there is only one site container, called Atlanta. Inside the Atlanta site container are further third-level directory objects (Get the picture? It's hierarchical!). Specifically, each site container generally contains two third-level containers, specifically:

- *Configuration*. This container contains all the directory objects that are used for configuring the properties of the site and its various Exchange servers.
- *Recipients*. This container contains all the mailboxes, distribution lists, and other recipient objects that you have created in the site.

We could go further still. Within the Atlanta site container is a container called Servers. This is a collection of containers representing individual servers within the site. In our example, the only Server container within the Servers container is the container called MICKEY, the only server in the Atlanta site at this point (yes, that's right—there is a *Servers* container and there are *Server* containers within it!) Within the MICKEY server container are the various configuration objects and recipient containers for that particular server. Eventually, the process comes to an end and we reach the end of the line, with only leaf objects at the tips of the directory tree's branches.

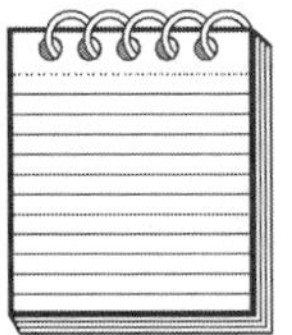

Permissions Flow

One thing we'll mention now is that permissions flow naturally down the Exchange directory hierarchy. In other words, if we assign the user Joan Smith the Permissions Admin *role on the Configuration container within a site, Joan can administer any object located within the branch of the directory hierarchy whose root is the site Configuration container and permissions flow down into all objects contained within the container and its subcontainers.*

Well, that's not completely true. There are some exceptions to this permissions flow issue, which will be discussed later. The topic of Exchange permissions is covered later in this chapter.

Using Exchange Administrator

The Exchange Administrator program is automatically installed on an Exchange Server when Setup is run in Typical mode, but you don't need to install it on every Exchange server in your organization. In fact, you can also use the Complete/Custom mode of Setup to install the Exchange Administrator program alone (without the Exchange Server services) on a Windows NT Workstation (or Windows NT Server) machine and use it to administer from one location Exchange Server in both your local site and in other remote sites of your organization. In fact, this is really a better way of doing things, since you avoid the overhead of having the Exchange Administrator program running on the server and can give higher priority to background processes like the Exchange services.

On the other hand, it might be a good idea to have a local copy of Exchange Administrator installed on each Exchange Server anyway, just in case the network goes down and you have to manage the servers interactively from their local consoles. The only requirement for administering an Exchange Server remotely from another machine is that there be RPC connectivity between your administrator workstation and the servers you are administering. In practice, having RPC connectivity simply means you need a common network protocol like TCP/IP.

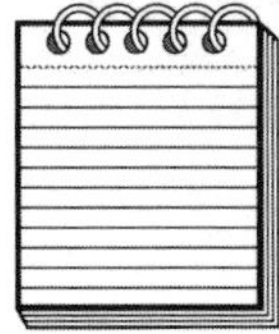

Permissions Admin Role

Simply having Exchange Administrator installed on a Windows NT workstation and having RPC connectivity with an Exchange Server doesn't enable you to administer that server. Even being a member of the Windows NT Domain Admins global group doesn't give you sufficient privileges to administer Exchange. You need to be explicitly assigned the Permissions Admin role to be able to use Exchange Administrator to administer sites and servers in an organization. This has to do with Exchange permissions, not Windows NT permissions, and is discussed later in this chapter.

You can also administer multiple Exchange Servers using a single Exchange Administrator workstation console, although you should always install Exchange Administrator on several machines in each site for redundancy purposes. When you first start the Exchange Administrator, you select an Exchange Server to connect to for obtaining the necessary directory information to display the Exchange directory hierarchy in the Exchange Administrator window. Then you can use Connect To Server from the File menu to open multiple windows, each based on a connection to a different Exchange Server and focused on a different portion of the directory hierarchy (note that if directory replication is not up-to-date in your organization, the objects displayed in each Exchange Administrator window could be different).

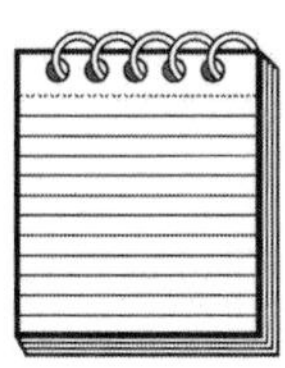

Platforms Supporting Exchange Administrator

You can install the Exchange Administrator program on Windows NT 4.0 Server or Windows NT 4.0 Workstation, but you cannot install it on Windows 98, 95, or 3.1. However, you could administer Exchange from a Windows 98 machine by installing remote-control software like PCAnywhere™ with the server portion of this tool running on a Windows NT machine that has Exchange Administrator installed and the client portion running on your Windows 98 machine.

To administer an object in the directory hierarchy (typically, both containers and leaf objects have configurable properties), you simply select the object in either pane and open the *property sheet* for that object. For example, Figure 5-2 shows the property sheet for the MICKEY server container that was previously selected in Figure 5-1.

This typical example of an Exchange property sheet consists of a number of tabs, each of which contains various controls (listboxes, checkboxes, option buttons, and so on) for configuring the various *attributes* (properties)

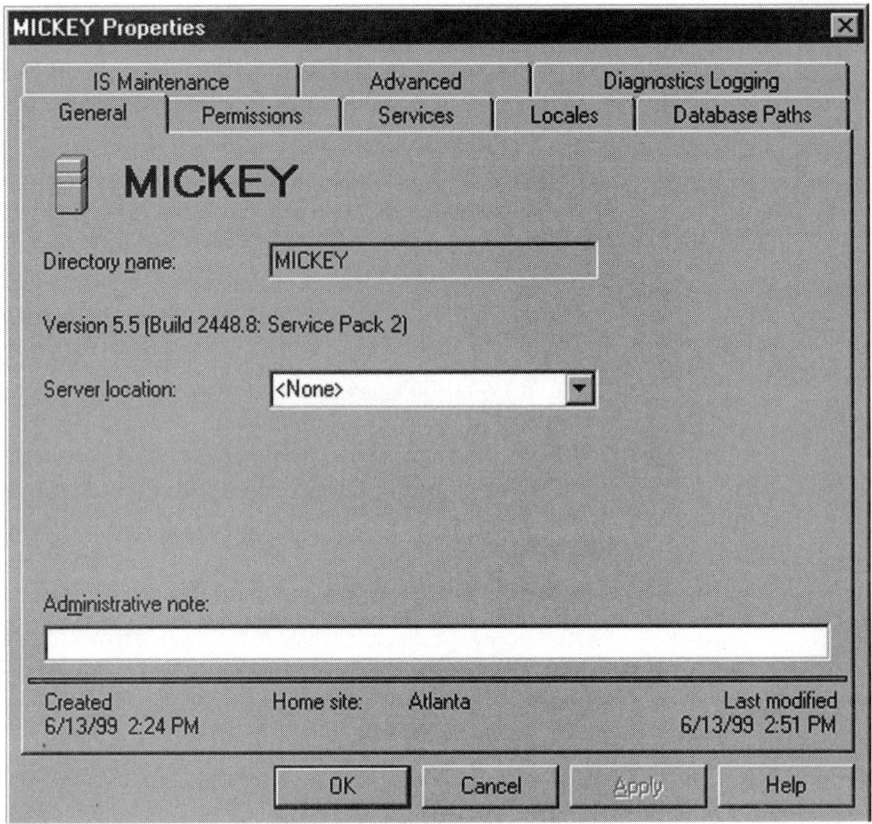

Figure 5-2 Property sheet for the MICKEY server container.

of the selected directory object. You will soon realize that what makes Exchange Server such a difficult product to get your head around is the vast number and large variety of different property sheets.

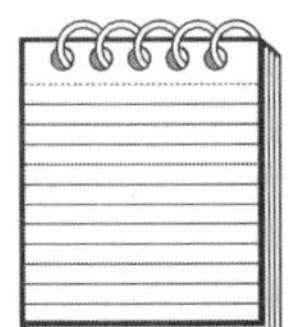

Opening Property Sheets

Note that you can't always open the property sheet of a directory object simply by double-clicking on it. This procedure works for leaf objects, but for containers it simply expands the container in the containers pane, showing any further containers underneath it. Neither can you right-click on an object to open a context menu and select Properties (bummer!). The best way to open an object's property sheet is to select the object in a pane and then either

- *Select Properties from the File menu,*
- *Click the Properties button on the toolbar, or*
- *Press the ALT + ENTER keystroke combination*

Command-Line Utilities

Although most Exchange administrative tasks are performed using the GUI tool Exchange Administrator, a number of command-line utilities are included with Exchange. These utilities are primarily intended for troubleshooting purposes, and although we will list them here, we will defer a close look at their operation until a later chapter. But for sake of completeness, here they are now:

- `Isinteg.exe`, which allows you to check the Information Store for errors and try to recover from them
- `Eseutil.exe`, a last-resort tool that allows you to defragment, repair, and perform an integrity check on the Exchange Directory and Information Store databases (this tool replaces the earlier `Edbutil.exe` tool that was included in versions 4.0 and 5.0 of Exchange)
- `Mtacheck.exe`, which allows you to fix or unblock corrupted queues if the MTA cannot be started

In addition to the above command-line utilities, the main Exchange GUI tools discussed previously (the Exchange Administrator, Performance Optimizer, and Migration Wizard) can also be started from the command-line using various switches and options that provide special functionality. We will only look at the command-line switches for the Exchange Administrator (`Admin.exe`) tool here and defer the others until later. Here are the various command-line options of `Admin.exe`, along with a description of what they are used for (you can get additional help on each command's syntax by running each command using the `/?` switch at the command-line).

`Admin /e` is used to export the attributes of the recipients on an Exchange Server into a comma-delimited (*.csv) text file. Its main use is to easily make bulk modifications to the attributes of a large number of recipients. For example, say that the company telephone number changes and you have 500 mailboxes that need this information updated. You could open the property sheet of each mailbox individually and change the phone number (ugh!), or you could use `Admin /e` to export the attributes of your mailboxes to a `*.csv` file, import this file into a spreadsheet program like Microsoft Excel, use a macro or some other procedure to change all the phone numbers at once, export the changed information from Excel into a new `*.csv` file, and then use Admin /i to import the new `*.csv` file into Exchange to make the changes to the recipients. We'll examine this in more detail in a later chapter. Note that running `Admin /e` from the command-line is the same as selecting Directory Export from the Tools menu in the Exchange Administrator program.

`Admin /i` is used to import the attributes of a group or some recipients into Exchange, provided the information is contained in a properly formatted `*.csv` file. In addition to being used in conjunction with the `Admin /e` command for making bulk modifications to Exchange recipients, this tool is often used for importing mailbox information exported from third-party mail systems when migrating from these systems to Exchange. Note that running `Admin /i` from the command-line is the same as selecting Directory Import from the Tools menu in the Exchange Administrator program.

`Admin /m` can be used to start a Server Monitor or Link Monitor from the command-line. You could use this in a logon script so that if the Exchange Server reboots, the specified monitor will automatically start running.

`Admin /r` is kind of deep; it opens the Exchange Administrator window in raw mode. This adds a new submenu item to the File menu called Raw Properties, which allows you to examine the raw directory information for any object in the Exchange Directory. It is generally used only in conjunction with Microsoft technical support to resolve problems with the directory, or for performing a few special tricks with Exchange. Stay away from this tool unless you know what you are doing, as you can easily render Exchange inoperable if you fool around with it in raw mode, sort of like fooling around with the Windows NT registry! Refer to Figure 3-9 for an example of what a raw mode property sheet looks like.

`Admin /s` can be used to start Exchange Administrator and have it connect to an Exchange Server you specify.

`Admin /t` is used when you want to temporarily shut down Server and Link Monitors to perform scheduled maintenance on the server. It prevents the monitors from generating unnecessary alerts and notifications while the server is offline and repairs are being done.

Running Exchange Commands

To run an Exchange command like `Admin /e` *from the command-line, open a command prompt window and change to the* `\exchsrvr\bin` *directory before running the command. You can also run some of the commands from the Start menu by clicking Start, then Run, entering the full path to the command along with optional switches, and clicking OK. For example, you might typically type* `C:\exchsrvr\bin\admin /e`.

Windows NT Tools

In addition to the GUI and command-line utilities included with Exchange, a number of Windows NT Server tools and utilities are useful in managing Exchange Servers. These include the following tools:

- *Event Viewer*. This Windows NT administrative tool enables you to view the Application Log where Exchange logs all of its error, warning, and information events. Get used to checking the Application Log frequently to check for problems that might have occurred or are in the process of happening. You can also use the Diagnostic Logging tab on the property sheet of the Directory Service, Message Transfer Agent, System Attendant, and other directory objects for Exchange services to set the level of detail for logging Exchange events to the Application Log.
- *Performance Monitor*. This Windows NT administrative tool is used to monitor the health of the processor, memory, disk, and network subsystems on a machine and the various services running on the machine. Installing Exchange adds a number of new objects and counters to Performance Monitor, and some pre-configured Performance Monitor charts can be accessed from the Start menu in the Exchange program group.
- *Registry Editor*. A tool for making modifications to the Windows NT registry, used with Exchange primarily for manual tuning of Exchange services (although the Performance Optimizer usually does a better job that you can do manually using Registry Editor).
- *Server Manager*. A Windows NT administrative tool that allows you to manage resources, services, and connections on both local and remote servers. This tool can stop and restart Exchange services on a remote Exchange Server computer.
- *Services in Control Panel*. A utility for stopping, starting, and pausing the services running on the local machine (use Server Manager for managing services on a remote machine).
- *Task Manager*. Useful for viewing the status of processes running on a machine and troubleshooting issues related to memory and disk paging. Table 5-1 shows the executable file names for some of the common Exchange services.
- *User Manager for Domains*. This tool allows you to create a mailbox for a new user at the time you create the user account—a great way of

Table 5-1

Process Names for Exchange Services.

Exchange Service	Process Name
Directory Service	`Dsamain.exe`
Directory Synchronization	`Dxa.exe`
Event Service	`Events.exe`
Information Store	`Store.exe`
Internet Mail Service	`Msexcimc.exe`
Message Transfer Agent	`Emsmta.exe`
System Attendant	`Mad.exe`

creating new mailboxes. Installing Exchange on a machine adds a DLL to the User Manager for Domains. We'll see how to use this in a later chapter.

- *Windows NT Backup*. This simplifies the process of backing up critical files on an Exchange Server. Installing Exchange on a machine adds a new DLL to Windows NT Backup

BackOffice Resource Kit (BORK) Utilities

The *BackOffice Resource Kit* (BORK) Part 2 has some valuable utilities for performing specialized tasks relating to Exchange. We'll just list some of the more useful ones here. Consult the BORK documentation for further information on how to use these tools.

- *Crystal Reports* is useful for creating reports from message tracking logs and other exported Exchange information.
- *Import Header Tool* is used in conjunction with `Admin /e` and `Admin /i` for performing Directory Export/Import. This tool is used to create the specific header fields needed for the `*.csv` file so that you can export/import only the directory information you need.
- *Mailbox Cleanup Agent* is used for deleting outdated messages from mailboxes or for moving them to another location.

- *MAPIsend* is a troubleshooting tool for sending a MAPI-based message using the command-line.
- *Profile Generator* is used for creating roaming profiles for Exchange users.
- *Unix Mail Source Extractor* is used for migrating users from Unix SMTP-based mail systems.

Exchange Permissions and Roles

One more preliminary item that we need to consider before we begin administering our Exchange organization is the issue of permissions. In addition to the standard Windows NT permissions that are used to control access to resources on Windows NT machines (NTFS and shared folder permissions), the Exchange administrator also needs to cope with Exchange permissions.

Exchange permissions are permissions that can be used to grant different levels of access to various portions of the Exchange directory hierarchy, including sites, servers, services, connectors, mailboxes, and other directory objects. Exchange permissions consist of a number of different Exchange *rights* that are grouped together into sets of pre-defined Exchange *roles*. For each object in the directory hierarchy, a user's Windows NT account can be granted access to that object by assigning the user a specific role on that object's Permissions page. As an example, Figure 5-3 shows the Permissions page for the Server object MICKEY, described earlier.

Permissions Tab

If the objects in your directory hierarchy don't have a Permissions tab, select Options from the Tools menu to make this tab visible.

In the figure, the top listbox shows which Windows NT accounts have received Exchange permissions on the directory object MICKEY by *inheritance* (that is, by having had permissions assigned to them on a parent container of MICKEY higher up in the directory hierarchy). We can see that two accounts have received permissions by inheritance:

- The Administrator account in the MTIT domain has inherited the Permissions Admin role from the Configuration container for the Atlanta site.

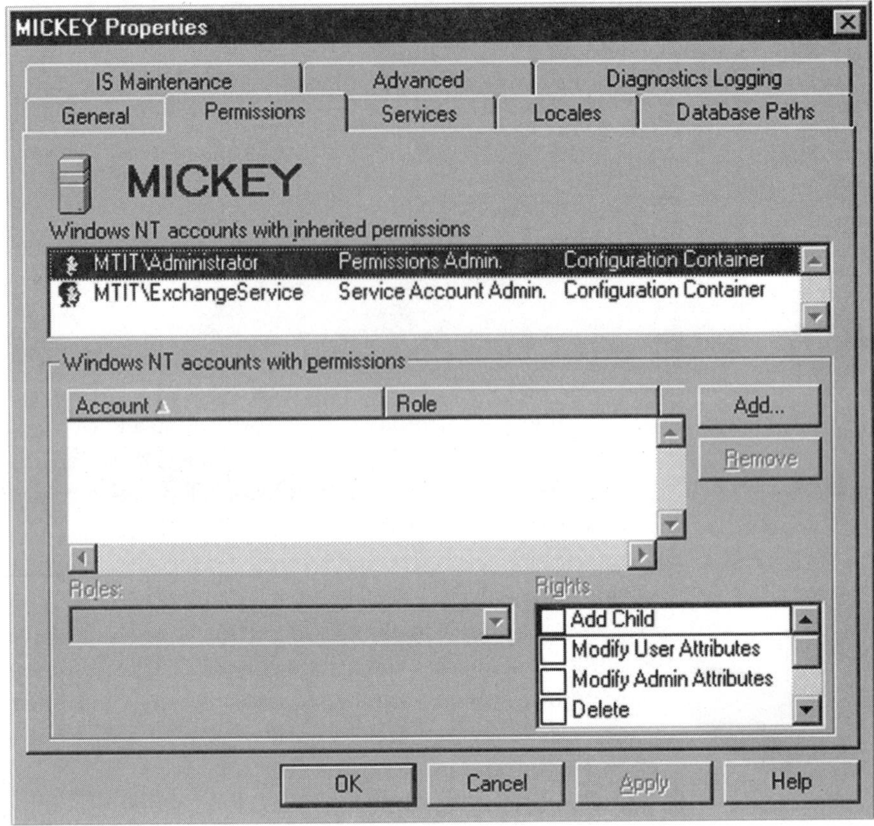

Figure 5-3
The Permissions tab on the property sheet for the Server object MICKEY.

- The ExchangeService account has inherited the Service Account Admin role from the Configuration container as well.

The middle listbox shows those Windows NT accounts that have been *explicitly* granted Exchange permissions on the directory object MICKEY. At this point, no user accounts have had Exchange permissions explicitly assigned to them for MICKEY. The bottom listbox (unavailable here because the middle listbox is empty) shows the role that has been explicitly assigned to the account selected in the middle listbox.

Table 5-2 summarizes the Exchange rights that can be selectively assigned or withheld from a user (not all of these rights may be available for a particular directory object).

In order to simplify the process of assigning Exchange permissions to users, the rights listed in Table 5-2 are consolidated into a number of predefined groupings of rights called roles. These roles are listed in Table 5-3 along with their associated individual rights (not all roles can be assigned

Table 5-2

Exchange Rights.

Right	Type of Permission Granted
Add child	Creates objects within a container
Modify user attribute	Modifies user-level attributes of an object
Modify admin attributes	Modifies administrator-level attributes of an object
Modify permissions	Modifies the permissions on the object
Delete	Deletes the object
Logon	Accesses the directory database*
Replication	Replicates directory information*
Mailbox owner	Reads and deletes messages in the mailbox
Search	Views the contents of the container
Send as	Sends a message using the sender's return address

*needed by the Exchange service account

Table 5-3

Exchange Roles.

Role	Rights						
	Admin	Permissions Admin	Service Account Admin	View Only Admin	User	Send As	Search
Add Child	√	√	√				
Modify User Attributes	√	√	√		√		√
Modify Admin Attributes	√	√		√			
Delete	√	√		√			
Logon	√	√	√	√			
Modify Permission	√	√					
Replication			√				
Mailbox Owner			√		√		
Send As			√		√	√	
Search							√

to users for any given directory object). In addition, you can create a custom role by selecting or deselecting any of the individual permissions assigned to an account.

One common reason for assigning permissions is when you want to grant another Windows NT user permission to use the Exchange Administrator program for administering a site in your organization. To do this, you need to grant the account the Permissions Admin role on both the Site and Configuration containers for the site. All other directory objects within the site will then inherit these permissions, enabling the user to use the Exchange Administrator program to manage any aspect of the site. Alternatively, if you only wanted to assign a user limited permissions so they could create new mailboxes for any server in a site but couldn't modify site configuration parameters, you could grant the account the Permissions Admin role on the Site container and the View Only Admin role on the Configuration container within the site.

Exceptions to Permissions Flow

The rule of permissions being inherited by all objects beneath them in the directory hierarchy has two exceptions:

- *If you modify the permissions assigned to the Organization container, the modifications are not inherited by any other objects in the directory hierarchy. In any case, there is generally no real reason for assigning anyone permissions to this container since it only allows one to modify the display name of the container.*
- *If you modify the permissions assigned to the Site container for a site, the modifications are inherited by the Recipients container for the site, the Address Book View container, and any Public Folder objects whose has that site as its home. What's significant is that modifications made to a Site container are* not *inherited by the Configuration container for that site. You must also explicitly assign a user permissions on a site's Configuration container if you want to enable them to administer all the directory objects within that site.*

Walkthrough: Using Exchange Administrator

Let's walk through some of the preliminary things you might want to do using Exchange Administrator before we actually start configuring our sites and servers, creating recipients, and so on.

Assigning the Permissions Admin Role

We'll begin by starting the Exchange Administrator program for the first time on our newly installed Exchange Server. The first thing that happens is that the program prompts you to select which Exchange Server you want to administer (see Figure 5-4).

The Connect To Server dialog box asks you to select which Exchange Server to which you want to connect. The server you select here will be the one from whose Directory Database you obtain information about the objects in the Exchange directory hierarchy and the attributes of these objects. If the directories of your various Exchange Servers are not up to date with each other due to delays or problems with the directory replication process, then the directory hierarchy information displayed in the Exchange Administrator program (once it has started) may depend on the server to which you have connected.

To connect to an Exchange Server, you can type the name of the server in the textbox or click the Browse button to find all the RPC-connected Exchange Servers in your organization, which at this point only consists of the server MICKEY in the site Atlanta (see Figure 5-5). After you select a server to connect to, you can also select the Set As Default checkbox and each time you open Exchange Administrator it will connect to the same server in your organization.

At this point, the main window of the Exchange Administrator program opens (see Figure 5-6). You may want to maximize the child window to allow you to see more objects in the directory hierarchy. The focus should be on the Configuration container of the new site you created.

The first thing we will do is assign suitable Exchange permissions to our friend Boris Zhivago, who is the Assistant Network Administrator in Atlanta for our company MTIT, and whose user account Boris is a member of the Domain Admins global group in the MTIT domain. Boris does not yet have a mailbox created for him on the Exchange Server; we will do that in a later chapter.

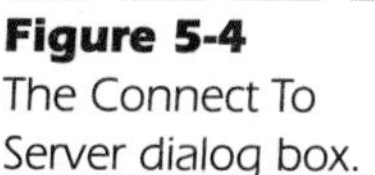

Figure 5-4 The Connect To Server dialog box.

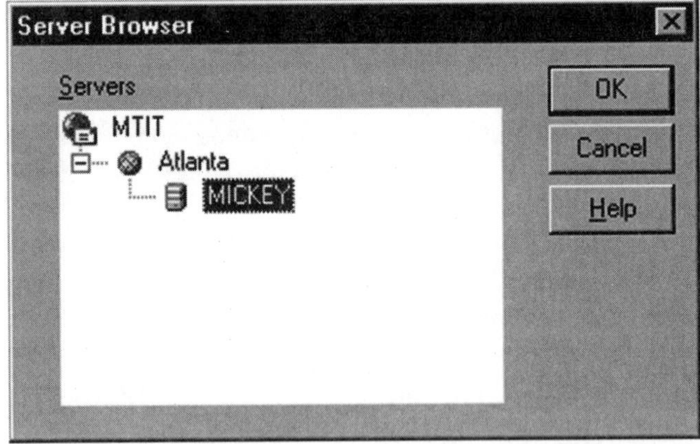

Figure 5-5 Selecting a server to connect to.

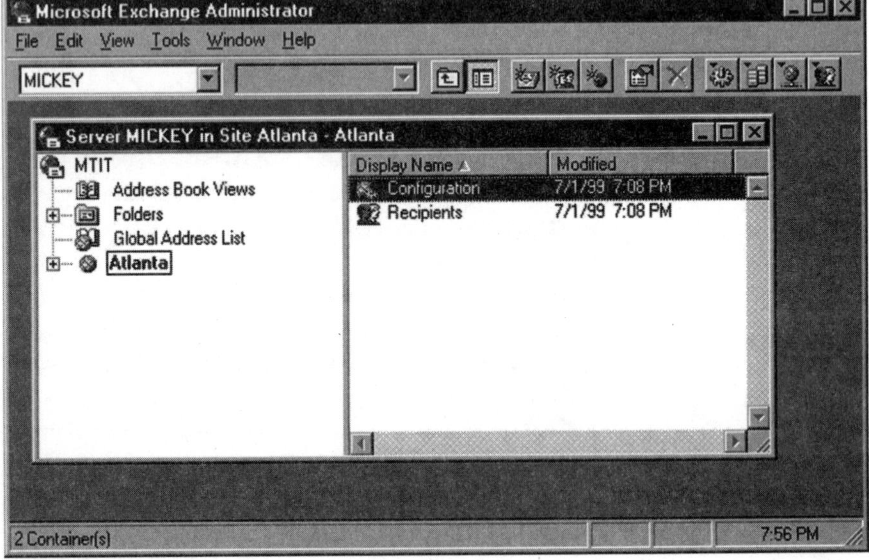

Figure 5-6 The Exchange Administrator main window.

We need to assign Boris the role of Permissions Admin. To do this, we first have to make the Permissions tab visible on all property sheets in Exchange Administrator. To do this, select Options from the Tools menu and select the Permissions tab on the Options property sheet (see Figure 5-7). This page shows which Windows NT domain will be the default domain that user accounts are drawn from when you want to assign Exchange roles, default settings for displaying Permissions tabs, and whether when you delete a mailbox its associated primary Windows NT account should be deleted as well. Select the following checkboxes:

- *Show Permissions page for all objects.* This will cause a Permissions tab to be added to the property sheet of objects in the Exchange directory hierarchy.
- *Display rights for roles on the Permissions page.* This will show the individual rights that belong to each role on a Permissions page and allows you to select or deselect individual rights to create Custom roles for users.

Click OK to return to Exchange Administrator. Now select the Atlanta container (our Site object) and press ALT+ENTER to open the property sheet for the container. Select the Permissions tab on the opened property sheet and note that only the Administrator and ExchangeService accounts from the MTIT domain have roles assigned to them for this container.

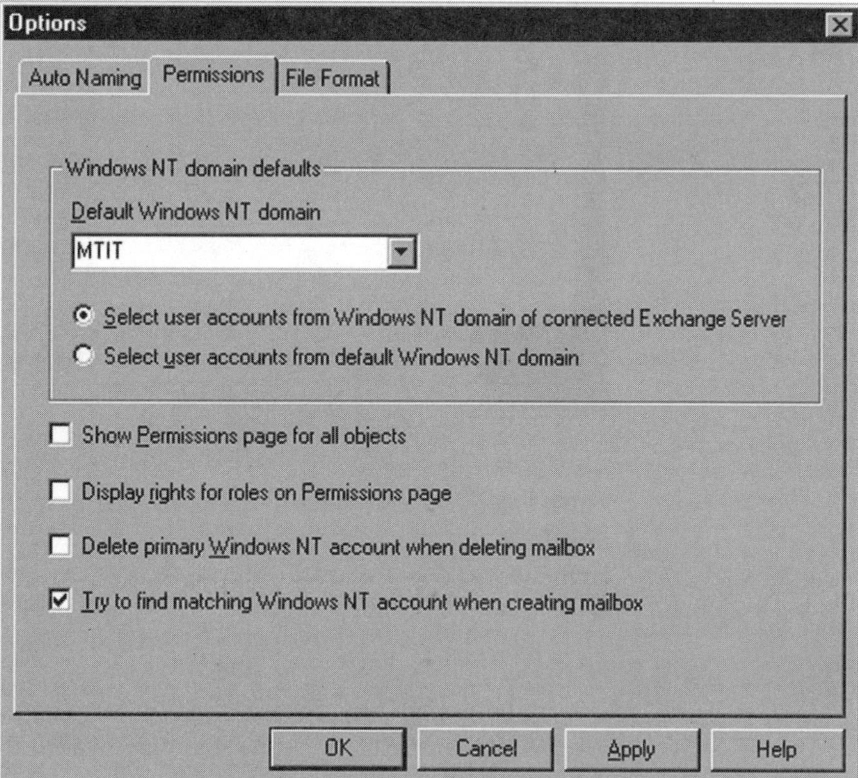

Figure 5-7 Toggling the Permissions tab on for property sheets.

Site Permissions

You may have also noted that there is no listbox on this property page for accounts that have received permissions by inheritance (refer to Figure 5-3). This is because site objects can only have permissions explicitly assigned to them and cannot inherit permissions from the parent organization container. It's these little inconsistencies that can make your head spin when you are learning to administer Exchange.

Click the Add button and select the user account Boris from the MTIT domain (see Figure 5-8). Click OK to return to the Permissions tab of the Atlanta property sheet. The MTIT\Boris account should be selected in the listbox on this page.

Now we want to grant Boris the Permissions Admin role on the container. Select the Permissions Admin role from the drop-down Roles listbox to do this (see Figure 5-9). Click OK to close the Atlanta property sheet. Just for interest's sake, open the property sheets for the Configuration and Recipi-

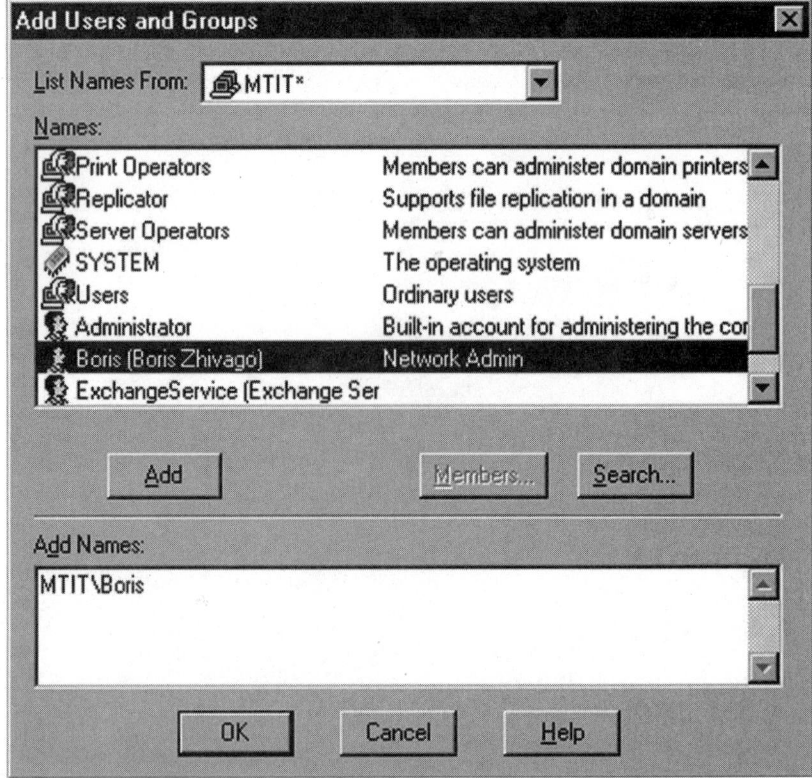

Figure 5-8
Selecting a user account that will be assigned an Exchange role.

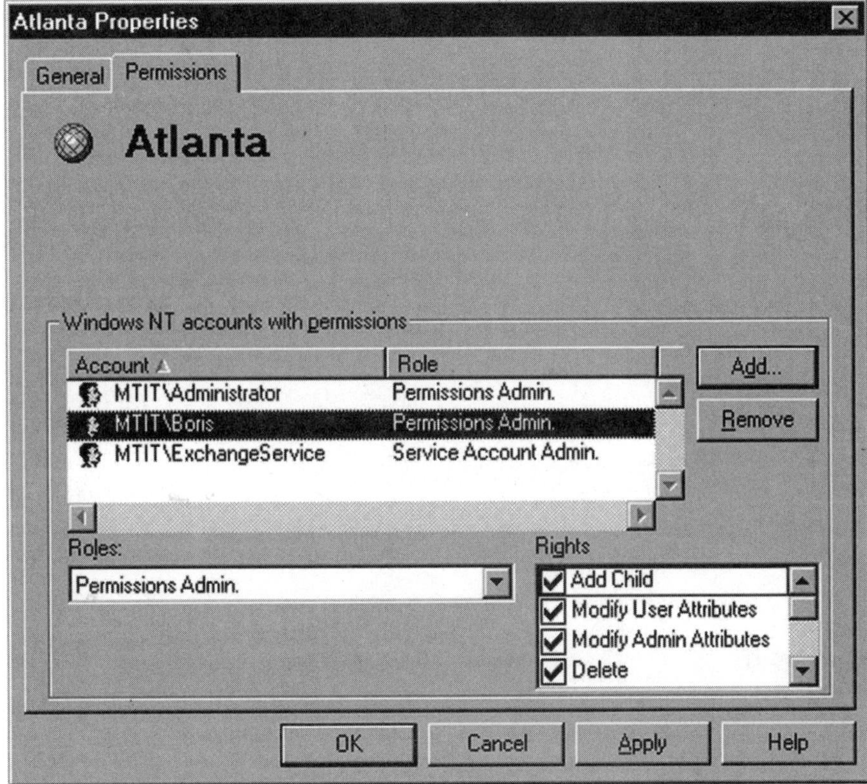

Figure 5-9 Assigning Boris the Permissions Admin role on the site container Atlanta.

ents containers within the Atlanta site container. You will notice that the Permissions tab on the Configuration property sheet shows that Boris does not have any permissions assigned to him yet. This means that Boris is not yet able to configure Exchange services for servers in the Atlanta site. The Permissions tab on the Recipients property sheet shows that Boris does have the Permissions Admin role on this container. This means that Boris can at least create and modify mailboxes and other recipients homed on servers in the Atlanta site.

To give Boris full administrative capability for the Atlanta site, we next need to open the Configuration container within Atlanta and assign him the Permissions Admin role on that container as well. We'll leave the steps to the reader to accomplish this. Once this is completed, try logging on as Boris and see if you can modify the attributes of some object in the directory hierarchy using Exchange Administrator (for example, have Boris assign the Permissions Admin role to Natasha for the site Atlanta). For comparison, you might also try logging on as another user who doesn't have this role and see if you can use Exchange Administrator. What happens when you try to do this? Does it make any difference whether the user account is a Domain Admins account or not? Try it out!

Specifying Auto Naming Conventions

The next thing we will do is specify our auto naming convention for new recipients we create. Select Options from the Tools menu of Exchange Administrator, and select the Auto Naming tab of the Options property sheet which appears (see Figure 5-10).

MTIT is a really trendy company (they develop e-commerce Web sites and all that), so most people's user accounts use their first name only as their username (Boris, Natasha, and so on). This way when they log on, they only have to remember their first name, which is usually easier after working all night and eating a lot of pizza.

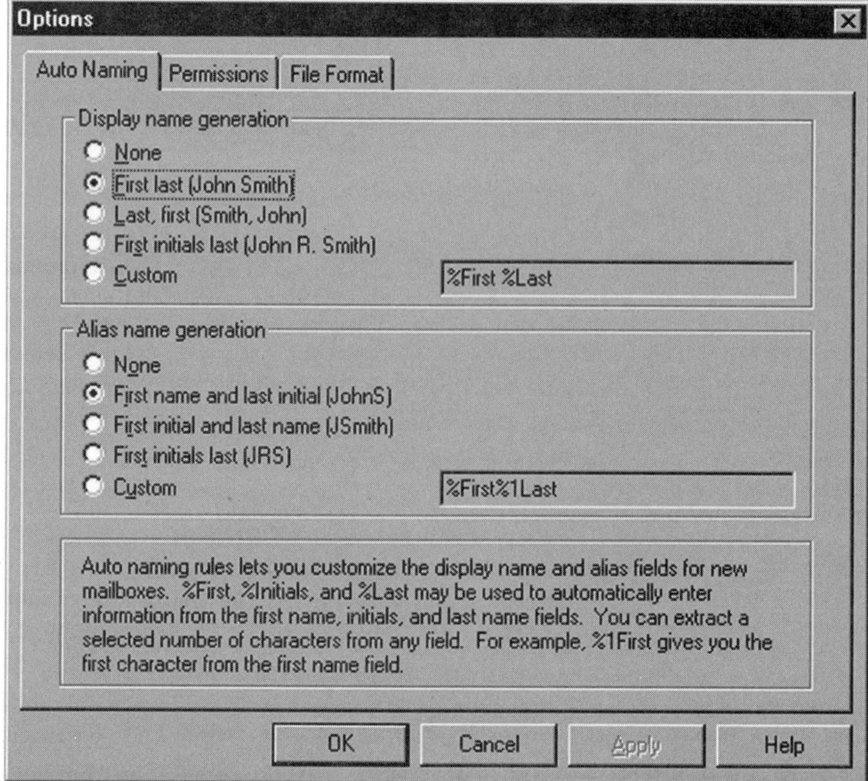

Figure 5-10 Specifying auto naming conventions.

As the mail administrator, however, you want to keep things a little more tidy and professional, so you decide on a naming convention for all Exchange Server mailboxes:

> The name of a mailbox shall consist of a string comprised of the first letter of the user's given name, together with the full surname of the user appended to the string.

This means you need to select the "First initial and last name (JSmith)" option on this page, but this option appears in two places. Why? The answer is that there are two types of names used to refer to objects in the Exchange directory:

- The *Display name*, which is the visible name of the object, as displayed in the Exchange Administrator window. Display names can be up to 256 characters in length and can include spaces and special characters. You can modify the display name at will, but you have to decide on an initial display name for a directory object when you first create it.
- The *Directory name*, which is the internal name for the object within the Directory Database. Directory names can be up to 64 characters in length and can include spaces and special characters. You specify both the display name and directory name when you create an object in the directory (such as a new connector or mailbox). You can modify the display name later, but you cannot modify the directory name. For recipient objects only (mailboxes and so on), the directory name goes by the name *Alias Name* instead. The reason is that this name is used for the user-specific (alias) portion of the user's email address. For example, the SMTP address of a user would be <Alias_Name>@<Domain_Name>.

Getting back to auto naming then, we want to select the "First initial and last name (JSmith)" option under Alias Name Generation in order to comply with the rule we have decided upon above. Click OK.

Miscellaneous Tasks

Let's do a few more tasks with Exchange Administrator before we finish this chapter. Select the Recipients container for the Atlanta site in the left-hand container pane (you may have to expand the Atlanta site by clicking on the plus sign beside it first; the directory hierarchy expands and collapses like Windows Explorer does). Examine the contents of this container by looking at the right-hand contents pane. You should see only one recipient there, namely the Microsoft Schedule+ Free/Busy Container (MICKEY) object (see Figure 5-11). This is a type of recipient called a mailbox agent, and it is used when you want to share scheduling information between an Exchange organization whose users are running Microsoft Outlook and a legacy MS Mail network whose users are running Microsoft Schedule+, the precursor to Outlook.

Let's configure Exchange Administrator so it will only show mailbox recipient objects, not all types of recipient objects (which is the default setting). Select Mailboxes from the View menu to toggle this feature on; the mailbox agent you saw previously in the Recipients container has vanished. Select View, All to toggle back and make all types of recipients visible again (we still have only one).

Now select View, Hidden Recipients to make any hidden recipients located in the Recipients container visible. You should now see objects like Offline Address Book-Atlanta and Schedule+ Free/Busy Information-Atlanta in the contents pane. These hidden recipients are used by Exchange to support different kinds of system functionality, and we don't want to disturb them, so toggle Hidden Recipients off using the View menu.

Now let's create a second Recipients container, which we will call "List." We will use this container for storing Distribution List recipients when we create them later, while we will store all mailboxes we create in the default Recipients container. To do this, select the Atlanta site object and choose File, New Other, Recipients Container from the Exchange Administrator menu bar. A blank property sheet will appear for the new container (see Figure 5-12). Type in "List" (without the quotes) for both the display name and directory name, an administrative note (if you like), and click OK. There should now be two Recipients containers visible within the Atlanta site container in the Exchange Administrator window. We'll use this new container later on in the book.

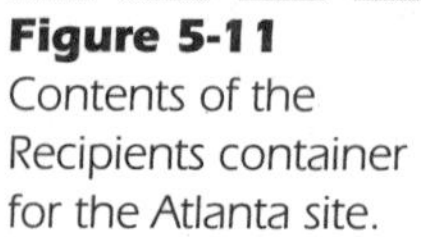

Figure 5-11 Contents of the Recipients container for the Atlanta site.

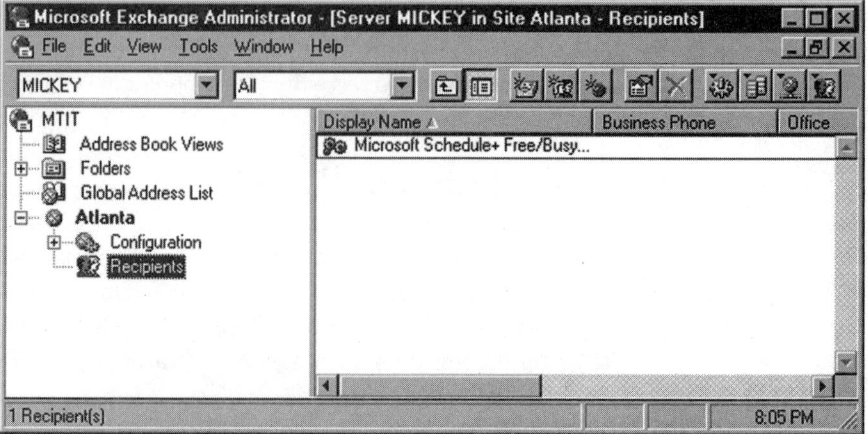

Figure 5-12 Blank property sheet for a new Recipients container.

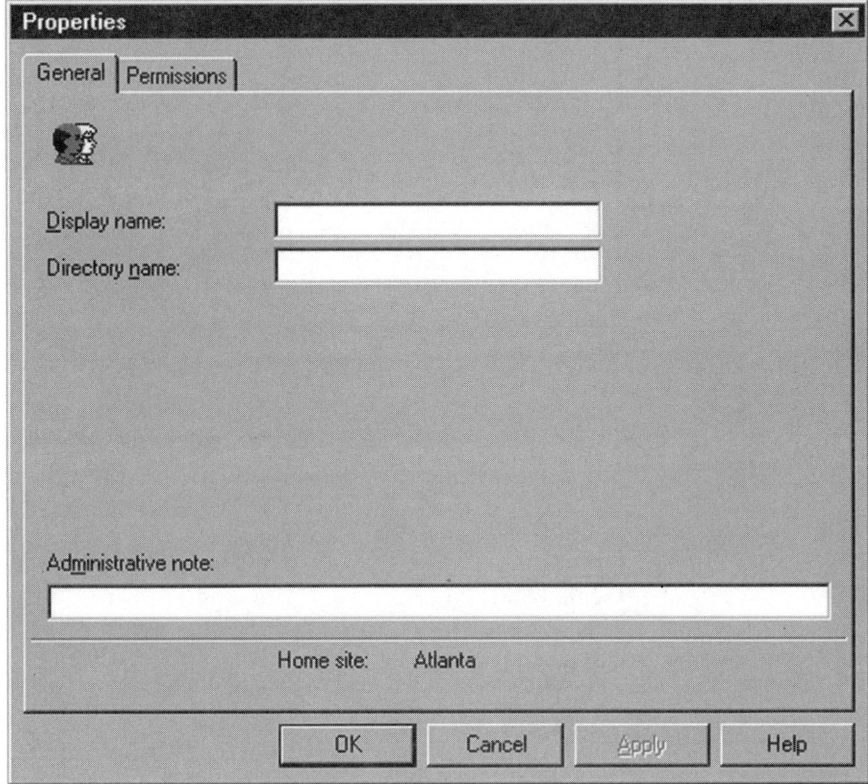

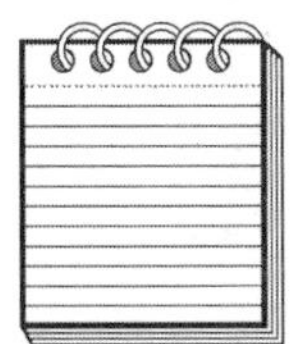

Recipients Containers

It's a good idea to use only a few Recipient containers and one might even be enough. Never create different recipient containers for each department within a company, since when a user moves from one department to another, you can't move their mailbox to the new recipients container simply by dragging or some other easy method. You will need to export the mailbox using Directory Export, delete the original mailbox, and then import the mailbox into the new container (ugh!). You should only create additional recipients containers for some specific function like storing all distribution lists in the company. Another reason might be if you need to create a number of virtual organizations, *that is, separate Exchange organizations for different companies that are all hosted on a single Exchange Server. If you need to do this, look up article Q182902 of the Microsoft Knowledge Base, which is included with your TechNet subscription (or is available on Microsoft's Web site if you don't have TechNet) to find out how to accomplish this task.*

Where Do We Go from Here?

In the next chapter, we will begin the job of administering our Exchange organization in earnest, starting with the job of creating new recipients. Specifically, we will look at how to create new mailboxes, distribution lists, and custom recipients. Then in the chapter following, we will install client software and test the recipients we have created.

For More Information

Other than the Exchange Server manuals (or Books Online), there's not much else available that's relevant to the general use of Exchange Administrator as discussed in this chapter. In particular, you might look at Chapters 3 and 4 in the *Getting Started* manual for more information about the Exchange Administrator program.

BORK2

The BackOffice Resource Kit Part 2 utilities are included on a CD as part of your Microsoft TechNet subscription if you have one, or they can be downloaded from the Microsoft Web site. Note that the BORK2 utilities are "not officially supported" by Microsoft, but some of them are extremely useful.

CHAPTER 6

Administering Recipients

In Chapter 5, we examined the different GUI and command-line tools that can be used to administer an Exchange organization. We looked in particular at the Exchange Administrator program, which is used for about 95 percent of all Exchange administration. The logical progression from this last chapter would actually be to configure the various site-level and server-level features of Exchange before we actually start creating and using recipients, but this would be a rather dry way to continue. Instead, we'll focus on creating Exchange recipients. After reading this chapter, you will have an understanding of

- The different types of Exchange recipients
- Creating and configuring mailboxes
- Creating and configuring distribution lists
- Creating and configuring Custom Recipients

This chapter contains three walkthrough exercises associated with creating and configuring each type of Exchange recipient described above.

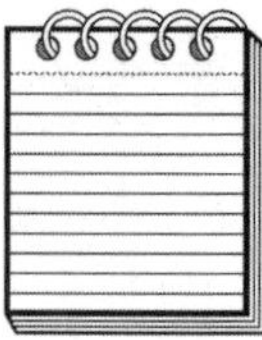

MTIT Topology

Note that for the purposes of the walkthroughs and examples in this chapter, we have installed a second Exchange Server into the Atlanta site of the MTIT organization, making the topology of MTIT a little more interesting. The new Exchange Server is a Windows NT member server called DONALD and is in the same Windows NT domain (MTIT) and Exchange organization (MTIT) as the Windows NT PDC and Exchange Server MICKEY, which we installed in Chapter 3.

Types of Exchange Recipients

A *recipient* is an entity in the Exchange directory where an email message can be addressed and delivered. Recipients are generally created in the Recipients container, one of the objects in the Exchange directory hierarchy, but if you've played around a bit with Exchange Administrator, you will have noticed that there are two Recipients containers in the directory hierarchy:

- There is a *Site Recipients* container for each Exchange site in your organization. These containers have the name "recipients" and are immediately beneath the Site container for each site. The Recipients container for a site contains all the recipients that have been created on all the Exchange Servers in that site. In Figure 6-1, you can see a Recipients container just beneath the Atlanta site container.

- A *Server Recipients* container exists for each Exchange Server in your organization. These containers have the name "<Server> Recipients" where <Server> represents the name of the Exchange Server they were created on. In Figure 6-1, you can see two of these containers, a "MICKEY Recipients" container on server MICKEY and a "DONALD Recipients" on server DONALD.

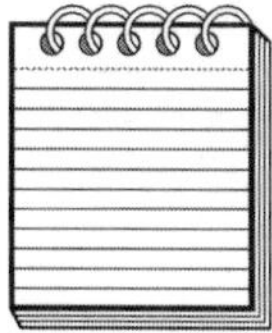

Creating Recipient Containers

Remember that we said in the previous chapter that you can create new Recipients containers using Exchange Administrator and that this is not generally a good idea except in a few situations. These additional Recipients containers can be named anything you want, like "Lists" for a container that holds distribution lists only, or "External" for a container that holds Custom Recipients only. You can also change the display name

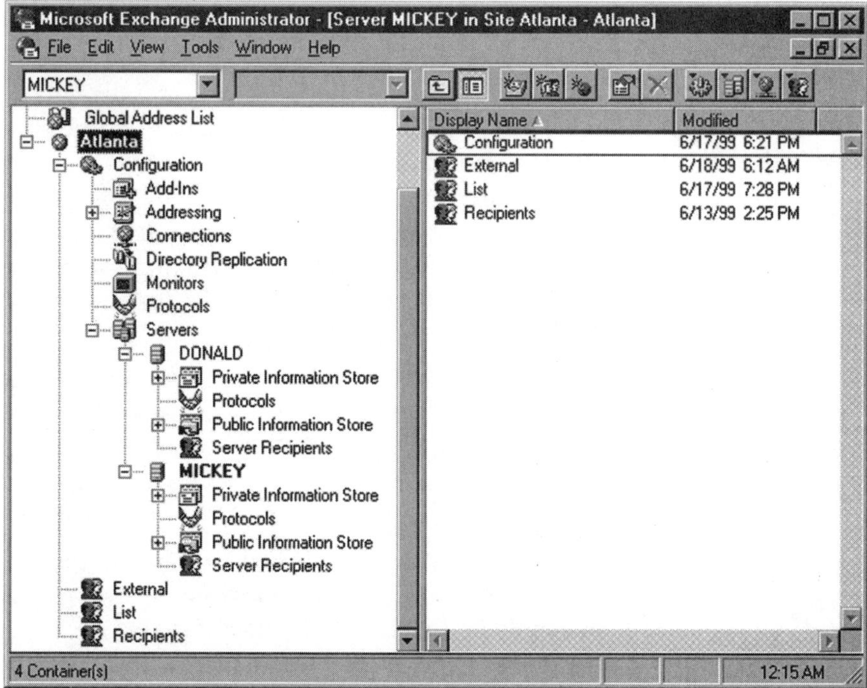

Figure 6-1
Different types of Recipients containers.

of both the Site Recipients and Server Recipients containers in your organization if you want to. The way you can tell that they are Recipient containers is from their icon in the directory hierarchy.

Five types of recipients can be created using Exchange Administrator:

- *Mailboxes*, which can hold messages and attachments that have been sent by other users. Since mailboxes actually hold messages, they occupy space within the Private Information Store on the Exchange Server on which they reside (the mailboxes are *homed* on a particular server). mailboxes are the most common type of recipient in an Exchange organization and are typically assigned one-to-one with the Windows NT user accounts in your company, each user having one and only one mailbox. However, it is possible for a user to have more than one mailbox or for several users to share one mailbox.
- *Distribution Lists (DLs)*, which are collections of recipients grouped together to facilitate mass mailings. DLs can contain mailboxes, Custom Recipients, and other DLs. If a message is sent to a DL, every recipient that is a member of the DL receives a copy of the message.
- *Custom Recipients*, which represent recipients that are not part of your Exchange organization and generally represent people outside your company. Custom recipients are essentially only a pointer to an address on a foreign mail system. Typically, you would create Custom Recipients for outside mail addresses to which your users frequently send mail. They are created as a convenience to your users so that if they want to send mail to someone outside the foreign mail system, they only need to select the particular custom recipient from the *Global Address List* (GAL) as their To: address, instead of having to remember and enter the address by hand.
- *Public Folders*, which are locations for storing messages and documents that you want to share with other users in your organization. Public Folders are thus a little different from the three types of recipients described above, in that they are not associated with particular users. We will be covering Public Folders in a separate chapter later on.
- *Mailbox Agents*, which are DLLs that can receive messages and then act on them in some fashion without any user intervention. An example is the Microsoft Schedule+ Free/Busy Agent, which receives messages from Microsoft Schedule+ running on legacy MS Mail systems and enables users to share their scheduling information

with each other. We will not cover this type of recipient here in this chapter.

In the rest of this chapter, we will be dealing with only the first three types of recipients listed above: mailboxes, distribution lists, and custom recipients.

Creating and Configuring Mailboxes

A *mailbox* is a recipient that enables a user to receive and store messages and their attachments. mailboxes store their contents in the Private Information Store on the Exchange Server where the mailbox is homed. Two main tools are used for creating mailboxes in Exchange:

- *Exchange Administrator*. Use this tool primarily if you want to create a new mailbox for a Windows NT user account that already exists (although you can also use it to create a mailbox and its associated user account at the same time). To do this, just select New mailbox from the File menu to open a blank property sheet for a new mailbox (see Figure 6-2). Fill in the user's personal attributes like Last Name, First Name, Address, Phone, and so on, then configure any additional settings you want to configure on the other tabs, and finally click OK. At this point, a dialog box will appear, prompting you to either select an existing Windows NT user account to associate with the new mailbox, or to create a new Windows NT user account based on an alias name you have specified on the mailbox property sheet.
- *User Manager for Domains*. Use this tool primarily if you want to simultaneously create both a new Windows NT user account and its associated mailbox. This is possible because installing Exchange Server on a Windows NT Server machine also installs an extension for User Manager that adds an additional menu item called Exchange. This new menu option can specify the Exchange Server where your new mailboxes will be created, the Recipients container on that server that will contain them, and whether to delete the mailbox when deleting the user account. You can also activate User Manager for Domains to open the property sheet for the mailbox associated with a user account.

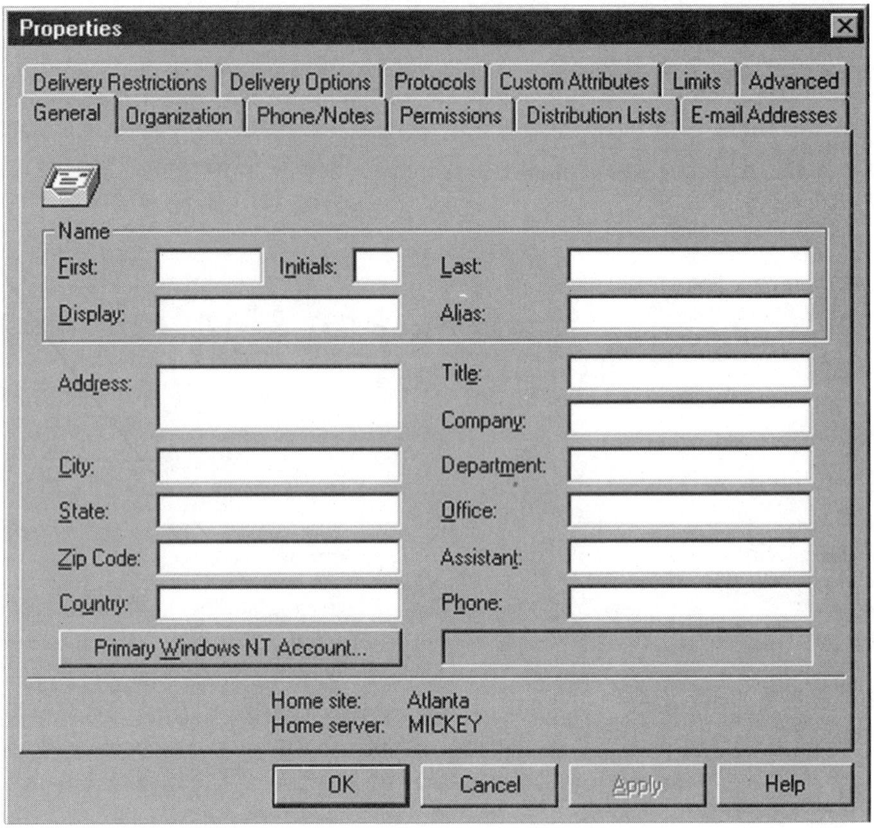

Figure 6-2
Blank property sheet for a new mailbox.

Creating Mailboxes from Accounts

You can also create new mailboxes by using the Windows NT or NetWare User Extraction utilities to extract all user account information from a Windows NT domain controller or NetWare server, and then import this information into Exchange to create mailboxes for the accounts you have extracted. Typically, you might do this if you have a large number of existing user accounts on your network and you want to create mailboxes for all of them. To use this utility, follow these steps:

1. *Select Extract Windows NT Account List (or Extract NetWare Account List) from the Tools menu of the Exchange Administrator program.*
2. *Specify the name of a Windows NT domain controller or NetWare server on the network that has the accounts you want to create mailboxes for, and specify a comma-delimited (`*.csv`) text file where the extracted account information is written.*

3. *Edit the* `*.csv` *file to remove any accounts that will not be needing mailboxes.*
4. *Then select Directory Import from the Tools menu to import the* `*.csv` *file into the Exchange Server your Exchange Administrator program is currently connected to (the mailboxes will be homed on the connected server), thus creating mailboxes for the accounts.*

The mailbox property sheet is a typical example of the property sheet for an Exchange directory object with lots of tabs, each having many different attributes (properties) you can configure. In fact, Exchange has over 70 different directory objects, each having its own property sheet with anywhere from two to a dozen different tabs, leaving you with something like four or five hundred different *property pages* (tabs on property sheets) to learn to configure. So there's always something new to learn about Exchange, and the hardest thing about administering it is remembering which property page has the setting you want to configure. There is some logic to the whole thing, but there are a lot of inconsistencies as well, so don't expect to master it all right away.

Let's look at the various property pages for the mailbox object. Some of them are obvious and self-explanatory, but others require some explanation to know what they are used for:

- *General*. This includes personal attributes of the user like first and last name, title, department, company, address, phone, and so on. There is also the *display name*, which we mentioned before, is the name by which the object is displayed in the Exchange Administrator window, and the *alias*, which is both a nickname and part of the user's email address as well as being the internal name or *directory name* by which the mailbox object is known within the Exchange directory. The display name and alias name are generated automatically from the first and last names you enter here, according to the auto naming settings you have established for your organization using Options from the Tools menu.

  The button labeled Primary Windows NT Account enables you to either associate an existing Windows NT user account with the mailbox (who will be the *owner* of the mailbox) or create a new Windows NT user account simultaneously with the new mailbox.

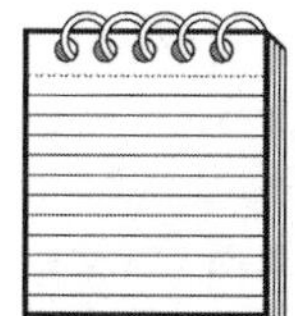

Changing the Alias

If you change the alias after the mailbox has been created, two things will not *happen:*

- *The internal name that the mailbox object is referenced by in the Directory will* not *change. It's still the original alias of the mailbox.*

- *The email addresses that are automatically generated for the mailbox when it was created are* not *updated. You must edit them manually using the Email Addresses property page.*

The same is true for other types of recipients like distribution lists and Custom Recipients.

- *Organization*. This page just lets you keep record of who the user reports to in the company, and who else in the company reports to the user.
- *Phone/Notes*. Pretty self-explanatory!
- *Permissions*. This page is only visible if you have toggled it on using the menu with Tools, Options. We covered the topic of permissions in the last chapter.
- *Distribution Lists*. This page lets you specify which *distribution lists* (DLs) to which the mailbox belongs.
- *Email Addresses*. This page shows the user's auto-generated MS Mail, SMTP, and X.400 email addresses (and also other addresses if other connectors such as the Lotus cc:Mail connector are installed). We looked at address types in Chapter 4. Exchange includes a set of DLLs called proxy generators, which automatically create several email addresses for each new mailbox you create, one address of each type that has been configured on the machine.

Distinguished Name (DN)

We mentioned in Chapter 4 that distinguished names *(DNs) are the internal address type used to route messages within the Exchange organization. The distinguished name of a mailbox is not shown on the Email Addresses property page. Instead, you have to start Exchange in raw mode using* `admin /r` *to be able to view the distinguished name of a mailbox.*

- *Delivery Restrictions*. This page enables you to specify the recipients from which the mailbox will accept or reject messages.
- *Delivery Options*. This page is used to give another user permission to send messages on behalf of the mailbox owner. For example, you might assign the executive assistant of the mailbox owner the Send On Behalf Of privilege. This means that messages they send will be identified in the message header as having originated from the

assistant on behalf of the owner. You can also specify an alternate recipient that will receive copies of all mail delivered to the mailbox. You might configure this if the owner is a temporary worker under someone else's supervision.

- *Protocols.* This page lets you specify which Internet protocols the mailbox can use when connecting to Exchange. We will cover Internet protocols later in this book.
- *Custom Attributes.* This page lets you specify values for any custom attributes that have been defined. Custom attributes can include things like a user's employee ID number, social security number, date of birth, favorite color, or anything else you want to include in the mailbox definition for users in your company. Before you can specify any values here, you must first use the Custom Attributes page of the DS Site Configuration object's property sheet to define the custom attributes you want to use for your organization. We'll look at this in our walkthrough.
- *Limits.* This page lets you specify deleted item retention time, disk storage limits, and the maximum message size for the mailbox. Deleted item retention time and disk storage limits are also defined globally for all mailboxes on the General page of the Private Information Store object's property sheet, but anything you specify here overrides those global settings. Note that message size limits can be set separately for incoming and outgoing mail. We'll look at these settings in more detail when we look at configuring the Private Information Store object in a later chapter.
- *Advanced.* This page includes a hodge-podge of different settings that are used in specific situations. These include the following:
  - *Simple Display Name.* This display name is used by systems that cannot interpret all the characters that may be used in the normal display name. You can usually leave this blank.
  - *Directory Name.* This shows the internal directory name used to represent the mailbox object in the Exchange directory hierarchy. It is also used within email addresses to route messages addressed to the mailbox. This is normally the same as the alias defined on the General page and cannot be changed.
  - *Trust Level.* This is used for directory synchronization with MS Mail systems and is discussed in a later chapter.
  - *Home Server.* The home server of the mailbox is the server in whose Private Information Store the mailbox contents (folders, messages, and

attachments) reside. If you change the home server here, it will move the mailbox to the Private Information Store of the server you specify.

- *Hide From address Book*. Makes the recipient a hidden recipient, which means that it doesn't show up in users' address books.
- *ILS Server and Account*. This allows users running Microsoft NetMeeting to connect to an ILS server and request an online meeting with the owner of the mailbox.
- *Outlook Web Access Server*. This is the server (if there is one) that is running Internet Information Server 3.0 or higher along with Active Server pages, which enable users to access their mailboxes using a standard Web browser like Internet Explorer.

Walkthrough: Creating and Configuring Mailboxes

Creating and configuring mailboxes is one of the most common (and time-consuming) jobs of the Exchange administrator. This walkthrough will take you through some of the different ways mailboxes can be created and configured.

Creating a Mailbox Using Exchange Administrator

Let's create a mailbox for Boris Zhivago, one of our network administrators for MTIT, and whom we previously assigned the Permissions Admin role so that he could administer any Exchange Server in the Atlanta site. Start the Exchange Administrator program and connect to the server MICKEY in site Atlanta. From the Exchange Administrator menu, select File, New mailbox to open up a blank property sheet for our new mailbox (refer to Figure 6-2). You can also use the keyboard shortcut CTRL+M to begin the process of creating a new mailbox. If the Recipients container for Atlanta doesn't have the focus in our Exchange Administrator window, you will be prompted to switch to that container (see Figure 6-3). Click OK to do so.

Enter "Boris" as the first name and "Zhivago" as the last name on the General page. This will automatically generate "Boris Zhivago" for the dis-

Figure 6-3 Recipients must be created in a Recipients container.

play name and "BZhivago" for the Alias fields, according to our previously defined auto naming convention. Enter the following additional information on this page:

Address: 15 AppleTree Lane

City: Atlanta

State: Georgia

Country: U.S.

Title: Assistant Network Admin

Company: MTIT

Department: Information Services

Skip ahead to the Email Addresses page and examine the auto-generated email addresses for Boris's mailbox (ssee Figure 6-4). Look back to Chapter 4 if you need to review the meaning of these address types.

Note that you can edit existing email addresses or even create a new email address (click the New button to see all the types of addresses Exchange will allow you to create). If you create a new email address of one of the types that has been auto-generated, you end up with two email addresses of the same type for Boris. In that case, you need to select one and click the Set As Reply Address button to specify which address will be used as the default Reply-To address when a user replies to a message sent by Boris by clicking the Reply button on their mail client program.

Since Boris likes to be known by his first name to his colleagues out there on the Internet, let's create an additional SMTP address for him. Click New to open the New Email Address dialog box, select Internet Address, and click OK. The Internet Address Properties dialog box appears. Enter the address `Boris@MTIT.com` into the textbox and click OK (see Figure 6-5). The new address should now appear in the listbox on the Email Addresses page. Select the new address and click the Set As Reply Address button to make

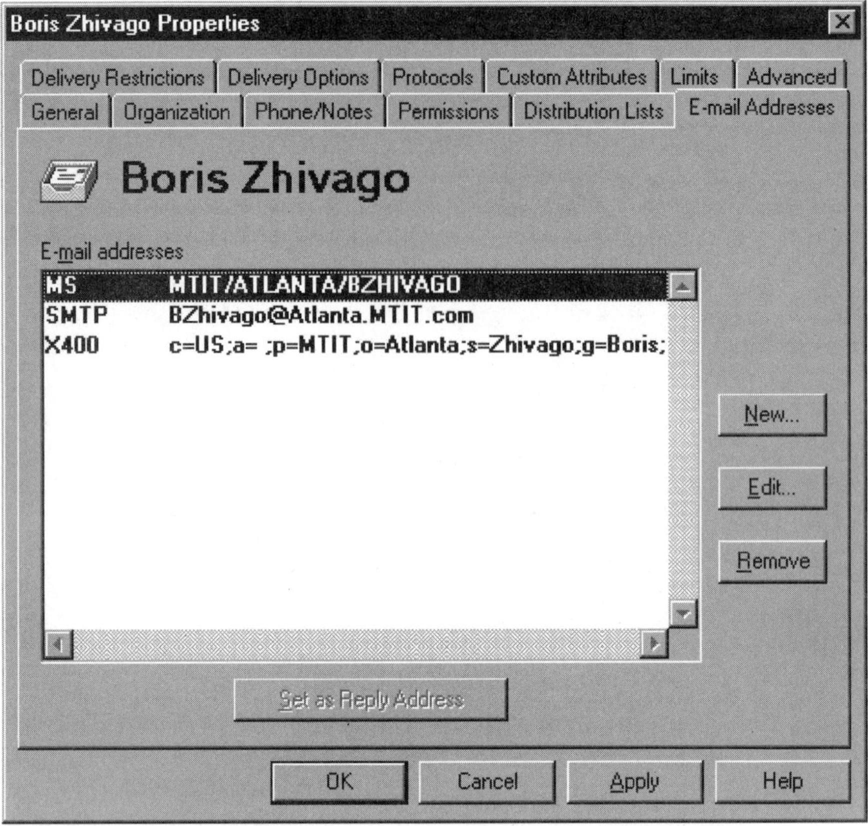

Figure 6-4 Email addresses generated for our new mailbox.

Internet Address Properties

General

E-mail address: Boris@mtit.com

OK Cancel Apply Help

Figure 6-5 Creating an additional SMTP email address for Boris.

this Boris's Reply-To SMTP address. We won't worry for now about the fact that the domain of this new address (`MTIT.com`) is different from the domain of the existing SMTP address (`Atlanta.MTIT.com`).

Deleting Email Addresses

You should generally not delete the default email addresses which Exchange generates for its mailbox recipients, as these may be used by different Exchange services. Deleting them can cause message delivery problems for that mailbox. This is especially true of the X.400 email address (also called the O/R address), since Exchange uses X.400 addresses as a backup when routing messages within an organization in case routing by the distinguished name *(DN) fails.*

Leave all the remaining settings on the various property pages as they are and click OK to create your new mailbox for Boris. At this point, a dialog box will appear, prompting you to make a choice (see Figure 6-6):

- Select an existing Windows NT account to be associated with the new mailbox (the default).
- Create a brand new Windows NT account simultaneously with the creation of the new mailbox.

Since Boris's account has already been created using User Manager for Domains, we'll accept the default option and click OK. From the list of accounts in the MTIT domain that next appears, double-click on Boris and click OK. The new mailbox has now been created and should show up within the Recipients container for the Atlanta site in the Exchange Administrator window.

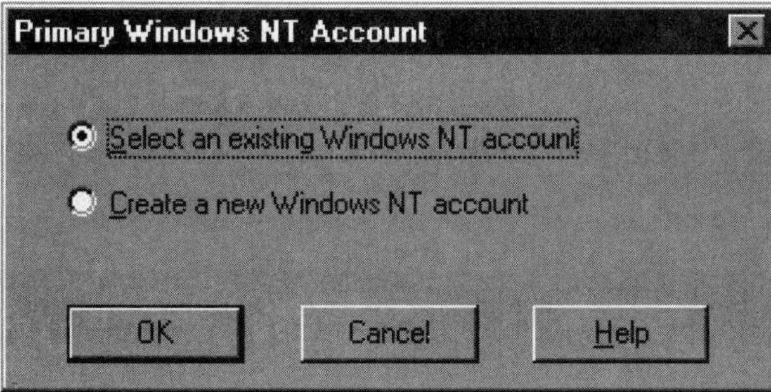

Figure 6-6 Associate a Windows NT account with the new mailbox.

Creating a Mailbox Using User Manager for Domains

Now let's use User Manager for Domains to create a new account and its mailbox simultaneously. We'll create an account for Natasha Smith, another new network administrator in MTIT, and also assign her the Permissions Admin role to administer the Atlanta site of MTIT.

Start User Manager for Domains from the Administrative Tools program group and select Exchange, Options from the menu to view the new options for configuring User Manager to work with Exchange (see Figure 6-7). Note that the default settings are provided to create new mailboxes when you create new user accounts and to delete the corresponding mailbox when you delete an account. The settings are also configured so that all new mailboxes that are created will be homed within the default Recipients container on the server MICKEY, which is fine for now.

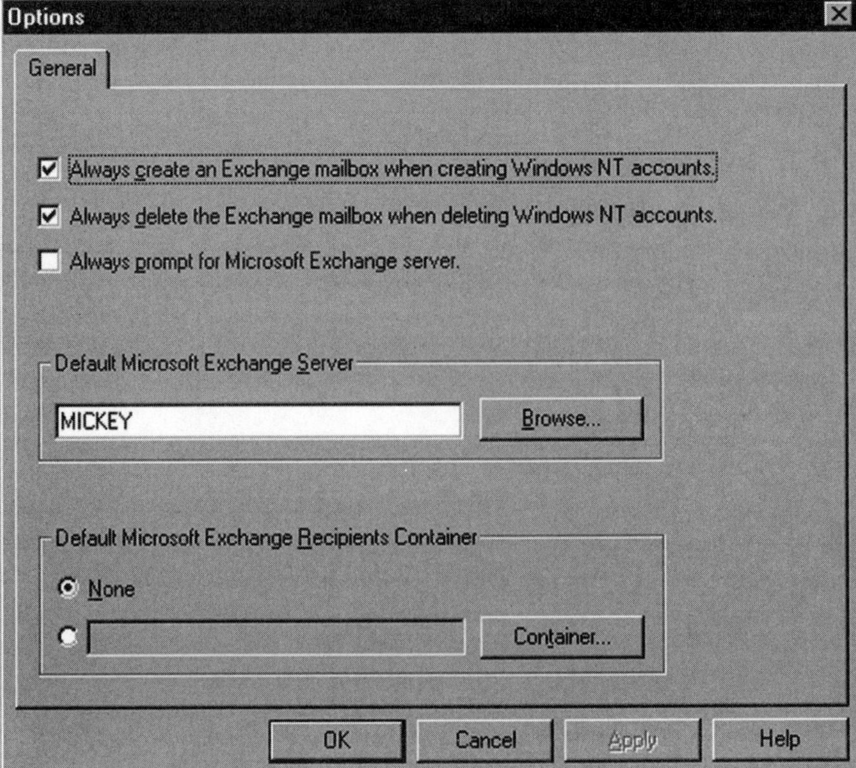

Figure 6-7 Exchange options for User Manager for Domains.

Close the Options box. Select the Boris account and choose Exchange, Properties from the menu. This opens the property sheet for Boris's mailbox and allows you to make changes to it if you will. Close the property sheet and let's go on to Natasha. Select User, New User from the menu and specify the following information for Natasha's new user account:

Username: Natasha

Full Name: Natasha Smith

Groups: add Domain Admins

plus anything else you want to specify (like a password and so on).

Once the account is configured, click the Add button to create the account. Instead of being returned to a blank New User dialog box at this point, the property sheet for Natasha's mailbox is now opened. Type in the necessary information, following Boris's account information listed above, and click OK. You should now see two mailboxes within the Recipients container (you may need to select Refresh from the Windows menu of Exchange Administrator to make her new mailbox visible, as Exchange Administrator refreshes automatically but not very well). Double-click on her mailbox to open its property sheet, and note that the Primary Windows NT Account for the mailbox is set to MTIT\Natasha as desired.

Using Mailbox Templates

As you can see, it can be pretty tedious creating mailboxes, especially if you have to create a lot of them. One way to speed the process is to use *mailbox templates*, which are mailboxes that have been pre-configured with default values for most of their attributes. Templates are useful when you need to create a lot of mailboxes that have similar values for their attributes, such as the same department, address, phone number, and so on.

Let's create a mailbox template for a default employee in the Information Services department of MTIT, and then use this template to create mailboxes and user accounts for a dozen new Information Services department employees. To do this, start the Exchange Administrator program and select File, New mailbox from the menu. Enter the following values in the property sheet:

Display Name: _IS Template

Alias: IS Template

Address: 15 AppleTree Lane

City: Atlanta

State: Georgia

Country: U.S.

Title: Technology Specialist

Company: MTIT

Department: Information Services

Phone: 222-3333

(The underscore in the display name makes the template appear at the top of the recipients list in the contents pane.) Click OK to create the mailbox. When prompted to create or select a Windows NT account, click Cancel, as this is a template mailbox that will be used to create other mailboxes and will not be used by any MTIT employee.

Now select the new template mailbox in the Contents pane of Exchange Administrator and choose File, Duplicate from the menu. A new mailbox property sheet appears (see Figure 6-8) whose attributes have the same val-

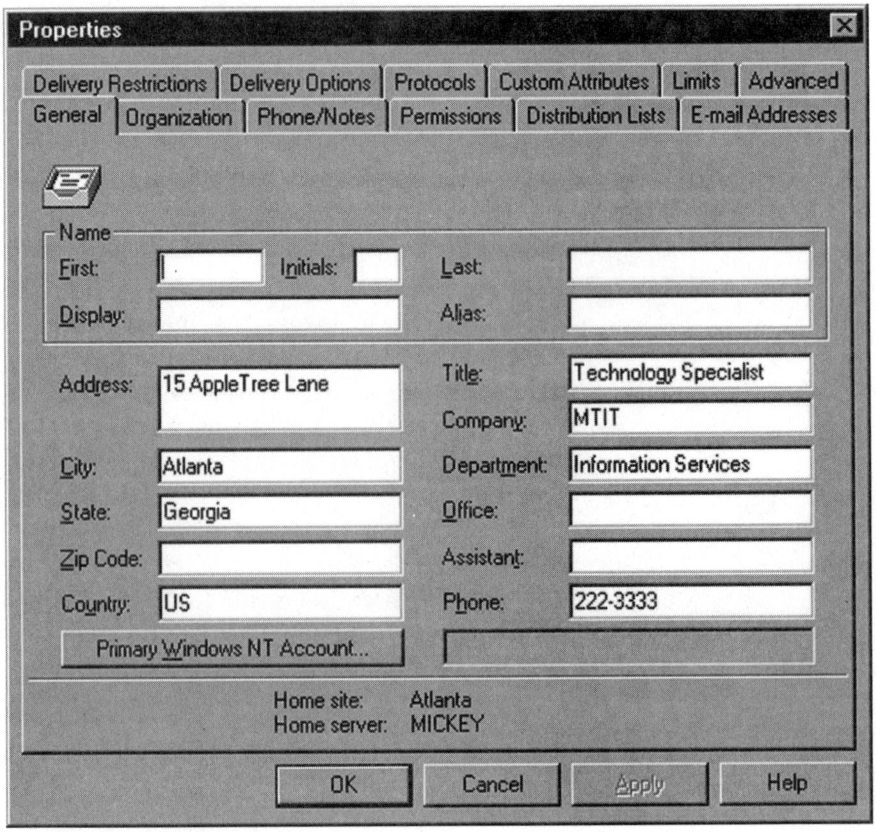

Figure 6-8 Using a template to create new mailboxes.

ues as those of the template mailbox, with the exception that the following attributes are blank (undefined):

First Name

Initial

Last Name

Display Name

Alias

Enter "Fred" for First Name, "Shakespeare" for Last Name, accept the auto-generated display name and alias, and click OK. Choose the option to create a new user account, accept the default username, and click OK twice (note that the new account is assigned a blank password and Fred will be required to change the password the first time he logs in). Voila! The new account and mailbox have been created. Reselect the template mailbox, select Duplicate from the File menu, and create a dozen new mailboxes/ accounts that all will use the template.

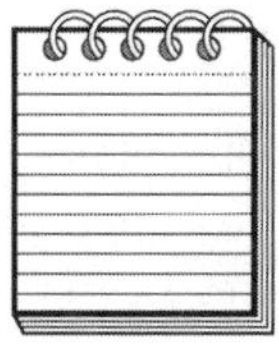

Using Mailbox Templates

You can create mailboxes a lot faster if you use the keyboard instead of the mouse for making menu and dialog box selections. To create a mailbox for a new user called Tom Jones using the keyboard, first use the up or down arrow keys to select the IS Template mailbox and press:

ALT

F

U

Tom

TAB

TAB

Jones

ENTER

DOWNARROW

ENTER

ENTER

ENTER

As a final step, let's hide the mailbox template from the recipients list so that ordinary users won't know of its existence or try to send an email to it (hiding the mailbox also removes it from the GAL so that it doesn't appear in the address book of client mail programs). To hide the mailbox template, open its property sheet, select the Advanced tab, and select the Hide From Address Book checkbox. To view the template in the Exchange Administrator window (to see which templates you have created for the mailboxes), select View, Hidden Recipients. Be sure to unhide the template when you plan to use it to create more mailboxes or the mailboxes you create will all be hidden as well.

Modifying Mailbox Settings

Management has struck again! The boss has decided that employees in the Information Services department who were previously called "technology specialists" will from now on be known as "information technology specialists." You've got 300 users who need the Title attribute of their mailboxes changed. What do you do?

The answer is to use the Directory Export and Directory Import menu options in Exchange Administrator. To modify the properties of a large number of mailboxes simultaneously, we will export the settings of the mailboxes to a comma-delimited (`*.csv`) text file, modify the settings using a spreadsheet program (Microsoft Excel), and import the modified file back into Exchange to make the changes. An essential adjunct utility to this process is the Import Header Tool (`Header.exe`) that is part of the *BackOffice Resource Kit* (BORK) Part 2 (why Microsoft didn't include this valuable tool together with Exchange is anybody's guess!) It is used to create the header record for the `*.csv` file that contains the names of the mailbox fields we want to export/import. We've already installed the BORK2 tools that come with Microsoft TechNet on our Exchange Server and are ready to proceed.

Click Start, Run, enter the path `C:\BORK\Exchange\Header.exe`, and click OK to start the Import Header tool. It takes a few seconds to read the Directory schema and be initialized (you need to have your monitor set to a minimum resolution of 800 × 600 to use this tool). Leave the mode set to Export and the object class set to mailbox (the defaults). Select all the bold attributes in the left listbox and add them to the right listbox (bold attributes are required). Also select the Title attribute in the left listbox and add it to the right listbox (the Title attribute is the one we want to change for the mailboxes that need to be modified). Click the File button and accept the default name for the `*.csv` file to be generated, which is `header.csv`. It is created in the root directory of the C: drive. Now click Open and the Directory Header Configuration dialog box will look like Figure 6-9.

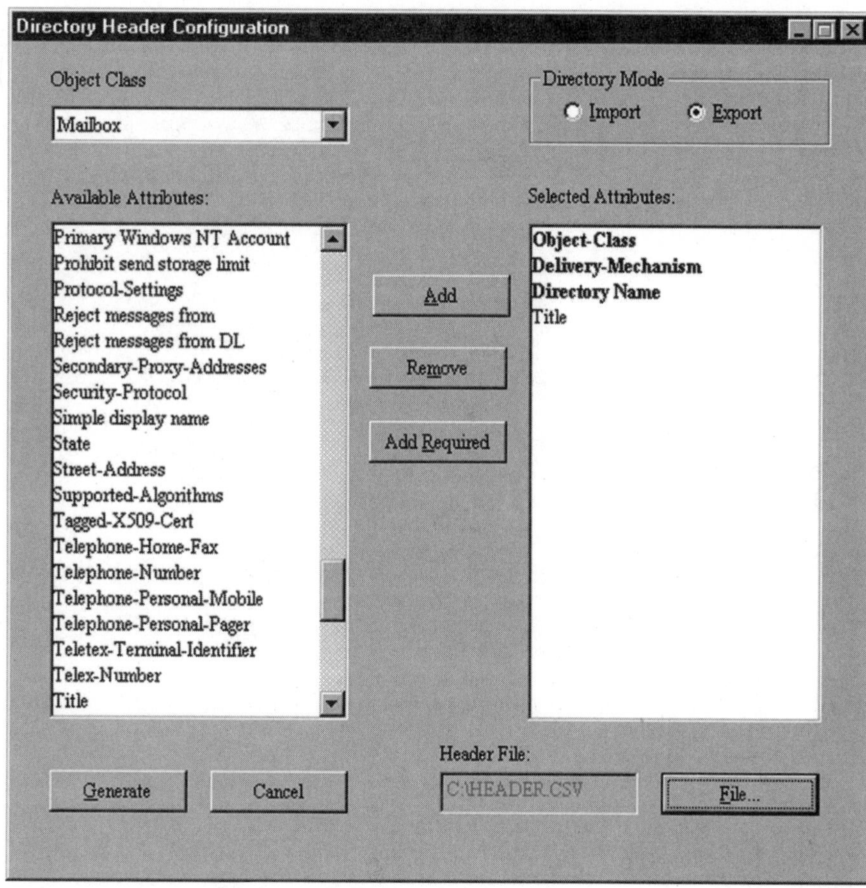

Figure 6-9 Using the Import Header tool.

Now click Generate to create the `header.csv` file. A dialog box will appear, informing you that the process was successful. Close the Import Header Tool and open `header.csv` using Notepad to see what it looks like. It should have only one line (record) in it:

```
Object-Class,Delivery-Mechanism,Directory Name,Title
```

This record is the header record for the export file we are now going to create, and it indicates which attributes (fields) will be exported. Start the Exchange Administrator program and select Directory Export from the Tools menu. Make the following selections on the Directory Export dialog box (see Figure 6-10):

MS Exchange Server: MICKEY

Home Server: MICKEY

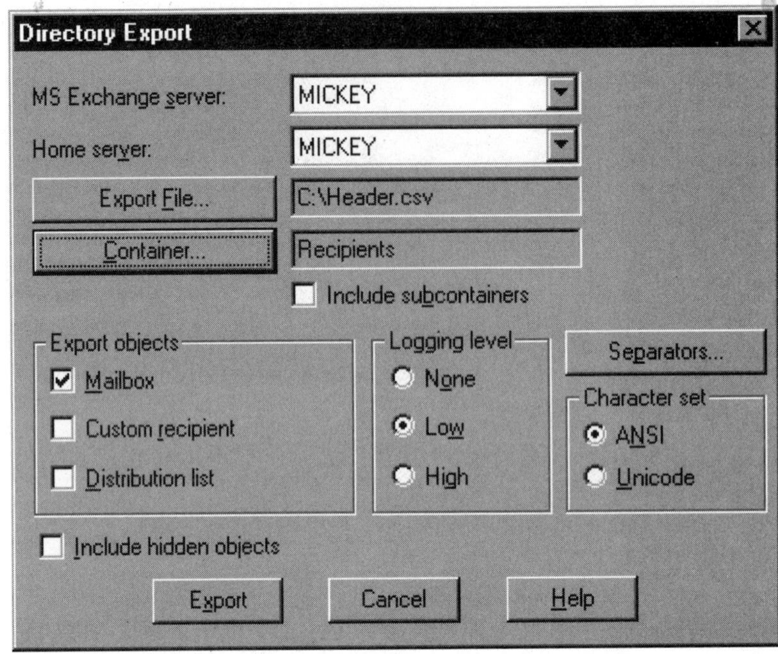

Figure 6-10 Exporting mailboxes to a header file.

Export File: `C:\header.csv`

Container: Recipients

Leave the remaining settings as they are. All the mailboxes we have created so far are homed on MICKEY, which will be our home server to export from. Click the Export button to export the mailboxes now. What this does is export the values of the attributes specified in the header record for each mailbox homed on MICKEY. What export does not do is export any messages contained in those mailboxes. Only directory information is exported, not information contained in the Information Store. After a moment, the export process is finished, our old `header.csv` file that had one record is renamed as `header.c01`, and our `header.csv` file now looks like this:

```
Obj-Class,Delivery-Mechanism,Directory Name,Title
mailbox,0,AMaupaissant,Technology Specialist
mailbox,0,BZhivago,Assistant Network Admin
mailbox,0,DDickens,Technology Specialist
mailbox,0,FShakespeare,Technology Specialist
mailbox,0,FWillow-Smith,Technology Specialist
mailbox,0,HSebastian,Technology Specialist
mailbox,0,JHemingway,Technology Specialist
```

```
mailbox,0,JLongfellow,Technology Specialist
mailbox,0,JRecca,Technology Specialist
mailbox,0,Natasha,Assistant Network Admin
mailbox,0,RKeats,Technology Specialist
mailbox,0,TJones,Technology Specialist
mailbox,0,ZHammerstein,Technology Specialist
```

Now we will make our modifications to the Title field of each record. Start Microsoft Excel, open the `header.csv` file, and walk through the steps of the Text Import Wizard to import the file into a spreadsheet (see Figure 6-11).

Do a search and replace to change all instances of "technology specialist" to "information technology specialist" in the spreadsheet. Once this is completed, save the file as `header.csv`, overwriting the old file.

All that remains is to import the `header.csv` file back into the Recipients container on MICKEY. In Exchange Administrator, select Directory Import from the Tools menu and specify the following settings in the Directory Import dialog box (see Figure 6-12):

MS Exchange Server: MICKEY

Container: Recipients

Import File: `C:\Header.csv`

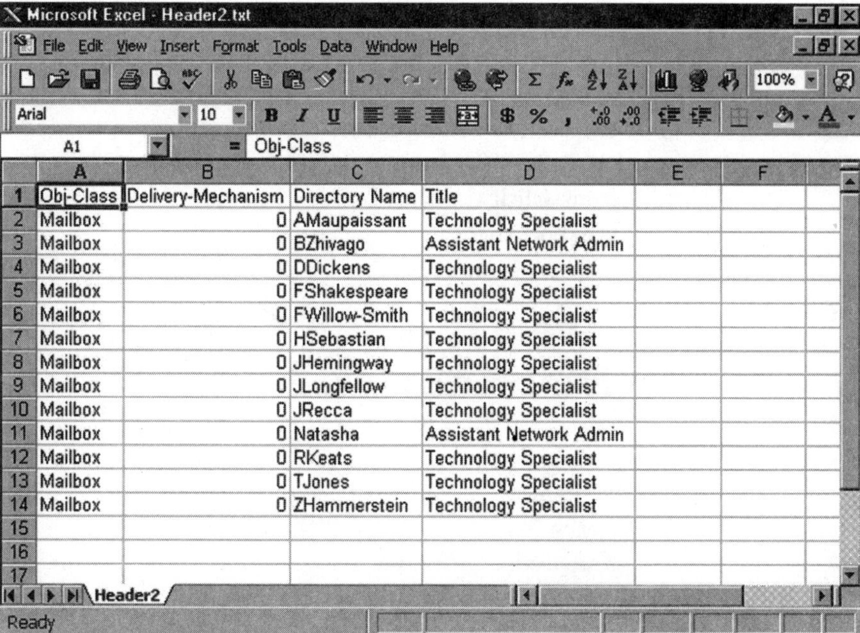

Figure 6-11 Using Excel to modify the header file.

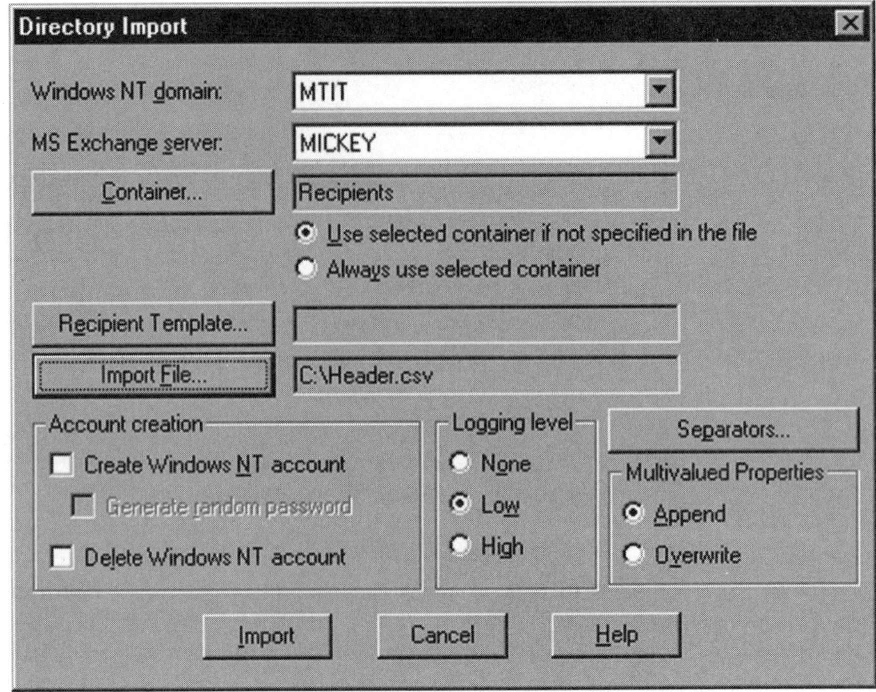

Figure 6-12 Using Directory Import to modify mailbox properties.

Leave everything else as it is, and click Import to import the information contained in the header file back into the directory, overwriting the old values for the existing mailbox settings. Once this process is complete, open the property sheet of each mailbox on MICKEY to make sure it worked successfully.

Creating and Configuring Distribution Lists

A *distribution list* (commonly abbreviated as DL) is essentially a collection of pointers to mailboxes, with a pointer for each mailbox that is a member of the list. DLs are typically used for announcements of meetings, events, and product offerings; mass mailings of marketing information; warnings of virus threats and other potential user problems; discussions relating to the topic of the list; and so on.

Distribution lists can only be created using Exchange Administrator, and creating and configuring them is a straightforward process, so we will look at DLs in the context of a walkthrough.

Walkthrough: Creating and Configuring distribution lists

Start the Exchange Administrator program and select File, New Distribution List to open a blank property sheet for a new DL. You can also use the keyboard shortcut CTRL+D to begin the process of creating a new DL. We'll create a list that is used only by network administrators (Boris, Natasha, and a new user called Igor Jones that we've created a mailbox for, duplicating Boris's mailbox to do this). This list will be used for discussions between the network administrators, so we'll call the list Talk-NetAdmin (it's often a good idea to give DLs some distinguishing name such as "Talk- . . ." to distinguish them from individual mailboxes). Let's fill in the various property pages for the DL. Many of these pages are similar to those for mailbox objects, so we won't duplicate what we've said before.

- General:
  - Enter "Talk-NetAdmin" as both the display and alias names (see Figure 6-13).
  - Make Boris the *owner* of the list. This means any *non-delivery reports (NDRs)* that are generated by users sending mail to the list will be delivered to Boris. It also gives Boris the right to modify the list's membership using a client program like Microsoft Outlook.
  - The *expansion server* is the Exchange Server that will be used to expand the list, that is, to create copies of the original message for each intended recipient. If you make heavy use of DLs in your organization, you will probably want to dedicate one of your Exchange Servers to the job of expanding DLs.
  - Click Modify and add Boris, Natasha, and Igor to the list membership.

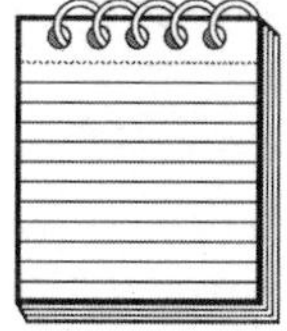

Alias Name

Be careful with the alias name that you choose for recipients! For example, if you are going to send SMTP mail to the recipient, the alias should not include any special characters that SMTP mail cannot use. In general, it's best to stick to letters, numbers, and dashes or underscores for aliases, and avoid spaces and other special characters.

Figure 6-13 Creating a new Distribution List.

- *Distribution Lists.* This tab indicates which DLs your DL belongs to (DLs can be nested in Exchange).
- *Email Addresses*. Same as for mailbox objects.
- *Delivery Restrictions*. Same as for mailbox objects.
- *Custom Attributes*. Same as for mailbox objects.
- *Advanced*. Same as for mailbox objects, except we will select the Lists container we created earlier as the container that stores the list, instead of the default Recipients container. This allows us to keep DLs separate from mailboxes as far as administrative purposes are concerned. We will also configure the various Distribution List options as follows:
- Report to distribution list owner (selected). This will cause NDRs and delivery notifications to be sent to Boris.

- Report to message originator (selected). This will cause NDRs and delivery notifications to also be sent to the message originator.
- Allow out of Office Messages to Originator (unselected). Selecting this will respond with an Out of Office message for any user who is a member of the list.
- Hide from address book (unselected). This will hide the list itself from the address book.
- Hide membership from address book (unselected). This will hide the list members from the address book and will override the Report to Message Originator option *if selected.*

Hidden Recipients

Remember that users can still send mail to a hidden recipient if they know the exact email address of the recipient.

Creating and Configuring Custom Recipients

Finally, let's consider creating and configuring Custom Recipients for our Exchange organization. *Custom Recipients* represent users that can receive mail but are not part of your Exchange organization. A Custom Recipient therefore occupies no space in the Information Store, since the user's Inbox and other folders are located on a different mail system than your Exchange organization. Custom Recipients only exist in the Exchange Directory, and normally do not have a Windows NT account associated with them.

A Custom Recipient is essentially specified by its email address. When you create a Custom Recipient, you must specify which type of email address the recipient will use. This depends on the type of mail system the user associated with the recipient resides on. For example, a Custom Recipient address could be

- The SMTP address of a user on the Internet
- The X.400 address of a user in a foreign X.400 mail system
- The cc:Mail address of a user on a foreign cc:Mail system

and so on.

Custom Recipients are not the only way that users in your organization can send email to users outside your organization. For example, when a user in your organization wants to use a client program like Microsoft Outlook to send a message to a user outside your organization, this can be done in three ways:

- The administrator can create a Custom Recipient for the foreign user. This Custom Recipient will appear in the GAL just like mailboxes and DLs, and to send a message to it, a user just selects it in their To: field from the GAL in Outlook. You can see that if you expect users in your organization to frequently send messages to a specific group of foreign users, creating Custom Recipients for these foreign users will make their lives easier.
- If, as an administrator, you don't want the hassle of creating Custom Recipients, but your users have certain foreign users they frequently send mail to, the users can enter email addresses for users directly into their personal address book in Outlook.
- For occasional mail sent outside the organization, users can create a *one-off address*, which is a one-time email address for sending a message to a user. In Outlook, you can either type the user's email address into the To: field in the new message window or select To:, click New, select an address type, and click Put This Entry In This Message Only to open the one-off address template. Fill in the template and then send the message.

Walkthrough: Creating and Configuring Custom Recipients

Let's create a Custom Recipient for an SMTP email address that will be commonly used by our MTIT employees. We'll say that this email address is `info@escape.com` (my ISP's email address) Here are the steps in the process:

1. Start the Exchange Administrator program and select File, New Custom Recipient. This opens the New Email Address dialog box, prompting us to choose which type of email address our recipient uses (see Figure 6-14).
2. Select Internet Address and click OK. The Internet Address Properties dialog box appears, into which we type the email address

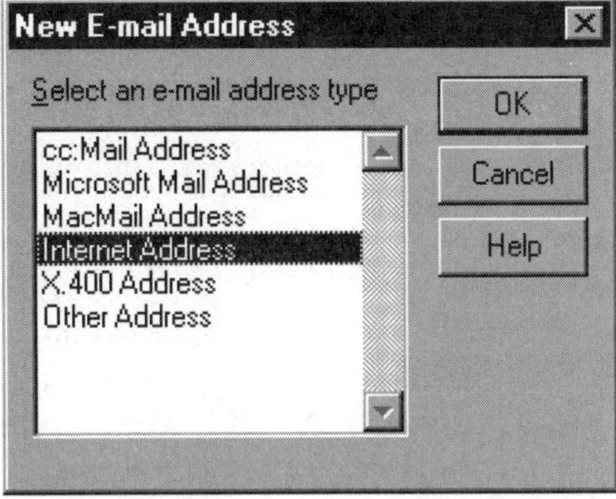

Figure 6-14 Selecting an email address type for a new Custom Recipient.

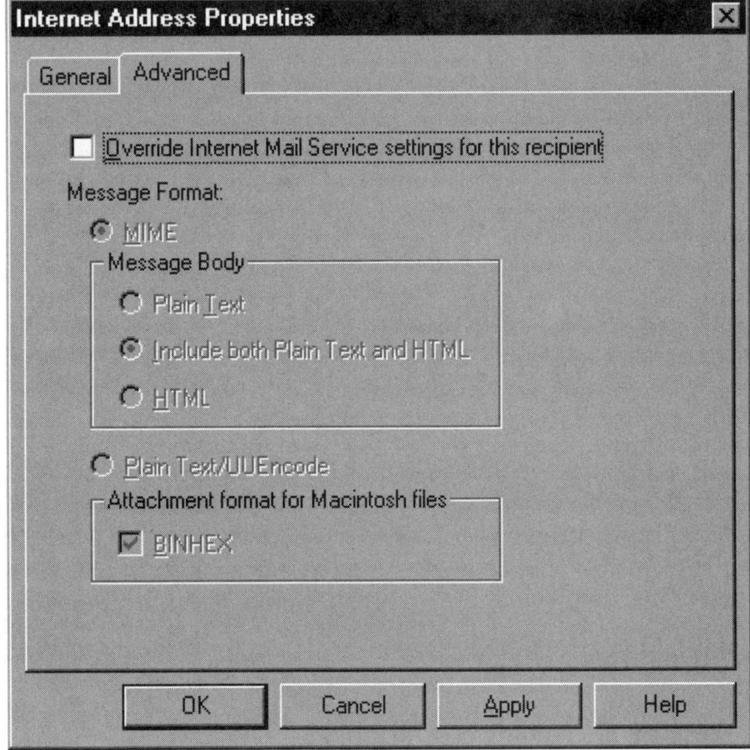

Figure 6-15 Encoding options for SMTP Custom Recipients.

of our Custom Recipient. Type `info@escape.com` as the email address and then select the Advanced tab (see Figure 6-15). This tab enables us to configure special settings for our Custom Recipient. In particular, by choosing to override the default settings of the

Internet Mail Service (IMS), we can specify whether outgoing messages with attachments will use one of the two choices:

- Multipurpose Internet Mail Extensions (MIME) for encoding the attachments and the type of format that will be used for the message body (plain text, HTML, or both)
- Uuencoding for encoding attachments, or BINHEX for Macintosh files

3. Alternatively, we can choose to go with whatever encoding method is specified in the settings for the IMS (which we haven't installed yet anyway). We'll make this choice and click OK.
4. At this point, a blank property sheet for a new Custom Recipient appears, which is similar to that of a mailbox. Specify the following information into this property sheet:
   - "Escape" for both Display Name and Alias on the General tab
   - External as the Container name on the Advanced tab (we decided in an earlier chapter to store all Custom Recipients in a separate recipients container called External)
   - Enable rich text in messages (selected) to use the Rich Text Format for sending messages to the recipient (the recipient's client program must support this feature)
5. Finally, click OK to create the new Custom Recipient.

Where Do We Go From Here?

Now that we've created some recipients, it's time to test sending mail to them. In the next chapter, we will look at the various client mail programs that can be used with Exchange and how to install and configure them.

For More Information

You can find more information on creating and configuring recipients in the Exchange Server manuals (or Books Online). In particular, take a look at Chapter 5 of the *Getting Started* manual and Chapter 1 of the *Operations* manual.

BORK2

`Header.exe` and other useful utilities can be found in the BackOffice Resource Kit (BORK) Part 2, which is included on the CD as part of the Microsoft TechNet subscription. They can also be downloaded from the Microsoft Web site. Note that the BORK2 utilities are "not officially supported" by Microsoft, but some of them are extremely useful.

CHAPTER 7

Administering Clients

In Chapter 6, we looked at the different kinds of Exchange recipients and how to create, configure, and modify them. Much of Exchange administration, once everything is set up and running, consists of managing issues relating to recipients. Now that we have some recipients defined, we will look now at the various types of mail clients that can be used together with Exchange. We won't go into any great depth about using these clients (that would take a whole book in itself), but after reading this chapter, you will have a basic understanding of the following:

- The different types of Exchange clients
- Installing Microsoft Outlook
- Configuring Outlook Profiles

Walkthroughs are included in this chapter for installing Microsoft Outlook 98 from a client installation point and for configuring and testing Outlook Profiles.

Microsoft Exchange Clients

Microsoft Exchange Server supplies only the back-end of an Exchange-based messaging system. Equally important in an Exchange implementation is selecting, installing, and configuring the front-end client software that users will employ for sending and receiving messages. Microsoft Exchange Server is designed to be compatible with a wide range of Microsoft and third-party client software. This section provides a brief overview of these different clients.

Microsoft Outlook

This is a full-featured desktop information management program that lets users:

- Send and receive email.
- Create and maintain lists of contacts.
- Post and read messages to Public Folders.
- Schedule appointments and meetings.
- Create and maintain task lists.

Microsoft Outlook is available in a 32-bit version for Windows 95/98 and Windows NT 4.0, a 16-bit version for Windows 3.x, and a Mac version for

Apple Macintosh computers. The 32-bit version of Outlook is available in several flavors:

- *Outlook 97* (or Outlook 8.0), which is included as part of the Microsoft Office 97 suite of office productivity applications.
- *Outlook 98* (or Outlook 8.5), which is included in the Exchange Server 5.5 Service Pack 2 (see Figure 7-1).
- *Outlook 2000,* which is included as part of the Microsoft Office 2000 suite (or can be purchased separately).

Microsoft Outlook clients use Microsoft's *Messaging Application Programming Interface* (MAPI) technology to exchange messages and other information with Microsoft Exchange Server computers. MAPI provides a uniform set of APIs for messaging functions, allowing developers to easily create client-side software for Exchange that supports messaging and information management functionality. MAPI essentially acts as a broker between Outlook client-side functions like reading messages or viewing the address book, and Exchange Server functions like accessing messages in

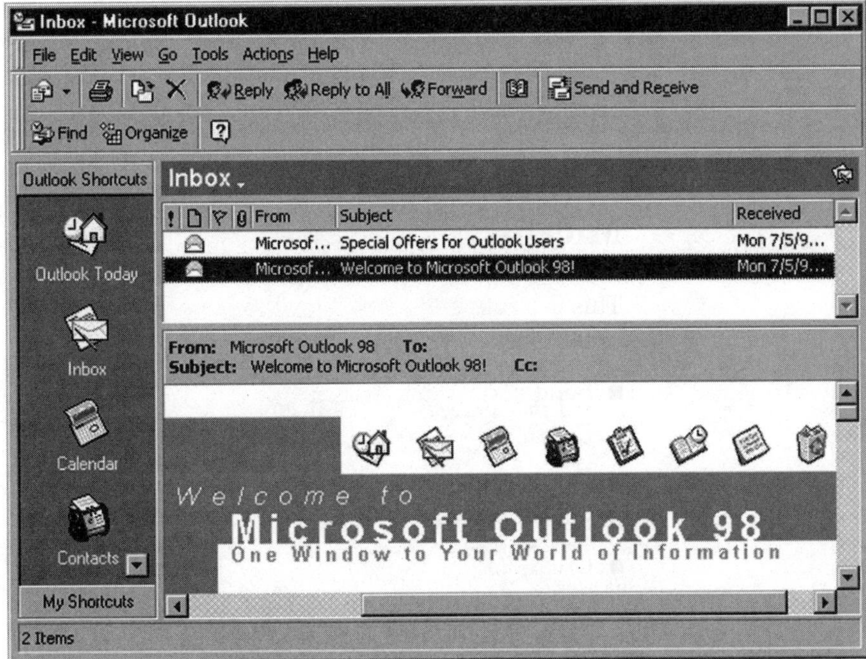

Figure 7-1 Microsoft Outlook 98 mail client and personal information manager.

the information store or creating address book views. Outlook uses MAPI calls to send messages through Exchange, read messages in the Exchange information store, access address lists, post messages to public folders, query Exchange for free/busy information of other users to book appointments, and interact with other Exchange Server functions. MAPI enables Exchange Server and Outlook to work together as a truly client/server application. Outlook uses Remote Procedure Calls (RPCs) to access MAPI functions on the Exchange server.

Microsoft Schedule+

Microsoft Schedule+ is an older Exchange client originally designed for Microsoft Mail 3.x messaging systems that provide similar but not as sophisticated scheduling capabilities as Microsoft Outlook does. Schedule+ was the precursor to Microsoft Outlook and went through several upgrades until its final release as part of the Microsoft Office 95 suite of office productivity applications.

A key consideration in any heterogeneous messaging environment where more than one type of client software is used is interoperability. Microsoft Outlook users can schedule meetings and send messages to Microsoft Schedule+ users and vice versa. Both client programs can also be used in a mixed Microsoft Exchange and Microsoft Mail network. These platforms are interoperable to a certain extent, but full functionality is best achieved by upgrading Schedule+ to Outlook and migrating MS Mail systems to Exchange. If Outlook and Schedule+ are both installed on users' computers, they can import their Schedule+ calendars into Outlook using the Import and Export command from the File menu in Outlook.

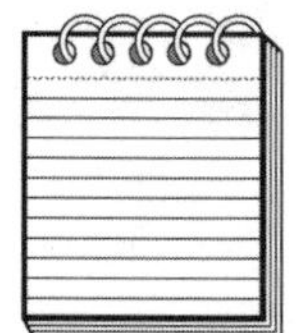

Free/Busy Information

Both Microsoft Outlook and Microsoft Schedule+ make use of the Schedule+ Free / Busy Connector in Microsoft Exchange to exchange free / busy information between users for making appointments. This connector is a type of Mailbox Agent and is found in the site Recipient's container. In addition, both Microsoft Outlook and Microsoft Schedule+ make use of the Schedule+ Free Busy Information system public folder, which needs to be replicated between all sites in an Exchange organization to allow users to make appointments and book meetings with other users in the organization.

Microsoft Outlook Express

Microsoft Outlook Express is a popular Internet mail and news client included with Microsoft Internet Explorer 4.0 or later. Microsoft Outlook Express supports Internet access only to Exchange servers, using the standard Internet protocols:

- SMTP for sending Internet mail.
- POP3 and IMAP4 for downloading Internet mail.
- NNTP for accessing USENET newsgroups.
- LDAP for accessing personal information about users stored in the Microsoft Exchange directory database.
- S/MIME for sending secure email using digital signatures and public-key encryption.
- HTML for sending and receiving rich text messages in HTML format.

Outlook Express is a messaging client designed for Internet SMTP mail and NNTP newsgroup access only. It does not support the desktop information management features of Microsoft Outlook. Outlook Express is included as part of the Microsoft Internet Explorer 4.0 or later suite of client-side Internet applications.

Outlook Express
To use Microsoft Outlook Express in your Exchange organization, you must have the Internet Mail Service installed on at least one Exchange server (see Figure 7-2). Internet access to Exchange is covered in later chapters of this book.

Microsoft Internet Mail and News

This was the precursor to Microsoft Outlook Express and was included as part of the Microsoft Internet Explorer 3.0 suite of client-side Internet applications. Microsoft Internet Mail and News has less functionality than Outlook Express and doesn't support IMAP4, LDAP, or S/MIME protocols. If you are still using this client, you should upgrade to Outlook Express.

Microsoft Outlook Web Access

This is a feature that uses Microsoft Exchange Server combined with Microsoft Internet Information Server version 3.0 or higher to provide

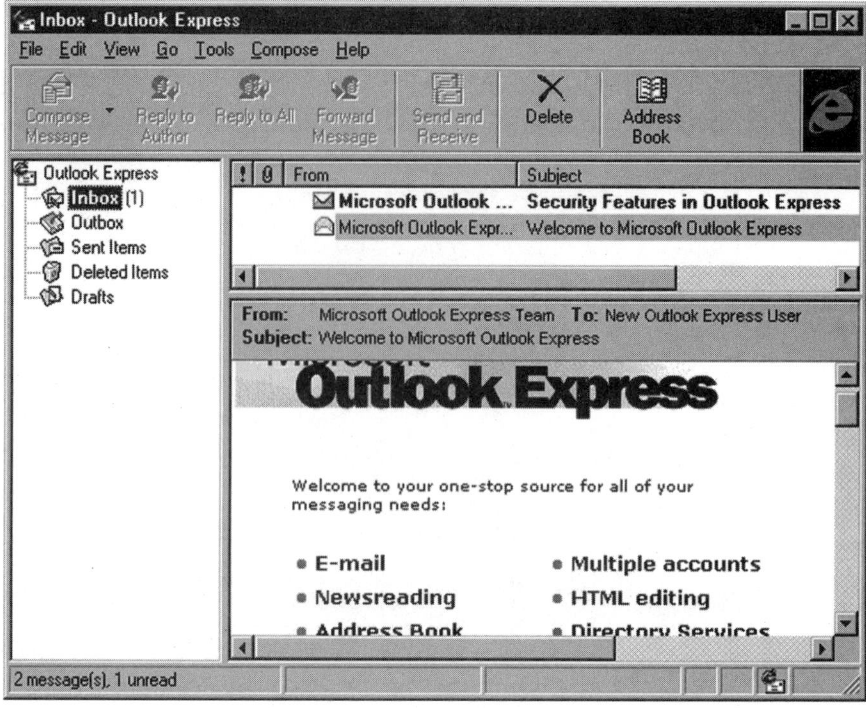

Figure 7-2 Microsoft Outlook Express Internet mail and news client.

client-side access to messaging functions using a standard Web browser like Microsoft Internet Explorer. Outlook Web Access allows users to use a standard Internet Web browser like Microsoft Internet Explorer to

- Securely access their email on Microsoft Exchange servers.
- Access the personal scheduling and collaboration functions of Microsoft Outlook that are supported by Exchange Server.
- Access public folders and the Global Address List (GAL).
- Accomplish these tasks using a standard Web browser running on any operating system platform.

Outlook Web Access

Before you install Outlook Web Access on an Exchange computer, you must have Microsoft Internet Information Server version 3.0 or higher installed on a computer, together with Active Server Pages *(ASP). Outlook Web Access is covered later in this book.*

Other Clients

Older Exchange clients include the MS-DOS- and Windows 3.x-based *Exchange Client*, and the *Windows Messaging* client originally included with Windows 95. These clients support limited MAPI-based email functions only, and since they are obsolete, they are not covered in this book.

Exchange also supports Internet SMTP messaging through any RFC-compliant POP3 or IMAP4 mail client such as *Eudora*. It enables the posting and reading of messages on Usenet newsgroups through any RFC-compliant NNTP news client such as *FreeAgent*. These third-party clients are also not covered in this book.

Installing and Configuring Microsoft Outlook

As we mentioned previously, this book cannot cover all aspects of client software for Exchange, partly because of the many different types of clients available (three versions of Outlook are probably the biggest headache for administrators) and because of the variety of ways they can be implemented with Exchange. For example, Outlook 97 can be implemented as a run-from-server application, making it unnecessary to install a local copy of Outlook on each client machine. However, this option is not possible with Outlook 98 or Outlook 2000.

Also, various interoperability issues arise when more than one version of client software is implemented in the same network, since the different versions of Outlook have different capabilities. These client-side issues could take a whole book to discuss, while our focus in this book is on the server-side implementation of Exchange messaging solutions. If you need more information than is provided for you in this chapter, see the section, "For More Information," at the end of the chapter for additional resources that might help you in implementing Exchange clients on your network (particularly Outlook).

Installing Outlook 97

Basically, Outlook 97 can be installed in two ways, through local and shared installations:

- *Local installation*. Install the Outlook 97 client software directly on the hard drive of the client computer. This option is available for all Outlook versions (16- and 32-bit) and platforms (PC and Mac). It requires only that sufficient disk space be available for the installation. You can perform a local installation by using the Outlook CD directly at each workstation (slow) or by creating a client installation point (shared folder containing the installation files) on a network server and having each client computer connect to the client installation point to run the `Setup.exe` program (fast). A client installation point is simply a shared folder on a network file server that users connect to, using a mapped drive or UNC path in order to run the Setup program. To create a client installation point, share a folder on the file server, insert the Outlook CD, and either run the `Ucsetup.exe` program from the CD (Outlook 97 only) or copy the entire contents of the Outlook CD to the shared folder, making sure you have made the hidden files visible in Windows Explorer so that these are copied as well (Outlook 98).

  As an administrator, you need Full Control permission on the share, but all other users should have only Read access to the share. The user then connects to the shared installation point using a UNC path or by mapping a drive letter to the share, running `Setup.exe` from the share, and selecting either the Typical or Custom Setup options to continue. We will walk through this process later in this chapter.

- *Shared Installation*. This installation method for Outlook 97 uses less disk space on the client computers by keeping most of the Outlook code in a read-only shared folder on a network application server. Multiple client computers can then connect to this shared folder and run Outlook remotely from their computers. The main disadvantage, of course, is that if the application server becomes unavailable, no one will be able to run Outlook from their computers. Another disadvantage is that this method only works with Outlook 97 and not later versions.

  To create a shared installation of Outlook, share a folder on the file server, insert the Outlook CD, and run `Setup /a` and follow the prompts to install the necessary Outlook program files in the network share on the server. The client computers then only need a minimal set of files installed on them in order to run Outlook directly from the server. The user simply connects to the server, runs `Setup.exe`, and selects the Run From Network Server option instead of the Typical or Custom options. This will install the minimum files necessary on the client to be able to run Outlook from the server.

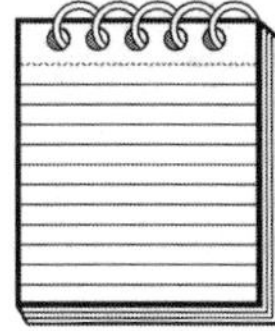

Anti-virus Software

Be sure to disable any anti-virus software before running Outlook Setup, as the anti-virus software might be triggered during Setup resulting in an aborted or incomplete installation.

The Outlook installation process is controlled by several kinds of setup files:

- `Setup.exe`, the actual Setup program.
- Information files (`*.inf`) including `Outlook.inf`, which supplies information concerning the location of program files that are to be installed on the machine, whether they are to be copied or renamed, and so on; and `Admin.inf`, which is used by the Setup program `Setup.exe` only when Outlook is installed from a network share point.
- The Setup Table file (`*.stf`), specifically the `Outlook.stf` file, which controls the logical flow of the Setup process. The `Outlook.stf` file is structured like a tree with multiple branch points. The path through which this tree of information is traversed depends upon the Setup environment and on which options the user selects during Setup. If you run Setup using the `/g` switch, a log file is created that records everything done during Setup, in effect tracing the path through the `Outlook.stf` file that is traversed during Setup.
- Additional Setup files, specifically the `Setup.lst` and `Setup.ini` files.

To modify the above installation files in order to install a customized version of Outlook 97 on your users' desktop machines, you can use the Microsoft Office Network Installation Wizard that is included with the Microsoft Office 97 Resource Kit. You should not modify these files directly using a text editor like Notepad, as a single misplaced tab or space character in these files can ruin the Setup process. The main use for this wizard is to modify the logical flow of Setup that is controlled by the `Outlook.stf` file by specifying the default answers for the various prompts, which are generated during the Setup process, although the wizard modifies the other Setup files as well. Specifically, you can use the wizard to specify:

- The default location where the Outlook program files will be installed on the machine.
- The default location of the Documents folder.
- The name of the log file tracking the Setup process.
- The Setup mode (Typical, Custom, or Run From Network Server).

- Which components to install.
- Questions relating to upgrading previously installed software like Schedule+ (if any).
- Start menu shortcuts and desktop icons to be created.
- Any additional Registry entries you want to modify during Setup (for advanced administrators only).

Once the Setup files have been modified appropriately, you can either:

- Run Setup in *interactive mode,* allowing users to supply answers to the various prompts (or simply accept the default answers specified in the Setup files).
- Run Setup in *batch mode* (using the `/q` switch) for unattended installation, using the default answers specified in the Setup files.

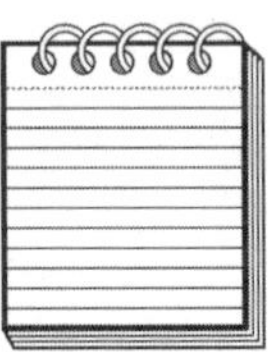

Network Installation Wizard

Here are a few more notes concerning the Network Installation Wizard:

- *The wizard ends by informing you of the command-line string that you need for running Setup using the modified installation files. This is necessary since the modified Setup files (namely the `*.stf`, `*.inf`, and `*.lst` files) created by the wizard are stored in a subfolder of the folder where `Setup.exe` itself is located. Copy down this string and use it to install Outlook on your client machines.*
- *If you want different customized Outlook installations for different groups of users (such as users in different departments), you can run the wizard several times to create several different subfolders with different sets of installation files, one for each group of user. Then use the appropriate command-line string for each group of installations you want to perform.*
- *If you are going use the wizard to modify the installation files, you obviously have to copy the various Outlook files from the CD to a shared network folder and make sure you have sufficient permissions for the wizard to write new versions of these files to the shared folder.*

Installing Outlook 98

Outlook 98 does not support the Shared Installation method supported by Outlook 97. In other words, you can only install and run Outlook 98 locally on client machines; you cannot run it from a single copy located on a network server.

Many network administrators said "bummer!" when they first heard of this change in Outlook 98, since server-based applications are so easy for them to configure and manage, especially if users are given diskless workstations to work on. Unfortunately, Microsoft chose to create dependencies between Outlook 98 and Active Setup used for installing Internet Explorer 4.0, with the result that the Run From Server or RNS configuration is not possible for Outlook 98. These dependencies also prevent you from running Outlook 98 directly from a CD-ROM like in earlier versions of Microsoft Office. If Internet Explorer 4.0 is not already installed, then installing Outlook 98 automatically installs Internet Explorer 4.0 as well on the machine.

In addition, you can install Outlook 98 in three different ways, depending on your users' messaging needs. These three installation methods are as follows:

- *Corporate or Workgroup* (CW). This method allows users to connect to a MAPI-based mail server such as Microsoft Exchange and make full use of its advanced capabilities. Using the Mail and Fax icon in the Control Panel (or by selecting Services from the Tool menu) after Outlook is installed, users can implement any of the following messaging services and functions:
- Microsoft Exchange Server
- Microsoft Fax
- Microsoft Mail
- Email
- Outlook Address Book
- Personal Address Book
- Personal Folders
- *Internet Mail Only* (IMO). This method only enables users to connect to Internet SMTP mail servers using protocols like POP3 and IMAP or to Internet LDAP directory servers. Instead of using Mail and Fax in the Control Panel, Internet account information is specified using Accounts from the Tools menu in Outlook after it is installed.
- *No Email*. This method can be used if Outlook is to be installed as a stand-alone personal information manager (PIM) client for storing scheduling information, contact lists, task lists, and so on.

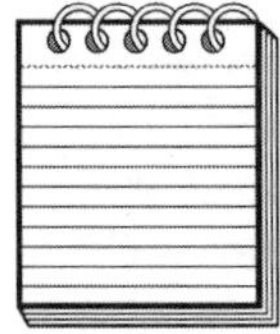

Outlook 98 Installation Methods

Outlook 98 will often try to guess which of the three methods you should choose for installation: CW, IMO, or No Email. For example, if you are upgrading from Outlook Express to Outlook, Setup will automatically choose the IMO method. If you want to override Setup in this regard, select None Of The Above when Setup displays the Email Upgrade Options dialog box, click Next, and select which of the three installation methods you want to use.

If you have installed Outlook 98 on a machine and can't remember which of the three installation methods you used, select About Microsoft Outlook from the Help Menu to find out.

When running Active Setup for Outlook 98, you have the following choices:

- *Standard Installation*. This includes either the IMO or CW installation method program files, the Help files, and the Outlook News Reader (a version of Outlook Express that only supports NNTP for accessing Usenet newsgroups).
- *Minimal Installation*. This is the same as the Standard Installation, except the Outlook Help files are not installed.
- *Full Installation*. Installs all components of Outlook 98.

We will walk through the process of installing Outlook 98 in a moment.

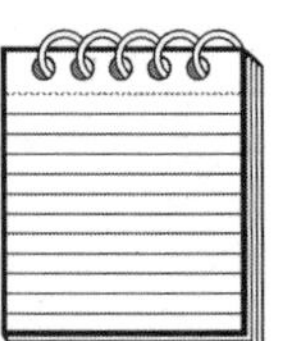

Installing Outlook 98

Here are other notes regarding installing Outlook 98 on client machines in your network:

- *You cannot install multiple copies of Outlook 98 on a single machine, so you can run both the CW and IMO installation methods of Outlook 98 on one machine.*
- *The CW installation method supports multiple mail profiles for different users that use the same machine. The IMO method does not support mail profiles, but you can create multiple Internet email accounts for Outlook on the machine, one for each user that uses the machine.*
- *If you already have Office 97 installed on your machines, make sure you install the Office 97* Service Release 1 *(SR-1) patch before installing Outlook 98.*

- *If you are installing Outlook 98 on a Windows NT 4.0 machine, make sure you install Windows NT 4.0 Service Pack 3 or higher first and make sure you are logged on as a user with administrative privileges, both during the installation and during the first logon after installation is complete.*
- *Finally, if you are installing the CW installation method of Outlook 98 on a Windows 98 machine, you must first install the Windows Messaging System on your machine before installing Outlook. To do this, follow these steps: Insert the Windows 98 CD. Click Start, then Run, and access the following file on the Windows 98 CD:* `\tools\oldwin95\message\us\wms.exe`. *Follow the steps in the wizard, restart your system, and then go ahead and install Outlook 98.*

Installing Outlook 2000

Since Outlook 2000 was released near the end of writing of this book, it is not covered in detail here. See Microsoft's Web site for more information on its features and for white papers, technical papers, and other useful information regarding its deployment and configuration.

Walkthrough: Installing Microsoft Outlook 98

Let's now walk through an installation of Outlook 98 on a Windows 98 machine. As per the previous note, we need to first install Windows Messaging on the Windows 98 machine before installing Outlook.

We begin by inserting the Windows 98 CD in the desktop machine called GOOFEY, which has Client for Microsoft Networks configured to enable users to log on to the MTIT domain where our Exchange Server MICKEY resides. If the Windows 98 installation screen appears, close it and click Start, then Run, access `\tools\oldwin95\message\us\wms.exe`, and click OK. A prompt appears asking if you are sure you want to install Windows Messaging. Click Yes to begin copying files to your hard drive, and then click OK when the process is complete. Don't forget to reboot your system (there is no prompt for doing so, unfortunately).

Next, we need to prepare a client installation point for doing a network installation of Outlook onto GOOFEY. We will create a folder called `\install` on the hard drive of a Windows NT file server called BLOOM, copy the entire contents of the Outlook 98 CD, which you obtained from

Microsoft, to the `\install` folder (since this is a test, I'll just copy the contents of the `\OL98` folder from my Exchange Server 5.5 Service Pack 2 CD). Finally, share `\install` with Read permission for Everyone and Full Control for Administrators.

Now we are ready to begin the installation. We log on to GOOFEY, click Start, then Run, enter the UNC path `\\BLOOM\Install\Setup.exe`, and click OK. The first screen of Outlook 98 Active Setup appears (see Figure 7-3).

Click Next, read and accept the license agreement, and enter your name, organization, and CD key (since this is a test, I'll use my Office 97 CD key, but when you obtain your Outlook CD from Microsoft, make sure you understand and comply with all licensing requirements). At this point, you are presented with the Installation Option screen (see Figure 7-4), prompting you to select either

- *Minimal Installation*. This includes Outlook 98 and Internet Explorer 4.01.
- *Standard Installation*. This includes Outlook 98, Internet Explorer 4.01, and Outlook Help.
- *Full Installation*. This includes Outlook 98, Internet Explorer 4.01, Outlook Help, NetMeeting, Office Assistants, PIM Converters, System Tools, and Additional Outlook Enhancements.

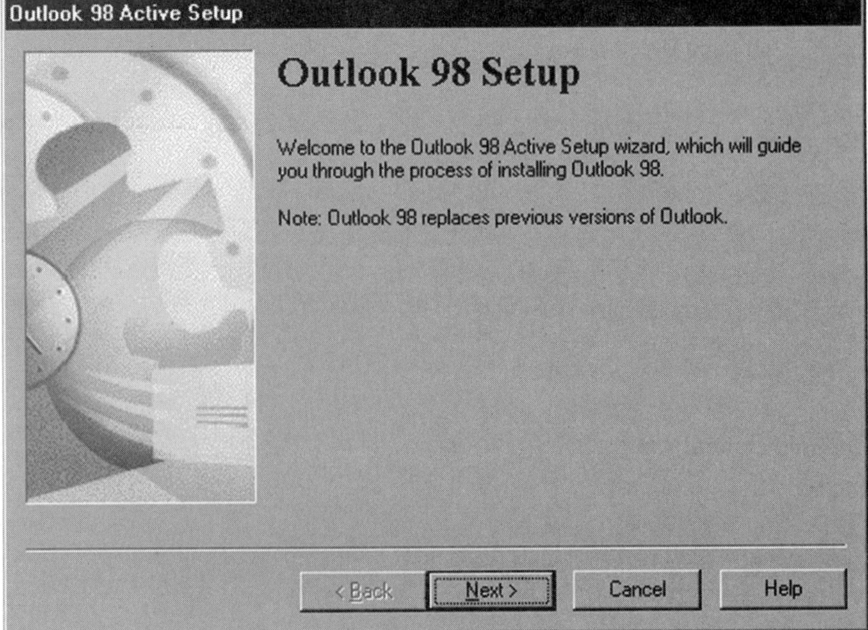
Outlook 98 Active Setup
Outlook 98 Setup
Welcome to the Outlook 98 Active Setup wizard, which will guide you through the process of installing Outlook 98.
Note: Outlook 98 replaces previous versions of Outlook.
< Back
Next >
Cancel
Help

Figure 7-3 Welcome to Outlook 98 Active Setup.

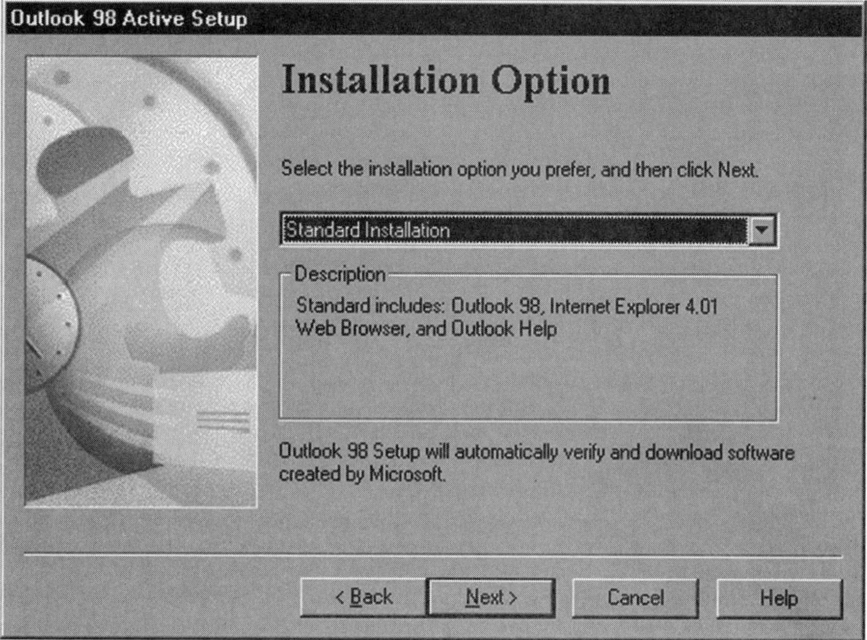

Figure 7-4 Selecting an installation type.

We'll just select Standard and click Next. The Email Upgrade Options screen appears next. Since we have installed Windows 98 on the machine, Outlook Express is already installed and we therefore have two upgrade options:

- Outlook Express
- None of the Above

We'll choose None of the Above, since if we choose the first option, Outlook will automatically install in IMO mode, while we would prefer to install it in CW mode instead. The next screen presents us with the three installation modes (see Figure 7-5):

- *Internet Only*. This mode supports SMTP messaging only.
- *Corporate or Workgroup*. The best choice when using Microsoft Exchange Server for your back-end messaging services.
- *No E-mail*. Used for stand-alone systems to install Outlook as a PIM.

We'll choose Corporate or Workgroup and click Next. Accept the default installation path, click Next, wait while Setup inspects your system, accept the digital signatures for the components installed by the Setup program

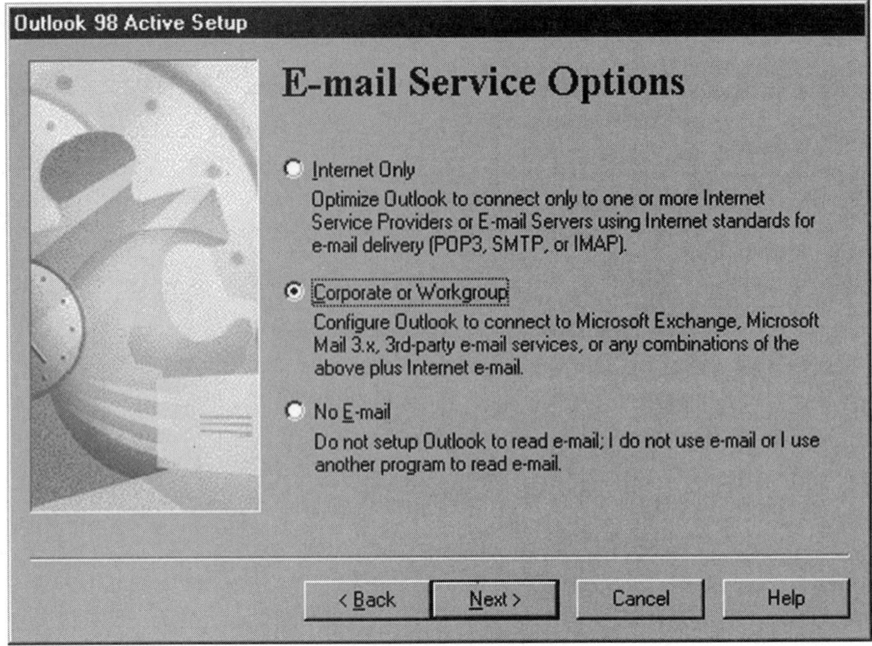

Figure 7-5
Select an installation mode.

(there may be many of them, with some appearing during copying of files later), and the copying of files shortly commences (go for coffee—it takes a while!). When the necessary files have all been copied, you are prompted to restart. Click OK and when the machine has restarted, log on as the same user and Windows updates its system settings and sets up Outlook and the other components you chose to install.

Outlook Profiles

After installation is finished, Microsoft Outlook clients need to have an Outlook Profile created for each user who uses the program in order for the Outlook program to function properly (sometimes it is referred to as a Windows Messaging Profile or simply a Messaging Profile). The Outlook Profile essentially specifies three things:

- *Which messaging services are being used* at the back-end of your messaging system. These include services like Microsoft Exchange Server, an Internet SMTP/POP3 server, a MS Mail post office, and so on.

- *Where incoming email is delivered and stored*. Possible choices include the user's own personal folders or the Information Store on an Exchange Server.
- *How outgoing email is addressed and delivered*. Possible choices include using the user's own Personal Address Book or the GAL on an Exchange Server.

Profiles

The Outlook Profile of a user is not the same as their Windows 98 or Windows NT user profile. A user's Outlook Profile is contained within their user profile. If all user profiles are stored on a Windows NT network file server in order to provide users with roaming profiles, then users will also be able to access their messages from any computer on the network using Microsoft Outlook.

Outlook Profiles can be created manually on computers where Microsoft Outlook has been installed by using the Mail (or Mail and Fax) utility in the Control Panel, or by selecting Services from the Tools menu in Microsoft Outlook. The Mail utility opens the Add Service to Profile dialog box (see Figure 7-6).

The explanation of these installable information services is as follows:

- The *Exchange Server* is used to configure a Microsoft Exchange Server as the back-end to a Microsoft Outlook-based messaging system.
- *Internet Mail* is used to configure an Internet SMTP/POP3 host as the back-end of a Microsoft Outlook-based messaging system.

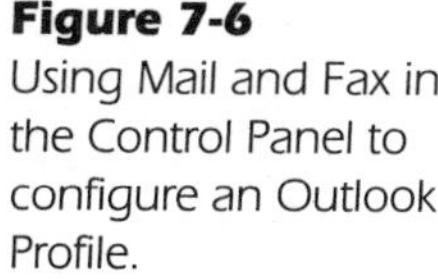

Figure 7-6
Using Mail and Fax in the Control Panel to configure an Outlook Profile.

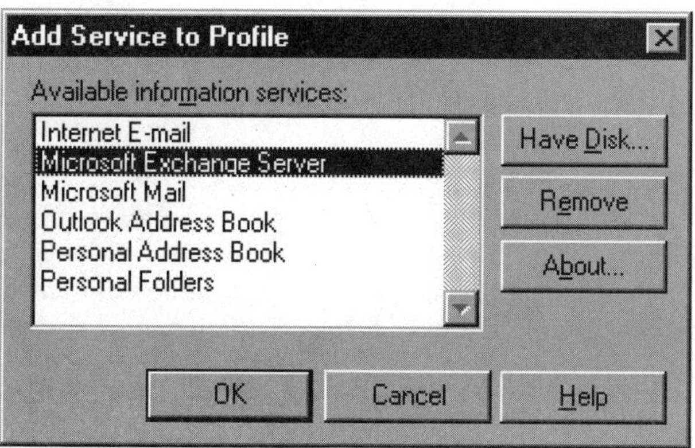

- *Microsoft Mail* is used to configure a Microsoft Mail 3.x post office as the back-end of a Microsoft Outlook-based messaging system.
- The *Outlook Address Book* supports the functions of the Outlook Contacts folder by storing email addresses of all entries in the Contacts folder.
- The *Personal Address Book* is a file with the extension `*.pab` that is usually located on the client computer that allows users to maintain their own personal address lists. Personal Address Books are an alternative to using the GAL and Address Book Views created by an Exchange Server.
- *Personal Folders* is a file with the extension `*.pst` that is usually located on the client computer that acts as a delivery point for incoming messages to be delivered. Personal Folders are an alternative to using the Information Store on an Exchange Server for storing users' messages.

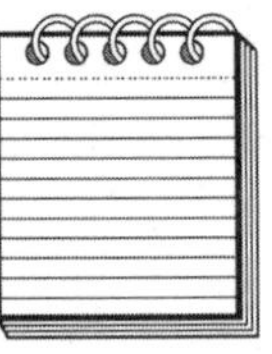

.pab and *.pst files

A user's Personal Address Book (`*.pab`) and Personal Folders (`*.pst`) files can be stored either on the client computer or on a network share. Placing them on a network share enables users to access them from anywhere on the network (roaming users). However, if the Exchange Server is your messaging system back-end, you should typically configure the Information Store on the Exchange Server as the location for storing users' messages and disable the use of Personal Folders for your users. One reason for doing this is that `*.pst` files have a maximum size of only 2 GB. Another reason is that `*.pst` files are password-protected by a password the user specifies. If the user forgets the password, there is no way to reset it; their messages are gone forever.

These `*.pst` files can be used if you are in the process of migrating a Microsoft Mail 3.x messaging system to Exchange. During the migration process, users may have both MS Mail mailboxes and Exchange mailboxes. To simplify access to their mail, you can configure Outlook to download their messages from both mail systems to a single location, a `*.pst` file either on the user's client machine or on a network file server. This way users can receive all their mail to a single location, instead of having to check for mail twice. This trick will work even if there is no messaging connectivity between the two mail systems during the migration process.

Walkthrough: Configuring and Testing Outlook Profiles

Now that we have installed Microsoft Outlook 98 on a desktop machine in CW mode, let's configure and test Outlook messaging profiles on the machine. We'll proceed as follows:

- Create messaging profiles for users Boris Zhivago and Natasha Smith.
- Have Boris use Outlook to send a message to Natasha and see if she receives it.

Log on to GOOFEY as an Administrator (if you are not already logged on as such), open up the Control Panel, and double-click on the Mail (or Mail and Fax) icon. The Mail dialog box will appear, showing no profiles set up for your computer (see Figure 7-7).

Click Add to open the Inbox Setup Wizard to create a new messaging profile. Select the Option button to manually configure Information Services

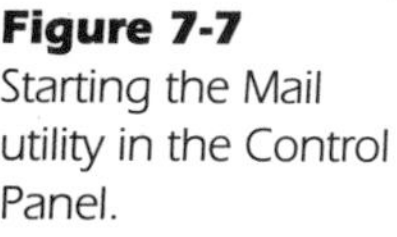

Figure 7-7 Starting the Mail utility in the Control Panel.

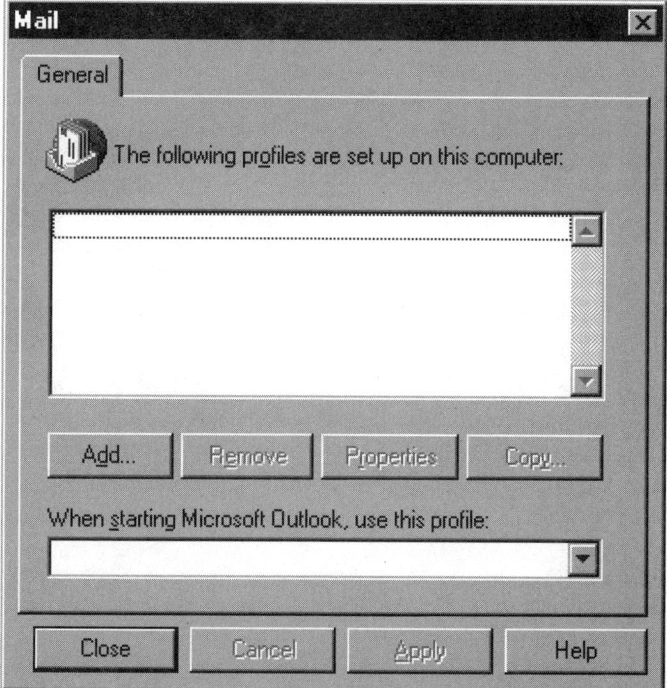

and click Next. Type "Boris Zhivago" (without the quotes) as the name of the messaging profile you want to create and click Next. The Boris Zhivago Properties box appears, displaying no information services, delivery options, or addressing options configured as of yet (see Figure 7-8).

Select the Services tab (if it isn't already selected) and click Add to display the available information services (refer to Figure 7-6). Select Microsoft Exchange Server and click OK. The Microsoft Exchange Server property sheet now appears (see Figure 7-9). Type MICKEY as the name of the Exchange Server and Boris Zhivago as the mailbox name; then click the Check Names command button. This will cause GOOFEY to try to connect to the GAL on MICKEY to verify that there is, in fact, a mailbox named Boris Zhivago ("Boris Zhivago" is the Display Name of the mailbox in the Exchange Administrator window on MICKEY). If it connects, the names MICKEY and Boris Zhivago will be underlined where you've entered them. If it fails, check your spelling and check the name of the mailbox using Exchange Administrator on MICKEY.

Leave everything else on the Microsoft Exchange Server property sheet as it is and click OK. The Microsoft Exchange Server should now be listed as the

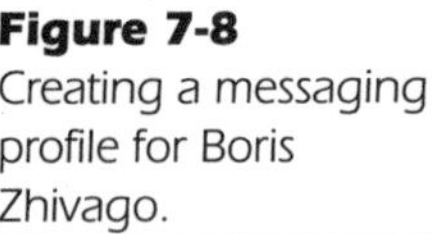

Figure 7-8
Creating a messaging profile for Boris Zhivago.

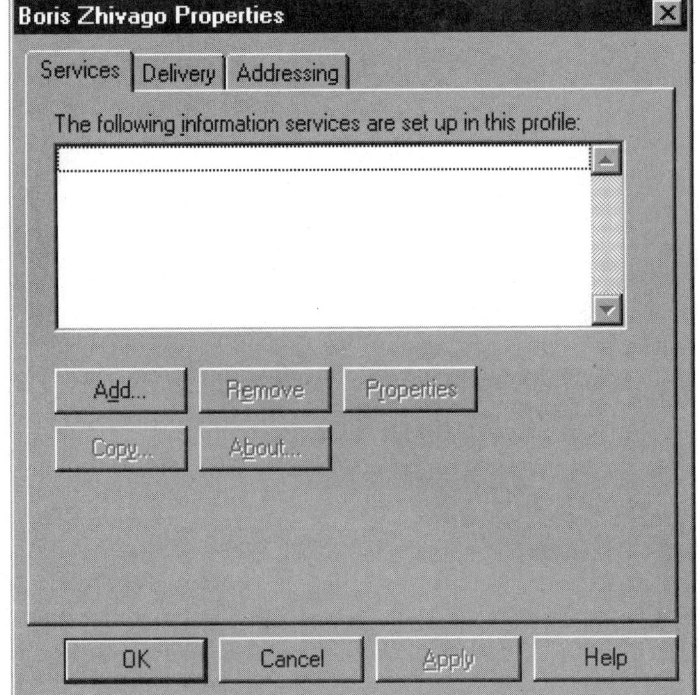

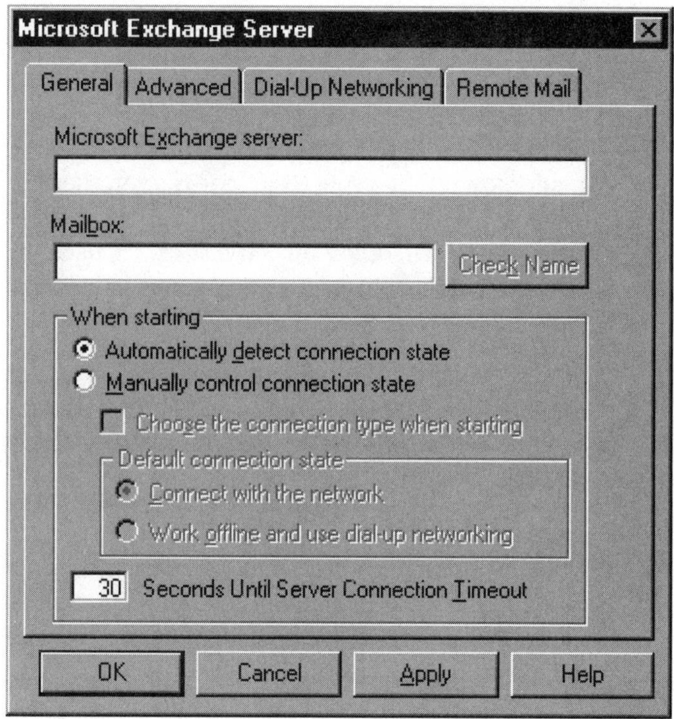

Figure 7-9 Configuring Microsoft Exchange as the mail server for the new messaging profile.

messaging service in the Boris Zhivago Properties dialog box (refer to Figure 7-8). Click OK to return to the Inbox Setup Wizard and Next your way to the Finish button, and you're back at the Mail dialog box (refer to Figure 7-7), which should now show a messaging profile for Boris Zhivago set up on GOOFEY. Now click Add again and create a similar messaging profile for Natasha Smith. When that is done, verify that Boris Zhivago is configured as the profile that will be used when Outlook is started (Boris will be logging on next), and close the Mail utility and log off from GOOFEY as Administrator.

Now let's test our messaging profiles. Log on to GOOFEY as Boris (the Windows NT user account for Boris Zhivago) and double-click the Microsoft Outlook icon on the desktop. Specify Location Information if prompted, register Outlook as your default manager for Mail, News, and Contacts if prompted, and get rid of the little Office Assistant if it bugs you. Read the Welcome messages if you like, and then select File, New, Mail Message to open an Untitled message window. Click the To button and select Natasha Smith as the recipient of the message, enter the subject "This is a test" and the text "Are we messaging yet?" in the body of the message, and click Send. To make sure the message is delivered immediately, click Send And Receive.

Now close Outlook, log off as Boris, and log on as Natasha. Before starting Outlook, however, open the Mail utility in the Control Panel. Notice that

- The property sheet that opens is called Boris Zhivago Properties, which is obviously wrong for Natasha.
- In addition to Microsoft Exchange Server, there is an additional messaging service installed called Outlook Address Book. This is automatically installed by Outlook and is used for maintaining Contacts lists.

Click the Show Profiles button to show the two profiles created on the machine. Select Natasha Smith at the bottom as the profile to be used when starting Outlook and click Close. Now start Outlook and the message from Boris should be visible in Natasha's Outlook window (see Figure 7-10).

User Profiles

The above walkthrough is only for learning how to configure and test messaging profiles. We've omitted one important preliminary step if we really want Boris and Natasha to share a single machine for their email: creating separate user profiles for them. Without this, Boris and Natasha

Figure 7-10
Message received!

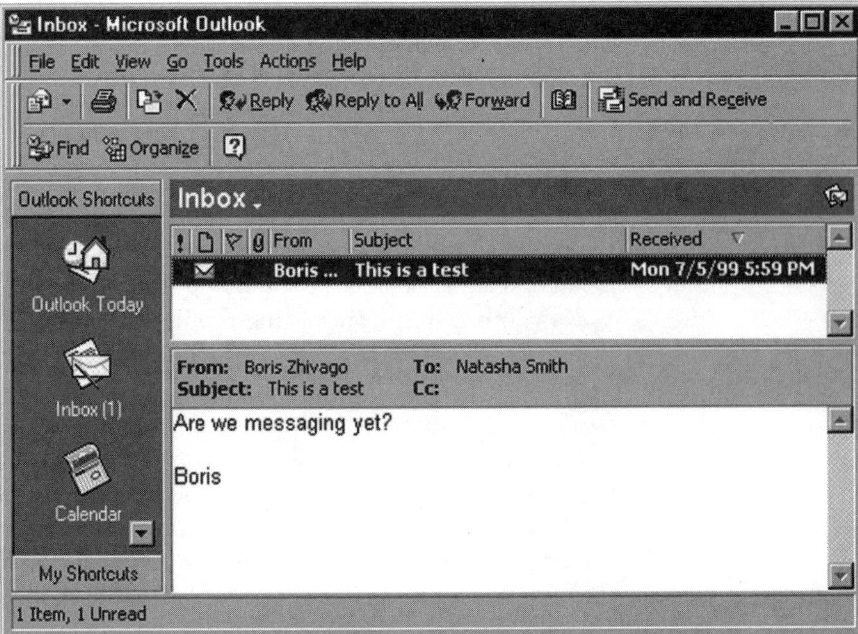

have to keep going back to Mail in the Control Panel and choosing their messaging profile each time they log on, or they might be reading each other's mail.

To implement user profiles, log on to GOOFEY as Administrator again and open the Users utility in the Control Panel. Type Administrator to create a user profile on GOOFEY for yourself as Administrator, enter your network password, Select all the personalization items displayed (Desktop, Start Menu, and so on), choose to create copies of the current items from the default user profile, and click Finish to create personalized settings for the Administrator. Restart Windows when prompted to do so and log on again as Administrator.

Now log off as Administrator and log on as Boris. You will be informed by a dialog box that you have not logged on to the computer before (you have, actually, but now Windows is configured to remember who logs on to it and maintains personalized settings for each user that logs on). Click Yes to retain your individualized settings for further logon sessions and Boris's desktop appears. Open Mail in the Control Panel, click Show Profiles, and select Boris Zhivago as the messaging profile to be associated with this user profile. Start Outlook and send another test message to Natasha.

Log off as Boris and log on as Natasha. Click Yes to get past the dialog box telling you this is the first time you have logged on as that user, open Mail in Control Panel, click Show Profiles, and select Natasha Smith as the messaging profile to be associated with this user profile. Start Outlook and check if the message from Boris came through. Reply to the message, log off as Natasha, and log on as Boris. You should then see the reply.

Of course, for better security, you would probably want to store all user profiles on a Windows NT Server, setting the permissions so that only Natasha can access her user profile, only Boris can access his user profile, and so on. Consult your Windows NT documentation for information on how to do that.

More on Installing and Configuring Outlook

There are some additional utilities from Microsoft that can be used by administrators to simplify the process of creating Outlook messaging profiles for users on the network. This section briefly reviews some of these tools.

Automatic Profile Generator (Outlook 97 Only)

Outlook 97 messaging profiles have their services, delivery, and addressing settings specified in a type of file called a Profile Descriptor File (`*.prf`). The Outlook 97 CD contains a default `.prf` file called `Outlook.prf`, which is typically installed by Setup in the `\Windows` directory. A unique `Outlook.prf` file is needed for every unique Outlook profile on a machine, each containing information such as the user's mailbox name and home server. Administrators can customize this file before installing Outlook on client machines.

Administrators can also use the Automatic Profile Generator (`Newprof.exe`) utility located in the `\Windows` directory after Outlook is installed, which can be used to automatically create Outlook profiles for each user when they install or first start Microsoft Outlook. `Newprof.exe` can be run from the command line and creates a default Outlook profile that contains those settings you specify in the `Outlook.prf` file. You can also run `Newprof.exe` during Setup so that you don't need to set up messaging profiles for individual users afterwards.

Microsoft also provides some additional `*.prf` files to simplify the customization process:

- `Exchange.prf`. This file can be found on the Microsoft Office 97 Resource Kit CD and should be used in place of `Outlook.prf` if your deployment of Outlook will be using Exchange Server as its messaging service. The reason for this is that the `Outlook.prf` file generates Outlook Profiles that specify each user's local Personal Folders (`*.pst`) file as their default message store, rather than using the Information Store on the Exchange server to store their messages. To use the `Exchange.prf` file, copy it to your client installation point, delete the `Outlook.prf` file and rename `Exchange.prf` to `Outlook.prf`. Then open it using Notepad and find the line:

  ```
  HomeServer =
  ```

  and add the name of the Exchange server on which the user's mailbox is homed.

- `None.prf`. An alternative for administrators is to replace the `Outlook.prf` file with a different file from the Microsoft Outlook CD, namely `None.prf`. When users first start Outlook on their computers, this will cause the Outlook Setup Wizard to start. Users should be provided with written instructions on how to complete the Wizard.

An alternative to using the above files is to use the Microsoft Exchange Roving User Profile Generator Program (`Profgen.exe`). This is an unsupported program from Microsoft that creates a new Outlook profile using a user's Windows NT account information and does not require creating custom `Outlook.prf` files for each user. In order for `Profgen.exe` to work, a user's Windows NT user name and their Exchange Server alias name must be the same.

Outlook 98 Deployment Kit (Outlook 98 Only)

Deployment is much easier with Outlook 98 than for Outlook 97. Microsoft has created an Outlook 98 Deployment Kit that contains a CD with documentation, tools, utilities, and various sample files to help you get Outlook 98 deployed quickly and easily. The most important of these is the Outlook 98 Deployment Wizard, which allows administrators to create custom installation packages of different Outlook components together with preset configurations of user preferences and profiles. You can obtain the Outlook 98 Deployment Kit through Microsoft's MSDN, Solution Provider, and other channels; unfortunately, it is not available for download from the Web.

The Outlook 98 Deployment Wizard replaces both the Network Installation Wizard of Outlook 97 and the various tools used to edit the Profile Descriptor files like `Outlook.prf` described earlier. This allows administrators to deploy and maintain Outlook installations from a single point on the network. The Deployment Wizard is similar to (and actually contains) the *Internet Explorer Administration Kit* (IEAK) Wizard that is used to create customized installation packages for Microsoft Internet Explorer (see Chapter 7 of my book *Administering IIS4* from McGraw-Hill for information on and a walkthrough of the IEAK). The Deployment Wizard employs the same Active Setup technology used to simplify the deployment of Internet Explorer on client machines in a network. Installation packages created using the Deployment Wizard can be stored on a network share for network installations or burned onto a CD for local installations. These packages can run as either interactive (requiring user responses to prompts generated during Setup) or quiet (no intervention required) installations, if you provide just the set of Outlook components the users need, contain information about the messaging profiles to be created, lock down desktop settings for greater security, and so on. The Deployment Wizard works in five stages:

1. *Stage 1: Gathering Information.* This portion prompts you for information such as your company name, the CD key, the language

for the custom installation package being created, and the destination folder on the network where your finished package will be stored.

2. *Stage 2: Specifying Active Setup Parameters*. This portion prompts you to select which Outlook components to include in your installation, together with up to 10 custom components (other software) you may want to bundle into your installation package.
3. *Stage 3: Customizing Active Setup*. This portion enables you to specify an Autorun splash screen, package title and version number, whether to run in interactive or quiet mode, which types of Setup to offer (for example, Minimum, Standard, and Full), and so on.
4. *Stage 4: Customizing Outlook 98 Setup Options and Internet Explorer*. This portion lets you customize various Outlook settings including installation mode, the Outlook bar, toolbars, menus, support for Schedule+, and various Internet Explorer settings.
5. *Stage 5: User Settings Customization*. This portion lets you customize user settings, user restrictions, mail and news servers, LDAP servers, and additional registry settings for custom components.

When the five stages of the Deployment Wizard are completed, the Wizard creates the customized Outlook installation package. By storing the package on a network share, users can connect to it and run `Setup.exe` to extract Setup files to a temporary directory, after which Active Setup runs to install Outlook on the client machines.

Miscellaneous Stuff

Once Outlook is installed, there are numerous ways that it can be configured, depending on users' needs and the network environment. Space doesn't permit complete coverage of all the various options, but here are a few that are worth mentioning (Some of these options apply to both Outlook 97 and Outlook 98, but the details of implementing them may differ between the two versions. Refer to the Outlook Help files for more specific information when required):

- *Offline Folders*. If you want to use Outlook to work with the contents of an Exchange Server-based folder while offline (disconnected from the Exchange server), you can use Offline Folders. Your Offline Folders are stored in a file formatted similarly to a `*.pst` file, except that it is called an Offline Store or `*.ost` file. To make a server-based folder available for offline use, open the property sheet of the folder in Outlook, select the Synchronization tab, and specify that the folder should be made available for offline use. This will copy the contents of the server-based folder to the local `*.ost` file on your hard drive.

Offline Folders are a good way of enabling users to access their mailboxes both locally when at work and remotely when travelling with laptop computers. When using Offline Folders, note that making any of the following folders available for offline use makes all of them available for offline use: Inbox, Outbox, Deleted items, Sent items, Contacts, Tasks, Journal, and Notes.

To make Public Folders available for offline use, they must first be identified as Favorites. You can do this by first copying these public folders to your Favorites folder in Microsoft Outlook and then specifying that the folder be available for both offline and online use by accessing the Synchronization tab of the folder's property sheet. When you modify the contents of folders identified for offline use, you need to synchronize these changes back to the server-based copies of those folders. Use the Synchronize option from the Tools menu to either:

- Manually synchronize Offline Folders with their server-based copies.
- Configure Offline Folders to be automatically synchronized each time the user exits Outlook.

Note that while a `*.pst` file can be copied to another computer and used, an `*.ost` file cannot.

- *Remote Mail*. When an Outlook client is configured to use Remote Mail, a user can establish a connection to an Exchange Server, view a list of messages waiting to be retrieved from the server, and select which of these messages the user wants to download to the client machine. Remote Mail is typically used when users dial-in remotely using laptops. This enables users to select which messages to download and which to leave unread on the server; typically, messages with large attachments or dealing with unimportant issues can be left unread on the server.

  To configure Remote Mail on an Outlook client, open the Outlook Profile using the Services option on the Tools menu, open the properties of the Microsoft Exchange Server information service, and then configure the settings on the Dial-Up Networking and Remote Mail tabs. Specifically, the Dial-Up Networking tab enables you to specify a

Dial-Up Networking (DUN) connection to be used for Remote Mail access, while the Remote Mail tab lets you specify whether to

- Download only mail items that you mark for retrieval.
- Filter items for retrieval by From or Subject fields, and whether the messages are directly addressed to the user or copied (cc'd). In addition, using the Advanced button, you can filter messages by size in KB, date received, importance, sensitivity, whether the messages contain attachments, whether the messages are unread, or messages that do not meet the selected criteria (logical NOT).
- Schedule when and how often Remote Mail should connect to download mail.

To start using Remote Mail, use Remote Mail from the Tools menu.

- *Delegate Access*. Sometimes you may want another user to create and send messages on your behalf, such as when you are going on a trip and want your assistant to send messages on your behalf. Microsoft Outlook enables you to configure several kinds of delegate access:
  - *Send On Behalf Of*. This places your delegate's name in the From field of the message, while indicating your own name as Sent On Behalf Of.
  - *Send As*. This is a little stronger. The message actually appears to be from you, and your delegate's name does not appear anywhere in the message.

  To configure Send On Behalf Of delegate access, you need to do two things:

  - Use the Options selection from the Tools menu, select the Delegates tab, and add your delegate from the GAL.
  - In the Delegate Permissions dialog box that appears next, specify which folders you want to make available to your delegate and what kind of access to those folders you want to grant to your delegate.

  To configure Send As delegate access, you need to do the following:

  - Access the property sheet of the Mailbox folder in Microsoft Outlook and select the Permissions tab.
  - Click Add to select your delegate from the GAL and then specify the level of permissions you want to grant to your delegate.

  Finally, for both kinds of delegate access, the delegate needs to add your own mailbox to their Exchange Server information service properties, which will allow them to see and access your mailbox according to the permissions you have granted them.

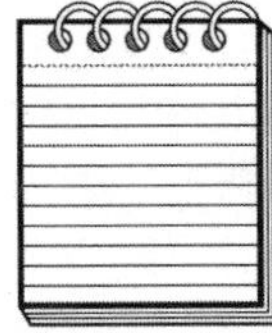

Delegation

The Exchange Administrator program can also configure Send On Behalf Of delegate access for a user by using the Delivery Options tab of the user's mailbox property sheet.

- *Assistants*. Microsoft Outlook includes two assistants:
  - *Inbox Assistant*. Use this to generally configure how incoming mail is handled. Note that in the more recent version of Outlook 98, this feature is replaced by the Rules Wizard.
  - *Out of Office Assistant*. Use this to specifically configure how incoming mail is handled when you are out of the office, such as when you are on vacation.

  These assistants handle incoming mail by using a series of rules you create. These rules examine aspects of incoming messages and process these messages accordingly. For example, you could create a rule that forwards a copy of all incoming mail to an SMTP host at your *Internet Service provider* (ISP) so you can access your work mail at home by dialing into your ISP.
- *Forms and Form Libraries*. Forms are a graphical interface presented to users for creating, viewing, or modifying messages. Forms are typically created as a user interface to public folders and allow information stored in these folders to be entered and displayed in a standardized format. Forms are used to build collaborative applications for multiple users to work together on a project. Examples of collaborative applications using forms include things like bulletin boards, purchase orders, help desk request forms, and so on.

  Microsoft Outlook includes an optional component called the Outlook Forms Designer for creating and configuring Outlook forms. Forms created by the Outlook Forms Designer can be saved as `*.oft` files and published to public folders. Outlook Forms can be designed by selecting forms from the Tools menu. Forms are stored in Forms Libraries on Exchange servers. There are several types of Forms Libraries:
  - *Organization Forms Library*. This contains forms that are accessible to anyone in the Exchange organization and is located in a Public Folder on an Exchange server. They should be replicated to all other sites in your organization. An Organization Forms Library can be

created using Forms Administrator from the Tools menu of the Exchange Administrator program. Usually, only administrators have the permission to install new forms in the Organization Forms Library. The Organization Forms Library is only accessible to users who are online.

- *Personal Forms Library*. These are forms that are only accessible to you as an Exchange user and are stored in your mailbox, that is, in the private information store of your home server. When Microsoft Outlook is installed and configured on a client machine, a Personal Forms Library is created for the user of that machine. A user's Personal Forms Library is accessible whether the user is online or offline.
- *Folder Forms Library*. These are forms that are installed on a particular public folder and are available to all users who have been granted access to that public folder.

RPC Binding Order

An important issue in heterogeneous networking environments where different network protocols are being run is the RPC binding order between Exchange Server and MAPI clients like Microsoft Outlook. The order in which Microsoft Outlook attempts RPC connections when trying to connect to an Exchange Server is as follows:

- *Local Procedure Call (LPC), which is used only when MAPI client is on the same machine that Exchange Server is installed on*
- *TCP/IP, which uses the Windows Sockets (WinSock over TCP/IP) interface*
- *SPX, which uses the Windows Sockets (WinSock over SPX) interface*
- *Named Pipes, which uses named pipes*
- *NetBIOS, which uses NetBIOS over the underlying network protocol (TCP/IP, IPX, or NetBEUI)*
- *VINES IP, which uses VINES IP*

In a heterogeneous environment, the responsiveness of Outlook when it is started (the time it takes to connect to Exchange) may be affected by this binding order. Improvements may be made, however, by rearranging the binding order. See the following article in Microsoft TechNet for more information: Q174701. XCLN: Troubleshooting RPC Problems for Exchange Clients.

Where Do We Go from Here?

Now that we've looked at the deployment and configuration of Exchange clients, we will next consider how to configure our Exchange services on a site-wide basis.

For More Information

Here are a few tips for further information regarding the deployment of messaging clients for Exchange Server, particularly Microsoft Outlook and its various incarnations.

TechNet

The best source of additional information on the deployment of Outlook is Microsoft TechNet. Some of the useful information on the monthly TechNet CD includes the following (as of June 1999):

- MS Outlook Manuals:
- Outlook 97 Administrator's Guide. This document contains six chapters of useful information for network administrators on installing and configuring Outlook 97.
- Outlook 98 Deployment Kit. This document contains five chapters walking you through using the Outlook 98 Deployment Wizard and other deployment tools.
- MS Outlook Technical Notes:
- Automate Outlook Profile creation using PRFPATCH
- Customizing Outlook installations
- Automating MS Outlook 97
- Knowledge Base articles, the most interesting of which are as follows:
- Q185357. OL98: Troubleshooting Active Setup Problems
- Q183775. OL98: Outlook Components Installed with Typical Setup
- Q182633. OL98: Summary of Outlook 98 Setup and Interoperability Issues
- Q184212. OL98: (CW) How to Install and Use the LDAP Service

- Q182693. OL98: Pre-installation Considerations
- Q182167. OL98: Installing and Using the Outlook Newsreader

Microsoft Web Site

Be sure to check out the home page for Outlook on Microsoft's Web site:

```
www.microsoft.com/office/outlook
```

This is probably the best source for information about the latest version (Outlook 2000), while TechNet is a better source for earlier versions.

Slipstick Systems has a useful FAQ on Outlook located at

```
www.slipstick.com/exchange/outlfaq.htm
```

Usenet

Check out the following Outlook-related newsgroups on Microsoft's public Usenet news server, `msnews.microsoft.com`:

- `microsoft.public.outlook.calendaring`
- `microsoft.public.outlook.contacts`
- `microsoft.public.outlook.fax`
- `microsoft.public.outlook.general` (by far the busiest)
- `microsoft.public.outlook.thirdpartyutil`

Also be sure to take a look at

```
microsoft.public.exchange.clients
```

CHAPTER 8

Administering Sites

In Chapters 6 and 7, we digressed from the process of configuring a new Exchange Server to look at creating new recipients and deploying mail client software. This chapter picks up where Chapter 5 left off, which introduced the main tool for administering an Exchange organization, the Exchange Administrator program. In this chapter, we will learn how to configure a new Exchange site, focusing on settings that are site-wide in scope. After reading this chapter, you will have a basic idea of the important site-level directory objects and how to configure them using Exchange Administrator. Coverage includes the following directory objects:

- Site configuration
- DS site configuration
- Information Store site configuration
- MTA site configuration
- Site addressing

The walkthrough in this chapter covers basic site configuration tasks such as creating offline address books, defining custom attributes, and specifying a container for storing public folders.

Configuring a Site

After you have installed a new Exchange Server to create a new site, you should take time to configure a number of directory objects at the site-level. In this chapter, we will consider only the most important site-level objects. Due to the huge number of property sheets in Exchange, we will only highlight the settings that might commonly need to be configured.

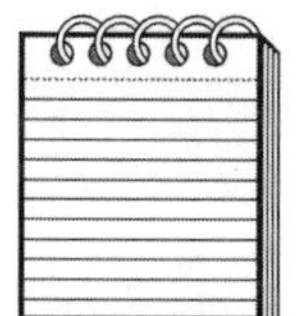

Directory Hierarchy

Note that the actual objects in the Exchange directory hierarchy (the tree-like hierarchy of Exchange directory objects, starting with the root Organization object) that are displayed in the Exchange Administrator window depend upon which additional Exchange components (connectors, gateways, and so on) are installed on your servers. As a result, the directory hierarchy for your machine may differ from that displayed in the screenshots for this chapter, so don't be confused.

Figure 8-1 shows the directory hierarchy for our Exchange organization MTIT, with the Configuration container for the site Atlanta having the

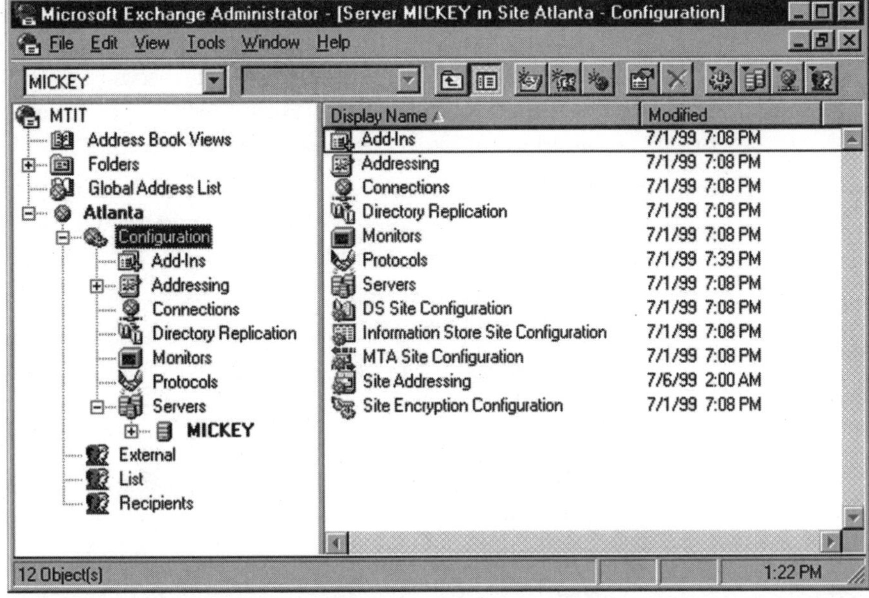

Figure 8-1 The Atlanta site configuration container and its contents.

focus in the container pane (left pane). The Configuration container for a site contains all the Exchange directory objects in the site with the exception of recipient objects, which are found in the default Recipients container and any other recipients containers you may have created (such as External for Custom Recipients and List for Distribution Lists for our organization).

As we examine this directory hierarchy, notice that the list of objects in the container pane (left pane) that is directly beneath the Configuration container is not exactly the same as the list of objects in the contents pane (right pane) when the Configuration container is selected. This seems a bit confusing until we realize that the container pane only shows containers, not leaf objects (it would have be nice if there was some easy way to tell the difference between the two types of objects. In the two-pane view of Windows Explorer, for example, containers (folders) are easy to identify by their folder icons, while leaf nodes (files) are anything else).

For our Atlanta site, which was created when we installed our first Exchange Server MICKEY in Chapter 3, "Installing Exchange," the Atlanta Configuration container includes the following container and leaf objects:

- *Containers*:
- *Add-ins*. This contains optional extensions and third-party services. There's nothing much for administrators to be concerned about here.

- *Addressing*. This contains Email Address Generators that are used to automatically generated email addresses for recipients as well as Details templates and One-Off Address templates that are used for customizing certain Microsoft Outlook dialog boxes associated with addressing, searching, and other functions.
- *Connections*. This contains connectors for establishing messaging with other sites and mail systems. Connectors will be covered in later chapters in more detail.
- *Directory Replication*. This contains the Directory Replication Connector that is used to replicate directory information between sites in an Exchange organization. We will look at directory replication in a later chapter.
- *Monitors*. This contains Server and Link Monitors for monitoring the health of Exchange servers and messaging links. Monitoring an Exchange organization is covered in a later chapter.
- *Protocols*. This contains objects for configuring Internet protocols such as HTTP, IMAP4, LDAP, NNTP, and POP3 at the site level. We will look at Internet protocols later in this book.
- *Servers*. This contains one server container for each Exchange server in the site. In this chapter, only the MICKEY server is present. (The DONALD server, which was added to the Atlanta site for Chapter 6, "Administering Receipts," has been removed. You will see a lot of servers coming and going in future chapters of this book. After all, the author only has so many electrical outlets in his office!) We will look at server-level configuration settings in the next chapter.

- *Leaf objects*:

- *DS Site Configuration*. This object is used to configure certain aspects of the directory service and database for all Exchange servers in your site. We will look at how to configure this object in this chapter.
- *Information Store Site Configuration*. This object is used to configure certain aspects of the information store for all Exchange servers in your site. We will look at how to configure this object in this chapter.
- *MTA Site Configuration*. This object is used to configure certain aspects of the message transfer agent (MTA) for all Exchange servers in your site. This object will be covered in this chapter.
- *Site Addressing*. This object is used to configure certain addressing and routing properties at the site level. We will look at how to configure this object in this chapter.

- *Site Encryption Configuration.* This object is used for configuring advanced security in conjunction with the Key Management (KM) Server and is discussed elsewhere.

For the rest of this chapter, we will focus on the DS Site Configuration, the Information Store Site Configuration, and the MTA Site Configuration. Site Addressing objects and how to configure them in a newly created Exchange site will also be covered. Note that the first three of these directory objects correspond to three of the core Exchange services described earlier in Chapter 4, "Under the Hood" (the System Attendant service is configured at the server level, not the site level). But before we look at these, let's first look briefly at the Site Configuration container itself.

Site Configuration Container

The Site Configuration container (called simply the Configuration container in the Exchange Administrator window) is really just a container for holding the various site-level directory objects that you need to configure (see Figure 8-2). Only a couple of useful things can be done using the property sheet for this object:

- *Permissions.* This tab lets you assign Exchange permissions to a Windows NT account or modify existing permissions on an account. For example, you might want to assign the Permissions Admin role to other administrators on the network in order to give them permission to administer the Atlanta site. How to do this was covered in a previous chapter.
- *Service Account Password.* This tab lets you change the password used by the Exchange service account for all servers in your site. Note that if you change the password here, it changes the password for the startup settings of Exchange services on all servers in your site, but it doesn't change the actual password of the service account itself; you need to also do that using User Manager for Domains. If you don't make this second change, Exchange services for servers in your site will fail to start.

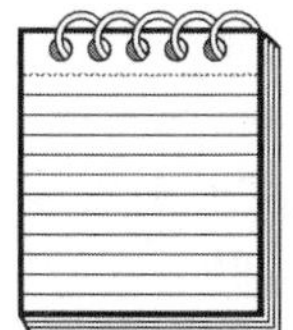

Changing the Service Account Password

If you ever need to change the service account password for security or other reasons, here are the exact steps to follow:

1. *Open the property sheet of the Configuration container for your site and select the Service Account Password tab.*

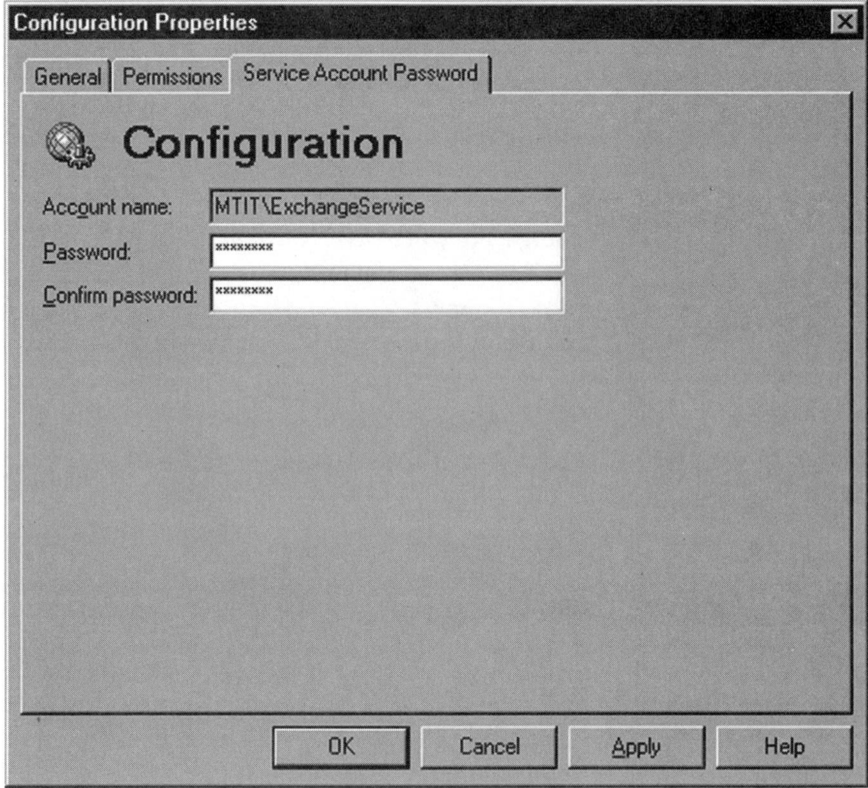

Figure 8-2
The Configuration container for the Atlanta site.

2. *Enter the new password twice and click OK.*
3. *A series of dialogs will appear, informing you as the new password information is updated for each Exchange server in your site. When this process is completed, the following message will appear:*

   This action has changed the password for the Windows NT Services installed by Microsoft Exchange Server. The password for the Service Account must also be changed in the Windows NT User Manager, or the Services will fail to start.
4. *Start User Manager for Domains and open the property sheet for your service account. Change the password here to match the change you made above and click OK.*
5. *Stop and restart the Exchange services for all Exchange Servers in your site. You can do this from a single location using the Windows NT administrative tool called Server Manager (select an Exchange Server and then choose Services from the Computer menu to open a Services dialog box for that server).*

Note that third-party Exchange utilities that use the service account may need to have their passwords changed manually.

Now let's go on and look at the main site-level directory objects that need to be configured when you create a new Exchange site.

DS Site Configuration

The DS (Directory Services) Site Configuration object is used to configure site-wide aspects of the Microsoft Exchange Directory service for all Exchange Servers in your site (see Figure 8-3). This can be important, since the Exchange directory database acts as a kind of central telephone book for all recipients and other objects in your organization. The Microsoft

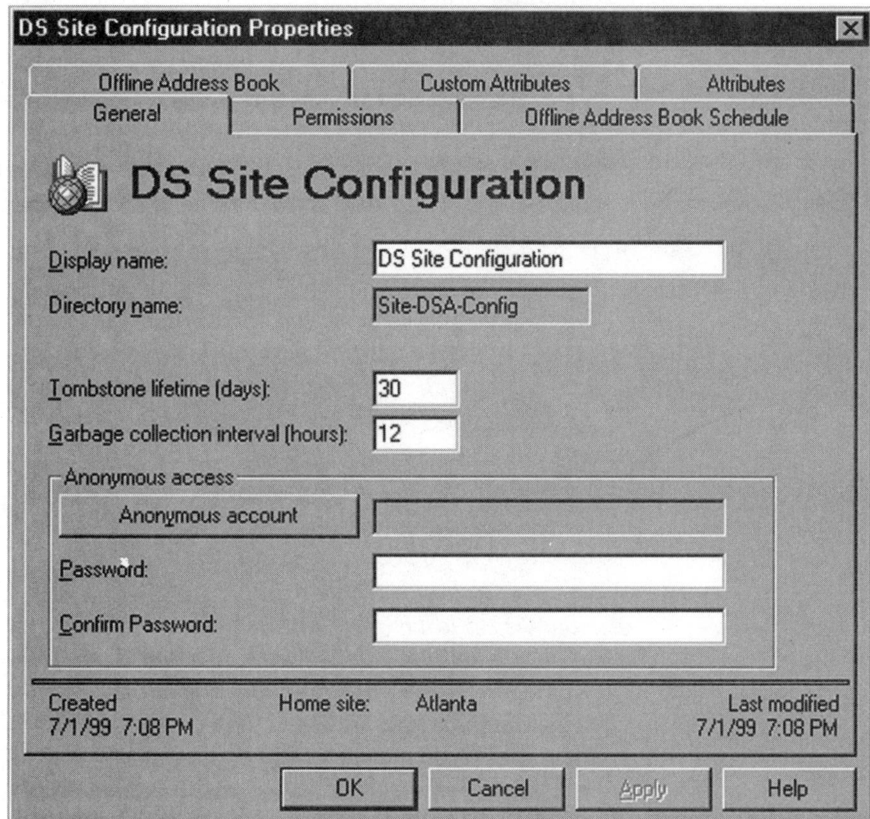

Figure 8-3 The DS Site Configuration object for the Atlanta site.

Exchange Directory service is implemented as a Windows NT service and is one of the four core components of every Exchange server.

Some of the more important settings you can configure using the property sheet for this object include the following:

- *Tombstone Lifetime* and *Garbage Collection Interval* (General tab). Recall that the Exchange directory database is replicated among all Exchange servers in an organization. If you just deleted an object from this directory, like the Mailbox object associated with user JohnS, the object might be deleted from the directory on the Exchange Server that you are currently connected to, but it still remains in the directory of all other Exchange Servers in your organization. This inconsistency in the directory database between different Exchange Servers could cause problems. The way Exchange resolves this is that when a directory object is deleted using Exchange Administrator, it is not really deleted from the directory at all. Instead, a tombstone property is added to the object that specifies a date and time stamp indicating when the object was deleted from the directory. Additionally, the "tombstoned" object is hidden from view in the Exchange directory hierarchy. The tombstoned object is then replicated to all servers in your organization through directory synchronization. Each Exchange Server regularly checks its own directory database according to a predefined garbage collection interval for any "tombstoned" objects that have expired, and if the server finds any tombstoned objects, it deletes them.

  By default, the tombstone lifetime is set to 30 days and the garbage collection interval to 12 hours. This means that an object that is "deleted" will be marked with a tombstone attribute for 30 days, after which the tombstone will be considered "expired." Every 12 hours Exchange checks its directory for "expired" objects and deletes them permanently.

Tombstone Problems

What actually happens when an object is "tombstoned" is that its IsDeleted attribute is set to TRUE. You can observe tombstoned objects and their attributes by running Exchange Administrator in raw mode using `admin /r` *from the command-line.*

Microsoft does not recommend lowering the tombstone lifetime, as this can result in a greater chance of directory objects being "orphaned." An orphaned object is a directory object that exists in some sites but not in others. Typically, this happens because of network connectivity problems between sites. For example, say you delete a Mailbox object in site A, causing it to be tombstoned, but before directory replication can take place with site B, the network link between them goes down. If the link stays down for a time interval longer than the tombstone lifetime, the tombstoned Mailbox object in site A will be scavenged by the garbage collection, while the copy of this object in site B remains unchanged. When the network link comes up again, you have a directory inconsistency: an orphaned object that exists in the directory of site B but not in site A, which directory replication cannot fix.

For more information on orphaned objects and how to fix them, see the following article in Microsoft TechNet: Q179573. XADM: Orphaned Objects and Exchange Server Directory.

- *Anonymous Account (General tab).* Sometimes you will want untrusted users (users from an untrusted Windows NT domain or from a non-NT network) to be able to have access to the contents of public folders. If so, you need to specify or create a Windows NT account as your anonymous account, and then open the property sheet for each public folder and grant some level of client permissions on that folder to the anonymous account you specified.
- *Offline Address Book settings (Offline Address Book and Offline Address Book Schedule tabs).* Offline address books are address lists that remote clients can download from your Exchange server so that they can keep a local copy on their computer. This is especially useful for users with laptops so they can address messages without having to dial in with their modems and then send them later. Offline address books can be based on the GAL, a particular recipients container, or an address book view. Once they are created, they are stored in hidden public folders.

  You can use the DS Site Configuration object to create a new offline address book by specifying which Recipients container it will be based upon. You can then configure a schedule for refreshing all the offline address books. The more often you add or delete recipients from your site, the more frequently you should schedule offline address books to be refreshed. If you click the Generate All button, the offline address books will be refreshed immediately.

  Offline address books are created and stored on a specific Exchange Server designated as the Offline Address Book Server. This should typically be a server that is not too busy doing other tasks, especially if your organization contains a lot of recipients and changes are frequently made to these recipients.

- *Custom Attributes tab*. Property sheets for mailboxes and other recipients enable you to store personal attributes about the recipients in the Exchange directory database. This includes information like the recipient's name, address, company, department, home phone number, and so on. But what if you want to configure additional attributes for recipients like their employee ID numbers or social security numbers? To do this, use this property sheet to define each custom attribute (up to 10 in all), which will be applied for all recipients in your organization. We will look at how to do this later in the walkthrough.
- *Attributes tab*. Here you can specify which attributes of the recipients can be viewed by both authenticated and anonymous clients. In order for client software to access these attributes, which are stored in the Exchange directory database, the client must support the Lightweight Directory Access Protocol (LDAP). Microsoft Outlook and Microsoft Outlook Express are two examples of LDAP clients.

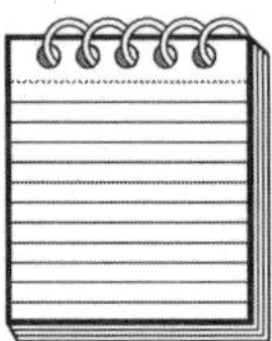

Replicating Attributes of Recipients

You can also use the Attribute tab of the DS Site Configuration property sheet to specify which attributes of directory objects are replicated to other Exchange sites in your organization. If your sites are connected by relatively slow WAN links, you can reduce replication traffic by only replicating necessary attributes and omitting others. Even with a fast WAN link, configuring only essential recipient attributes to be replicated between sites can save on disk space.

Information Store Site Configuration

The Information Store Site Configuration object is used to configure site-wide aspects of the information store for all Exchange servers in your site (see Figure 8-4). This can be important, since the information store acts as a repository for mailboxes and public folders created on your server. The Microsoft Exchange Information Store service is implemented as a Windows NT service and is one of the four core components of every Exchange server.

Some of the more important settings you can configure using the property sheet for this object include the following:

- *Public Folder Container (General tab)*. This lets you select the default recipients container within which new public folders will be created.

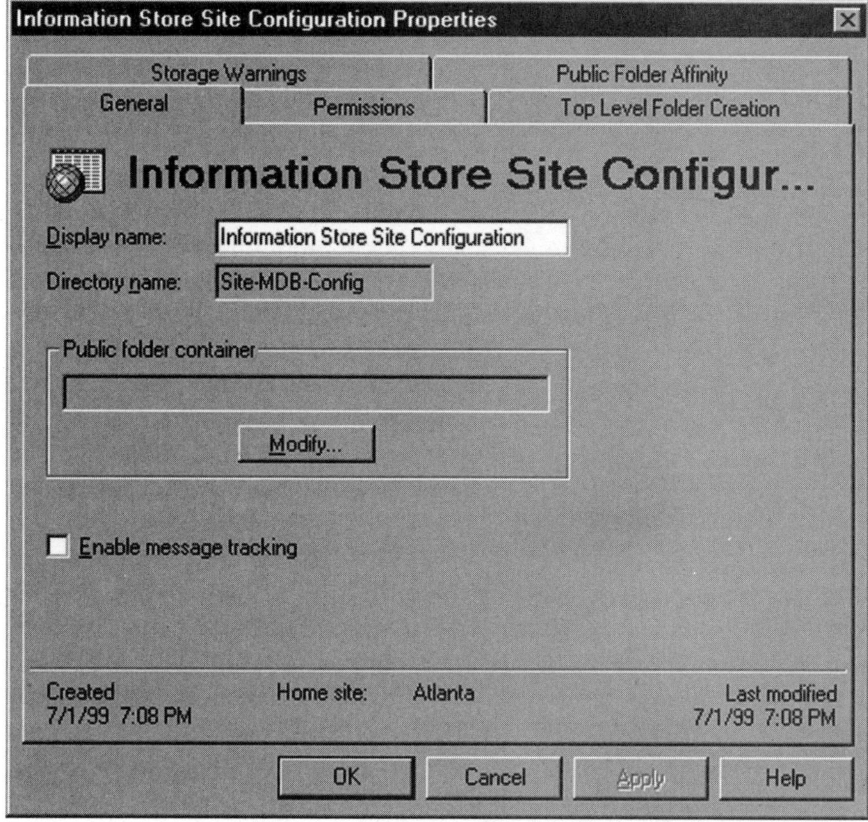

Figure 8-4
The Information Store Site Configuration object for the Atlanta site.

For example, you may want to create one recipients container solely for public folders, just as previously we created separate recipients containers for distribution lists and for custom recipients. We'll look at public folders in a later chapter.

- *Enable Message Tracking (General tab)*. This lets you enable Exchange's message tracking function on the Information Store component of all Exchange Servers in your site (after enabling this setting, you must stop and restart the Microsoft Exchange Information Store service in order for message tracking to begin to function). If you do this, the Microsoft Exchange System Attendant service will create a daily log file containing routing information for all messages processed by the information stores on Exchange Servers in your site. These log files are stored in the directory `\exchsrvr\tracking.log` and can be analyzed using the Message Tracking Center, as described in a later chapter.

- *Top-level Folder Creation tab*. Here you can specify which users have permissions to use Microsoft Outlook to create top-level Public Folders (and a hierarchy of subfolders beneath them) in your site. Such users will also have the right to assign client permissions to other users for controlling access to the folder hierarchy they create. You should be sparing in your assignment of this privilege or you might end up with too many top-level Public Folders in your address book (notice that the default setting enables all users to create top-level Public Folders, which is certainly not a desirable setting). Public Folders are examined further in a later chapter.
- *Storage Warnings tab*. If a user exceeds their mailbox disk space quota, a notification message is sent to them, according to the schedule you specify here. Similarly, if a public folder becomes full, a notification will be sent to the public folder contact person. This schedule page is similar to many other schedule pages in Exchange property sheets and enables you to specify the following trigger times:
  - *Always*. Send notifications every 15 minutes if the conditions occur.
  - *Never*. Suspend all notifications.
  - *Selected Times*. Click and drag to select times as desired. Use the Detail view to specify either a one-hour or a 15-minute grid.

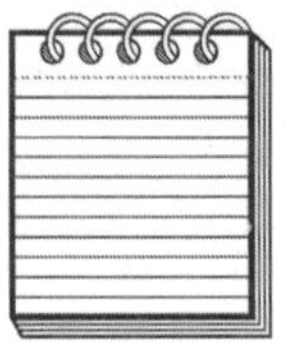

Storage Warnings

Storage warnings configured on this tab are site-wide and apply to all Exchange Servers in the site and all mailboxes and Public Folders homed on those servers. To override these settings for a specific server, use the General tabs on the Private Information Store or Public Information Store objects (see the next chapter). To override settings for a particular mailbox or Public Folder, use the Advanced tab on the property sheet for that mailbox or Public Folder object.

- *Public Folder Affinity*. This will be covered in a later chapter.

MTA Site Configuration

The MTA (Message Transfer Agent) Site Configuration object is used to configure certain aspects of the Exchange MTA for all Exchange servers in your site. This can be important, since the MTA on each server is responsible for routing messages to MTAs or information stores on other Exchange Servers, to connectors, and to any third-party gateways you have installed. The Microsoft Exchange MTA service is implemented as a Windows NT service and is one of the four core components of every Exchange server.

Some of the more important settings you can configure using the property sheet for this object include the following:

- *Enable Message Tracking (General tab).* This lets you enable Exchange's message tracking function on the message transfer agent component of all Exchange Servers in your site (after enabling this setting, you must stop and restart the Microsoft Exchange MTA service in order for message tracking to begin to function). If you do this, the Microsoft Exchange System Attendant service will create a daily log file containing routing information for all messages processed by the information stores on Exchange Servers in your site. These log files are stored in the directory `\exchsrvr\tracking.log` and can be analyzed using the Message Tracking Center, as described in a later chapter.

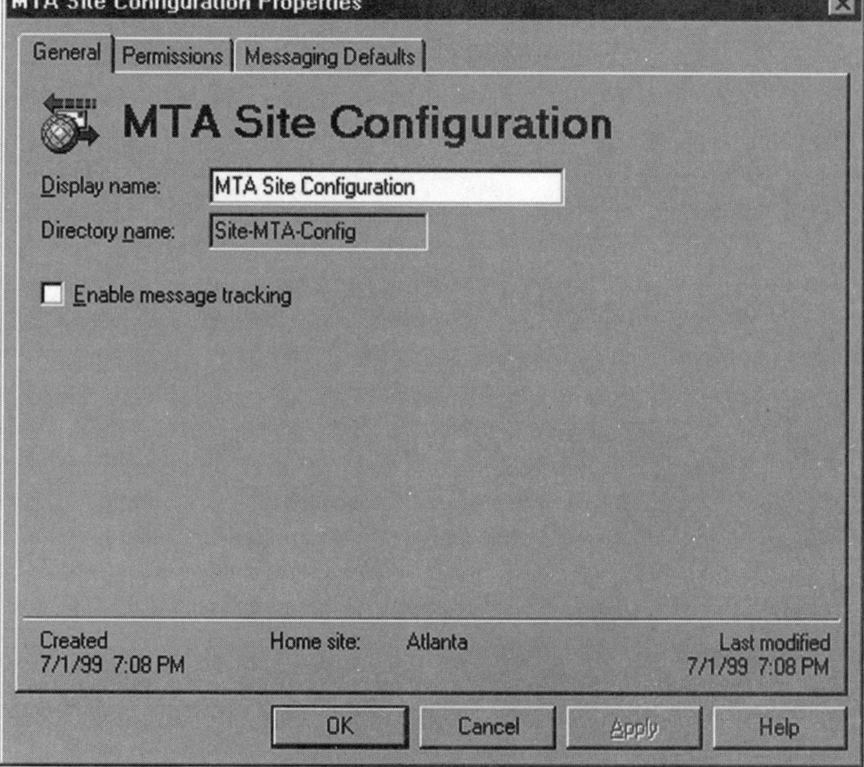

Figure 8-5 The MTA Site Configuration object for the Atlanta site.

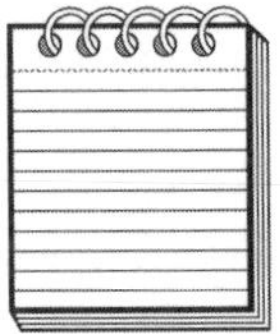

Enabling Message Tracking

Haven't we seen this somewhere before? Enabling message tracking for the MTA is different from enabling it for the information store, as discussed in the previous section. The MTA and Information Store represent two different core components of an Exchange server, and although both are involved in messaging, they have different functions. If you enable message tracking on the MTA but not on the information store, the message tracking log will record the routing activities of the MTA but not the information store for each server in your site. Microsoft Exchange enables you to separately enable or disable message tracking on each of the following Exchange components:

- *Information Store site configuration (use General tab)*
- *MTA site configuration (use General tab)*
- *System Attendant (use General tab)*
- *Internet Mail Services (use Internet Mail tab)*
- *Microsoft Mail Connector (use Interchange tab)*
- *Connector for cc:Mail (use Post Office tab)*

The reason for this flexibility is that message tracking adds a performance hit to an Exchange Server, so it should only be selectively enabled as needed for troubleshooting message routing problems and then disabled once the problem is resolved. We'll look some more at message tracking when we have some connectors installed, as it's not much fun tracking message flow within a single site.

- *RTS Values (Message Defaults tab).* RTS stands for Reliable Transfer Service, and these settings can be modified to ensure reliable messaging takes place. When Exchange is sending messages, it transfers them as a stream of bytes with checkpoints inserted at regular intervals. These checkpoints are acknowledged by the receiving server to ensure reliable transmission. If a network error (like a dropped packet) occurs at some point, instead of restarting the whole message stream, it is restarted from the last checkpoint transmitted. If your network connection is noisy or routers are dropping packets, decrease the checkpoint size (KB between checkpoints) to improve speed. This happens because now smaller portions of the data stream are retransmitted when errors occur. If you decrease the checkpoint size on a reliable connection, however, transmission speed will be reduced slightly because more checkpoints need to be inserted into the data stream. Recovery timeout is how long the MTA waits before establishing a new network connection and starting the message transfer all over again from the beginning. On unreliable networks, you may want to increase this parameter, since if the connection times out, the data stream must be restarted from the beginning again.

Window size is how many unacknowledged checkpoints can be transmitted before Exchange stops sending data and waits out the recovery timeout. If your network connection is reliable, you may want to try setting the window size to zero to get the fastest transmission speeds. If you do this, Exchange keeps sending data whether acknowledgements are received or not and assumes that acknowledgements will eventually come.

- *Association Parameters (Message Defaults tab).* An association is a messaging path that has been opened up to another system. Associations are contained within connections, and one connection can contain multiple associations. Lifetime specifies how long you want to keep an association open after sending a message, just in case you want to send another message a short time later. Disconnect is how long your server waits before disconnecting from a remote system, after it has informed the remote system that it wants to disconnect. Threshold is the maximum number of messages that can be queued by the MTA before being sent over an association. If this number is exceeded, another association is opened.
- *Connection Retry Values (Message Defaults tab).* These settings have to do with opening and closing network connections to remote systems for sending messages. Max open retries is the number of connection attempts that will be made before a non-delivery report (NDR) is returned to the sender. Max transfer retries is the number of attempts that will be made to send a message once a connection has been opened with the remote server. Open interval is how long Exchange waits before trying to open a new connection after an error occurs with the existing one. Transfer interval is how long Exchange waits before attempting to resend a message over a connection if the previous attempt failed.
- *Transfer Timeouts (Message Defaults tab).* These are the timeouts (in sec/KB) that Exchange recognizes before sending NDRs, depending on whether the message priority is Normal, Urgent, or Non-urgent.

Site Addressing

The Site Addressing object is used to configure addressing and routing properties for all Exchange servers in your site (see Figure 8-6). This can be important, since messages need to be successfully delivered from your site to other sites or other mail systems.

Some of the settings you can configure using the property sheet for this object include the following:

- *Routing Calculation Settings (General, Routing, and Routing Calculation Server tabs)*. Routing is the process by which Exchange determines how to deliver messages to another site or foreign mail system. To control the routing of messages you create address spaces, which are the ranges of email addresses and the cost of delivering messages to recipients within these ranges. The routing calculation server is the Exchange Server in your site that is assigned the job of constructing the Gateway Address Routing table or GWART. The

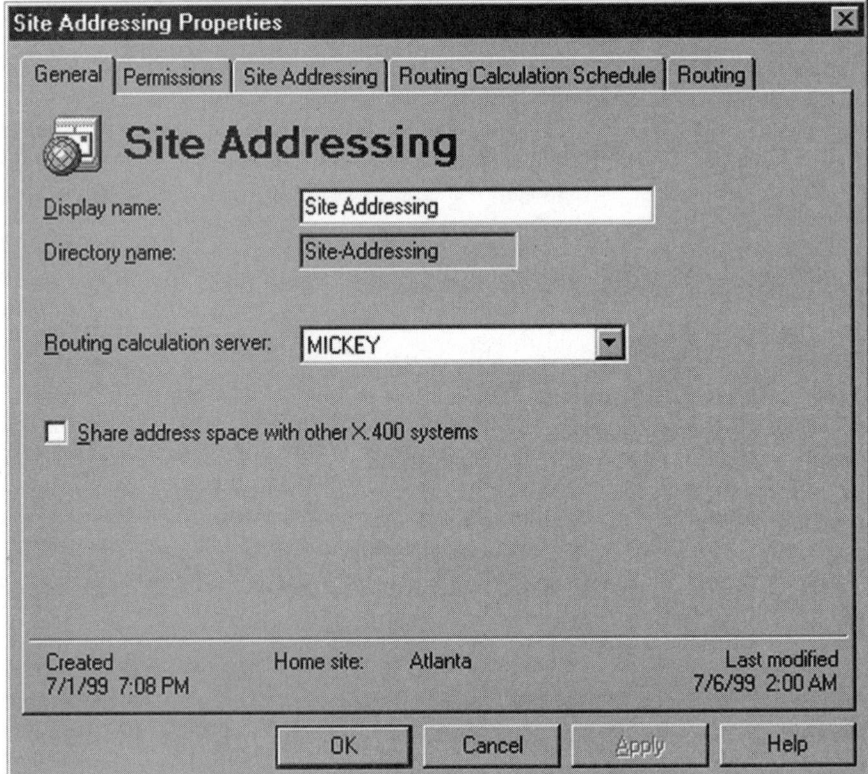

Figure 8-6 The Site Addressing object for the Atlanta site.

GWART is replicated to all Exchange Servers in an organization by the directory replication process. The GWART contains information regarding the various connectors and gateways in your site that can act as doorways for delivering messages to locations outside your site, that is, to other sites and to foreign mail systems like the Internet. The GWART needs to be recalculated whenever a connector or gateway is added or removed. This recalculation can take place in three ways:

- Exchange automatically initiates a recalculation when you add or remove a connector (but this may not take place immediately).
- You can schedule when recalculation takes place using the Routing Calculation Schedule page.
- You can force an immediate recalculation by selecting the Recalculate Routing button on the Routing page.

We'll look more at message routing and the GWART later on in this book.

- *Site Addressing tab*. This tab displays the various partial email addresses that Exchange has generated for your site. A partial email address contains enough address information to route a message to your site, but not to route a message to any particular recipient in your site. By default, Exchange always generates three different partial email addresses for your site (the abbreviation for each type is shown in parentheses):
  - *Microsoft Mail (MS)*. The partial email address of your site as far as MS Mail 3.x mail systems are concerned.
  - *Internet Mail (SMTP)*. The partial email address of your site as far as Internet SMTP mail servers are concerned.
  - *X.400 (X400)*. The partial email address of your site as far as X.400-based mail systems are concerned.

  Other types of partial email addresses (such as Lotus cc:Mail) can be generated if the appropriate connectors are installed. Table 8-1 shows the partial email addresses for the site Atlanta that is part of the organization MTIT.

Table 8-1

The Default Partial Email Addresses for the Site Atlanta Within the Organization MTIT.

Address Type	Partial Email Address
MS	`MTIT/ATLANTA`
SMTP	`@atlanta.mtit.com`
X400	`C=US;a= ;p=MTIT;o=Atlanta`

By clearing any of the checkboxes on the Site Addressing tab, you can disable the automatic generation of addresses of that type. For example, if you clear the SMTP checkbox, when you create new mailboxes or custom recipients, they will not automatically have an SMTP address generated for them. Disabling unnecessary address types can reduce network traffic and save disk space when creating mailboxes, but it also prevents users from sending mail to mail systems based on that address type.

Walkthrough: Configuring a Site

We'll now walk through a basic configuration process for the site Atlanta and test the configuration where feasible in our single-site setup.

Creating and Downloading Offline Address Books

Let's start with the DS Site Configuration object. We'll create an offline address book that's based on the GAL and contains information about all recipient objects in our site. To do this, open the property sheet for the DS Site Configuration object and select the Offline Address Book tab. Select the Recipients address book, click Remove to remove it, and then click Add to open the Offline Address Book Container dialog box (see Figure 8-7).

This dialog box enables us to create a new offline address book based on any of the following containers:

- An address book view
- The GAL
- Any recipients container in the site Atlanta

Select the GAL and click OK to create a new offline address book based on the contents of the GAL. Then click the Generate All button, which creates the new offline address book immediately, instead of waiting until the time specified on the Offline Address Book Schedule tab. What actually happens is that the contents of the GAL are converted by Exchange into a specially formatted data file, which is stored in a hidden public folder that can be accessed by client programs like Outlook. A dialog box indicates when the generation process is complete.

Let's now test our new offline address book. Log on as Boris to the Windows 98 machine GOOFEY and start Outlook 98, which we installed on it in the last chapter. Select Tools, Synchronize, Download Address Book to open the Download Offline Address Book dialog box (see Figure 8-8). Clear

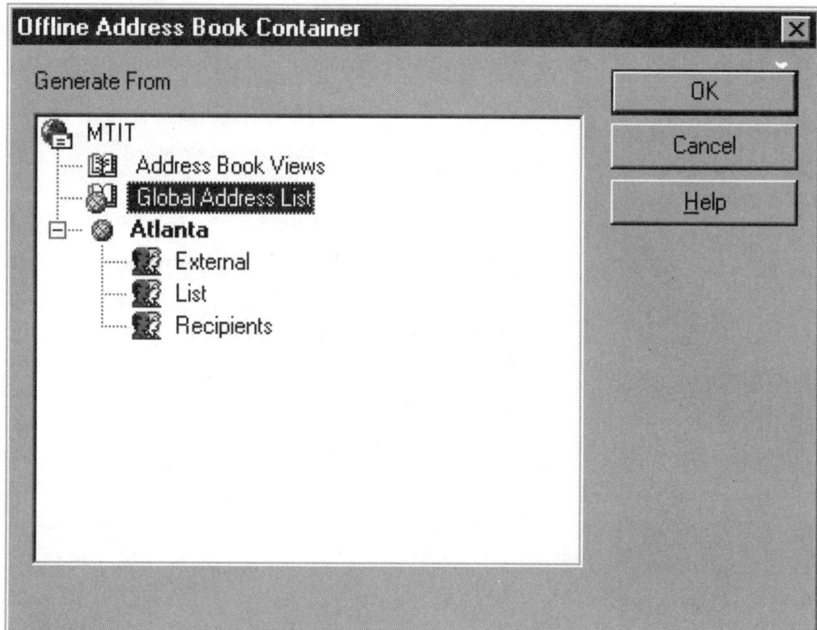

Figure 8-7 Selecting a container to generate an offline address book.

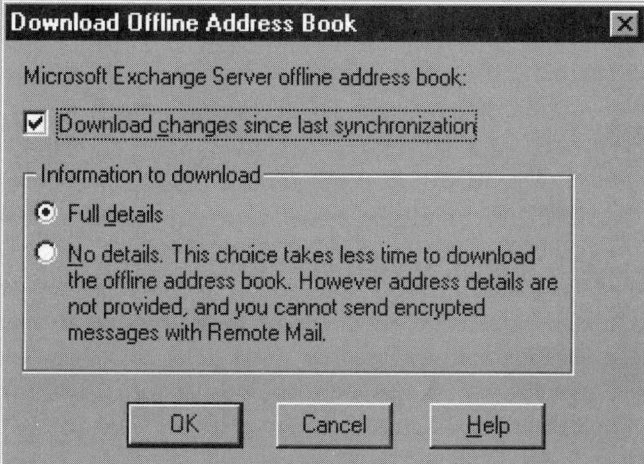

Figure 8-8 Downloading an offline address book using Microsoft Outlook 98.

the Download Changes Since Last Synchronization checkbox to force Outlook to download the entire offline address book, but leave the Information To Download setting at Full Details in order to download detailed information about Exchange recipients such as their titles, departments, phone numbers, and so on. Click OK to download the offline address book from MICKEY to GOOFEY.

Now let's configure Outlook to use offline folders. Outlook can be used in two different ways when you need to use it at a remote location, such as when you are using a laptop. These two methods are

- *Remote Mail*. This is a good method if you want to minimize your connection time when dialing in to collect your messages. It is especially useful when connecting to a non-Exchange server like an Internet SMTP/POP3 mail server at your ISP.
- *Offline Folders*. This method is recommended if you use Exchange Server as your company's back-end messaging platform and enables you to synchronize the contents for your folders on both the remote computer and the server. You can download address books, schedules, contacts, task lists, and so on.

We'll choose the second option for our remote connectivity option, namely Offline Folders. To configure this option, we need to create an Offline Folder (`*.ost`) file on our Outlook machine. To do this, select the Inbox folder and choose Services from the Tools menu. Double-click Microsoft Exchange Server, which is listed as the default information service on the Services tab, and the Microsoft Exchange Server property sheet appears. Select the Advanced tab of this property sheet (see Figure 8-9).

Click the Offline Folder File Settings command and verify that a path has been specified to an `*.ost` file (if not, specify a path within the folder where Boris's user profile is located, namely `\Windows\Profiles\Boris\`). Return to the Advanced tab and select the checkbox labeled Enable Offline Use. Click OK twice and exit Outlook. Now disconnect GOOFEY from the network and start Outlook again. Outlook will try first to connect to MICKEY since that is its default Exchange Server, but it will soon give up and start in offline mode (notice the icon in the bottom right corner of Figure 8-10).

Click the Address Book icon on the toolbar to open the address book and double-click one of the listed recipients to display its attributes (see Figure 8-11). The offline address book has obviously been downloaded from Exchange, which was our original purpose of this exercise. Close Outlook and reconnect GOOFEY to the network.

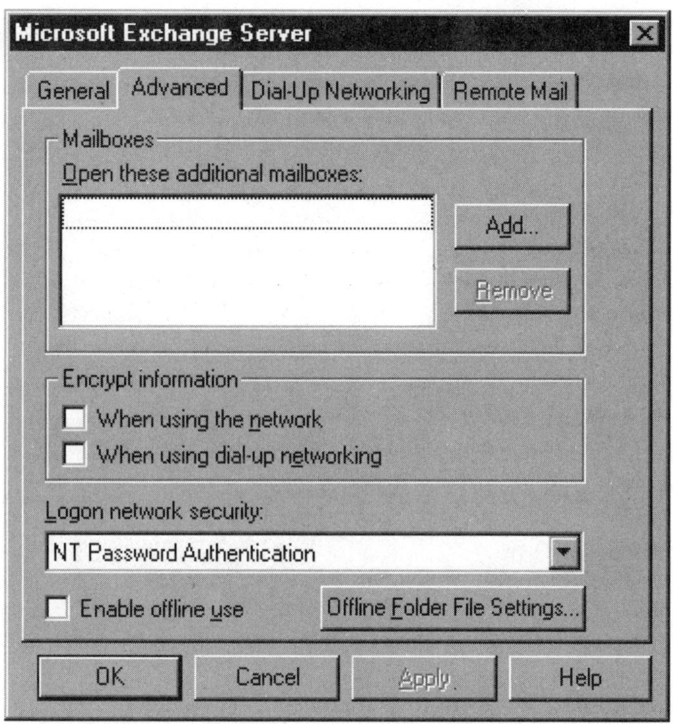

Figure 8-9 Enabling Outlook for Offline Folders.

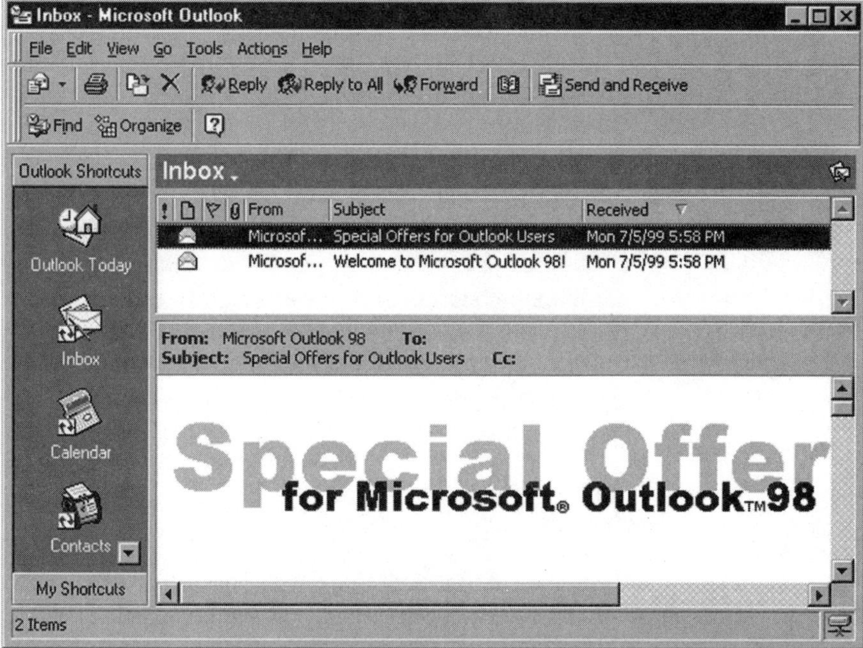

Figure 8-10 Outlook running in offline mode.

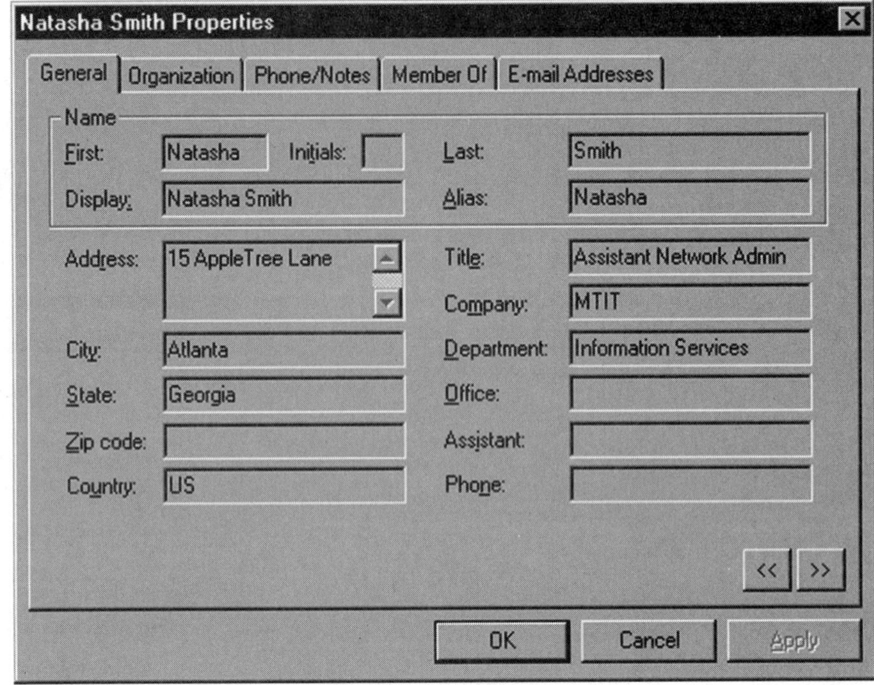

Figure 8-11 Attributes of a recipient as displayed by Outlook from the downloaded offline address book.

Defining Custom Attributes

Continuing with the DS Site Configuration object, let's define a new attribute for all recipients called Employee ID. Select the Custom Attributes tab of the DS Site Configuration property sheet and enter "Employee ID" (without the quotes) into the field labeled Custom Attribute 1. Click OK to apply the change and close the property sheet.

Now select the Recipients container for Atlanta and double-click on the mailbox belonging to Boris Zhivago to open its property sheet. Select the Custom Attributes tab and notice that the first field on this sheet is labeled Employee ID. Enter an Employee ID for Boris and click OK to close the sheet (see Figure 8-12). If you like, you can fill out the Employee ID field for every recipient in your site now.

Public Folder Creation Settings

Select the Atlanta site object in Exchange Administrator and create a new recipients container called Pub, which we will use later for storing all public folders we create in Atlanta. Once this is done, select the Atlanta Site Con-

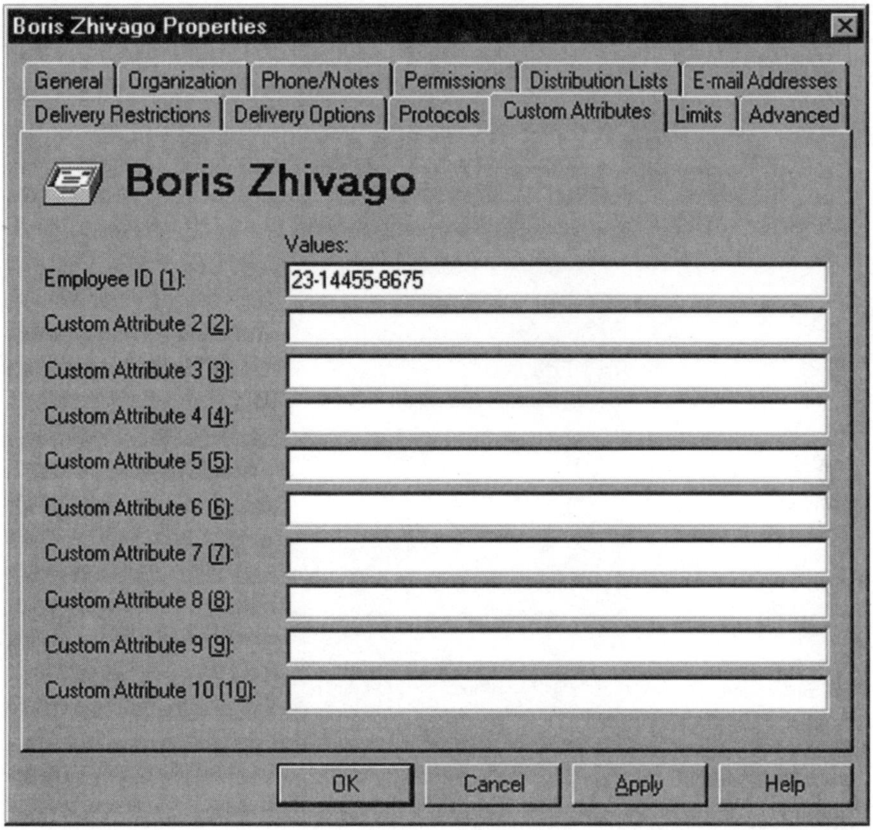

Figure 8-12 Specifying an Employee ID for Boris.

figuration container and open the property sheet for the Information Store Site Configuration object. On the General tab, click the Modify button and specify Pub as the container for holding public folders in Atlanta. Switch to the Top-Level Folder Creation tab and specify Boris and Natasha as the only users who are allowed to create top-level folders (see Figure 8-13). This automatically prevents all other users from creating top-level folders in Atlanta. Click OK to close the property sheet and apply the changes.

Where Do We Go from Here?

Having looked at how to configure site-wide parameters for an Exchange site, in the next chapter we will consider configuration parameters that are specific to individual Exchange Servers themselves. Once that is done, we will have fully configured the basic aspects of a single Exchange site, at

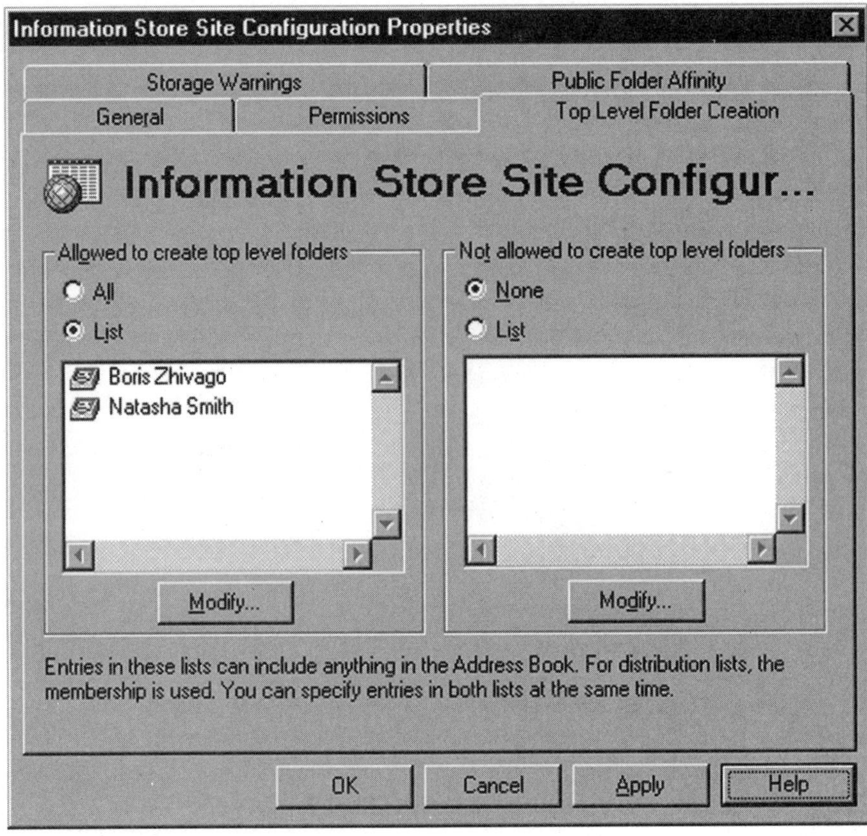

Figure 8-13 Restricting top-level folder creation.

which time we will begin to investigate options for establishing messaging connectivity with other sites and with foreign mail systems.

For More Information

For further information on site configuration options, see Chapter 7 of the *Getting Started* manual for Exchange, which can be found in Books Online.

Microsoft TechNet

A useful article you might want to read in TechNet is entitled "Configuring and Tuning the MS Exchange Server 5.5 MTA." The article refers to the settings on the Messaging Defaults tab of the MTA Site Configuration property sheet and covers these settings in some detail.

CHAPTER 9

Administering Servers

In the previous chapter, we looked at how to configure the site-wide aspects of an Exchange site. This chapter continues by looking at the various directory objects that can be used to configure server-level Exchange settings. After reading this chapter, you will have a basic understanding of how to configure individual Exchange Servers within a site. Coverage includes the following directory objects:

- Configuring a server
- Server and Server containers
- Directory Service
- Message Transfer Agent (MTA)
- Private Information Store
- Public Information Store
- System Attendant

The walkthrough in this chapter covers basic server configuration tasks such as disabling circular logging, configuring deleted item recovery, and configuring mailbox storage limits.

Configuring a Server

After you install a new Exchange Server, whether it joins an existing site or creates a new one, you should take time to configure a number of directory objects at the server level. We will consider here only the most important server-level objects in this chapter. Due to the large number of property sheets in Exchange, we will only highlight those settings that might commonly need to be configured. Remember, the actual objects displayed in the directory hierarchy depend upon the additional Exchange components that are installed. For example, some of the server-level objects mentioned below will only be present if additional Exchange components are installed (for example, the MTA Transport Stack for RAS component is only installed if you install the Dynamic RAS Connector component).

Figure 9-1 shows the directory hierarchy for our Exchange organization MTIT, with the MICKEY container for the site Atlanta having the focus in the left container pane. The MICKEY container is an example of a Server container, and there is only one Server container in the figure because there is only one Exchange Server in Atlanta at this point. Note, however, that the Server container MICKEY is itself contained within the Servers container above it in the hierarchy. In other words, each site like Atlanta has one

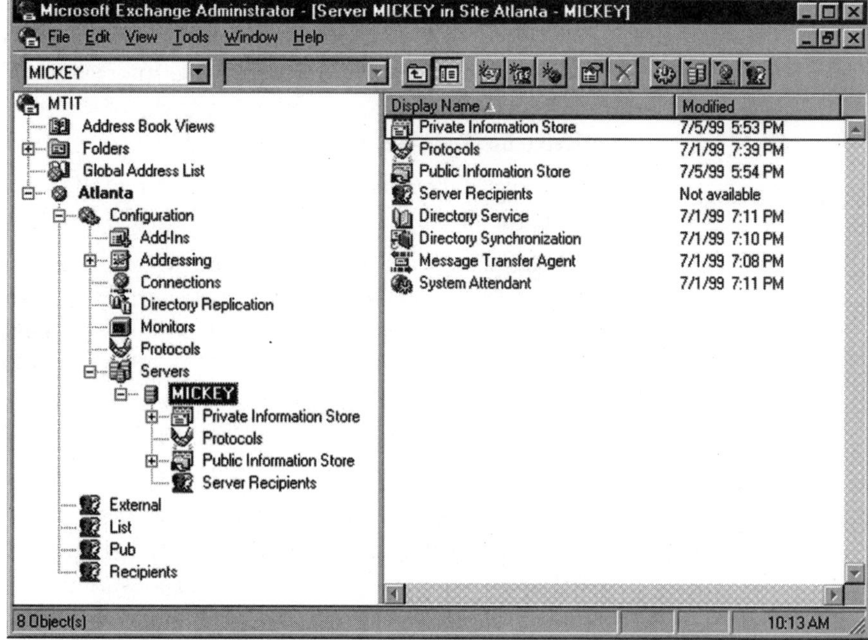

Figure 9-1
The MICKEY Server container and its contents.

Servers container that only holds the individual Server containers representing the Exchange Servers in that site. It is the Server containers (not the Servers container) that hold the various server-level directory objects which we will learn how to configure. It's easy to get confused with Exchange!

As we examine the directory hierarchy displayed in the figure, we notice, as in the previous chapter, that the list of objects in the left container pane that is directly beneath the MICKEY container is not exactly the same as the list of objects in the right contents pane when the MICKEY container is selected. This is because the container pane shows containers but not leaf objects, while the contents pane shows both types of directory objects.

For our server MICKEY, which was installed in Chapter 3, the MICKEY container has the following containers and leaf objects:

- *Containers*:
  - *Private Information Store*. This component is both a database and a service. The private information store database contains the contents (personal folders, messages, and attachments) of all mailboxes that are homed (located) on that particular server, while the private information store service allows Exchange to read/write to this database and is

responsible for local message delivery (when the sender and receiver of a message have their mailboxes homed on the same server). You will use the property sheet of the Private Information Store object to configure certain server-specific aspects of the private information store on the server, as we shall soon see.

- *Protocols*. This contains objects used for configuring various Internet protocols and is covered in a later chapter.
- *Public Information Store*. This component is also both a database and a service. The public information store database contains the contents (messages, attachments, and other documents) of all public folders that are homed on that particular server, while the public information store service enables Exchange to read/write to this database. You use the property sheet of the Public Information Store object to configure certain server-specific aspects of the public information store on the server.
- *Server Recipients*. This contains all recipients that are homed on the particular server, including mailboxes, distribution lists, public folders, custom recipients, and mailbox agents. Note that only recipients that are contained in the site's default Recipients container can be present in the Server Recipients container (in other words, the Server Recipients container is a subset of the Recipients container).

- *Leaf objects*:

- *Directory Service*. This object is used to configure the server-specific aspects of the MS Exchange Directory service, a core component of Exchange and a Windows NT service running on Exchange servers.
- *Directory Synchronization*. Contrary to what you might expect, this object is not used to configure directory replication between Exchange Servers within a site or between different sites. Instead, it has to do with configuring directory synchronization between an Exchange Server and a legacy MS Mail 3.x mail system and is covered elsewhere.
- *Message Transfer Agent (MTA)*. This object is used to configure certain aspects of the MS Exchange MTA service, a core component of Exchange and a Windows NT service running on Exchange servers.
- *System Attendant*. This object is used to configure certain aspects of the MS Exchange System Attendant service, a Windows NT service running on all Exchange Servers and a core component of Exchange. The System Attendant functions as a maintenance service that must first be running in order for all other Exchange services to run.

For the rest of this chapter, we will focus on the Directory Service, the MTA, and Public and Private Information Stores. We'll also cover System

Attendant objects and how to configure them on a newly installed Exchange Server. Note that these objects correspond to the four core components of an Exchange Server, which were described in Chapter 4, and are all implemented as Windows NT services. But before we look at these, let's briefly look at the properties of Server containers like MICKEY and the Servers container that holds them.

Server and Servers Containers

The Servers container is simply a container for holding the directory objects that represent the various Exchange Servers installed in your site and has no interesting configurable properties. On the other hand, Server containers like MICKEY are more interesting and have various settings you can configure (see Figure 9-2).

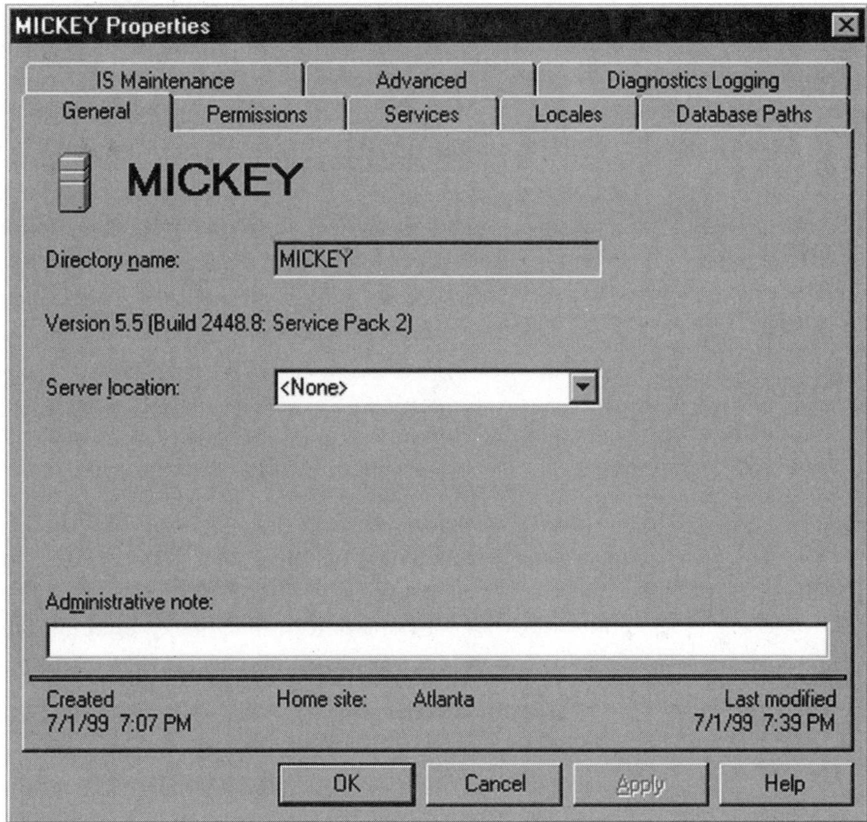

Figure 9-2 Properties of the MICKEY Server container.

Some of the more important settings you can configure using the property sheet for a Server container like MICKEY include the following:

- *Location (General tab)*. Exchange Servers in an organization are grouped into sites, but servers within a site can be further grouped into what are called locations. This feature is useful for controlling access to public folders and is discussed in a later chapter.
- *Services tab*. If you want to use a Server Monitor to monitor Windows NT services on your server, you can specify which services will be monitored here. Server monitors are discussed in a later chapter.
- *Locales tab*. Locales are different from locations, which were mentioned above. Locales have to do with foreign languages and enable currency, date, and time information to be displayed according to each language's conventions. Don't use these unless absolutely necessary, as they add a strain to the server's performance.
- *Database Paths tab*. This property page displays the locations of your various Exchange database files (database files were discussed earlier in Chapter 4). You can also use this page to move the files to other locations, such as if you install an additional hard drive. However, it is better not to do this manually but instead to run the Performance Optimizer tool from the Start menu and let Exchange decide where to locate the database files.
- *IS Maintenance tab*. This tab lets you schedule online maintenance for your server's information store (IS), which includes deleting expired messages from mailboxes and public folders and performing other system tasks. Maintenance should be scheduled when server load is low, since the information store runs more slowly during maintenance periods.
- *Circular logging (Advanced tab)*. Circular logging was discussed in Chapter 4.
- *Consistency Adjuster (Advanced tab)*. This button runs the DS/IS Consistency Adjuster tool (see Figure 9-3). DS stands for Directory Service, while IS stands for Information Store. The raison d'être for this tool is that certain objects like mailboxes and public folders are actually located in two different places on an Exchange server.

  For example, a user's mailbox exists in two locations:

  - The *contents* of the mailbox (the personal folders, messages, and attachments) are located on the user's home server (the Exchange Server on which the mailbox was created) and are stored in the private information store on that server.

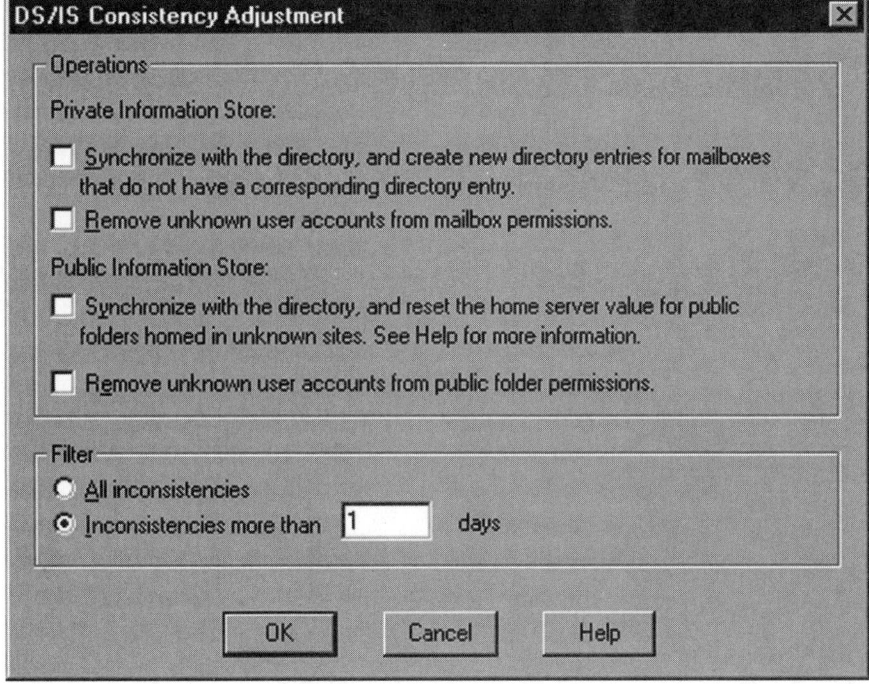

Figure 9-3 Running the DS/IS Consistency Adjuster tool.

- The *properties* of the mailbox are stored in the Exchange directory database, which is replicated to all Exchange Servers throughout the organization.

What happens then if an inconsistency occurs between these two locations, such as if you restored the private information store from a tape backup and this resulted in a mailbox existing in the information store but not in the directory database? In this case, the DS/IS Consistency Adjuster tool creates the necessary directory object for the mailbox so it exists properly in both locations. Some of the settings you can configure for the DS/IS Consistency Adjuster include the following:

- A Mailbox directory object can be created if the Adjuster finds a mailbox in the Private Information Store that doesn't have an associated directory object. Note that if there is a Mailbox directory object without a corresponding mailbox in the information store, it doesn't delete the directory object.
- A Public Folder directory object can be created if the Adjuster finds a public folder in the public Information Store that doesn't have an associated directory object. Note that if there is a Public Folder

directory object without a corresponding Public Folder in the information store, it deletes the directory object. Also, if it finds Public Folders in the information store that are homed in an unknown site, it homes them on the server where the DS/IS Consistency Adjuster is being run.

- You can remove any users that are no longer valid from either Information Store folder permissions.
- You can also reconcile either all inconsistencies or only those greater than a specified number of days (the latency period). Use the latter to preserve directory and information store entries when restoring a database from a tape backup.

DS/IS Consistency Adjuster

Do not run the DS / IS Consistency Adjuster if

- *You have deleted a directory replication connector to another site, unless you never plan to reconnect the sites again.*
- *You have just joined a site and directory replication has not yet occurred.*

- *Diagnostic Logging tab*. This lets you configure the logging levels for different types of Exchange Server events that are logged in the Application log and can be viewed using the Event Viewer. To configure this, select an Exchange service, specify an event category, and configure a logging level for that category. None means no events are logged for that category, while Maximum means practically everything having to do with that category is logged. Avoid too much logging unless you are troubleshooting specific Exchange services, since excessive logging can slow server performance and eat up mountains of disk space. Diagnostic logging can also be configured for the directory service, MTA, and the private and public information stores discussed below.

Directory Service

The Directory Service object is used to configure certain aspects of the Microsoft Exchange Directory service, a Windows NT service that is one of the core components of Microsoft Exchange servers (see Figure 9-4). The

DS is responsible for maintaining and replicating information in the Exchange directory database (see Chapter 4 for more details).

Here are some of the settings you can configure using the property sheet for this object:

- *Update Now (General tab).* All Exchange Servers in a given site replicate their directory databases with each other every five minutes, but you can manually force replication to occur at any time by clicking the Update Now button. This causes your server to immediately request any outstanding directory updates from other servers in your site.
- *Check Now (General tab).* What happens if an Exchange Server is down when a new server or site is installed in your organization? When you bring the downed server back online, it will have no knowledge that the new server or site was installed. To remedy this,

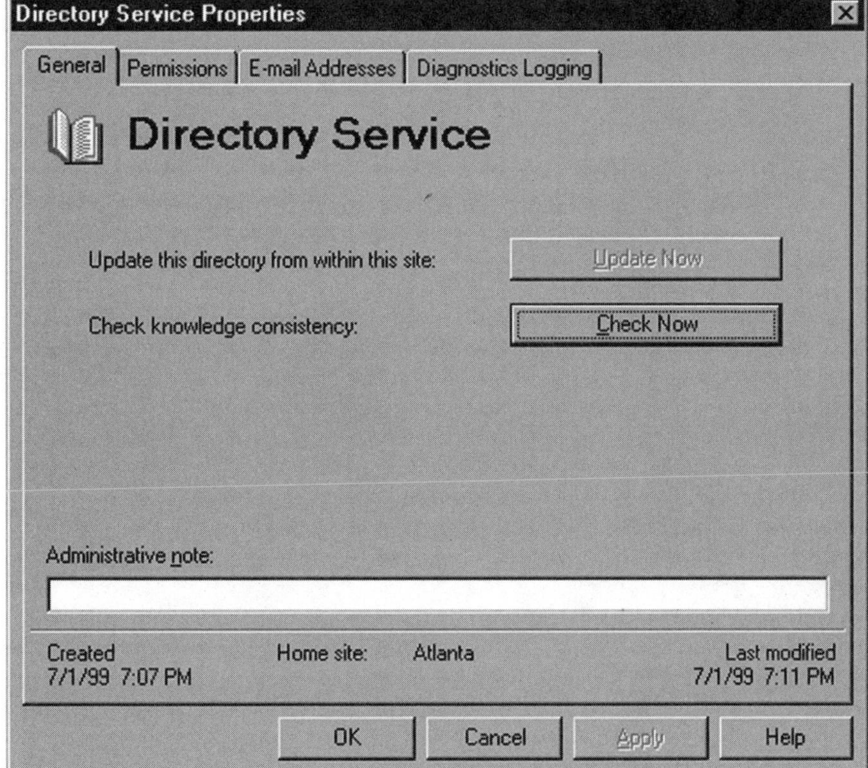

Figure 9-4 The property sheet for the Directory Service object.

Exchange Servers automatically check once a day for knowledge consistency, that is, they check that the directory databases on all servers in the organization are consistent with each other. The Check Now button included here enables you to force a *knowledge consistency check* (KCC) to occur immediately, instead of later. If you perform a KCC on a server you brought back online and discover a new server or site that your server was previously unaware of, you should do the following:

1. Select the Update Now button on this property page to update the directory database on your server.
2. Select the Recalculate Routing button (see the section below on the MTA in this chapter) to rebuild the routing table on your server.

- *Email Addresses tab*. This tab lists the various email addresses for the directory service on your Exchange server. For example, the SMTP address for the *Directory Synchronization Agent* (DSA) on server MICKEY in site Atlanta of organization MTIT would be

```
MICKEY-DSA@atlanta.mtit.com
```

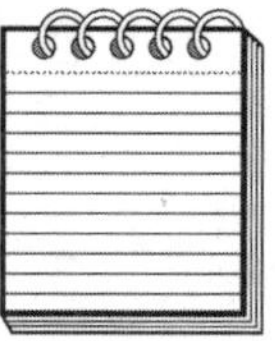

Changing Email Addresses

Since replication between sites usually takes place by means of email messages sent through connectors, it is important for each of the core components of the Exchange Servers to have its own email address for sending and receiving messages. You should generally not modify the email addresses of Exchange components like the directory service, as this may cause the service to fail and can affect other services as well (Exchange services use their email addresses to communicate with each other). For example, changing the address of the above directory service would cause the directory replication to fail with other servers in the site.

Message Transfer Agent

The MTA object is used to configure server-specific aspects of the Microsoft Exchange Message Transfer Agent service, a Windows NT service that is one of the core components of Microsoft Exchange servers (see Figure 9-5).

The MTA and the Information Store (IS) are both responsible for delivering messages and perform this task as follows:

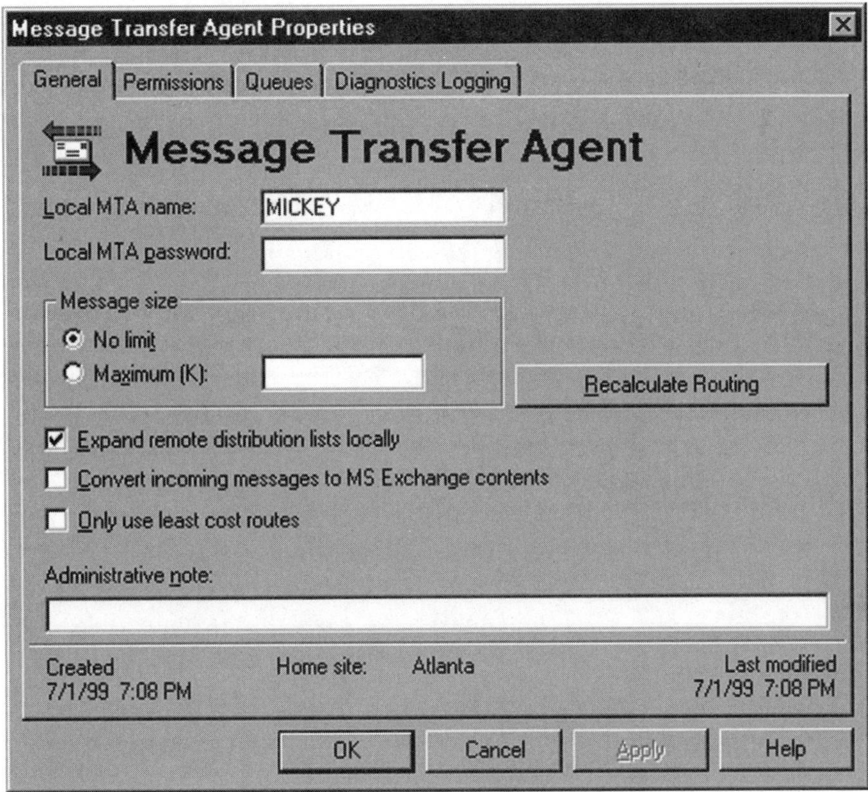

Figure 9-5
The property sheet for the MTA object.

- If a message is sent from one recipient to another on the *same server*, the Information Store on that server delivers the message directly. The MTA is not involved in this transfer.
- If a message is sent from one recipient to another on a *different server in the same site*, the MTA on the sender's server gives the message to the MTA on the receiver's server, which then delivers it to the receiving server's information store.
- If a message is sent from one recipient to another recipient in *another site or a foreign mail system*, the MTA on the sender's server determines which connector to use to route the message to the remote site or mail system, and then gives the message to the selected connector, which then routes the message towards its destination.

For more information on the operation of the MTA and IS, see Chapter 4. Some of the settings you can configure using the property sheet for this object include the following:

- *Local MTA Name and Password (General tab).* If you are routing messages to a foreign X.400 mail system, you may need to make the MTA name and password match those of the foreign system.
- *Message Size Limits (General tab).* This lets you specify a maximum message size in KB that the MTA can handle. Anything larger is returned to the sender with a *non-delivery report* (NDR).
- *Recalculate Routing (General tab).* This forces the routing table to be recalculated. Refer to information on the Site Addressing object in Chapter 8 for more information.
- *Expand Remote Distribution Lists (DLs) Locally (General tab).* Remote DLs are those that were created in a different site. If this option is selected (and it is by default) and a user in the local site sends a message to the remote DL, the DL is expanded on the server to which the user is currently connected.
- *Convert Incoming Messages to Microsoft (MS) Exchange Contents (General tab).* This changes the format of the address and content of incoming messages to one that is compatible with the MAPI interface of the underlying architecture of Exchange.
- *Only Use Least Cost Routes (General tab).* This causes the server's MTA to only attempt to route messages using the least cost route. If that fails, other possible routes will not be attempted and an NDR will be returned. Message routing is discussed in a later chapter.
- *Queues tab.* Depending on the number of servers in the site and the number of installed connectors and gateways, several different queues may be holding messages waiting to be delivered by the MTA. If you select a queue here, you can
- See how many messages are waiting to be delivered in that queue.
- View the sender's address, message ID, submission time, and the size and priority of each message in that queue.
- Change the priority of a message (but you cannot do this for messages in the Internet Mail Service and MS Mail Connector queues).
- Delete a message in the queue.

With no connectors installed for the site, the only queues listed here are those for the private and public information stores, which are used for local message delivery.

- *Diagnostic Logging tab.* See the section entitled "Directory Service" earlier in this chapter.

Private Information Store

The Private Information Store object is used to configure server-specific aspects of the MS Exchange Information Store service, a Windows NT service that is one of the core components of Exchange servers (see Figure 9-6). The Private Information Store stores the contents of all mailboxes for users that are homed on that server, including the user's personal folders, messages, and attachments. Some of the settings you can configure using the property sheet for this object include

- *Item Recovery (General tab)*. Exchange Servers can retain messages for a period of time even after users delete them from their mailboxes. You can specify either
- A retention time in days, after which the items are permanently deleted.

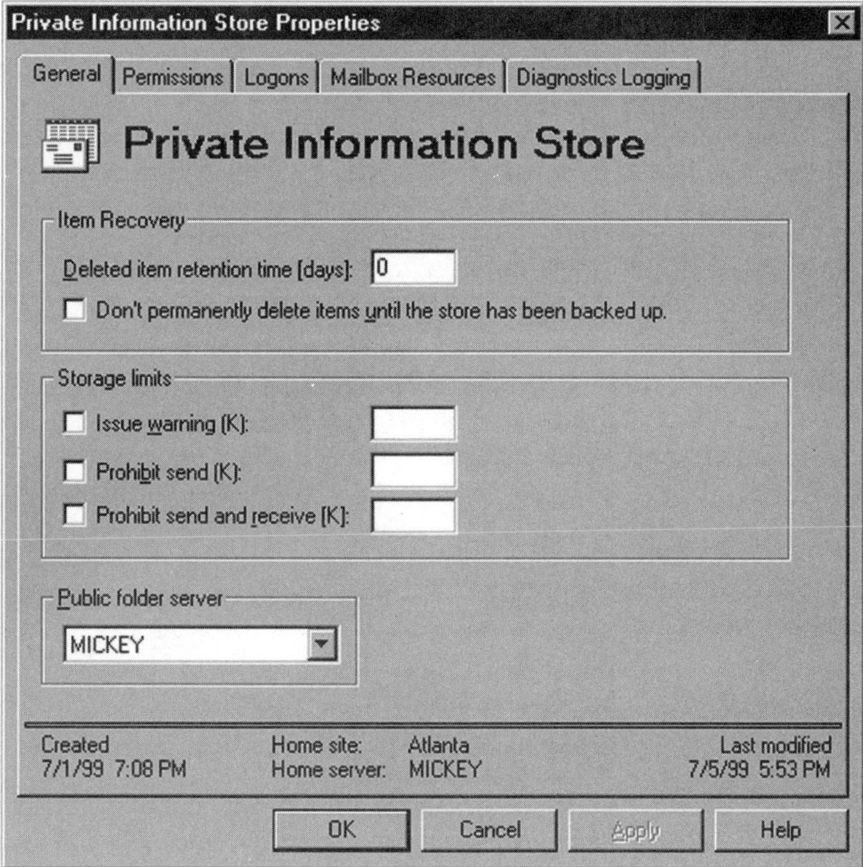

Figure 9-6 The property sheet for a Private Information Store object.

- Not to permanently delete items until after the information store has been backed up to tape, since they can then be recovered later by restoring the information store from tape.

Using MS Outlook, a user can recover a deleted item by selecting the Deleted Items folder and then choosing Recover Deleted Items from the Tools menu.

- *Storage Limits (General tab).* This lets you specify the maximum amount of disk space a mailbox can occupy in the private information store (these limits can be overruled for any particular mailbox by using the Limits page of the property sheet for that mailbox). If the limit is reached, a notification is sent to the mailbox owner. You can also specify separate (larger) limits that, once reached, prohibit the user from sending messages or receiving messages.

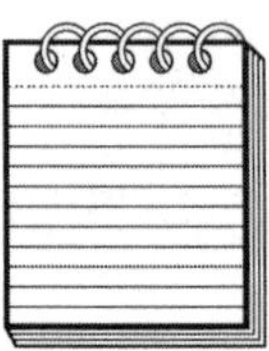

Prohibit Send

The Prohibit Send option is supported by MAPI clients like MS Outlook, but not by POP3 or IMAP4 clients like MS Outlook Express.

- *Public Folder Server (General tab).* This tab lets you specify the Exchange Server where users homed on this server can create Public Folders, which is the users' own home server by default. If you want to force users homed on your server to create their Public Folders on a different server in your site, specify that server here.
- *Logons tab.* This tab lets you find out which users and Exchange services are currently logged on to the private information store. Services log on using the service account for the site. Select the Columns button to customize which properties are displayed for logons shown in the listbox.
- *Mailbox Resources tab.* This tab lets you find out how much disk space is being used by mailboxes homed on this server, how many messages are in their mailboxes, and so on. Select the Columns button to customize which properties are displayed for mailboxes shown in the listbox.

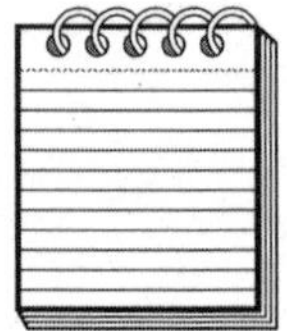

Logons and Mailbox Resources

You can also view the users that are currently logged on to the private information store and the disk space currently used by each user for their mailbox by expanding the plus sign beside the Private Information Store object in the container pane of Exchange Administrator and then selecting either Logons or Mailbox Resources in the container pane to view the corresponding information in the contents pane. The columns shown in the contents pane are the same as those you have selected to display on the Logons and Mailbox Resources tabs of the Private Information Store object's property sheet.

- *Diagnostic Logging tab*. See the section entitled Directory Service earlier in this chapter.

Public Information Store

The Public Information Store object is used to configure server-specific aspects of the MS Exchange Information Store service, a Windows NT service that is one of the core components of Exchange servers (see Figure 9-7). The Public Information Store contains the contents of all Public Folder hierarchies and Public Folder replicas homed on that server, including the messages and documents users have posted to these folders. We'll review these properties only briefly here as we will return to the topic of public folders in a later chapter.

Some of the settings you can configure using the property sheet for this object include

- *Item Recovery (General tab)*. Exchange servers can retain postings for a period of time even after users delete them from public folders. You can specify either
- A retention time in days, after which the items are permanently deleted.
- Not to permanently delete items until after the information store has been backed up to tape, since they can then be recovered later by restoring the information store from tape.

Using MS Outlook, a user can recover a deleted item by selecting the Public Folder and then choosing Recover Deleted Items from the Tools menu.

- *Storage Limits (General tab)*. This lets you specify the maximum amount of space the Public Folder can occupy in the information store. If this limit is reached, a notification is sent to the Public Folder contact.
- *Age Limits tab*. This tab lets you set expiration time limits for Public Folders, after which postings are deleted.

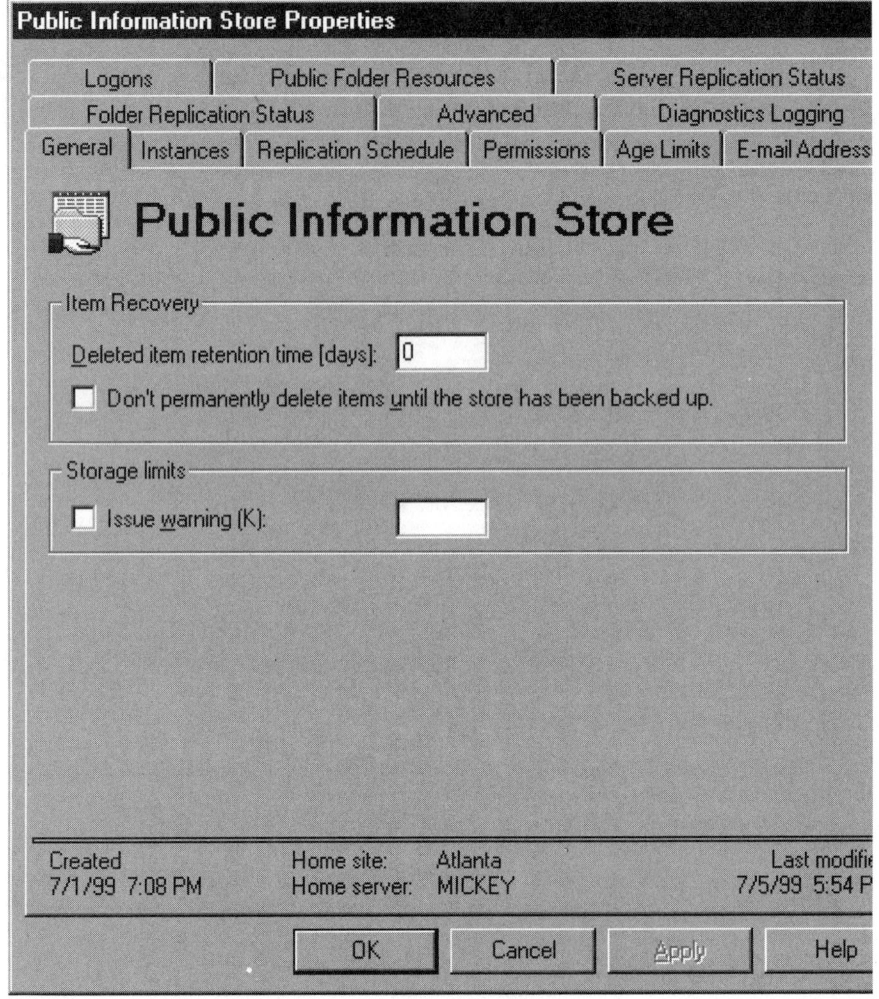

Figure 9-7 The property sheet for a Public Information Store object.

- *Email Addresses tab*. See the section on Directory Service earlier in this chapter.
- *Logons tab*. This tab lets you find out which users and Exchange services are currently logged on to the Public Information Store. Services log on using the service account for the site.
- *Public Folder Resources tab*. This lets you find out how much disk space is being used by Public Folders homed on this server, how many postings and documents are in the folders, and so on.
- *Instances, Replication Schedule, Advanced, Folder Replication Status, and Server Replication Status tabs*. These settings are used to create

and manage replicas of public folders on other servers and are discussed further in a later chapter.

System Attendant

The final server configuration object we will look at in this chapter is the System Attendant (see Figure 9-8). This object is used to configure server-specific aspects of the MS Exchange System Attendant service, a Windows NT service that is one of the core components of Exchange servers.

The system attendant is a maintenance service that must be running in order for other Exchange services to run and is responsible for tasks such as

- Generating email addresses for new recipients.
- Maintaining logs for message tracking.
- Monitoring the connection status between Exchange servers.

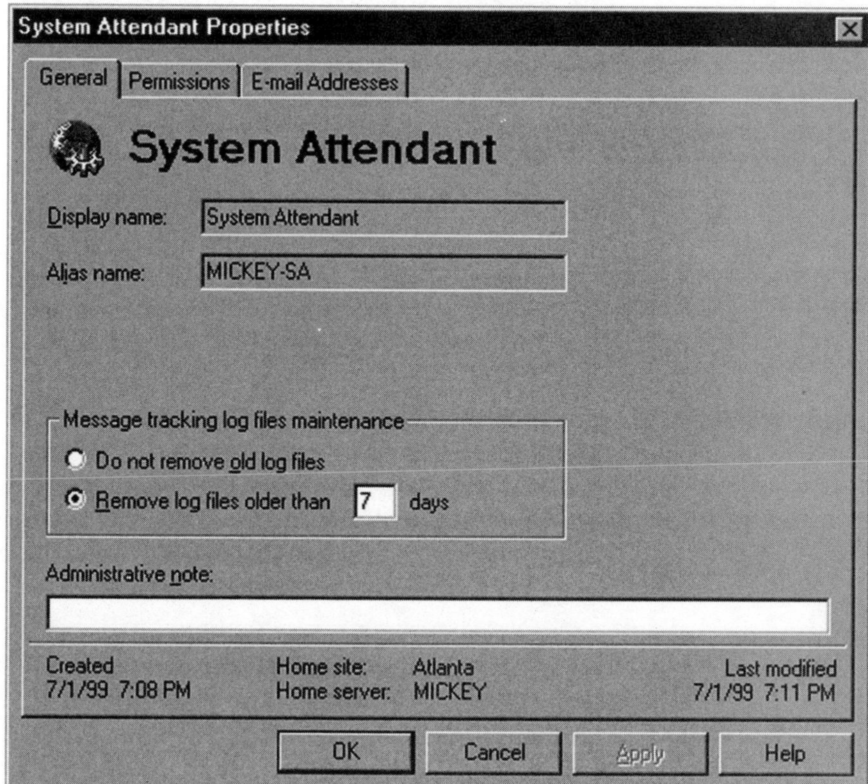

Figure 9-8 The property sheet for a System Attendant object.

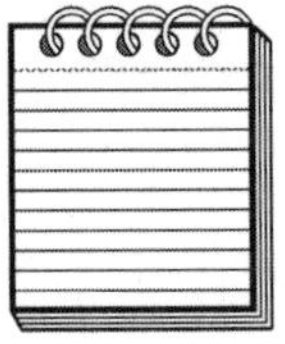

System Attendant

If you try to use the Exchange Administrator program to connect to a remote Exchange server like DONALD on which the System Attendant service is not running, you will get the error message: "A connection could not be made to the MS Exchange Server computer DONALD. The MS Exchange Server computer does not respond."

Only a couple of settings can be configured using the property sheet for this object:

- *Message Tracking Logs (General tab).* This lets you specify whether to keep old message tracking log files or discard them when they reach a certain age (in days).
- *Email Addresses tab.* See the section on Directory Service earlier in this chapter.

Walkthrough: Configuring a Server

Now let's walk through some basic configuration tasks for the server MICKEY in the site Atlanta and test the configuration where feasible in our single-site setup.

Disable Circular Logging

The first thing we'll do is turn off circular logging for the Directory and Information Store databases, something that we recommended earlier in Chapter 4. Using Exchange Administrator, open the property sheet for the MICKEY Server object, select the Advanced tab, and clear the two checkboxes to disable circular logging. Click OK to apply changes and close the property sheet. A message appears saying, "In order to save the database circular logging settings on server MICKEY, the corresponding service(s) will be restarted. Are you sure you want to save the circular logging settings?" Click Yes, after which the MS Exchange Directory Service (MSExchangeDS) is stopped and then restarted. That wasn't hard!

Configuring Deleted Item Recovery and Mailbox Storage Limits

Open the property sheet for the Private Information Store object and select the General tab. Make the following changes to the settings displayed:

- Set the deleted item retention time to seven days.
- Select the storage limit issue warning and set its size to 4,000 KB.
- Select the storage limit prohibit send and set its size to 8,000 KB.
- Select the storage limit prohibit send and receive and set its size to 12,000 KB.

Click OK to apply changes and close the property sheet. Now let's see if we can test our new settings. On GOOFEY (or any other machine that has MS Outlook 98 installed), create a junk file with a size of approximately 1,000 KB:

1. Open WordPad (Notepad can only create files up to 64 KB in size, while WordPad can be used to create files up to 16 MB).
2. Type in the string 1234567890 (a length of 10 characters equals 10 bytes). Select the string and choose Cut from the Edit menu to copy it to the clipboard. Paste it 10 times, giving you a new string with a length of 100 characters or 100 bytes. (Use CTRL+V to paste as it's much faster.)
3. Press CTRL+A to select the 100-byte string, cut it to the clipboard, and paste it back 10 times. The document is now 1,000 bytes in size (almost 1 KB).
4. Repeat until you have a 1,000 KB document (there will be some extra bytes of file overhead for WordPad files and mine came out to 1,359 KB in size. I probably pasted too many times!). Save it with the name `junk.doc` in a folder somewhere on your hard drive (My Documents is a good choice) and close WordPad.

Now log on as Boris and start Outlook 98 (if Outlook is still configured for Offline Folders, disable this feature by using Tools, Services, Advanced, and clearing the checkbox; see Chapter 7). Let's test Exchange's deleted item recovery feature first, which we configured above for the Private Information Store. You should still have a couple of Welcome to Outlook messages in your Inbox from before (if not, have Natasha send Boris a test message or have Boris send a message to himself). Select these messages and use the Delete button on the toolbar to delete them from the Inbox. Scroll down the Outlook Shortcuts bar on the left and click on the Deleted Items folder. You can see that deleting an item from the Inbox merely moves the item into the Deleted Items folder; it's not really deleted from your mailbox.

Select Options from the Tools menu to open the Options property sheet. Select the Other tab and place a checkmark beside Empty The Deleted Items Folder Upon Exiting. Click OK and exit Outlook.

Now start Outlook again and select the Deleted Items folder in the Outlook Shortcuts bar. It should still be empty. Select Recover Deleted Items from the Tools menu and the Recover Deleted Items From - Deleted Items dialog box should appear (see Figure 9-9).

Select a deleted message to recover and click the Recover Selected Items button on the toolbar of this dialog box. The dialog box closes and you are returned to Outlook, where you should see the recovered message in your Deleted Items folder. You could now copy it to a different folder to store it safely so it won't be deleted again seven days later.

Now let's test our message limit settings. In Exchange Administrator, select and expand the MICKEY Server object in the left container pane, expand the Private Information Store object beneath it, and select the Mailbox Resources object to view how much disk space is currently being used by users' mailboxes homed on MICKEY. Note the amount of space used by Boris's mailbox (see Figure 9-10). I have 74 KB stored as 16 different items.

We also need to configure a schedule for the warning messages that will be issued when we exceed our mailbox storage limits. Open the property sheet for the Information Store Site Configuration container (see Chapter 8), select the Storage Warnings tab, and choose Always. This will cause storage warning notification messages to be generated every 15 minutes (if conditions warrant it). If we don't do this step, we'll have to wait until the next day to receive our notification messages, which would make our walk-through a bit boring.

Now go back to GOOFEY, select the Inbox folder in the Outlook Shortcuts bar, and click the New Mail Message button (or select File, New, Mail

Recover Deleted Items From - Deleted Items

Subject	Deleted On	From	Received
RE: ddddddd	7/7/1999 12:48 PM	Natasha Smith	7/5/1999 6:23 PM
RE: This is a test	7/7/1999 12:48 PM	Natasha Smith	7/5/1999 6:08 PM
Special Offers for Outlook Users	7/7/1999 12:48 PM	Microsoft Outlook 98	7/5/1999 5:58 PM
Welcome to Microsoft Outlook 98!	7/7/1999 12:48 PM	Microsoft Outlook 98	7/5/1999 5:57 PM
Synchronization Log: C:\WINDOWS...	7/7/1999 12:48 PM	Boris Zhivago	7/5/1999 5:57 PM
Synchronization Log: C:\WINDOWS...	7/7/1999 12:48 PM	Boris Zhivago	7/5/1999 6:24 PM
Synchronization Log: C:\WINDOWS...	7/7/1999 12:48 PM	Boris Zhivago	7/6/1999 8:30 PM
Synchronization Log: C:\WINDOWS...	7/7/1999 12:48 PM	Boris Zhivago	7/6/1999 8:30 PM
Synchronization Log: C:\WINDOWS...	7/7/1999 12:50 PM	Boris Zhivago	7/7/1999 12:53 PM
test	7/7/1999 12:52 PM	Boris Zhivago	7/7/1999 12:52 PM

Figure 9-9 Recovering deleted items in Outlook 98.

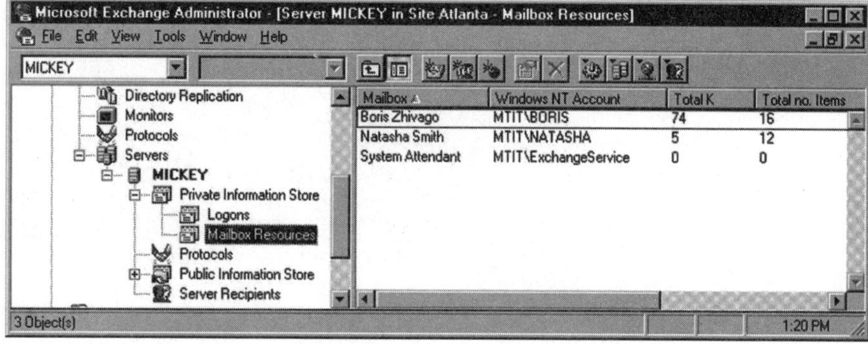

Figure 9-10 Disk space used by mailboxes on MICKEY.

Message from the menu bar) to open an untitled message window. Address the message to yourself (Boris), enter the subject "Testing message limits" as the subject, attach the 1359-KB `junk.doc` file to the message, and send it. It should appear in your Inbox in a moment. Go back to MICKEY and select Window, Refresh from the menu of Exchange Administrator. The disk space used by the mailbox should have increased dramatically, and the total number of items should have increased as well. Actually, my disk space usage increased by 2,718 KB and the number of messages stored increased by two to 18. This is because Outlook is configured by default to save copies of messages you send in your Sent Items folder. Space is filling up fast!

Send another test message to yourself with the junk file attached. You should immediately receive a warning message from Exchange that your second message could not be delivered (it actually says that it was sent by the "System Administrator"), along with the undeliverable message attached to it (see Figure 9-11).

Refresh the Mailbox Resources for MICKEY in Exchange Administrator and you'll see that you've exceeded 4,000 KB, our Issue Warning storage limit (mine shows 5,522 KB).

Try sending a third test message with the junk file attached. A dialog box now appears saying, "You have exceeded the storage limit on your mailbox. Delete some mail from your mailbox or contact your system administrator to adjust your storage limit." Exchange is getting nasty—all you want to do is send some mail! Click OK and you are returned to your new message window—the message could not be sent because of the Prohibit Send storage limit configured on MICKEY. I'll leave it up to you to figure out how to test the Prohibit Send and Receive storage limit on your server.

By the way, when 15 minutes has elapsed since you received the first storage limit warning, a second warning is sent to you that has "Your mailbox is closed" for the subject and the following message body:

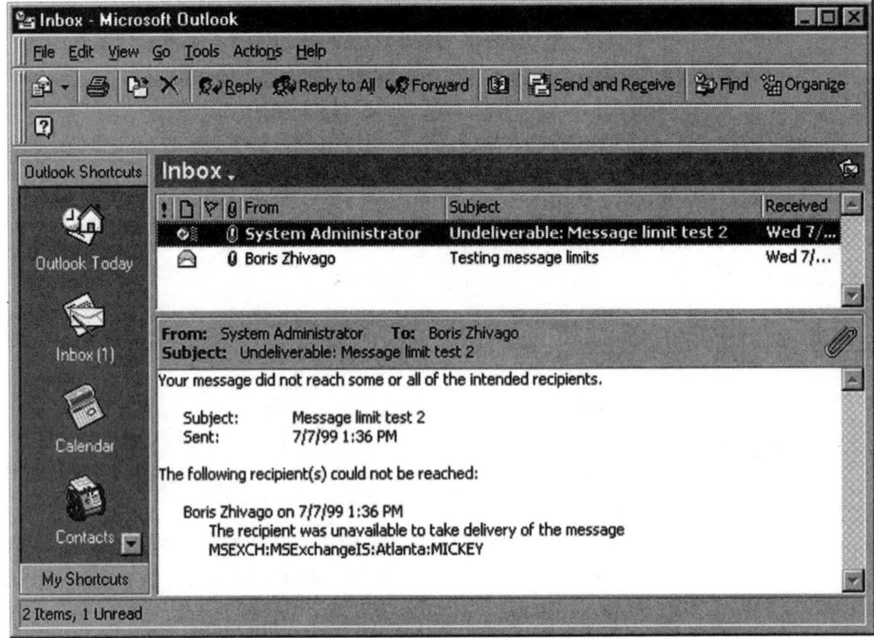

Figure 9-11 Storage limit warning issued to Boris.

```
Your mailbox has exceeded one or more size limits set by your
administrator.
Your mailbox size is 5,521 KB.
Mailbox size limits:
  You will receive a warning when your mailbox reaches 4,000 KB.
  You cannot send or receive mail when your mailbox reaches 1,200 KB.
You may not be able to send or receive new mail until you reduce
your mailbox size. To make more space available, delete any items
that you are no longer using or move them to your personal folder
file (.pst). Items in all of your mailbox folders including the
Deleted Items and Sent Items folders count against your size limit.
You must empty the Deleted Items folder after deleting items or the
space will not be freed.
See client Help for more information.
```

You better delete some messages from your mailbox; otherwise, a warning will arrive in your Inbox every 15 minutes indefinitely!

Where Do We Go from Here?

It's time now to start expanding our Exchange organization by adding other sites. We'll begin this in the next chapter, where we look at the Site Connector, the easiest way of joining two Exchange sites together for messaging connectivity.

For More Information

For further information on server configuration options, see Chapter 8 of the *Getting Started* manual for Exchange, which can be found in Books Online.

CHAPTER 10

Administering Site Connectors

In the previous two chapters, we considered how to configure site-level and server-level settings for Exchange in a single-site scenario. We move on in this chapter to begin considering multi-site implementations of Exchange. We start with the simplest situation, establishing messaging connectivity between two sites using the Site Connector. After reading this chapter, you will have an understanding of

- The different types of Exchange connectors
- The Connections Container
- The Site Connector

The walkthrough in this chapter covers creating, configuring, and testing a Site Connector. Using the Clean Mailbox command is also included for interest's sake.

Exchange Connectors

Connectors are components of the Microsoft Exchange Server that can be used to establish messaging connectivity between one Exchange site and another site in the same organization, or between one Exchange organization and a foreign mail system. Foreign mail systems can refer to

- A different Exchange organization.
- A Microsoft Mail 3.x messaging system.
- A Lotus cc:Mail messaging system.
- A public X.400-based messaging system (more common in Europe).
- A mainframe-based messaging system such as PROFS and SNADS.
- The SMTP mail system of the Internet.

When a connector is installed on an Exchange server, the connector acts as a kind of funnel or gateway for routing messages of a particular type to another site or mail system. When connecting Exchange sites together, creating a connector really means creating a pair of connectors: one in the local site and one in the remote site. Each connector in a pair of connectors must be configured properly in order for messages to pass between the sites. Connectors can be differentiated according to

- The kind of *network connectivity* they establish (a permanent or dial-up network connection).
- The type of *email addresses* they can handle (SMTP, X.400, MS Mail, and so on).

- Whether they can be used to connect Exchange *sites* together, connect to a *foreign* mail system, or *both*.

Table 10-1 shows the common types of Exchange connectors and what they can be used for (we omit the PROFS and SNADS connectors that require understanding IBM's System Network Architecture (SNA) to install and configure, something that is beyond the scope of this book). We'll consider only the Site Connector in this chapter and defer looking at the other connectors until later chapters.

Connections Container

First, we will note that any connectors that are installed in an Exchange site reside within the Connections container, which is in the Configuration container for that site. Figure 10-1 shows the Connections container selected in the left container pane of Exchange Administrator.

The right contents pane shows that two connectors are installed in the site Atlanta:

- *MS Mail Connector (MICKEY)*, which can be used for establishing messaging connectivity with a Microsoft Mail 3.x mail system. This connector was automatically created by Exchange when we chose to install the MS Mail component during Setup when we installed Exchange Server on MICKEY in Chapter 3.
- *Site Connector to Chicago*, a Site Connector that we will install in the walkthrough later in this chapter.

Table 10-1

Types of Exchange Connectors and Their Uses.

Connector	Can be used to connect to . . .	
	Another site	A foreign mail system
Site Connector	√	
Dynamic RAS Connector	√	
X.400 Connector	√	√
Internet Mail Service	√	√
Connector for cc:Mail		√
MS Mail Connector		√

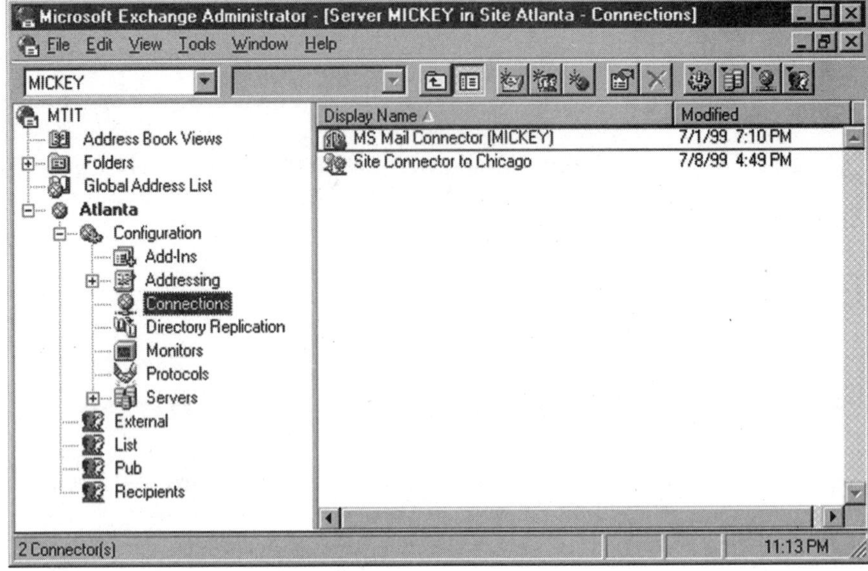

Figure 10-1 The Connections container in the Atlanta site.

The property sheet for the Connections container has no interesting properties; the Connections container simply serves to group together all the connectors installed in the site, so we won't consider it any further and move on to considering the Site Connector.

Site Connector

The Site Connector is the easiest way of connecting different Exchange sites together to establish messaging connectivity between them (see Figure 10-2). Site Connectors require a permanent high-speed LAN or WAN connection between sites, since they use Remote Procedure Calls (RPCs) to transport messages between sites. A Site Connector essentially establishes a direct connection between an Exchange server in the local site (called the messaging bridgehead server for that site) and a target server or servers in the remote site. Like all Exchange connectors, both ends of the connector must be created and configured for messaging to work via the connector. With the Site Connector, this requirement is simple; when you finish configuring the local side of the connector, a dialog box appears, asking you if you want Exchange to automatically create and configure the remote side of the connector in the other site.

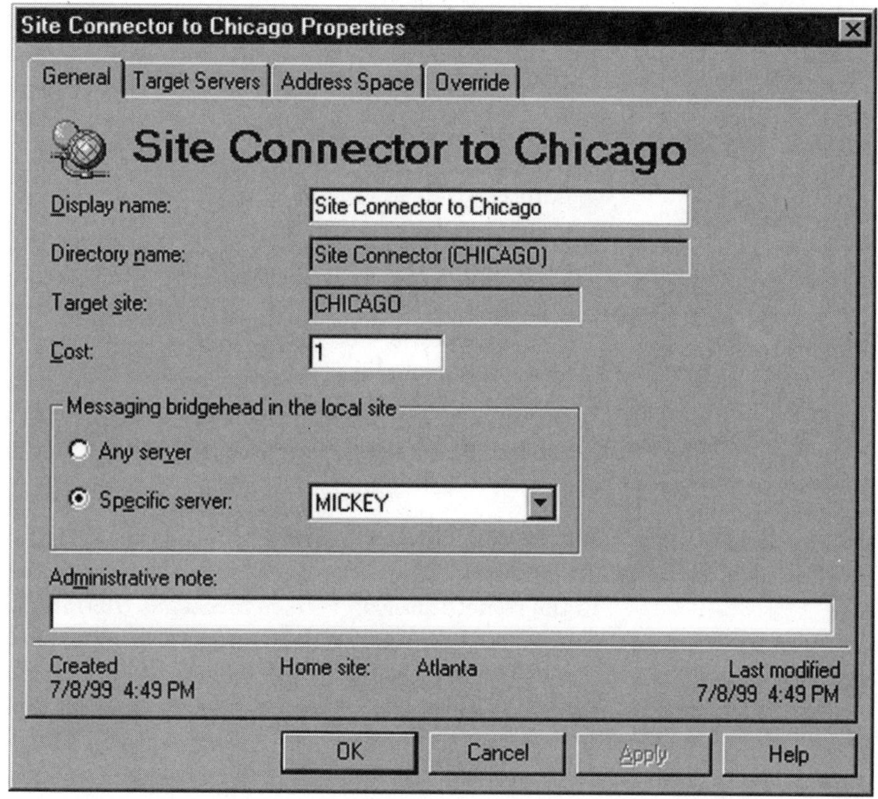

Figure 10-2 The Site Connector in the Atlanta site, which provides messaging connectivity with the Chicago site.

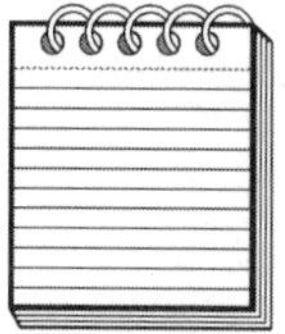

Site Connectors

Site Connectors can only be used to connect different sites in the same Exchange organization together for messaging connectivity. They cannot be used to establish messaging connectivity with foreign mail systems or other Exchange organizations.

The following settings can be configured when creating (or modifying) a Site Connector:

- *Target Site (General tab).* This is the remote site that the connector is establishing messaging connectivity with and is specified at the time the connector is created.
- *Cost (General tab).* This is a number from 1 to 100 that indicates the preference for using this connector when there are other possible messaging routes from the local to the remote site. If two different

routes are possible to the same remote site, the one with the lowest cost is chosen. The default setting here is 1. We'll talk more about message routing in a later chapter.

- *Messaging Bridgehead Server (General tab)*. This is a server in the local site that is used for forwarding messages to the remote site. The default setting is to enable any server in the local site to forward messages to the remote site, but it is often better to establish one specific server in each site as a dedicated messaging bridgehead server, especially in larger enterprises having many sites each with many servers and a lot of messaging traffic. You only have two choices here:
  - *All servers* in the local site can send messages to the remote site (no dedicated messaging bridgehead server).
  - A dedicated *messaging bridgehead server* can send messages to the remote site (only one is allowed).
- *Target Servers tab*. This tab lets you designate which Exchange Servers in the remote site can receive messages from the local site using the Site Connector. You can designate one or more servers in the remote site as target servers, and for each target server you can specify a target server cost from 0 to 100. When a message needs to be routed to the remote site using the Site Connector, an RPC connection to each of the servers in the target servers list is attempted one at a time, starting with those having a target server cost of 0 until a connection can be established and the message routed. If two target servers have the same target server cost, connection attempts will be load-balanced between the two target servers.

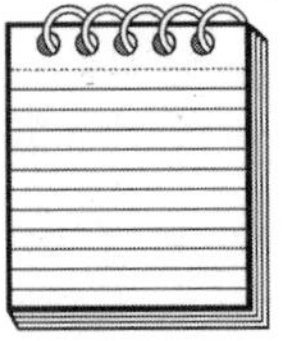

Topology of the Site Connector

You can see from the above explanation of messaging bridgehead servers and target servers that the messaging topology established by a Site Connector between two sites can vary considerably. What this means, for example, is that if Site A connects to Site B using a Site Connector and if each site has multiple Exchange Servers, then possible messaging topologies between the sites can be summarized as follows.

One of the following must be true:

- *Any single bridgehead server in Site A → Any group of one or more target servers in Site B*
- *All servers in Site A → Any group of one or more target servers in Site B*

Also one of the following must be true:

- *Any single bridgehead server in Site B → Any group of one or more target servers in Site A*
- *All servers in Site B → Any group of one or more target servers in Site A*

- *Address Space tab.* This specifies the address spaces for the local side of the Site Connector. An address space is essentially a range of email addresses to which the connector is allowed to forward messages. Any messages that are not within the address spaces specified for the connector cannot be routed by the connector. You can use address spaces to control whether the connector can forward messages to a location, a site, or an organization, and address spaces can be of type X.400, SMTP, MS Mail, and so on. Exchange automatically creates an X.400 type of address space for the Site Connector when you create it. This default address space allows users anywhere in the Exchange organization to use the connector to forward messages addressed with an X.400 address to which the recipient in the remote site is being connected. By creating additional address spaces for the connector, it can be used to route messages of different address types and to different destination sites. We'll look at address spaces in more detail when we consider message routing in a later chapter.
- *Override tab.* This tab can be used to override any problems that can occur when the two sites being connected belong to two different Windows NT domains. This is especially important when there is no trust relationship between the domains.

Walkthrough: Creating and Configuring a Site Connector

Let's examine the process of creating and testing a new Site Connector between two Exchange sites, and then test messaging connectivity between the sites. For the purposes of this walkthrough, we have already installed a second Exchange Server called BUGS, creating during the setup of a new site called Chicago that is part of the same organization MTIT that MICKEY in site Atlanta belongs to. The server in Atlanta belongs to a Windows NT domain called MTIT. We decided to call the Windows NT domain in Atlanta "MTIT" instead of "ATLANTA" simply because the company headquarters is in Atlanta, so the name of the domain there is chosen to be the same as the Exchange organization name MTIT, instead of only the site name Atlanta. The server BUGS in Chicago belongs to a different Windows NT domain called CHICAGO.

A trust relationship has also been established between the two domains such that the CHICAGO domain trusts the MTIT domain. This trust relationship has been established for administrative purposes to enable network administrators in Atlanta to be able to administer servers in Chicago. In addition, a separate Exchange service account called Exsrv has been created in the CHICAGO domain to enable Exchange services on BUGS to run in the context of an account from BUGS' own domain. It would have been quite possible using the trust relationship between the domains to have BUGS use the same service account as MICKEY uses, namely the account ExchangeService from the MTIT domain where MICKEY is a member. However, there is good reason for using a separate service account for each Exchange site. If the WAN link between the sites went down, Exchange Servers would be unable to run except in the domain where the original service account resides. Furthermore, if we plan to add additional Exchange Servers to either site, we must remember that all Exchange Servers in the same site must use the same service account in order to communicate with each other.

Finally, we still have Outlook 98 installed on a machine called GOOFEY in Atlanta for purposes of sending and receiving test messages. We've now also installed Outlook 2000 on a machine in Chicago for testing purposes. The installation was simple, but we haven't configured any messaging services on the machine yet; we'll do that later in the walkthrough. We've created a couple of user accounts and mailboxes in Chicago for network administrators to use there also.

If all this seems confusing, Table 10-2 should clarify things a bit.

Table 10-2

Summary of Sites and Domains for the Walkthrough.

Geographical Location	Atlanta	Chicago
Company Function	Headquarters	Branch Office
Windows NT Domain	MTIT	CHICAGO
Trust relationship	Trusted Domain	Trusting Domain
Exchange Organization	MTIT	MTIT
Exchange Site	Atlanta	Chicago
Exchange Server	MICKEY	BUGS
Exchange Service Account	MTIT\ExchangeService	CHICAGO\Exsrv

Preliminary Stuff

The first thing we'll do is create a new site connector, establishing messaging connectivity between the Atlanta and Chicago sites. Before attempting this, however, we need to ensure that the network administrator that will perform this action has the necessary administrative privileges in both Atlanta and Chicago. This means both Windows NT administrative privileges and Exchange administrative privileges must be assigned to that user's account. Since Atlanta is company headquarters and is the trusted Windows NT domain, we'll assign these privileges to our senior network administrator located there, namely Boris Zhivago.

First, let's confirm Boris has the necessary privileges for Atlanta. Start User Manager For Domains on a domain controller in Atlanta, open the property sheet for Boris' user account, click the Groups button, and verify that Boris is a member of the Domain Admins global group for the MTIT domain in Atlanta.

Next, start Exchange Administrator on MICKEY and make sure that the account MTIT\Boris has been assigned the Permissions Admin role on the Permissions tab for the property sheets of following three containers:

- MTIT (Organization container)
- Atlanta (Site container)
- Configuration (within the Atlanta Site container)

Previously in Chapter 5 we had granted Boris the Permissions Admin role on the second and third containers listed above, namely the Site and Configuration containers for the Atlanta site, which allowed Boris to make any changes he wanted to the configuration of Exchange Servers in Atlanta. By also assigning Boris the Permissions Admin role on the Organization container, we are giving him carte blanch permission to do anything he likes in his Exchange organization and all its sites, existing and future. If you can't remember how to assign the Permissions Admin role to an object, refer back to Chapter 5.

Now log on as the Administrator to a domain controller in the CHICAGO domain and start User Manager For Domains. Remember, since CHICAGO trusts MTIT, this means that a user logging on to a Windows NT machine in Chicago has a choice of logging on either to the CHICAGO or MTIT domain. Make sure you are logged in as the Administrator for the CHICAGO domain and open the property sheet for the Administrator local group. The members of this group are currently the default Administrator account and the Domain Admins global group, both of which belong to the CHICAGO domain (see Figure 10-3).

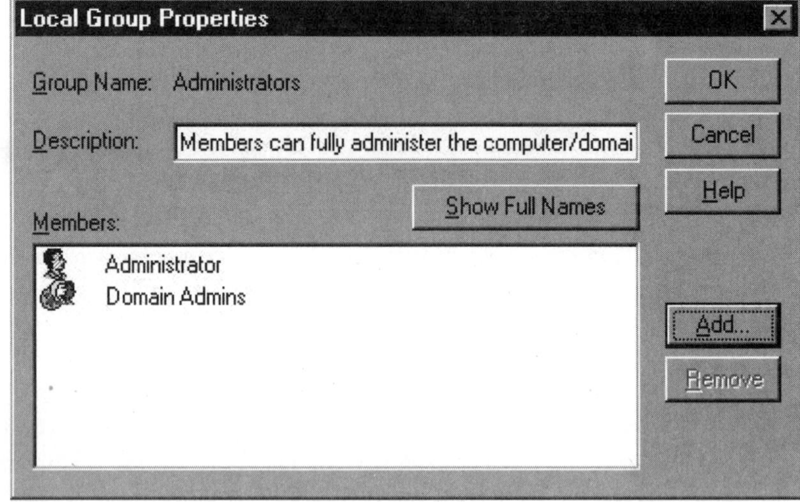

Figure 10-3 Membership in the Administrators local group for the CHICAGO domain.

Click the Add button to open the Add Users and Groups dialog box. We want to make Boris, whose account is in the MTIT domain in Atlanta, a member of the Administrators local group in the CHICAGO domain in Chicago. The standard way to do this in Windows NT administration is to use groups; we'll add the Domain Admins global group for MTIT to the Administrators local group for CHICAGO (something we can do because of the trust relationship established). Select the MTIT domain from the List Names From drop-down box to show the global user and group accounts from the MTIT domain in the Names listbox. Select Boris from the Names listbox and click the Add button to add his name to the Add Names listbox (see Figure 10-4).

Click OK to return to the property sheet for the Administrators local group in CHICAGO. Notice that the Administrators local group for CHICAGO now contains the Domain Admins global groups for both the CHICAGO and MTIT domains. In other words, any user that is a member of either Domain Admins groups in either domain now has the privilege to administer servers in the CHICAGO domain. The trust relationship allows administrators in the trusting domain CHICAGO to grant administrative privileges on their domain to administrators in other trusted domains like MTIT. This is because CHICAGO "trusts" MTIT, meaning the administrators in CHICAGO are willing to trust their equipment to their counterparts in MTIT.

Actually, it's even more complicated than that (which is why we're going to so much effort concerning this trust issue, which so many administrators have trouble with when working with Windows NT). By adding the

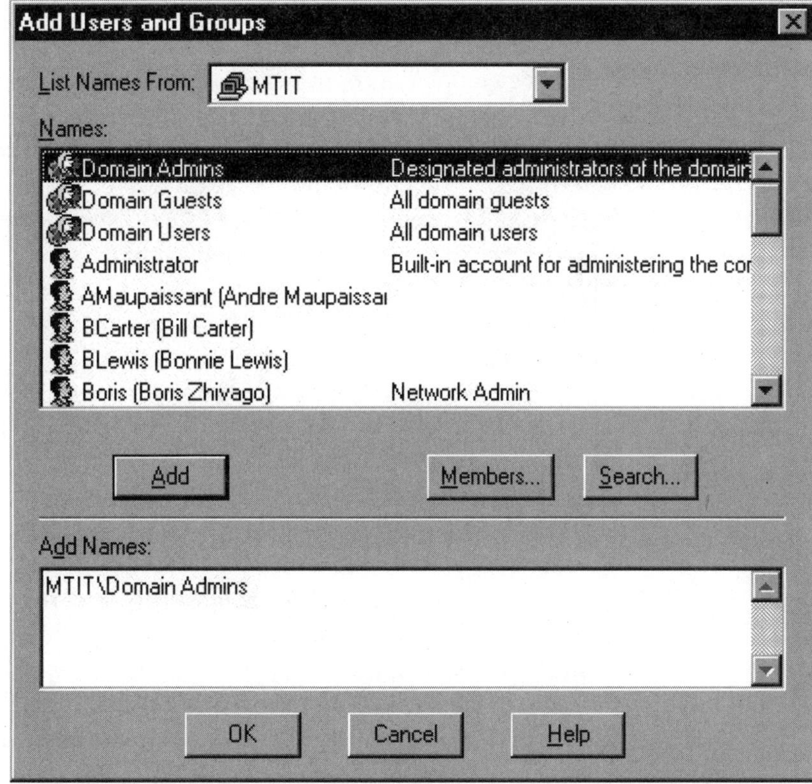

Figure 10-4 Adding the Domain Admins global group of the MTIT domain to the Administrators local group of the CHICAGO domain.

MTIT\Domain Admins global group to the CHICAGO\Administrators local group on a domain controller in CHICAGO, we've given MTIT administrators the power to administer domain controllers in CHICAGO, but not member servers in CHICAGO. This is because the Administrators local group on domain controllers is different from the Administrators local group on member servers. All Windows NT domain controllers share the same local groups, while Windows NT member servers and Windows NT workstations each have their own local groups. So if our Exchange Server BUGS in CHICAGO is a domain controller, everything is OK, but if it is a member server, you should log on to it as the Administrator and add the MTIT\Domain Admins global group to its Administrators local group.

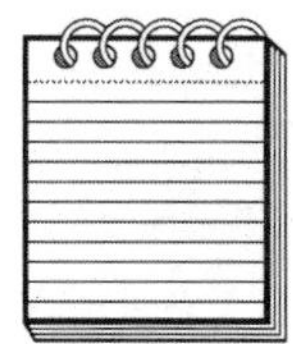

Windows NT User Administration

Administering Windows NT accounts can be frustrating and confusing. For example, if you use User Manager For Domains on a domain controller in CHICAGO (the trusting domain) and open the property sheet for the Administrators local group, you can see that one of the members of this *group is now the Domain Admins global group in the MTIT domain (signified as MTIT\Domain Admins). But if you use User Manager For Domains on a domain controller in MTIT (the trusting domain), there is no obvious way to tell that the MTIT\Domain Admins global group is indeed a member of the CHICAGO\Administrators local group. However, there is actually a way. You need to choose Select Domain from the User menu, select the CHICAGO domain, click OK, open CHICAGO\Administrators, and you can view it there. The system of domains and trusts used by Windows NT is complicated to administer, unless you use only one domain for your whole enterprise, which unfortunately doesn't scale very well past several thousand users. Windows 2000 with its Active Directory will be more straightforward for administering accounts in an enterprise once we've unlearned everything we've learned about domains and trusts in Windows NT and learned the new meaning of these terms in Windows 2000.*

Finally, we need to assign Boris the Permissions Admin role for the Organization, Site, and Configuration containers in Chicago. Start the Exchange Administrator program on BUGS, open the property sheet for each of these containers in turn, and select their Permissions tab (you may have to use Tools, Options to make this tab visible first). On each Permissions tab, click Add, select the MTIT domain in the List Names From drop-down box, double-click on Boris (we'll assign the Permissions Admin to his individual account, instead of MTIT\Domain Admins this time), and set his role to Permissions Administrator for each of the three containers.

Boris is now a Windows NT administrator for both domains and an Exchange Permissions Administrator for both sites and the Exchange organization. Boris can therefore administer all aspects of the enterprise from his administrative workstation in Atlanta. It's now time to create the Site Connector.

Creating a Site Connector

Log on to MICKEY as Boris, start Exchange Administrator, and note that there is only one Site container visible, namely Atlanta. This is because there is no connector installed yet to join the Atlanta site to the Chicago site, so MICKEY knows nothing of BUGS at this time. And even once we install the Site Connector, MICKEY will only know how to send mail to BUGS. The directory hierarchy on BUGS won't appear on MICKEY until we create a Directory Replication Connector in the next chapter.

Select File, New Other, Site Connector from the menu. A dialog box may appear, informating you that "Connections cannot be created in the selected parent container. Do you want to switch to the 'Connections' container of site 'Atlanta'?" Click OK to close the box and the New Site Connector dialog box now appears (see Figure 10-5).

Note that you cannot browse to a server in the site you want to connect to; instead, you must manually enter the name of an Exchange Server in the target site. Type "BUGS" without the quotes and click OK. A dialog box will flash, saying that MICKEY is attempting to connect to the remote server, and if the connection succeeds, the initial property sheet for the Site Connector (CHICAGO) appears (see Figure 10-6).

New Site Connector

Enter the name of a server in the target site:

OK

Cancel

Help

Figure 10-5 Creating a new Site Connector.

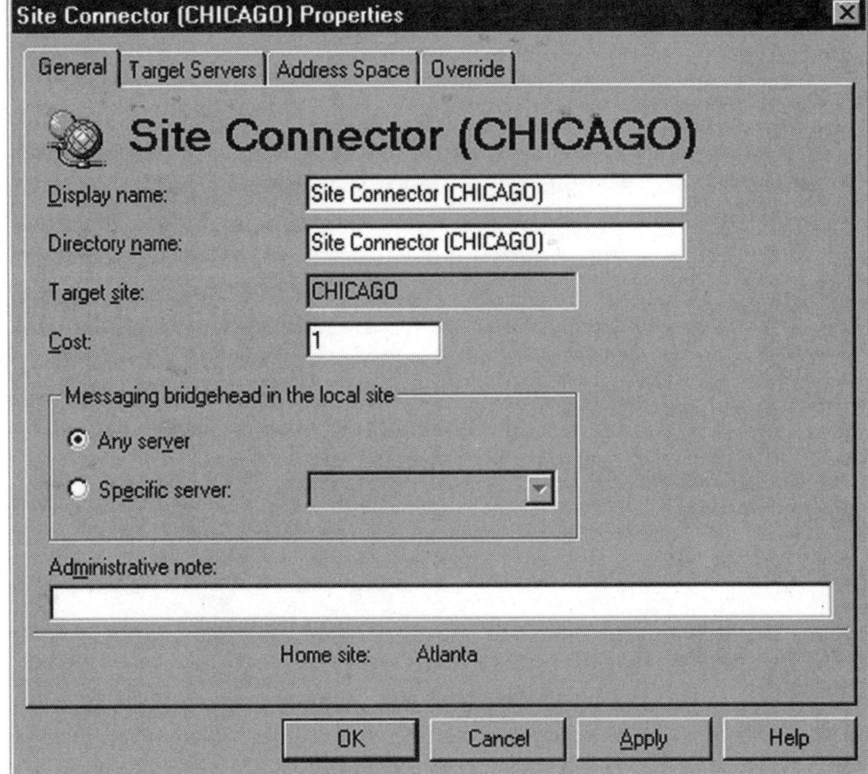

Figure 10-6 Initial property sheet for the new Site Connector, which is in the process of being created.

The name "Site Connector (CHICAGO)" might confuse you. After all, isn't Boris currently connected with Exchange Administrator to the server MICKEY, which is in site Atlanta? What "Site Connector (CHICAGO)" actually means is that you are creating a Site Connector in Atlanta that will provide messaging connectivity with an Exchange server located in the Chicago site (not the CHICAGO domain, but it's the same thing here anyway). To make this crystal clear for ourselves, let's change the display name from "Site Connector (CHICAGO)" to "Site Connector to Chicago." We only have one Exchange Server in the Atlanta site (MICKEY), but let's specify MICKEY anyway as the messaging bridgehead server in the local site using the option button and drop-down box on the General tab. Leave the Cost at 1 since there will only be one path for messages to be routed between the sites for now.

Move to the Target Servers tab. Since we initially specified BUGS as the target server in the remote site Chicago, BUGS shows up in the Target Servers listbox on the right. If there were other Exchange Servers in Chicago, these would show up in the Site Servers listbox on the left. Since there is only one possible target server for now, we can leave the Target Server Cost at the value 1 as well.

Go to the Address Space tab and view the address space for the remote site you are connecting to, which should look something like this:

```
X400    c=US;a= ;p=MTIT;o=CHICAGO;    1    Organization
```

What this means is that this Site Connector we are creating can be used by anyone in the entire Exchange organization, even users in sites other than Atlanta and Chicago (if we had any), in order to route messages with an X.400 destination address that are located in the Chicago site. In other words, at this point, the connector can only be used to send messages to Chicago (not any other sites, if we had them) and only if you use the X.400 address of the target recipient (using SMTP or MS Mail addresses won't work). Thus, we could use this connector to send a message to a recipient in Chicago that had the X.400 address:

```
c=US;a= ;p=MTIT;o=CHICAGO;s=Smith;g=John;
```

but the connector can't handle an X.400 address like

```
c=US;a= ;p=MTIT;o=MIAMI;s=Jones;g=Mary;
```

or any SMTP address such as

```
jsmith@chicago.mtit.com
```

By default, when we create a new Site Connector, an X.400 address space to the remote site is created automatically for the connector. We could create additional address spaces for the connector if we would like to enable it to forward messages to other target sites or use other types of email, but we'll leave this topic for a later chapter when we look at message routing.

Now go to the Override tab. Since the service account for Atlanta lacks Service Account permissions in the remote site (we could have assigned such permissions earlier when we were using Exchange Administrator on BUGS, but we didn't), we'll have to enter the service account information into this tab for the remote Chicago site, namely the account name Exsrv, the password, and the domain name CHICAGO (see Figure 10-7).

It's time to finish the process. Click OK to close the Site Connector to the Chicago property sheet. A dialog box appears saying, "Should a site connector be created in the remote site 'CHICAGO'?" Of course! That's why we gave Boris the necessary Windows NT and Exchange permissions in the

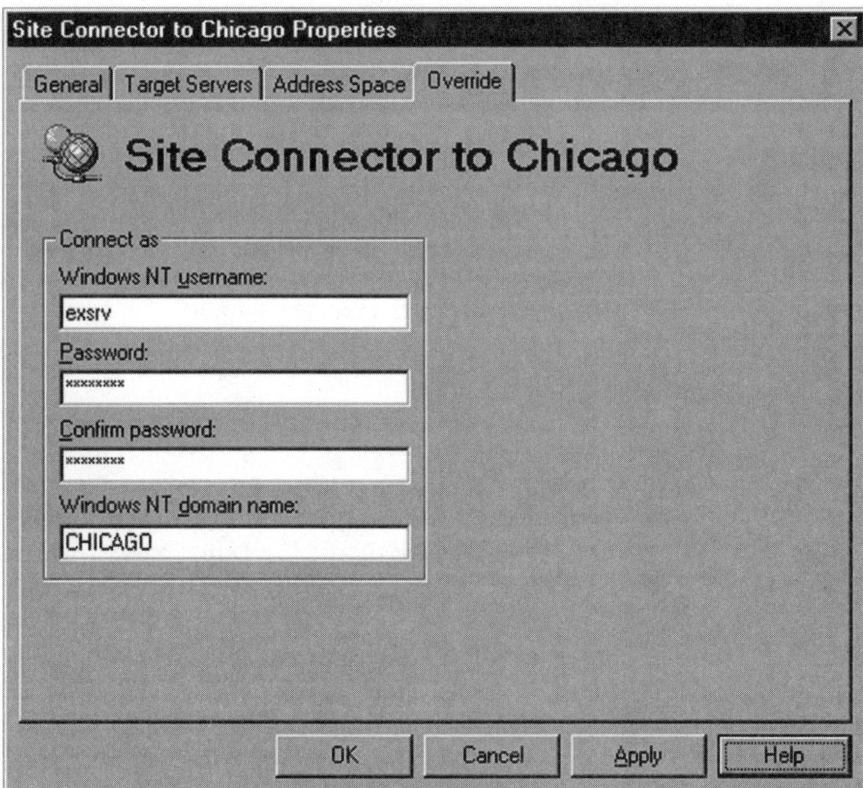

Figure 10-7 Overriding the local service account.

first place, so everything could be administered by Boris from a single location in Atlanta. If we click No, then an administrator in CHICAGO with the Permissions Admin role for Chicago would have to create and configure the other side of the Site Connector we are creating.

So click Yes, which opens the Site Connector (Atlanta) initial property sheet. We are now configuring the other side of the Site Connector between Atlanta and Chicago. Change the display name to "Site Connector to Atlanta," specify BUGS as the messaging bridgehead server, then go to the override, enter the service account ExchangeService for the MTIT domain, and click OK. The Site Connector has now been created.

Testing the Site Connector

Let's see if it works. First, let's get Outlook 2000 working on the machine we installed it on in Chicago (we actually installed it on BUGS prior to installing Exchange on the machine). Log on to BUGS with one of the administrator accounts you created in CHICAGO. We'll chose PJames, which is the account we created for Peter James, a member of the CHICAGO\Domain Admins global group. Start Outlook 2000 for the first time. Windows Installer will initialize and a wizard called Outlook 2000 Startup will guide you through the process of configuring Outlook. (In other words, we don't have to use the Mail utility in the Control Panel to create a Windows Messaging Profile for Peter prior to running Outlook; the wizard will guide us through this process.) Click Next and select Corporate or Workgroup (this choice allows Exchange to function as our back-end messaging service; refer back to Chapter 7 for more information). Click Next and a User Name dialog box will appear, prompting you for the user's full name and initials (see Figure 10-8).

Click OK and the Microsoft Outlook Setup Wizard opens. This is the same wizard that would have appeared had we used the Mail utility in the Control Panel to previously create a Windows Messaging profile for our user. Select the option to Manually Configure Information Services and click Next. Give the profile the name Peter. Click Next and then add and select Microsoft Exchange Server as the information service you want to add. Click OK and specify BUGS for the Exchange Server and Peter James for the mailbox, which will be associated with the new messaging profile. Click the Check Name button, and if you didn't enter a typo, the two entries should now be underlined. Click OK twice, followed by Finish, and you're done creating a messaging profile for Peter James. At this point, a dialog box may appear saying, "Outlook is not currently your default manager for

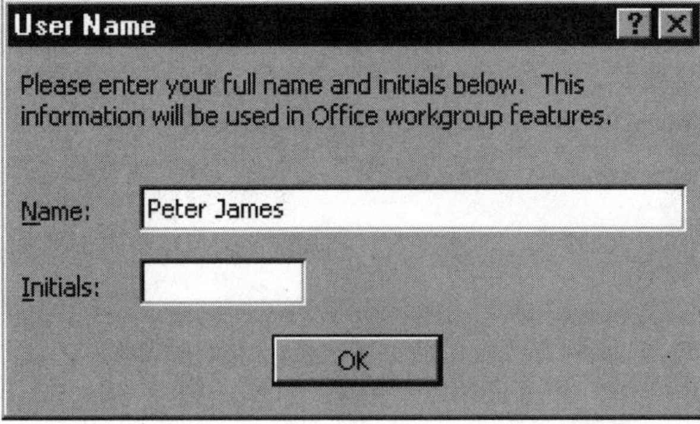
User Name
Please enter your full name and initials below. This information will be used in Office workgroup features.
Name:
Peter James
Initials:
OK

Figure 10-8
Enter the full name and initials of the Outlook 2000 user.

Mail. Would you like to register Outlook as the default manager?" Click Yes and Outlook 2000 is up and running. Test it by having Peter send a message to himself.

Now we want to see if Peter can send a message to Boris in Atlanta. Click the Address Book button on the toolbar and notice that Boris is not listed. In fact, no recipient from Atlanta is listed. Why? Because directory replication has not yet been set up between the two sites, so each site maintains its own separate copy of the Exchange directory, and each site's directory only contains information about that site alone. To have Peter send a message to Boris, we'll have to manually enter Boris' address, using what is called a one-off address (use it once and send it off).

To determine Boris' address, go to MICKEY in Atlanta, start Exchange Administrator, open the property sheet for Boris' mailbox, and switch to the E-mail Addresses tab. You'll see Boris' various email addresses listed there. We'll use his X.400 address (because the Site Connector we created has an X.400 address space configured for it) that should look something like this:

```
C=US;a= ;p=MTIT;o=Atlanta;s=Zhivago;g=Boris;
```

Note the space after the `a=` part of the address. Double-click on this X.400 address to open the X.400 Address Properties sheet, which shows the fields of this address in more detail (see Figure 10-9).

Go back to Outlook 2000 on BUGS and click the New button on the toolbar to open an untitled new message window. Click the To button to open the Select Names dialog box, and there click the New button to open the New Entry dialog box. To create a one-off address, select the In This Message Only option under Put This Entry, and highlight X.400 Address as the type of one-off address we will create (see Figure 10-10).

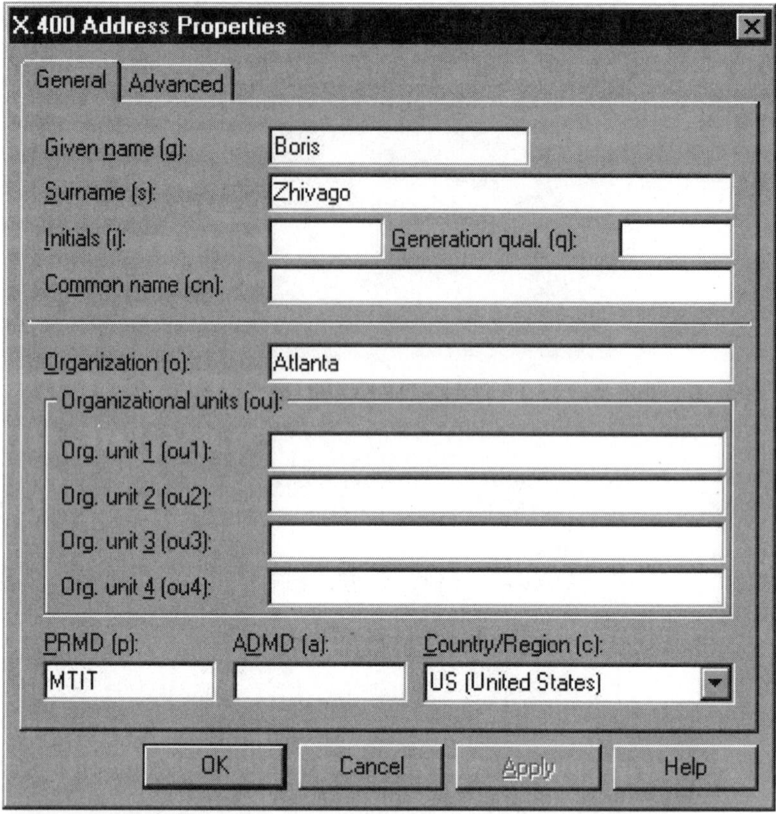

Figure 10-9 The X.400 Address Properties for Boris Zhivago.

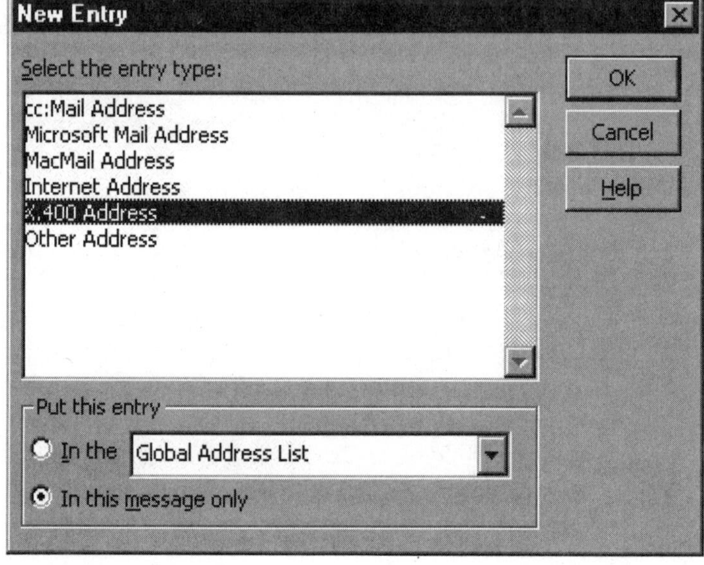

Figure 10-10 Choosing the type of one-off address to create in Outlook 2000.

Click OK to open the New X.400 Address Properties sheet. Fill in this sheet the same as the X.400 Address Properties sheet for Boris, shown in Figure 10-9 (don't forget the single space character in the ADMD field), giving it the display name "Boris in Atlanta." Then click "Add to: To" at the bottom to place this address in the To field of Peter's new message. Add a Subject like "Hi from Chicago" and add a short message like "Hope this dang connector thing works!" Then click the Options button on the toolbar and mark the checkbox to request a delivery receipt of the message. Now send Peter's message from Boris and if messaging connectivity through the Site Connector works, you should see a delivery recipient in Peter's inbox (see Figure 10-11). If you want to confirm this, log on to GOOFEY as Boris and start Outlook 98 and you should see Peter's message.

Cleaning Mailboxes

To finish things off, let's clean up Boris' mailbox by deleting unnecessary messages from it. This can be done by logging on to GOOFEY, starting Outlook, and deleting any unnecessary messages. However, there is another way mailboxes can be cleaned up: using Clean Mailbox from the Tools menu

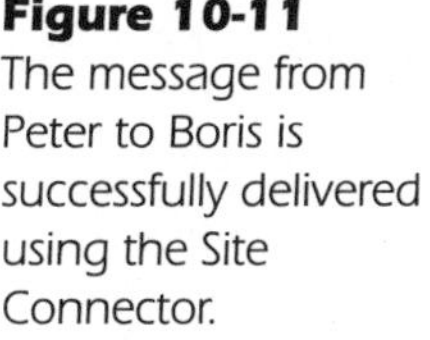

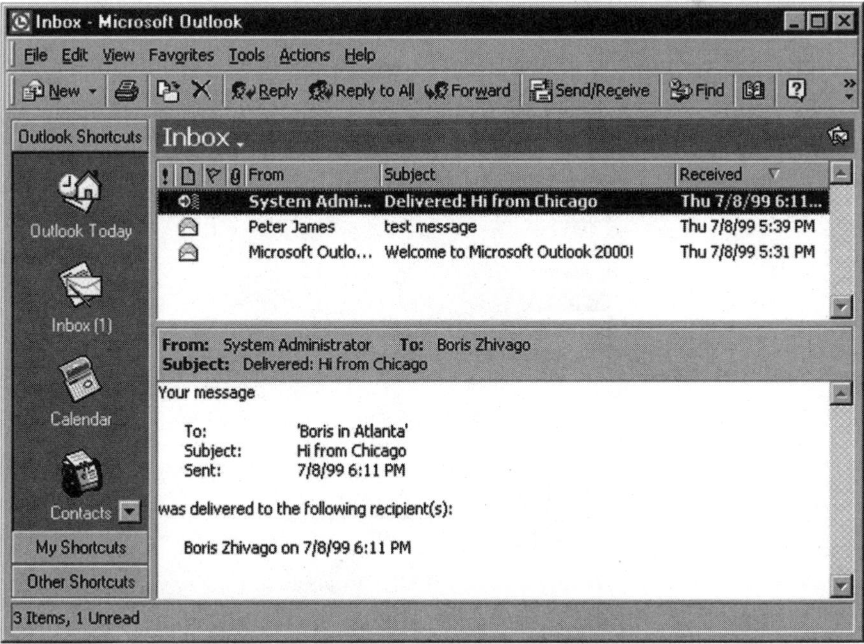

Figure 10-11 The message from Peter to Boris is successfully delivered using the Site Connector.

in Exchange Administrator (see Figure 10-12). Clean Mailbox gives administrators the power to wreak havoc with users' messages, so use it wisely and sparingly. One reason for using this tool might be to free up space in the private information store when disk space becomes low. A better solution would probably be to add an additional disk or configure mailbox quotas.

Start Exchange Administrator, select Boris Zhivago from the Recipients container, and select Clean Mailbox from the Tools menu. This opens the Clean Mailbox dialog box. Just to be ruthless, let's clean all the messages out of Boris' mailbox, so select the following settings:

- Delete messages older than 0 days (Received date) and greater than 0 K
- Both read and unread items
- All sensitivities
- Delete folder information
- All default types
- All custom message types
- Delete items immediately

Clean Mailbox

Messages
Older than (in days): 0
Based on:
Last modified date
Received date
Greater than (K): 0

Default types
Calendar
Journal
Notes
Contacts
Tasks
E-Mail messages

Read items
Read items
Unread items
Both read and unread items

Custom message types
None
All
User defined

Sensitivity
Normal
Private
Personal
Confidential

Action
Delete items immediately
Move items to deleted items folder

Delete folder associated information

OK Cancel Help

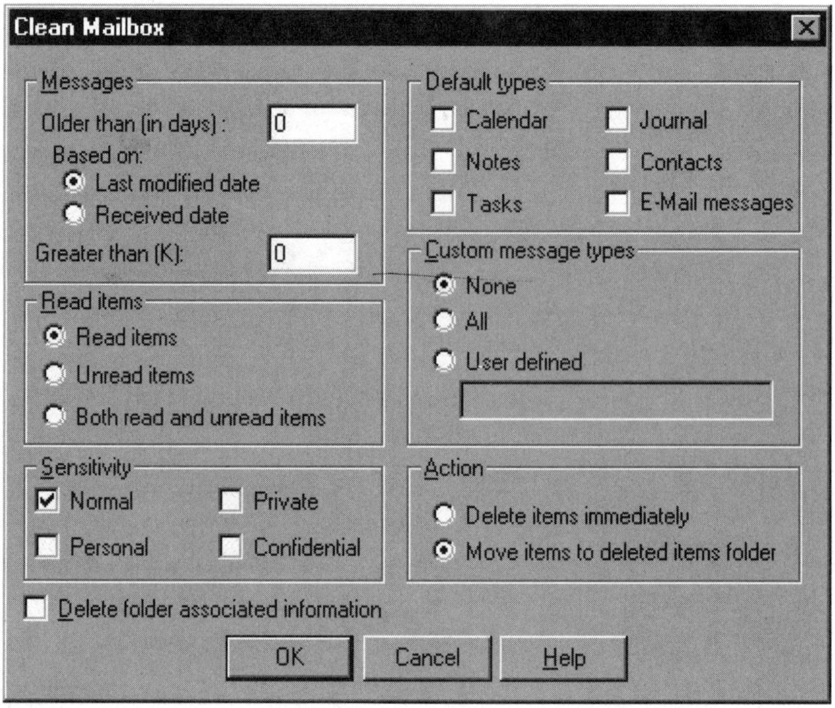

Figure 10-12 The Clean Mailbox command in Exchange Administrator.

Click OK to clean Boris' mailbox of all messages. Start Outlook as Boris and verify that all personal folders are empty of messages, contacts, tasks, and appointments.

Where Do We Go from Here?

Now that we have established messaging connectivity between two sites, our next task is to set up directory replication between the sites. This is the topic of the next chapter.

For More Information

The Site Connector is covered in some detail in Chapter 6 of the *Operations* manual, which is part of Exchange Books Online.

TechNet/Microsoft Web Site

A few articles in the Microsoft Knowledge Base cover the Site Connector (some of these articles apply specifically to Exchange version 4.0 but may nevertheless be of some help with version 5.5):

- Q165324. XCON: Basic Site Connector Troubleshooting Checklist
- Q190022. XCON: Comparison of X.400 and Site Connectors
- Q191594. XCON: Site Connector Not Usable Through a Firewall
- Q154624. XCON: Configuring the Site Connector Between Untrusted Domains

CHAPTER 11

Administering Directory Replication

In the previous chapter, we looked at how to establish messaging connectivity between two Exchange sites using the Site Connector. In this chapter, we consider the next logical step: establishing directory replication between two connected sites. After reading this chapter, you will have an understanding of

- The directory replication process
- The Directory Replication Connector
- Using the Exchange Performance Optimizer

The walkthrough in this chapter covers creating, configuring, and testing a Directory Replication Connector. We will also use the Message Tracking Center to track messages as they travel through our Exchange organization.

Directory Replication

We introduced the Exchange directory service and its associated directory database in Chapter 4 when we looked at the architecture and operation of the Exchange Server. For increased fault-tolerance and reliability, the Exchange directory is distributed, rather than located on a single directory server. The process by which updates to the directory on one server are copied to other servers is called directory replication.

This directory replication process for Exchange follows what is known as a multi-master model. This means that there is no master copy of the directory database located on a master server. Instead, each Exchange server is a peer with every other Exchange server with regard to directory replication, and each Exchange Server maintains a complete copy of the entire directory database for the organization. In addition to providing fault-tolerance, directory replication reduces network traffic produced by directory lookups. For example, if you were going to send mail to a recipient in a remote site, you could look up the email address of the recipient from an Exchange Server in your local site, instead of having to waste valuable inter-site WAN bandwidth looking up the address from a server in the remote site. In fact, without directory replication, there would be no way to look up the address of a recipient in a remote site at all.

Another major advantage of directory replication is that it allows administrators to manage Exchange Servers in remote sites using the Exchange Administrator program. In fact, if configured correctly, a world-wide multi-site Exchange messaging system could be managed from a single location using an administrator console running the Exchange Administrator program.

Directory Replication Models

The Exchange multi-master model for directory replication is different from the master/slave model used by the underlying Windows NT operating system itself. In this model, the database of authorized network users is managed by a single master authentication controller called a Primary Domain Controller *(PDC) and copies of this database are replicated to slave authentication controllers called* Backup Domain Controllers *(BDCs). However, the upcoming Windows 2000 operating system will use a multi-master model for directory replication between domain controllers running the active directory.*

When a change is made to the directory on one Exchange Server, that change must be passed on to all other Exchange Servers in the organization so that each server can have a complete, up-to-date copy of the entire Exchange directory for that organization. Changes are made to the directory in the following instances when

- Recipients are added, modified, or deleted
- Connectors are installed, configured, or removed
- New servers are added to existing sites
- New sites are added to the organization
- Address book views are created

and just about anything else you can do using the Exchange Administrator program. Updates to the directory are made in two different ways, however, depending on when replication takes place within a site (intra-site replication) or between sites (inter-site replication):

- *Intra-site directory replication*. Replication between servers in the same site takes place automatically about every five minutes and cannot be configured using the Exchange Administrator program. Updates are sent between servers using encrypted Remote Procedure Calls (RPCs).
- *Inter-site directory replication*. Replication between different sites is not automatic and must be configured before it will take place. A connector like the Site Connector must first be created and configured to establish messaging connectivity between the two sites. This is because Exchange sends system email messages for directory updates between sites, instead of using RPCs, as it does within a site. To enable directory replication between two connected sites, a Directory Replication Connector must be created and configured appropriately. The next section looks at how to do this.

Directory Replication Connector

Directory Replication Connectors are contained within the Directory Replication Container for a site. That's a bit confusing, but the Directory Replication Container (which itself is contained within a site's configuration container) is simply a holder for any Directory Replication Connectors you might create for establishing directory replication between that site and other sites. The Directory Replication Container itself has no interesting properties (like the connections container in the last chapter) so we'll move right on to the Directory Replication Connector itself (see Figure 11-1).

The Directory Replication Connector object is used to configure directory replication between different Exchange sites. Ensuring that the directory is up-to-date in every site is important. For example, if you create a new mailbox in your site and this information is not replicated to other sites, users

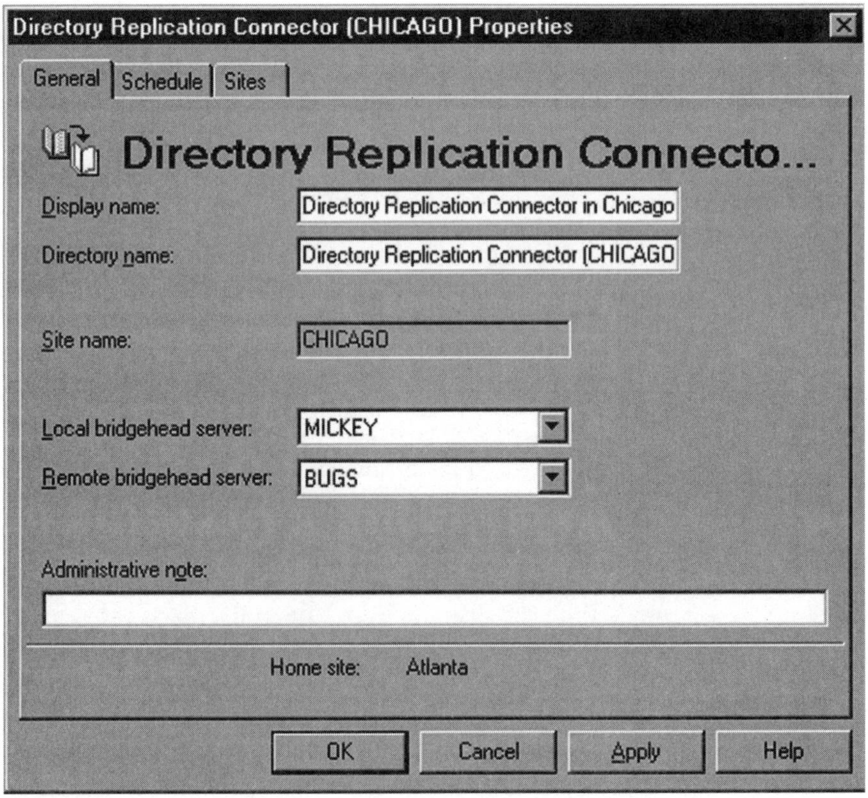

Figure 11-1 The Directory Replication Connector.

in other sites will be unaware of the existence of the new mailbox, since it won't show up in the Global Address List (GAL) for their site. Some of the settings you can configure using the property sheet for this object include the following:

- *Local and Remote Bridgehead Servers (General tab).* A bridgehead server is an Exchange server that acts as a funnel for messages going from one site to another. We used the term "messaging bridgehead server" in the previous chapter with respect to the Site Connector. In this property page, the term refers specifically to a "directory replication bridgehead server," that is, a server responsible for processing directory updates with another site, both outgoing and incoming directory replication update messages. The bridgehead server in your local site is called the Local Bridgehead Server, while the one in the other site connected to it by the Directory Replication Connector is called the Remote Bridgehead Server. A bridgehead server is the Exchange Server that makes the actual requests for directory updates from the other site, and as we mentioned previously, these inter-site directory updates actually travel from one site to the other in the form of system email messages. Once directory updates have been received by a bridgehead server, the server then distributes the updates to all other Exchange Servers in its own site using RPCs.

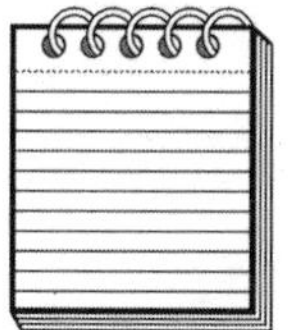

Bridgehead Servers

Note that from the point of view of an administrator in the other site, these two roles are reversed; the local server in one site is the remote server in the other site and vice versa (if you change the name of the local bridgehead server in one site, you must therefore make the same change to the remote server in the other site). Note also that there is a one-to-one correspondence between the local and remote bridgehead servers used for directory replication. You cannot have multiple target servers as you could with the Site Connector.

- *Schedule tab.* This tab lets you schedule when and how often directory replication takes place between sites. It works similarly to the Schedule tab for the Site Connector discussed in the previous chapter. If you frequently create or modify recipients, you should replicate the directory between your sites frequently, but be aware that if sites are connected by slow WAN links, then too much directory replication traffic may cause a bottleneck.

Directory Replication Schedule
You should consider the scheduling of your messaging connector when configuring a schedule for the Directory Replication Connector between two sites. For example, the Site Connector cannot be scheduled, so it doesn't matter when or how often you schedule directory replication to occur; no conflict is possible. The Dynamic RAS (DRAS) Connector can be scheduled, however, and directory replication should therefore be scheduled to occur during times when the DRAS Connector is available. Otherwise, replication will never occur.

- *Inbound and outbound sites (Sites tab).* Inbound sites are the remote sites from which your local site will be requesting the updated directory information. Outbound sites are the sites to which your site is sending directory updates (which includes your own site). These listboxes are populated automatically. Note that inbound sites include not only those remote sites that are directly connected to the local site but also remote sites that are indirectly connected through other sites.
- *Request Now (Sites tab).* This button sends a message to the selected inbound site basically saying, "If you have any directory updates, please send them to me now!" You might use this, for example, if your local site was down while changes were made to the configuration of other sites, and you want to have that information replicated immediately as soon as your local site comes back online.

Performance Optimizer

We'll now return here to briefly examine the Exchange Performance Optimizer tool first mentioned in Chapter 5. When you first install Exchange Server on a machine, you are prompted to run the Performance Optimizer utility at the end of the setup. Performance Optimizer considers the intended role of your server in your organization, analyzes your machine's hard disk subsystem and other hardware, writes optimized values of certain settings to the registry, and suggests where various Exchange Server database files should be located (see Figure 11-2).

In addition to running the Optimizer when you first install Exchange, you should also run it again whenever you

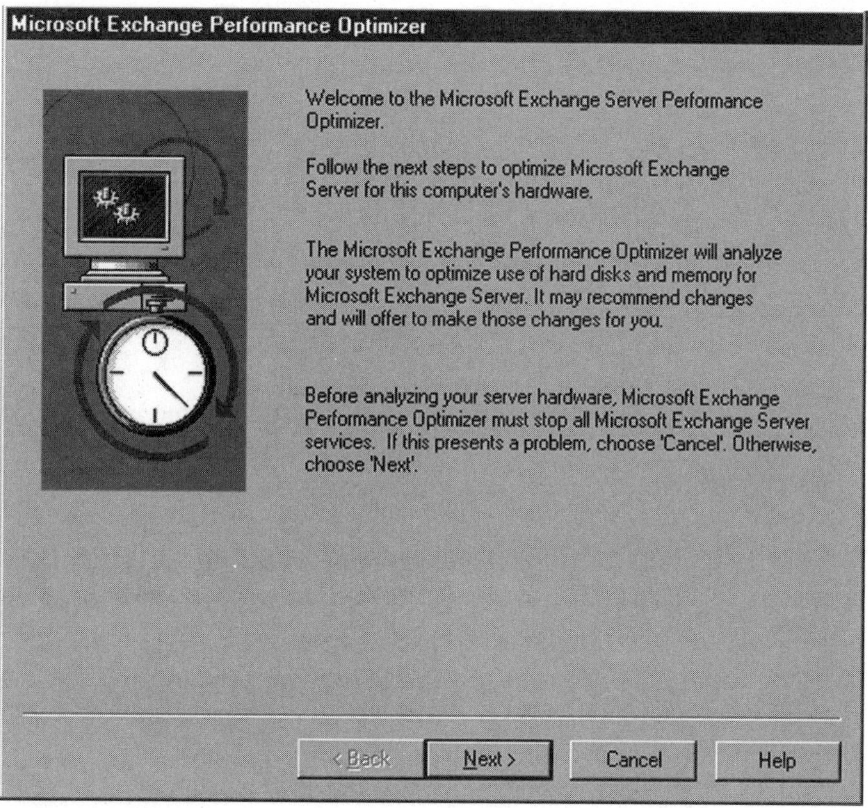

Figure 11-2 The Exchange Performance Optimizer.

- Add or remove hard disks.
- Add another CPU.
- Add more RAM.
- Add or remove a connector or gateway.
- Change the server's role, for example, making it a dedicated Public Folder Server.
- Change the server's expected load, for example, if you formerly optimized it for 500 users, but now you expect to add another 500 more.

Note that since we just installed a Site Connector in the previous chapter and will be installing a Directory Replication Connector later in this chapter, we'll need to run the Performance Optimizer afterwards, which is why we included this particular section in this chapter.

Performance Optimizer runs as a wizard that leads you step-by-step through the optimization process. We'll briefly summarize the steps involved in running this tool and will discuss it again later in this chapter's walkthrough.

After the introductory screen (refer to Figure 11-2), Performance Optimizer begins by stopping all Exchange services on the machine. The next screen of the wizard asks for input regarding the role, configuration, and expected load of the server. The settings you can select on this screen are as follows:

- Specify the number of mailboxes that will be homed on this server.
- Specify the total number of mailboxes in the entire organization.
- Specify the intended role(s) of the server by clearing or selecting checkboxes, specifically:
  - *Private Store*. This indicates that the server will host mailboxes.
  - *Public Store*. This indicates that the server will host public folder replicas.
  - *Connector/Directory Import*. This indicates that the server will be used as a backbone or bridgehead server for connecting sites together or for establishing messaging connectivity with foreign mail systems. It also indicates that the server may be used for bulk imports or exports of directory information, such as during a migration from some legacy or third-party mail system.
  - *Multiserver*. This indicates that other Exchange servers are in the organization. Only clear this option if you are running a single Exchange server for your company.
  - *IMAP4/POP3/NNTP Only*. This indicates that the server is being used for Internet mail and news only. Don't select this option if you are using MAPI clients like Microsoft Outlook.

By default, Exchange uses all available memory on the server. If you have another application running on the server, you can limit the amount of memory used by Exchange using the setting at the bottom of this screen.

After completing the wizard, Exchange services are restarted and the results of running Performance Optimizer are saved in the log file called `perfopt.log`, which is located in

```
C:\winnt\system32\perfopt.log
```

Advanced Use of Performance Optimizer
If you run Performance Optimizer in verbose mode by typing perfwiz –v at the command prompt, you will have six additional dialog boxes to play with. This is for advanced users only and is not discussed in this chapter, but sources of information covering this option can be found in the "For More Information" section at the end of this chapter.

Walkthrough: Creating and Configuring a Directory Replication Connector

Let's now walk through the process of creating and configuring a Directory Replication Connector to establish directory replication between two sites. In the last chapter, we installed a Site Connector in the Atlanta and Chicago sites and tested messaging connectivity by creating a one-off message that used an X.400 address. We will install the Directory Replication Connector in these two sites now.

First, start Exchange Administrator on MICKEY in the Atlanta site. Note that even though messages can be sent between Atlanta and Chicago, neither site has any knowledge of the other's directory. This is evident because Exchange Administrator on MICKEY shows only the Atlanta site in its directory hierarchy; the Chicago site is not visible.

To create a new Directory Replication Connector, select File, New Other, Directory Replication Connector from the menu bar. A dialog box may appear saying, "Directory Replication Connectors cannot be created in the selected parent container. Do you want to switch to the 'Directory Replication' container of site 'Atlanta'?" Click OK and the New Directory Replication Connector dialog box appears (see Figure 11-3).

The drop-down box enables us to choose the name of the remote site with which we want to establish directory replication (Chicago is the only choice here, since we only have two sites). We need to manually type in the name of a server in the remote site we want to connect to. This remote server will be the one from which MICKEY will obtain directory information concerning the remote site Chicago. The name of the remote server we will use is BUGS, our Exchange Server in Chicago. We also have to specify whether BUGS is currently on or off the network. Specifically, if BUGS is currently online, then you have the option of being able to create and configure both ends of the Directory Replication Connector in one shot, just like for the Site

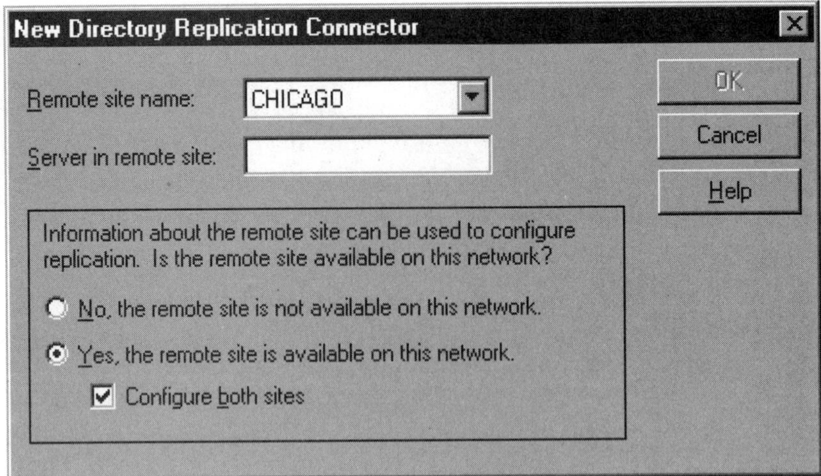

Figure 11-3 Creating a new Directory Replication Connector.

Connector in the previous chapter. If it is offline, then you can only configure the local side of the Directory Replication Connector here in the Atlanta site, and you will have to manually configure the remote side of the connector in Chicago later.

Type BUGS as the name of the remote server, choose Yes that BUGS is currently available on the network, make sure the checkbox is checked, and click OK. A new "Directory Replication Connector (CHICAGO)" property sheet opens up, so that you can configure the local side of the connector here in Atlanta (refer to Figure 11-1). Change the display name on the General tab to "Directory Replication Connector with Chicago" to make it a bit more meaningful. Note that in Atlanta the local bridgehead server will be MICKEY and the remote bridgehead server will be BUGS. It is just the opposite for the other side of the connector in Chicago. The local bridgehead server there will be BUGS, while the remote bridgehead server will be MICKEY.

Switch to the Schedule tab (see Figure 11-4) and note that directory replication between sites is configured by default to occur every three hours starting at 1 A.M. (actually 12:45 A.M. if you switch to the 15-minute view on the chart). For purposes of this walkthrough, select Always to force replication to occur every 15 minutes.

Switch to the Sites tab and notice that no inbound or outbound sites are currently defined. You don't have to specify inbound or outbound sites; these list boxes will be populated automatically once directory replication starts to occur. Click OK to create the new connector. Now wait 15 minutes (go have a mineral water or something).

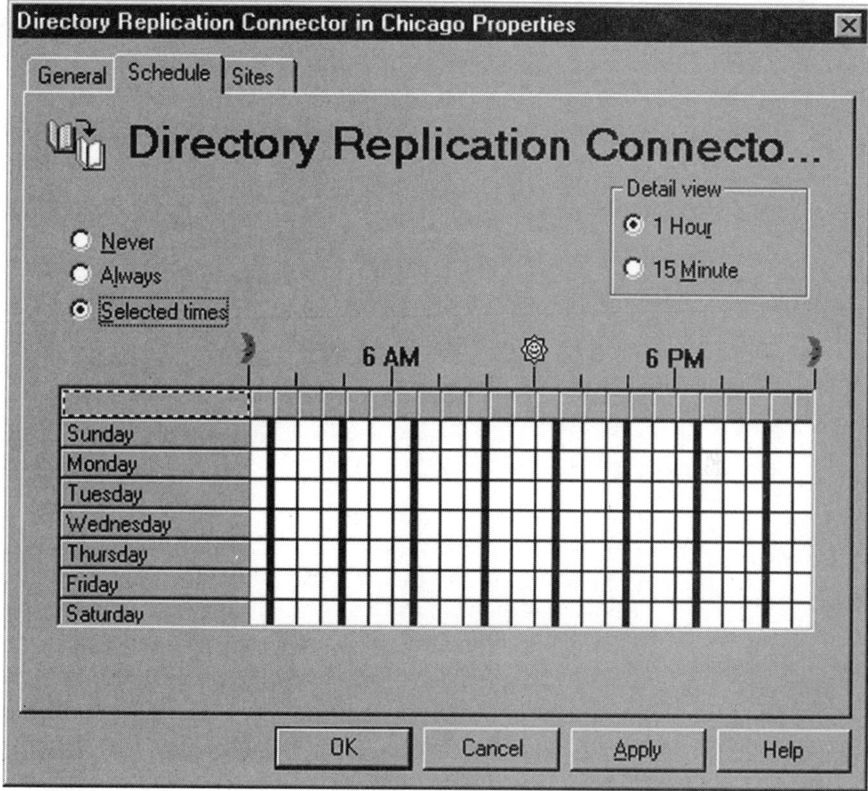

Figure 11-4 Configuring a directory replication schedule.

After a while, you may hear activity on your hard drive as the replication process starts and the directory database information is exchanged between MICKEY and BUGS. Exchange Administrator will soon automatically refresh itself, and you will now have both the Atlanta and Chicago sites visible in the Exchange directory hierarchy (see Figure 11-5).

This doesn't mean directory replication is finished. You may get an error if you try to open a property sheet in the remote site. In fact, the Exchange Administrator may get a bit sluggish as initial directory replication takes place, since a lot of database information is being replicated between the sites and your CPU is very busy because of it. Wait a few more minutes until the replication process finally completes.

Testing Directory Replication

Note in Figure 11-5 that the Atlanta site is in bold typeface, while the Chicago site is not. That means that Exchange Administrator is currently

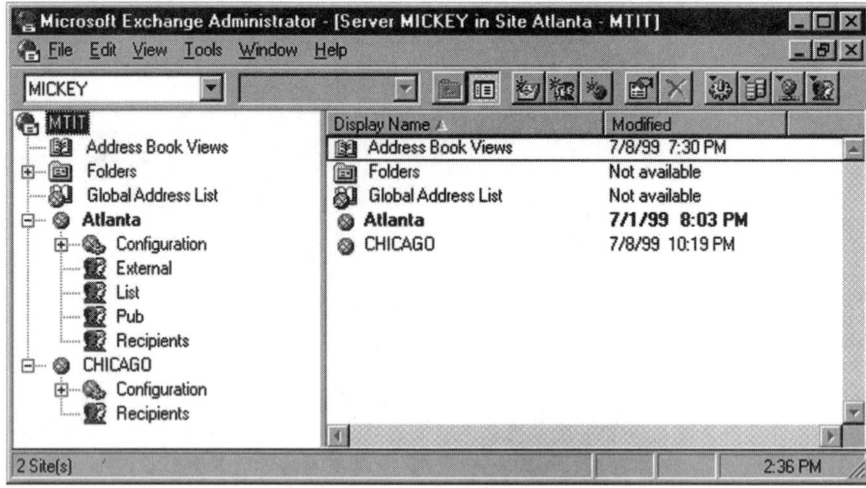

Figure 11-5 Changes to the Exchange directory hierarchy.

connected to the Atlanta site and is displaying the directory information it is obtaining from the server (MICKEY) in the local site Atlanta (see the title bar of the window as well for this information). This also means that you can only administer directory objects and their attributes within the site Atlanta using this window. You can display directory objects and their attributes also from Chicago, but you can't modify them using this window.

To see this, select the Recipients Container for Atlanta and open the property sheet for Boris Zhivago. You should be able to make changes to this property sheet, because the Exchange Administrator window you are currently using is connecting with MICKEY in Atlanta and Boris' mailbox resides in Atlanta also. Then select the Recipients Container for Chicago and open the property sheet for Peter James (or anyone else). You will get a warning first that "no mapping between account names and security IDs was done," which is generated because the Windows NT user account for Peter James is in a different Windows NT domain than the one MICKEY is in. When you click OK to close the dialog box, the property sheet for Peter James opens, but everything is grayed out and you can't modify any of the mailbox attributes. Furthermore, the primary Windows NT account for Peter is listed as \Unknown.

So why did we say earlier in this chapter that administrators could manage an entire multi-site Exchange organization from a single console running the Exchange Administrator program? You can if you open a second Exchange Administrator child window that connects to the server BUGS in the remote site Chicago. To do this, select Connect To Server from the File menu, click Browse, and select BUGS to connect with. Click OK and a second child window opens up, which obtains its directory information from BUGS, instead of MICKEY. Cascade the two windows so they look something like Figure 11-6.

Select the Recipients container in the "Server BUGS in Site CHICAGO" child window and open the property sheet for Peter James' mailbox again. This time you can modify the attributes of the mailbox in the remote site, and the primary Windows NT account shows up correctly as CHICAGO\PJames. Thus, we really can do multi-site administration from a single administrative console.

As a final test, go to the workstation in Chicago that had Outlook 2000 installed on it (this was BUGS in our setup) and start Outlook (make sure you log on as Peter James or whoever you used in Chapter 10). Click the New button to open a new untitled message window and click the To button to see who is listed in the address book. Select the Show Names drop-down box at the top right and you can see that you can select recipients from either site to send messages to (see Figure 11-7). In other words, Peter doesn't have to manually enter an X.400 one-off address for Boris in Atlanta if he wants to send Boris a message, since Boris' name shows up in the GAL, the address list for all recipients in the entire organization. Peter can also use the Show Names drop-down box to select the Recipients container in Atlanta so he won't need to scroll through names from both sites, as he does when he uses the GAL. Select Boris' name and send him a message. Then check to see if he received the message.

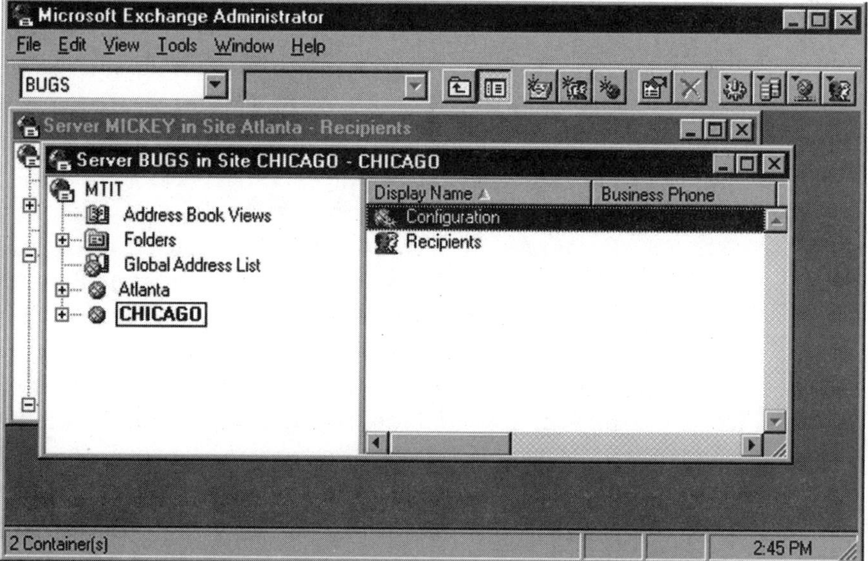

Figure 11-6 Administering both sites using Exchange Administrator.

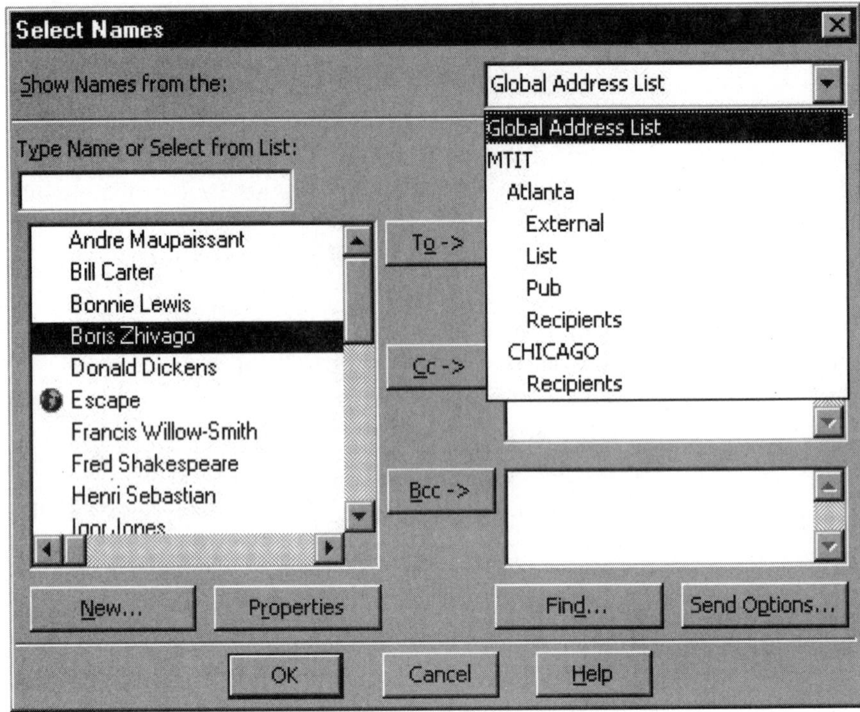

Figure 11-7 Accessing the GAL in Outlook.

Running Performance Optimizer

We should run Performance Optimizer now, since we have installed two new connectors on our servers in this chapter and the last. Installing connectors means the servers have different optimal system requirements, and the Optimizer will tune our system so it performs best on its existing hardware.

Go to MICKEY and click Start, Programs, Microsoft Exchange, Microsoft Exchange Optimizer to start the wizard. Click Next to stop the Exchange services on MICKEY and the screen shown in Figure 11-8 will appear next.

We've already explained the various options earlier in the chapter. The only change we really need to make is to select the Connector/Directory Import checkbox, but you also can modify other settings like the number of users in the site or organization. Click Next and Exchange analyzes your hard drives to determine if any changes need to be made to the location of Exchange database files. Click Next when the analysis is complete and accept the changes (if there are any) by clicking Next twice and then Finish to restart Exchange services on the machine. Run the Optimizer on BUGS as well.

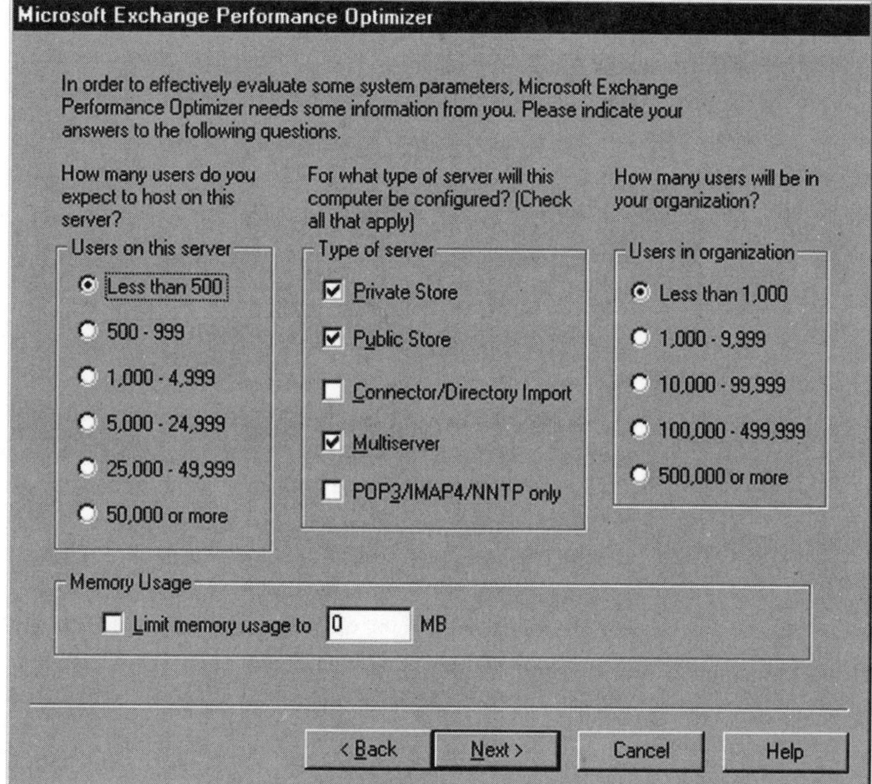

Figure 11-8 Running the Exchange Performance Optimizer.

Message Tracking

Exchange enables administrators to track messages as they travel through connectors from site to site within your organization and as they move through connectors and gateways with foreign mail systems. This lets administrators accomplish tasks like locating a specific message that might have gone astray, tracking down slow or failed connectors, determining reasons for messaging delays over specified routes, troubleshooting Exchange services and directory replications, or hunting down and deleting spam and other forms of unauthorized messages.

To track messages on Exchange, you first need to enable message tracking on the components of the servers whose activities you want to keep track of. Message tracking can be enabled on any or all of five different components on an Exchange Server (provided these components have been installed), namely on the following:

- The Information Store, using the Information Store Site Configuration object (General tab)
- The Message Transfer Agent, using the MTA Site Configuration object (General tab)
- The Internet Mail Service, using the Internet Mail Service object (Internet Mail tab)
- The Microsoft Mail Connector, using the Microsoft Mail Connector object (Interchange tab)
- The Connector for cc:Mail, using the Connector for cc:Mail object (Post Office tab)

In addition, the System Attendant object (General tab) can be used to specify how long message tracking log files are kept on a server.

When you enable message tracking on one of these components, the Exchange System Attendant service records all the component's activity in a log file covering all servers that have message tracking enabled. These tracking logs are saved with the name `yyyymmdd.log` and are located in the directory `\exchsrvr\tracking.log` on each server for which message tracking is enabled.

To analyze these tracking logs, use the Message Tracking Center. Let's open this now on MICKEY using Track Message from the Tools menu on Exchange Administrator. You are prompted to connect to an Exchange Server, so select MICKEY and set it as the default. The Message Tracking Center window opens in Exchange Administrator, and immediately a Select Message To Track dialog box appears. Cancel the dialog box to return to the main Message Tracking Center window (see Figure 11-9).

We'll look at the Message Tracking Center window in a moment, but first we must configure message tracking on some Exchange components. Using Exchange Administrator, enable message tracking on the following directory objects in both the Atlanta and Chicago sites:

- The Information Store Site Configuration object (General tab)
- The MTA Site Configuration object (General tab)

Now let's create some messages to track. Log on to GOOFEY as Boris, start Outlook 98, and have Boris send messages with the subject "Hello!" to the following recipients:

- Natasha Smith in Atlanta
- Peter James in Chicago

Now return to the Message Tracking Center and click the Search button to open the Select Message To Track dialog box again (see Figure 11-10).

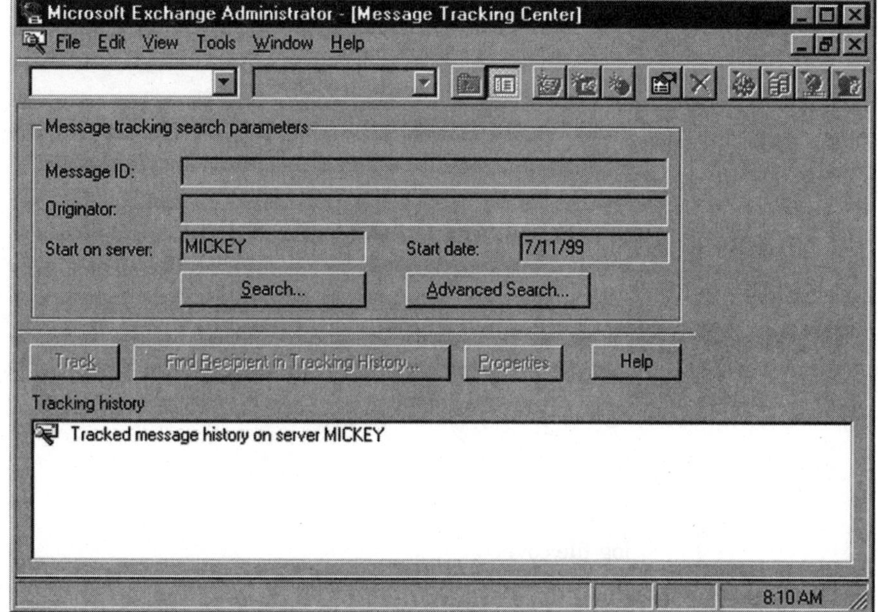

Figure 11-9 The main Message Tracking Center window.

Let's track the message to Natasha first. Click the From button and select Boris; then click the Sent To button and select Natasha. Then select Look Back 0 days, since the message was sent today. If you try to look back one day, you will be informed that a one-day-old message tracking log does not exist, but if you then click OK, it will check the current day's log and find the message. Leave Search On Server set to MICKEY (you select the server where the message you want to track originated, since that is the server where the tracking information is stored in a message tracking log) and click Find Now. The message from Boris to Natasha should show up in the listbox on the Select Message To Track dialog box, showing the date and time it was sent, its size in KB, the number of recipients, and the names of the recipients. Select the message and click Properties to open the Message Properties dialog box for the message (see Figure 11-11).

Note the information stated in this dialog box:

- *Event Type: Local Message Delivery*. The message tracking event was generated by the process of local message delivery (both Boris and Natasha have their mailboxes homed on the same server, MICKEY).
- *Transferred To: Private Information Store on MICKEY*. The message received from Boris was transferred to the Private Information Store on MICKEY.

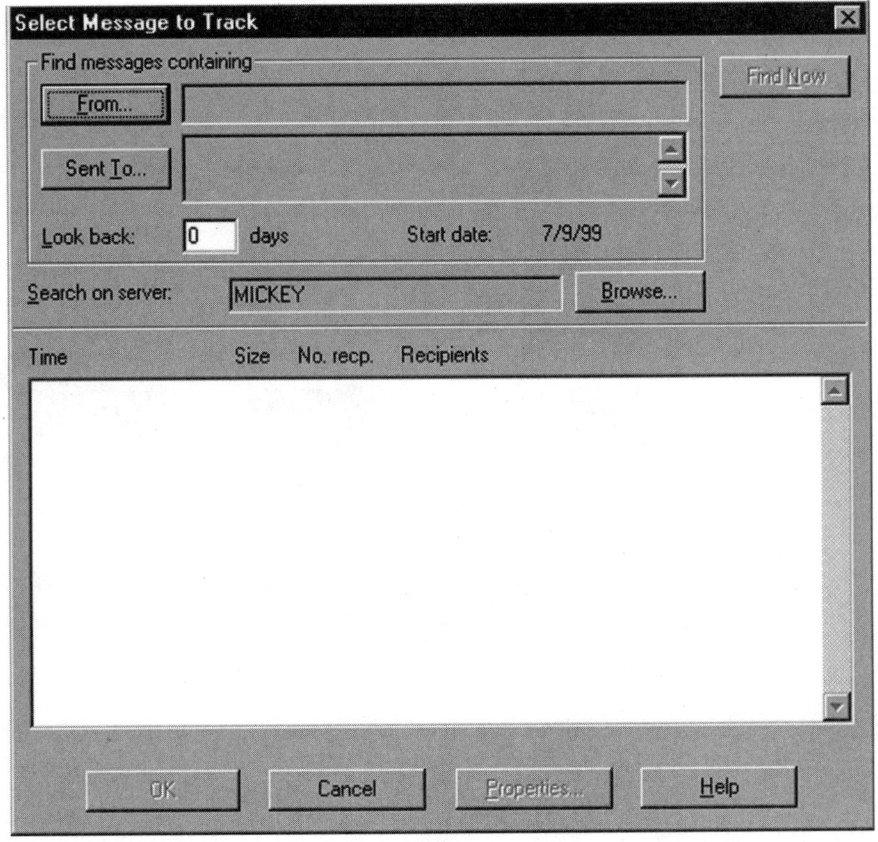

Figure 11-10 The Select Message To Track dialog box.

Refer back to Chapter 4 and you can see that this agrees with what we described concerning the process of single-server message flow. Close the Message Properties dialog box to return to the Select Message To Track box, and change the Sent To field from Natasha Smith to Peter James. Then click Find Now to locate message tracking information regarding Boris' message to Peter. Once you find the message, open its Message Properties dialog box and note that this time the following information is stated:

- *Event Type: Message Submission*. The message tracking event was generated by the process of the message from Boris being submitted for delivery to the remote recipient. (Boris and Peter have their mailboxes homed on different servers located in different sites).
- *Transferred To: Private Information Store on MICKEY*. The message received from Boris was transferred to the Private Information Store on MICKEY.

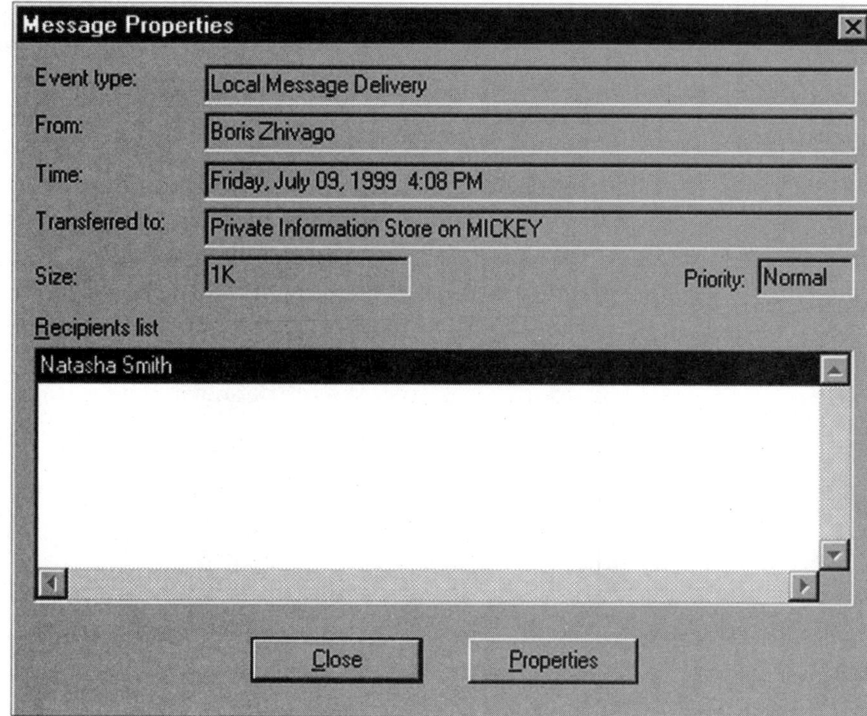

Figure 11-11 Message Properties of the message from Boris to Natasha.

We remember from Chapter 4 that when a message is sent to a recipient in a remote site, it is (1) first passed to the local Information Store (IS), which (2) passes it to the local message transfer agent (MTA), which (3) then uses a connector or gateway to forward it to an MTA in the remote site, which (4) finally transfers it to the IS on the server where the remote recipient's mailbox is homed. The information in the Message Properties dialog box shows only step 1 taking place in the above four-step process.

How do we follow the message on the rest of its route? Click the Close button on the Message Properties box to return to the Select Message To Track box, and there click OK to return to the main Message Tracking Center window, shown previously in Figure 11-9. Note that the window now displays new information regarding the message that Boris sent to Peter, specifically the Message ID of the message, a long string of characters that uniquely identifies the message to the system. A Message ID is generated by Exchange for each message routed through the mail system and remains with the message from its point of origin until it is either delivered somewhere in the Exchange organization or is passed to a gateway or connector that connects with a foreign mail system. The Message Tracking Center uses the Message ID to track the path of the message through the organization (Exchange cannot track messages after they leave the organization and enter a foreign mail system).

In the main Message Tracking Center window where the Message ID for Boris' message to Peter is displayed, click the Track button. In a few moments Exchange will have tracked the path that the message followed as it traveled from MICKEY in Atlanta to BUGS in Chicago (see Figure 11-12).

Five lines in the listbox describe the path of the message through the system (the first line is really just the title, while the remaining four lines describe the actual message history as it moves through the system). If you select each line and click Properties to open the Message Properties dialog box, you can construct the full details of the message history as follows:

- Message submitted by Boris Zhivago:
  - Event Type: Message Submission
  - Transferred To: Private Information Store on MICKEY
- Message transferred to the MTA on BUGS:
  - Event Type: Message Transfer Out

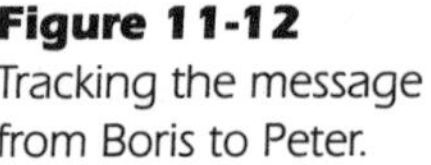

Figure 11-12 Tracking the message from Boris to Peter.

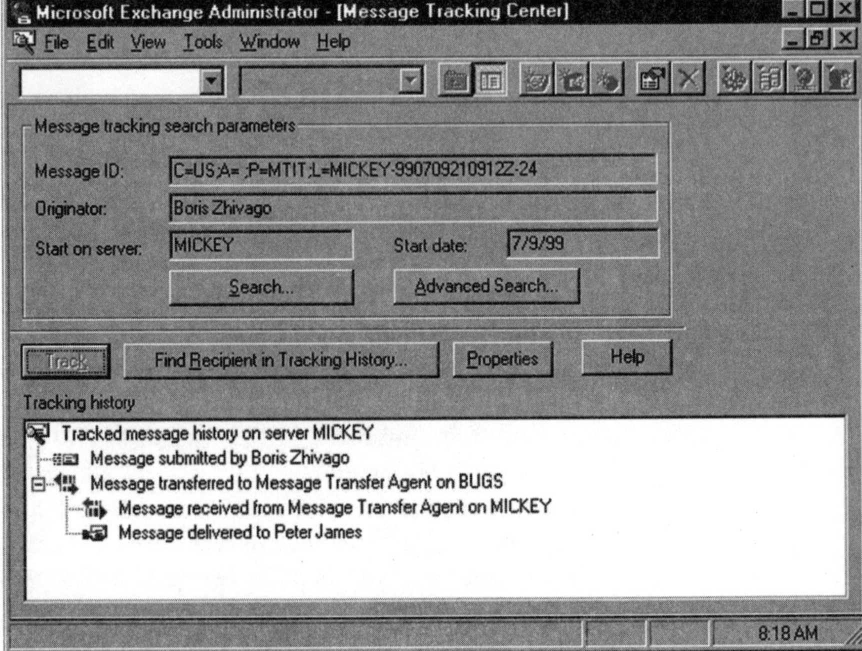

- Transferred To: MTA on BUGS
- Message received from MTA on MICKEY:
- Event Type: Message Transfer In
- Transferred To: MTA on MICKEY
- Message delivered to Peter James:
- Event Type: Message Delivery
- Transferred To: Private Information Store on BUGS

Note that these four lines correspond to the four-step delivery process described previously for a message sent from one site to another.

Advanced Message Tracking

The main Message Tracking Center window has an Advanced Search button that enables you to perform additional search functions. If you click Advanced Search, you are presented with three choices:

- *Find message sent by Microsoft Exchange Server*. This enables you to search for system messages sent by different Exchange components like the directory, Information Store, System Attendant, and so on. Using this, you could track directory replication messages if there is a problem with directory replication.
- *Find message transferred into this site*. This lets you track messages that enter your site via a connector or gateway from a foreign mail system.
- *Find message by Message ID*. This enables you to track a message that has a Message ID you specify. You can find the Message ID in Microsoft Outlook by opening the message in a separate message window, selecting Properties from the File menu to open the property sheet for the message, and selecting the Message ID tab.

Let's see if we can track directory replication messages, which we can create by forcing a directory replication to occur between Atlanta and Chicago. In Exchange Administrator, switch to the main window using the Window menu, find the Directory Replication Connector with the Chicago object in the directory hierarchy, open the property sheet for this connector, and select the Sites tab (see Figure 11-13).

Select the only inbound site displayed (Chicago) and click the Request Now button to force a directory update to occur (see Figure 11-14). You now are presented with two choices.

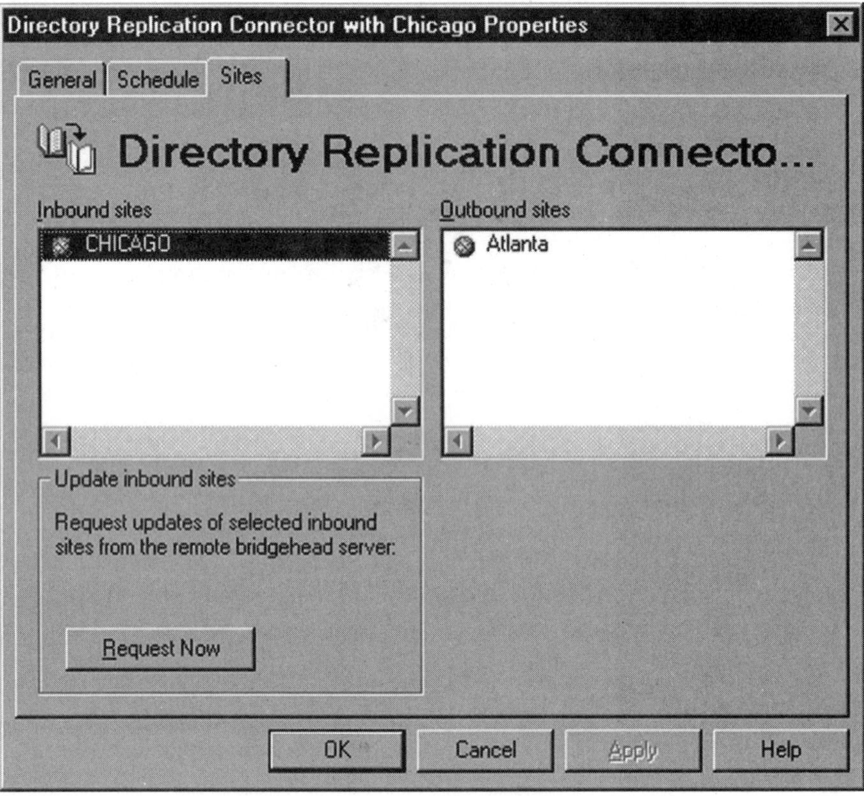

Figure 11-13 The Sites tab of the Directory Replication Connector with Chicago.

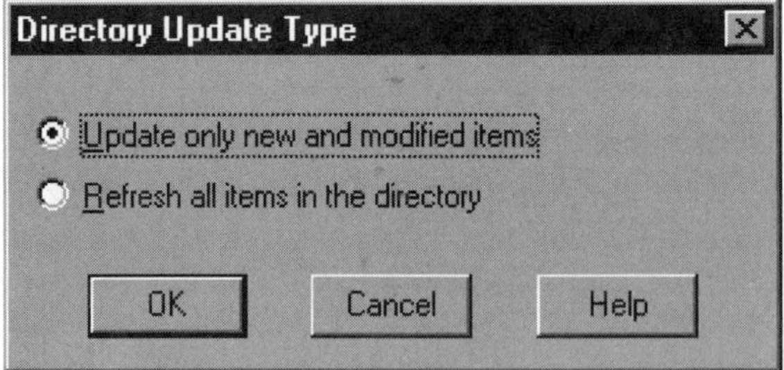

Figure 11-14 Forcing a directory replication to occur.

- You can request any updates to the directory that Chicago may have.
- You can request that Chicago replicates a complete copy of its directory with the local site.

We'll select the second option, Refresh All Items In The Directory, and click OK. A message will appear saying, "This will cause a new copy of every item for all selected inbound sites to be replicated to the local bridgehead server. The operation may take several hours to complete." However, with the single server BUGS in the remote site and only a few recipients created on it, the process will only take a few seconds. Click OK and note as the replication process takes place that the time is displayed. Make note of the time, which was 12:29 P.M. on my system.

Now close the property sheet. After a few seconds, the hard drive will stop thrashing, indicating that the process is complete. Open the Message Tracking Center, click the Advanced Search button, and select Find Message Sent By Microsoft Exchange Server to open the Select System Message To Track dialog box. In the From field, select the Microsoft Exchange Directory, leave Look Back set at 0 days, and click Find Now. Scroll down the list of directory service system messages found, and you should find some that match the time when you forced the directory replication to occur, which in my case was 12:29 P.M. (see Figure 11-15).

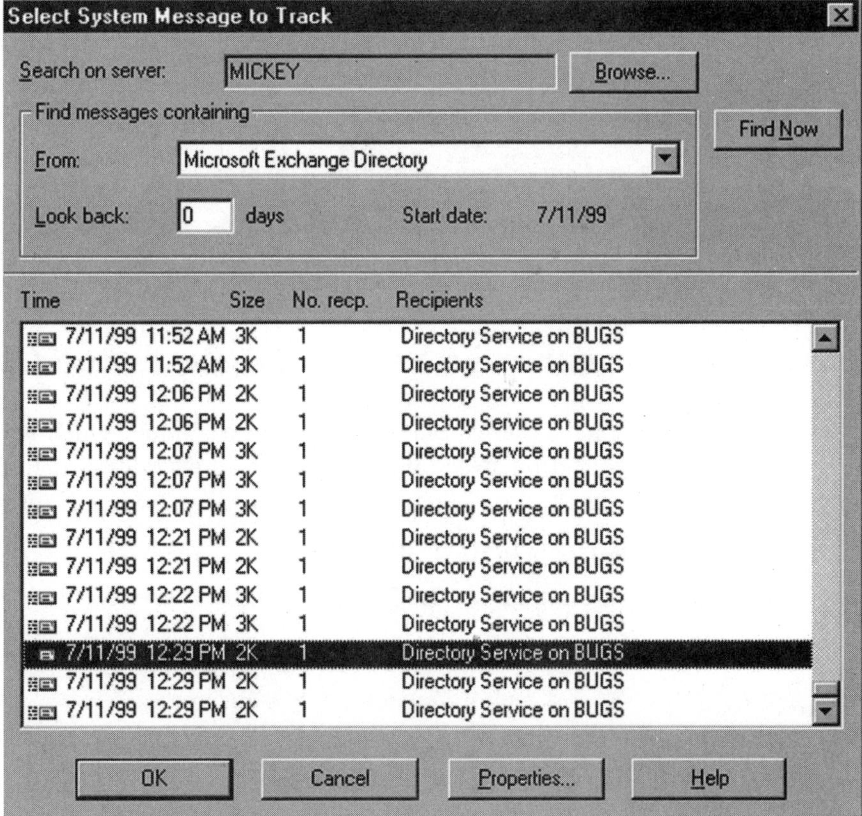

Figure 11-15 Finding directory replication messages.

Select one of the 12:29 P.M. messages, click OK to return to the main Message Tracking Center window, and click the Track button to display the message history. You should be able to trace the message, starting from the directory service on BUGS, to the MTA on BUGS, to the MTA on MICKEY, and finally to the directory service on MICKEY.

Where Do We Go from Here?

Having established messaging connectivity and directory replication between two sites in this chapter and the last, we will next move on to creating, viewing, and replicating Public Folder information between sites.

For More Information

The topic of directory replication is briefly covered in two Exchange manuals that are included in Books Online:

- *Getting Started*: Chapters 8 and 10
- *Concepts and Planning*: Chapter 7

In addition, message tracking is covered in detail in Chapter 4 of the *Maintenance and Troubleshooting* manual in Books Online.

Exchange Server 5.5 Resource Guide

The Exchange Server 5.5 Resource Guide, which is currently included as part of TechNet, contains some valuable information about topics covered in this chapter. In particular, study the following chapters:

- Chapter 10, "Optimizing Performance"
- Chapter 15, "MS Exchange Server Directory and Directory Replication"

TechNet

The Technical Notes section for MS Exchange in TechNet includes some useful articles you might want to look at. Here are the relevant titles:

- How to Replicate Exchange Server Directories Using the Internet Mail Service
- Understanding the MS Exchange Server Performance Optimizer
- MS Exchange Inter-Organization Directory Synchronization Planning Guide

CHAPTER 12

Administering Public Folders

In the last few chapters, we looked at creating and configuring Exchange sites and connecting them using the Site Connector and Directory Replication Connector. This chapter draws upon our knowledge of creating, managing, accessing, and replicating Public Folders in a multi-site Exchange organization. After reading this chapter, you will have an understanding of the following topics:

- Creating and Configuring Public Folders
- Configuring Public Folder client permissions
- Implementing Public Folder replication
- Implementing Public Folder affinity

The walkthrough in this chapter covers creating and testing Public Folders, configuring Public Folder affinity, and implementing Public Folder replication between sites.

Public Folders

A Public Folder is a recipient object in Exchange that can be used for sharing information with other users. Whereas mailboxes are usually owned by a single user, Public Folders are generally accessible to all users, or at least to specific groups of them. Thus, they can post messages with attached documents to Public Folders so others can read, modify, or delete them, depending on the client permissions assigned to the folder.

Although a mailbox resides within the private Information Store of the specific server on which the mailbox is homed, a Public Folder can have several replicas (copies) that reside in the public Information Stores of several servers in your organization. Public Folder content can be replicated between these servers so that when a user posts a message to one replica, it is soon copied to all replicas of the Public Folder throughout the organization.

Like mailboxes that exist both in the directory (where the properties of mailbox objects are stored) and in the private information store of the user's home server (where the mailbox content is stored), Public Folders also exist in two places in Exchange:

- The *Public Folder hierarchy*, which consists of top-level Public Folders and their subfolders, exists within the directory on every Exchange server in the organization (provided directory replication is configured properly).

- The *Public folder content*, which comprises the messages and attached documents that are posted to Public Folders, exist within the public information store of the server where the Public Folder was created and on other servers if replicas of the folder have been created.

Figure 12-1 shows the Exchange Administrator program running on MICKEY with the root container of the Public Folder hierarchy selected. This root container is called Public Folders and is contained within the Folders container, which itself is directly beneath the root Organization container for MTIT. Within the Public Folders container are two top-level Public Folders:

- IS-Talk, which has three sub-folders beneath it
- Sales-Talk, which has two sub-folders beneath it

You can create deeper Public Folder hierarchies with Exchange, but two levels is generally sufficient.

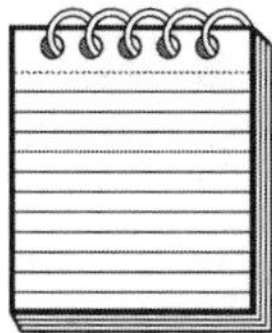

Hidden Folders

Public Folders are also contained within each site's Recipients container as hidden objects. You can make these objects visible by selecting Hidden Recipients from the View menu. The disadvantage of this view of Public Folders is that it does not show the hierarchical relationship between the folders, but instead lists them all in whatever sort order you have selected using Sort By from the View menu.

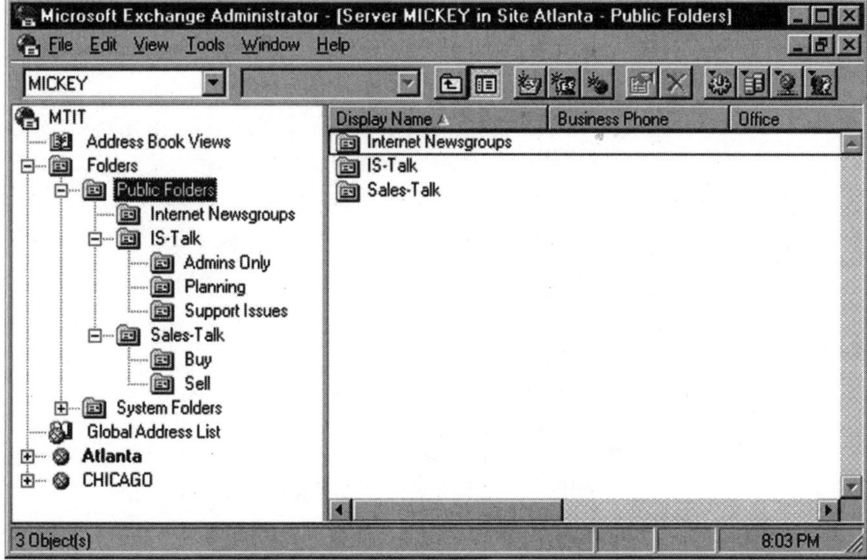

Figure 12-1
A hierarchy of Public Folders in the MTIT organization.

One thing that may seem surprising at first is that there is no facility in the Exchange Administrator program for creating Public Folders. To create a Public Folder, you have to use a client program like Microsoft Outlook. Once the folder has been created, it can be configured and managed using Exchange Administrator, although some aspects of it can also be configured using Outlook. We'll look at how to create Public Folders using Outlook later in the walkthrough of this chapter.

Public Folder Servers
Companies that make heavy use of Public Folders often configure specific Exchange Servers as Public Folder Servers. To do this, you typically delete the private information store from the server by selecting it in Exchange Administrator and clicking the Delete button on the toolbar. You would also refrain from installing any connectors or gateways on the server. Make sure you run Performance Optimizer after doing these things.

Properties of a Public Folder

Unlike mailboxes, which can essentially be completely configured using their property sheets, several different directory objects need to be used for configuring the properties and behavior of Public Folders. Figure 12-2 shows the property sheet for a Public Folder called IS-Talk, which we will create later on in this chapter.

Some of the settings you can configure using the property sheet for this object include the following:

- *Folder Name (General tab).* This is the folder's name in the directory hierarchy that is visible in Exchange Administrator and is the name given to the folder when it was created using Outlook.
- *Address Book Display Name (General tab).* This is name by which the folder appears in a client address book. It can either be the same as its Folder Name above or you can specify something different for it here.
- *Alias Name (General tab).* This is the name that can be used in the To: field of an email message for posting the message to the folder. For example, using SMTP, a client could post a message to the folder IS-Talk by sending it to the address

  `IS-Talk@Atlanta.MTIT.com.`

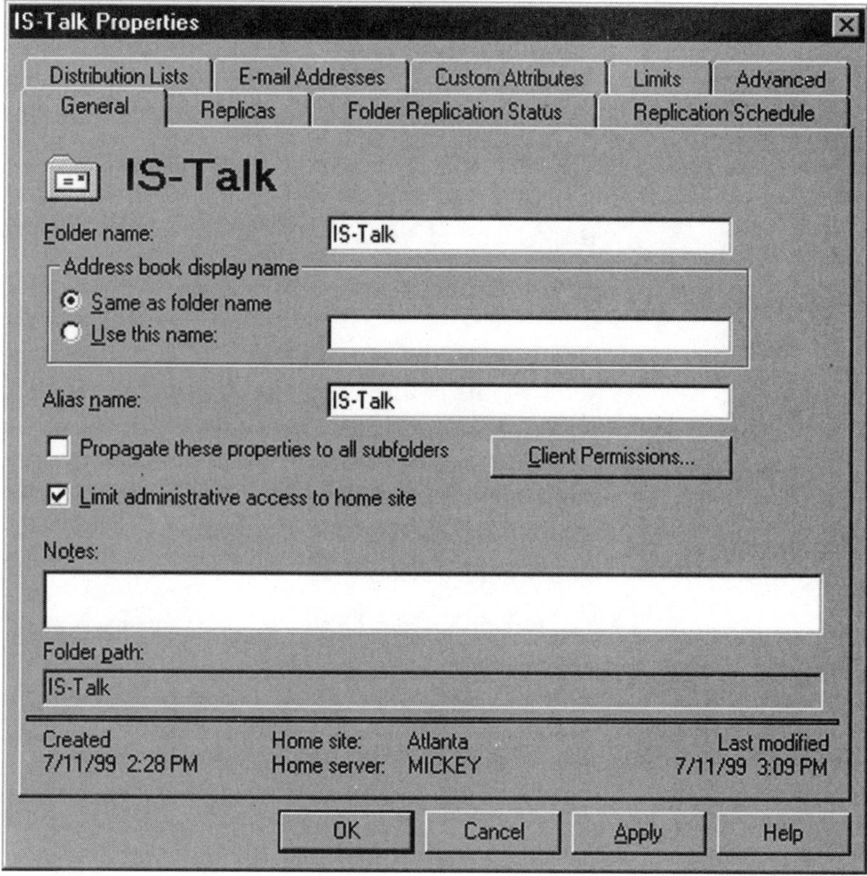

Figure 12-2 Property sheet for IS-Talk.

- *Client Permissions (General tab)*. This button enables you to set permissions for controlling access to the folder by recipients. We'll examine these in more detail in a moment.
- *Propagate these properties to all subfolders (General tab)*. Regardless of whatever changes have been made to the tab settings in a Public Folder's property sheet, selecting this checkbox can cause subfolders to inherit the attributes of their parent folder. We'll use this feature in the walkthrough.
- *Limit Administrative access to home site (General tab)*. Selecting this checkbox prevents administrators in other sites from rehoming a Public Folder from your site to theirs. It's a "hands-off" sort of setting.
- *Replicas, Folder Replication Status, and Replication Schedule tabs*. These tabs are discussed later in this chapter when we consider Public Folder replication.

- *Advanced tab*. This tab lets you configure advanced options such as the following:
  - Hide the Public Folder from the address book or unhide it if it is hidden.
  - Specify the folder's home server, which is the server on which it was created. Click the drop-down box to see the location of all replicas of this folder and specify which server will be the folder's home server.
  - The Trust level is discussed in a later chapter when we discuss Microsoft Mail connectivity.
  - Configure the priority level for replication messages used to replicate the contents of this folder to other servers. Options include Normal, the default priority; Urgent, which specifies that replication messages for that Public Folder are to be prioritized as urgent; and Not Urgent, which specifies that replication messages will have a low priority.
  - Container Name is the name of the recipients container where the Public Folder is located.

The remaining tabs on this property sheet are similar to those of mailbox objects and are easily understood. Refer back to Chapter 6 if you have any questions regarding them.

Client Permissions

Client permissions determine which users are allowed to access Public Folders and what level of access they will have. Client permissions are different from the administrative permissions discussed in Chapter 5 that govern access to the properties of directory objects in Exchange Administrator. The client permissions for a Public Folder can be viewed and modified in two different ways:

- Select the folder in the Exchange Administrator window, switch to the General tab, and click the Client Permissions button (see Figure 12-3).
- Right-click on the folder in the Folder List window in Microsoft Outlook, select Properties to open its property sheet, and switch to the Permissions tab.

To grant client permissions to recipients, click the Add button, which opens a list of all the recipients in the Global Address List (GAL) of your organization, and assign the recipient a role. These roles are different from

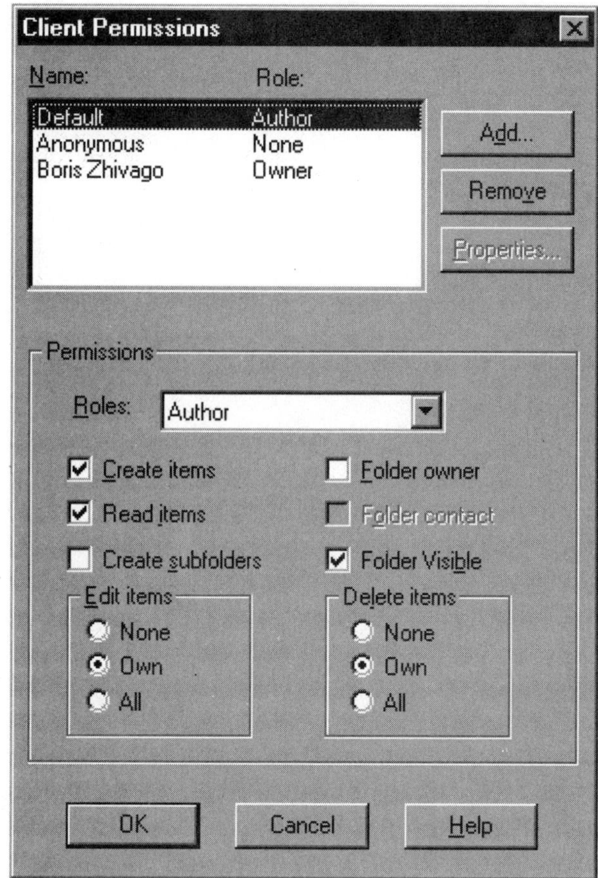

Figure 12-3 Client permissions dialog box.

the roles described in Chapter 5 and are summarized in Table 12-1. The roles are comprised of different sets of raw client permissions, which are summarized in Table 12-2. You can also define a custom role for a recipient by individually specifying the raw client permissions for a recipient. We'll look at client permissions again in the walkthrough for this chapter.

Public Folder Replication

When users in your organization try to connect to a Public Folder and read messages posted to it, they may have to cross site boundaries or even slow WAN links to access the contents of the Public Folder. For this reason, it is

Table 12-1 Roles for Client Permissions.

Role	Client Permissions							
	Create items	Create subfolders	Folder owner	Folder contact	Folder visible	Read items	Edit items	Delete items
Owner	√	√	√	√	√	√	All items	All items
Publishing Editor	√	√			√	√	All items	All items
Editor	√				√	√	All items	All items
Publishing Author	√	√			√	√	Own items	Own items
Author	√				√	√	Own items	Own items
Non-editing Author	√				√	√		Own items
Reviewer					√	√		
Contributor	√				√			
None					√			

Table 12-2 Individual Client Permissions.

Client Permission	Allows users to . . .
Create items	Create items in the folder
Create subfolders	Create new subfolders in the folder
Folder owner	Be the folder's owner
Folder contact	Be the recipient contacted when notification messages are generated for the folder by the information store
Folder visible	View the folder in the folder hierarchy
Read items	Read items in the folder
Edit items items)	Edit items in the folder (either All items or the user's Own
Delete items	Delete items in the folder (either All items or the user's Own items)

sometimes advantageous to create replicas of Public Folders. A replica is a copy of the contents of a Public Folder that is stored on a different server's public information store. If a Public Folder has replicas, then the original Public Folder is also called a replica. In other words, there is no master replica of a Public Folder. Replicas are maintained across different servers within a site and across different sites by the process called Public Folder replication, which is similar to directory replication.

Creating replicas for Public Folders can have some advantages, allowing you to

- Load-balance access to several Public Folder servers.
- Distribute Public Folder content to other geographical locations.
- Provide a hot backup of Public Folder contents.

Creating and managing replicas of Public Folders in Exchange can be done in two different ways:

- *Globally* for all Public Folders using the Public Information Store property sheet
- *Individually* for each Public Folder using the Public Folder's own property sheet

Let's first consider how to globally configure Public Folder replication using the Instances, Replication Schedule, Folder Replication Status, Server Replication Status, and Advanced pages of the Public Information Store object that was previously mentioned in Chapter 9. Specifically, the significant settings are as follows:

- *Instances tab*. This creates a replica of a Public Folder on a different server within the public Information Store of the server selected in the Exchange Administrator window. Just select the site where the folder is located, choose a folder in that site, and click Add (see Figure 12-4). The right-hand listbox shows all Public Folders that have replicas in the public Information Store of the selected server, while the left-hand listbox shows folders in different sites that do not have replicas on the selected server.
- *Replication Schedule tab*. This tab governs the schedule for replicating Public Folder replicas in the selected server's public Information Store.
- *Age Limits*. This tab lets you configure a maximum duration for how long items remain in Public Folders, after which they are deleted. This prevents Public Folders from getting clogged with tons of old information that nobody uses.

Figure 12-4
The Instances tab on the Public Information Store property sheet on MICKEY.

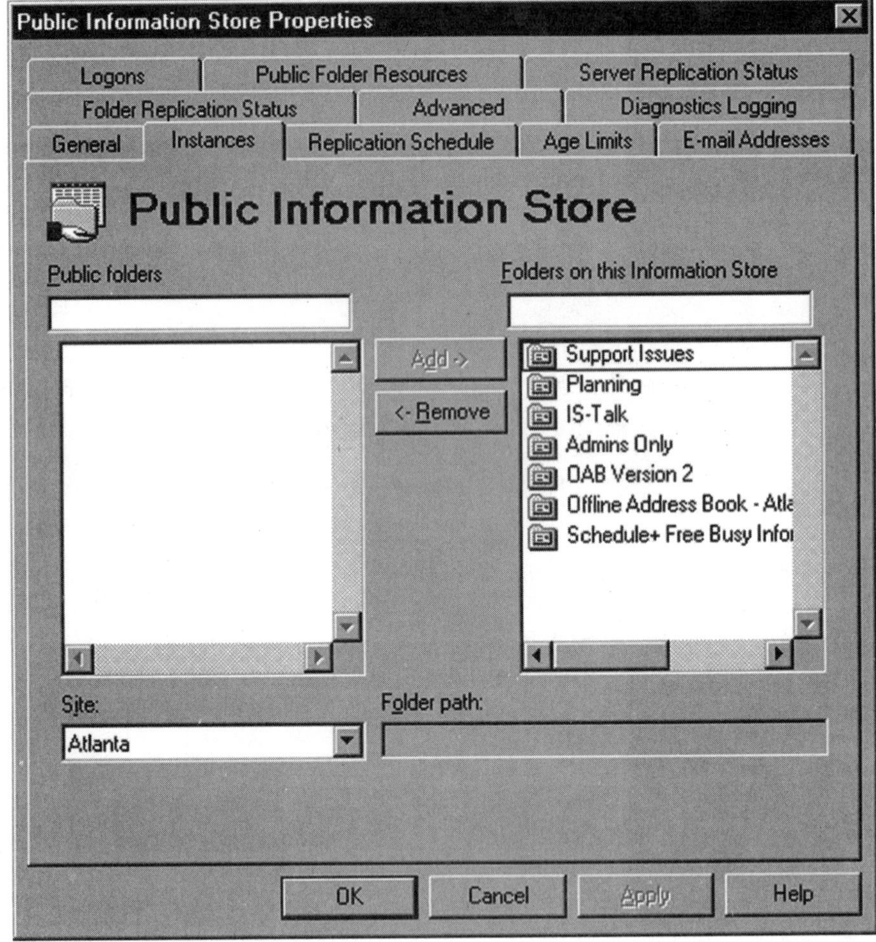

- *Logons*. This displays which users are currently logged on to Public Folders. You can also view this information by selecting Logons under the Public Information Store object in the container pane of Exchange Administrator and reading the status information in the columns of the contents pane.
- *Public Folder Resources*. This tab shows the number of items in each Public Folder and the total space in KB occupied by these items. You can also view this information by selecting Public Folder Resources under the Public Information Store object in the container pane of Exchange Administrator and reading the information in the contents pane.

- *Server Replication Status tab.* This tab lets you view the replication status (In Sync or Local Modified) of all servers in your organization that contain Public Folder replicas in their public Information Stores. Server replication status is listed for a folder as either
  - *In Sync.* This means that no changes have been made to the replica since the last updates were replicated; that is, no new messages have been posted, none deleted or modified, and so on.
  - *Local Modified.* This means that the local replica has been modified and its updates have not yet been replicated throughout the organization.
- *Folder Replication Status tab.* This tab lets you view the replication status of all Public Folders in the selected server's public Information Store, that is, whether the replicas are up to date or not. You can also view this information by selecting Folder Replication Status under the Public Information Store object in the container pane of Exchange Administrator, and reading the status information in the columns of the contents pane. Server Replication Status is listed for a folder as either In Sync or Local Modified.
- *Advanced tab.* This lets you specify the smallest time interval for Public Folder replication and the maximum message size that can be used for Public Folder replication messages.

If instead you want to individually configure Public Folder replication settings for specific folders, you would use the Replicas, Replication Schedule, and Folder Replication Status property tabs of the property sheet for that folder (refer to Figure 12-2). Note that, where applicable, these settings override those configured using the Public Information Store object described previously. Here are the important tabs:

- *Replicas tab.* Use this to create a replica of the selected Public Folder on a specific server. To do this, select the site where you want to create a new replica, choose the server you want to create a new replica on from the left-hand listbox, and then click Add (see Figure 12-13). The right-hand listbox displays the locations of all replicas of the Public Folder in the organization.
- *Replication Schedule tab.* This tab governs the time schedule allotted for replication of the selected Public Folder.
- *Folder Replication Status tab.* This tab shows the replication status (In Sync or Local Modified) for all servers that contain replicas of the selected Public Folder in their public Information Stores.

In the walkthrough for this chapter, we will step through the process of replicating Public Folders between servers in different sites.

Public Folder Affinity

Finally, if users need to access Public Folders in sites other than their own but you don't want to replicate the contents of these folders to their sites, you can get around implementing Public Folder replication by configuring Public Folder affinity instead. Public folder affinity is a way of specifying which remote sites a user can connect to in order to access Public Folders within those sites. A cost value can also be associated with each replica, so that if a client needs to access replicas of a Public Folder located in several different sites, it can try accessing these replicas in a specific order, taking advantage of which network connections are best or load-balancing between equally good connections. The cost value determines the order in which connections are attempted with replicas in remote sites, with lower cost values being attempted first.

To configure Public Folder affinity for a site, use the Information Store Site Configuration object that was described previously in Chapter 8. The Public Folder Affinity tab on the property sheet for this object lets you specify a cost value for each site you create an affinity for. When this tab is configured, the right-hand listbox shows all the remote sites that users in your site can potentially use for accessing Public Folder replicas outside their own site. When Public Folder affinity is configured and Public Folder replicas exist, the order of steps a user must take to access a Public Folder are as follows:

1. If the user's home server has a replica of the desired Public Folder, a connection to the home server's public information store is attempted first.
2. If a connection to the home server cannot be made, or if there is no replica on that particular server, attempts are made to connect to replicas on servers that are in the user's location. This takes place one at a time until a connection succeeds or until all attempts fail.
3. If no connections to servers in the user's location can be made, or if no replicas are in the user's location, attempts are made to connect to replicas on other servers in the same site but in different locations. This takes place one at a time until a connection succeeds or until all attempts fail.

4. If no connections can be made to servers in the user's site, connections with servers in remote sites are attempted using Public Folder affinity and each remote site's cost values. Sites with the lowest cost values are attempted first. Sites without Public Folder affinity are not attempted at all.

Locations
A location is a sub-grouping of servers in a site used primarily to control access to Public Folder replicas in that site. A user's location is the location specified for that user's home server. You can specify the location for a server using the General tab of the specific Server object's property sheet (see Chapter 9).

Walkthrough: Creating and Testing Public Folders

In this series of walkthroughs, we will step through a number of scenarios relating to Public Folders in both single-site and multi-site scenarios.

Creating a Public Folder

Let's start Exchange Administrator on MICKEY; our Exchange Server is in the Atlanta site. We want to create Public Folders in Atlanta, but the first thing we should do is step back for a moment and see who we have granted privileges to for creating top-level Public Folders (a top-level Public Folder is one that is directly beneath the Public Folders container in the Exchange Administrator program). Open the Information Store Site Configuration object within the Atlanta site's Configuration container, and select the Top Level Folder Creation tab (see Figure 12-5).

Notice that only Boris and Natasha, the two network administrators in Atlanta, have the necessary privileges for creating new top-level Public Folders in Atlanta. It is generally a good idea to restrict who can create top-level folders; otherwise, the Public Folder hierarchy within the site might become complex for users to navigate.

Let's now have Boris create a top-level folder. This is going to be called IS-Talk, because it will be used as a discussion group for members of the Information Services department, which Boris heads. Log on as Boris to

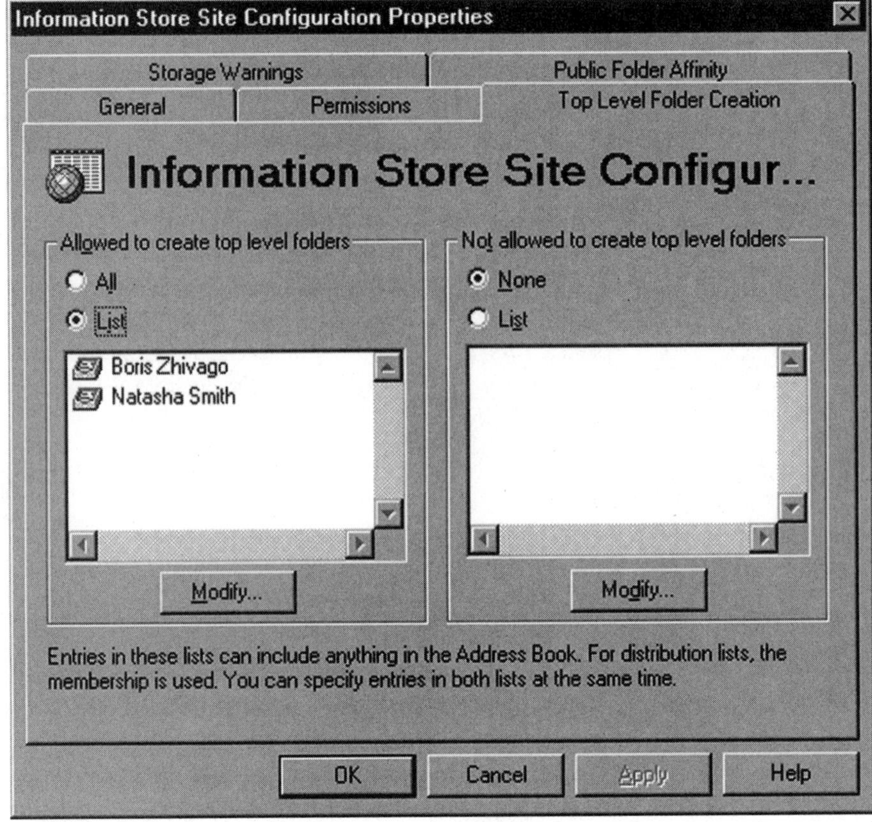

Figure 12-5 Displaying who has top-level Public Folder creation privileges on MICKEY.

GOOFEY, our Windows 98 machine running Microsoft Outlook 98 that is in the MTIT domain in Atlanta. Change the view using the View menu to get rid of the Outlook Shortcuts bar and display the Folder List. Expand the Folder List to show the All Public Folders folder icon (see Figure 12-6).

Select File, Folder, New Folder from the Outlook menu to open the Create New Folder dialog box (see Figure 12-7).

Type "IS-Talk" (without the quotes) for the name of the new top-level folder. Next, we need to specify the type of folder to be created. The various types are related to the different kinds of activities you can perform using Outlook and include types that will contain one of the following kinds of items:

- Appointments
- Contacts
- Journal entries

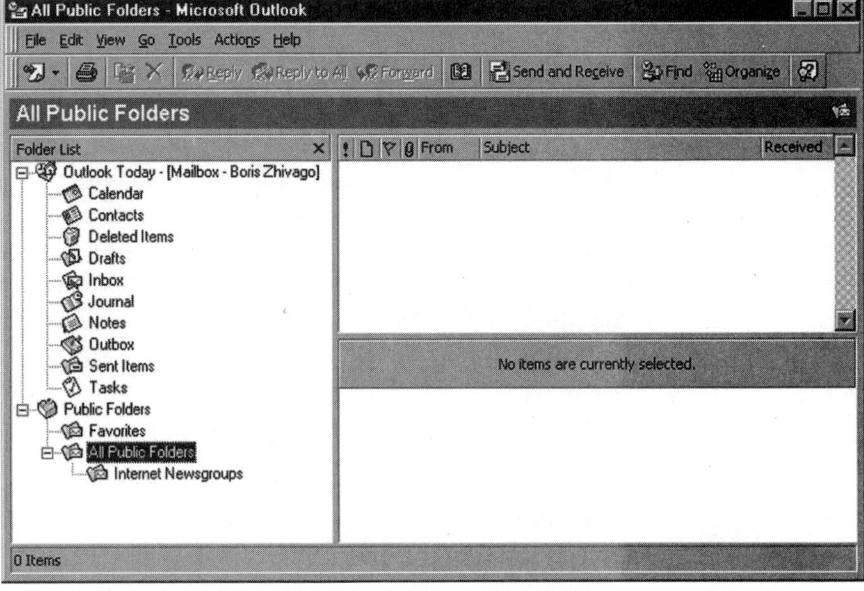

Figure 12-6 Displaying the All Public Folders folder in Outlook 98.

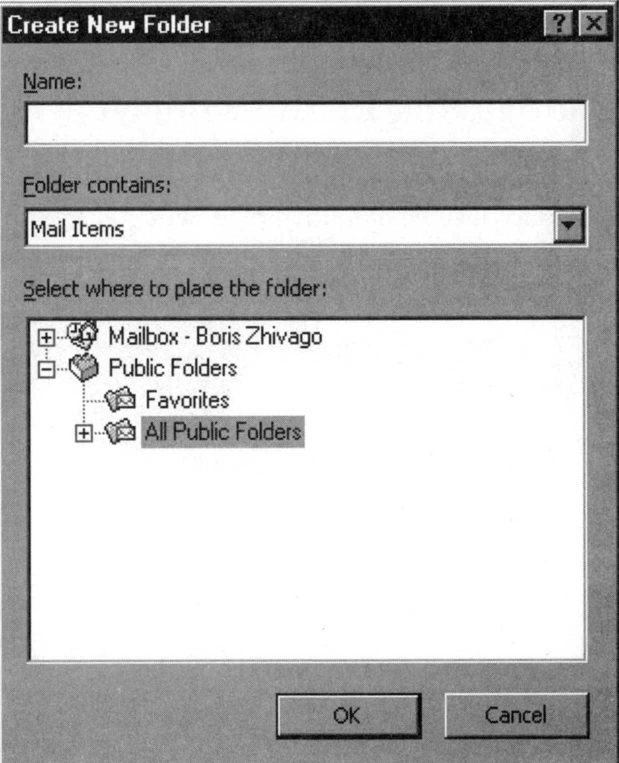

Figure 12-7 Creating a new Public Folder.

- Mail messages
- Notes
- Tasks

We'll choose the default, Mail Items. Finally, we need to indicate where in the Outlook folder hierarchy the new folder will be created. All Public Folders should already be highlighted and is the usual choice. Click OK to create the new folder, return to Exchange Administrator on MICKEY, and refresh the view by pressing the F5 function key on the keyboard. Select the Public Folders container in the container pane and you should see the IS-Talk folder listed in the contents pane (see Figure 12-8).

Go back to GOOFEY as Boris and create three new subfolders for Mail items beneath the IS-Talk folder, namely:

- Support Issues
- Planning
- Admins Only

Check your new Public Folder hierarchy if it was created in the Folder List window of Outlook and in Exchange Administrator on MICKEY.

Configuring Public Folder Permissions

While still logged on to Outlook as Boris, select the IS-Talk folder in the Folder List window; then right-click and select Properties to open the IS-Talk Properties sheet. We won't be able to cover each aspect of this prop-

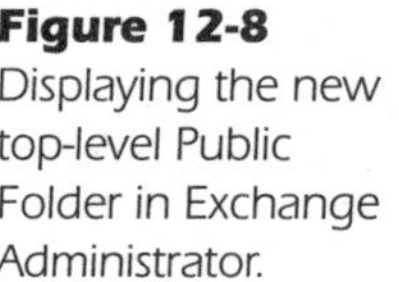

Figure 12-8 Displaying the new top-level Public Folder in Exchange Administrator.

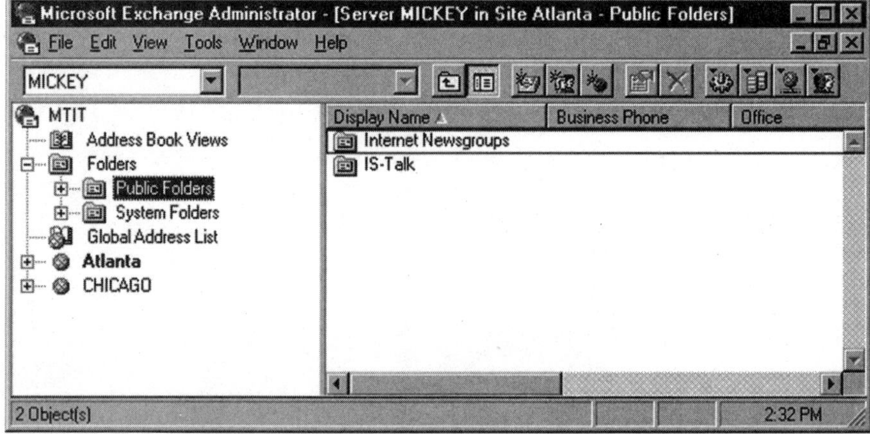

erty sheet (that relates more properly to a book on Outlook than Exchange), but one thing we need to do is configure client permissions on the folder, that is, which clients are allowed to access the folders and what level of access they can have. Select the Permissions tab to see the default client permissions assigned to the folder (see Figure 12-9).

We want only the members of the *Information Services* (IS) department to be able to post messages to the IS-Talk Public Folder hierarchy. The default setting, however, is to assign Default the author role, which means that any recipient in the organization can create and read items in this folder hierarchy. We want to restrict author permission to members of the IS department only, and the easiest way to do this is to switch back to Exchange Administrator on MICKEY and create a new Distribution List

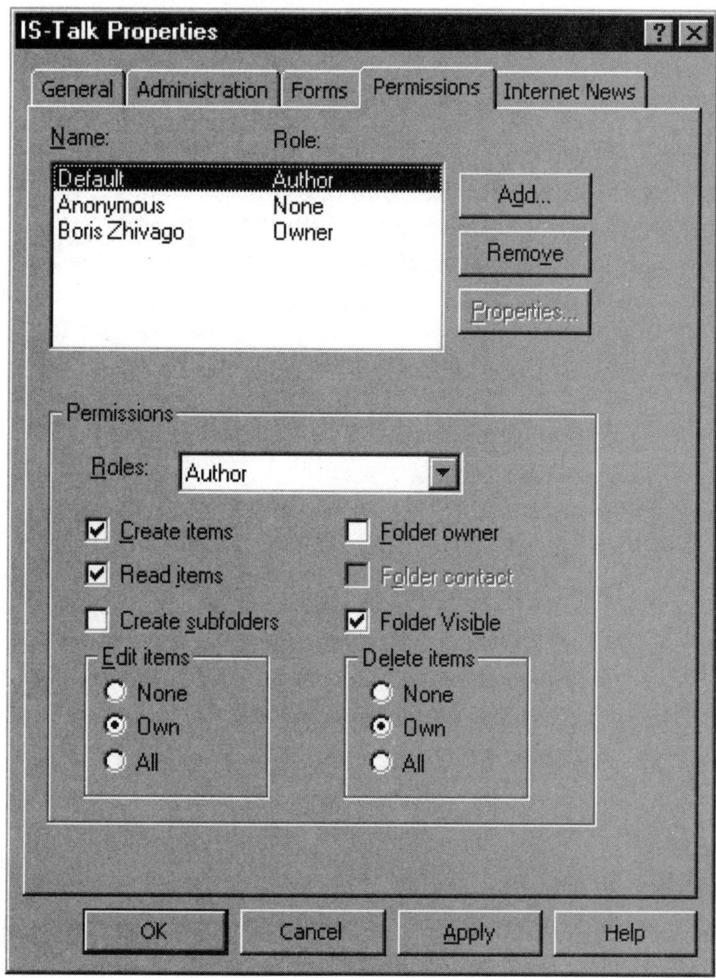

Figure 12-9 Displaying the default client permissions assigned to the IS-Talk Public Folder.

that contains only members of the IS department. We'll call that list the Nerds List, and we'll include Peter James and any other IS people in Chicago as well on this list.

Returning to Outlook on GOOFEY, change the role of Default to None to prevent non-IS users from reading or posting messages in the folder. Then click Add, select the Nerds List, and assign members of that list author permission on the folder. Click OK to close the IS-Talk Properties sheet.

Select one of the subfolders under IS-Talk and open its property sheet. Switch to the Permissions tab and note that the permissions we assigned to the parent folder were not inherited by the child folders. Rather than assign the permissions for IS-Talk to each of its child folders individually, let's return to Exchange Administrator on MICKEY and continue there. (This is one of the things that is a bit awkward about Public Folders with Exchange; some aspects can be administered using only Outlook, some using only Exchange Administrator, and some using both tools.)

Open the property sheet for IS-Talk in Exchange Administrator (refer to Figure 12-2). Click the Client Permissions button on the General tab and you will see that you can configure client permissions on a Public Folder using Exchange Administrator, not by just using Outlook, as we did above. Select the checkbox labeled Propagate These Properties To All Subfolders and click Apply. This opens the Subfolder Properties dialog box (see Figure 12-10).

We can propagate some or all of the various properties of a parent folder to its child folders. We'll select only the checkbox for Client Permissions and click OK. If you now return to Outlook on GOOFEY and open the property sheet for a child folder of IS-Talk, you should see that the permissions on the parent folder have been inherited by the child folders, as expected.

Let's try posting to a Public Folder. Have Boris select the Planning folder in the Public Folder hierarchy and then click the New Post In This Folder button on the toolbar to open an untitled discussion window. Enter the subject, "Year 2000 planning," type a message, and click the Post button on the toolbar to post the message to the folder. The post should work fine. Log off as Boris and log on as Natasha and reply to Boris' message in the Planning folder (select the message Boris posted to this folder, right-click, and select Post Reply To This Folder).

Configuring Public Folder Affinity

Now have Peter James log on to the Outlook 2000 machine in Chicago (the machine BUGS in our case) and try to view the IS-Talk Public Folder hierarchy and the contents of its folders. You should get an error like that shown in Figure 12-11.

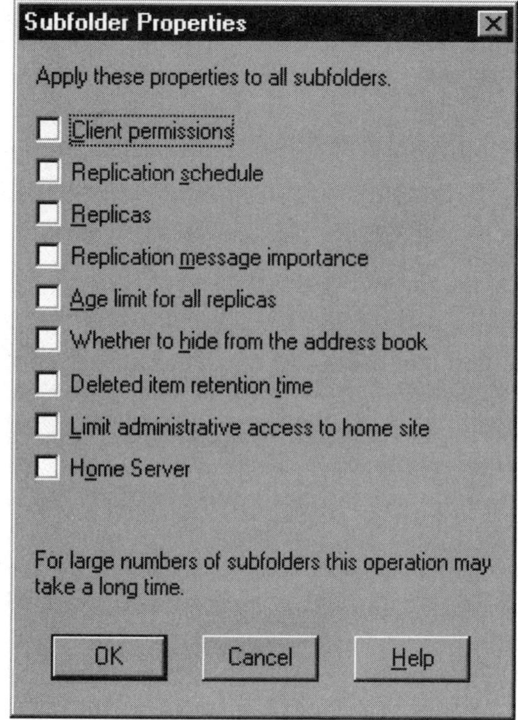

Figure 12-10 Propagating Public Folder settings to child folders beneath a parent folder in a Public Folder hierarchy.

Actually, you may not even be able to see the IS-Talk Public Folder hierarchy on BUGS unless directory replication has taken place between Atlanta and Chicago, since the folders were created (remember that we configured directory replication to take place every 15 minutes for the purposes of our walkthroughs, so you might have to wait a few minutes and then try starting Outlook again).

In any case, Peter, who is himself a network administrator in Chicago and a member of the IS department in MTIT, will not be able to view or post messages to the Public Folder hierarchy we created in Atlanta unless one of two things is done:

- *Public folder affinity* on the Public Folder hierarchy in the Atlanta site is configured to enable users in the Chicago site to access the contents of Public Folders that are homed on MICKEY in Atlanta.
- *Public folder replication* is configured so that a copy of the folders is replicated to the public information store on BUGS in Chicago.

Let's choose the first option: configuring Public Folder affinity on the folder hierarchy. Return to Exchange Administrator on MICKEY in

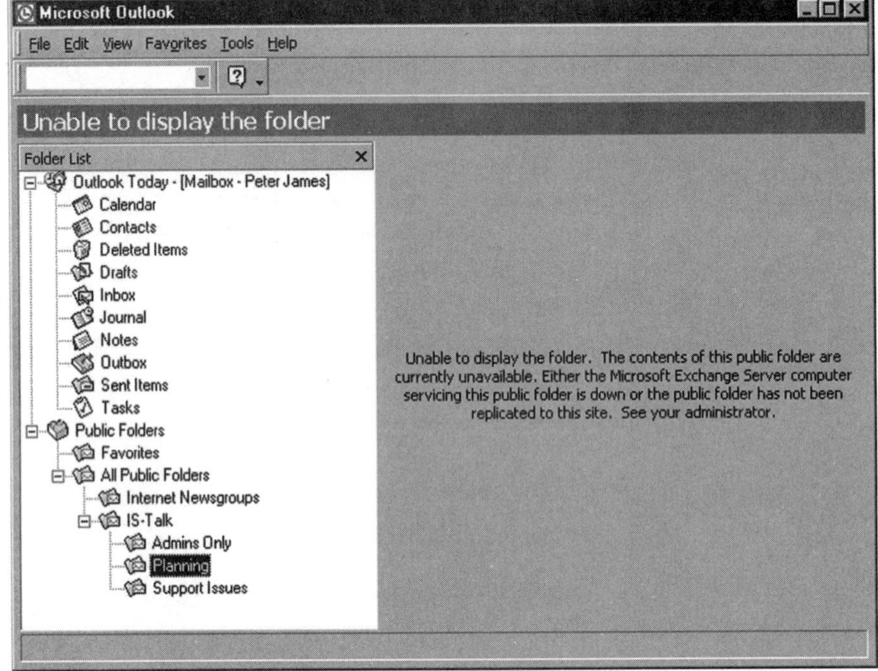

Figure 12-11 Peter in Chicago cannot view the contents of the Planning Public Folder.

Atlanta, connect to the server BUGS in Chicago to administer directory objects in Chicago, and open the property sheet for the Information Store Site Configuration in Chicago. (Alternatively, we could have logged on to BUGS in Chicago as an administrator and run Exchange Administrator from there, but we are trying to do all of our administration from a single administrator console in Atlanta that is running the Exchange Administrator program.) Select the Public Folder Affinity tab on this property sheet (see Figure 12-12).

We will use this Public Folder Affinity tab to configure Exchange Servers in Chicago so they can access Public Folders in Atlanta. Select Atlanta in the Sites listbox on the left and click Add to move it over to the Public Folder Affinity listbox on the right. There is no point configuring a connected site cost, since there is only one other site that is connected to Chicago in our setup so far, namely Atlanta. Click OK to apply the changes and close the property sheet and return to Exchange Administrator. Start Outlook on BUGS as Peter James and you should be able to view the messages posted by Boris and Natasha to the Planning Public Folder.

For an additional exercise, configure Public Folder affinity using the Information Store Site Configuration object in Atlanta to allow users in Atlanta to access Public Folders homed on servers in Chicago. Have Peter

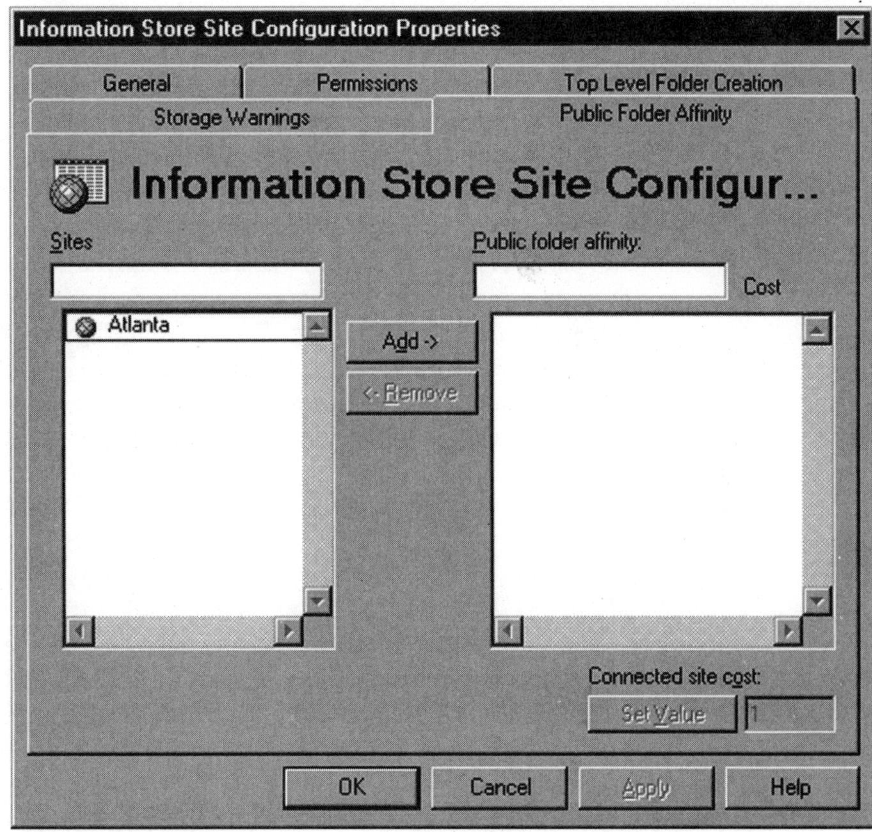

Figure 12-12 Configuring Public Folder affinity for the Chicago site.

in Chicago create a top-level Public Folder called Sales-Talk and post a message to it. Then see if Boris can read the message from Atlanta.

Synchronizing Server Clocks
If directory replication seems to behave unpredictably or takes longer than you expect it to work, it may be due to the clocks between servers being off in the local and remote sites. Exchange uses Greenwich Mean Time (GMT) internally for time-sensitive operations. Make sure that all server clocks are properly synchronized throughout your organization.

Replicating Public Folders

Public Folder affinity is often not the best way of allowing users to access Public Folder contents in other sites. You need a permanent network connection that supports RPCs to enable Public Folder affinity to work. In addition, if users make heavy use of Public Folders, then Public Folder affinity can contribute significantly to inter-site WAN link traffic. It is often a better idea to configure Public Folder replication so that the actual contents or replica of remote Public Folders can be placed on a server in the local site. That's what we will try doing next. But first, disable Public Folder affinity for both sites using the Information Store Site Configuration object in both sites, and then wait until directory replication brings everything up to date or forces each site to update its directory from the other site. Now try accessing IS-Talk from Chicago. You shouldn't be able to do so, since Public Folder affinity is now off.

As we mentioned previously, we can configure Public Folder replication either globally for all Public Folders on a server using the Public Information Store object or on an individual basis for a specific Public Folder on a server using the property sheet of that Public Folder. Let's choose the second method. Open the property sheet for the IS-Talk Public Folder object using Exchange Administrator (make sure you are currently connected to MICKEY) and select the Replicas tab (see Figure 12-13).

Note on this tab that there is currently only one replica of IS-Talk, that being the original replica located within the public Information Store on MICKEY in Atlanta. Select Chicago from the site's drop-down box to show Exchange Servers in Chicago. BUGS should appear in the server's listbox on the left. Select BUGS and click Add to move it over to the Replica Folders To dialog box on the right (it enters the box as Chicago\BUGS to indicate that it is the server BUGS in the site Chicago).

Now move to the Replication Schedule tab and select Always to cause the IS-Talk folder to be replicated every 15 minutes (to speed things up for the purposes of our walkthrough).

Return to the General tab and select the checkbox labeled Propagate These Properties To All Subfolders. Click OK to bring up the Subfolder Properties dialog box, which we saw previously in Figure 12-10. Make sure that the Replication schedule and Replicas options are checked (this will cause the subfolders Planning, Customer Support, and Admins Only to also have replicas created for them in Chicago) and click OK to return to the IS-Talk property sheet. Then wait a few minutes . . .

Switch to the Folder Replication Status tab of the IS-Talk property sheet to see what's going on. Click the Columns button and remove the Average Transmission Time column from those being displayed and click OK. If both MICKEY and BUGS are listed as being In Sync, that means that the new replica has been created on BUGS and both replicas of the folder are synchronized and have the same contents (see Figure 12-14).

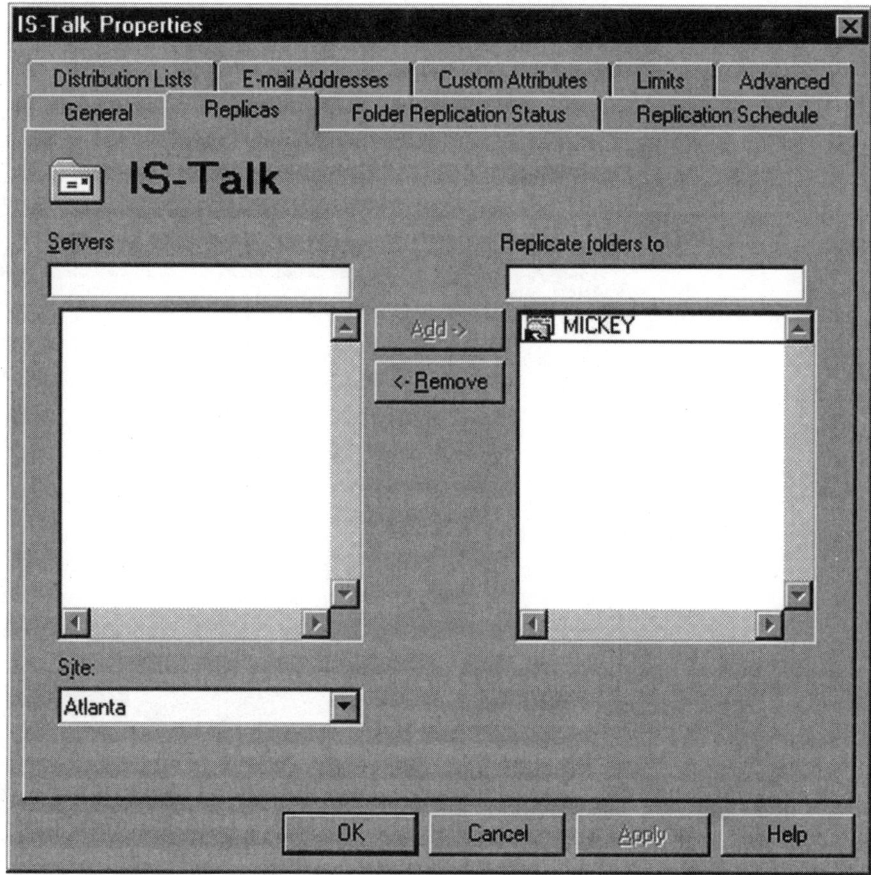

Figure 12-13 Creating a new replica of the IS-Talk Public Folder.

Try posting a new message to the IS-Talk Public Folder as Boris in Atlanta. Check the Folder Replication Status tab immediately for the IS-Talk property sheet on MICKEY; the server BUGS should be listed as Local Modified, meaning that messages have been posted to the replica of IS-Talk located on BUGS in Chicago and have not yet been replicated to the replica of IS-Talk located on MICKEY in Atlanta. After a short time, the message should be accessible by Peter in Chicago.

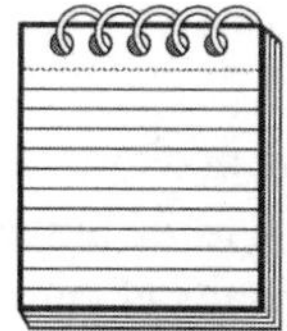

In Sync

Just because a Public Folder replica shows up as In Sync doesn't actually mean the replication process is complete. If the message hasn't appeared in the remote site yet, try connecting to the Public Folder server in the remote site using Exchange Administrator and select Public Folder Resources in

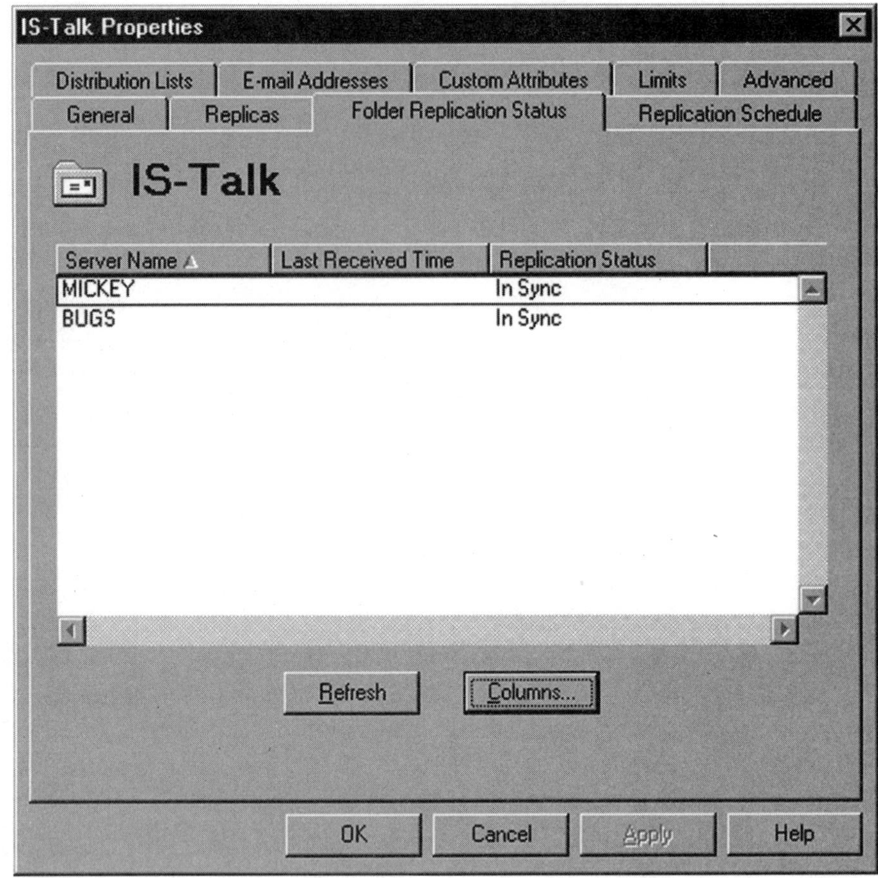

Figure 12-14 Replicas are up to date.

the contents pane (this is under the Public Information Store object on the remote server). Examine the number of messages in the Public Folder replica on the remote server. Press the F5 function key every minute or so until you see the number of messages suddenly increase. This indicates the actual replication process is underway, copying messages between the replicas to ensure they are up to date.

Where Do We Go from Here?

In the next chapter, we will consider how creating address book views eases the task of managing addressing for users sending mail within an Exchange organization. After that, we will return to the topic of connectors and look at various other Exchange connectors in succeeding chapters.

For More Information

You can find some good information concerning managing Public Folders in the Exchange manuals and their Books Online equivalents. Specifically refer to

- *Getting Started*: Chapters 6 and 9
- *Concepts and Planning*: Chapter 2

Exchange Server 5.5 Resource Guide

This guide is currently included with TechNet and Chapter 6 contains useful material on managing Public Folders.

TechNet

The Technical Notes section for MS Exchange contains a few useful articles, including

- Building MS Exchange and Outlook Solutions
- MS Exchange Server: Planning for Routing and Public Folders

CHAPTER 13

Administering Address Book Views

This chapter looks briefly at how to make life easier for users in your Exchange organization by providing customized address lists for them called address book views. After reading this chapter, you will have an understanding of the following topics:

- Global Address List (GAL)
- Address book views

The walkthrough in this chapter takes you through creating and testing various types of address book views. The Find Recipients tool of Exchange Administrator is also covered.

Global Address List (GAL)

When users in your Exchange organization want to send messages using client software like Microsoft Outlook, they need a simple way of addressing those messages. They could manually type in the destination address each time, creating what are called one-off addresses, but this would be tedious. They could create their own personal address books, but this too is a lot of work. Instead, Exchange makes life simple for users by creating a single GAL that contains all recipients (mailboxes, custom recipients, and Distribution Lists) that are defined in the organization. Outlook users can access the GAL and select recipients from it. The GAL is a container located directly beneath the Organization container in the Exchange directory hierarchy (see Figure 13-1). Unlike most other Exchange directory objects, the GAL has no property sheet and cannot be directly configured.

The GAL is fine and dandy if your Exchange organization only consists of a few dozen users, but if your organization has thousands of recipients, the GAL then becomes impractical as a tool for addressing messages. This is because users are presented with one long list of recipients in their Outlook address book, and they would have to do a lot of scrolling to find the recipient they need. To simplify the process of addressing messages, administrators can create address book views for their users.

Address Book Views

An address book view is a grouping of Exchange recipients according to common attributes. Address book views can group recipients according to any of the following eight recipient attributes:

Figure 13-1
The Global Address List or GAL.

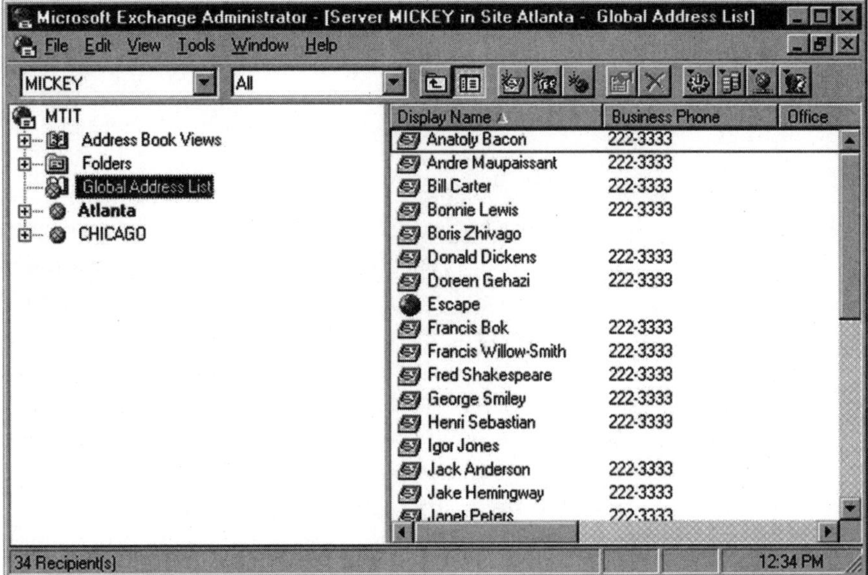

- City
- Company
- Country
- Department
- Home Server
- Site
- State
- Title

or by any of the 10 custom attributes you can define using the DS Site Configuration directory object (see Chapter 8). You can also create address book views that group recipients by more than one attribute. For example, you could create an address book view that groups recipients first by country and then by state. In this case, the structure of the address book view might be something hierarchical like this:

Address Book View
  Country#1
    State#1
    State#2
  ...

Country#2

State#1

State#2

. . .

. . .

Address book views can be created using hierarchical groupings of up to four different properties. These hierarchical groupings are displayed as containers in the Exchange Administrator window, and they are also displayed in hierarchical fashion in the Outlook address book with the associated recipients in each container. The result is that instead of just having one GAL container with hundreds or even thousands of recipients listed in it, you have an address book view consisting of a hierarchy of different containers, each having much fewer recipients in it. Provided users know which state or city their intended recipient is located in, address book views enable them to find and select recipients much faster for addressing their messages.

Rather than just talk about address book views, let's go ahead and create one and see how it works.

Walkthrough: Creating an Address Book View

Let's walk through the process of creating and testing some address book views for our organization MTIT. Begin by adding some additional recipients to the following departments:

- Information services
- Sales
- Accounting

Use mailbox templates to speed up the mailbox creation process. List the employees in various states and cities, so that you end up with a distribution of employees something like the following:

- The state of Georgia has employees in the cities of
- Atlanta
- Augusta
- Savannah

- The state of Illinois has employees in the cities of
- Chicago
- Peoria

We will first create an address book view that groups employees first by state and then by city. Connect to MICKEY in Atlanta using Exchange Administrator and select File, New Other, Address Book View from the menu. A blank property sheet opens for the new address book view (see Figure 13-2).

Enter "By State and City" (without the quotes) as both the display name and directory name for this new address book view. You can actually use something different for the directory name if you like, since the directory name is only used internally by the Exchange directory service, but it's easiest just to make the two names agree.

Select the Group By tab on the property sheet. Note that you can create address book views with up to four nested layers of attributes. In other

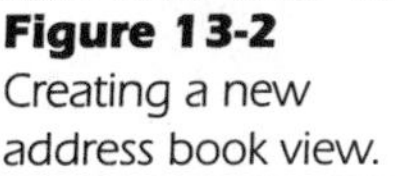

Figure 13-2 Creating a new address book view.

words, we could create an address book view that grouped recipients hierarchically starting with country, then state/province, then city, and finally department if we liked. However, using more than two levels of grouping tends to make address book views unwieldy for users, so we'll just stick to two.

Select the first Group Items By drop-down box and set it to show State as its attribute. After you set the first Group Items By box, the second one now becomes available (you can't set a second-level attribute if you haven't chosen a first-level attribute). Set the second box to display City (see Figure 13-3).

Move to the Advanced tab of the property sheet (see Figure 13-4). The settings on this tab are as follows:

- *Promote entries to parent containers.* If this checkbox is selected (and it is by default), then recipients will appear in multiple containers of an

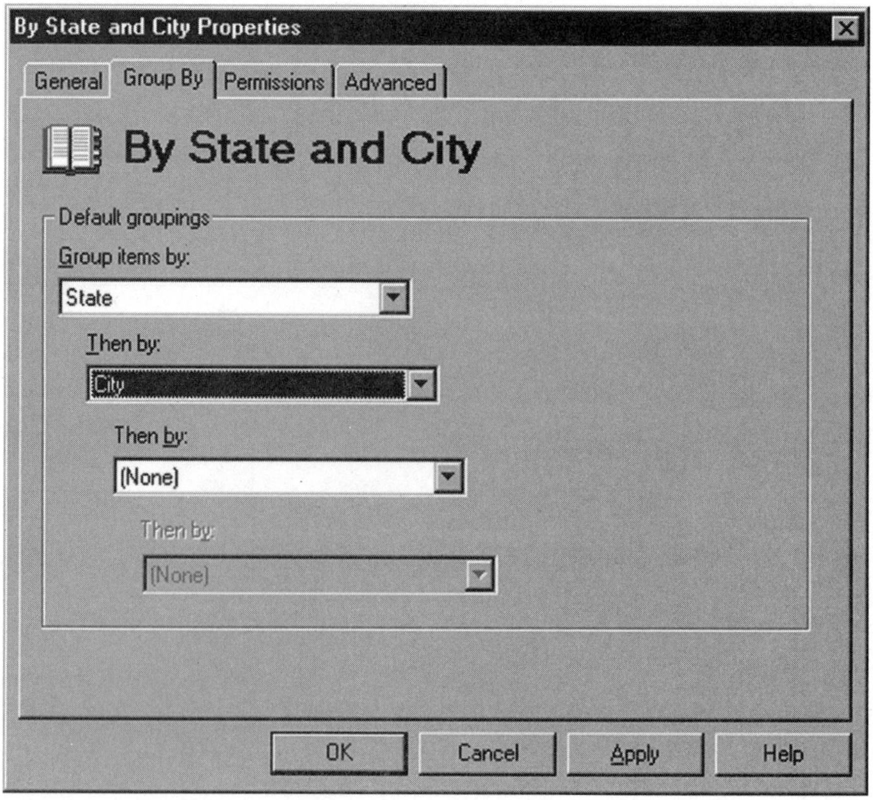

Figure 13-3 Setting the Group Item By attributes for an address book view.

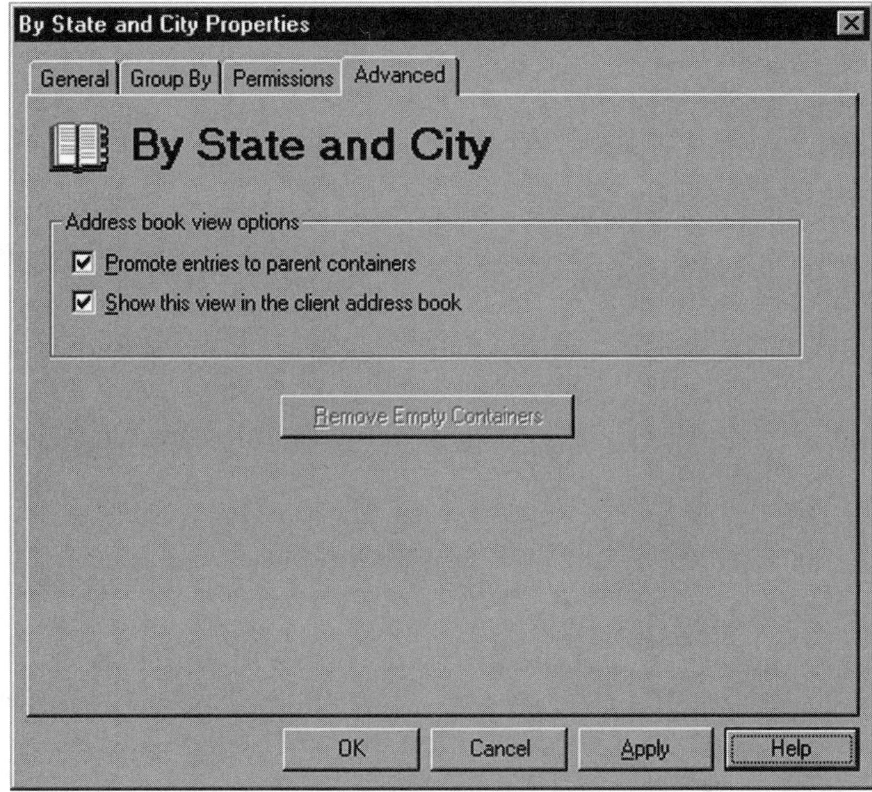

Figure 13-4 Advanced tab of a new address book view.

address book view. For example, a recipient that works in Savannah, Georgia will be listed in both the Savannah city-level container and the Georgia state-level container. This will enable Outlook users to see all recipients in the city of Savannah and all recipients in the state of Georgia. On the other hand, by clearing this checkbox, the above recipient will only show up in the Savannah container, while the Georgia container will only contain the various city subcontainers for the state of Georgia. It's your call which you prefer to implement for your users.

- *Show this view in the client address book*. If this checkbox is checked (and it is by default), the address book view you are creating will show up in client address books, such as the Microsoft Outlook address book. This is probably what you want to do. After all, address book views are created for clients, aren't they?

Exporting Address Book Views

Actually, address book views also have a use for administrators, not just for ordinary users. You can export the recipients in an address book view using Directory Export form the Tools command. This is probably the only reason why you might want to hide an address book view from users by using the Advanced tab, such as if you created an address book view solely for administrative purposes so you could export a group of recipients for migration or some other purpose.

- *Remove Empty Containers*. This button can only be used once the new address book view has been created. By default, empty containers created while generating an address book view are not deleted. For example, if you created an address book view that grouped users first by city and then by department, it might be that there is a sales department in Atlanta, but not currently one in Chicago. Nevertheless, there will be a Sales subcontainer beneath the Chicago container in your new address book view, even through it is empty. The point is that you might want to later move some sales people to Chicago. If these empty containers are cluttering up your address book view, you can use the Remove Empty Containers button to delete them.

  On the other hand, what if you don't have any users yet in Athens, Georgia, but you still want to have an empty city-level container for them anyway in the address book view you are creating? We'll see how to handle that situation in a moment.

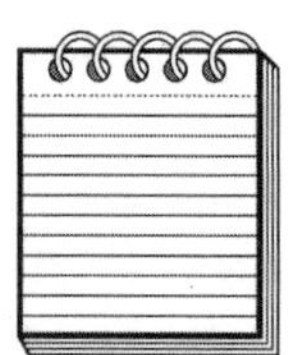

Advanced Tab

The Advanced tab is only visible on the property sheet of the parent Address Book View container, not on the sheets of the automatically generated containers and subcontainers within the address book view.

It's time to generate the By State and City address book view. Click the OK button and a message appears saying, "A process has been started to update the address book view." If your organization has thousands of recipients in it, this process may take a little while. For our setup, it should take only a few seconds to generate the new address book view.

Figure 13-5 shows the result. As expected, the new address book view called By State and City has two state-level containers beneath it, Georgia and Illinois. The Georgia container has three city-level subcontainers, Atlanta, Augusta, and Savannah, while the Illinois container has two city-

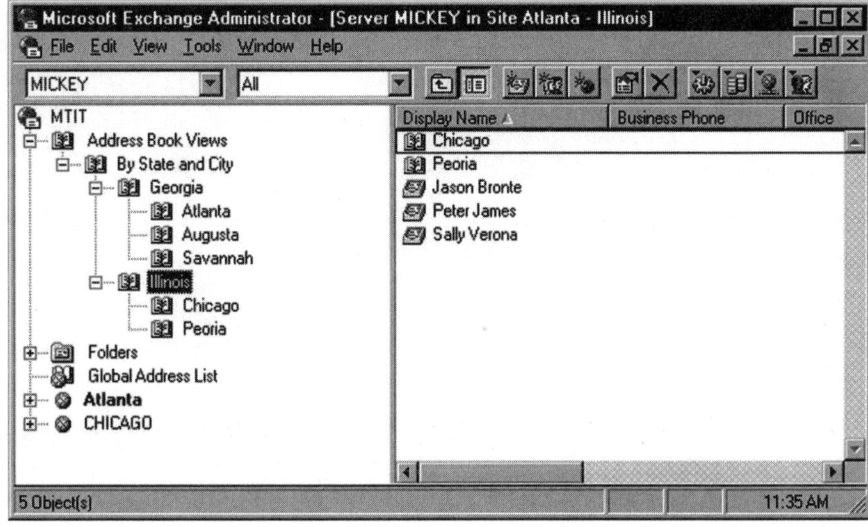

Figure 13-5 The new By State and City address book view.

level subcontainers, Chicago and Peoria. The Illinois container is selected in the container pane, showing both its two city-level subcontainers and all Illinois recipients in the contents pane.

If you open the property sheet for the Illinois container, you will see that it looks a bit different from the property sheets for the parent By State and City address book view. The Illinois container property sheet has no Advanced tab, and the Group By tab shows the following:

- Groupings for this container: State
- Groupings for subcontainers: City
- Grouping value: Illinois

Testing the Address Book View

To test the new By State and City address book view, log on to GOOFEY as Boris and start Outlook 98. Click the Address Book button on the toolbar to open the Outlook Address Book, and click the Show Names drop-down box to show the structure of the address book. The result should look something like Figure 13-6.

The structure of our Outlook Address Book looks like the following:

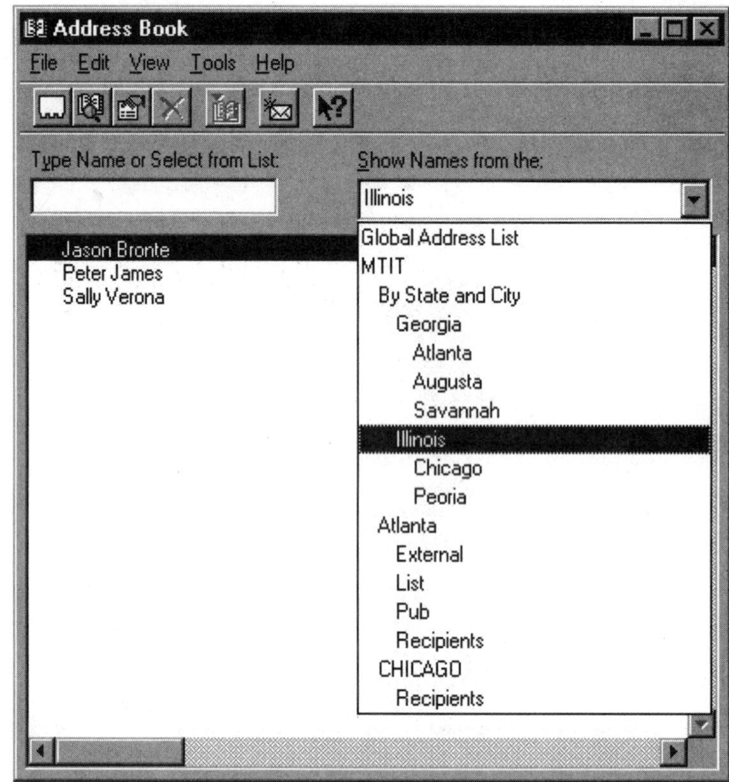

Figure 13-6 Testing an address book view in Outlook.

Global Address List: Shows all recipients in the organization MTIT

MTIT: Contains all address lists in the organization MTIT

- By State and City: The address book view we just made
  - Georgia: Contains recipients from state of Georgia
    - Atlanta: Contains recipients from city of Atlanta
    - Augusta: Contains recipients from city of Augusta
    - Savannah: Contains recipients from city of Savannah
  - Illinois: Contains recipients from state of Illinois
    - Chicago: Contains recipients from city of Chicago
    - Peoria: Contains recipients from city of Peoria
- Atlanta: Contains all recipients containers in the Atlanta site
  - External: Contains all custom recipients in the Atlanta site
  - List: Contains all distribution lists in the Atlanta site
  - Pub: Contains all public folders in the Atlanta site
  - Recipients: Contains all mailboxes in the Atlanta site
- Georgia: Contains all recipients containers in the Georgia site
  - Recipients: Contains all recipients in the Georgia site

Adding a Recipient

What if . . .

- You add a new recipient to your company? The recipient is automatically added to the address book view in the appropriate container or subcontainer.
- You modify a recipient's property sheet so that it acquires a new value for an attribute that defines it as being part of an address book view? Exchange then automatically updates the address book view with this information. For example, if Donna Smith originally had no State attribute specified and you modified her property sheet to specify her State as Georgia, she will appear in the Georgia container of the By State and City address book view.
- You created a new recipient in Illinois in which their City attribute has the value Springfield? If you did this, a Springfield subcontainer would automatically be created under the Illinois container to accommodate the new city.

Try out the above procedures. It may take a minute or so before the address book view is actually updated.

Moving a Recipient

If you select a recipient in Exchange Administrator and move the recipient from one address book view container to another using Add to Address Book View from the Tools menu, the recipient acquires those attributes that define the new container. For example, if Bob Thomson is moved from the Atlanta to the Savannah subcontainer, his City attribute is automatically updated from Atlanta to Savannah on his mailbox property sheet. Try it!

Creating an Empty Container

What if you plan to move some employees to Athens, Georgia? You can prepare for the move by creating an empty Athens city-level subcontainer beneath the Georgia state-level container of the By State and City address book view. To do this, select the Georgia container of the By State and City address book view in Exchange Administrator and then choose

File, New Other, Address Book View Container from the menu. Then enter the following:

Display name = Athens

Directory name = Athens

Click OK twice and you should now have four city-level subcontainers beneath the Georgia state-level container. Try it!

Modifying an Address Book View

We will add a third level to our By State and City address book view, which groups recipients according to department. This will make the address book view somewhat unwieldy, but we'll do it just for demonstration purposes.

Open the property sheet for the By State and City address book view and make the following modifications:

- In the General tab, change the display name to "By State, City, and Department" (without the quotes).
- In the Group By tab, select Department in the third drop-down box.

Now click OK. A message appears saying, "The address book view must be rebuilt to complete the changes you have requested. Do you want to continue?" Click Yes. After the process completes, view the results in Exchange Administrator. Click F5 to refresh if necessary. It may take a few minutes to update the view. The result should look something like Figure 13-7.

Check the modified address book view in Outlook as well. Once you have examined it, change it back to the two-level By State and City address book view we defined earlier by opening the Group By tab on the property sheet for the address book view and setting the third drop-down box back to None.

Restricting Access to Address Book View Containers

When an address book view has been created, any user in your organization can access it, but this may not be what you intend. For example, if you are hosting recipients for two different companies on your Exchange Server, you can create an address book view called By Company that has two con-

Figure 13-7 A three-level address book view.

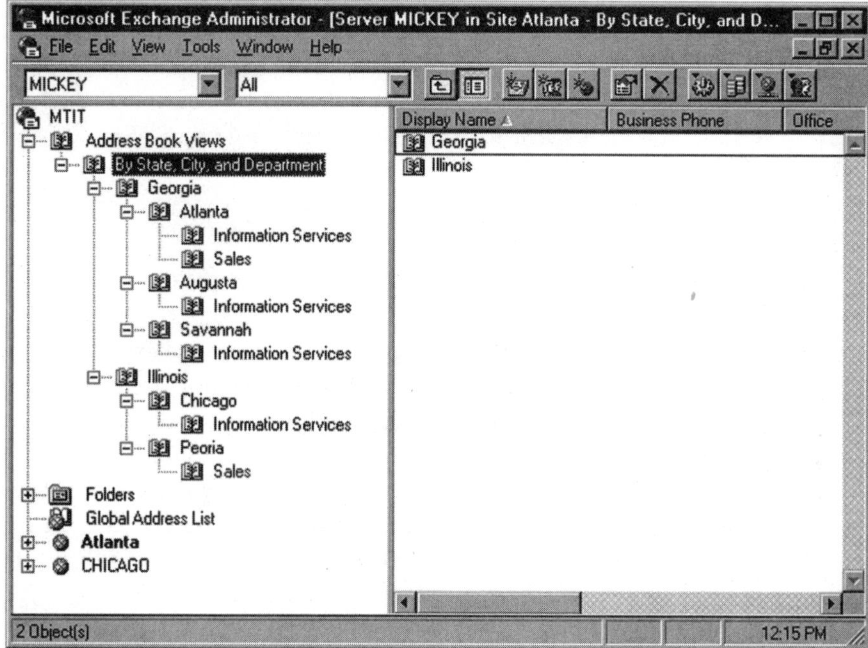

tainers within it, one for each company's recipients. You can then restrict recipients in one company from accessing recipients in the other company's client address book. This way, recipients will only be able to see recipients from their own company in their client address book. To accomplish this, you might do the following:

1. Create two Windows NT global groups, one for company A containing all users in Company A, and one for company B containing all users in Company B.
2. Select the Company A container within the By Company address book view and open its property sheet. Select the Permissions tab and assign the Company A global group the Search role.
3. Do the same with Company B.

Once you have completed the above procedure, recipients will only have access to those containers within the By Company address book view for which they have the Search role assigned. I'll leave this procedure to you as an exercise to try out yourself!

Anonymous Access to Address Book Views

If you want to give anonymous users access to an address book view, assign the Search role to the anonymous account specified in the DS Site Configuration property sheet (see Chapter 8).

Finding Recipients in Exchange Administrator

An address book can also make it easier to find recipients in Exchange Administrator. Select Find Recipients from the Tools menu in Exchange Administrator, and the Find Recipients dialog box appears (see Figure 13-8).

Note that you can search for recipients in the GAL by first name, last name, department, and so on, but you cannot search by city or state. By selecting the Container button, however, you open the Find Container dialog box (see Figure 13-9) that allows you to select any of the following containers for restricting your search:

- GAL
- Any container or subcontainer of any address book view
- Any recipients container of any site

Figure 13-8 Finding recipients in Exchange Administrator.

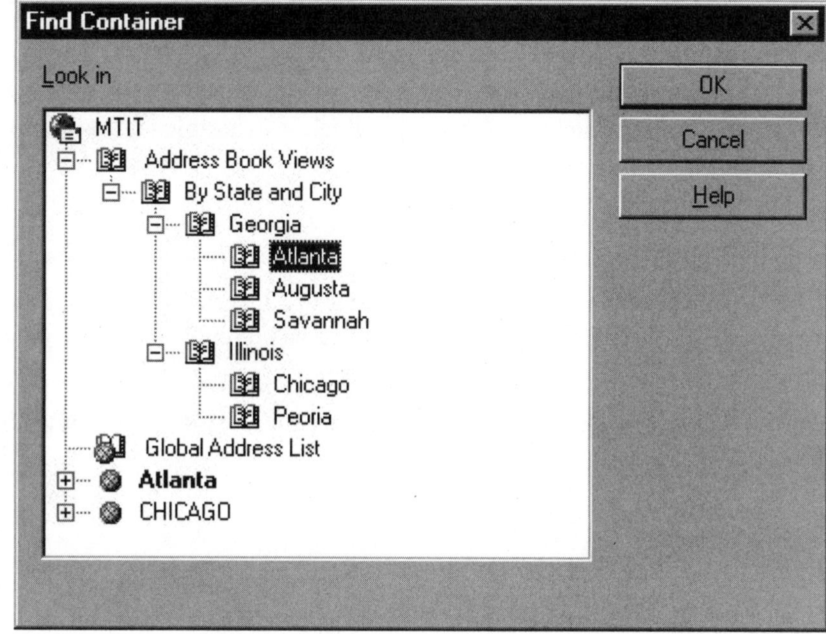

Figure 13-9 Selecting a container to restrict your search for recipients.

You could then enter "d" into the First Name field and click Find Now to display all recipients whose first name starts with "d" and whose City attribute has the value Atlanta.

Finding Recipients in Outlook

You can also use the Find button when you open the address book in Outlook to find recipients within the GAL or a selected address book view or recipients container.

Where Do We Go from Here?

Earlier we introduced our first connector for establishing messaging connectivity between Exchange sites, the Site Connector. In the next few chapters, we will return to the topic of connectors and introduce some of the other connectors available with Exchange.

For More Information

Further information on address book views can be found in the *Operations* manual for Exchange, which is available on Books Online.

TechNet

If you want to dig deeper into address book views, a couple of articles in the Microsoft Knowledge Base cover TechNet and can be found on the Microsoft Web site:

- Q.180141. XADM: Recurring Address Book Views in Exchange Server
- Q193423. XADM: Address Book Views Not Updated After Correct Interval

CHAPTER 14

Administering X.400 Connectors

In the last two chapters, we took a detour and looked at administering public folders and address book views. Here we will pick up where we left off in Chapter 10, "Administering Site Connectors," and Chapter 11, "Administering Directory Replication," and continue with our study of Exchange connectors. The focus of this chapter is the X.400 Connector. After reading this chapter, you will have an understanding of the following topics:

- X.400 messaging standards
- X.400 addressing
- MTA transport stacks
- X.400 Connectors

The walkthrough in this chapter will take you through creating and configuring an X.400 Connector for establishing messaging connectivity between two Exchange sites.

X.400 Messaging Standards

The Enterprise Edition of Exchange Server 5.5 includes the X.400 Connector, which is based on the X.400 messaging standards of the *Comité Consultatif International Télégraphique et Téléphonic* (CCITT), now the *International Telecommunications Union* (ITU). This X.400 Connector can be used in several ways:

- To provide messaging connectivity between an Exchange organization and a public or private X.400 messaging system
- To link Exchange sites in different locations together using a public or private X.400 communications carrier as the messaging system backbone
- As an alternative to the Site Connector for joining sites together in an Exchange organization

Before we look in detail at how the connector works, let's get some background on the X.400 messaging standards.

What is X.400?

X.400 is a series of standards and recommendations first published by the ITU in 1984 in their Red Book. X.400 standards describe a way of creating a global messaging system that is structured hierarchically in a way that is similar to the Domain Name System (DNS) used in the Internet. X.400 is designed to embrace all types of messaging services including email, voice and fax communications, telex and telegraph, Electronic Data Interchange (EDI), and even good-old hand-delivered "snail mail." In order to be able to embrace such a wide range of delivery mechanisms, X.400 is quite complex, both in its addressing scheme and in its implementation.

Being developed in Europe, it has been embraced there by governments and public carriers. X.400 also has a wide implementation through various *Post, Telephone, and Telegraph* (PTT) carriers all over Europe and in parts of Asia as well. X.400 has never caught on much in the United States or Canada, however, where the Internet's SMTP mail system predominates.

The ITU has continued to refine X.400 recommendations, and in 1988 the original Red Book recommendations were augmented by a newer Blue Book set of standards. Both sets of standards are intimately bound to the seven-layer OSI model for networking developed by the *International Standards Organization* (ISO), and in fact, X.400 messaging was originally intended to run on the OSI protocol stack. However, the OSI protocol stack has remained largely theoretical in nature with few working implementations, and X.400 has since been broadened to run on other protocol stacks, particularly on TCP/IP. X.400 can also run on X.25 packet-switching networks as well. Exchange supports all three protocols for running X.400, namely OSI, X.25, and TCP/IP.

How X.400 Works

An X.400 *Message Handling System* (MHS), which can be either a public or private messaging system, is essentially modular in structure and consists of the following five basic components:

- *User Agent* (UA). A user interacts with an X.400 MHS through a User Agent (UA), which represents software installed on a terminal or workstation that enables the user to send and receive X.400 messages. UAs can support text, voice, fax, or any combination or number of messaging services.
- *Message Store* (MS). This component provides a temporary message storage facility in a "store-and-forward" messaging processing fashion. An incoming message for a user would be held at an MS until the UA could connect to it to download the message.

- *Message Transfer Agent* (MTA). This is the main active component and is responsible for routing messages to their destination. MTAs can communicate with each other, with MSs, and with UAs.
- *Message Transfer System* (MTS). A collection of MTAs and MSs functioning together under a single administrative umbrella (private or public) from an MTS. An MTS is thus the backbone of an MHS.
- *Access Unit* (AU). This is essentially a gateway to another messaging system, such as the SMTP mail system of the Internet. Gateways must be able to translate between different addressing schemes and repackage messages into a form acceptable to the other system.

X.400 contains other components as well, but these five are the main ones that make up an MHS. Another helpful component is the *Remote User Agent* (RUA), which provides messaging capabilities for a UA when it is offline from the MHS. The RUA acts as a spool for outgoing messages and supports dial-up messaging connections.

In addition to the components described above, an X.400 MHS also uses a number of special X.400 messaging protocols, of which the following are the most important:

- *P1 protocol*. This protocol defines the format for communications between a UA and an MTA, and between two MTAs. Also known as the Message Transfer Protocol, P1 defines the format of an X.400 message "envelope" that contains the necessary routing information for an X.400 MTA to know how to route a message to its destination.
- *P2 protocol*. This protocol defines the format for communications between two UAs in an MHS. The 1988 Blue Book revised this protocol, calling it P2 Version 2 or P22 for short.
- *P3 protocol*. This protocol defines the format for communications between an MTA and an MS.
- *P7 protocol*. This protocol defines the format for communications between a UA and an MS.

There are many more P-series protocols, some of them arrived after the 1988 Blue Book, such as the P35 protocol for Electronic Data Interchange (EDI), but the ones listed above are the basic ones.

So how do all these different components and protocols work together to create a messaging system? A typical X.400 messaging session might look something like this:

- UA1 submits message to MTA1 using P1
- MTA1 forwards message to MTA2 using P1

- MTA2 forwards message to MTA3 using P1
- MTA3 delivers message to MS2 using P3
- UA2 connects to MS2 to download message using P7

From the perspective of the user, however, it looks much simpler:

- UA1 sends message to UA2 using P22.

Simple, isn't it?

X.400 Addressing

If you think the architecture and operation of an X.400 messaging system is complex, wait until you look at its addressing scheme. We've already looked briefly at X.400 addresses in Chapter 4, where we called them Originator/Recipient Addresses or O/R Addresses. What makes this addressing system so complex is that it was designed from the start to be global and encompass all forms of messaging media (email, voice, fax, EDI, post, telex, and so on). As a result, an O/R address can get rather long, since it has to uniquely define a recipient somewhere in the world.

An O/R address typically consists of a string of name/value pairs, each one delimited by a semicolon or other delimiting character. Table 14-1 shows the various fields that can be used in an O/R address. Only one attribute listed below is case-sensitive: the *Domain Defined Attribute* (DDA).

Table 14-1

Possible Field Names in an O/R Address.

Name of Field	Abbreviation	Label	Max. Length
Given Name	Given Name	G	16
Initials	Initials	I	5
Surname	Surname	S	40
Generation Qualifier	Generation	Q	3
Common Name	Common Name	CN	32
X.121 Address	X.121	X.121	15
UA Numeric ID	N-ID	N-ID	32
Terminal Type	T-TY	T-TY	3
Terminal Identifier	T-ID	T-ID	24
Organization	Organization	O	64

Table 14-1

Continued.

Name of Field	Abbreviation	Label	Max. Length
Organizational Unit 1	Org.Unit.1	OU1	32
Organizational Unit 2	Org.Unit.2	OU2	32
Organizational Unit 3	Org.Unit.3	OU3	32
Organizational Unit 4	Org.Unit.4	OU4	32
PRMD Name	PRMD	P	16
ADMD Name	ADMD	A	16
Country	Country	C	2
Domain Defined Attribute	DDA	DDA	8,128

A typical name/value pair would be `c=US`, which indicates that the Country is the United States of America, US being the international two-letter code for that country. A typical X.400 address consists of a series of name/value pairs strung together. For example, the following might be the O/R address of the network administrator for MTIT in our trendy Paris site:

```
c=FR;a=ATLAS;p=MTIT;o=Paris;s=Sartre;g=Jean-Paul;
```

Let's decipher this address:

- `c=FR;` tells us that the country of the recipient is France.
- `a=ATLAS;` tells us that the ADMD is ATLAS, a major public X.400 service provider in France. ADMD stands for Administrative Management Domain and represents an MHS that is managed by a registered telecommunications company, the equivalent of Sprint or AT&T in the states.
- `p=MTIT;` tells us that the PRMD is MTIT, the name of our dummy company in this book. (My own company is actually called MTIT Enterprises and is registered on the Internet as mtit.com. Check out my Web site sometime at `www.mtit.com` to find out about all the great books I have written—just thought I'd mention it!) PRMD stands for Private Management Domain and represents an individual subscription to an ADMD. In other words, the PRMD registers itself with the ADMD, just like a subscriber registers itself with AT&T. Two PRMDs can communicate with each other by using the interconnected global X.400 network of ADMDs. The PRMD typically represents the

name of the company to which the user belongs, specifically the highest-level name of the business enterprise.

- `o=Paris;` tells us that the organization is called Paris. In X.400 terminology, an Organization (O or o) represents the name of the network within the company on which the user resides. It typically represents the name of a state, city, department, or branch of the company.
- `s=Sartre;g=Jean-Paul;` tells us that the user's given name is Jean-Paul and surname is Sartre. MTIT attracts only the best people.

Note that many O/R attributes have not been included in the above address. That's because an O/R address only needs the minimum number of name/value fields necessary in order to uniquely specify the intended recipient. If, for example, we had two Jean-Paul Sartres in Paris, one in the IS department and one in Sales, we could use an additional field called Organizational Unit 1 to specify the department of the intended recipient, whose address might then become:

```
c=FR;a=ATLAS;p=MTIT;o=Paris;ou1=IS;s=Sartre;g=Jean-Paul;
```

To create a valid O/R address, the following two attributes are required:

- Country
- ADMD

while at least one of the following attributes must also be included:

- PRMD
- Organization
- Organizational Unit
- Common Name
- Surname

If we are working solely within an Exchange organization (for example, if we are using an X.400 connector to join the sites together in our organization), then the addressing is the same as above, but it is interpreted a little differently:

- The ADMD field is typically represented by a single blank space character.
- The PRMD field is the name of the Exchange organization.
- The Organization field is the name of the Exchange site in which the recipient resides. (the Organization field is *not* the name of the Exchange organization).

Take a look, for example, at the following O/R address:

```
c=US;a= ;p=MTIT;o=Atlanta;s=Zhivago;g=Boris;
```

The above address represents the O/R address of Boris Zhivago, the network administrator for the Atlanta site of MTIT. If you open the property sheet for Boris' mailbox in Exchange Administrator and switch to the E-mail Addresses tab, you'll see that this is so (see Figure 14-1).

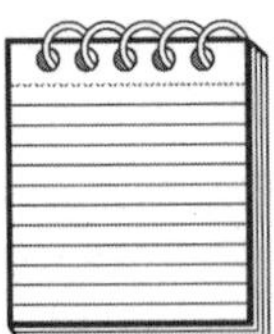

X.400 vs. SMTP

You've probably guessed why X.400 never really caught on in our country: it's too complex! Imagine having to memorize the following address for sending email to the President of the United States:

```
c=US;a=MCI;p=Washington DC;Whitehouse;s=Clinton;g=Bill;
```

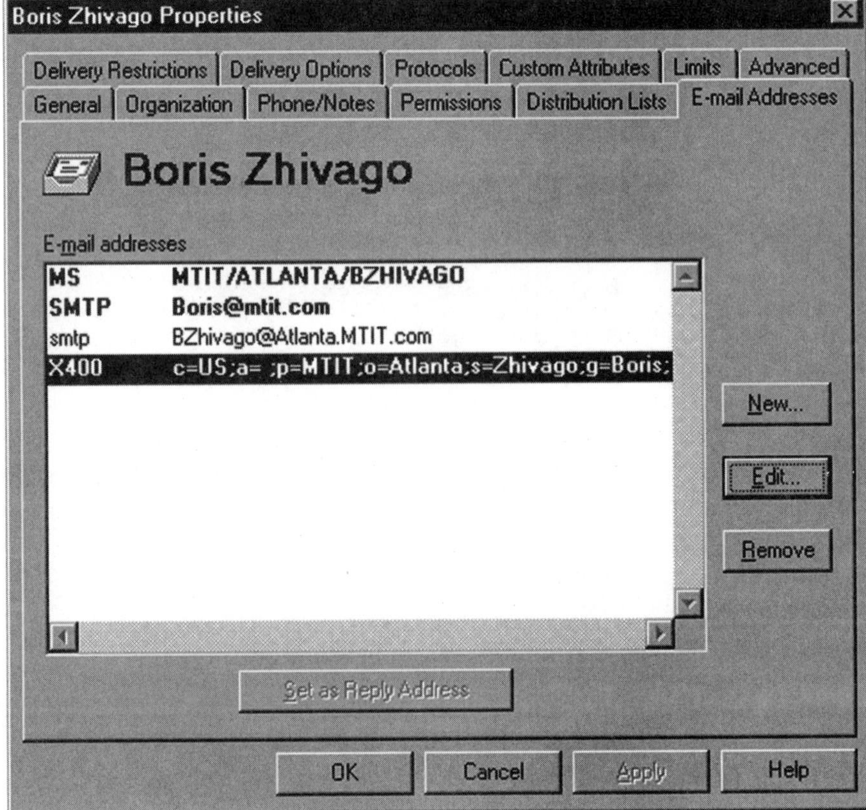

Figure 14-1 The O/R address for Boris Zhivago's mailbox in Atlanta.

It's much easier to use the SMTP address

```
president@whitehouse.gov
```

Another reason that X.400 never caught on was that software developers had to pay to purchase the X.400 standards documents from the ITU, whereas the IETF's Request For Comment (RFC) documents outlining the operation of SMTP and other Internet protocols are available for free on the Internet. Neither system is perfect. On the one hand, you have the complex, bureaucratic nature of X.400, which parallels the centuries of civil service bureaucracy in European nations, while the wild, wild west nature of the Internet appeals more to American freedom and individualism. Nevertheless, almost a dozen carriers still support some level of interconnected X.400 MHS service in North America. Because of this, Exchange Server includes support for interoperability with both types of messaging systems, SMTP and X.400.

MTA Transport Stack

Before we look at the X.400 Connector in detail, we first need to consider the MTA Transport Stack. An MTA Transport Stack is a special protocol stack residing above the normal network protocol, which enables message transports for an X.400 Connector. (A specific type of MTA Transport Stack is also required if you are going to use the Dynamic RAS Connector also.) Four types of MTA Transport Stacks can be installed with Exchange, and these types are summarized in Table 14-2. In addition, certain hardware and software may need to be installed on a machine before these transport stacks can be installed, and this is summarized in Table 14-3.

We'll look at how to install and configure an MTA Transport Stack later in this chapter during the walkthrough.

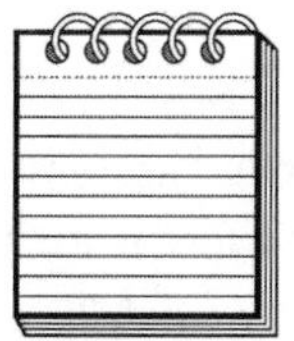

Deleting an MTA Transport Stack

Because the operation of an X.400 Connector depends on the presence of an underlying MTA Transport Stack, if you delete the MTA Transport Stack, it will automatically delete any X.400 Connectors that use it as well, along with any unsent messages waiting in the X.400 Connector message queue.

Table 14-2

Types of MTA Transport Stacks for Exchange.

Transport Stack	Supported Connector	Explanation
TCP/IP	X.400 Connector	Can be used on any dedicated network connection that has TCP/IP for its network protocol to provide X.400 messaging connectivity over TCP/IP.
X.25	X.400 Connector	Can be used with Eicon X.25 port adapters over either dedicated or dial-up connections.
TP4	X.400 Connector	Can be used on networks that use the connectionless Transport Class 4 (TP4) OSI transport layer protocol.
RAS	Dynamic RAS Connector	Can be used with modems, ISDN, or X.25 for connecting to remote sites using Windows NT RAS and works with either TCP/IP or NWLink.

Table 14-3

Hardware/Software Requirements for Different MTA Transport Stacks.

Transport Stack	Hardware and Software Required
TCP/IP	TCP/IP networking protocol and network interface card.
X.25	Eicon X.25 port adapter with associated software, plus a connection from an X.25 service provider.
TP4	Network interface card that supports TP4, a connection from a TP4 service provider, and the TP4 driver from the Windows NT CD. Use the Control Panel to configure the Network Service Access Point (NSAP) address for TP4.
RAS	Windows NT Remote Access Service together with either a networking protocol like TCP/IP or NWLink, an ISDN terminal adapter, or an X.25 PAD.

X.400 Connector

We mentioned at the beginning of this chapter the three uses of an X.400 Connector in an Exchange organization. Let's focus for a moment on the idea of using the X.400 Connector instead of the Site Connector for linking different sites together. Each type of connector has its own advantages and disadvantages in this regard, which are summarized in Table 14-4.

Table 14-4

A Comparison of the X.400 Connector vs. the Site Connector for the Purpose of Linking Exchange Sites Together.

X.400 Connector	Site Connector
Fast and reliable message delivery	Same.
Requires a permanent LAN or WAN connection that supports RPCs.	Same.
Somewhat complex to install and configure, but offers many configuration options.	Very easy to install and configure, but offers few configuration options.
Will work even if both sites are in different domains with no trust relationship between them (does not use Windows NT Challenge/Response authentication).	Requires that both sites either be in the same Windows NT domain, or that they be in separate domains with a trust relationship between them (uses Windows NT Challenge/Response authentication).
Requires an MTA Transport Stack to be previously installed and configured.	Does not require an MTA Transport Stack.
Uses Remote Procedure Calls (RPCs) to transfer messages.	Does not use RPCs.
Supports TCP/IP, TP4, and X.25 protocols. protocols.	Supports TCP/IP, IPX/SPX, and NetBEUI
Requires a minimum of 56 Kbps available network bandwidth and generally performs better than the Site Connector in low bandwidth environments.	Requires a bare minimum of 56 Kbps available network bandwidth but only minimal message traffic can be supported at this speed. Sharing a 56-Kbps messaging link with file-transfer applications may result in unreliable messaging. A minimum of 128 Kbps is recommended.
Can schedule the time and frequency of message transfers to take advantage of slow periods of network traffic.	Cannot schedule message transfers but instead is always active.
Can control the maximum size of messages being transferred, which is useful in low-bandwidth environments.	Cannot control message size.
The messaging bridgehead servers can become a bottleneck because of the point-to-point messaging topology of the connector.	Supports more flexible messaging topologies and is less likely to experience bottlenecks, since instead of specifying a bridgehead server, you can enable any server in the local site to initiate connections with servers in the remote site.

Looking at Table 14-4, we might ask when we would prefer the Site Connector over the X.400 Connector. The general rule of thumb is to use a Site

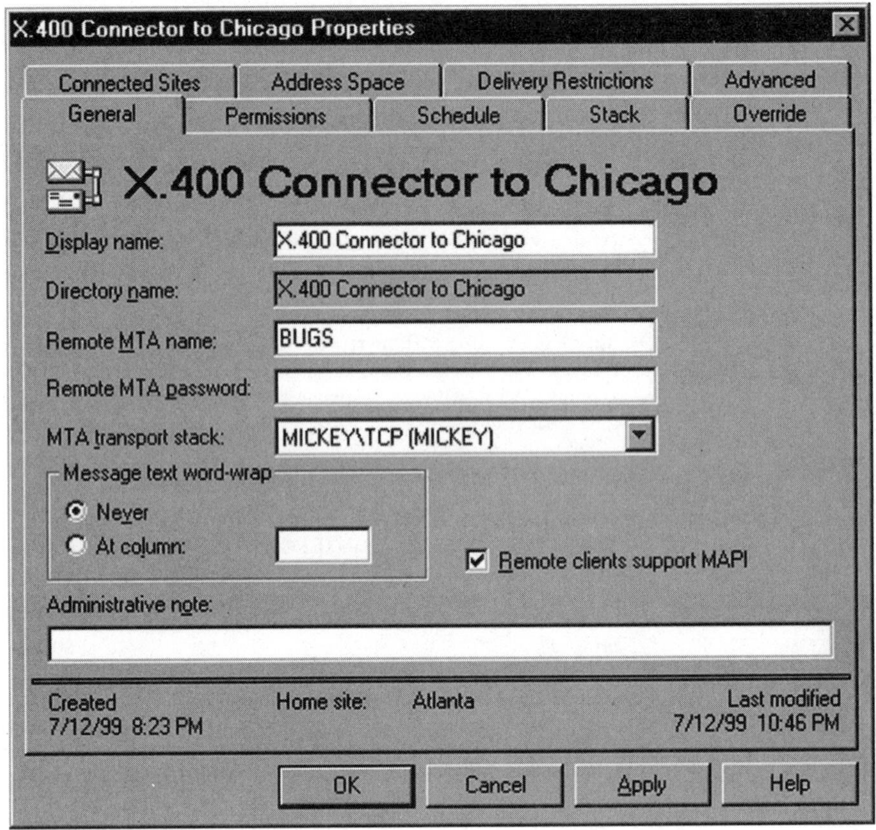

Figure 14-2 Configuring an X.400 Connector.

Connector instead of an X.400 Connector for linking Exchange sites together if the following two conditions apply:

- There is at least 128 Kbps of available dedicated network bandwidth between the two networks.
- The two networks can authenticate each other using Windows NT Challenge/Response authentication.

Let's now look at the various tabs and their configuration settings on the property sheet for the X.400 Connector (Figure 14-2):

- *Remote MTA name and password (General tab).* To find the name of the remote MTA, start Exchange Administrator on the server that you are going to connect to in the remote site, open the property sheet for the MTA that is located in the Server container, select the General tab, and use the Local MTA name and password displayed here. The purpose of the password is because the X.400 Connector does not use Windows NT Challenge/Response (NTLM) authentication, so you can put a password on the MTA for security reasons. You should do this especially if you are connecting to a public X.400 messaging service.

- *MTA Transport Stack (General tab).* Here you select the appropriate installed MTA Transport Stack, which will be associated with the connector. There is usually only one MTA Transport Stack installed, however.
- *Message Text Word-Wrap (General tab).* Leave this at Never usually, unless the foreign X.400 messaging system you are connecting to requires word-wrap to occur at a specific column.
- *Remote Clients Support MAPI (General tab).* Leave this checked if you are connecting to another Exchange site.
- *Schedule tab.* This tab lets you schedule when (for how long and how often) the connector is active for transferring messages. The X.400 Connector can be scheduled to deliver mail to other sites in four different ways:
  - *Always* means the connector to be active continually. (Online Help says that Always means the connector is active every 15 minutes, but this is wrong.)
  - *Selected Times* means the connector is scheduled to transfer mail to the remote site at the time specified in either hourly or 15-minute blocks.
  - *Remote Initiated* means that any messages queued for delivery at this end of the connector will only be delivered when the remote end of the connector initiates a connection. If you choose Remote Initiated at one end, do not make the same choice at the other end or messages will never be delivered. Also, make sure you have configured both connectors as a two-way alternate on the Advanced tab as well.
  - *Never* disables the connector.
- *Stack tab.* This tab lets you specify the transport address information of the X.400 Connector or remote X.400 MTA you are connecting to. The displayed form of this property page depends on the type of transport stack installed. For a TCP/IP-type X.400 Connector and a MTA Transport Stack, you can either specify the IP address, the fully qualified DNS host name, or the NetBIOS name of the remote machine with which you are connecting. The OSI address information on this tab may be required when connecting to foreign X.400 mail systems

(check with your X.400 service provider for information on how to configure this if required).

- *Override tab*. This tab can be used to override the settings on the Messaging Defaults tab of the MTA Site Configuration object for your local site (but only for messages routed through this connector). They should match the settings on the MTA Site Configuration object for the remote site. You can generally leave these as they are.
- *Connected Sites tab*. If you are using this connector to link two sites together in your Exchange organization, use this tab to specify the name of the remote site you are connecting to. This is explained in more detail in the walkthrough later.
- *Address Space tab*. If you are using this connector to provide messaging connectivity with a foreign X.400 messaging system, you need to specify an address space for the foreign X.400 MTA, that is, a path to route messages from your site to the foreign messaging system. Obtain this information from your X.400 service provider.
- *Delivery Restrictions tab*. This tab lets you restrict who you will accept or reject messages from (to prevent spam).
- *MTA conformance, X.400 link options, and so on (Advanced tab)*. Talk to your X.400 service provider to configure these settings. If you are just using the connector to link Exchange sites together in your organization, leave the defaults as they are.
- *Message Size (Advanced tab)*. The X.400 Connector lets you limit the maximum message size that the connector will pass. This can be useful if you are in a limited bandwidth situation. It is different from setting a message limit on the MTA object, which limits message size over *all* installed connectors for the site.

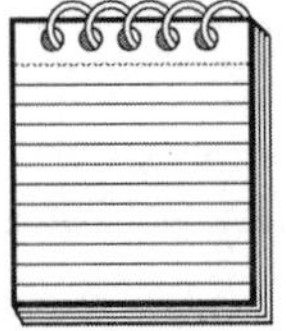

X.400 Connectors and Directory Replication
Here's a planning issue for your consideration. Let's say that you have three sites in your organization called A, B, and C. Sites A and B are linked together using an X.400 Connector, and sites B and C are linked using an X.400 Connector. How should you configure directory replication to occur between your sites? Should you have A replicate with B, B with C, and C with A? That scenario results in a waste of bandwidth. It's better to simply have B replicate with both A and C in order to do the job most efficiently. We'll look more at scenarios with more than two sites in a later chapter.

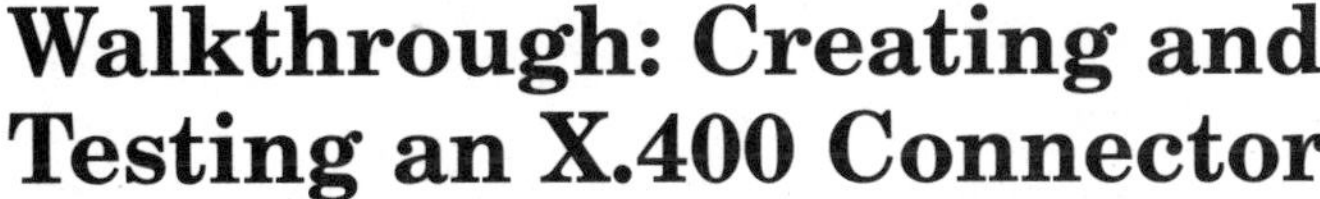

Walkthrough: Creating and Testing an X.400 Connector

Now let's walk through the process of establishing messaging connectivity between two sites using the X.400 Connector. We'll use our Atlanta and Chicago sites, which are currently joined together using the Site Connector that we installed in Chapter 10 and are sharing directory information using the Directory Replication Connector installed in Chapter 11. We'll first remove these two connectors in order to completely restore the sites back to their original state before we joined them together.

Removing Existing Connectors

Begin by starting Exchange Administrator on MICKEY and selecting the Directory Replication Connector with Chicago that is located in the Directory Replication container in the Atlanta site. Click the Delete button on the toolbar to remove the connector. A message appears saying, "Deleting the directory replication connector that connects with site 'Chicago' will stop replication with that site. To re-establish replication with that site, you must add a new directory replication connector. Are you sure you want to delete the directory replication connector?" Click Yes, and another message appears, saying "Should the Directory Replication Connector with Chicago in the remote site 'Chicago' be deleted also?" Click Yes, and another message appears, saying, "The directory replication connector has been deleted from both the local site and the remote site. Allow up to an hour for replicated data to be completely deleted." Click OK and another message appears (see Figure 14-3).

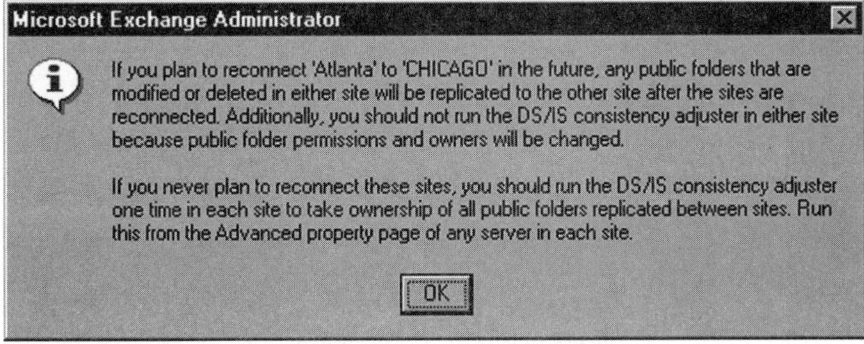

Figure 14-3 Warning after deleting a Directory Replication Connector.

You can see from this message that creating and deleting Directory Replication Connectors can potentially cause problems unless you're careful. In a real Exchange implementation, you wouldn't install and remove components as freely as we are doing in our test implementation.

Now select the Site Connector to Chicago, which is located in the Connections container for the Atlanta site. Delete it. You are prompted to confirm your action. Note that when you delete one end of the Site Connector, it does not delete the other end, so now you have to go to Chicago site and start Exchange Administrator on BUGS to delete the other half of the Site Connector.

Go make yourself a latte. When you come back, the directory service in each site should have processed the above actions, and the sites will be totally disconnected and know nothing about each other's directory.

Now let's create the X.400 Connector in Atlanta. Select File, New Other, X.400 Connector from the menu. Instead of starting the process of creating a new X.400 Connector, a message appears saying, "Before you can configure an X.400 connector, you must use the New Other MTA Transport Stack command on the File menu to install an MTA transport stack." Oops, I forgot!

Installing an MTA Transport Stack

So let's install an MTA Transport Stack first. We'll install one of the types suitable for use on a TCP/IP network. Select File, New Other, MTA Transport Stack from the Exchange Administrator menu to open the New MTA Transport Stack dialog box (see Figure 14-4).

We'll select the TCP/IP MTA Transport Stack and install it on the server MICKEY in Atlanta. (If there is more than one Exchange Server in our site, the one we select will be the one through which the X.400 Connector will route all X.400 messages; that is, it will be the Message Bridgehead Server for the connector.) Click OK to open a property sheet for our new transport stack, which by default has the display name "TCP (MICKEY)" (see Figure 14-5).

We don't need to configure anything here. If we had other X.400 applications on the server that used this transport stack, we might need to configure the OSI address information parameters. Fortunately, we don't need to understand that stuff if we just want to use the transport stack to install the Exchange X.400 Connector on our system. Just click OK, and a new directory object named "TCP (MICKEY)" appears within the MICKEY Server container in the Exchange Administrator window. "TCP (MICKEY)" is our new MTA Transport Stack on MICKEY.

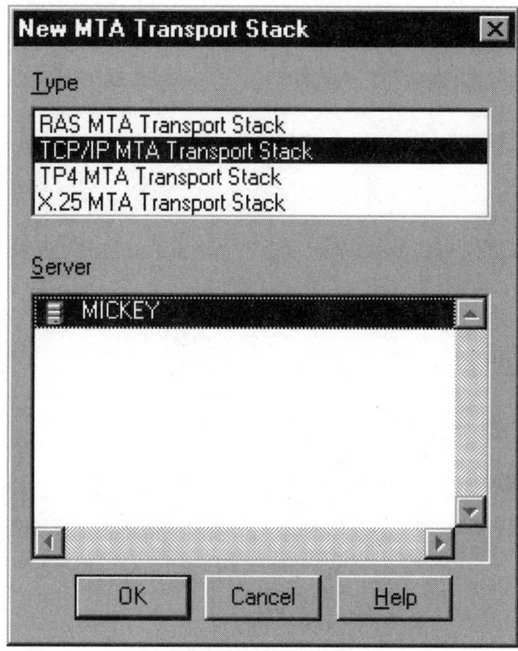

Figure 14-4 Specifying the type of MTA Transport Stack to install.

Creating an X.400 Connector

Now let's go back to creating an X.400 Connector on MICKEY. Select File, New Other, X.400 Connector from the menu. The New X.400 Connector dialog box appears, asking us to select the type of X.400 Connector we want to install. Each type of X.400 Connector depends on its corresponding MTA Transport Stack, so there are three possible types of X.400 Connectors:

- X.25 X.400 Connector
- TCP/IP X.400 Connector
- TP4 X.400 Connector

Since we have only installed the TCP/IP type of the MTA Transport Stack, only the middle choice above appears in the New X.400 Connector dialog box (see Figure 14-6).

Click OK. You may be prompted to switch to the Connections container, and click OK to this as well. A blank property sheet for a new X.400 Connector appears so we can configure our new connector (see Figure 14-7).

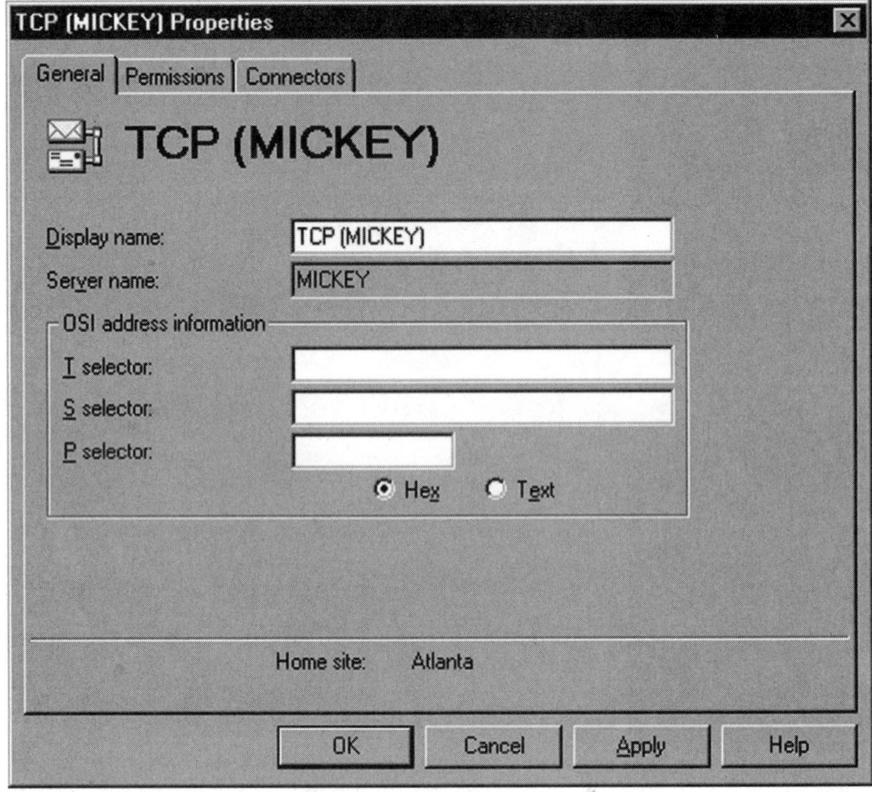

Figure 14-5 Configuring a new MTA Transport Stack.

Enter the following on the General tab:

Display Name = X.400 Connector to Chicago

Directory Name = X.400 Connector to Chicago

Remote MTA Name = BUGS

Note that the Remote MTA Name is shown as the Local MTA Name on the General tab of the MTA object for the server you are trying to connect to in the remote site.

Switch to the Schedule tab and make sure that Always is selected. This makes the X.400 Connector continually active. Note that you can schedule the X.400 Connector; you couldn't do this with the Site Connector we installed in Chapter 10.

Switch to the Stack tab. Here we are required to only enter the address of the server in the remote site, which will have the other half of the X.400 Connector installed on it. We could enter either

- The fully-qualified DNS name of the remote host, provided we have a DNS server configured somewhere on the network

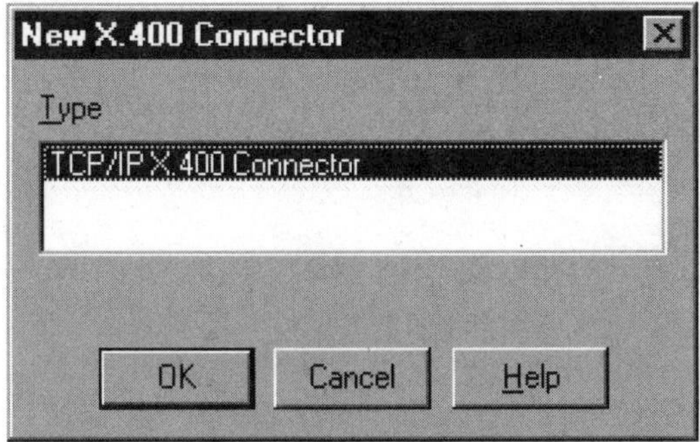

Figure 14-6 Specifying the type of X.400 Connector to create.

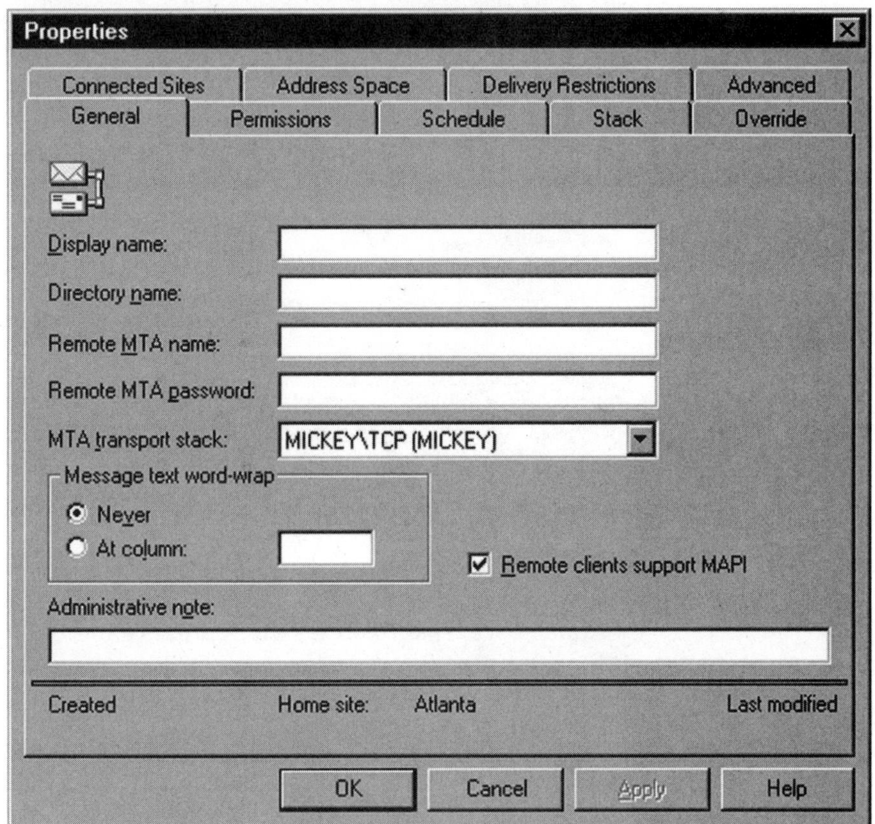

Figure 14-7 Configuring a new X.400 Connector.

- The NetBIOS name of the remote host if we are using a WINS server
- The IP address of the remote host

We'll use the third option. Select the IP Address button and enter the IP address of BUGS (see Figure 14-8). You can use `ipconfig` from the command-line on BUGS to determine this address. Again, we can ignore all the OSI addressing here.

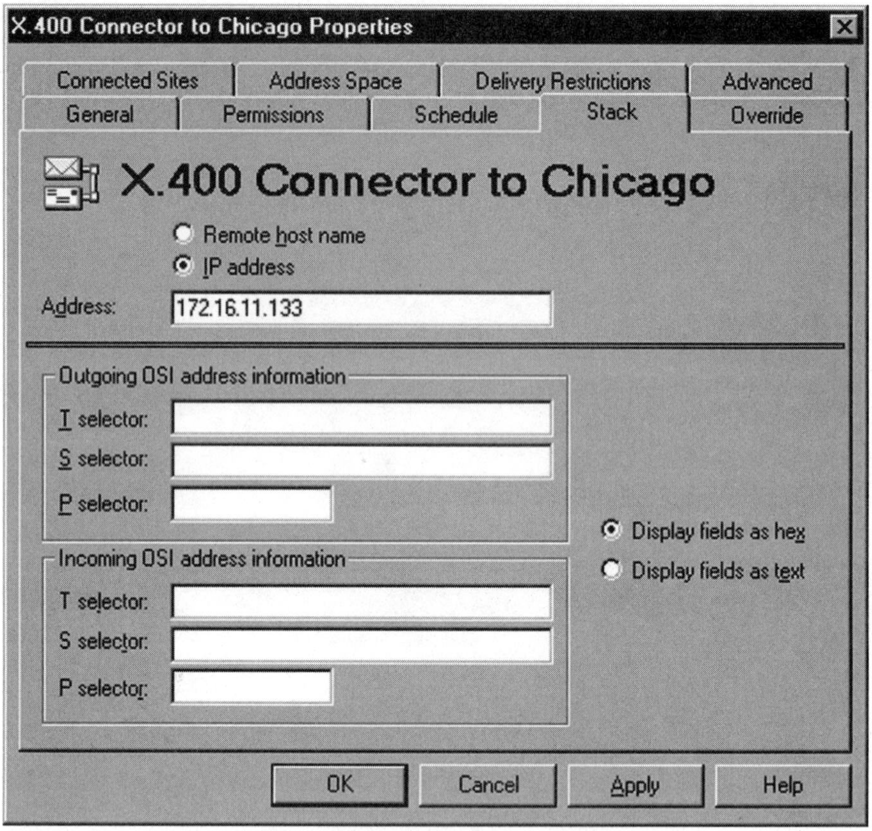

Figure 14-8 Configuring the address of the remote server.

Finally, we need to either configure a connected site on the Connected Sites tab or an address space on the Address Space tab so the X.400 Connector knows how to route messages to the remote site. Since we are connecting to another site in our Exchange organization MTIT, we'll use the Connected Sites tab. Switch to this tab now (see Figure 14-9).

Click the New button on this tab to open a Properties sheet (rather a vague name) for specifying the connected site (see Figure 14-10).

On the General tab of this Properties sheet, the Organization should be listed as MTIT. Enter "Chicago" (without the quotes) for the name of the Site, and switch to the Routing Address tab (see Figure 14-11). Note the various name/value pairs of the O/R address for the remote site that are visible in this tab. We don't actually have to configure anything here, so just click OK to return to the Connected Sites tab of the X.400 Connector to

Figure 14-9 Configuring a connected site.

Chicago property sheet. The listbox in the Connected Sites tab should show the following routing information for our new X.400 Connector:

Organization = MTIT
Site = CHICAGO
Routing address = `X400:c=US;a= ;p=MTIT;o=CHICAGO;`
Cost = 1

We're done with the Atlanta side of the connector. Click OK and a message appears saying, "You must configure both sides of this connection before messages can be sent successfully. If you are connecting to another Microsoft Exchange site, then ensure that a properly configured connector exists in that site."

Now start Exchange Administrator on BUGS in Chicago and install a new MTA Transport Stack of type TCP/IP, accepting the default name of

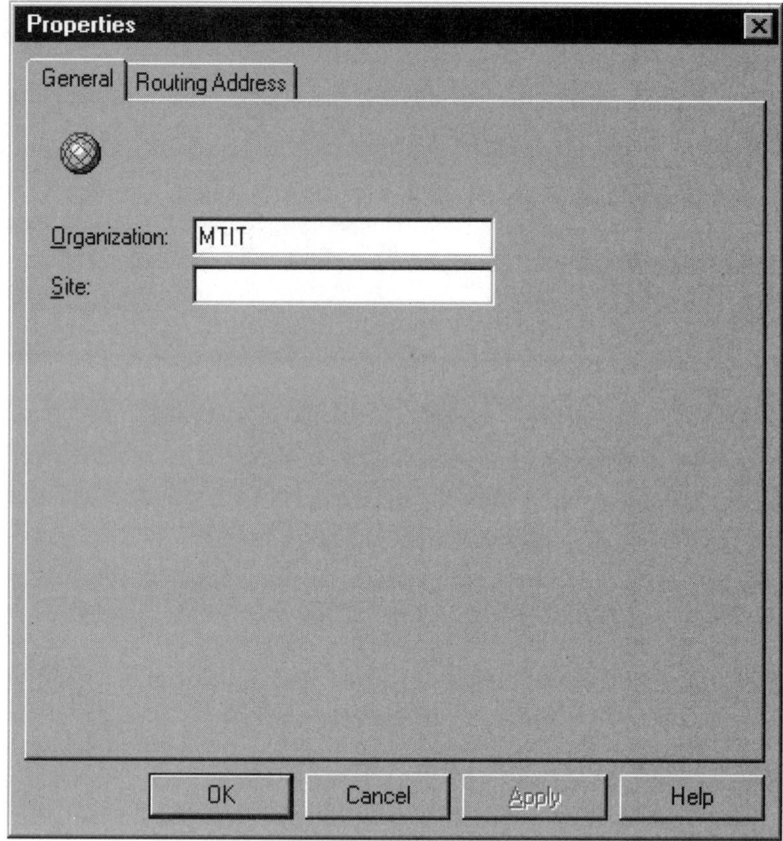

Figure 14-10 Specifying a connected site.

"TCP (BUGS)." Then install a new TCP/IP X.400 Connector on BUGS and configure it as follows:

- Display Name = X.400 Connector to Atlanta
- Directory Name = X.400 Connector to Atlanta
- Remote MTA Name = MICKEY
- IP address = (enter MICKEY's IP address here)
- On the Connected Sites tab, add the site Atlanta, which will enter the following routing information into the listbox:

  Organization = MTIT
  Site = Atlanta
  Routing address = `X400:c=US;a= ;p=MTIT;o=Atlanta;`
  Cost = 1

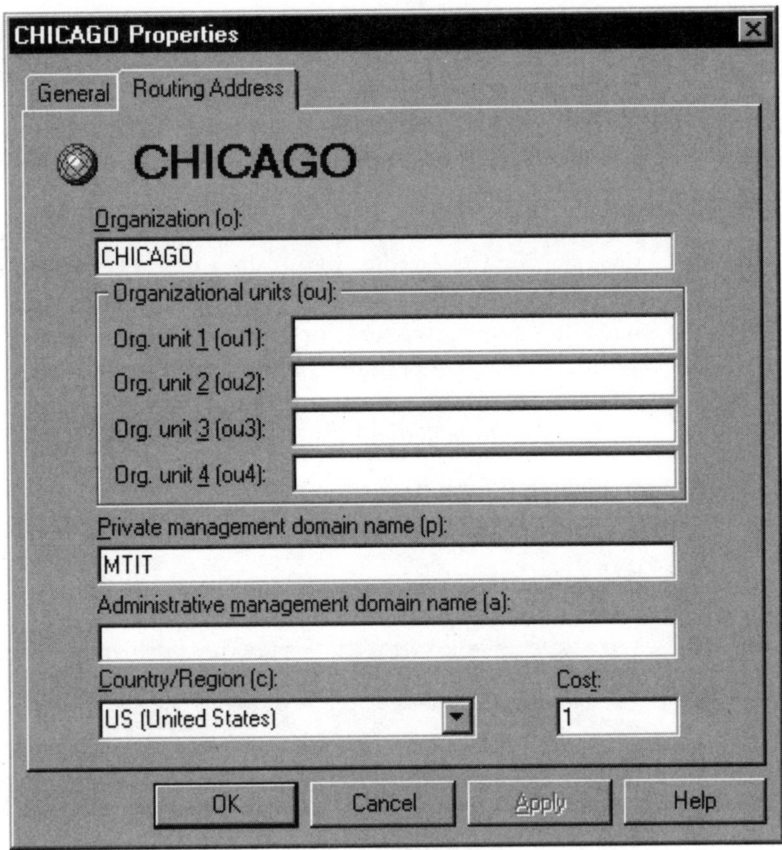

Figure 14-11 Specifying a connected site (continued).

Testing the X.400 Connector

We should now have both ends of the X.400 Connector configured properly. To test the connector, send a one-off message using the X.400 address to a recipient in the other site (see Chapter 10's walkthrough for details on how to do this). I tried this, sending a message as Boris on GOOFEY in Atlanta to Peter James on BUGS in Chicago. Peter James' O/R address is

```
c=US;a= ;p=MTIT;o=Chicago;s=James;g=Peter;
```

(By the way, instead of always entering one-off O/R addresses into Outlook to test connectors, you could create an X.400-type custom recipient in Atlanta for Peter James in Chicago, and Boris could send his test messages to this custom recipient instead).

Anyway, if the test message doesn't work, check the Remote MTA Name, IP address, and routing information on the Connected Sites tabs of each X.400 connector to make sure they are entered properly. After you've got it working and played with it, remove the connector from both sites since we are going to try a different connector in the next chapter (you can leave the transport stack installed if you like).

If you like, try changing the X.400 Connector schedule to send messages at a specific time of day, like from 3 to 4 A.M. Wait a few minutes for the change to take effect and send another test message using Outlook. Then open the property sheet for the MTA object on MICKEY in Exchange Administrator (see Figure 14-12). The Queues tab on this property sheet lets you check for messages queued up for delivery on MICKEY. Three queues should be listed in the Queue Name drop-down box:

- Private Information Store
- Public Information Store
- X.400 Connector to Chicago

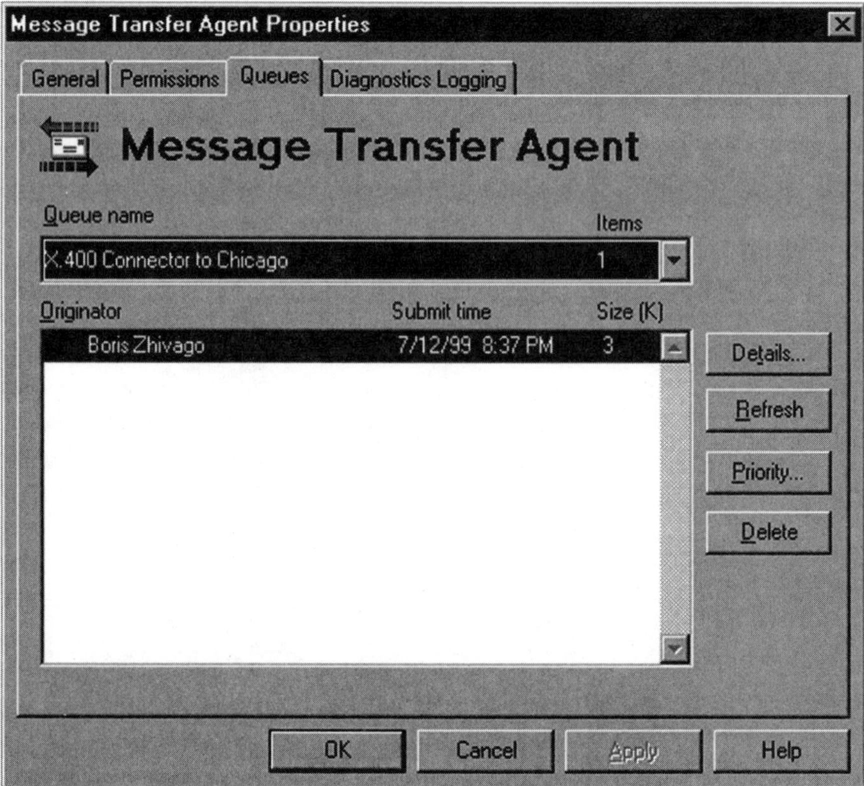

Figure 14-12 A message from Boris to Peter queued for delivery by the X.400 Connector on MICKEY.

The queue for the X.400 Connector to Chicago shows the message from Boris to Peter waiting in the queue until the connector is activated to deliver it.

Where Do We Go from Here?

In the next few chapters, we will continue looking at other types of connectors that can be used for linking sites in an Exchange organization and establishing messaging connectivity with legacy and third-party mail systems.

For More Information

You can find some information on configuring MTA Transport Stacks and X.400 Connectors in Chapter 7 of the *Operations* manual for Exchange, which is included in Books Online.

TechNet

A number of useful resources regarding X.400 can be found on the monthly TechNet CD. Of particular interest are the following:

- From the *Technical Notes* section on MS Exchange Server:
- X.400 Concepts and Terminology
- MS Exchange and X.400
- Configuring and Tuning the MS Exchange Server 5.5 MTA
- From the *Microsoft Knowledge Base* on MS Exchange Server:
- Q190022. XCON: Comparison of X.400 and Site Connectors
- Q174756. XADM: X.400 Connector Enabled on Standard Version of Exchange
- Q175483. XCON: Configuration Sample—Exchange X.400 Connector and Infonet
- Q196381. XCON: Messages Queue Over X.400 Connectors Through Firewall
- Q184662. XADM: Messages Not Rerouted Between 2 X.400 Connectors in Site

- Q177862. XCON: Messages Fail Downgrade, Bounce Between X.400 Connectors
- Q215472. XFOR: How the X.400 Connector Handles High-Priority Mail
- Q165279. XCON: X.400 First Contact Form for X.400 Connector Problem

And if you're wondering about those four-letter X prefaces at the beginning of Knowledge Base articles on Exchange, you can find out what they mean by reading Q140950. XGEN: How to Search for Microsoft Exchange Articles by Topic.

CHAPTER 15

Administering MS Mail Connectors

In the last chapter, we looked at how to create and configure X.400 Connectors, which can be used either for linking sites in an Exchange organization or for establishing messaging connectivity with a foreign X.400 messaging system. In this chapter, we will look at another kind of connector called the Microsoft Mail Connector, which is designed to provide messaging connectivity between an Exchange organization and a legacy Microsoft Mail 3.x messaging system. After reading this chapter, you will have an understanding of the following topics:

- Microsoft Mail
- Microsoft Mail Connector
- Directory Synchronization

The walkthrough in this chapter takes you through the process of establishing messaging connectivity with a Microsoft Mail 3.5 postoffice server.

Microsoft Mail

Microsoft Mail (MS Mail) is a legacy mail system that has now been superseded by Microsoft Exchange Server. MS Mail was actually developed by Consumer Software Inc. in the 1980s and was called Network Courier 2.0 when Microsoft acquired it in 1991, renaming it Microsoft Mail for PC Networks 2.0. Microsoft then revised and enhanced the product and produced several more versions, culminating in MS Mail 3.5, which was soon superseded by Exchange 4.0. MS Mail was designed to run on the Microsoft LAN Manager Server, the precursor to Microsoft Windows NT Server, although it could also run on Windows for Workgroups (WFW) 3.11 and even Windows NT machines as well. There was also a version of MS Mail for AppleTalk networks called Microsoft Mail for AppleTalk Networks or QuarterDeck Mail.

MS Mail is different from Exchange; it was intended primarily as a LAN-based messaging system that operated on a store-and-forward mail transfer mechanism. What this basically meant was that an MS Mail Server (called a postoffice) was basically nothing more than a passive file server with a hierarchy of mail folders. All processing of messages was done by the client. For example, to send a message, the client basically copied the message to the destination recipient's mail folder on the server. The destination recipient's mail client regularly polled the postoffice for new mail, and if some was found, it was downloaded by the client. In essence, MS Mail was a proprietary implementation of the X.400 messaging standards, since X.400 was also designed to operate on a store-and-forward mechanism.

This is quite different from Exchange, which operates as a client/server messaging system where the Outlook client and the Exchange Server function together as a whole by using Remote Procedure Calls (RPCs). With an Outlook/Exchange combination, the client and the server share the processing of messages. The destination client does not need to poll the Exchange Server to see if there is new mail waiting for it; Exchange automatically connects with the destination client to transfer mail to it.

MS Mail was bigger than just a single-server messaging system. You could have multiple postoffices on your network, which could be connected together using a MTA called the External program. In addition, a process called directory synchronization could copy address information between postoffices to create a single Global Address List (GAL) for all users on the network. Finally, various gateways were provided for establishing messaging connectivity between an MS Mail network and foreign messaging systems like SMTP, X.400, or mainframe-based PROFS and SNADS. In all, MS Mail was pretty ambitious for a product that started out as a LAN-based messaging system. Its performance in large-scale implementations left something to be desired, however, and administration was DOS-based and tedious to perform. Hence, Microsoft Exchange.

We won't be covering MS Mail in detail in this book; it's probably not worth the bother. Instead, we will focus on the basic issue of how to establish messaging connectivity between your Exchange organization and a legacy MS Mail system using the Microsoft Mail Connector, so that users in either system can exchange messages with those in the other system. A better long-term solution to the problem of coexistence between Exchange and legacy messaging systems, however, is migration, which will be covered in a later chapter.

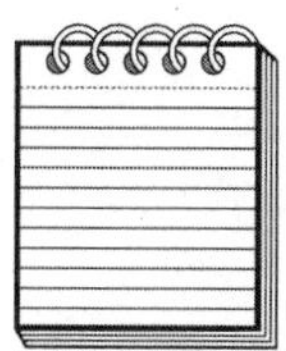

MS Mail Addressing

You should be familiar with the topic of MS Mail addresses. We covered this briefly in Chapter 4, and you should refer back to that chapter if necessary before proceeding further here.

Microsoft Mail Connector

The MS Mail Connector enables messages to be exchanged between an Exchange organization and a legacy Microsoft Mail 3.x postoffice server (see Figure 15-1). The MS Mail Connector can function over a dedicated LAN, an asynchronous modem, or X.25 network connections.

When configuring messaging connectivity between an Exchange organization and an MS Mail system, you basically need to do two things:

- Configure the MS Mail postoffice server to be able to route messages to external MS Mail recipients.
- Configure the MS Mail Connector on the Exchange Server to connect to the MS Mail postoffice for transferring mail between them.

In this section, we will only summarize the configuration settings of the Exchange side of the connection, namely the MS Mail Connector. In the walkthrough later in this chapter, however, we will consider both sides of the configuration process.

Let's now look at the tabs of interest on the property sheet for the MS Mail Connector (some of these settings will be discussed in more detail during the walkthrough):

Figure 15-1 The property sheet for the Microsoft Mail Connector.

- *General tab*. Note that you can specify a maximum message size that can be routed through the connector.
- *Address Space tab*. This tab shows address spaces for the connector, that is, paths over which the connector is able to route messages. We'll look at this more later.
- *Diagnostic Logging tab*. This tab controls which types of events related to this connector are logged to the Application Log. The meanings of the different categories listed here are as follows:
  - *MSExchangeMSMI* is the MS Mail Connector Interchange service.
  - *MSExchangePCMTA* is the MS Mail for PC Networks Connector MTA service.
  - *MSExchangeATMTA* is the MS Mail for AppleTalk Networks Connector MTA Service.
- *Interchange tab*. This is where you configure the MS Mail Connector Interchange service, We'll look at the important settings on this tab later during the walkthrough.

Operation of MS Mail Connector

Two kinds of Exchange services are associated with the operation of the MS Mail Connector:

- MS Mail Connector Interchange service. *This is a Windows NT service on an Exchange Server that is responsible for routing messages between the Exchange Server MTA service and a temporary MS Mail postoffice located on the Exchange Server called the Shadow Postoffice.*
- MS Mail for PC Networks Connector MTA service. *This is a Windows NT service that is responsible for routing the messages between the shadow postoffice (called the local postoffice on the MS Mail Connector property sheet) and a postoffice on an actual MS Mail server. This service is created when the MS Mail Connector is configured, has whatever name you assign to it when you create it, and will have multiple instances if you are establishing connections with multiple MS Mail postoffices.*

In other words, Exchange implements messaging connectivity with MS Mail servers in a multi-step process. For example, let's say a user on the Exchange system wants to send a message to a user on the MS Mail system. Here's an outline of how it would work:

1. *The Exchange user sends the message, which is passed from the Outlook client program to the Information Store on the Exchange Server.*

2. *The Information Store recognizes that the destination recipient is not on the Exchange system, so it passes the message to the Exchange MTA to route it outside of the system.*
3. *The Exchange MTA recognizes that the message needs to be routed to an external MS Mail postoffice, so it hands the message off to the MS Mail Connector Interchange service.*
4. *The MS Mail Connector Interchange service places the message in the shadow postoffice (temporary postoffice), which is located in the MAILDAT$ share on the Exchange Server.*
5. *The MTA Connector service polls the shadow postoffice from time to time and notices that mail is waiting to be delivered to an external MS Mail postoffice.*
6. *The MTA connector transfers the message to the local postoffice on the MS Mail server.*
7. *The destination recipient's mail client program polls the local postoffice of the MS Mail server from time to time and notices that there is mail waiting to be downloaded.*
8. *The destination recipient's mail client program downloads the message sent to it.*

- *Local Postoffice tab*. This specifies the network and postoffice names of the local postoffice, which is created on the Exchange server when the MS Mail Connector is installed. The local postoffice is used for processing mail in transit through the connector and identifies the Exchange Server to the MS Mail system. (From the point of view of the MS Mail servers, the Exchange Server on which the MS Mail Connector is installed looks just like another MS Mail server.)
- *Connections tab*. This tab is used to establish a connection to MS Mail postoffice servers and displays the postoffices with which you are currently connected. You can also use the Queue button to view messages waiting in the MS Mail Connector message queue and either delete them or return them to the sender.
- *Connector MTAs tab*. This tab is used to create and configure the MS Mail for PC Networks Connector MTA service described previously. You must create and configure a separate instance of this service (a separate Connector MTA) for each remote MS Mail postoffice you are connecting to. We'll look at this in more detail during the walkthrough.

Directory Synchronization (Dirsync)

Directory synchronization is a process in which MS Mail servers exchange directory (addressing) information with each other on an MS Mail network. This process is outlined in this section.

Each postoffice in a MS Mail messaging system functions as a Directory Requestor postoffice, except for one that functions as a Directory Server postoffice. A Directory Requestor postoffice periodically checks to see if there are any changes to the GAL on its server. If there are any address changes, it sends these changes to the Directory Server postoffice and requests any additional address changes that the Server postoffice might have. By changes to the GAL, we mean modifications to any information about recipients in the GAL, such as email addresses, telephone numbers, departments, or whatever else is stored in the MS Mail or Exchange directories. This also refers the addition of new recipients or the deletion of obsolete ones.

The Directory Server postoffice collects all address changes sent to it by Directory Requestor postoffices on the MS Mail network and distributes these changes back to the Requestor postoffices. The Directory Server postoffice acts as the central clearing house for changes to the GAL, making sure that all MS Mail postoffice servers have up-to-date addressing information for all MS Mail users. The Dirsync process for Microsoft Mail is a scheduled process that makes use of MS Mail messages to exchange addressing updates between the Server postoffice and the Requestor postoffices. In a typical MS Mail network, each Requestor postoffice might send its update message to the Server postoffice once a day.

For a Microsoft Exchange organization to synchronize its GAL with that of an MS Mail network, the same basic mechanisms must be used. In this context, the term directory synchronization also refers to the exchange of directory information between a Microsoft Exchange organization and a legacy MS Mail system. This is analogous to what we did in Chapter 10 and Chapter 11, where we first established messaging connectivity between two sites using the Site Connector and then established directory replication between the two sites using the Directory Replication Connector. In a similar fashion, once you first establish messaging connectivity with an MS Mail system using the MS Mail Connector, you can then exchange directory information between the two systems by establishing directory synchronization between the two messaging systems. The catch is that Exchange and MS Mail use totally different directory systems, so it's not that simple to exchange directory information between them. In fact, to implement directory synchronization, you use a whole raft of different Exchange directory objects, including

- Directory Synchronization objects
- Dirsync Server objects
- Dirsync Requestor objects
- Remote Dirsync Requestor objects

Directory synchronization can also be implemented in a number of different ways. Most of this stuff is beyond the scope of this chapter, which is only concerned with establishing messaging connectivity between the two systems, but we will review some of the basics concerning these different objects.

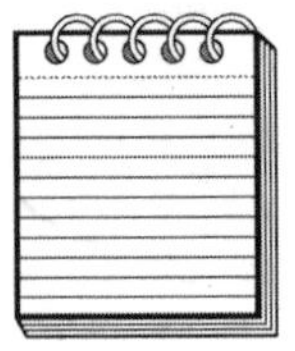

Implementing Directory Synchronization

Everything depends on the MS Mail Connector, which is the focus of the walkthrough later in this chapter. If this connector fails, all the other Exchange components that establish Dirsync with MS Mail systems will also fail to work. This is because they all depend on the MS Mail Connector for establishing messaging connectivity between Exchange sites and MS Mail systems.

Dirsync Requestor

When this component is installed on an Exchange server, the server can act as a Directory Requestor postoffice as far as an MS Mail network is concerned. In other words, a Dirsync Requestor periodically checks with the Exchange server it is installed on to see if there are any updates to the Exchange organization's GAL. If changes are found, the Dirsync Requestor uses the MS Mail Connector to send these updates to an MS Mail Directory Server postoffice according to the specified schedule. If the Server postoffice has any additional changes, it returns these to the Dirsync Requestor on the Exchange server and these changes then propagate throughout the Exchange organization. In this scenario, you might have one MS Mail Server postoffice receiving and distributing GAL updates from three MS Mail Requestor postoffices and one Exchange server with a Dirsync Requestor installed on it.

Dirsync Server

When this component is installed on an Exchange Server, this server can act as a Directory Server Postoffice as far as an MS Mail network is concerned. In other words, MS Mail Directory Requestor postoffices periodically check with the servers they are installed on to see if there are any updates to the MS Mail system's GAL. If changes are found, each Requestor Postoffice sends these updates to a Microsoft Exchange server with a Dirsync Server installed on it according to the specified schedule. If the Exchange server has any additional changes, it returns these to each Requestor postoffice on the MS Mail network. In this scenario, you might have one Exchange server with a Dirsync Server installed on it, receiving and distributing GAL updates from a group of MS Mail Requestor postoffices. Things can get more complicated than this, obviously!

One thing to note, however, is that an Exchange server can have a Dirsync Server or a Dirsync Requestor installed, but not both. Even if there are two different legacy MS Mail networks in your company, an Exchange server can't participate in Dirsync with more than one MS Mail network at a time.

Remote Dirsync Requestor

When you want an Exchange server to handle MS Mail directory synchronization by having a Dirsync Server installed on it, you must configure the Exchange server to replace the existing MS Mail Directory Server postoffice computer. In order to do this, you must create a Remote Dirsync Requestor for each MS Mail Directory Requestor postoffice on the MS Mail network. For example, if you want your Exchange server to perform Dirsync for an MS Mail network consisting of one Directory Server postoffice and three Directory Requestor postoffice computers, configure your Exchange server to replace the Directory Server postoffice by installing the Dirsync Server component on it and then install three Remote Dirsync Requestor components on your Exchange server, one configured for each of the three Directory Requestor postoffices in the MS Mail network.

Directory Synchronization

Finally, once you have all the MS Mail Connectors, Dirsync Servers, Dirsync Requestors, and Remote Dirsync Requestors installed and configured on your Exchange servers (pretty much in that order), you still need to configure one more component on the server: the Directory Synchronization object, which is located within the Server container. This should be on a different server than where the Dirsync Requestors or Servers have been installed.

Walkthrough: Configuring a Microsoft Mail Connector

Let's walk through the process of establishing messaging connectivity between an Exchange Server and an MS Mail 3.5 postoffice server. Our test setup has four machines in it, so we'll summarize the configuration and roles of these machines here (see Figure 15-2).

Our four machines, which are all in the Windows NT domain called MTIT, are configured as follows:

- MICKEY
  - Windows NT 4.0 with Exchange Server 5.5
  - Role: Exchange Server in site Atlanta of organization MTIT; it has MS Mail Connector installed with temporary postoffice `MTIT/ATLANTA`
- GOOFEY
  - Windows 98 with Outlook 98
  - Role: Machine for Boris' email (Exchange administrator in Atlanta)

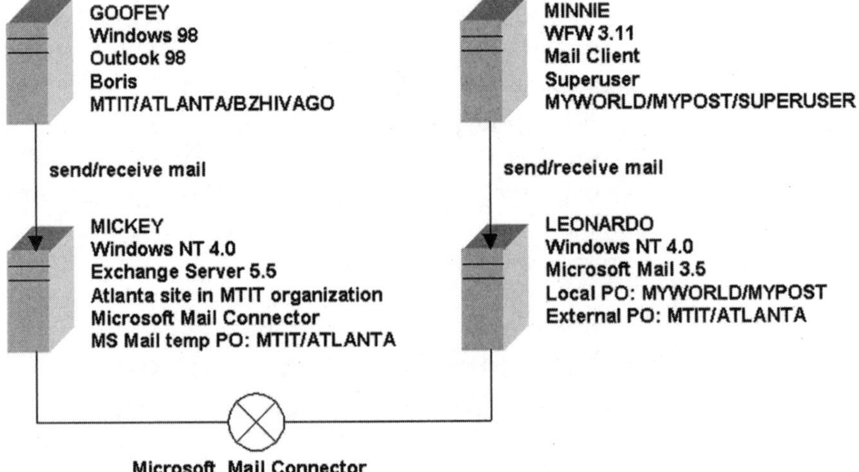

Figure 15-2 Testbed layout for establishing connectivity between Exchange and MS Mail servers.

- LEONARDO
  - Windows NT 4.0 with Microsoft Mail 3.5
  - Role: MS Mail postoffice MYPOST on MS Mail network MYWORLD; the local postoffice is `\\LEONARDO\PODATA`
- MINNIE
  - Windows for Workgroups 3.11 with Mail client
  - Role: Machine for Superusers' (MS Mail administrator) email; also used by Superuser to run the MS Mail Administrator program for administering the postoffice `MYWORLD/MYPOST` on LEONARDO

Microsoft Mail 3.5 was installed on LEONARDO by running the MS Mail Setup program on MINNIE, a 486 computer with Windows for Workgroups. The MS Mail network name is MYWORLD and the postoffice name is MYPOST. In other words, the MS Mail address for LEONARDO's postoffice is `MYWORLD/MYPOST`, while the MS Mail address for Superuser, the MS Mail administrator, is `MYWORLD/MYPOST/SUPERUSER`.

LEONARDO has two folders on it that have been shared on the network:

- PODATA, which is where the mail folders for MS Mail are located
- POEXE, which is where the executables for MS Mail are located, including the MS Mail Administrator program `admin.exe`

MINNIE has a drive letter mapped to each of the above two shares on LEONARDO as follows:

- M: on MINNIE maps to `\\LEONARDO\PODATA`
- F: on MINNIE maps to `\\LEONARDO\POEXE`

'Nuff said. Now let's walk through the process of configuring messaging connectivity between MICKEY and LEONARDO so Boris can send messages to the Superuser and vice versa. We'll begin by configuring an external postoffice on LEONARDO so that mail can be routed from the local MS Mail postoffice `MYWORLD/MYPOST` on LEONARDO to the temporary MS Mail postoffice (shadow postoffice) `MTIT/ATLANTA` located on MICKEY (for more on temporary or shadow MS Mail postoffices, see the Note earlier in this chapter). We'll then configure the MS Mail Connector on MICKEY so that mail can be transferred between the shadow postoffice on MICKEY and the local postoffice on LEONARDO. Finally, we'll test connectivity by sending a message from Boris on GOOFEY to Superuser on MINNIE and then in the reverse direction.

First, Superuser starts the MS Mail Administrator program by opening a full-screen command-prompt session on MINNIE, switching to the root of

F: drive, typing `admin`, and pressing ENTER. The MS Mail Administrator program requests the name of an administrator mailbox, so Superuser enters `SUPERUSER` and `PASSWORD` and presses ENTER. The top-level menu for the MS Mail Administrator program is then displayed onscreen (see Figure 15-3). Note that MS Mail Administrator is a typical, classy looking MS-DOS program.

Navigation through this program is accomplished using the arrow keys, page up/down, ESC, and ENTER. Use the left arrow key to select External-Admin in order to create an external postoffice on LEONARDO, which is essentially an address space or route to a local postoffice on another MS Mail server. In other words, we need to tell LEONARDO how to route mail outside of itself to the temporary postoffice located on MICKEY. Click ENTER to open the External-Admin submenu, select Create, and click ENTER. Then enter the following information one line at a time (see Figure 15-4):

Network name = MTIT
Postoffice name = ATLANTA
Route type (select "DIRECT" here)
Direct connection via (select "MS-DOS Drive" here)

The above information can be obtained from the Local Postoffice tab of the property sheet for the MS Mail Connector object located in the Connections container on MICKEY.

Click ENTER twice and you have now finished configuring your MS Mail postoffice to route mail to the shadow postoffice located on Exchange Server MICKEY.

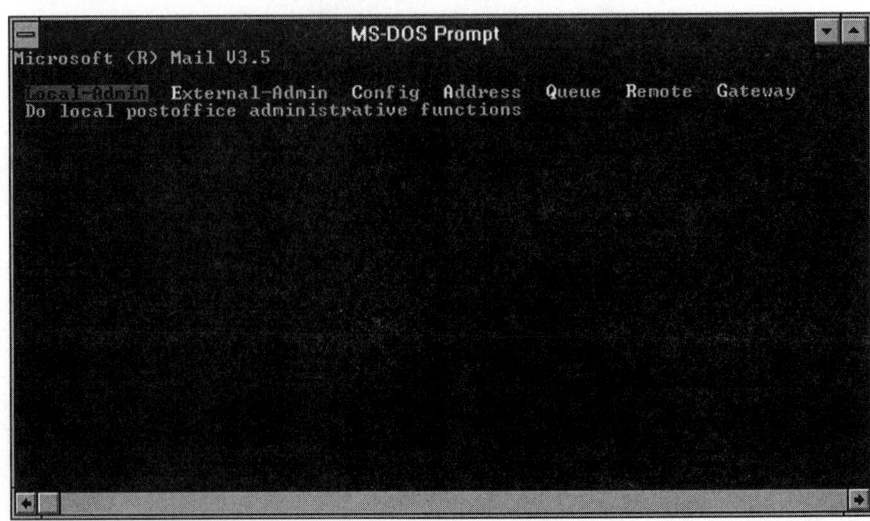

Figure 15-3 The MS Mail Administrator program running on MINNIE and connected to the postoffice on LEONARDO.

Before we exit the MS Mail Administrator program, let's check the configuration info we need for configuring our MS Mail Connector on MICKEY to exchange mail with LEONARDO. Press ESC to return to the main menu of the MS Mail Administrator program and select Config. Press ENTER to go to the Configure Directory Synchronization submenu and select Password. Press ENTER to display the network and postoffice names for your MS Mail server and make a note of them (see Figure 15-5). Press ESC three times and click ENTER to exit the MS Mail Administrator program. Then exit the command prompt session on MINNIE.

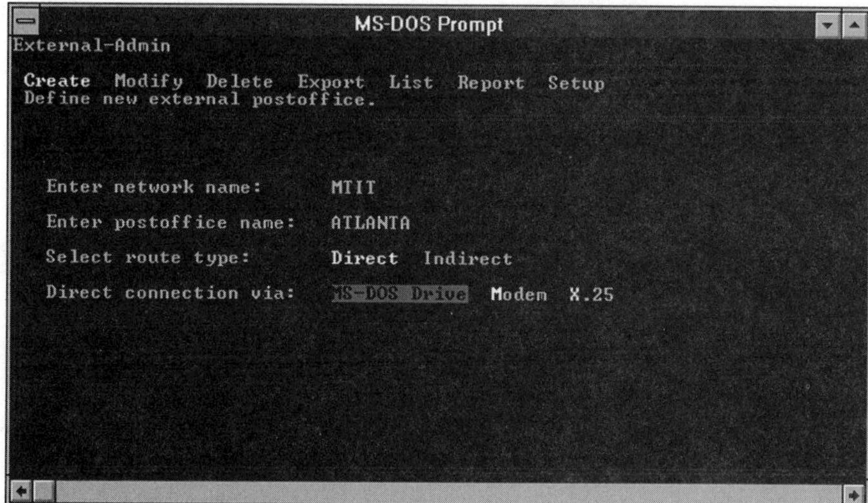

Figure 15-4 Creating an external postoffice on LEONARDO using the MS Mail Administrator program.

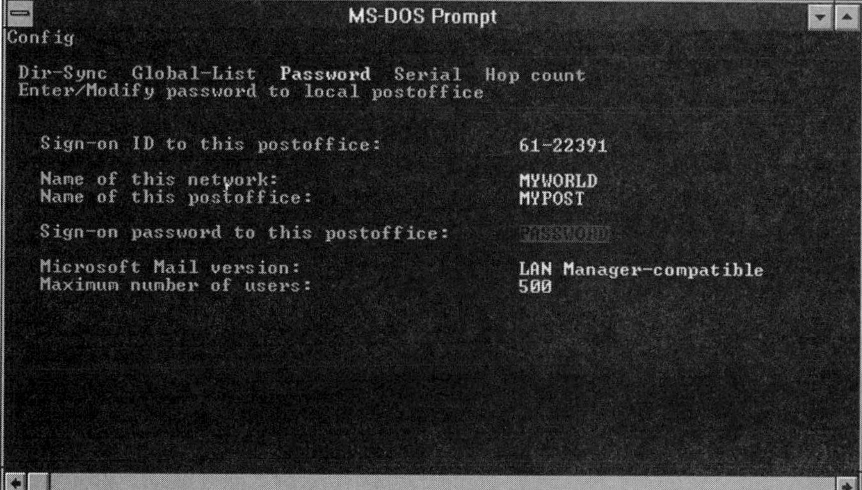

Figure 15-5 Displaying the network and postoffice names for the MS Mail postoffice on LEONARDO.

Now let's configure the MS Mail Connector on MICKEY. First, make sure you can connect to LEONARDO (try mapping drive letter M: to `\\LEONARDO\PODATA`). Open the property sheet for MS Mail Connector (MICKEY), which is found in the Connections container of site Atlanta on MICKEY. (We chose during Exchange Setup to include the MS Mail Connector in our initial Exchange installation, so an MS Mail Connector was automatically created for us during Setup, but we still need to configure it.) The Interchange tab should have the focus on the property sheet. Click the Change button and select Boris as the user who will receive administrative messages from the MS Mail server (refer to Figure 15-1). The other settings on this tab can be left as they are. (You could enable message tracking if you want to view the route over which MS Mail messages travel through your system using the Message Tracking Center.) Move next to the Connections tab (see Figure 15-6).

The tab already shows the MS Mail shadow postoffice `MTIT\ATLANTA` on MICKEY, which you cannot delete or modify. What we need to do is to estab-

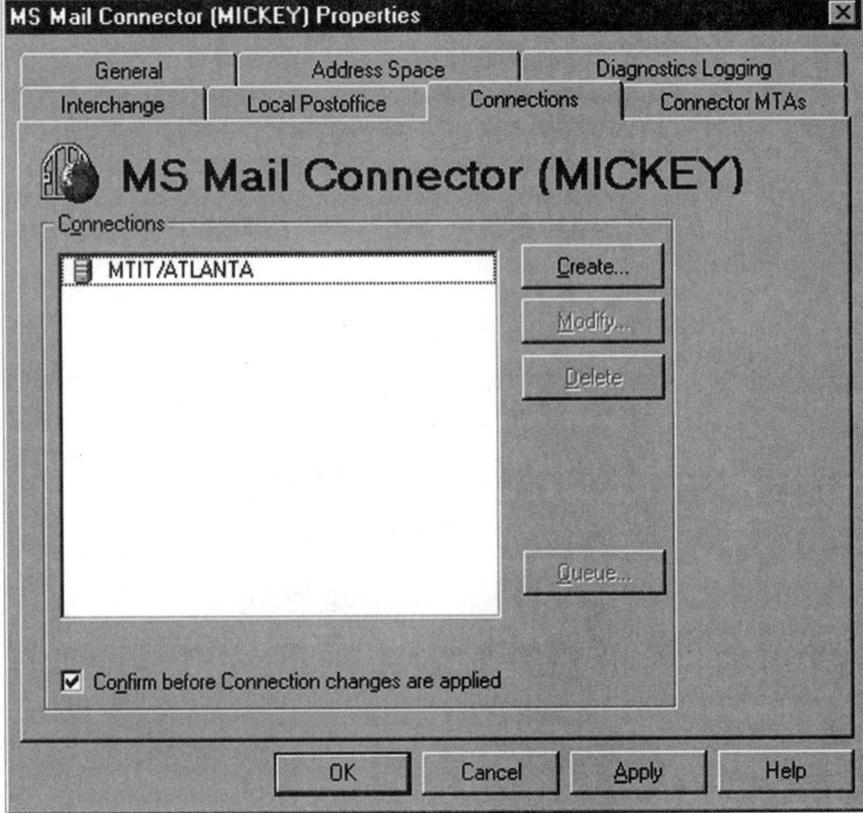

Figure 15-6 The Connections tab for the MS Mail Connector.

lish a connection between this local shadow postoffice and the postoffice MYWORLD/MYPOST located on the MS Mail server LEONARDO. Click the Create button to open the Create Connection dialog box (see Figure 15-7).

Leave the Connection Parameters set to LAN, since we are making a direct network connection and not using a modem or packet-switching network to connect to LEONARDO. Also leave Connection Attempts set to 3. We need to populate the dialog box with the network name and postoffice name of the MS Mail server LEONARDO. To do this, click the Change button to open the Postoffice Path dialog box (see Figure 15-8).

Enter the following path `\\leonardo\podata` to the postoffice located on the MS Mail server LEONARDO. You can leave the Connect As and Password fields blank, since these are only needed if the MS Mail postoffice you are

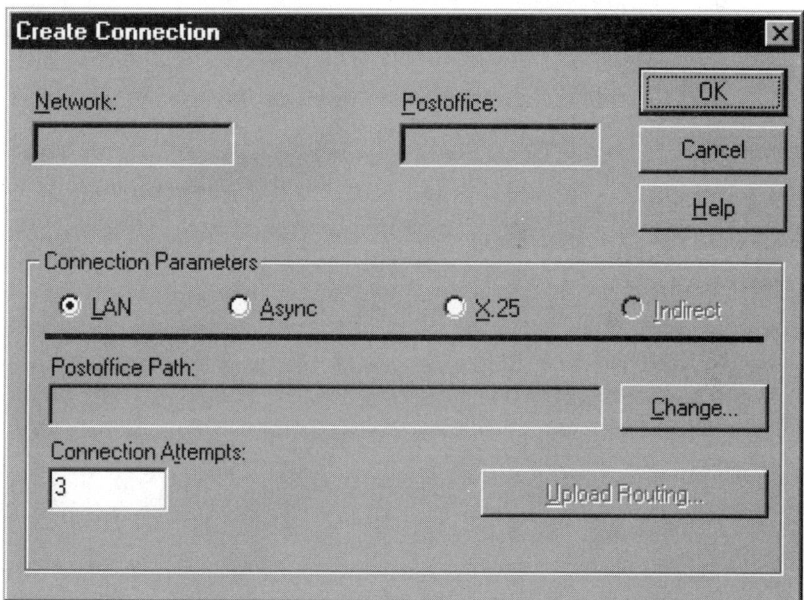

Figure 15-7 Creating a new connection to an MS Mail postoffice.

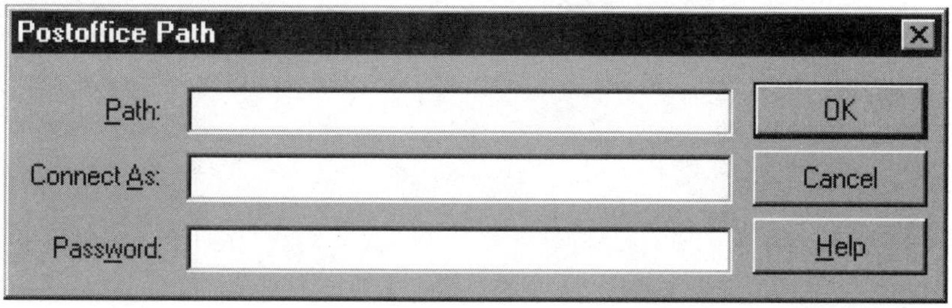

Postoffice Path
Path:
Connect As:
Password:
OK
Cancel
Help

Figure 15-8 Specifying the path to the postoffice on the MS Mail server.

connecting to is located in a non-trusted Windows NT domain or if the Exchange service account is not valid on the MS Mail server. Click OK to return to the Create Connection dialog box. Check to make sure that the Network and Postoffice names for the MS Mail server you are connecting to are correctly displayed in the dialog box (see Figure 15-9).

Click OK and then OK again to apply changes. You are returned to the Connections tab that now shows a connection between the two postoffices, the shadow postoffice `MTIT/ATLANTA` on the Exchange Server MICKEY and the postoffice `MYWORLD/MYPOST` on the MS Mail server LEONARDO (see Figure 15-10).

Now switch to the Connector MTAs tab and click New to create a new Connector MTA. This Connector MTA we are going to create will be a new Windows NT service on the Exchange Server MICKEY and will be responsible for transferring mail between the shadow postoffice on MICKEY and the postoffice on LEONARDO. Clicking the New button opens the New MS Mail Connector (PC) MTA Service dialog box (see Figure 15-11).Enter the following information into this dialog box:

- Service Name = My MS Mail MTA (We can name the new Connector MTA anything we want, and whatever name we choose will show up in the Services utility in the Control Panel.)

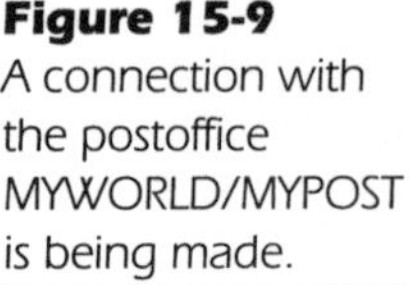

Figure 15-9 A connection with the postoffice MYWORLD/MYPOST is being made.

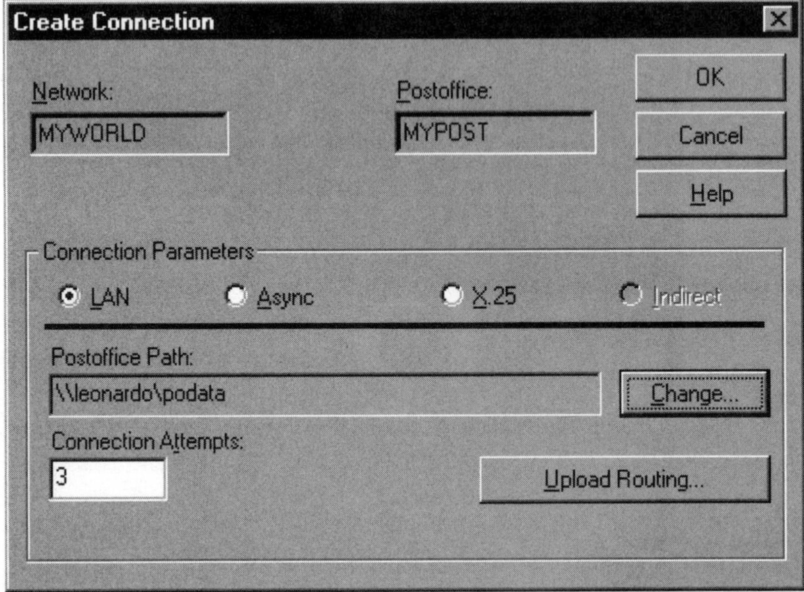

Figure 15-10 The connection has been established.

- Log Messages (Leave both checkboxes checked, so that any routing problems with the new MTA Connector will appear in the Application Log of Event Viewer.)
- Update configuration every = 1 minute (We'll have the new Connector MTA poll both postoffices—the shadow postoffice on MICKEY and the postoffice on LEONARDO—every minute in case the user or network information has been modified.)
- Check for mail every 1 minute (The new Connector MTA will poll both postoffices every minute for messages that need to be delivered. We are choosing this small time interval for demonstration purposes only for this walkthrough.)
- Connection Parameters (Leave LAN selected since the postoffices are connected by a permanent LAN connection.)

Click OK to create the new Connector MTA called "My MS Mail MTA" and be returned to the Connector MTAs tab on the MS Mail Connector (MICKEY) property sheet. If you take a moment now to start the Services utility in the Control Panel, you will see that you have a new Windows NT service listed there called "My MS Mail MTA" (see Figure 15-12).

Figure 15-11 Creating a new Connector MTA.

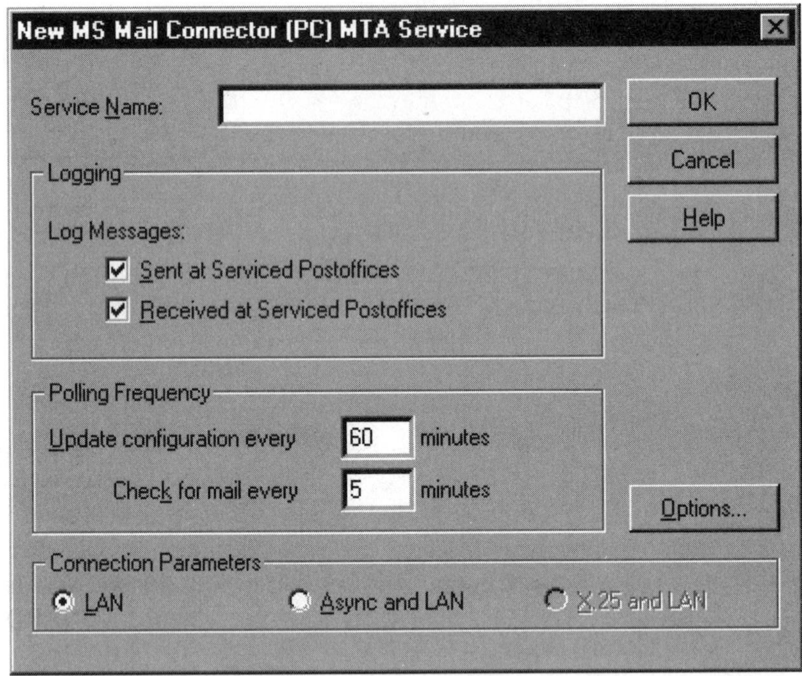

Figure 15-12 A new Windows NT service has been created on MICKEY.

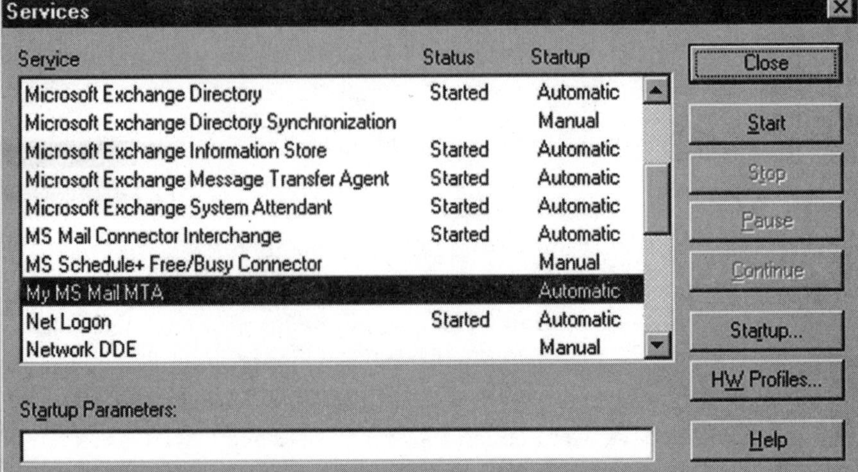

Returning to the Connector MTAs tab on the property sheet for the MS Mail Connector (MICKEY), we now need to configure the MS Mail postoffice that will be serviced by the new Connector MTA we have created. Click the List button to open the Selected LAN Postoffices dialog box (see Figure 15-13).

Select `MYWORLD\MYPOST` in the left listbox and click Add to move it to the right listbox. Click OK to return to the Connected MTAs tab and it should now look like Figure 15-14.

Click OK to close the MS Mail Connector (MICKEY) property sheet as we are finished configuring the connector.

Finally, go to the Control Panel and start these two services:

- MS Mail Connector Interchange
- My MS Mail MTA

If you want these services to restart automatically after a reboot, change their Startup setting from Manual to Automatic.

Testing the Connector

Now let's test our new MS Mail Connector. We'll send a message from Boris in Atlanta, who will be using Outlook 98 on GOOFEY, to Superuser, who will be using the *Windows for Workgroups* (WFW) Mail client program on MINNIE to connect to the MS Mail server LEONARDO.

First, start Exchange Administrator and create a new custom recipient for Superuser on the MS Mail server LEONARDO. Select File, New Custom Recipient to open the New E-mail Address dialog box. Select Microsoft Mail Address and click OK to open a blank MS Mail Address Properties dialog box. Fill it out as shown in Figure 15-15 and click OK.

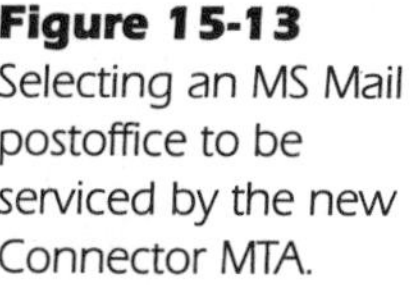

Figure 15-13 Selecting an MS Mail postoffice to be serviced by the new Connector MTA.

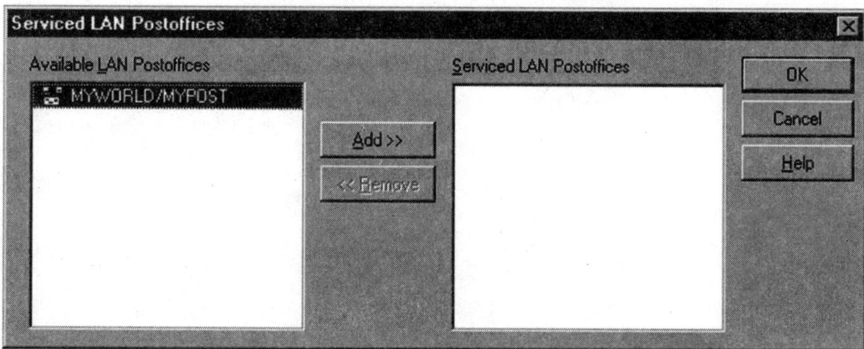

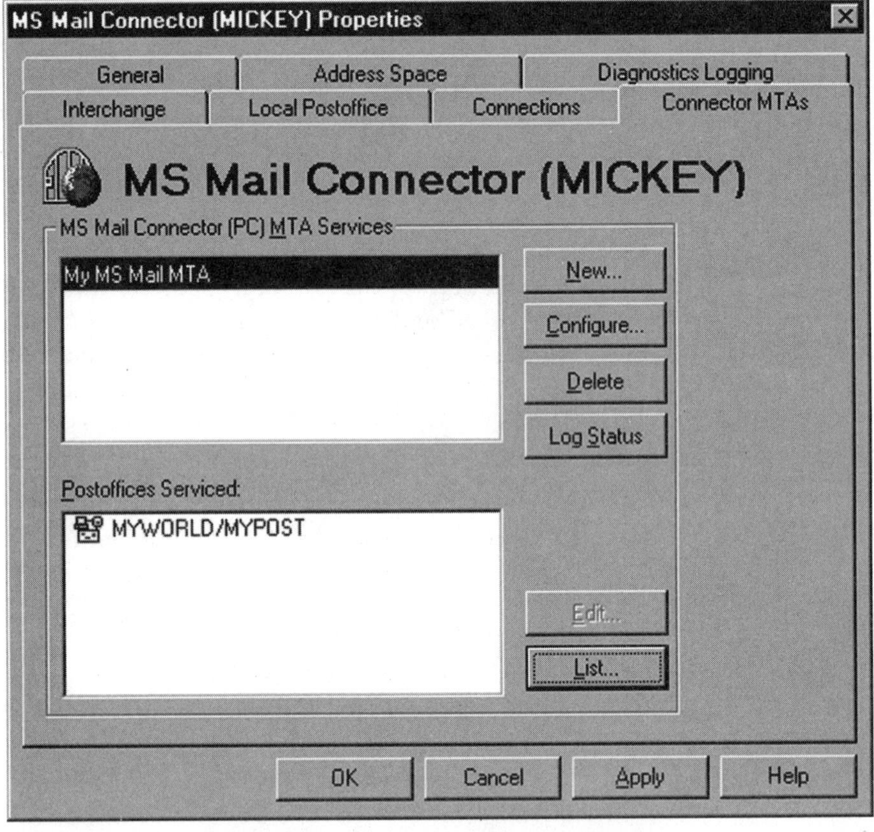

Figure 15-14 The new Connector MTA has been configured to service the postoffice MYWORLD/MYPOST.

Figure 15-15 Creating a custom recipient of type MS Mail.

Enter "Superuser" (without the quotes) for both the display and alias names on the blank property sheet for the new custom recipient and click OK to create the custom recipient. Now anytime Boris wants to send mail to Superuser at `MYWORLD/MYPOST`, Boris just addresses the message be selecting Superuser from the address book. Now log on to GOOFEY as Boris and start Outlook 98. Create a new message from Boris to Superuser similar to Figure 15-16.

Before you click the Send button to send Boris' message to Superuser, go to MICKEY and open the property sheet for the MS Mail Connector. Switch to the Connections tab, select the `MYWORLD/MYPOST` connection in the listbox on this tab, and click the Queue button to open the Messages Queued For `MYWORLD/MYPOST` dialog box. It should be empty of queued messages.

Now click Send on GOOFEY and then click Refresh on the Messages Queued dialog box on MICKEY and you should see the message from Boris sitting in the MS Mail Connector queue waiting to be delivered to Superuser on the MS mail server LEONARDO (see Figure 15-17). You may have to click Refresh several times until the message appears in the queue. Keep clicking Refresh every 10 seconds until the message leaves the queue and is delivered to LEONARDO.

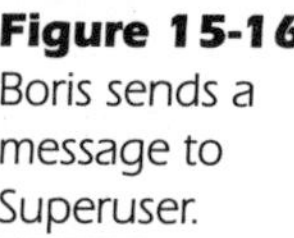

Figure 15-16 Boris sends a message to Superuser.

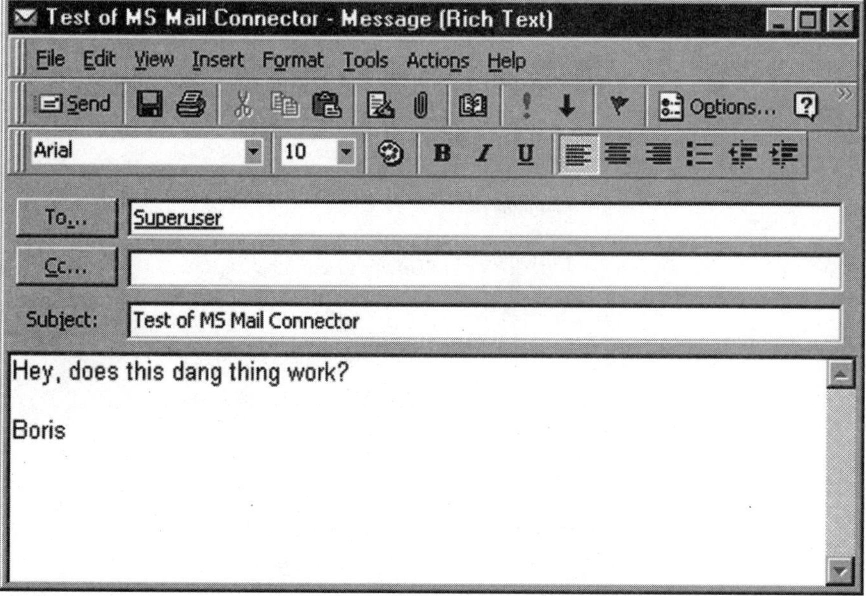

Now start the Mail client program on MINNIE and log on as Superuser with password PASSWORD. In a few moments, the message from Boris should appear in your Inbox (see Figure 15-18).

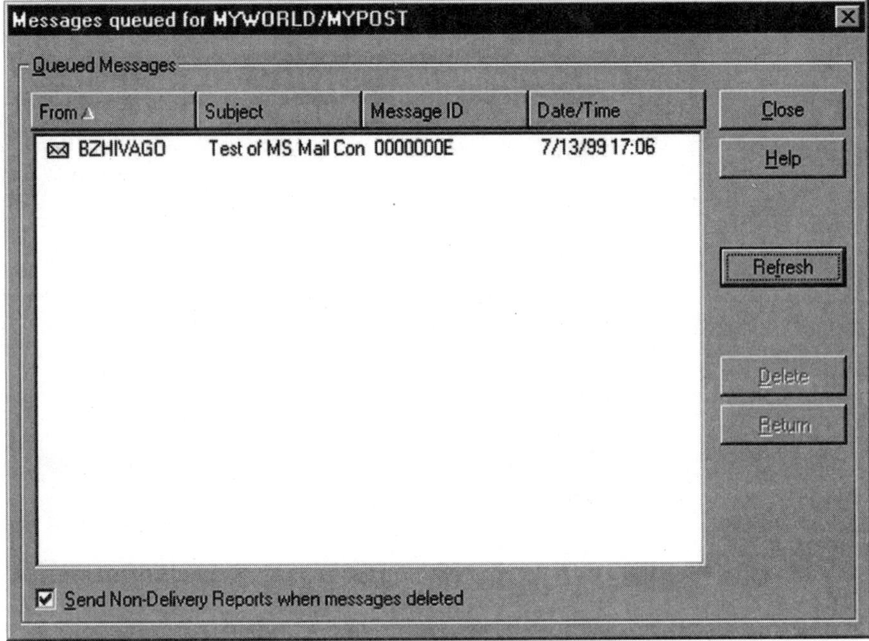

Figure 15-17 Boris' message to Superuser is queued for delivery in the MS Mail Connector queue.

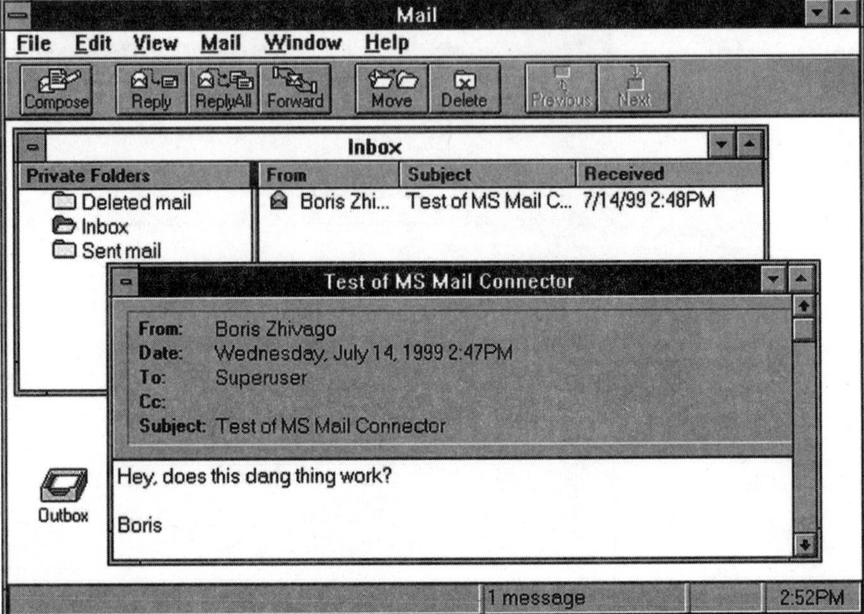

Figure 15-18 Boris' message has been received by Superuser.

Try replying to Boris to make sure that connectivity works the other way as well.

Troubleshooting

Things can go wrong! After I configured the MS Mail Connector in the above walkthrough, I found that I could send mail from Boris to Superuser but not in the reverse direction, from Superuser to Boris. I used the MS Mail Administrator program to check the configuration of the external postoffice created on LEONARDO, but everything looked OK. I checked the Application Log in Event Viewer, but the only Warning messages was a cryptic one that looked like Figure 15-19.

It took me a while to figure out that the message was telling me that there was a clock off somewhere by over 10,080 minutes. It turned out that

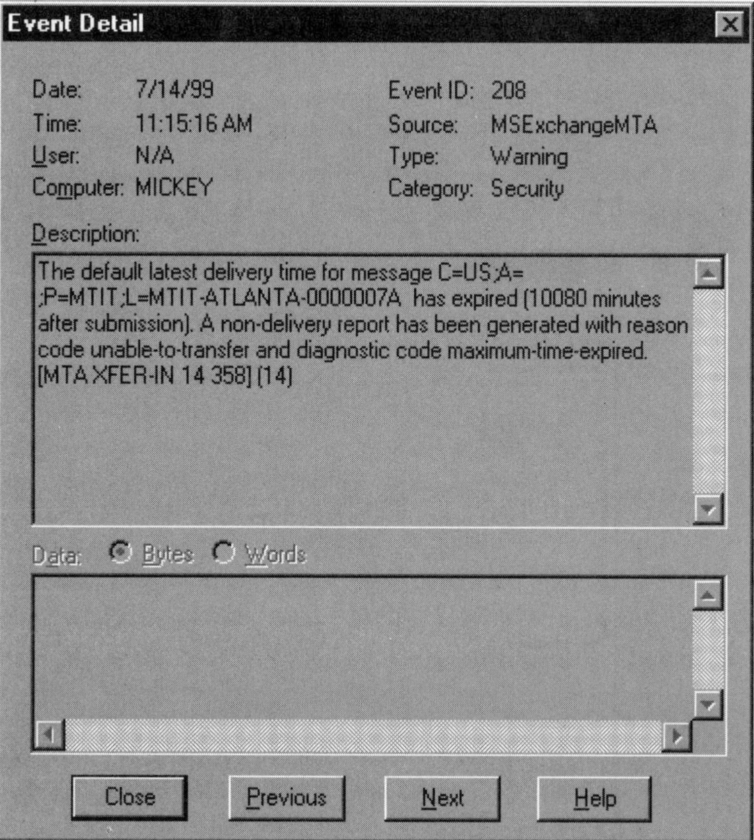

Figure 15-19 Cryptic message in the Application Log.

MINNIE's system clock was set more than a month behind the clocks of the other machines and that this was what was causing a *non-delivery report* (NDR) to be returned to Superuser when he tried to reply to Boris' message. Once the clock was fixed, messaging worked both ways through the connector. Aren't computers fun!

Where Do We Go from Here?

In the next chapter, we will continue looking at Exchange connectors by considering Internet protocols and configuring the Internet Mail Service.

For More Information

For information on administering Microsoft Mail 3.x, see the *Microsoft Mail for PC Networks Administrator's Guide*. For more information on the MS Mail Connector, see Chapter 10 of the *Operations* manual, which is included in Books Online. For information on how to configure directory synchronization between an MS Mail network and an Exchange organization, see Chapter 11 of the *Operations* manual for Exchange. You will also need a fair bit of knowledge of Microsoft Mail to get this to work.

TechNet

The Technical Notes section of the MS Exchange section may be of some help. It contains the article, How to Configure the MS Exchange Server MS Mail Connector. Also see the MS Mail section of TechNet and the Knowledge Base for troubleshooting information.

CHAPTER 16

Administering Internet Services

In the previous few chapters, we looked at various connectors for establishing messaging connectivity between Exchange sites and in foreign mail systems. One of the most important foreign mail systems is the SMTP mail system of the Internet, and connecting this with Exchange is the subject of this chapter. After reading this chapter, you will have an understanding of the following topics:

- Internet protocols
- Configuring Internet protocols
- The Internet Mail Service (IMS)
- The Internet News Service

The walkthrough in this chapter leads you through the steps of establishing messaging connectivity between an Exchange Server and an Internet SMTP host.

Internet Protocols

Let's start with a brief review of the Internet and its many different protocols. The Internet is the worldwide TCP/IP internetwork that grew out of the ARPANET project of the U.S. Department of Defense in the 1970s. In fact, the development of the TCP/IP protocol suite was itself closely tied to the development of the Internet. The Internet can rightly be considered the "network of networks," and its importance to business, commerce, and communications has rapidly grown in the last few years. Because of this, the latest version of Exchange supports the most popular Internet protocols, including DNS, SMTP, POP3, IMAP4, MIME, S/MIME, NNTP, LDAP, HTTP, and SSL. We will briefly examine the nature and function of each of these protocols and to what extent they are implemented in Exchange. Then we will look at how to configure these protocols on Exchange.

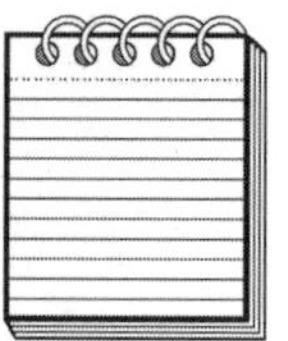

Another Great Book!

For more information on many of the Internet protocols discussed in this section, you might try picking up a copy of a book I have written called Administering IIS4 *(McGraw-Hill Professional Publishing, 1998). Just thought I'd mention it!*

DNS

The *Domain Name System* (DNS) is a worldwide hierarchical naming scheme that allows dotted names to refer to computers on the Internet, instead of numeric IP addresses. Using DNS, computers on the Internet can be given friendly, easily remembered names called *Fully Qualified Domain Names* (FQDNs). An example from our walkthroughs in this book would be

```
bugs.chicago.mtit.com
```

It is much easier to remember the FQDN for a host instead of trying to remember its numeric IP address:

```
172.16.11.133
```

Client computers that connect to the Internet can then use DNS servers called Name Servers to resolve a host's FQDN into its IP address. This name resolution process is essential for network communications to take place between the client and the host. Exchange Server fully supports DNS since DNS is implemented in the underlying Windows NT Server operating system on which Exchange runs.

SMTP

Simple Mail Transfer Protocol (SMTP) is the mail protocol used on the Internet to send and receive email messages. Exchange supports SMTP through the IMS, an installable connector for Exchange. Using the SMTP protocol, one SMTP host can forward email to another SMTP host. An SMTP host is any computer connected to the Internet and running an SMTP service or daemon (the Unix equivalent of a Windows NT service, which runs in the background continually to perform some function). The term "host" refers to any computer running TCP/IP that is connected to the Internet, but this term is more commonly used in the Unix world than in the Windows world.

SMTP hosts communicate with each other by first establishing a session using TCP port number 25. SMTP hosts then use a series of simple commands like HELO, MAIL FROM, RCPT TO, DATA, and QUIT to initiate the sending and receiving of messages. To troubleshoot an SMTP host, you can use a Telnet client to connect to the host on port 25 and manually type these commands and examine how the host responds (we'll try that later).

What is important to realize is that SMTP has no provision for the creation of personal mailboxes for individual users. SMTP is simply a mechanism for moving mail from one place to another, sort of like moving "snail mail" from one postal station to another. Also, for SMTP to work, a host needs to be continuously connected to the Internet (although the IMS on

Exchange can actually be configured to dial up an SMTP host at an Internet Service Provider to download mail from it, but then it isn't really functioning as an SMTP host). If the host is down when mail is being transferred in, the mail will bounce back to the sender or disappear into nana land. This may have been OK in the early 70s when the Internet consisted of a few thousand high-powered systems that were continually online, but today millions of people use the Internet for SMTP mail, most of them having PCs or laptops that establish temporary dial-up connections to download their mail. That's where two other Internet mail protocols come in: POP3 and IMAP4.

POP3

Post Office Protocol version 3 (POP3) is an Internet mail protocol supported by Exchange that describes how to implement a maildrop service that can hold mail received through SMTP at a POP3 server until an agent (client program or computer) can call in to collect it. The POP3 server can be a different machine than the SMTP host, or both services can be installed on the same machine as in the case of Exchange. If they are implemented on different machines, the SMTP machine is responsible for accepting outgoing messages submitted by clients and forwarding them to their destination, while the POP3 machine is responsible for accepting incoming mail from an SMTP machine and storing the received mail in the recipient's mailbox until the user dials in to retrieve it. Think of SMTP as the sending service/protocol, and POP3 as the receiving service/protocol. The mail itself is referred to as SMTP mail, however.

POP3 also supports various authentication methods so that a user can only access the mailbox that contains mail intended for him or her. This enables multiple users to privately access SMTP mail received by a single POP3 host. POP3 (and IMAP4 discussed later), as implemented on Exchange, supports the following user authentication methods:

- *Basic Authentication*. In this method, user passwords are transmitted as clear text. This method is supported by almost all mail client software, Microsoft or otherwise.
- *Windows NT Challenge/Response*. Also known as NTLM (for *Windows NT Lan Manager*) authentication, this is a secure authentication method in which a user's password is not actually transmitted over the network. However, this method is supported nearly by Windows NT clients only.

- *Microsoft Commercial Internet Server* (MCIS) *Membership System*. This method is used primarily for creating membership lists for anonymous users connecting over the Internet, such as a membership list for an online bookstore.
- *Secure Sockets Layer* (SSL) *protocol*. This method encrypts transmissions using public key cryptography. Note that the SSL protocol can be optionally applied on top of the other three authentication methods described here. That is, you can have Basic Authentication with SSL or without SSL, and so on. Thus, six different authentication methods for Internet protocols can be supported by Exchange.

POP3 mail clients like Outlook Express and some versions of Outlook communicate with POP3 servers by establishing a session using TCP port number 110 to retrieve messages from their personal mailbox. To send a message, a POP3 client uses SMTP on port 25 to connect directly to an SMTP server. POP3 clients and servers use a series of simple commands like USER, PASS, STAT, LIST, RETR, and QUIT to enable users to download messages from their mailboxes.

Exchange fully supports the POP3 protocol. In fact, POP3 is integrated within the core components of Exchange, so that Exchange can act as a POP3 server, regardless of whether the IMS is installed to enable it to support SMTP as well (though POP3 is generally useless without additional SMTP functionality).

One disadvantage of POP3, however, is that when a user connects to a POP3 server to retrieve their mail, they must download all of it. In other words, POP3 doesn't let users leave some of their mail on the server. This can be a problem for users who use more than one computer to access their mail, such as someone who accesses their mail using a PC at work and using a laptop when they travel. This problem can be solved by using the IMAP4 protocol.

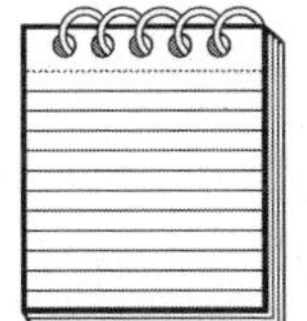

Outlook and Outlook Express

Outlook 97 (version 8.0.3) supported only SMTP and POP3. Outlook 98 (version 8.5) and Outlook 2000 (version 9.0) support SMTP, POP3, IMAP4, LDAP, NNTP, and S/MIME. Outlook Express (all versions) support SMTP, POP3, IMAP4, LDAP, and NNTP.

IMAP4

Internet Mail Access Protocol version 4, revision 1 (IMAP4rev1) is an Internet mail protocol supported by Exchange that expands on the functionality of POP3. Like POP3, IMAP4 enables IMAP4 mail clients like Outlook Express to retrieve their SMTP mail from an IMAP4-compliant server. Like POP3, IMAP4 is used only to retrieve mail; SMTP is still used to send it.

IMAP4 incorporates all the features of POP3 plus these additional enhancements:

- Users can choose which mail they want to download from the server and leave the rest.
- Users can read the headers or a part of a message without downloading the entire message.
- Users can create a hierarchical collection of folders on the server for storing and classifying their messages.
- Users can search for messages on the server based on information in the header, subject, or body of the message.

IMAP4 clients communicate with IMAP4 servers by establishing a session using TCP port number 143 to retrieve messages from their mailbox. To send a message, IMAP4 clients use SMTP on port 25. IMAP4 clients and servers use a series of simple commands like LOGIN, SELECT, FETCH, STORE, LIST, and CLOSE to download messages from their mailbox.

MIME

Multipurpose Internet Mail Extensions (MIME) is a method for sending non-text information using SMTP mail that is supported by Exchange. SMTP was originally designed as a text-only messaging protocol, but early on, users saw the advantage of being able to send binary attachments to SMTP messages. These binary files can include image files, sound files, movies, word processing documents, spreadsheets, executable programs, and so on.

An early method of encoding these binary files so that they could be transmitted as text was Uuencode, which stands for Unix-to-Unix Encoding. In the Macintosh world, this was known as BinHex. Uuencode was a simple method of converting binary eight-bit data into ASCII seven-bit data, so it could be sent as text using SMTP.

MIME is an improvement on Uuencode since it provides message headers that indicate the content type of each attachment as well as a multiple encoding method for different kinds of content. MIME enables email messages to be constructed of several parts, each of which contains data encoded using a different method. MIME enables users to create email messages that contain *Rich Text Format* (RTF) information including images, sounds, and other multimedia and binary content. MIME also enables users to create messages using character sets other than the US-ASCII character set. Exchange also supports both MIME and Uuencode for sending attachments with messages.

The main thing to remember is that an attachment must be encoded in a way that the recipient at the other end can decode it. If you encode a message using MIME but the recipient of the message is using older mail software that only supports Uuencode, they won't be able to read your attachment.

S/MIME

Secure Multipurpose Internet Mail Extensions (S/MIME) is an extension to MIME supported by Exchange that enables messages and attachments to be encrypted using public key cryptography. This ensures messaging privacy and verification of the sender's identity using digital signatures.

NNTP

Network News Transfer Protocol (NNTP) is an Internet news protocol supported by Exchange that established the worldwide news and bulletin board system known as Usenet. The Usenet system consists of tens of thousands of newsgroups covering very topic imaginable under the sun. NNTP is a client-server protocol in which

- NNTP hosts (news servers) replicate newsgroups and their messages to other NNTP hosts around the world using newsfeeds (or simply feeds).
- NNTP clients (news readers) connect to an NNTP host to download a list of newsgroups, download messages for a selected newsgroup, and read or post new messages to a newsgroup.

NNTP clients like Outlook Express communicate with NNTP servers by establishing a session using TCP port number 119 to download newsgroups and post new messages to them. NNTP clients and servers use a series of simple commands like LIST, GROUP, ARTICLE, POST, and QUIT to download newsgroups, read messages, and post new ones. Exchange also supports NNTP through the Internet News Service, an installable component of Exchange.

LDAP

Lightweight Directory Access Protocol (LDAP) is an Internet directory protocol supported by Exchange. LDAP enables clients like Outlook Express and some versions of Outlook to connect to an LDAP-compliant directory service, like the Exchange directory, in order to search for, view, add, modify, and delete information contained in the directory, depending on what permissions the user has been granted. For example, you can use Outlook Express to connect to an Exchange Server and use LDAP to view the telephone numbers and other information for recipients created on that server. LDAP thus provides a kind of white pages access to information about recipients stored in an organization's directory.

LDAP is a simplified version of X.500, an International Telecommunications Union (ITU) recommendation for the design and operation of a global directory service (similar to the way X.400 is an ITU standard for a global messaging service). The Exchange directory database and directory service are modeled after LDAP, which itself is an offshoot of the X.500 recommendations.

LDAP clients communicate with LDAP-compliant directory servers like Exchange by establishing a session using TCP port number 389 to access directory information on the server. LDAP clients and servers use a series of simple commands like BindRequest, SearchRequest, ModifyRequest, and AddRequest to search the directory, add new information, view existing information, or delete information from the directory. LDAP also uses the same authentication methods that POP3 and IMAP4 employ.

HTTP

Hypertext Transfer Protocol (HTTP) is the Internet protocol upon which the World Wide Web is based. HTTP is a client/server protocol in which HTTP clients called Web browsers send request commands to HTTP servers called Web servers using TCP port number 80. The server then responds by sending the client the requested file or document, usually called a Web page.

Microsoft Exchange does not in itself support HTTP as a method of transporting information over the Internet, apart from sending SMTP messages in HTML format. However, combined with Microsoft *Internet Information Server* (IIS) version 3.0 or higher, Exchange supports access to users' mailboxes and to public folders using an optional Exchange component called Outlook Web Access.

SSL

The *Secure Sockets Layer* (SSL) protocol is an Internet security protocol supported by Exchange that enables messages to be signed using digital signatures and encrypted using public key cryptography. This allows the recipient of a message to be sure of the sender's identity and ensure the privacy of the communication.

SSL works on top of the other Internet protocols described above. For example, SSL can provide secure, encrypted transmission for SMTP messaging to guarantee message authenticity and integrity. SSL uses a pair of asymmetric keys to encrypt and decrypt messages. The private key is known only to the client program, while the public key is free to anyone. SSL signs messages using X.509 digital certificates, which can be validated by a public *Certificate Authority* (CA) like Verisign Inc. This enables recipients to verify the identity of the sender of a message.

In order to use SSL, you need access to a CA who can issue certificates to identify servers and/or clients. You also need to install the *Key Manager* Server (KM) component on one Exchange server in your organization. This creates two new directory objects called the Site Encryption Configuration object and the CA object that can be used to enable SSL and other advanced forms of security for your organization. This topic is beyond the scope of this book, however.

Firewall Issues

Most networks these days are connected to the Internet through a firewall, a program or device whose main purpose is to prevent unauthorized users from accessing your network through your Internet connection. A firewall is like a gateway between your network and the Internet that enables your users to freely access Internet services and resources while preventing access in the opposite direction.

A simple form of firewall is to use a machine with two network interface cards in it. This dual-homed machine acts as a router and separates the network outside (the Internet) from the network inside (your corporate network). All communications between the two networks take place through this machine. Its routing table can be configured to block access over certain TCP and UDP ports in certain directions, if it is sophisticated enough to handle this. In addition, proxy software is often installed on the machine that receives packets from one network and then forwards them to the other network while masking the identity of the sending host from the receiving host.

We can't get into a lot of detail about firewalls here. What we will point out is that any firewall can be configured to allow or deny packets the right to traverse it, based on either the packet's IP address (source or destination) and the TCP or UDP port used by the packet. In this context, you should be familiar with the standard (default) port numbers for the various Internet protocols and services supported by Exchange, as shown in Table 16-1. Using this table, we can see, for example, that if we want to allow an LDAP client like Outlook Express to connect to an Exchange server beyond a firewall to obtain directory information, we need to keep port 389 open on the firewall to allow incoming packets on this port.

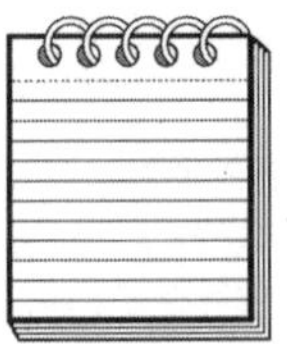

RPC Connectivity

If you can't connect to an Exchange server on the far side of a firewall using the Exchange Administrator program, your firewall is probably configured to block traffic on port number 135. This port must also be open between Exchange Servers in the same site to enable RPC connectivity between them for exchanging messages and directory information.

Table 16-1

Default Port Numbers for Internet Protocols Supported by Exchange.

Protocol	Port Number	Port Number with SSL
SMTP	25	N/A
POP3	110	995
IMAP4	143	993
NNTP	119	N/A
LDAP	389	636
HTTP	80	443
RPC connectivity	135	N/A

Configuring Internet Protocols

Exchange enables you to configure certain aspects of the five Internet protocols POP3, IMAP4, NNTP, LDAP, and HTTP at three different levels:

- The *Site-level Protocols container* is located within the Configuration container for a site and can be used to configure all five of these protocols at the site level, that is, for all objects within the site (see Figure 16-1). For example, you could enable NNTP for any Exchange server in your site using the NNTP Protocols object in the Protocols container. Both the Protocols container itself and the individual Protocol objects within it have configurable settings on their property sheets.
- The *Server-level Protocols container* is located within the various Server containers within a site and can be used to override the defaults set for POP3, IMAP4, NNTP, or LDAP at the site level. For example, you can disable NNTP for a particular Exchange Server if it is enabled by default for all servers in the site. Both the Protocols container itself and the individual Protocol objects within it have configurable settings on their property sheets. Note that you cannot configure HTTP at the server level.
- The *Protocols tab* can be used to override the site- and server-level defaults set above for any protocol. It can be found in the property

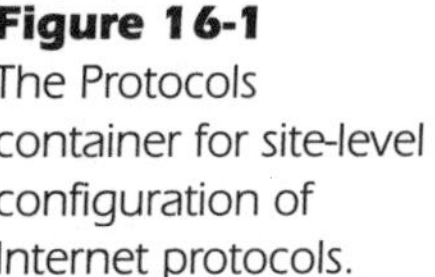

Figure 16-1
The Protocols container for site-level configuration of Internet protocols.

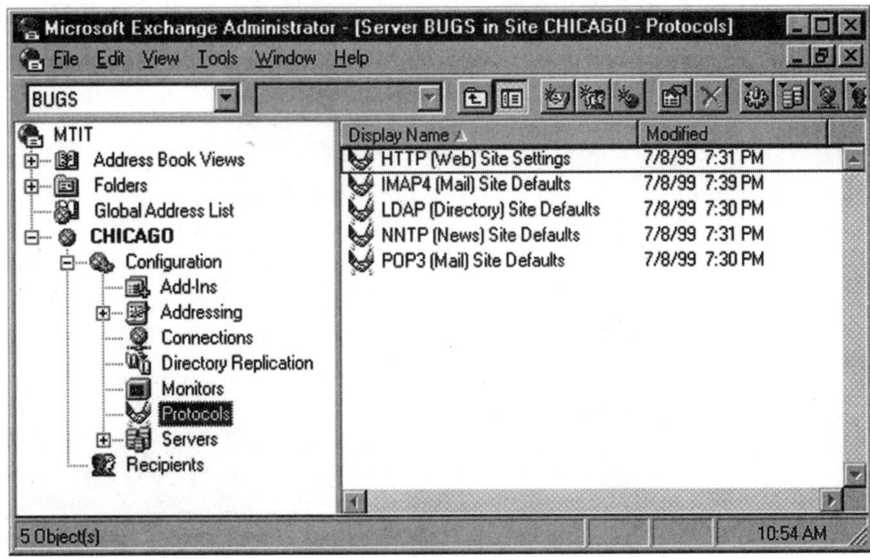

sheet for an individual Mailbox or Custom Recipient object. For example, you could prevent a particular recipient from using NNTP to connect to Usenet using this tab.

Protocols Containers

Using the site- and server-level Protocols containers, you can configure default settings for Internet protocols as follows:

- The *Outlook Web Access Server name (General tab)* is used to specify the name of the server on which the optional Outlook Web Access component of Exchange has been installed.
- The *Connections tab* lets you accept or reject TCP/IP connections to your site or server based on the IP address of the remote client (see Figure 16-2). This feature only works with the POP3, NNTP, and LDAP

Figure 16-2
Configuring the Protocols container.

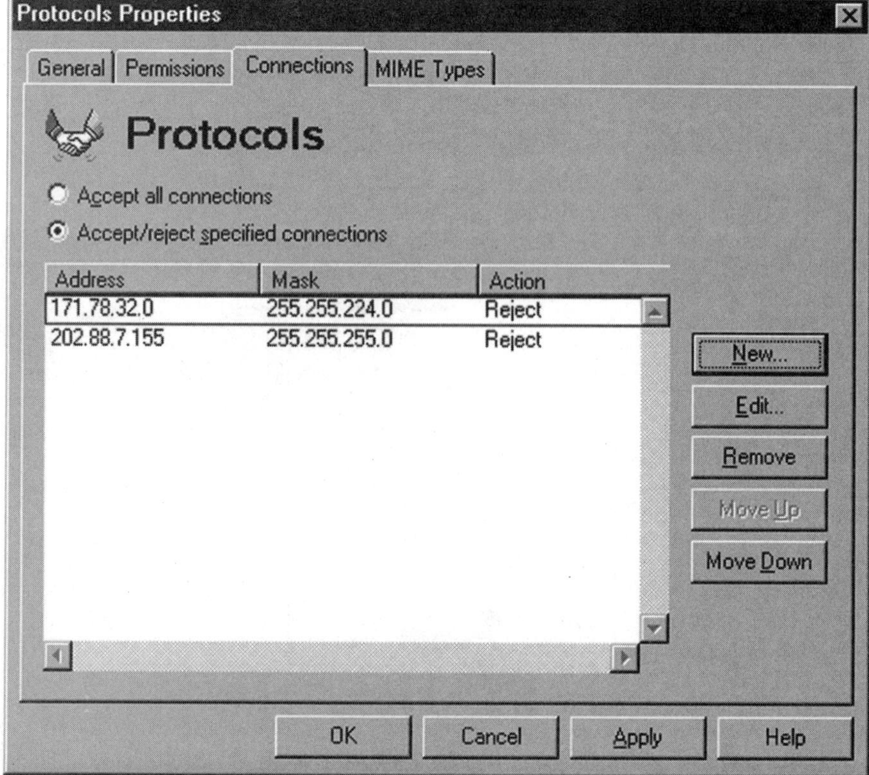

protocols and is a good way to block attacks from hackers. You can accept or reject any number of individual IP address or IP subnetworks by specifying an IP address and subnet mask.

- The *MIME Types tab* lets you configure the file extensions that will be mapped to different MIME types for attachments to incoming messages and the MIME types that will be assigned for attachments to outbound messages based on their file extensions. This is used to create a set of mappings between the applications used to create and display attachments and the MIME types used to encode those attachments.

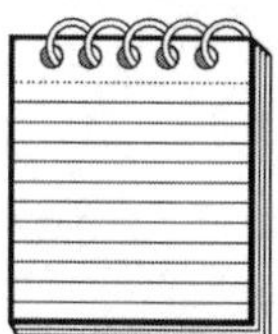

Outlook Web Access

If you want to accept or reject HTTP connection attempts to your Outlook Web Access server based on the IP address of the remote client, you can do this using the Internet Service Manager tool on the server where Microsoft Internet Information Server (IIS) is installed.

Protocol Objects

Five different Protocol objects exist at the site level and four can be found at the server level that can be configured on Exchange. These are named differently according to whether they exist at the site or server levels. Here are some examples:

- The site-level POP3 Protocol object, which is contained within a site's Configuration container, is called the POP3 (Mail) Site Defaults object (see Figure 16-3).
- The server-level POP3 Protocol object, which is contained within a Server container, is called the POP3 (Mail) Settings object.

The absence or presence of these different Protocol objects at the site and server levels is summarized in Table 16-2. Note that server-level objects always override site-level objects in the way they are configured.

You can configure various settings using the property sheets for each of these protocols. Table 16-3 summarizes the general configuration options you can configure for each type of Protocol object.

Most of these settings are fairly self-evident in their application. We'll just mention here that the message-encoding settings specify the encoding method that incoming SMTP messages are converted to when a POP3 client connects to Exchange to retrieve its mail. Exchange stores incoming messages in native Exchange format, and these messages are

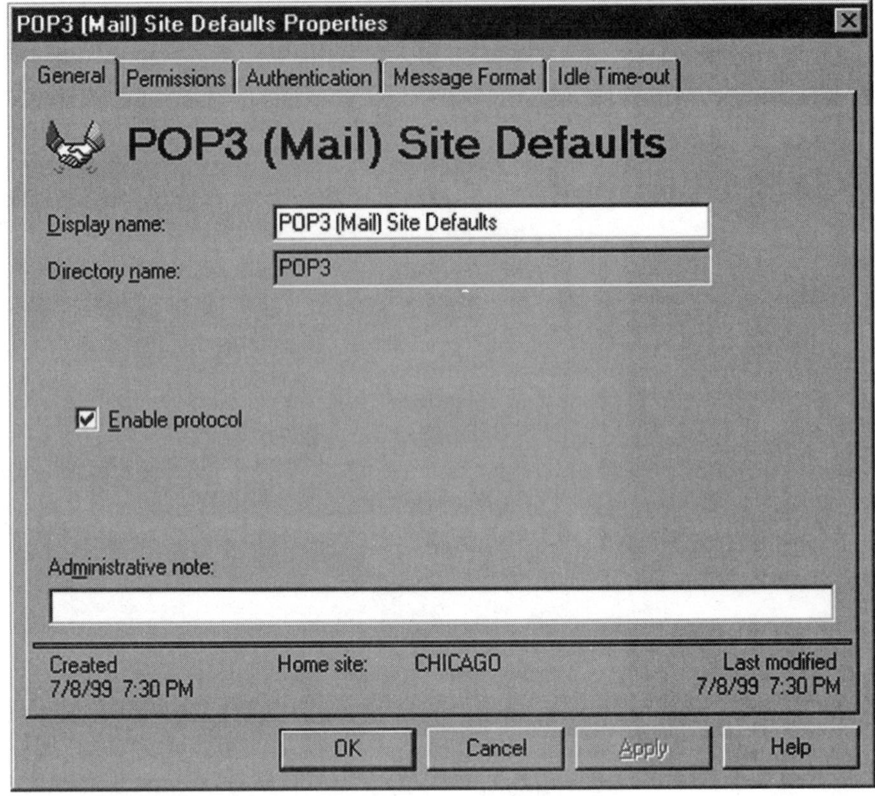

Figure 16-3 The POP3 Protocol object at the site level.

Table 16-2 Types of Protocol Objects at the Site and Server Levels.

Protocol	Site Level	Server Level
POP3	√	√
IMAP4	√	√
LDAP	√	√
NNTP	√	√
HTTP	√	none

then converted to the appropriate format for the client. However, this is only true for messages sent from other users in the organization. If a message comes in from the Internet, Exchange stores it in its native message format and does not convert it.

Table 16-3

Configuration Options for Protocol Objects.

Configuration Option	HTTP	IMAP4	LDAP	NNTP	POP3
Enable/disable protocol	√	√	√	√	√
Enable client access				√	
Specify authentication method		√	√	√	√
Allow anonymous access	√	√	√	√	
MIME message encoding		√		√	√
Uuencode message encoding				√	√
Support S/MIME signatures				√	
Specify Character set		√			√
Use RTF		√			√
Specify TCP port number			√		
Idle time-out		√	√	√	√
Close idle connections		√	√	√	√

In addition to the general configuration options listed in Table 16-3, some of the protocol objects have more specific settings that can be configured:

- *HTTP*. You can create Public Folder shortcuts to enable Public Folders to be accessed using a standard Web browser through Outlook Web Access. You can also selectively allow anonymous access to anonymous Public Folders, the Global Address List (GAL), and how many address list entries are returned to the client.
- *IMAP4*. You can enable fast message retrieval, which causes Exchange to estimate the approximate size of messages on the server, instead of determining their correct size. You can also specify a Windows NT account to be used for anonymous access to Exchange by IMAP4 clients.
- *LDAP*. You can configure how LDAP clients can use substrings when searching for information in the Exchange directory and how many results should be returned per search query. You can also configure Exchange to redirect an LDAP client to a different Exchange organization if the desired information cannot be found by the client.

- *NNTP*. You can view the properties of newsfeeds created on the server and accept or delete NNTP control messages waiting in the queue. NNTP control messages are used when one NNTP host replicates with another.

Protocols Tab

Finally, using the Protocols tab on the property sheets for Mailbox and Custom Recipient objects, you can configure how individual recipients interact with Exchange using the HTTP, IMAP4, LDAP, NNTP, and POP3 protocols (see Figure 16-4). Table 16-4 shows the configuration options available for these protocols at the recipient level.

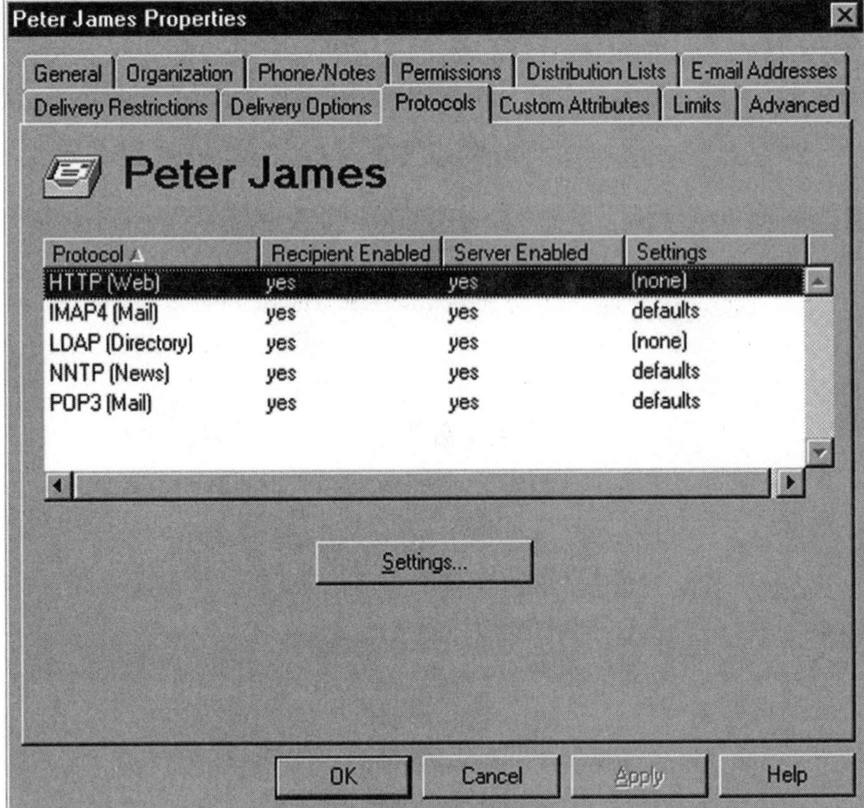

Figure 16-4 The Protocols tab on a Mailbox object.

Table 16-4

Configuration Options for the Protocol Tab.

Configuration Option	HTTP	IMAP4	LDAP	NNTP	POP3
Enables/disables protocol	√	√	None	√	√
Uses protocol default settings from site and server levels		√		√	
MIME message encoding		√		√	√
Uuencode message encoding				√	√
Specifies character set		√			√
Uses RTF		√			√
Includes all public folders when a folder list is requested		√		√	√
Allows user to act as a delegate		√		√	√

The Internet Mail Service

It's time to move on to the fun stuff: the IMS on Exchange. The IMS enables Exchange to send and receive SMTP mail over the Internet, in effect acting as a gateway between your normal MAPI-based Exchange mail system and the Internet's SMTP mail system. But you could also use the IMS as your sole messaging service on Exchange or you could use it to connect your remote Exchange sites together using the Internet as your messaging backbone. Our focus here is on the main use of the service: as an SMTP gateway between Exchange and the Internet.

We're also going to do things a bit differently in this chapter. We'll do the walkthrough first and then look at the various configuration settings afterwards.

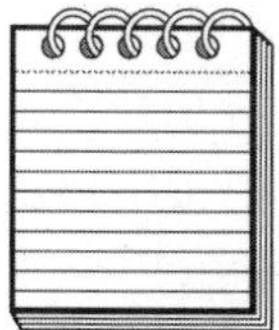

Service or Connector?

By the way, why is it called the IMS instead of the Internet Mail Connector? Actually, the second name was used in the earlier version Exchange 4.0, but for some reason Microsoft changed it.

Walkthrough: Installing and Testing the IMS

In this walkthrough, we'll go through the steps of getting an Exchange Server connected to an Internet SMTP host using the IMS on Exchange. It's surprisingly easy—almost! But first I'd like to thank my Internet Service Provider (ISP), *Escape Communications Corp* (www.escape.ca), for allowing me to bring in an Exchange Server and connect to their SMTP host to take the screenshots for this chapter (after all, you can't expect a poor author like me to have a dedicated T-1 connection in his home). Thanks especially to Jill Lampi (blackcat@escape.ca), a DNS/System Administrator at Escape, for her help in getting things working from their side.

Scenario

Here's the setup:

- *Exchange Server*. My Exchange Server machine is named BUGS and is located in the Atlanta site of my Exchange organization MTIT. The machine is installed as a PDC to make the walkthrough more self-contained. The machine is running Exchange Server 5.5 with Service Pack 2 and Windows NT 4.0 with Service Pack 4, plus Outlook 2000 for testing messaging connectivity. A fixed IP address of 207.161.116.92 is assigned to the machine by Jill. I logged on to BUGS using the account CHICAGO\pjames, who is a member of the Domain Admins group for the CHICAGO domain and has been assigned the Permissions Admin role on the Organization, Site, and Server containers using Exchange Administrator.
- *SMTP Host*. My ISP's Unix mail server is running Sendmail 8.9.1a. The IP address of the machine is 198.163.232.249. In addition, to enable their SMTP host to accept connections with my Exchange Server BUGS, Jill added two DNS resource records to the zone file for the mtit.com domain on their BIND name server:

```
bugs.chicago    IN      A       207.161.116.92
chicago IN      MX      10      bugs.chicago
```

Note that our original DNS setup used only the A record shown above, which caused some problems that will be described later in this walkthrough. The MX record was then added to make things work.

Installing the IMS

Installing the IMS is straightforward because unlike most other Exchange components, the IMS is installed using a wizard. To start this wizard, open Exchange Administrator and select File, New Other, Internet Mail Service from the menu. This opens the initial screen of the Internet Mail Wizard (see Figure 16-5).

Click Next and read the next screen, which contains some information about configuring TCP and DNS to enable the IMS to work properly on your machine (see Figure 16-6). Note that you must specify both a hostname and a domain name for your machine on the DNS tab of the TCP/IP property sheet. You can open this property sheet by using the Network utility in the Control Panel.

Click Next and select which Exchange Server you want to install the IMS on (see Figure 16-7). Since only one server, BUGS, is in this site, there is nothing to select here. Note, however, the option for allowing Internet mail to be downloaded using a dial-up connection (you must have the Windows NT Remote Access Service installed on your machine prior to selecting this option). We are using a direct LAN connection in this walkthrough, which is essentially the same as using a high-speed leased line connection

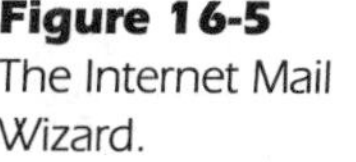

Figure 16-5 The Internet Mail Wizard.

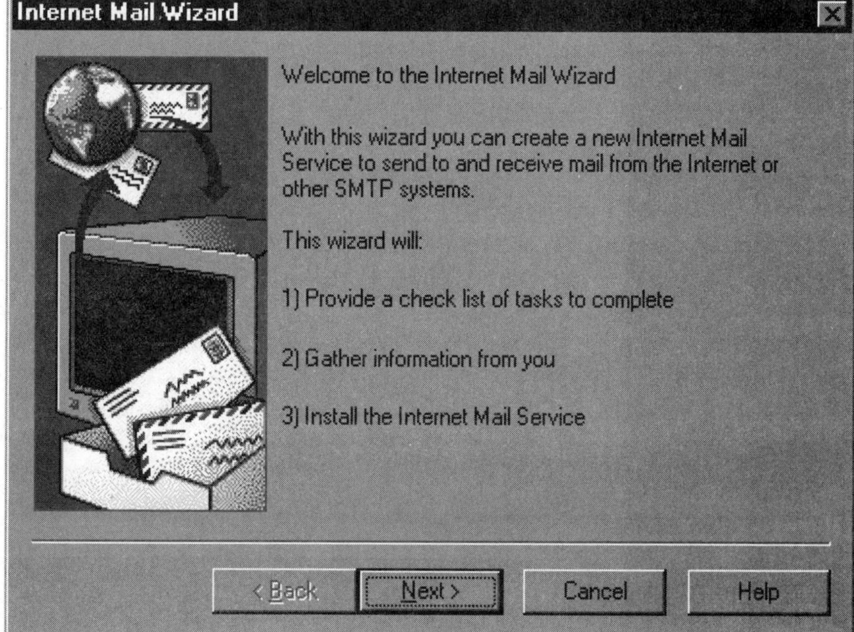

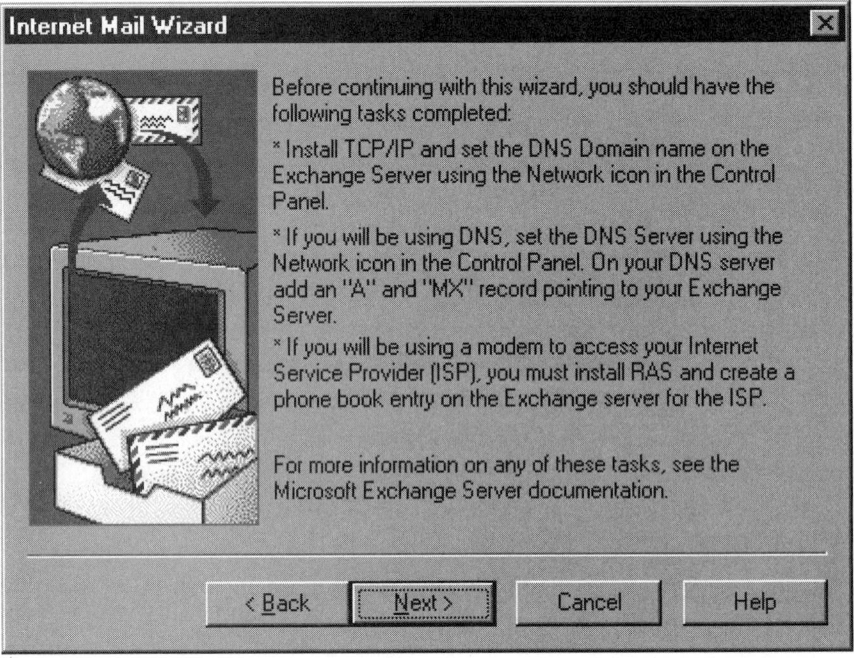

Figure 16-6 Preliminaries before installing the IMS.

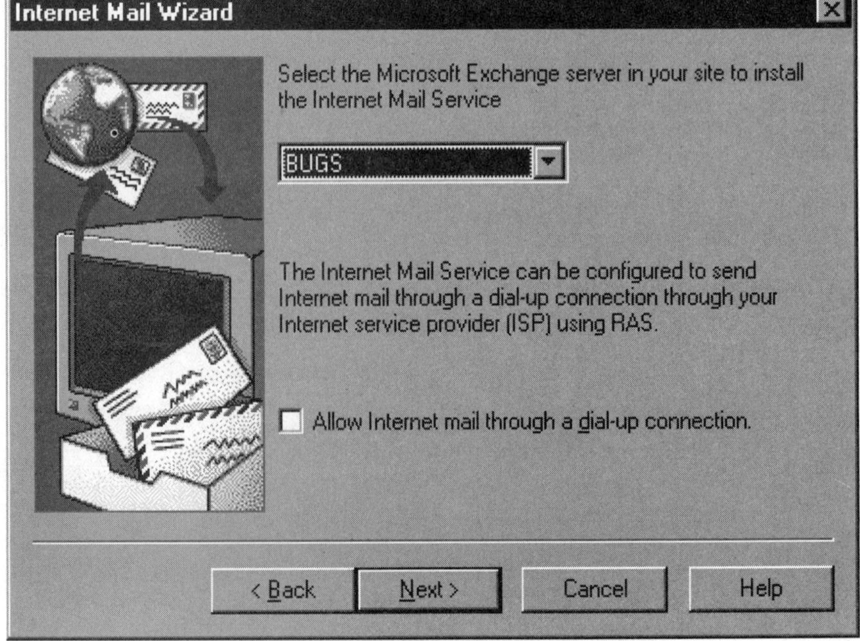

Figure 16-7 Specifying which server to install the IMS on.

like a T-1 line for a WAN link, but if you are interested in dial-up usage of the IMS, see the section entitled "For More Information" at the end of this chapter for a useful article on this topic in Microsoft TechNet.

Click Next and choose whether your Exchange Server with IMS will be allowed to relay Internet SMTP mail or not (see Figure 16-8). Relaying mail is generally a bad idea, as it opens your server up to abuse by spammers (companies who send junk mail over the Internet). Exchange does give you some control over who is allowed to relay mail through your machine, however, but for the purpose of this walkthrough, we selected the default No in this screen of the wizard to prevent our server from being used to relay mail.

If you plan to allow POP3 or IMAP4 clients to send SMTP mail to recipients outside of your Exchange organization, then you need to enable SMTP mail relaying using the Yes option here. In that case, you need to open the Routing tab of the property sheet for your Internet Mail Service object once the wizard is finished. Then set the mail relay restrictions to prevent your IMS from being abused. I chose "No" here for the sake of simplicity and because I'm using the MAPI client Outlook instead of the "pure" POP3 client Outlook Express. Exchange performs the necessary protocol conversion internally.

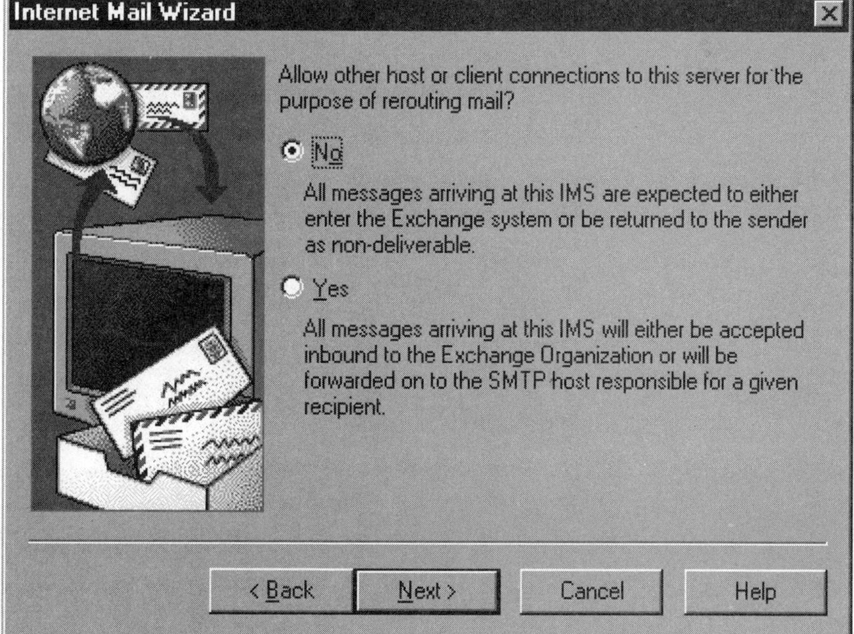

Figure 16-8 Disabling relaying of SMTP mail.

Click Next and type in the IP address of your ISP's mail server to specify it as an SMTP smart host (see Figure 16-9). A "smart host" is an SMTP host where your mail server forwards all the SMTP mail. In other words, if a user in your organization wants to send an email to someone on the Internet, your Exchange organization routes the message through the IMS directly to the smart host at your ISP, which then routes it from there. A smart host acts as a kind of external gateway to the rest of the Internet.

The alternative to specifying the IP address of a smart host at your ISP is to select the Use Domain Name System (DNS) To Send Mail option. If you select this option, your IMS will bypass your ISP's SMTP mail server when it has mail to deliver. The IMS will try to connect directly with the SMTP host managing the domain of the intended recipient (unless the intended recipient is located within the local domain of your ISP).

I choose Route All Mail Through A Single Host and specified the IP address of my ISP's Sendmail host here, since I only wanted to test connectivity with their machine and exchange mail with users in their domain. If I change my mind later, I could change this setting using the Connections tab on the property sheet for the IMS object after the wizard is finished.

Click Next and specify which Internet mail addresses your IMS will be permitted to send mail to (see Figure 16-10). The typical setting here is All Internet Mail Addresses, which enables your Exchange recipients to send

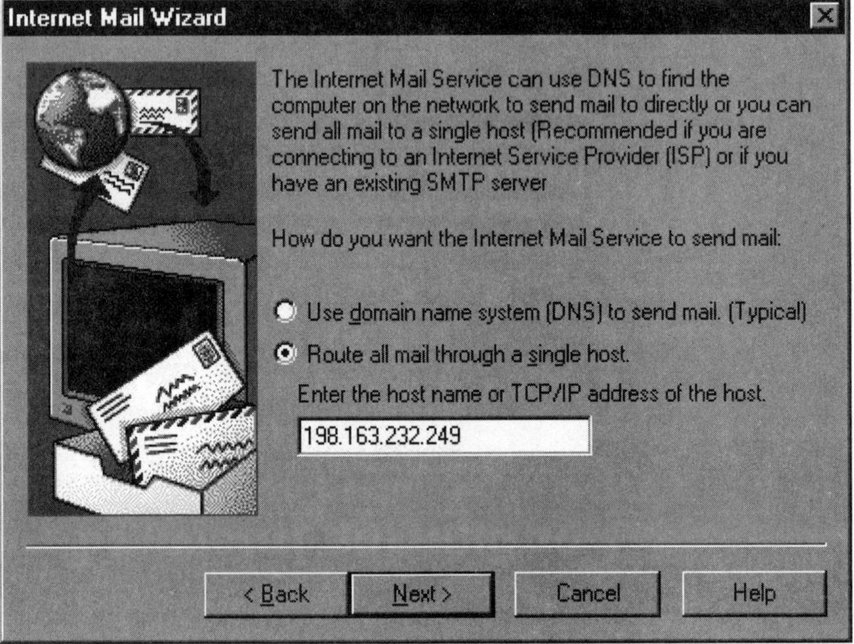

Figure 16-9 Specifying the DNS name or IP address of your provider's SMTP host.

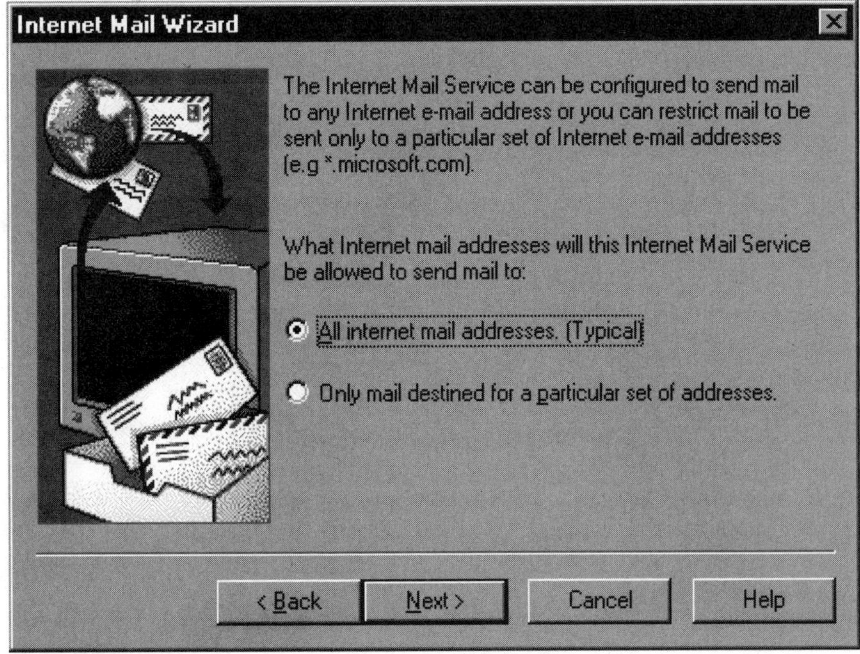

Figure 16-10 Specifying the users on the Internet to which your Exchange recipients are allowed to send SMTP mail.

SMTP mail to anyone on the Internet. The alternative is to restrict your IMS to a particular set of IP addresses. For simplicity, I just selected All here, but if I changed my mind later, I could restrict the SMTP mail to specific SMTP addresses by opening the Address Space tab on the IMS property sheet once the wizard is finished and specifying the address spaces to which users can send SMTP mail. Address spaces are explained in more detail in Chapter 18, "Administering Message Routing."

Click Next and you are asked to specify the SMTP site address that will be used to generate SMTP addresses for your users (see Figure 16-11). By default, the following entry should appear in the textbox:

```
@<site_name>.<org_name>.com
```

Whatever you type here will also appear on the Site Addressing tab of the property sheet for the Site Addressing object in Exchange Administrator. If you change the default address here, once you finish the wizard, a message will appear saying, "A process has been started to update the Recipient E-mail Addresses." This process will automatically update the SMTP-type address for all recipients in your site. I accepted the default address displayed here, which is:

```
@chicago.mtit.com
```

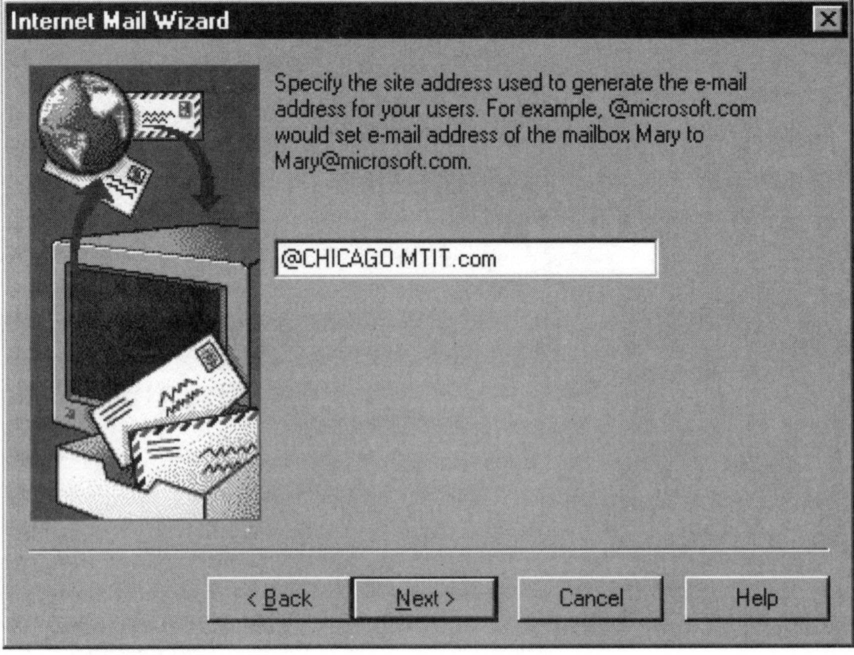
Internet Mail Wizard
Specify the site address used to generate the e-mail address for your users. For example, @microsoft.com would set e-mail address of the mailbox Mary to Mary@microsoft.com.
@CHICAGO.MTIT.com
< Back
Next >
Cancel
Help

Figure 16-11 Specifying the SMTP partial address of your Exchange site.

Click Next and select a mailbox or distribution list that any notifications generated by the IMS will be sent to, such as non-delivery reports (NDRs) and other system messages (see Figure 16-12). You could also create a mailbox for the default administrator account if you need to, but if you are working with a real-world Windows NT-based network, you probably renamed that account anyway. I selected the mailbox for Peter James, MTIT's network administrator in Chicago.

Click Next and specify the password for the Exchange service account for your site. Just a precaution! (See Figure 16-13.)

Click Next and then click Finish to close the wizard, install the service, update the registry, start the service, and create your new IMS directory object. The new object is created in the Connections container for your Exchange site. A dialog box appears to recommend that you run the Exchange Performance Optimizer once you are finished configuring the new service, which we'll skip here.

Testing the IMS

I first tried sending a test message using Outlook to Jill at Escape. To simplify the test process, I created a custom recipient for Jill named

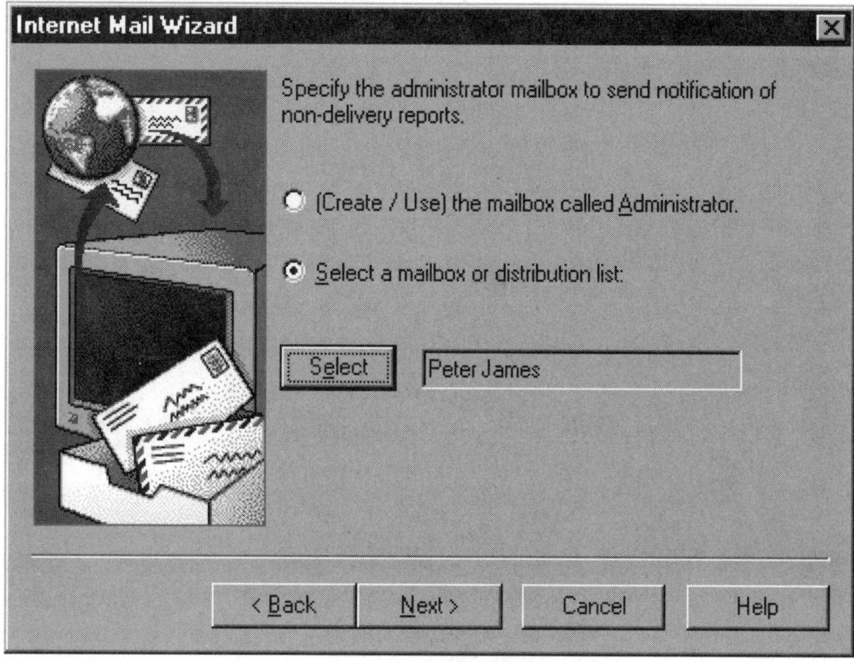

Figure 16-12 Specifying the SMTP administrator mailbox.

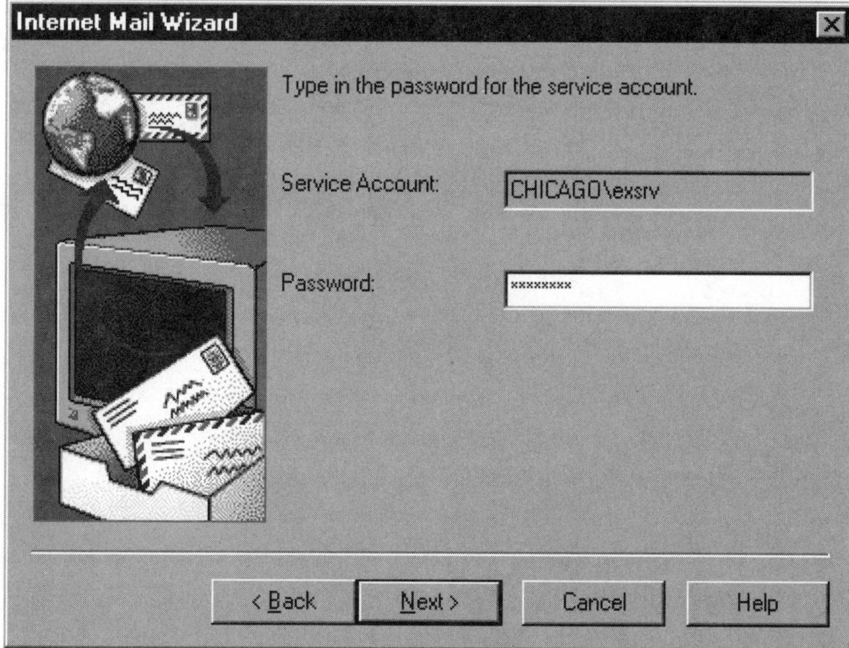

Figure 16-13 Specifying the service account password.

Black Cat of type Internet Mail and assigned this recipient the SMTP address:

```
blackcat@smtp.escape.ca
```

Logged on to BUGS as Peter James (`pjames@chicago.mtit.com`), I created a test message and sent it Black Cat, but unfortunately she didn't receive it. I opened the property sheet for the IMS on BUGS and switched to the Queues tab to see if the message was stuck in the IMS outbound message queue. Sure enough, it was there (see Figure 16-14).

What went wrong? Was it a problem with my IMS configuration or something to do with my ISP's setup? I selected the displayed message and clicked the Details button to open the Details box for the stuck message (see Figure 16-15).

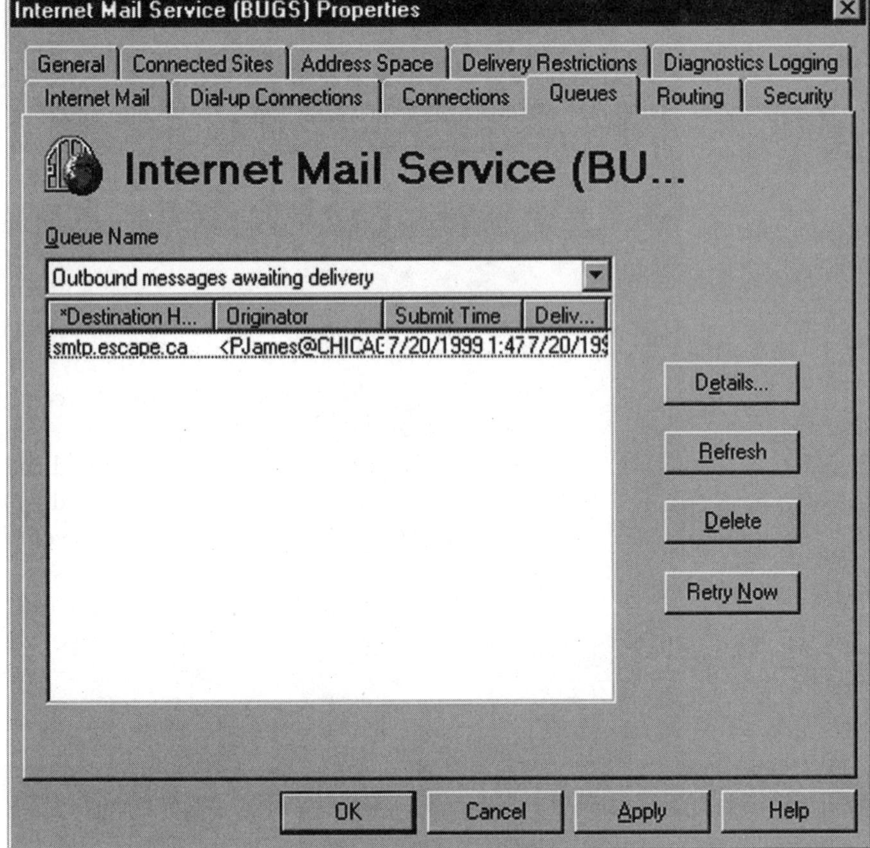

Figure 16-14 An outbound message stuck in the queue.

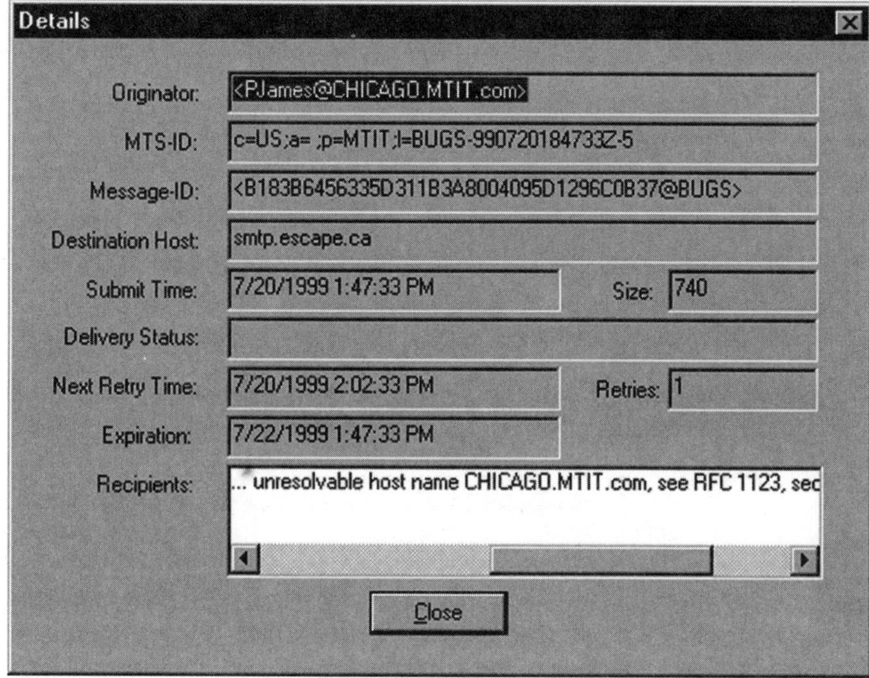

Figure 16-15 Details of the outbound message stuck in the queue.

The problem is indicated in the Recipients field on this dialog box. The text indicates that the ISP's Sendmail server could not resolve the domain name `chicago.mtit.com` of my Exchange Server. Basically, this told us that it was a security issue associated with how their Sendmail server was configured. Jill then edited the DNS zone file for my `mtit.com` domain on their BIND name server to include the MX record listed at the beginning of this walkthrough (we had only entered the A record for my server at that point). Once the zone file was updated, I deleted the stuck message from the queue (which caused an NDR to be returned by the IMS to Outlook), created another test message to Black Cat, and sent it, which worked (see Figure 16-16).

For interest's sake, here is the SMTP header of the message, as viewed at the client station where Jill received the message:

```
Return-Path: <PJames@CHICAGO.MTIT.com>
Received: from wpg-06.escape.ca ([198.163.232.249]) by wpg-
10.escape.ca
 (Netscape Messaging Server 3.61) with ESMTP id AAA674B
 for <blackcat@escape.ca>; Tue, 20 Jul 1999 14:23:34 -0500
Received: from bugs.chicago.mtit.com (bugs.chicago.mtit.com
[207.161.116.92])
```

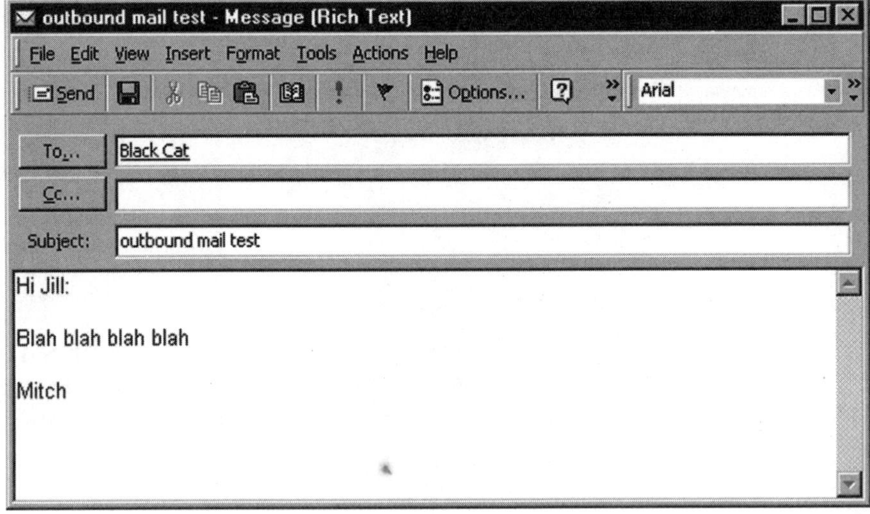

Figure 16-16 Test message to Black Cat.

```
 by wpg-06.escape.ca (8.9.1a/8.8.8) with ESMTP id OAA03836
 for <blackcat@smtp.escape.ca>; Tue, 20 Jul 1999 14:23:32 -
0500 (CDT)
Received: by BUGS with Internet Mail Service (5.5.2448.0)
 id <PJZRGGYS>; Tue, 20 Jul 1999 14:23:32 -0500
Message-ID: <B183B6456335D311B3A8004095D1296C0B3C@BUGS>
From: Peter James <PJames@CHICAGO.MTIT.com>
To: Black Cat <blackcat@smtp.escape.ca>
Subject: testing
Date: Tue, 20 Jul 1999 14:23:31 -0500
MIME-Version: 1.0
X-Mailer: Internet Mail Service (5.5.2448.0)
Content-Type: text/plain;
 charset="iso-8859-1"
```

Configuring the IMS

We'll conclude this section with an overview of the various tabs on the property sheet for the IMS. The IMS object is located in the Connections container for the site where it was created.

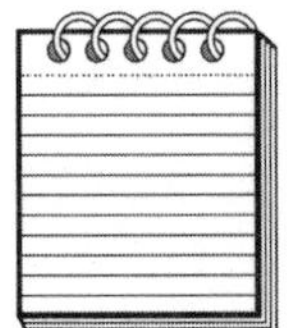

Modifying IMS Settings
Unlike other Exchange connectors, you need to use Services in the Control Panel to stop and restart the IMS after modifying the settings on its property sheet.

Let's examine some of the most important configuration options on the property sheet of this IMS object:

- The *General tab* lets you specify a maximum limit for message size of the IMS.
- The *Connected Sites tab* displays other Exchange sites your IMS is connected to, if you are using the IMS for connecting different sites together in your organization. If you are only using the IMS to provide an SMTP gateway to the Internet as in the walkthrough above, this tab can be ignored.
- The *Address Space tab* lets you specify which SMTP addresses your server can process for outbound mail. If you specify only the wildcard character (*) for the address, this means the IMS will allow recipients in your organization to send SMTP mail to anyone on the Internet (see Figure 16-17). This is actually the setting we chose when we ran the

Figure 16-17 Address Space tab of IMS property sheet.

Internet Mail Wizard in the walkthrough (refer to Figure 16-10). If, however, you only wanted to allow your recipients to send SMTP mail to users in the `.com` domain, then you would specify `*.com` here. You can specify as many address spaces as you want and assign a cost and scope to each one. Address spaces are discussed more in Chapter 18.

- The *Delivery Restrictions tab* lets you accept or reject SMTP messages sent by any recipient in your organization. Use this to prevent certain recipients in your organization from sending SMTP mail to people outside your organization. Settings on this tab do not affect incoming SMTP mail, however.
- The *Internet Mail tab* configures message encoding for outbound attachments, character sets, S/MIME, message tracking, an SMTP mail administrator's mailbox, and other general settings related to the sending and receiving of SMTP mail over the Internet (see Figure 16-18). Most of this stuff is pretty self-explanatory.

Figure 16-18 Internet Mail tab of the IMS property sheet.

Problems Decoding Attachments

If users in your organization regularly send Internet mail to users outside your organization and the recipients complain that the attachments to your users' messages come out garbled, try changing the Attachments (Outbound) setting here from MIME to Uuencode, since Uuencode is sometimes used by Unix SMTP hosts on the Internet.

- The *Dial-up Connections tab* specifies *Remote Access Service* (RAS) phonebook entries and scheduling options when you are using the Windows NT RAS to dial up an SMTP host in order to use the IMS for SMTP mail capabilities. Chapter 17, "Administering Dynamic RAS Connectors," will cover more information regarding RAS.
- The *Connections tab* contains a lot of stuff you can configure as far as how your IMS connects to remote SMTP hosts, almost too much for a single tab (see Figure 16-19). We'll review some of the more important settings:
  - The *Transfer mode* specifies whether to only accept inbound messages, only send outbound messages, do both, or do neither and just flush the IMS message queues. Clicking Advanced lets you specify the maximum number of inbound and outbound connections and other options.
  - *Message Delivery* lets you specify whether to use DNS to connect to remote SMTP hosts, forward all outbound SMTP messages to an SMTP smart host, or specify a RAS connection for the Dial-up Connections tab described earlier. Select the Email Domain button if you want to restrict sending to specific DNS domains.
  - *Accept Connections* lets you specify whether to accept unauthenticated inbound connections to port 25 from any SMTP host or to accept connections from only a specific group of hosts using some form of authentication. Use the Hosts button to specify the IP addresses of specific SMTP hosts or networks from which you want to accept or reject connections.
  - *Service Message Queues* specifies retry intervals and message timeout settings.
- The *Queues tab* shows the contents of the IMS message queues. We looked at this during the walkthrough.
- The *Routing tab* lets you choose whether or not to allow rerouting of incoming SMTP mail (see Figure 16-20). If you choose to allow this, you must specify what to do with incoming SMTP mail addressed to different domains. For example, the default routing entry here is

Figure 16-19 Connections tab of IMS property sheet.

```
chicago.mtit.com        <inbound>
```

This means that if we turned on rerouting by selecting the second option button on this tab, any inbound mail of the form

```
<recipient>@chicago.mtit.com
```

would be routed to the IMS as inbound, while all other inbound mail would be rerouted outbound.

Rerouting

The IMS must be configured to reroute mail if you want to enable users to email recipients outside your Exchange organization. If you select Do Not Reroute Incoming SMTP Mail, your users will only be able to send SMTP mail to recipients in the GAL of your organization.

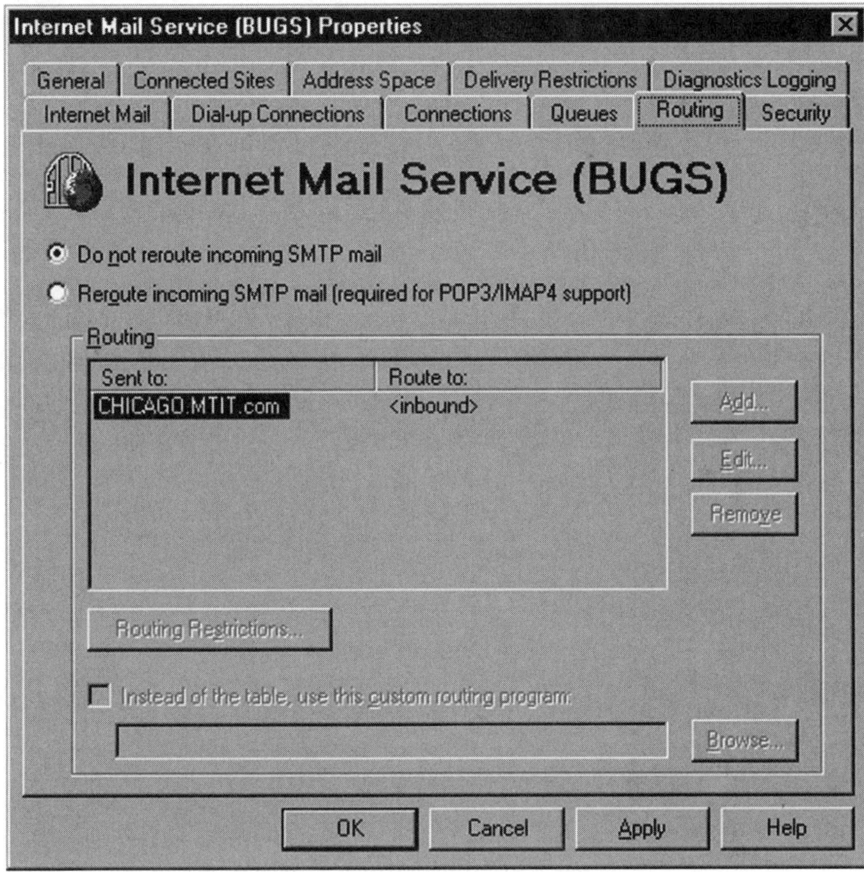

Figure 16-20
Routing tab of IMS property sheet.

- The *Security tab* is used to configure SSL or Windows NT Challenge/Response security for specific email domains.

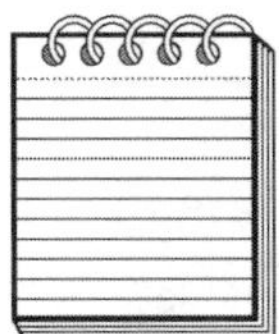

SMTP Addressing

Consider the two sites Chicago and Atlanta in our Exchange organization MTIT. Users in the Chicago site will, by default, have SMTP email addresses of the form

```
user@chicago.mtit.com
```

while users in the Atlanta site will have addresses in the form

```
user@atlanta.mtit.com
```

What if you want to make life easier for all your users by allowing them to send and receive SMTP email using an address of the simpler form

```
user@mtit.com
```

In other words, you'll want to hide the site portion of the DNS domain name for users' email addresses. Here's what you can do to accomplish this:

1. *Modify the MX record for the DNS server that is servicing your organization so that it points to your Exchange Server that is running the IMS using the* `mtit.com` *domain designation.*
2. *Use the Routing tab on the IMS property sheet to specify that all mail inbound to the domain* `mtit.com` *is routed as* `<inbound>`.
3. *Open the Site Addressing tab of the Side Addressing directory object for each site in your organization and add an SMTP proxy address of the form* `@mtit.com`.

The Internet News Service

We will end this chapter with a brief look at another Exchange service that provides connectivity with the Internet, the Internet News Service. The Internet News Service has nothing to do with mail at all. Instead, it enables an Exchange Server to act as an NNTP host and participate in the worldwide Usenet news system. Using the Internet News Service, Exchange can exchange newsfeeds with other NNTP hosts on the Internet and enable NNTP clients like Outlook Express to connect and download newsgroups and read or post messages to these groups. This is rather a specialized service and beyond the needs of most mail administrators, so we'll provide only a brief overview of this service.

To install and configure the Internet News Service on an Exchange Server, you create a newsfeed on that server using File, New Other, Newsfeed from the Exchange Administrator program menu. This starts a long and somewhat complicated wizard called the Newsfeed Configuration Wizard that we won't discuss here. These newsfeeds are of two types, depending on which side initiates the NNTP connection:

- *Push feeds*. These are when your Usenet service provider's NNTP host machine initiates the connection with your Exchange Server and sends newsgroup information to your server on a schedule determined by the provider. Push feeds are typically used when the newsfeeds are large, such as when you want to download a full Usenet newsfeed.

- *Pull feeds*. These are when your Exchange Server initiates the connection with your provider's NNTP host and accepts selected newsgroup content from the host on a schedule that you determine. Pull feeds are used for smaller, select feeds that you control.

Newsfeeds can be classified in two other categories, however:

- *Inbound feeds*. These are feeds received by your Exchange server from a Usenet provider's NNTP host. Inbound feeds are typically used when you want to host Usenet content on your Exchange Server.
- *Outbound feeds*. These are feeds generated and sent by your Exchange Server to your provider's NNTP host. For example, you might create a hierarchy of public folders and then send it to your provider in the form of a newsgroup hierarchy to propagate elsewhere.

Thus, a newsfeed can function in one of six ways:

- Inbound pull feed
- Inbound push feed
- Outbound pull feed
- Outbound push feed
- Inbound and outbound pull feed
- Inbound and outbound pull feed

The last two are the most common. Use an inbound/outbound push feed only if you have gigabytes and gigabytes of free space on your Exchange Server, since a full Usenet feed nowadays is huge and typically contains over 40,000 different newsgroups.

Once a Newsfeed object is created, it can be configured by opening its property sheet (see Figure 16-21). Newsfeed objects are located in the Connections container along with the various mail connectors installed in your site. Like the IMS, newsfeeds are implemented as a Windows NT service called the Internet News Service.

Let's look at some of the settings you can configure on the tabs of a Newsfeed property sheet:

- The *General tab* displays the type of newsfeed you created when you ran the Wizard, which cannot be changed. You can also disable your newsfeed using the checkbox.
- The *Messages tab* lets you specify message size limits for incoming and outgoing messages.

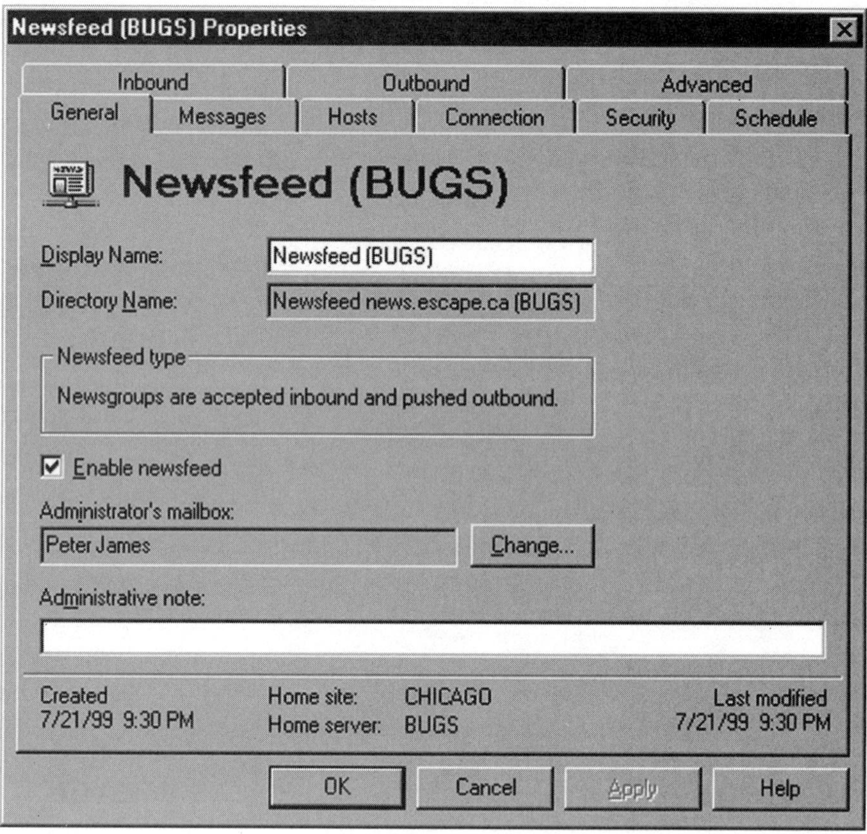

Figure 16-21 Newsfeed property sheet.

- The *Hosts tab* is where you can specify the site and host names of the remote NNTP host you are receiving your Usenet feed from.
- The *Connection tab* lets you specify whether you are connecting to the remote NNTP host using a LAN or a RAS connection.
- The *Security tab* is where settings can be configured if your provider's NNTP host requires authentication in order to be accessed.
- The *Schedule tab* lets you specify when and how often you connect to your provider's NNTP host (if you have created a pull feed).
- The *Inbound tab* is where you can specify which newsgroups to receive and have replicated to your server if your server receives inbound feeds from your provider.

- The *Outbound tab* specifies any Exchange public folders you want to replicate to your provider's Usenet host if you created an outbound feed.
- The *Advanced tab* contains a button that lets you mark all newsgroup messages as having already been delivered.

Where Do We Go from Here?

In the next chapter, we will look at another connector that can be used for establishing messaging connectivity between Exchange sites: the Dynamic RAS Connector.

For More Information

You can find some useful information on Exchange Internet services in the *Operations* manual, which is included in Books Online.

Exchange Server 5.5 Resource Guide

Chapter 11 of this guide contains information on troubleshooting the IMS. This resource guide is currently included in TechNet.

TechNet

The Technical Notes in the MS Exchange section of TechNet include two useful articles:

- Dial-up Internet Mail Service Host Configuration
- How to Replicate Exchange Server Directories Using the Internet Mail Service

The Third-Party Information section of the MS Exchange section contains the article, Configuring Internet Mail Service on MS Exchange Server 5.5. The Knowledge Base articles on IMS, however, are too numerous to list here.

CHAPTER 17

Administering Dynamic RAS Connectors

The last few chapters covered various connectors that can establish messaging connections between Exchange sites and between Exchange Servers and foreign mail systems. We'll now look at the last of these connectors that this book will cover, the *Dynamic Remote Access Service* (DRAS) Connector.

The walkthrough in this chapter takes you through installing and configuring the Windows NT RAS, as well as the RAS MTA Transport Stacks and the DRAS Connectors.

DRAS Connector

The most common way of connecting two sites together in an Exchange organization is to use the Site Connector, which is easy to install and configure. A close second is the X.400 Connector, which has certain advantages over the Site Connector in terms of limiting message size and scheduling message transfers during periods of slow WAN traffic. However, both of these two connectors require that you have a permanent high-speed LAN or WAN connection between your two sites, which is the best solution, although it is also a costly one.

If the messaging connectivity needs of your Exchange sites are only occasionally required, you can use the DRAS Connector to establish dial-up connectivity between your Exchange sites. This dial-up connectivity can use an ordinary modem and telephone line and can either be activated on demand (when messages are queued to be sent over the connector) or scheduled to occur at specific times or intervals (such as every three hours or only at 2 A.M.).

The DRAS Connector is the only choice you have for establishing asynchronous connectivity between your Exchange sites; it makes use of the Windows NT RAS to accomplish this. You might use this connector to connect a remote branch office to headquarters using an asynchronous device like a modem, an ISDN terminal adapter, or an X.25 *Packet Assembler/Disassembler* (PAD), especially if the messaging traffic is low and a certain amount of messaging latency (delay) is acceptable for users. The DRAS Connector is also useful as a backup connection between sites, in case the permanent network link goes down, causing the Site Connector or X.400 Connector to fail.

Remote Access Service

This chapter assumes that you have some familiarity with the Windows NT RAS. However, the walkthrough includes steps for installing and configuring RAS in the context of preparing to install a DRAS Connector.

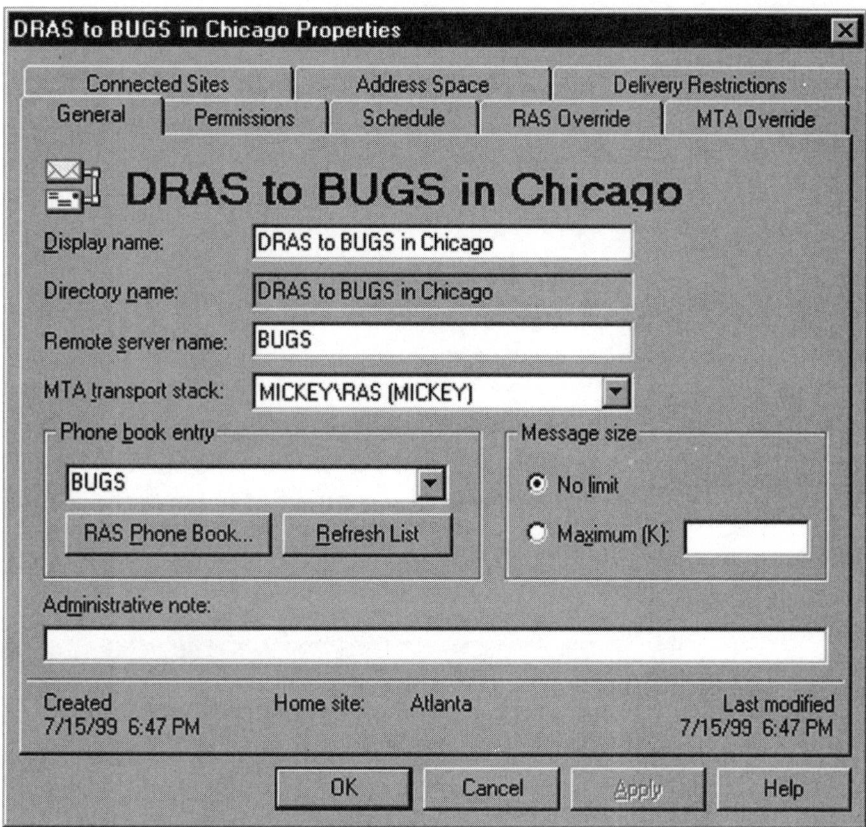

Figure 17-1
The DRAS Connector.

Now let's consider some of the configuration settings for the DRAS Connector. Some of these settings will be covered again during the walkthrough later in this chapter:

- *General tab*. The important settings on this tab are as follows (see Figure 17-1):
- *Remote Server Name*. This is the name of the Exchange Server in the remote site where the mirror DRAS Connector is installed.
- *MTA Transport Stack*. Here you select a RAS MTA Transport Stack that will be used by the connector. Refer to Chapter 14, "Administering X.400 Connectors," for more on MTA Transport Stacks.
- *Phone Book Entry*. This is the RAS client phone book entry that is used when the connector initiates a dial-up connection. We'll look at how to create this phone book entry in the walkthrough.
- *Message Size*. We can configure a maximum message size that can be routed through the connector.

- *Schedule tab*. The DRAS Connector can be scheduled to deliver mail to other sites in different ways (see Figure 17-2):
  - *Remote Initiated* causes the local side of the DRAS Connector never to initiate a RAS connection to the remote site. Instead, it waits for the remote site to connect to it, whereupon messages waiting in queues are sent both ways. Do not configure both connectors as Remote Initiated, or the mail will never be transferred between the sites.
  - *Never* disables the connector.
  - *Always* causes the connector to initiate a RAS connection to the remote site whenever an outbound message is waiting in the local MTA queue. You would use this only if message traffic is low and message latency cannot be tolerated.
  - *Selected Times* can be used to schedule RAS connections to the remote site at selected times specified in hourly or 15-minute intervals.

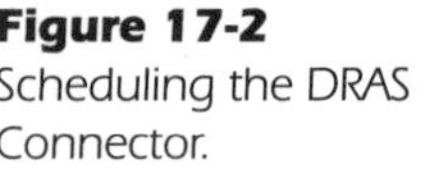

Figure 17-2 Scheduling the DRAS Connector.

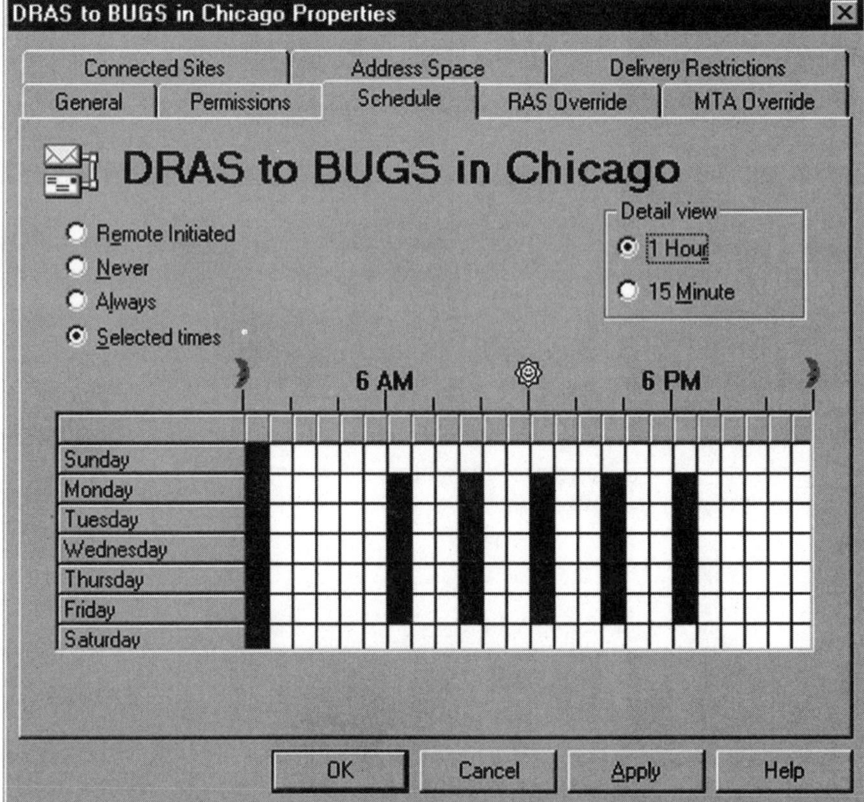

- *RAS Override tab*. This tab is used to specify the Windows NT user account in the remote site that the connector uses to establish a RAS connection. This account must have suitable Exchange permissions in the remote site and must be configured as a dial-in user account. See the walkthrough for how to do this. You also can use this tab to specify a phone number for RAS callback for greater security when using RAS.
- *MTA Override tab*. This tab can be used to override the settings on the Messaging Defaults tab of the MTA Site Configuration object for your local site (but only for messages routed through this connector). They should match the settings on the MTA Site Configuration object for the remote site. You can generally leave these settings as they are.
- *Connected Sites tab*. Use this tab to specify the name of the remote site to which you are connecting. Configuring a connected site's entry with the remote site is also required to enable directory replication to take place with the remote site. By default, the DRAS Connector uses the X.400 address (O/R address) of the remote site for message routing. Configuring this tab is explained in more detail in the walkthrough later.
- *Address Space tab*. If you want the DRAS Connector to route messages to the remote site using address types other than X.400 addresses, specify these address spaces here.
- *Delivery Restrictions tab.* This tab enables you to accept or reject outbound messages according to who sends them.

Walkthrough: Creating and Testing a DRAS Connector

Here we'll walk through the process of installing and configuring a DRAS Connector. Because a prerequisite for DRAS is to have the Windows NT Remote Access Service up and running, we'll include a walkthrough of how to install and configure Windows NT RAS for readers who aren't familiar with this. We'll begin with an overview of our networking scenario.

The Scenario

We have two Windows NT domains, the domain MTIT in Atlanta and the domain CHICAGO in Chicago. Each city has one Exchange Server with the following configuration:

- Atlanta site
  - Exchange Server MICKEY

- IP address = 172.16.11.24
- Chicago site
- Exchange Server BUGS
- IP address = 172.16.11.133

Both servers are PDCs for simplicity. In addition, Atlanta has a Windows 98 machine called GOOFEY that Boris uses to send messages using Outlook 98. Peter in Chicago uses BUGS to send messages using Outlook 2000. By the way, you may want to delete any existing connectors and MTA Transport Stacks installed on MICKEY and BUGS to make the following walkthrough a clean one.

Installing and Configuring the RAS

We'll begin by installing the RAS on our Windows NT Server MICKEY, which is our Exchange Server in the Atlanta site. Start by logging on as Administrator, open the Network utility in the Control Panel, select the Services tab, and click Add. Select Remote Access Service from the Select Network Service dialog box (see Figure 17-3).

Click OK, and if you have no modem installed on your machine, a dialog box will appear saying, `There are no RAS capable devices to Add. Do you want RAS setup to invoke the Modem installer to enable you to add a`

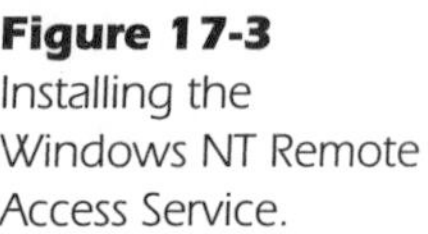

Figure 17-3 Installing the Windows NT Remote Access Service.

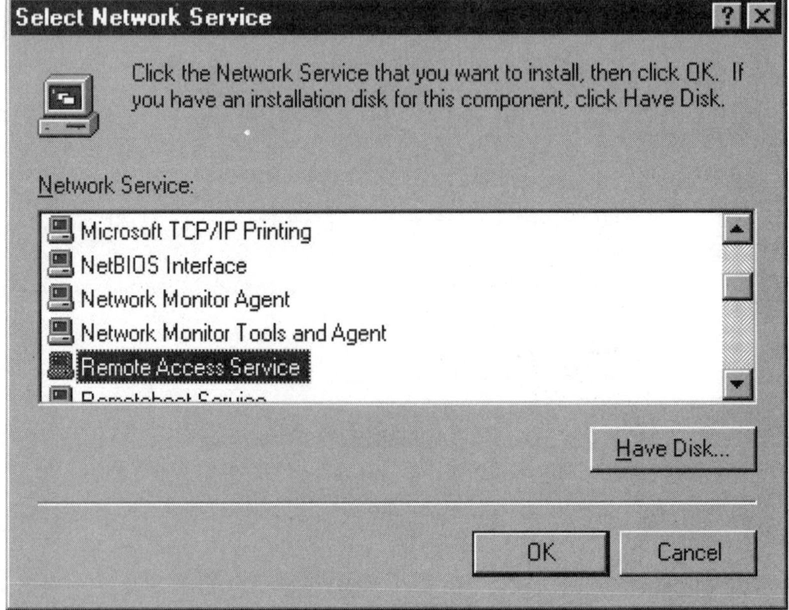

`modem?` Click Yes to open the Install New Modem wizard. Because we are doing a testbed setup using a null modem cable, select the checkbox so that the wizard will allow you to specify the modem from a list, instead of trying to detect one, and click Next. From the Manufacturers listbox, select Standard Modem Types, and from the Models listbox, select Dial-Up Networking Serial Cable Between 2 PCs. Click Next and select COM2 (or whichever unused serial port you plan to use). Click Next and specify country and area code information for your default TAPI location. Click Next and then Finish to exit the wizard and return to installing and configuring RAS. The Add RAS Device dialog box now appears (see Figure 17-4).

Make sure that the Dial-Up Networking Serial Cable is selected as your RAS-capable device and click OK. This will take you to the Remote Access Setup dialog box, which is the main starting point for configuring the RAS on Windows NT (see Figure 17-5). (If you need to return to this dialog box later on, just start the Network utility in the Control Panel again, select the Services tab, and double-click on the Remote Access Service entry in the listbox.)

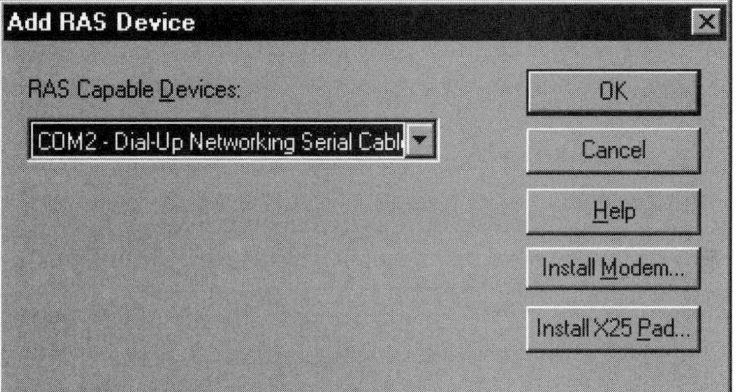

Figure 17-4 Selecting a RAS-capable device.

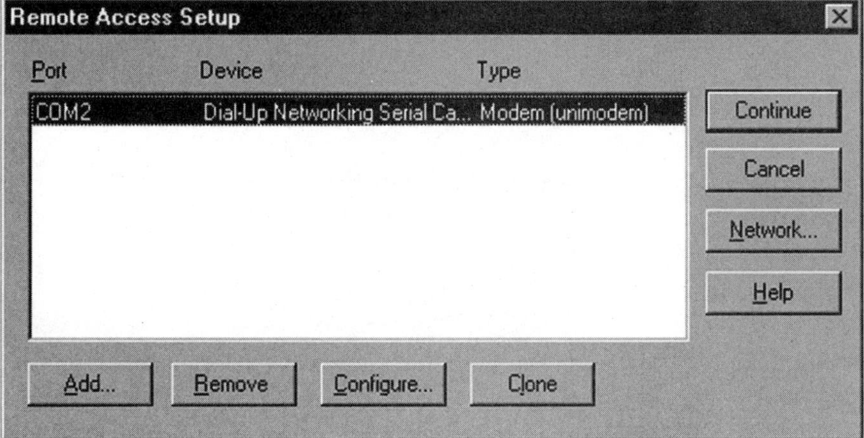

Figure 17-5 The Remote Access Setup dialog box.

Select the Configure button to open the Configure Port Usage dialog box. This is where we can specify whether the RAS is allowed to only receive calls, initiate calls, or do both. We should select Dial Out and Receive Calls in order for the DRAS Connector to work properly, so select this option (see Figure 17-6).

Click OK to return to the Remote Access Setup box. Now we have to configure the network protocols that RAS will use, so click the Network button to open the Network Configuration dialog box (see Figure 17-7).

Because we have configured our RAS port to be able to both dial out and receive calls, our computer will be functioning as both a RAS client and a RAS server. This means we have to specify one or more networking protocols that will be used, both for the client and server side of RAS. Note that TCP/IP is automatically selected for both roles, since this is our primary network protocol. For security reasons, leave the Encryption Settings configured as Require Microsoft Encrypted Authentication.

We still have some important configurations to do on the server side of RAS. Click the Configure button beside TCP/IP under Server Settings. This will open the RAS Server TCP/IP Configuration dialog box (see Figure 17-8).

We need to create a pool of IP addresses that can be used by RAS. This pool should have at least two IP addresses in it, one for the RAS client and one for the RAS server. To keep the routing simple, the IP address for the network interface card (NIC) in the machine MICKEY is `172.16.11.24`, and the IP address for the NIC in BUGS is `172.16.11.133`, which means that both machines are on the same subnet. We'll choose our pool of RAS addresses from the same subnet as well, so select Use Static Address Pool and specify the following range:

Begin = `172.16.11.240`

End = `172.16.11.241`

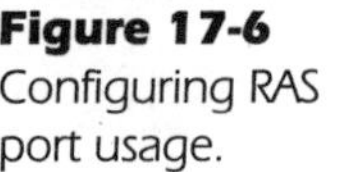

Figure 17-6
Configuring RAS port usage.

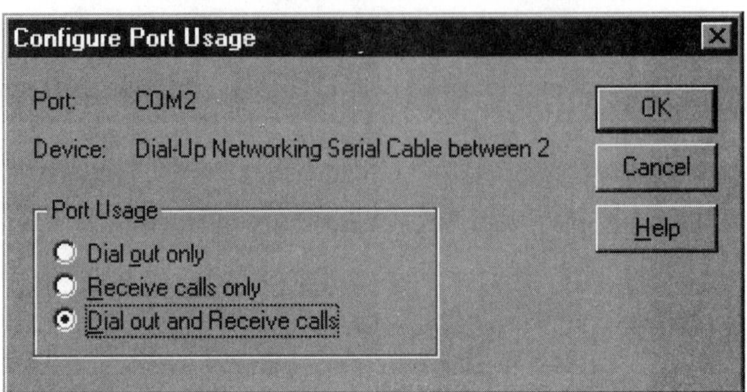

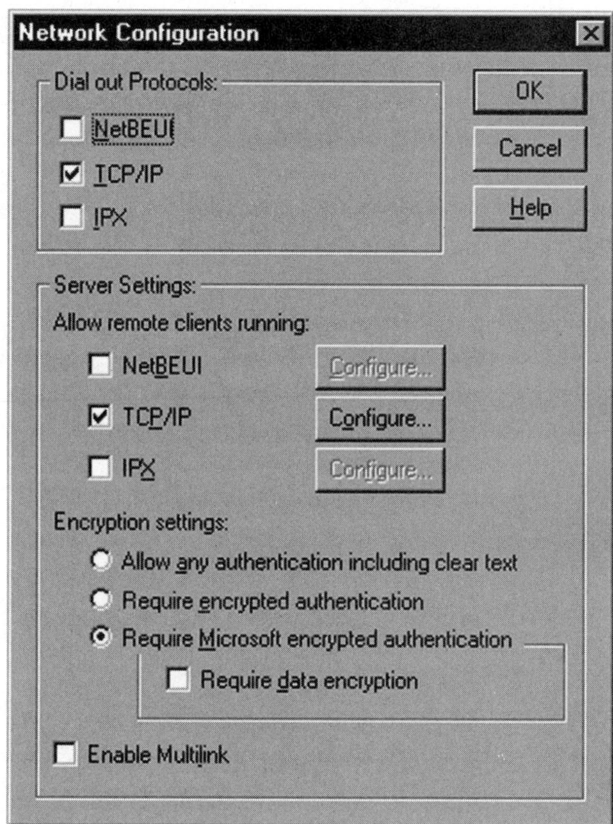

Figure 17-7 The RAS Network Configuration dialog box.

This will cause RAS on MICKEY to select RAS client and RAS server addresses from the range `172.16.11.240` to `172.16.11.241` (two IP addresses). Typically, the higher of the two addresses will be assigned to the RAS server on MICKEY, while the lower address will be assigned to the RAS client on the machine that dials in to MICKEY, namely BUGS.

RAS Routing

For more complicated setups in which the RAS servers are in different subnets, you may need to configure the RAS clients to request a specific IP address from the server and use the Route Add command to configure the routing table appropriately. See the section, "For More Information," at the end of this chapter regarding this kind of situation.

Click OK twice to return to the Remote Access Setup box and click Continue to finish installing RAS on the machine. A dialog box will appear,

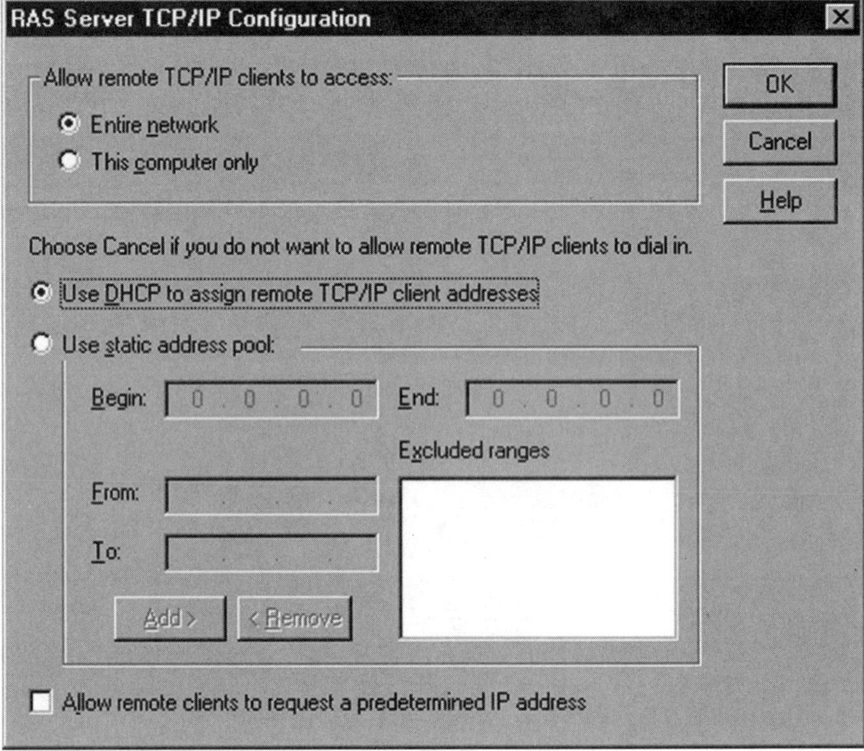

Figure 17-8 Configuring RAS server TCP/IP settings.

indicating that the service has been successfully installed. Click OK twice to close the Network utility from the Control Panel. Bindings will now be configured, and you will be prompted to reboot. Choose Yes and remember that it takes a while to reboot an Exchange Server because the Exchange services have to be properly shut down during the process.

After your system reboots and you have logged on again as Administrator, reinstall your latest Windows NT 4.0 service pack again on the machine. You need to reapply your latest service pack to a machine whenever you add or remove a component of Windows NT. Service Packs for all Microsoft products are included in a subscription to Microsoft TechNet.

Next we need to configure name resolution so that the two Exchange Servers connecting via RAS can properly resolve each other's name into its associated IP address. We'll use the LMHOSTS file for this, which allows us to manually specify NetBIOS names to IP address mappings for our servers. (You also can use the HOSTS file for name resolution as an alternative to LMHOSTS.) To enable LMHOSTS name resolution, start the network utility in the Control Panel again, switch to the Protocols tab, and double-click on TCP/IP Protocol to open the Microsoft TCP/IP Properties box. Switch to the WINS Address tab and make sure that the checkbox labeled Enable LMHOSTS Lookup is selected (see Figure 17-9). If it is already selected, click Cancel twice to return to the desktop; otherwise, select the option, click OK, close it, and reboot your machine again.

We'll now create an LMHOSTS file for our server MICKEY, which will enable RAS on MICKEY to resolve the name of our other server BUGS into its IP address. Open Notepad and enter the following two lines:

```
172.16.11.133       BUGS      #PRE      #DOM:MTIT
172.16.11.133       "CHICAGO            \0x1b" #PRE
```

Make sure that the second line has exactly 20 characters within the double quotes. After typing the preceding lines, click the Enter key three or four

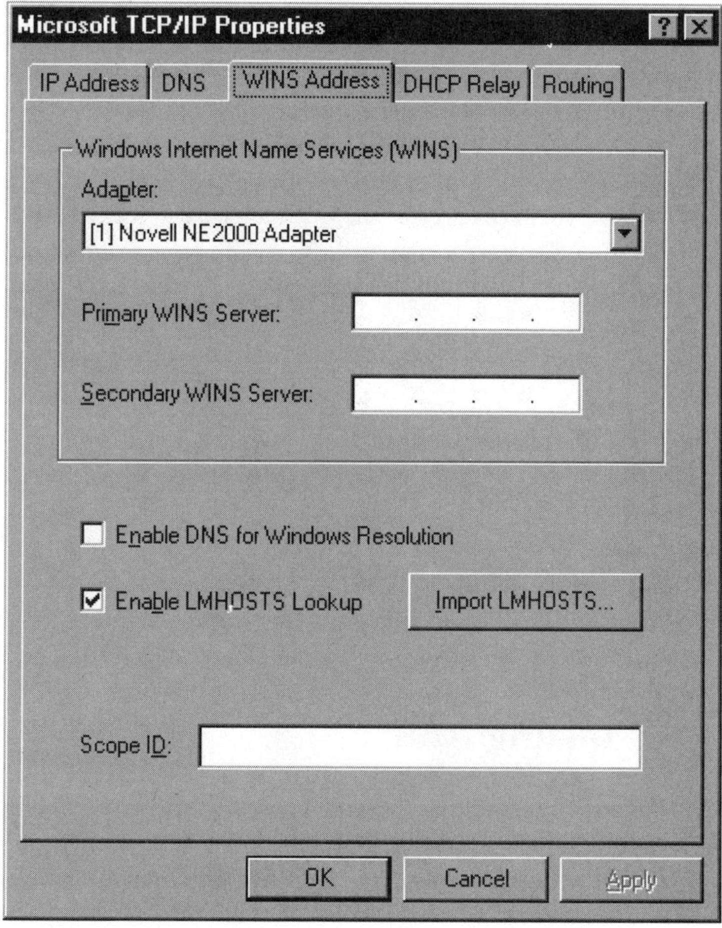

Figure 17-9 Configuring Windows NT to use LMHOSTS for TCP/IP over NetBIOS name resolution.

times to add some blank lines at the end of the file. Save the file with the name LMHOSTS with no file extension in the directory:

```
\Winnt\System32\Drivers\Etc
```

Do *not* select the checkbox labeled Save As Unicode when you are saving the file! Go to the preceding directory and make sure that the LMHOSTS file has no file extension; remove it if there is one. A sample LMHOSTS file is in this directory called LMHOSTS.SAM, which you can read for more information about creating LMHOSTS files.

The explanation for these lines in the LMHOSTS file on MICKEY is that they enable MICKEY to resolve the name BUGS into its associated LAN IP address. The #PRE entry causes the mapping to be preloaded into the NetBIOS name cache upon bootup, and the #DOM:MTIT identifies BUGS as a domain controller in the domain MTIT. The second line specifies that CHICAGO is the name of the domain to which BUGS belongs.

Now we need to create a RAS phone book entry so MICKEY can dial up BUGS. On MICKEY, start Dial-up Networking in the Accessories program group. A dialog box opens saying, `The phonebook is empty. Press OK to add an entry.` Click OK to start the New Phonebook Entry Wizard. Give the new phonebook entry the name BUGS and click Next three times, followed by Finish to end the wizard. This leaves you with the Dial-Up Networking dialog box (see Figure 17-10). Note that we do not need to enter a phone number for calling BUGS, because we are using a null modem serial cable.

Click Close, and we're finished installing and configuring RAS on MICKEY. Now go to BUGS and repeat the preceding steps with the following differences:

- Specify the range `172.16.11.250` to `172.16.11.251` for the static pool of IP addresses that RAS can use on BUGS.
- Use the following for the LMHOSTS file entries on BUGS:

```
172.16.11.24      MICKEY      #PRE      #DOM:CHICAGO
172.16.11.24      "MTIT                \0x1b" #PRE
```

- Create a new phonebook entry called MICKEY on BUGS.

Testing RAS

Now connect a null modem (file transfer) serial cable between BUGS and MICKEY and make sure that they do not share a common LAN connection (The easiest way to test them is to disconnect them both from the LAN and have them connect to each other via a serial connection.) Then reboot both

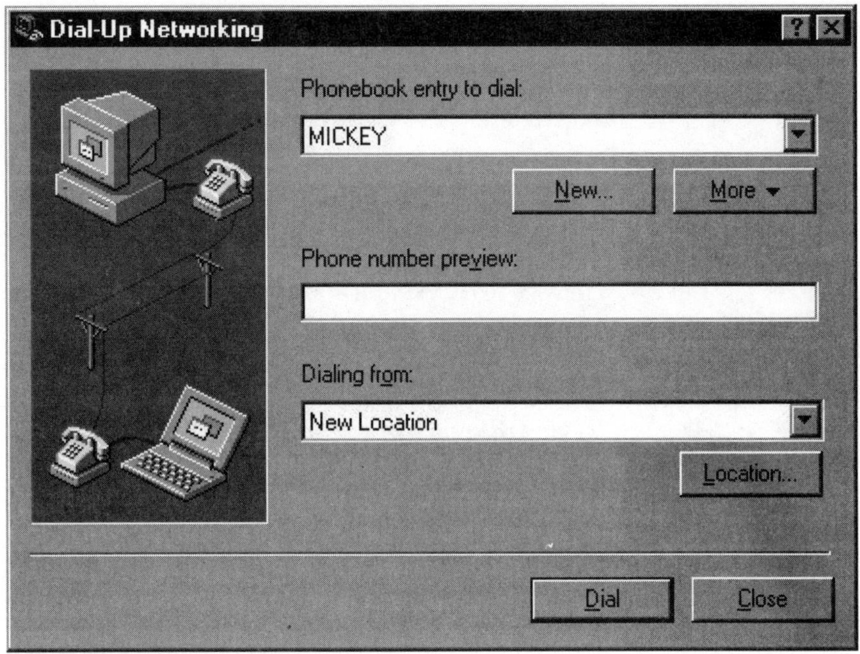

Figure 17-10 Creating a phonebook entry for BUGS on MICKEY.

machines. When MICKEY comes up, log on as Administrator and open a command-prompt window and type the following command:

```
nbtstat -c
```

This will display the NetBIOS name cache on MICKEY. The LMHOSTS entry for BUGS should have been preloaded into the cache, so the results of entering the preceding command on MICKEY should display something like this:

```
C:\>nbtstat -c
Node IpAddress: [172.16.11.24] Scope Id: []
                  NetBIOS Remote Cache Name Table
Name                 Type         Host Address     Life [sec]
------------------------------------------------------------
BUGS           <03>  UNIQUE       172.16.11.133       -1
BUGS           <00>  UNIQUE       172.16.11.133       -1
BUGS           <20>  UNIQUE       172.16.11.133       -1
CHICAGO        <1C>  GROUP        172.16.11.133       -1
CHICAGO        <1B>  UNIQUE       172.16.11.133       -1
```

Let's check whether RAS works before creating a DRAS Connector to link the Atlanta and Chicago sites. Remember that the CHICAGO domain in which BUGS resides trusts the MTIT domain where MICKEY resides, so BUGS should be able to dial in to MICKEY using an account in the MTIT domain, provided that the account has RAS dial-in permissions. Go to MICKEY and start User Manager for Domains, open the property sheet for the user account Boris, and click the Dial button to open the Dialin Information dialog box for Boris. Select the checkbox labeled Grant Dialin Permission to User (see Figure 17-11) and click OK twice. This gives the account `MTIT\Boris` permission to dial in to MICKEY using RAS.

Now go to BUGS and start Dial-up Networking from the Accessories program group. The Dial-Up Networking dialog box appears (refer to 17-10 again). Click Dial to open the Connect to MICKEY dialog box. Enter the credentials for the account `MTIT\Boris`, as shown in Figure 17-12.

Click OK, and a series of dialog boxes will flash by until a Connection Complete dialog box appears, saying that you have successfully connected to the remote server. If you want, try opening a command-prompt window on BUGS and typing `ipconfig` to display the TCP/IP configuration for the LAN and RAS interfaces on BUGS, followed by `route print` to display the routing table on BUGS (routing entries for RAS interfaces are present in this table only when a RAS connection is active). Then try using the `ping` command to test network connectivity with MICKEY via the null modem serial cable connection. The output of such a command prompt session should look something like the following:

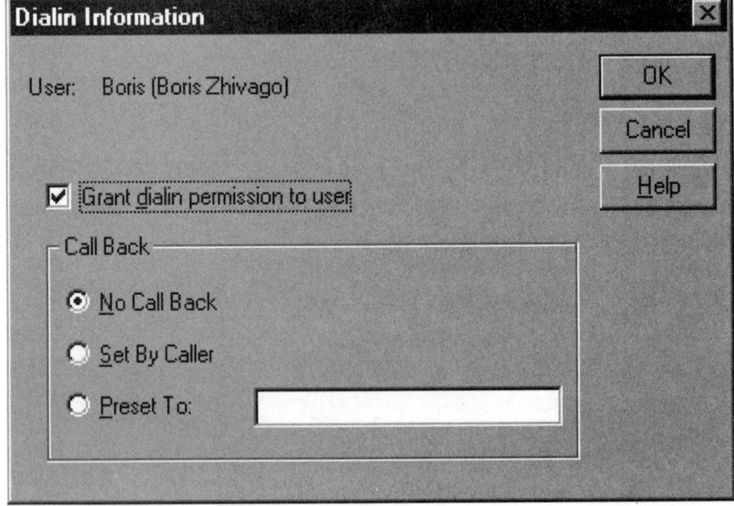

Figure 17-11 Granting RAS dial-in permission to the user account Boris on MICKEY.

Figure 17-12 Dialing up MICKEY using Boris's credentials.

```
C:\>ipconfig

Windows NT IP Configuration

Ethernet adapter NE20001:

        IP Address. . . . . . . . . : 172.16.11.133
        Subnet Mask . . . . . . . . : 255.255.255.0
        Default Gateway . . . . . . : 172.16.11.133

Ethernet adapter NdisWan5:

        IP Address. . . . . . . . . : 172.16.11.241
        Subnet Mask . . . . . . . . : 255.255.0.0
        Default Gateway . . . . . . : 172.16.11.241

Ethernet adapter NdisWan4:

        IP Address. . . . . . . . . : 0.0.0.0
        Subnet Mask . . . . . . . . : 0.0.0.0
        Default Gateway . . . . . . :

C:\>route print
===========================================================================
Interface List
0x1 ........................... MS TCP Loopback interface
0x2 ...00 40 95 d1 29 6c ...... Novell 2000 Adapter.
0x3 ...00 01 90 27 85 80 ...... NdisWan Adapter
0x4 ...00 00 00 00 00 00 ...... NdisWan Adapter
===========================================================================
===========================================================================
Active Routes:
Network Destination        Netmask          Gateway       Interface  Metric
          0.0.0.0          0.0.0.0    172.16.11.133   172.16.11.133       2
          0.0.0.0          0.0.0.0    172.16.11.241   172.16.11.241       1
        127.0.0.0        255.0.0.0        127.0.0.1       127.0.0.1       1
```

```
           172.16.0.0        255.255.0.0  172.16.11.241  172.16.11.241       1
          172.16.11.0      255.255.255.0  172.16.11.133  172.16.11.133       2
          172.16.11.0      255.255.255.0  172.16.11.241  172.16.11.241       1
        172.16.11.133    255.255.255.255      127.0.0.1      127.0.0.1       1
        172.16.11.241    255.255.255.255      127.0.0.1      127.0.0.1       1
       172.16.255.255    255.255.255.255  172.16.11.133  172.16.11.133       1
            224.0.0.0          224.0.0.0  172.16.11.133  172.16.11.133       1
            224.0.0.0          224.0.0.0  172.16.11.241  172.16.11.241       1
      255.255.255.255    255.255.255.255  172.16.11.133  172.16.11.133       1
===============================================================================

C:\>ping 172.16.11.24

Pinging 172.16.11.24 with 32 bytes of data:

Reply from 172.16.11.24: bytes=32 time=71ms TTL=128
Reply from 172.16.11.24: bytes=32 time=20ms TTL=128
Reply from 172.16.11.24: bytes=32 time=20ms TTL=128
Reply from 172.16.11.24: bytes=32 time=20ms TTL=128

C:\>ping mickey

Pinging mickey [172.16.11.24] with 32 bytes of data:

Reply from 172.16.11.24: bytes=32 time=30ms TTL=128
Reply from 172.16.11.24: bytes=32 time=21ms TTL=128
Reply from 172.16.11.24: bytes=32 time=20ms TTL=128
Reply from 172.16.11.24: bytes=32 time=20ms TTL=128

C:\>
```

Creating a RAS Override Account

Before we can install and configure DRAS Connectors on MICKEY and BUGS, we need to consider what user credentials these servers will use to log on to each other using RAS. RAS will generally try to form a connection using the credentials of the currently logged-on user. In the case of Exchange Server, however, the DRAS Connector must use an account that has the capability to access the directory database on the remote Exchange Server with full permissions. The Exchange service account on the remote machine is one possibility, but Microsoft recommends creating a separate RAS Override account in each domain with the necessary RAS and Exchange permissions.

So here's what we'll do: start User Manager for Domains on MICKEY and create a new user account in the MTIT domain with the account name RASCON and some secure password of your choice. Make sure that this account never expires and use the Grant Dialin Permission to User option to grant the account RAS dial-in permissions (refer to Figure 17-11). Click Add, and when a blank Mailbox property sheet for the new account opens up, just click Cancel, since you don't want a mailbox associated with this new account.

Now start Exchange Administrator on MICKEY and open the property sheet for the Server container MICKEY in the Atlanta site. Switch to the Permissions tab and assign the Service Account Admin role to the account MTIT\RASCON (see Figure 17-13).

Now go to BUGS and create an account with the same name and password for the CHICAGO domain and the same role for the Server container BUGS in the Chicago site. We will use these two accounts on the RAS Override tabs of our DRAS Connectors when we create them shortly.

Installing a RAS MTA Transport Stack

Before we install a DRAS Connector on an Exchange Server, we need to install and configure a RAS MTA Transport Stack on the machine. A RAS MTA Transport Stack essentially performs the same function as an X.400 MTA Transport Stack does for the X.400 Connector (refer to Chapter 14).

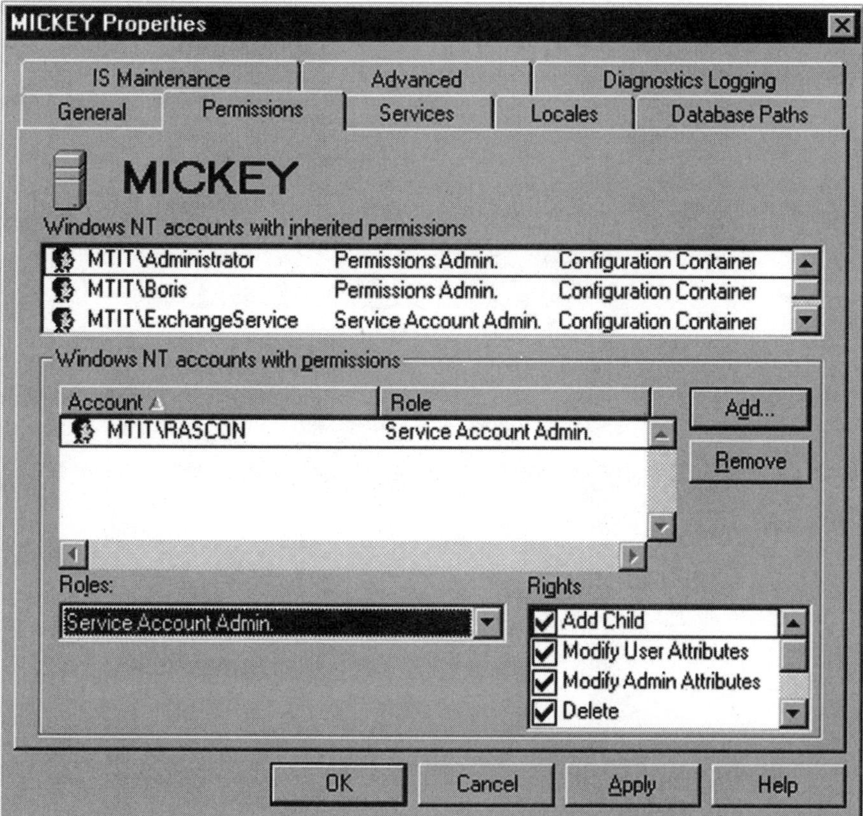

Figure 17-13 *Assigning the Service Account Admin role to the account MTIT\RASCON.*

Installing and configuring a RAS MTA Transport Stack is a straightforward process. Log on to MICKEY as Boris (or any other user with the Permissions Admin role in the Atlanta site) and start Exchange Administrator. Select File, New Other, MTA Transport Stack from the menu to open the New MTA Transport Stack dialog box (see Figure 17-14).

Select RAS MTA Transport Stack and click OK to open a blank property sheet for the new RAS MTA Transport Stack. By default, the new transport stack you are creating on MICKEY is given the name RAS (MICKEY). This is fine, so click OK to accept the defaults and close the property sheet. (We could configure a callback phone number for greater security between our two RAS servers.) Now go to BUGS and create a new RAS MTA Transport Stack there also.

Creating and Configuring a DRAS Connector

Return to MICKEY and select File, New Other, DRAS Connector from the menu to open a blank property sheet for a new DRAS Connector (see Figure 17-15).

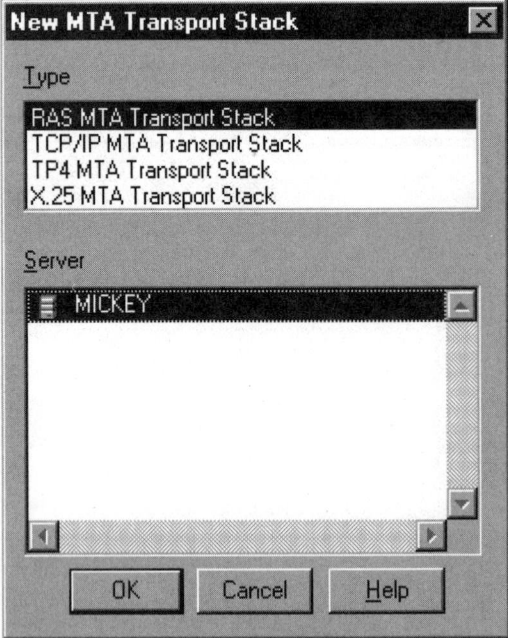

Figure 17-14 Creating a new MTA Transport Stack of type RAS.

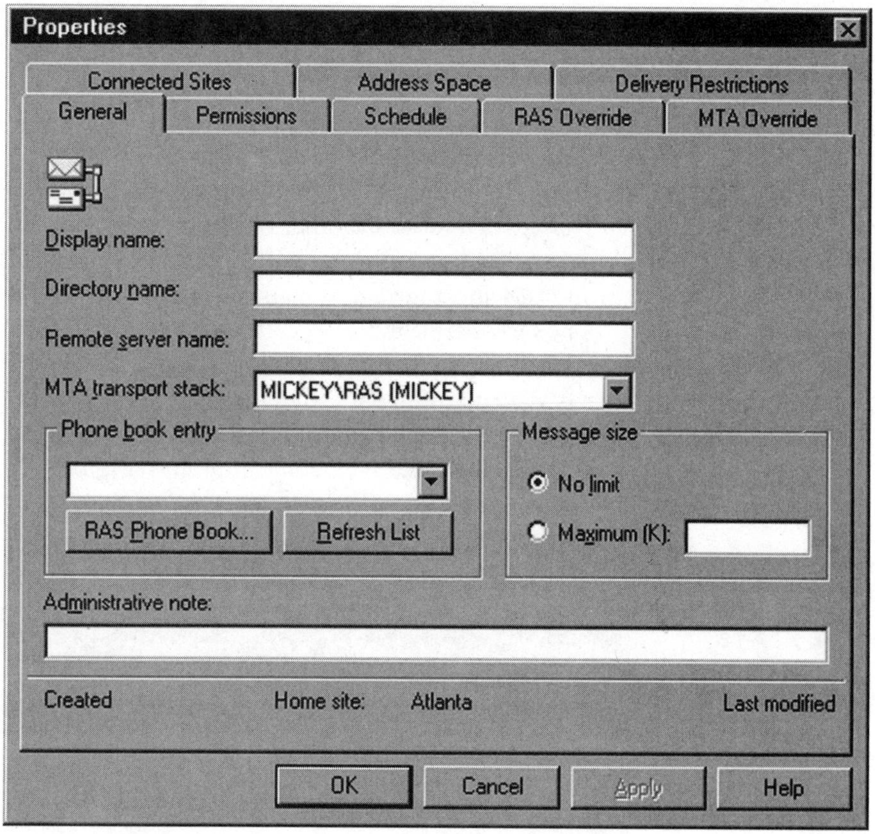

Figure 17-15 Creating a new DRAS Connector on MICKEY.

Specify the following settings on the General tab of the property sheet for the new connector:

Display name = DRAS to BUGS in Chicago

Directory name = DRAS to BUGS in Chicago

Remote server name = BUGS (This entry is case-sensitive!)

MTA Transport Stack (select MICKEY\RAS (MICKEY))

Phone book entry = BUGS

Switch to the Schedule tab and select Always. This will cause the connector to immediately dial up the remote machine BUGS whenever there is a message queued to be sent over the connector to BUGS. We'll choose Always simply for testing purposes. Normally, you would most likely schedule the connector to run every few hours or so.

Switch to the RAS Override tab and enter the credentials for the RAS Override account we created in the other Chicago site earlier (see Figure 17-16). This specifies that when using RAS to dial in and connect to the remote server BUGS in the CHICAGO domain, the Windows NT account CHICAGO\RASCON is used, which has both the necessary RAS and Exchange permissions to enable the connector to work.

Now switch to the Connected Sites tab to specify a routing address to the remote site Chicago where BUGS resides. Click the New button to open a Properties sheet for a new connected site (see Figure 17-17).

The Organization field is already specified as MTIT, so you must enter the name of the remote site here, namely `Chicago`. Enter this and switch to the Routing Address tab and verify the O/R address to the remote site. Click OK to return to the Connected Sites tab of the connector's property sheet, which should look something like Figure 17-18.

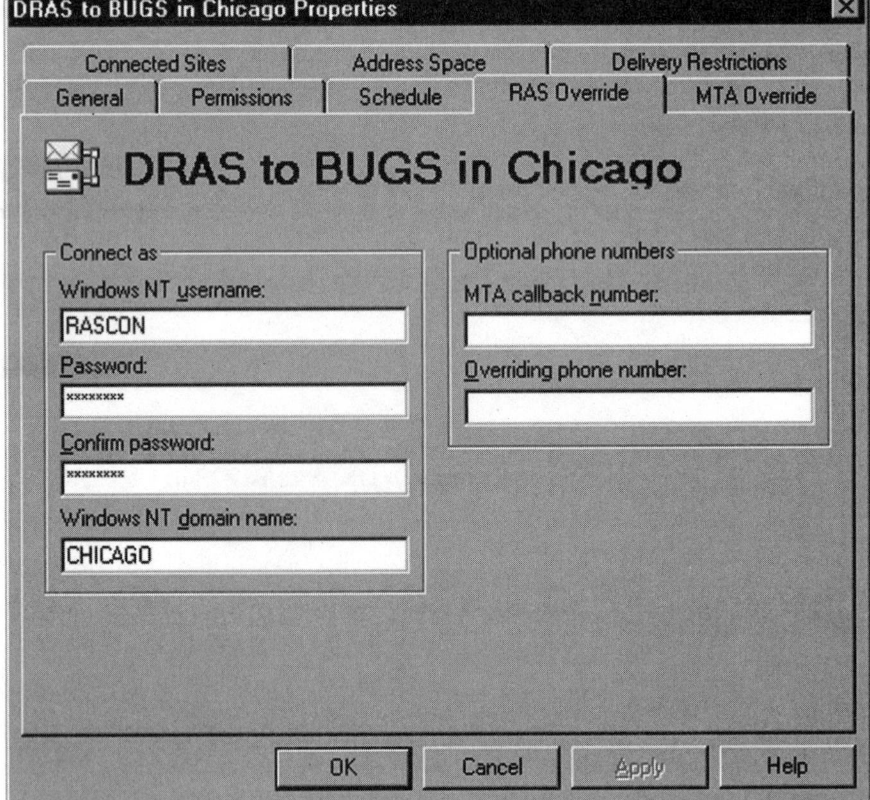

Figure 17-16 Specifying the RAS Override account for the remote site.

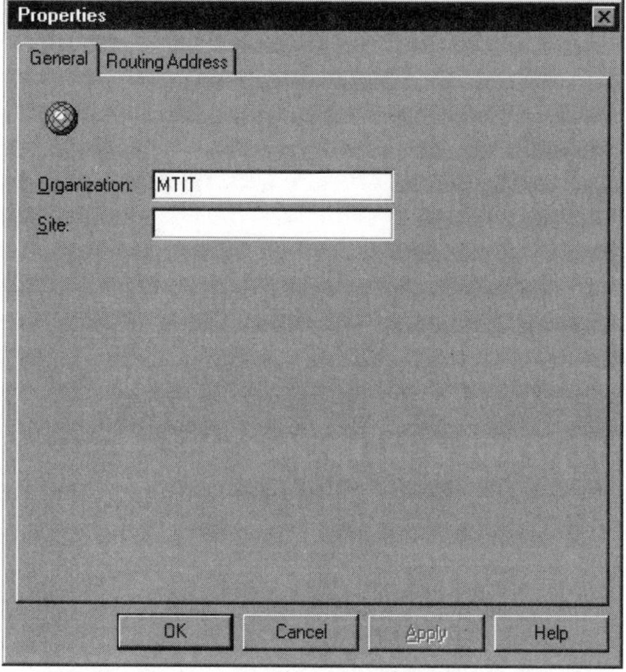

Figure 17-17 Specifying a new connected site.

Figure 17-18 Chicago has been specified as a connected site.

Click OK, and a dialog box informs you that you need to configure a similar DRAS Connector in the remote site. Move to BUGS and follow the preceding steps to accomplish this.

Testing the DRAS Connector

We're ready for the test. Make sure that there is no active RAS session between the two sites. (Use the Dial-Up Monitor utility in the Control Panel to hang up any active RAS session, and you can leave this utility open if you want to view the status of RAS sessions on your machines.)

Now log on to GOOFEY in Atlanta as Boris, start Outlook 98, and send a test message to Peter James (or whomever) in Chicago. You can either use an X.400 custom recipient if you created one for Peter in Atlanta, or you can create a one-off message to Peter using his O/R address. (Because our connected sites use O/R addresses for routing messages through the DRAS Connector, we need to use this type of address for our test messages. However, in a real situation, once connectivity is established between the two sites, we should create and configure a Directory Replication connector to make the addressing of messages between the two sites simpler.)

Anyway, send the message from Boris to Peter. This should automatically initiate a RAS connection between MICKEY and BUGS, with MICKEY dialing in to the RAS server on BUGS to transfer mail. After a short time, the connection will terminate. Log on to BUGS in Chicago as Peter, start Outlook 2000, and the message from Boris should be waiting in the Inbox. Try sending a message in the reverse direction. It should work.

On Your Own

Try installing a Directory Replication Connector on each server and see whether you can get directory replication to occur between sites using the DRAS Connector. It's quite straightforward.

Where Do We Go from Here?

In the next chapter, we will expand on our understanding of Exchange connectors by considering message routing in a multisite Exchange organization.

For More Information

You can find some useful information on installing and configuring DRAS Connectors in Chapter 5 of the *Operations* manual for Exchange Server, which is included as part of Books Online or can be purchased separately from Microsoft.

TechNet

The Technical Notes of the MS Exchange section of TechNet contains a useful article on TCP/IP routing issues related to using the DRAS Connector, "How to Configure the DRAS Connector over TCP/IP."

Here are a few useful articles from the Knowledge Base on Windows NT RAS, LMHOSTS, and the DRAS Connector:

- Q128647." Troubleshooting TCP/IP LAN and RAS Routing Issues"
- Q162293. "Troubleshooting RAS Client Issues in Windows NT 4.0"
- Q178205. "Connecting to a Server Is Slow over RAS Using LMHOSTS File"
- Q102725. "LMHOSTS File Information and Predefined Keywords"
- Q180099. "Troubleshooting LMHOSTS Name Resolution Issues"
- Q180094. "How to Write an LMHOSTS File for Domain Validation"
- Q162071. "LMHOSTS IP Address Should Refer to Network Interface Card"
- Q178538. "Configuring DRAS with Reserved IP Address for Private Networks"
- Q191397. XCON: "During DRAS Call, Server Unavailable on the Local Network"
- Q170274. XCON: "How to Configure DRAS Between Different Organizations"

CHAPTER 18

Administering Message Routing

In the previous chapter, we finished looking at the various types of Exchange connectors that are covered in this book. In this chapter, we consider how messages are routed through an Exchange organization and to foreign mail systems. After reading this chapter, you will have an understanding of the following topics:

- Message routing
- The GWART
- Connected sites
- Address spaces
- Route selection

The walkthrough in this chapter covers how messages are routed through an Exchange organization consisting of four different sites and what happens when different routing costs are assigned to the connectors.

Message Routing

Message routing is the process by which a message moves throughout an Exchange organization or to a foreign mail system. When a recipient sends a message to another recipient in the organization or to a recipient on a foreign mail system, Exchange has to concern itself with a number of things, such as

- What is the best route for the message to travel to its destination?
- What alternate routes can be used if the best route fails?
- What happens if no route can be found to deliver the message to its destination?
- Is the message address and/or content in a format that the destination recipient can understand, or does some form of message conversion have to take place first?

Messaging routing takes all these different questions into consideration in order to make messaging efficient and successful. Although message routing is primarily the concern of the Message Transfer Agent and various connectors, other Exchange components can be involved in various situations. We looked briefly at Exchange message flow in Chapter 4, and here it will be examined in more detail.

Single Server Routing

Recall that mailboxes have a home server, namely the server where the contents of the mailbox are stored. If one recipient on an Exchange Server sends a message to another recipient on the same server, the Exchange Information Store service makes use of the target recipient's *distinguished name* (DN) to route the message to the destination mailbox. We looked at distinguished names in Chapter 4 when we considered Exchange address types. The DN of a mailbox is essentially an X.500 address and is the native or internal addressing format that is used by Exchange for addressing messages. Exchange always attempts to send a message using the DN address of the recipient first; if that fails, it tries the X.400 or O/R address of the recipient, which is why it is never a good idea to delete the O/R addresses that are automatically generated when you create mailboxes on Exchange. Note that in this scenario the Message Transfer Agent (MTA) is not used in the routing process.

Single-Site Routing

If the target recipient is homed on a different server in the same site, the MTA uses the destination recipient's DN to route the message to the Information Store service on the destination recipient's home server, which then moves the message to the destination recipient's mailbox. If the DN is wrong or cannot be obtained, the O/R address is used instead.

Routing to Other Sites and Mail Systems

Messages sent to recipients in other sites or in foreign mail systems must be delivered by connectors. A typical Exchange organization may use a combination of Site Connectors, Dynamic RAS Connectors, Internet Mail Service (IMS), and other connectors for establishing messaging connectivity between sites that are connected by dedicated high-speed WAN links such as leased T-1 lines or dial-up RAS connections using modems or ISDN. Connectors also are used to establish connectivity with legacy MS Mail systems, foreign X.400 systems, or with external messaging systems such as the Internet or an X.400 messaging system. When you send a message to one of these sites or mail systems, Exchange must determine which routes (messaging paths) can be used to route the message and which order should attempt these routes. Typically, what happens during message routing is that messages move from

- MTA to MTA to travel from server to server within a site
- MTA to a connector to leave a site and travel to another site or foreign mail system
- Connector to Exchange MTA to enter a site from another site or from a foreign mail system
- Connector to foreign MTA to enter a foreign mail system from an Exchange organization

The question is, if Exchange MTAs and connectors need to select the best path for routing a message, how do the MTAs and connectors know the possible paths from which to choose? The answer lies in the GWART.

The GWART

The *Gateway Address Routing Table* (GWART) is an internal message routing table maintained by a server in each Exchange site, which contains all known information about possible messaging paths (routes) through the organization and to foreign mail systems. Each route has a specified cost that determines which route should attempt to deliver the message. In particular, the MTA on an Exchange Server looks at the GWART to determine which connectors and gateways can be used to deliver the message. The MTA is processed in the GWART line by line, applying a specific set of rules to select the best route (these rules are described later in this chapter). If no route can be found in the GWART to deliver the message to its destination, the MTA returns a nondeliver report to the sender.

Figure 18-1 shows an example of a GWART as displayed on the Site Addressing Routing tab of the Exchange server JR in the site Dallas. Each line in the GWART represents a different possible messaging path through the system. Lines are processed from top to bottom by the MTA as it looks for possible routes to its target destination for sending the messages. For example, the first line in the displayed GWART says:

```
EX    /O=MTIT/OU=ATLANTA;    2    Site Connector (Atlanta)
```

Here is an explanation of each of the four columns of this GWART:

- The first column displays the address type for the route, which here is type EX, meaning that a DN must be used in the destination address

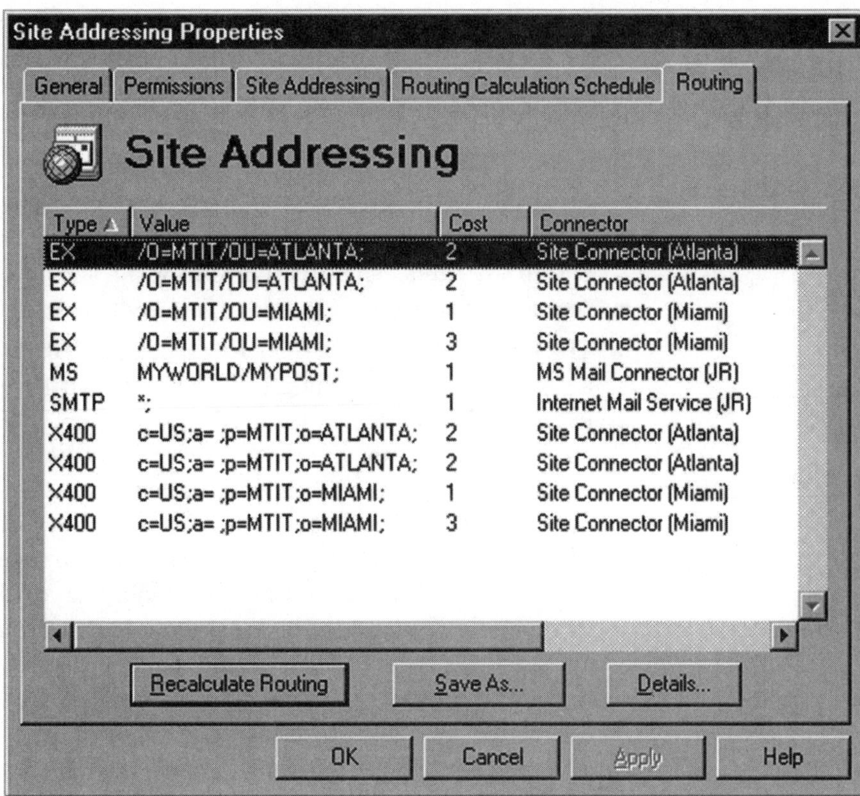

Figure 18-1
The Gateway Routing Table or GWART.

of the message for this route to be used. Possible address types for entries in the GWART include

- *EX*. This stands for *Exchange* and refers to the DN addressing scheme used internally by Exchange. This kind of route is used only if the destination recipient exists in the Exchange directory and has a valid DN. If you are sending email to a recipient in a foreign mail system using a one-off address, for example, the MTA would ignore EX entries in the GWART when determining how to route the message to its destination.
- *MS*. This stands for *Microsoft Mail* and is used primarily when messages are sent to or received from a legacy MS Mail 3.x network using the MS Mail Connector (see Chapter 15).
- *SMTP*. This stands for *Simple Mail Transfer Protocol* or Internet mail and is used primarily when messages are sent to or received from a connected Internet SMTP mail system (see Chapter 16).

- *X400.* This stands for the O/R addresses that are automatically generated for new recipients and function as a backup for distinguished name addresses.
- The second column displays the DN of the destination site, which here is site Atlanta in our Exchange organization MTIT. Remember that the message sender is in the Dallas site, and we are looking at the GWART as it is displayed on the Routing tab of the Site Addressing object within the Dallas site. In other words, the address tells us that this particular route starts in Dallas and ends in Atlanta.
- The third column gives the cost associated with this route, which has a cost value of 2. The meaning of different cost values is covered later in the walkthrough. All we need to know now is that, generally speaking, the larger the cost value, the less likely the route will be used. Costs can be arbitrarily assigned to routes to force messages along certain paths, but it is best if the cost reflects some real aspect of the WAN link underlying the messaging connection. For example, a 1.544-Mbps T-1 line might be assigned a low cost, while a 64-Kbps Frame Relay link might be assigned a high cost. In this way, preference is given to the T-1 line when messages need to be routed through connectors, which is good because of the large amount of bandwidth available for the line.
- The final column displays the name of the adjacent connector, which is the start of the route through the system. In this case, it is the Site Connector (Atlanta) that can be found in the Connections container within the Dallas site.

Figure 18-2 shows the result when we select the second line of the GWART in Figure 18-1 and click the Details button. This provides us with a Routing Details dialog box that displays more information about the selected route. In particular, we can see that the selected route, which starts in the Dallas site and ends in the Atlanta site, actually consists of two hops (it is read from the bottom up):

- The Site Connector (Miami) in the Dallas site takes the message from Dallas to Miami.
- The Site Connector (Atlanta) in the Miami site takes the message from Miami to Atlanta.

We'll return to the GWART later during the walkthrough in this chapter, but now let's find out how the GWART is constructed.

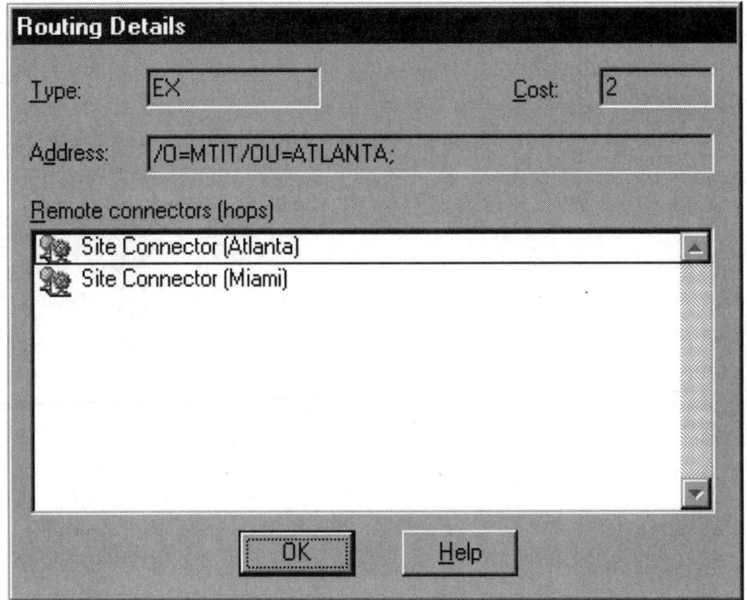

Figure 18-2 Detail of a route in the GWART.

Connected Sites

Two sources of information are taken into account for the calculations that are done to generate the GWART: connected sites and address spaces. We will look at the first of these here.

Connected sites are other sites in your Exchange organization that are linked to the present site using connectors. Figure 18-3 shows the General tab for the Site Connector (Atlanta), which was installed on the server JR in Dallas. The Target Site listed here is the connected site for this connector. Other types of connectors, specifically the X.400 Connector, Dynamic RAS Connector, and the IMS, all have a tab called Connected Sites that lists the sites directly adjacent to the present site and that are linked to it by the connector. You specify a connected site when the connector is created (see the walkthrough in Chapter 14, "Administering X.400 Connectors," for an example). This connected sites information then is used in calculation of the GWART.

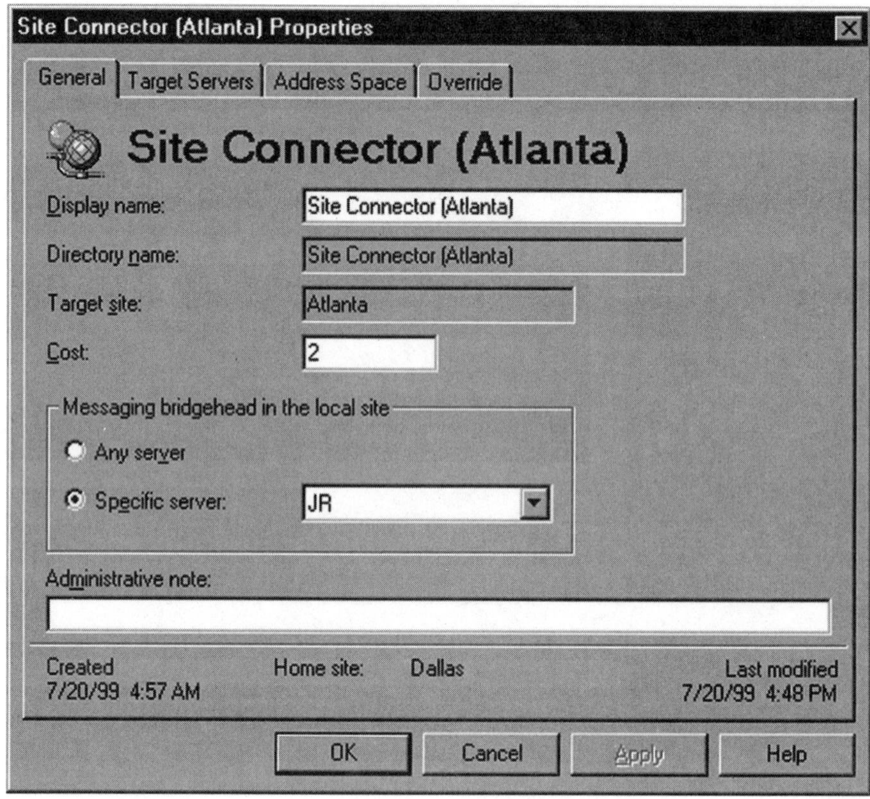

Figure 18-3 General tab of the Site Connector (Atlanta) showing the Target Site Atlanta.

Address Spaces

Whereas connected sites specify information on how a connector can be used to route a message to a different site in the same Exchange organization, address spaces are primarily (but not exclusively) used to specify information on how a connector can be used to route a message to a foreign mail system. An address space is essentially part of an email address—just enough to tell the connector how to deliver a message to the target mail system, but not enough to deliver it to any specific recipient of that system. An address space for a connector thus identifies the type of recipient address that can be routed through the connector. Connectors can have one or more address spaces associated with them, and these are defined using the Address Space tab on the connector's property sheet.

At the least, address space for a connector must be specified when you create the connector (unless you are connecting to another Exchange site, in which case it is sufficient to specify a connected site instead). Address spaces are specified using the Address Space tab on the property sheet for the connector. This tab can be found on the property sheet for the Site Connector, X.400 Connector, Dynamic RAS Connector, and IMS. Figure 18-4 shows the Address Space tab for the Site Connector (Atlanta) in the Dallas site discussed previously.

Note that a single address space is listed on this tab. It is of type X.400 and represents the following:

- The X.400 address of the Atlanta site to which the connector is able to route messages
- The cost of this route
- The scope of this route

In other words, messages sent from anywhere in the Exchange organization can be routed through this connector to target recipients in the Atlanta site, provided that the message uses the X.400 O/R address of the

Figure 18-4 Address Space tab of the Site Connector (Atlanta).

target recipient. If a message uses an address of type SMTP or MS, then this connector cannot route it, as there is no address space to Atlanta of that type, unless we create a new address space for the connector of the appropriate type using the New button on this property sheet.

If you click Edit, you can edit the properties of the address space displayed on the tab. This opens the X.400 properties box, which has two tabs, the first showing the O/R address of the address space and the second showing the restrictions that are in place for the address space (see Figure 18-5).

Three possible values can be configured for the restrictions on the scope of an address space:

- *Organization*. Any recipient in the Exchange organization can send messages through this connector.
- *This Site*. Only recipients in the local site can use this connector.

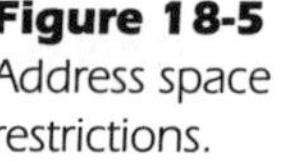

Figure 18-5 Address space restrictions.

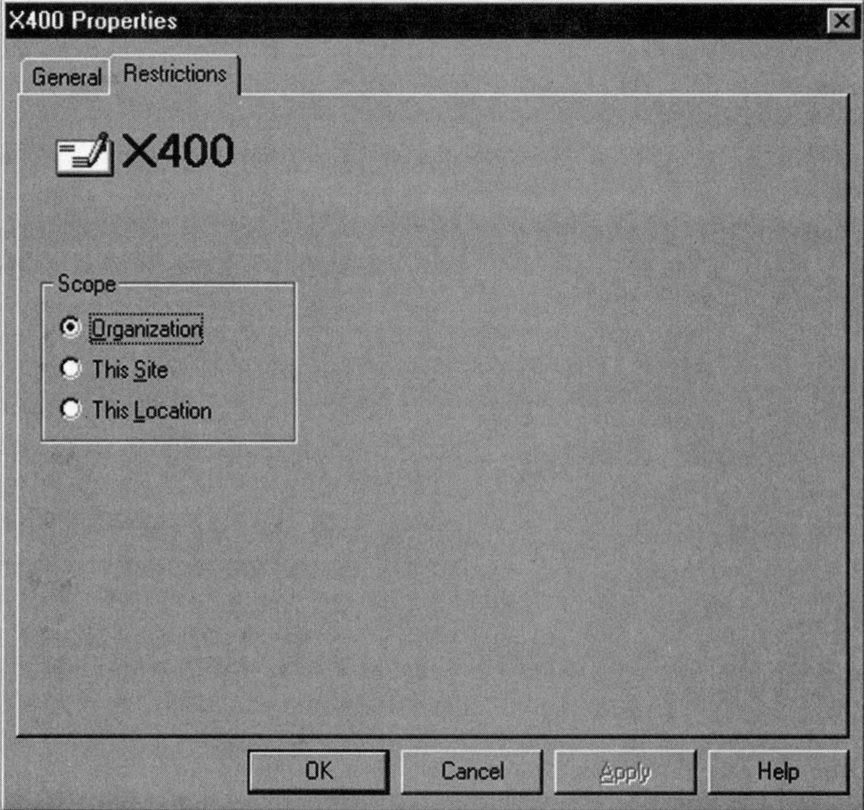

- *This Location*. Only recipients in the same location as the server where the connector is installed can use this connector (see the General tab of the Server container's property sheet).

Exchange then uses all of the defined address spaces for all of the installed connectors together with connected sites' information to enable the GWART to be calculated.

Route Selection

After the GWART for an organization has been calculated using the connected sites and address space information from its connectors and gateways, the GWART then can be used to route messages throughout the organization and to foreign mail systems. When a message is submitted to the MTA for delivery, the MTA follows a multistep process for determining which route (GWART entry) to use for routing the message, or, in other words, which connector to which to forward the message. Here are the steps that the MTA follows when a message is submitted to it for delivery and when the message needs to be routed outside the site to another site or a foreign mail system:

1. If the message was delivered to the MTA by a connector, any route using the same connector is eliminated from consideration. This is necessary to prevent messages from looping endlessly.
2. If any connectors have the parameter Retry Count equal to Max Open retries, then those connectors are eliminated from consideration. Max Open retries can be configured globally for all connectors on the Messaging Default tab of the property sheet for the MTA Site Configuration object. This value also can be overridden for X.400 and DRAS Connectors. If this value is exceeded, the connector may be too busy or may not be functioning properly, and so it is eliminated from consideration as delivery agents.
3. If any connectors have message size limits or delivery restrictions that apply to the message, the connectors are eliminated from consideration.
4. Active connectors are now selected. The Site Connector, IMS, and MS Mail Connectors are always active, so if any of these have routes to the destination, then they are selected. If no active connectors are available, then scheduled connectors like the X.400 and DRAS Connector are selected. If there are no active or scheduled connectors, then remote initiated connectors are selected.

5. The list of possible routes/connectors has been narrowed down somewhat, so the MTA now selects connectors that have a Retry Count of zero. In other words, it selects connectors that are not currently attempting the delivery of another message.
6. Routing costs are considered next. The connectors with the lowest cost are selected. Several connectors may have the same cost.
7. Connectors that are local with respect to the MTA are selected next.
8. At this point, if there is still more than one route/connector left, the MTA randomly load-balances between them.
9. If all connectors are attempting to retry delivery of another message, the one that has the lowest value of the Retry Counter is used.

Simple, isn't it!?

Walkthrough: Understanding Message Routing

The best way to learn about message routing and how the GWART works is to work through an example in some detail. Let's begin!

Scenario

For the purposes of this walkthrough, we have created an Exchange organization that consists of four different sites. Each site has a single Exchange Server in it, which, by the way, is a Windows NT Primary Domain Controller (PDC) that minimizes the number of machines we have to set up. In other words, each site has its own Windows NT domain.

Figure 18-6 shows the four different domains and the Exchange Server in each of them. These four domains are as follows:

- *MTIT*. This is the domain in Atlanta with the Exchange Server MICKEY in it. The network administrator in Atlanta is Boris Zhivago.
- *CHICAGO*. This is the domain in Chicago and has the Exchange Server BUGS in it. The network administrator in Chicago is Peter James.

- *MIAMI*. This is the domain in Miami and has the Exchange Server SNOOPY in it. The network administrator in Miami is Ingrid van Gogh.
- *DALLAS*. This is the domain in Dallas and has the Exchange Server JR in it. The network administrator in Dallas is Bobby Oohing.

Each network administrator is a member of the Domain Admins for their own domain. In addition, each network administrator has been assigned the Permissions Admin role on the Organization, Site, and Configuration containers for their own Exchange site, enabling them to run the Exchange Administrator program on their server. Finally, each server has some version of Microsoft Outlook installed on it, and a mailbox and Windows messaging profile has been created for each network administrator so they can send and receive messages from each other.

Note also in Figure 18-6 that trust relationships are configured between the various domains:

- CHICAGO trusts MTIT
- MIAMI trusts MTIT
- DALLAS trusts MTIT

In other words, MTIT is the trusted domain, while the other three are trusting domains. The reason for setting up the trust relationships this way

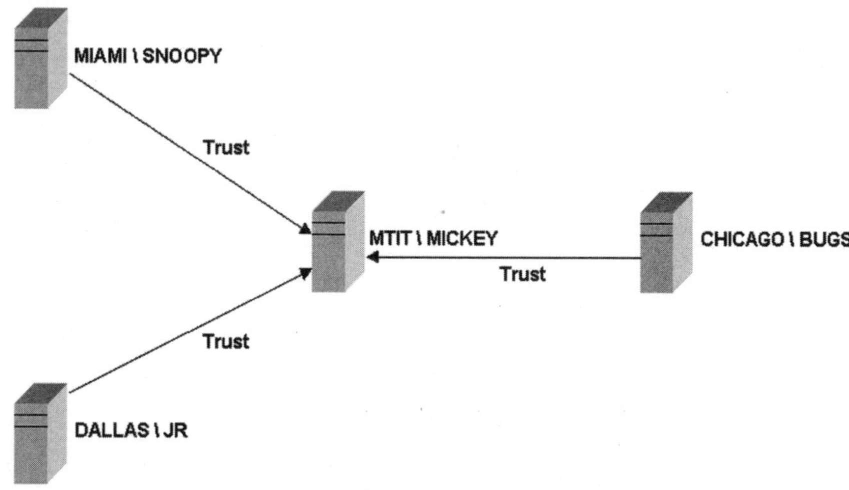

Figure 18-6 Domain setup for the walkthrough.

is that the MTIT domain in Atlanta represents company headquarters for MTIT Enterprises. If you are familiar with enterprise-level implementations of Windows NT, this is called a *master domain model*. Here MTIT is the master domain, while the other three domains are the resource domains.

Each domain has its own separate Exchange service account. The default Administrator account in the trusted MTIT domain has been assigned to the Administrators local group in each trusting domain, so that the Administrator in Atlanta can manage all aspects of Windows NT Servers in every domain throughout the enterprise. The default Administrator account in the trusted MTIT domain has also been assigned the Permissions Admin role on the Organization, Site, and Configuration containers in each trusting domain, so that the Administrator in Atlanta can also manage the Exchange Servers in the trusting domains by simply connecting to the server in the remote site using Exchange Administrator.

Figure 18-7 shows the four different Exchange sites and the server within each of them. Also shown are the Site Connectors that have been installed to provide messaging connectivity between the different sites. For the purposes of this walkthrough, the sites are all on the same LAN, but we can think of them as being joined together by high-speed, dedicated WAN links such as T-1 lines.

This kind of implementation is called a *hub and spoke model* and is more common in enterprise-level implementations of Exchange than the free-for-all mesh model, which tends to generate extremely large message routing tables. In our hub and spoke model, the Atlanta site is at the center and is

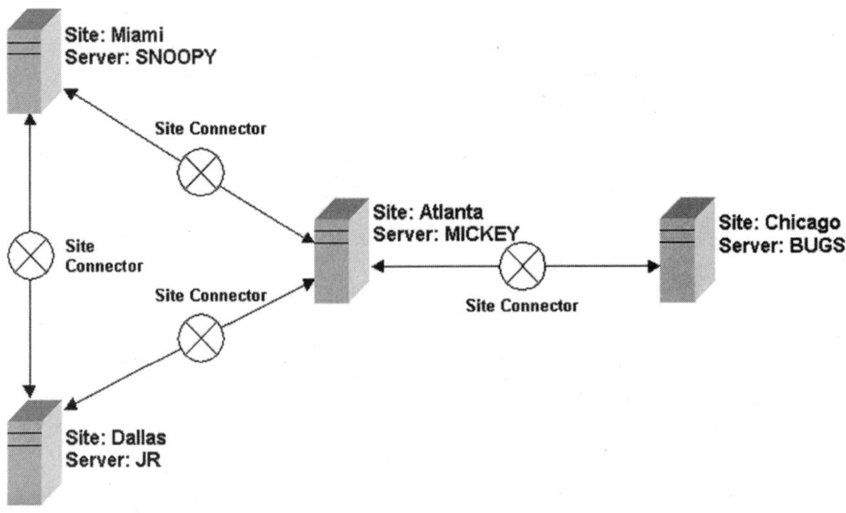

Figure 18-7 The Site Connector setup for the walkthrough.

connected to each of the other sites by Site Connectors. These Site Connectors were installed by logging on as an Administrator to MICKEY in Atlanta and creating them from there, supplying the Exchange service account information for the remote sites using the Override tab of the Site Connector property sheet (see Chapter 10, "Administering Site Connectors"). Because the MTIT\Administrator account in Atlanta has full Windows NT administrative privileges and the Exchange Permissions Admin role in each of the trusting domains, it is easy to create both sides of each Site Connector from Atlanta.

It is a little more tricky creating a Site Connector to link Miami and Dallas, however, as these domains do not trust one another. Here is how this was done:

1. A user account called `xservice` was created in both the MIAMI and DALLAS domains and assigned the same password.
2. The `MIAMI\xservice` account was assigned the Service Account Admin role for the Organization, Site, and Configuration containers on the Exchange Server SNOOPY in Miami. Similarly, the `DALLAS\xservice` account was assigned the Service Account Admin role for the Organization, Site, and Configuration containers on the Exchange Server JR in Dallas.
3. We then logged on using the `MIAMI\xservice` account to SNOOPY in Miami and created the Site Connector to join Miami and Dallas together, specifying the `<Other_Domain>\xservice` account on each Override tab.

The reason for creating this additional redundant Site Connector between Miami and Dallas is so that we have two possible paths for messages traveling between Dallas and Chicago.

Finally, Figure 18-8 shows the Directory Replication Connectors that have been installed to replicate directory information throughout our Exchange organization. All three Directory Replication Connectors with the three trusting sites are installed in the Atlanta trusted site while logged on as an Administrator. The replication schedule for these connectors is configured on the Schedule tab of each connector's property sheet. Leave the replication schedule for the directory Replication Connectors on each of the three trusting sites set to the default schedule of replicating every three hours starting at 12:45 A.M. However, configure the replication schedule for each of the three Directory Replication Connectors installed on MICKEY in Atlanta (the hub site) to occur one hour earlier, namely in 15-minute intervals three hours apart starting at 2:45 A.M. (See Figure 18-9.) You will have to select the 15-Minute Detail View in order to do this, because if you leave

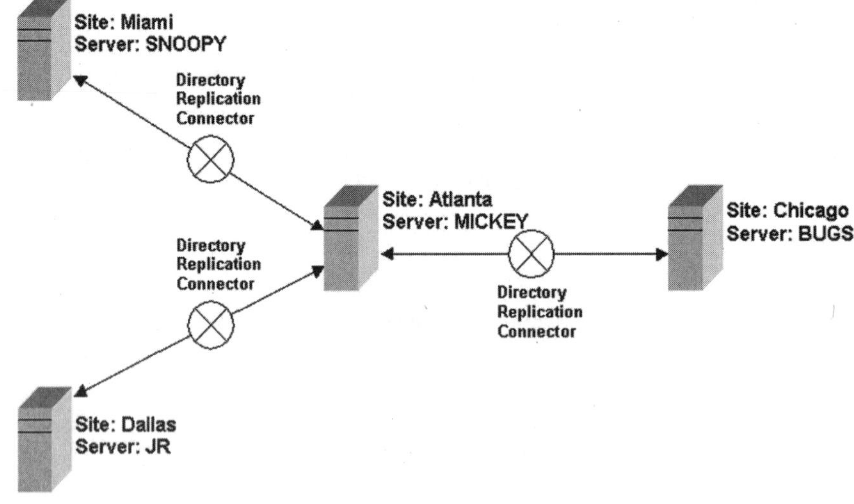

Figure 18-8 Directory Replication Connectors for the walkthrough.

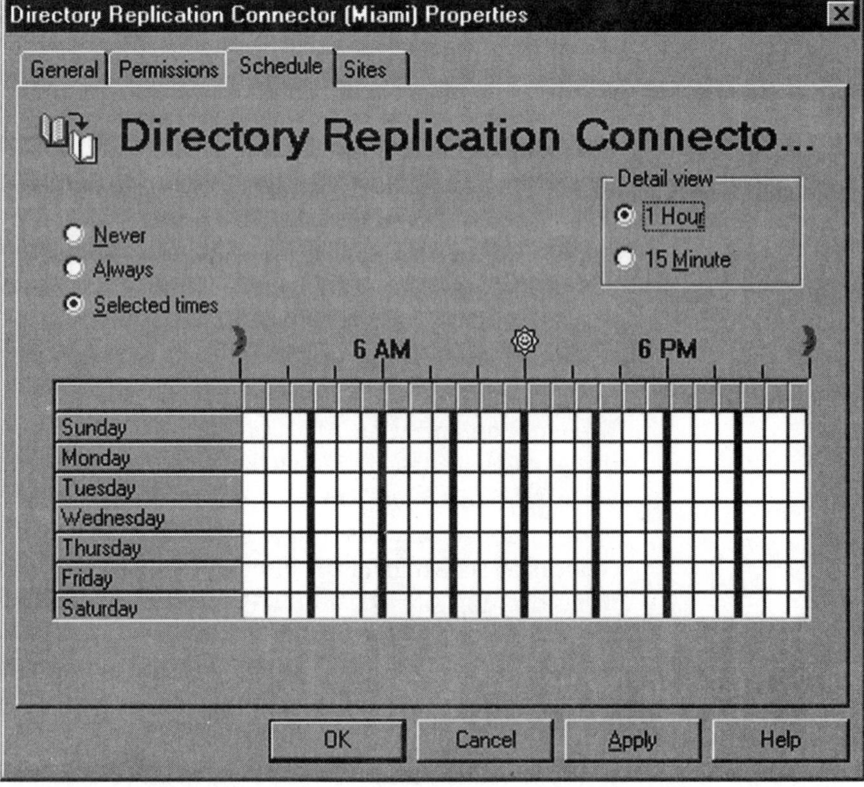

Figure 18-9 The schedule for Directory Replication Connectors in hub site Atlanta.

the Detail View set to 1 Hour, you will be blocking out one-hour intervals during which the connector is active. Since it activates every 15 minutes, it will replicate four times per blocked out hour.

What's the reason for staggering the replication schedules so that the Directory Replication Connectors in the hub site always replicate one hour earlier than those in the spoke sites? This way, the hub site will have time to gather directory information about all the spoke sites before the spoke sites request directory information from the hub site. The result is that directory information is up to date everywhere, give or take a few hours.

After the initial replication has occurred between each pair of connected sites, go to each trusting site, open the property sheet for the Directory Replication Connector, switch to the Sites tab, and click the Request Now button to speed up the process by which the trusting sites obtain complete directory information for the entire organization. (The Atlanta site, which is the Inbound site for each of the trusting sites, has the complete directory information for the entire organization because it replicates directly with every other site.)

Next, enable Message Tracking on the following directory objects on each Exchange site in your organization:

- MTA Site Configuration (General tab)
- Information Store Site Configuration (General tab)

We'll need Message Tracking enabled because we want to trace the routes of messages as they travel through our Exchange organization.

Finally, go to every site in the organization, open the property sheet for the Site Addressing object, select the Routing Calculation Schedule tab, and select Always (see Figure 18-10). This ensures that the GWART is recalculated every 15 minutes and is thus always up to date. We choose this only for the sake of the walkthrough; in real life, we would typically leave this setting to Selected Times and have recalculations occur every night by default at 2 A.M. After configuring this setting, switch to the Routing tab and click Recalculate Routing to force a recalculation immediately. Make these changes on the machines in each site.

Shortly, the Exchange Administrator on each machine should show the same directory hierarchy consisting of all four Exchange sites: Atlanta, Chicago, Miami, and Dallas.

Let's now examine the GWART for our organization, which is used by Exchange to decide how to best route messages throughout the organization. The GWART can be viewed by opening the property sheet for the Site Addressing object in a site and selecting the Routing tab on this property

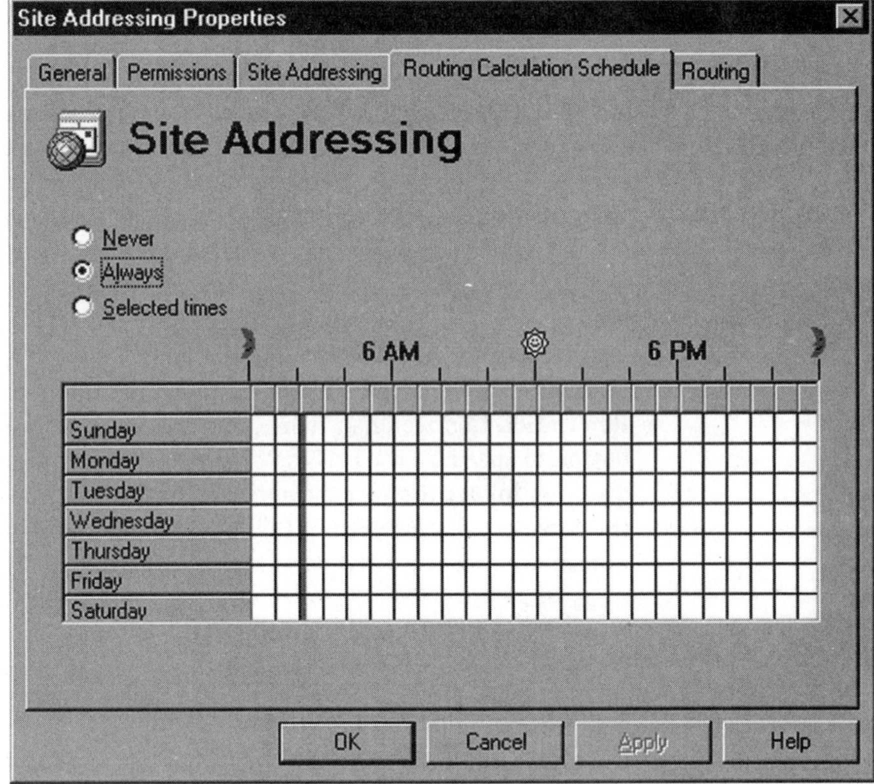

Figure 18-10 Specifying the schedule for recalculating the GWART.

sheet. In Figure 18-11, we see the GWART as it is displayed in the Site Addressing object on the server JR in the site Dallas. Note that the GWART may look different in different sites because each Site Addressing object displays from the perspective of messages originating in that site and propagating throughout the organization. We will consider only the GWART on JR in Dallas because our test messages will all originate from Bobby Oohing, the network administrator in Dallas.

Let's examine this GWART one line at a time. Remember, this representation of the GWART is for routing messages that are submitted for delivery in the Dallas site (which is why the Dallas site doesn't show up in any of the entries in this GWART). Note that some of the information for these entries has been obtained by selecting the entry and clicking the Details button.

```
EX    /O=MTIT/OU=ATLANTA;    1    Site Connector (Atlanta)
```

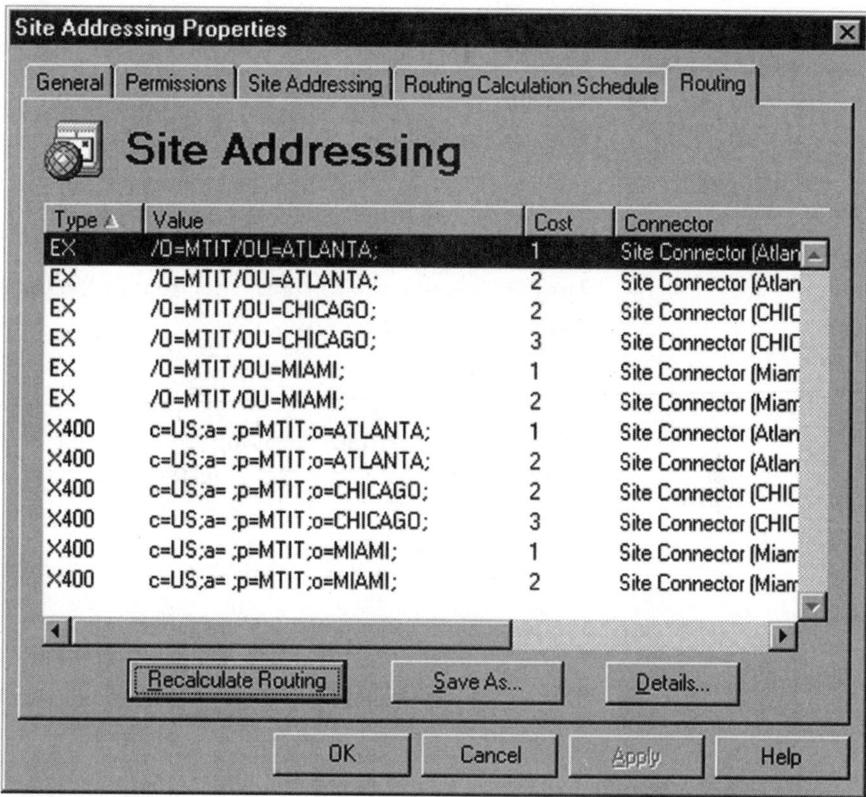

Figure 18-11 The GWART as displayed on JR in Dallas.

Routes messages directly: Dallas → Atlanta
The distinguished name of the destination recipient is used.
The cost of the route is 1.

```
EX    /O=MTIT/OU=ATLANTA;    2    Site Connector (Atlanta)
```

Routes messages indirectly: Dallas → Miami → Atlanta
The distinguished name of the destination recipient is used.
The cost of the route is 1+1 = 2.

```
EX    /O=MTIT/OU=CHICAGO;    2    Site Connector (CHICAGO)
```

Routes messages directly: Dallas → Atlanta → Chicago
The distinguished name of the destination recipient is used.
The cost of the route is 1+1 = 2.

```
EX    /O=MTIT/OU=CHICAGO;    3    Site Connector (CHICAGO)
```

Routes messages indirectly: Dallas → Miami → Atlanta → Chicago
The distinguished name of the destination recipient is used.
The total cost of the route is 1+1+1 = 3.

```
EX    /O=MTIT/OU=MIAMI;    1    Site Connector (Miami)
```

Routes messages directly: Dallas → Miami
The distinguished name of the destination recipient is used.
The cost of the route is 1.

```
EX    /O=MTIT/OU=MIAMI;    2    Site Connector (Miami)
```

Routes messages indirectly: Dallas → Atlanta → Miami
The distinguished name of the destination recipient is used.
The cost of the route is 1+1 = 2.

```
X400    c=US;a= ;p=MTIT;o=ATLANTA;    1    Site Connector (Atlanta)
```

Routes messages directly: Dallas → Atlanta
The O/R address of the destination recipient is used.
The cost of the route is 1.

```
X400    c=US;a= ;p=MTIT;o=ATLANTA;    2    Site Connector (Atlanta)
```

Routes messages indirectly: Dallas → Miami → Atlanta
The O/R address of the destination recipient is used.
The cost of the route is 1+1 = 2.

```
X400    c=US;a= ;p=MTIT;o=CHICAGO;    2    Site Connector (CHICAGO)
```

Routes messages directly: Dallas → Atlanta → Chicago
The O/R address of the destination recipient is used.
The cost of the route is 1+1 = 2.

```
X400    c=US;a= ;p=MTIT;o=CHICAGO;    3    Site Connector (CHICAGO)
```

Routes messages indirectly: Dallas → Miami → Atlanta → Chicago
The O/R address of the destination recipient is used.
The total cost of the route is 1+1+1 = 3.

```
X400    c=US;a= ;p=MTIT;o=MIAMI;    1    Site Connector (Miami)
```

Routes messages directly: Dallas → Miami
The O/R address of the destination recipient is used.
The cost of the route is 1.

```
X400    c=US;a= ;p=MTIT;o=MIAMI;    2    Site Connector (Miami)
```

Routes messages indirectly: Dallas → Atlanta → Miami
The O/R address of the destination recipient is used.
The cost of the route is 1+1 = 2.

Now let's perform some tests to observe how messages are actually routed through our organization. We will vary some of the routing costs for the connectors and observe the results. Check back with the GWART entries to make sure that you understand how the contents of the GWART are related to the results of each test.

Test One

Let's start by sending some messages between Dallas and Chicago. We will leave our routing costs set at their defaults, as in Figure 18-12.

Log on as Bobby to server JR in Dallas and start Outlook. Send a message to Peter in Chicago and repeat this process five times. Log on as Peter to server BUGS in Chicago, start Outlook, and verify that all five messages have arrived in Peter's inbox.

Now log on as Boris to server MICKEY in Atlanta and start Exchange Administrator, which is connected to MICKEY. Select Tools, Track Message to open the Message Tracking Center, which is connected to BUGS during the process.

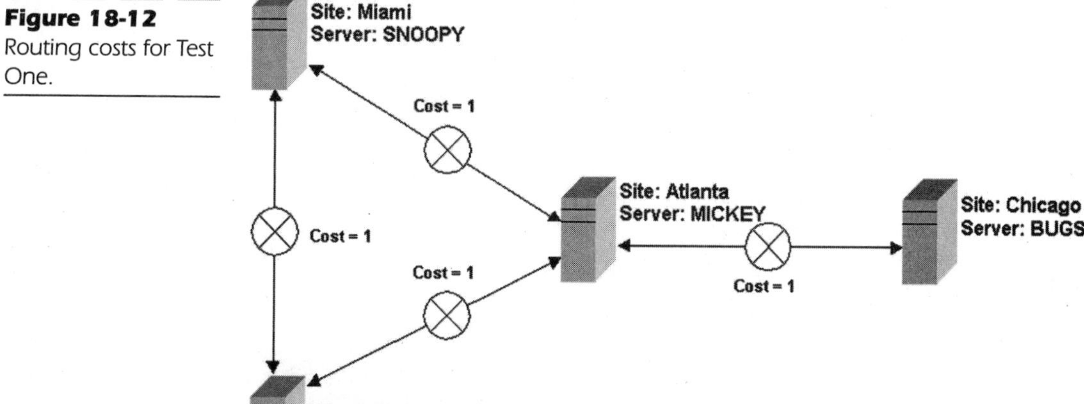

Figure 18-12 Routing costs for Test One.

In the Select Messages to Track box, configure the following search parameters:

From = Bobby Oohing

Sent to = Peter James

Look back = 0 days

Search on server = JR

Note that we have selected JR as the server whose message tracking logs we want to examine; you select the server where the messages were sent from to track the messages. Click the Find Now button, and you should see the five messages from Bobby to Peter listed in the listbox (see Figure 18-13).

Select the first message (sent at 9:10 A.M.) and click OK to return to the main Message Tracking Center window. Click the Track button, and the history of this message is displayed in the Tracking History listbox (see Figure 18-14).

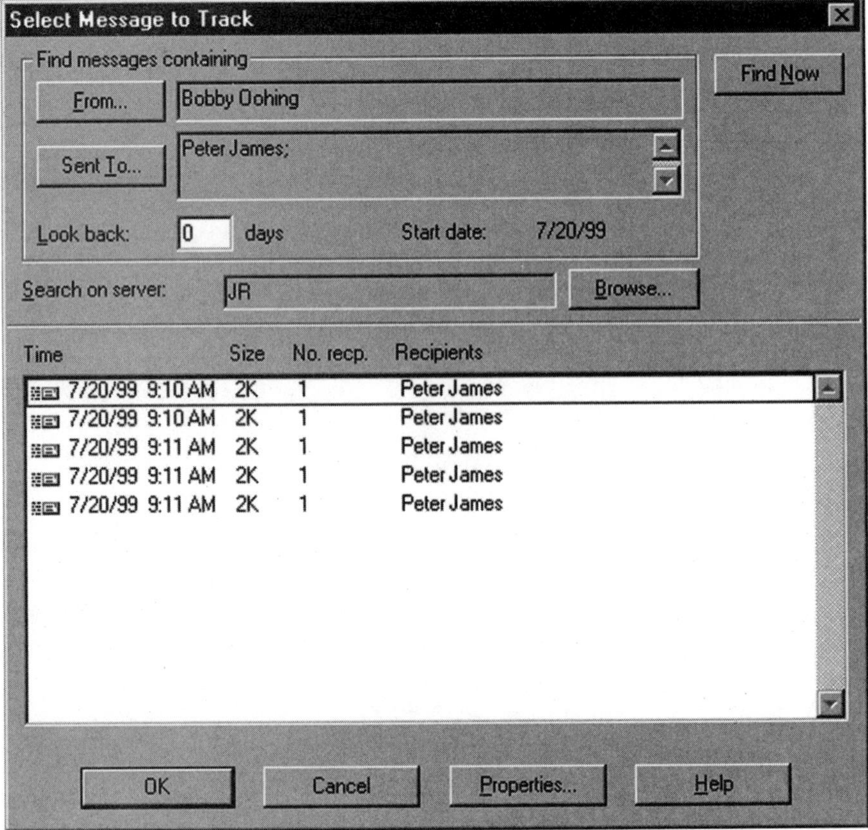

Figure 18-13 Searching for messages from Bobby to Peter.

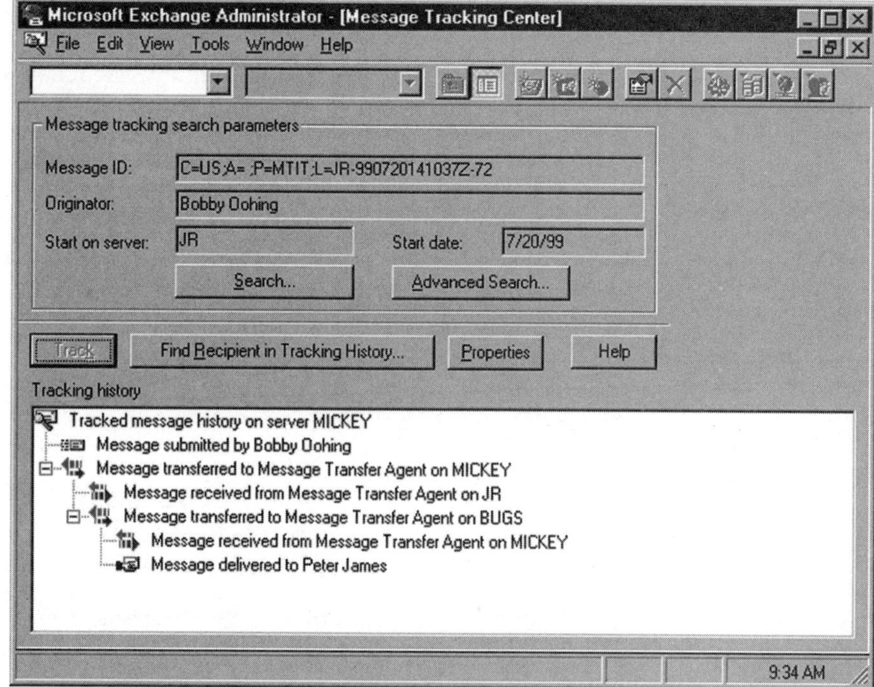

Figure 18-14 Tracking the history of a message from Bobby to Peter.

Click the Search button and enter the same search parameters listed previously (From Bobby, Sent to Peter, Look back 0 days, Search on server JR) to find the same five messages again, only this time select the second message, click OK, and click Track to display its tracking history. Do this with each of the five messages Bobby sent to Peter.

Each of the messages should have followed the same path through your organization. This path is shown in the tracking history for the first message, as shown in Figure 18-14. This path is as follows (IS means *Information Store* and MTA means *Message Transfer Agent*):

IS (JR) → MTA (JR)

MTA (JR) → MTA (MICKEY) via Site Connector (cost = 1)

MTA (MICKEY) → MTA (BUGS) via Site Connector (cost = 1)

MTA (BUGS) → IS (BUGS)

Looking at the second line, we might ask, why did all the messages get routed directly (one hop) from JR to MICKEY, instead of some of them being routed indirectly (two hops) from JR to SNOOPY to MICKEY? The answer lies in the cost associated with each Site Connector, which is found on the General tab of the connector's property sheet. The cost between each pair of Site Connectors as presently configured is 1, and a cost value of 1 means that that connector is preferred over higher cost routes 100 percent of the time (see Table 18-1). Thus, we have the following:

- The total cost from JR to MICKEY via Site Connector = 1
- The total cost from JR to SNOOPY to MICKEY = 1+1 = 2

So all messages sent from JR to MICKEY (and hence from JR to BUGS because there is only one messaging path from MICKEY to BUGS) get sent via the route that has a cost equal to 1, or directly from JR to MICKEY via the Site Connector between them.

Test Two

Let's change the routing costs now. Configure the Site Connector between JR and MICKEY to have a cost of 5, instead of 1. We now have the following routes between JR and MICKEY with their costs (see Figure 18-15):

- The total cost from JR to MICKEY via Site Connector = 5
- The total cost from JR to SNOOPY to MICKEY = 1+1 = 2

What do these changes mean? Because the indirect route (two hops) from JR to SNOOPY to MICKEY has a lower routing cost than the direct route (one hop) from JR to MICKEY, all messages sent from Dallas to Atlanta (or to Chicago) should be routed through Miami.

Select the Recalculate Routing button on the Routing tab of each Site Addressing object to bring the GWART up to date on all sites if necessary. After a few minutes, the GWART on MICKEY should look like Figure 18-16.

Let's try sending half a dozen messages from Bobby in Dallas to Peter in Chicago again. After this has been done, open the Message Tracking Center and track the path of each of the messages. You can distinguish which messages they are from their sending time, which should be different from the

Table 18-1

Explanation of Routing Costs for Connectors.

Cost	Meaning
1	Use this route 100% of the time
2-99	Use the lowest cost route first
100	Use this route only if no other routes are available

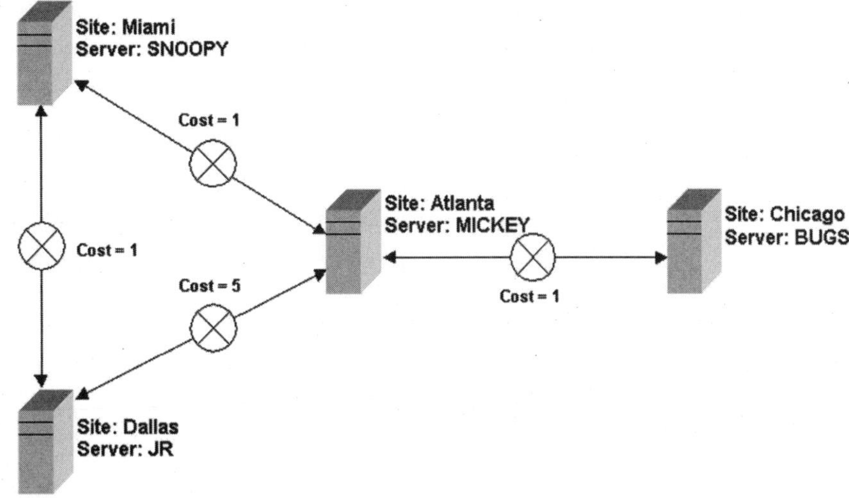

Figure 18-15
Routing costs for Test Two.

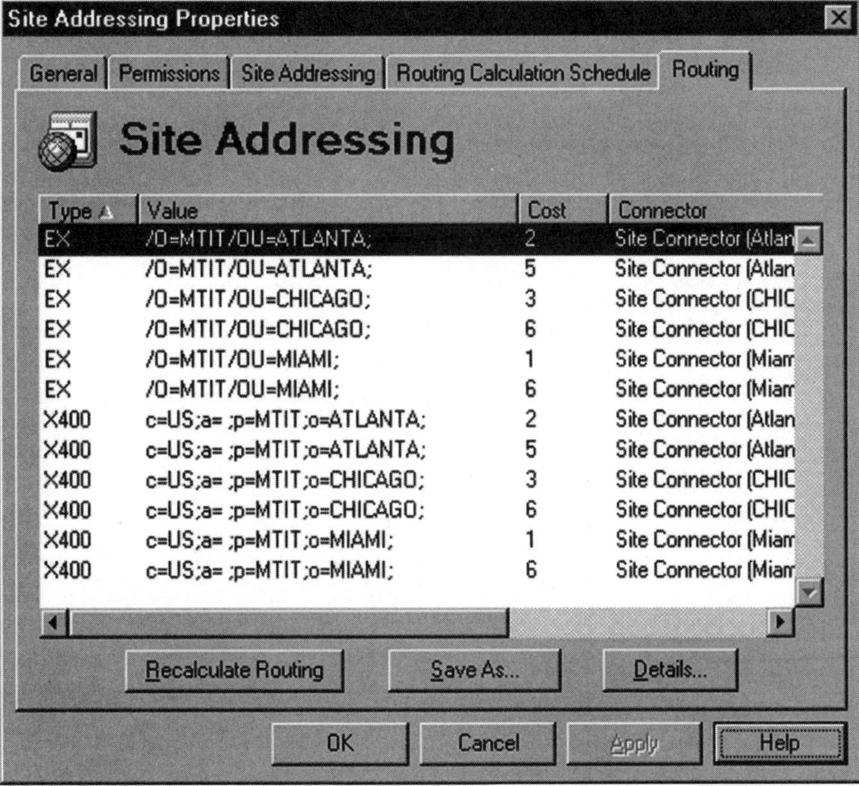

Figure 18-16
The GWART after specifying a routing cost of 5 between JR and MICKEY.

first set of messages sent in Test One. All six messages should have been routed as follows:

IS (JR) → MTA (JR)

MTA (JR) → MTA (SNOOPY) via Site Connector (cost = 1)

MTA (SNOOPY) → MTA (MICKEY) via Site Connector (cost = 1)

MTA (MICKEY) → MTA (BUGS) via Site Connector (cost = 1)

MTA (BUGS) → IS (BUGS)

This is just as we predicted.

Test Three

Let's change the costs again. Configure the Site Connector between JR and MICKEY to have a cost of 2, instead of 1. We now have the following routes between JR and MICKEY with their costs (see Figure 18-17):

- The total cost from JR to MICKEY via Site Connector = 2
- The total cost from JR to SNOOPY to MICKEY = 1+1 = 2

What does this mean? Because the indirect route (two hops) from JR to SNOOPY to MICKEY has the same routing cost as the direct route (one hop) from JR to MICKEY, the Site Connectors should load-balance the routing of messages between Dallas and Atlanta (and hence between Dallas

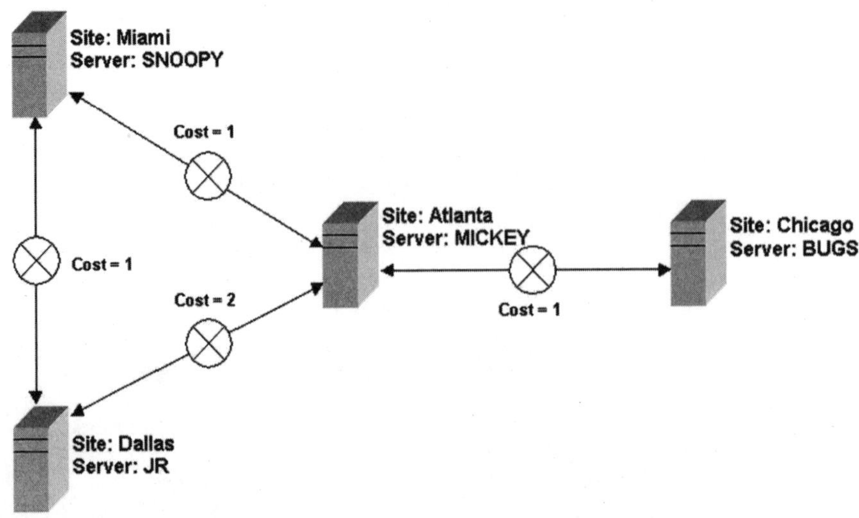

Figure 18-17 Routing costs for Test Three.

and Chicago). Approximately half the messages sent from Dallas to Atlanta (or to Chicago) should be routed through Miami, while the rest are routed directly from Dallas to Atlanta.

Select the Recalculate Routing button on the Routing tab of each Site Addressing object to bring the GWART up to date on all sites if necessary. Then try sending a dozen messages from Bobby in Dallas to Peter in Chicago again. After this has been done, open the Message Tracking Center and track the path of each of the messages. You can distinguish which messages they are from their sending time, which should be different from the first set of messages sent in Test One. About half of the messages should have been routed as follows:

IS (JR) → MTA (JR)

MTA (JR) → MTA (MICKEY) via Site Connector (cost = 2)

MTA (MICKEY) → MTA (BUGS) via Site Connector (cost = 1)

MTA (BUGS) → IS (BUGS)

The other half should have been routed as follows:

IS (JR) → MTA (JR)

MTA (JR) → MTA (SNOOPY) → MTA (MICKEY) (cost = 2)

MTA (MICKEY) → MTA (BUGS) via Site Connector (cost = 1)

MTA (BUGS) → IS (BUGS)

This is just as we predicted.

Where Do We Go from Here?

In the next chapter, we will look at how the status of servers and messaging links in an Exchange organization can be monitored using Server Monitors, Link Monitors, and the Windows NT administrative tool, Performance Monitor.

For More Information

Chapter 9 of the *Concepts and Planning* manual provides more information on message routing.

Exchange Server 5.5 Resource Guide

Chapter 5 of this guide is entitled "Addressing and Routing" and contains some details on Exchange message routing, probably more than you'll want to understand!

TechNet

Check out the following articles from the Knowledge Base. Note that some of this stuff applies to earlier versions of Exchange, but it still is helpful in understanding the current version to an extent:

- Q182128. XCON: "Site Connector Address Spaces Do Not Appear in GWART"
- Q149121. XCON: "Gateway Address Routing Table Information"
- Q193322. XCON: "Route Selection Criteria"
- Q182798. XADM: "Routing Calculation Fails Across Entire Organization"
- Q154624. XCON: "Configuring the Site Connector Between Untrusted Domains"

CHAPTER 19

Monitoring Exchange

The last few chapters have covered establishing messaging connectivity between Exchange sites and foreign messaging systems and also have examined message routing in an Exchange organization. In this chapter, we will examine how to monitor the health and status of servers and connectors in an Exchange organization. After you have read this chapter, you will have an understanding of the following topics:

- Server Monitors
- Link Monitors
- Performance Monitor

The walkthroughs in this chapter lead you through the steps of implementing Server and Link Monitors in an Exchange organization.

Server Monitors

When your Exchange organization is up and running, you need to monitor its health and status on an ongoing basis to ensure that your implementation is performing the way you expect. Exchange provides several tools for doing this, which we will examine in this chapter.

The first tool we will look at is an installable Exchange component known as the Server Monitor. Server Monitors verify that essential Exchange services and other Windows NT services are properly running on specified Exchange Servers. If these services are not functioning, appropriate actions can be taken, such as

- Generating a Windows NT administrative alert
- Sending an email notification to an administrator
- Restarting the stopped services
- Rebooting the Exchange Server

Server Monitors can also be used to check whether a remote Exchange Server's system clock is properly synchronized with the local server and can reset a clock that is off.

Server Monitors don't require any special permissions to monitor the status of services on Exchange servers or to send notifications of problems, but they do require RPC connectivity with the servers they are monitoring. Permissions may need to be assigned, however, if you want the monitor to be able to restart services, reboot computers, or reset system clocks.

Server Monitors are created within the Monitors container of the Configuration container for your site. Let's look at the settings we can configure on a Server Monitor property sheet, shown in Figure 19-1 (we'll look more at many of these settings during the walkthrough later in this chapter):

- *Polling Interval (General tab).* The polling interval specifies how frequently the Server Monitor checks the services on the designated Exchange servers. You can specify two separate polling intervals:
  - *Normal.* This specifies how often the monitor checks servers whose services are running properly. The default is every 15 minutes.
  - *Critical Sites.* This specifies how often the monitor checks servers whose services are detected as having a problem, such as when an essential Exchange service has stopped on the server. The default is every five minutes.
- *Log File (General tab).* You can have the monitor create an additional log file that records the status of the services on the monitored Exchange Servers.

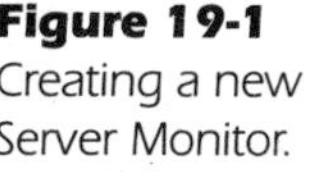

Figure 19-1 Creating a new Server Monitor.

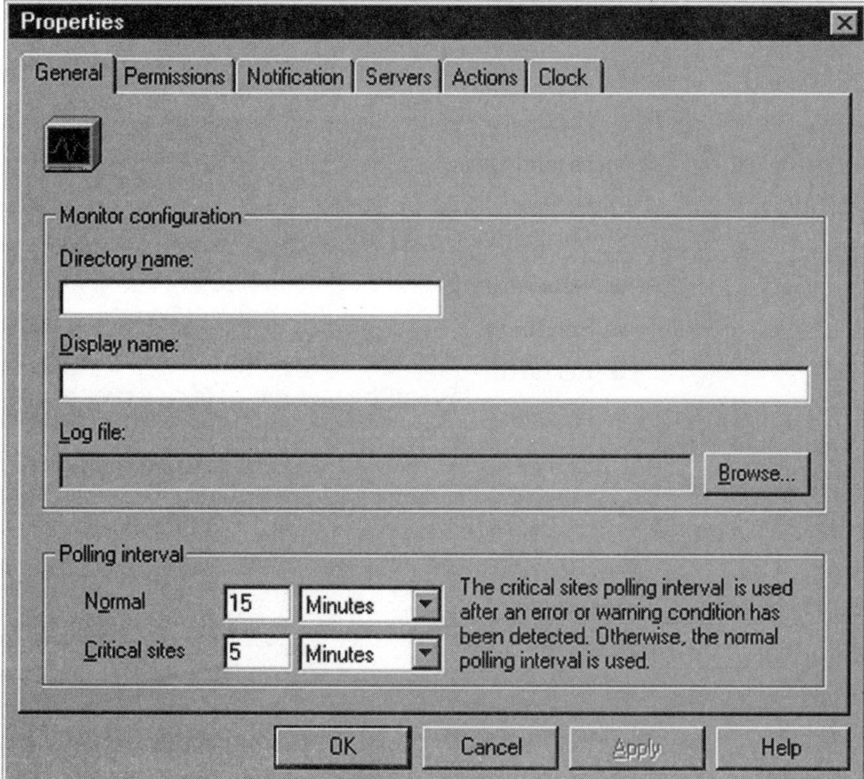

- *Notification tab*. Use this tab to specify the series of notification actions that should occur when a server becomes unstable. This series of notifications is called an Escalation Path. The times you specify for each notification are the time between the condition being recognized by the monitor and the time when the notification action is performed. Possible notification actions can include
  - Sending an email notification to an administrator
  - Generating a Windows NT alert
  - Running any executable, such as a program to notify a pager or a batch file to perform some administrative action

  When you create a new notification action, you can specify whether this action should apply to servers that are
  - Either in a Warning state or an Alert state
  - In an Alert state only

  The meaning of these two states is as follows:
  - An *Alert* state (red triangle) means a serious condition exists, such as the server is not responding, a service is not working, or the server's clock is way off for some reason.
  - A *Warning* state (red exclamation point) means a possible problem exists, such as the server's clock is off slightly or the server has not been checked recently.
- *Servers tab*. Use this tab to specify which Exchange Servers in your organization will be monitored using the Server Monitor and which Windows NT services will be monitored on these servers. By default, the Exchange services monitored are the ones associated with the directory, Information Store, and MTA.
- *Actions tab*. Use the Actions tab to specify what series of steps should be followed when the monitor detects a problem on a monitored Exchange server. These different actions are called Escalation Actions. You can select from three different kinds of actions:
  - Do nothing.
  - Attempt to restart the service.
  - Attempt to reboot the server.

  You can configure the monitor to make three attempts to remedy the problem. For example, you could try to restart the service twice, and if that fails, you could try to reboot the server. If you configure the monitor to reboot the server, you should specify a restart message here that will appear on the Exchange server's console, and a delay time for this message will be displayed before the reboot attempt takes place, to give time for anyone working at the server's console, to save their work. Restart the server only as a last resort.

- *Clock tab*. Use this tab to specify how far the server's clock needs to be off before it is considered to be in an Alert state or a Warning state. If you select the checkboxes here, you can have the Monitor synchronize the server's clock if it falls into either of these two states.

Running a Server Monitor

Several Server Monitors can be created if you need them, each one with specified escalation paths and actions as it monitors a group of servers. After you configure a new Server Monitor, you still need to start it. This can be done in one of two ways:

- The *Manual Start*: Select the Server Monitor in the Exchange Administrator program, select an Exchange server to run the monitor, and then choose Start Monitor from the Tools menu. The monitor's status window will open, displaying the status of a monitored Exchange server by the symbol in the first column of the monitor's status window:
  - Green triangle: Everything is OK.
  - Red exclamation: Warning!
  - Red triangle: Alert!!
  - Blue question mark: Not sure what's happening.

  Note that if you close the Exchange Administrator program, the monitor stops running.
- The *Automatic Start*: To automatically start a Server Monitor when the Exchange server is booted, you can create a shortcut to the executable for the Exchange Administrator program `admin.exe` using the `/m` switch as follows:

  ```
  /admin /m site_name\monitor_name\server_name
  ```

  This starts the Exchange Administrator program and runs the specified monitor using the specified Exchange server. You can then place this shortcut in the Startup program group, so it will start automatically when the administrator logs on to the server. Finally, you can configure a Windows NT `AutoAdminLogon` registry setting to have the server automatically log on using the administrator account when a reboot occurs. Make sure that you have your server securely locked away if you plan to use this feature!

You can find more information about the status of a monitored server in Exchange Administrator by double-clicking on the server's name. This opens a property sheet that provides information concerning the services running on the server. We'll see how to do this in the walkthrough.

Scheduling Maintenance

If you are going to perform scheduled maintenance on an Exchange server, you should run the `admin.exe` *command with the appropriate* `/t` *switch options prior to taking the server offline. This puts the server into maintenance mode and stops monitoring actions for the server so the monitor won't get confused and think the server is in a problem state. The various options for the* `/t` *switch are as follows:*

- `/t n` *puts the server into maintenance mode and stops notifications from being generated by monitors, but if the monitor wants to initiate a repair action (like trying to restart a stopped service), it will do so.*
- `/t r` *puts the server into maintenance mode and allows monitors to generate notifications concerning the state of the server, but it stops them from initiating any repair actions.*
- `/t nr` *puts the server into maintenance mode and stops monitors from either generating notifications or initiating repair actions concerning the server (preferred).*
- `/t` *takes the server out of maintenance mode and into normal mode again.*

You can remember this `/t` *switch as "t"ake the server offline for maintenance! You can also use the Maintenance Status tab on a running Server Monitor to perform these actions (see the following walkthrough).*

Walkthrough: Installing and Testing a Server Monitor

Let's now create a new Server Monitor and test its operations. We will work with our two Exchange Servers:

- MICKEY in site Atlanta
- BUGS in site Chicago

The servers are connected using a Site Connector, and a Directory Replication Connector has been installed to synchronize the directories on the two servers.

Let's work on BUGS in Chicago, where Peter James is the senior network administrator. Log on to BUGS as Administrator and start the Exchange Administrator program. Then select File, New Other, Server Monitor from the menu. If a message appears saying, `Monitors cannot be created in the select parent container. Do you want to switch to the 'Monitors' container of site 'Chicago'?`, click OK. This opens up a blank property sheet for the new Server Monitor (see Figure 19-2).

Enter the following information on the General tab of this property sheet:

- Directory name = Server Monitor on BUGS
- Display name = Server Monitor on BUGS

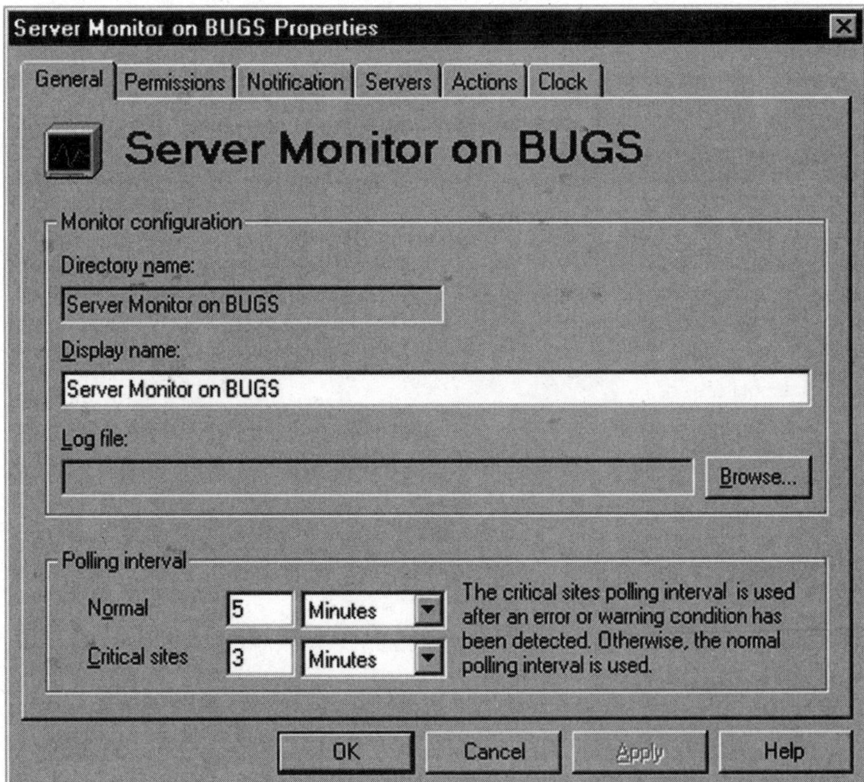

Figure 19-2 Property sheet for a Server Monitor.

- Polling intervals:
  - Normal = 5 minutes (we'll check running services every five minutes for the purposes of this walkthrough)
  - Critical Sites = 3 minutes (same reason)

Switch to the Notification tab, and we will create a series of notification events to establish an escalation path for the monitor. Click New to open the New Notification dialog box (see Figure 19-3).

Select Mail Message and click OK to open the Escalation Editor (Mail Message) dialog box (see Figure 19-4).

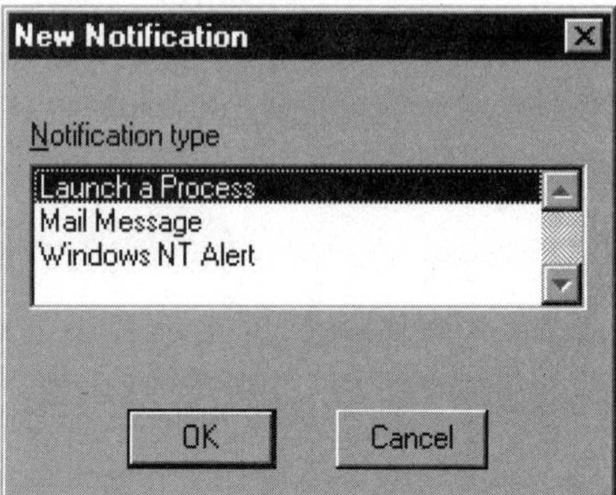

Figure 19-3 Creating a new notification for a Server Monitor.

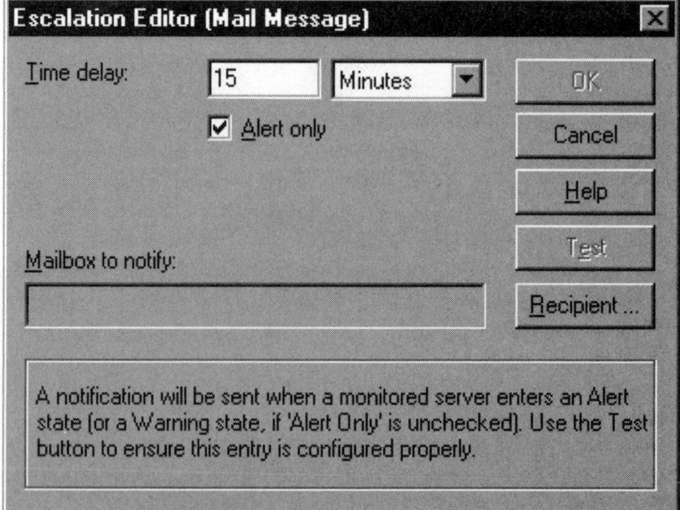

Figure 19-4 The Escalation Editor dialog box for creating a new Mail Message notification.

Specify a time delay of one minute, clear the Alert so that only mail message notifications will be sent if the monitored server enters a Warning state (otherwise, a notification would be sent only if the server enters an Alert state), and specify Peter James in Chicago as the mailbox to notify when the monitor is tripped. Click the Test button and check whether Peter receives a test message when logged on to GOOFEY and running Outlook 98 on that machine. Note that the test message is sent by the System Attendant service on BUGS. (You may need to create a Windows messaging profile for Peter James on GOOFEY and then log on to GOOFEY as PJames and start Outlook.)

Click OK to close the Escalation Editor dialog box, and a message appears saying, `Notifications for server/link monitors will be sent only during the next polling interval after the notification time has expired.` Select the Don't Tell Me Again checkbox and click OK to return to the Server Monitor on the BUGS properties sheet.

Now let's create two more new notifications as follows:

- Type = Windows NT Alert
  - Time Delay = Two minutes
  - Alert Only (Selected)
  - Computer to Alert = GOOFEY (Make sure that WinPopUp is running on GOOFEY to receive the Windows NT alert, because GOOFEY is a Windows 98 machine. Then click Test to check that Peter on GOOFEY receives the alert message.)
- Type = Launch a Process
  - Time Delay = Five minutes
  - Alert Only (Selected)
  - Launch Process = `C:\Winnt\System32\Calc.exe` (just to have something to start on the machine, but you are more likely to run some batch file instead)

The Notification tab of the Server Monitor on the BUGS properties sheet should now look something like Figure 19-5.

Switch to the Servers tab. We'll use this Server Monitor to monitor both BUGS in Chicago and MICKEY in Atlanta, so follow these steps:

1. Select the Chicago site in the drop-down box at the bottom, and BUGS should be displayed in the Servers listbox on the left-hand side (this is the default situation anyway). Select BUGS and click the Add button to move BUGS to the Monitored Servers listbox on the right-hand side.

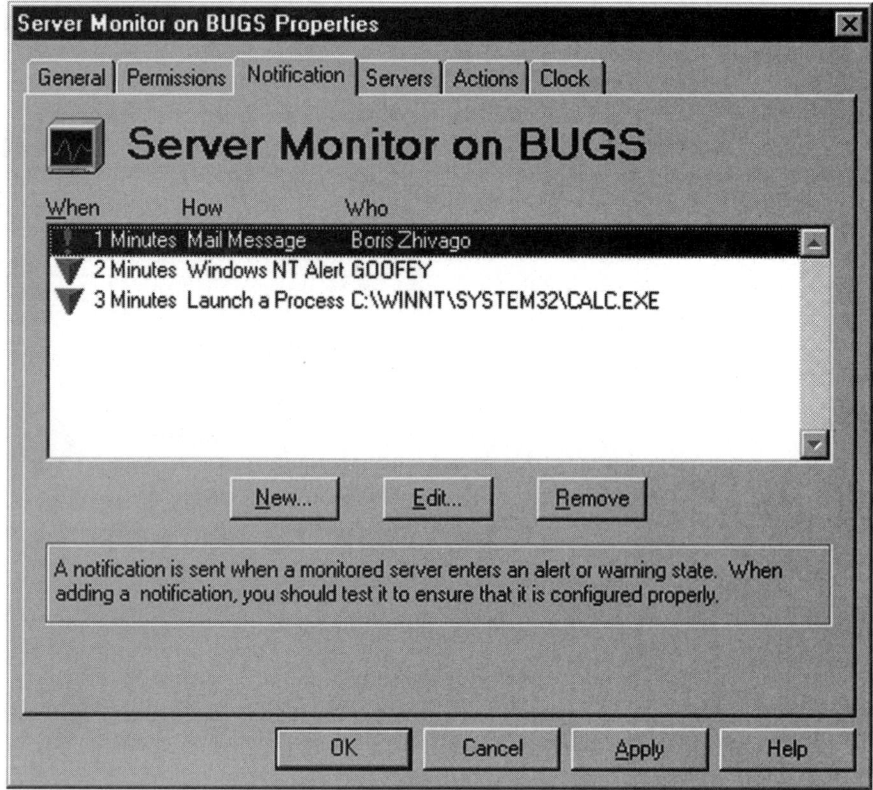

Figure 19-5 The escalation path for the new Server Monitor.

2. Select the Atlanta site in the drop-down box at the bottom, and MICKEY should be displayed in the Servers listbox on the left-hand side. Select MICKEY and click the Add button to move MICKEY to the Monitored Servers listbox on the right-hand side.

The Servers tab should look something like Figure 19-6.

We've selected the servers to monitor, but we haven't specified which services we will be monitoring on them. Select BUGS in the Monitored Servers listbox of the Server tab and click the Services button to open the BUGS Properties dialog box. This dialog box lists the installed Windows NT services on BUGS (whether they are running or not) and also which of these services is currently being monitored (see Figure 19-7). Three of the core Exchange services are being monitored on BUGS by default, and that's enough for us, so click OK to close the box. (There is no need to monitor the System Attendant service, because if that service stops, the other three core Exchange services will also stop, due to their dependencies on the System Attendant service.)

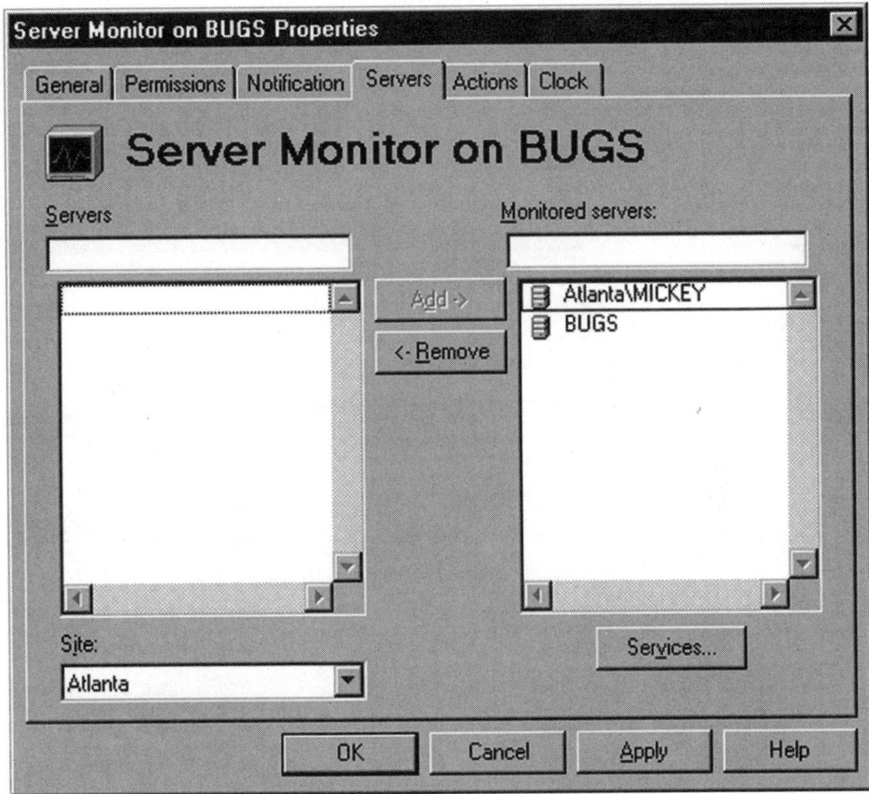

Figure 19-6 Specifying BUGS and MICKEY as monitored servers.

Move on to the Actions tab. Specify the following escalation actions to occur if a monitored service is stopped on a monitored machine:

- First attempt = Take no action
- Second attempt = Restart the service
- Third attempt = Restart the computer
- Restart delay = 15 seconds
- Restart message = Run for the hills, the server is restarting!!

Move on to the Clock tab and view the settings. Click OK to close the Server Monitor on the BUGS properties sheet and return to the Monitors container in Exchange Administrator, which should now contain a Server Monitor with a BUGS object within it.

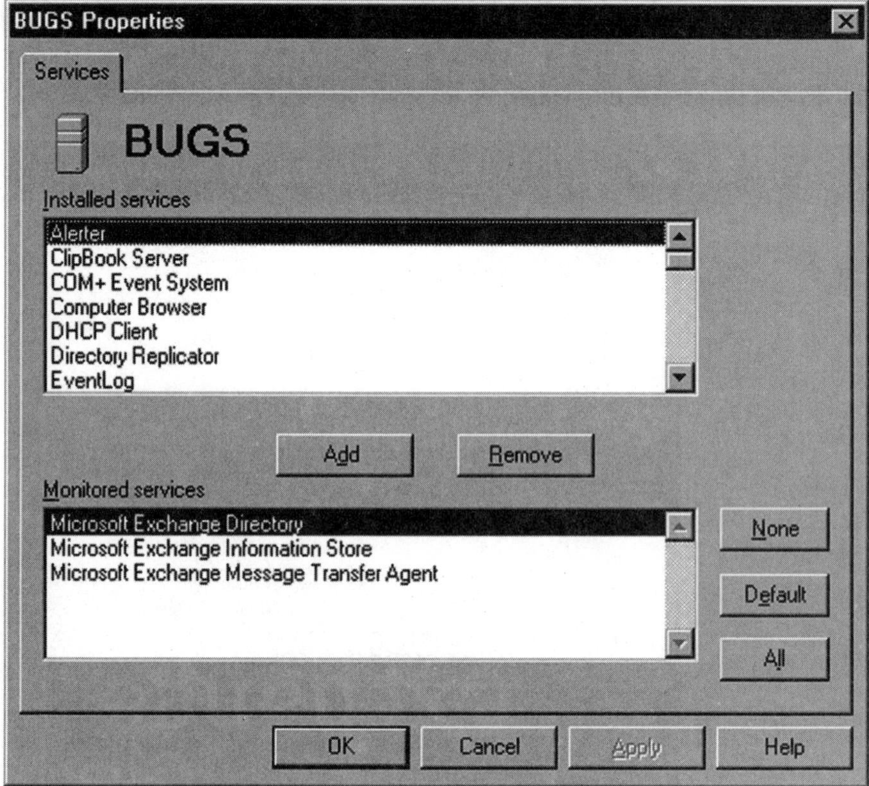

Figure 19-7 Specifying which Windows NT services to monitor on BUGS.

Testing the Server Monitor

Start the monitor by selecting it in the contents pane of the Exchange Administrator and choosing Start Monitor from the Tools menu. Specify BUGS as the server to be connected to (the server on which the monitor is run) and click OK. A new child window is displayed in the Exchange Administrator titled Monitor Server Monitor on BUGS (BUGS). Both monitored servers should be displayed with upwards-pointing green triangles beside them, indicating that the servers are running properly (see Figure 19-8).

In the Server Monitor window, double-click on server Atlanta\MICKEY to open the Atlanta\MICKEY Properties dialog box (see Figure 19-9). Here you can view the following status information about MICKEY:

- The *Actions tab* displays the version and status of monitored services on MICKEY and enables you to stop and start these services.
- The *Clock tab* displays the clock offset between MICKEY and the server that the monitor is running (BUGS) on as well as various time zone and daylight savings information.

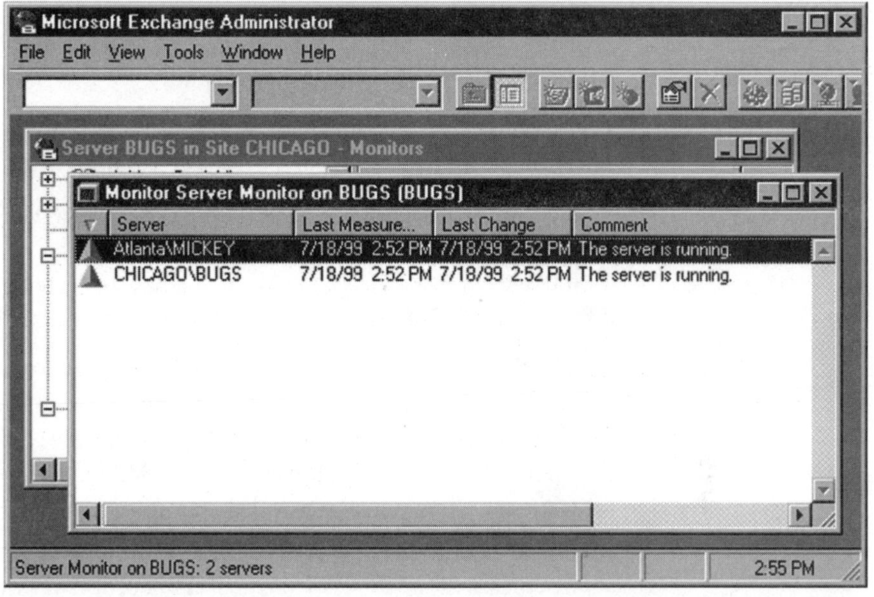

Figure 19-8 The Server Monitor on BUGS is running and displays that both BUGS and MICKEY are running properly.

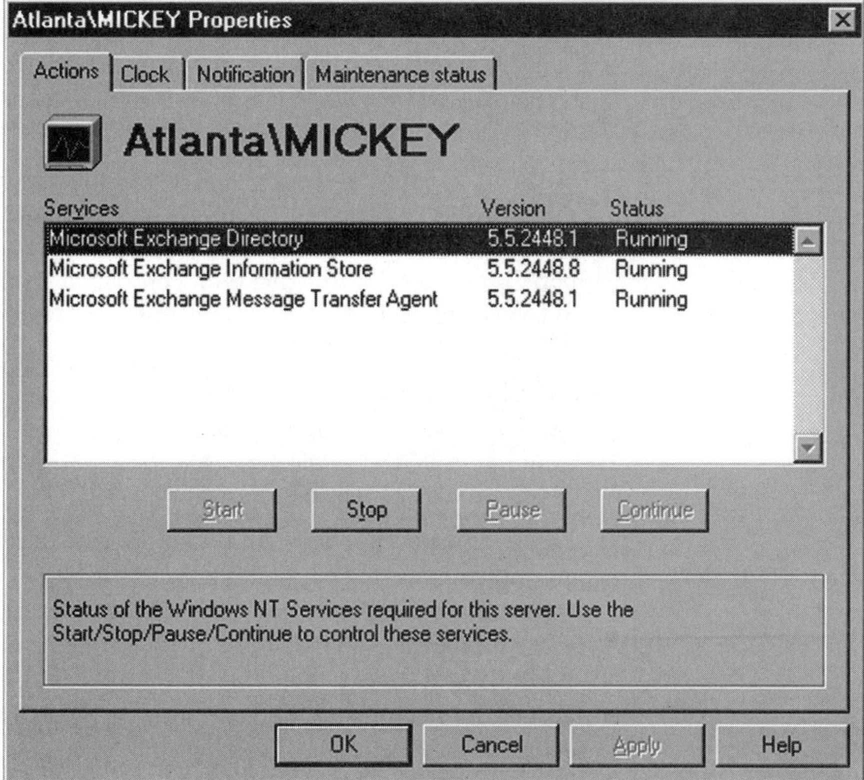

Figure 19-9 Viewing status information concerning MICKEY.

- The *Notification tab* shows any notifications that have been sent by the monitor, when, how, and to whom. This listbox should be empty at this point, because there are no problems with MICKEY.
- The *Maintenance Status tab* shows the current maintenance status on the machine and the time of the last modification.

Click OK to close the Atlanta\MICKEY Properties dialog box and return to the running Server Monitor window on BUGS.

Now let's cause a problem. We are going to stop the Microsoft Exchange MTA service on MICKEY, but before we do, let's consider what will happen:

1. The Server Monitor on BUGS is currently checking the status of core Exchange services on BUGS every five minutes (the normal polling interval is set on the General tab of the property sheet for the Server Monitor on BUGS). After we stop the MTA service on MICKEY, it may take up to five minutes until the monitor notices the failed service.
2. Once it notices the problem, the monitor will enter an Alert state because a stopped service is a serious problem (a warning state is entered only when a minor problem occurs, such as the clock being off a little). The monitor then will start checking the services on MICKEY every two minutes (the critical sites polling interval is set on the General tab). In addition, the monitor makes a first attempt to correct the problem on MICKEY, which in this case is Take No Action (the first stage of the escalation actions is set on the Actions tab).
3. Meanwhile, one minute after the monitor enters the Alert state, a mail message will be sent to Peter James by the System Attendant on BUGS, telling him of the problem (the first stage of escalation path, set on the Notification tab). Peter should receive this message in Outlook 98, which should be running on GOOFEY for the test.
4. Two minutes after the monitor enters the Alert state, it sends a second notification, this time a Windows NT alert sent to GOOFEY, which should be received by Peter in WinPopUp that should be running on GOOFEY (select Start, Run, type WinPopUp, and click OK to start this program).
5. Three minutes after the monitor enters the Alert state, the second attempt is made to correct the problem, which in this case is to restart the failed service on MICKEY (this occurs because the polling interval is now three minutes and that much time has elapsed since the last time the monitor polled the services on MICKEY). This should be successful, and so a third notification (starting Calculator on BUGS) should not occur.

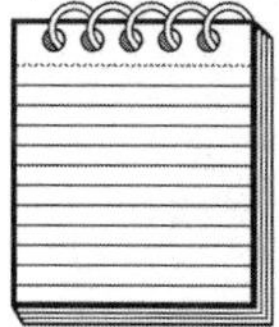

Running Server Monitors

*Now here's a trick: Normally, this attempt by the Server Monitor on BUGS to restart the failed service on MICKEY will run into a problem, namely that the service account on the two machines is different. Thus, BUGS won't have sufficient permissions to restart services on MICKEY; in fact, BUGS won't have sufficient permissions even to monitor those services! We are taking advantage of a security loophole in Windows NT; we are running the Server Monitor on BUGS while logged on as the default Administrator account for the CHICAGO domain where BUGS is located. Because our default Administrator account for the MTIT domain where MICKEY is located has the **identical** account name and password, the credentials of the logged-on user on BUGS are accepted by MICKEY, and the monitor can work across sites and in a different domain (this works for identical credentials even if there is no trust relationship between the two domains). In general, though, you would monitor servers in your own domain and your own Exchange site or use a single domain and a single service account for both sites. Otherwise, getting these monitors to run can be a bit tricky.*

Let's try it! Go to MICKEY and open the Services utility in the Control Panel, stop the Microsoft Exchange MTA service, and close the Services utility. Go back to the Server Monitor in the BUGS window in Exchange Administrator on BUGS to watch what happens. Here's what should happen:

1. First, the upwards-pointing green arrow beside Atlanta\MICKEY in the monitor window should change into a downward-pointing red arrow (this may take several minutes). The comment beside this entry should read `The service MSExchangeMTA is not available. Its status is Stopped.`
2. Next, the message shown in Figure 19-10 should appear in Peter's inbox in Outlook 98.
3. Next, a message should arrive for WinPopUp running on GOOFEY saying something like this:

```
From: Microsoft Exchange Administrator at \\BUGS
To: GOOFEY
Subj: **USER NOTIFICATION**
Date: 8/18/99 3:51 PM
MICKEY Alert since 7/18/99 3:49 PM The service MSExchangeMTA is
not available. Its status is Stopped.
```

4. Shortly after this, the service should be restarted and a second email message and second alert will be sent informing Peter of this.

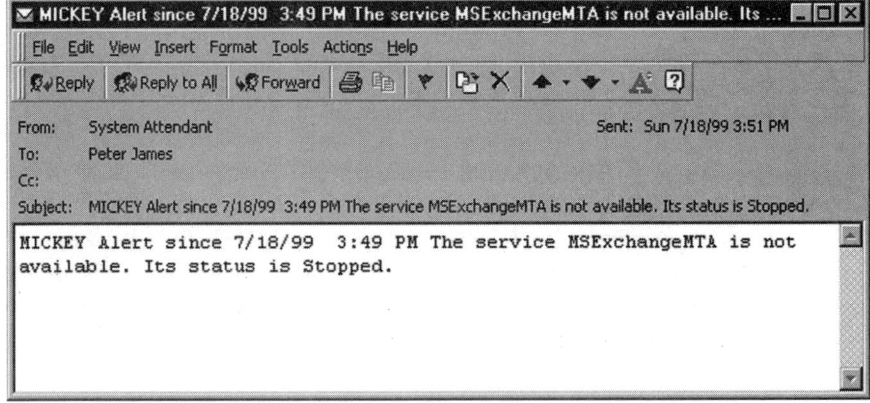

Figure 19-10 Email notification from Server Monitor on BUGS.

On Your Own

Try this if you like: Stop the Microsoft Exchange MTA service on MICKEY and set its Startup setting to Disabled. What do you think will happen, given the way we have configured the Server Monitor?

Link Monitor

Link Monitors are different from Server Monitors, but they share many of the same configuration settings and display their status information in a similar way, so we will cover them a little more quickly than we did Server Monitors. Link Monitors verify that messaging is functioning between Exchange Servers in your organization and between your organization and a foreign mail system with which you have established messaging connectivity. Link Monitors accomplish this by periodically sending messages to the specified Exchange or foreign mail servers and looking at the reply message or non-delivery report (NDR) generated, observing also the round-trip time taken by the process in order to determine whether the messaging link is functioning up to par or not (see Figure 19-11). If something is wrong with the link, appropriate actions can be taken, such as

- Generating a Windows NT administrative alert
- Sending an email notification to an administrator
- Restarting services on the remote server
- Rebooting the remote server

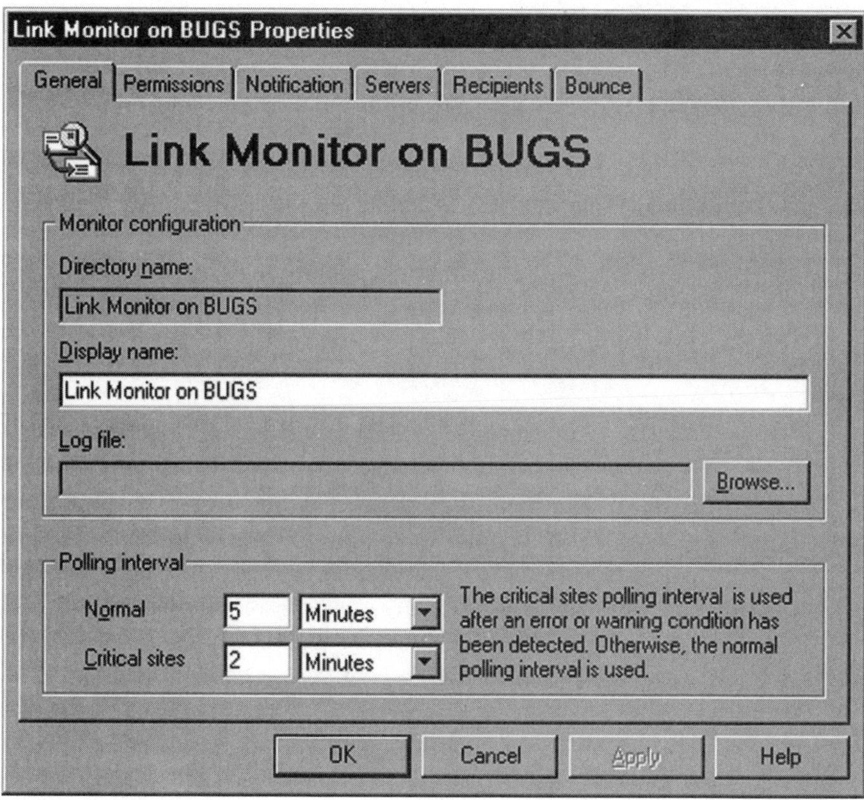

Figure 19-11 Property sheet for a Link Monitor.

Link Monitors are located in the Monitors container, which is in the Configuration container for your Exchange site. When you create a Link Monitor object, here are some of the important settings that need to be configured on its property sheet (many of these settings are similar to those for Server Monitors already described):

- *Polling Interval (General tab)*. This setting specifies how frequently the Link Monitor sends a test email message to check for messaging connectivity with the designated remote Exchange Servers or foreign mail systems. The two polling intervals mean the same as for Server Monitors.
- *Notification tab*. This is used to specify an escalation path of notifications and is just like the tab for Server Monitors.
- *Servers tab*. If you want to monitor the messaging links with another Exchange Server within your organization, specify servers from remote sites here that you want to monitor. For monitoring messaging links with foreign mail systems, see the following discussion of the Recipients tab.

- *Recipients tab*. To monitor connectivity with foreign mail systems, you must first create a custom recipient that does not exist on the foreign mail system, but that otherwise has the correct addressing information. For example, if you want to use a Link Monitor to test connectivity with an X.400 mail server whose O/R address is

  ```
  c=FR;a=ATLAS;p=Le MTIT;o=PePeLePhew;
  ```

  you could create a custom recipient with the following nonexistent O/R address on the remote X.400 mail server:

  ```
  c=FR;a=ATLAS;p=Le MTIT;o=PePeLePhew;s=Le Bounce;
  ```

  You must make sure that this recipient does not exist on the foreign mail system, as you want the link to bounce in order to test it. When the Link Monitor sends a message to this address, the foreign mail system should receive it, recognize that it is a nonexistent recipient, and return a non-delivery report (NDR) to the Link Monitor. The NDR then confirms that the link is operational, if it is returned in the expected bounce time. This Recipients tab is where you specify the custom recipient that you created.
- *Bounce tab*. Here you specify which round-trip (bounce) times will be considered acceptable as far as the messaging link is concerned and which times will cause the link to be considered in an Alert or Warning state.

Running a Link Monitor

After you configure your new Link Monitor (and you can create several of them on one server if you want to), you need to start it. Just like for Server Monitors, you can start a Link Monitor two ways: manually or automatically. Starting a Link Monitor opens the Link Monitor's status window, which is similar to the status window for a Server Monitor. This window enables you to see the status of your messaging links using the symbols in the first column of the window together with the comments in the Comments column. Just like a Server Monitor, if you observe that a monitored link is in a problem state in the monitor's status window, you can double-click on the link to open a property sheet that provides more information concerning the problem link. This is covered in the following walkthrough.

Walkthrough: Installing and Testing a Link Monitor

Let's now create a new Link Monitor and test its operation. We will work with the same two Exchange Servers we have already used, namely MICKEY in Atlanta and BUGS in Chicago.

First, let's create a custom recipient on BUGS that maps to a nonexistent recipient on MICKEY. Log on to BUGS as Administrator and start the Exchange Administrator program. Select File, New Custom Recipient and create a custom recipient of type X.400 with the following O/R address entered into the fields on the X.400 Address Properties dialog box:

```
c=US;a= ;p=MTIT;o=Atlanta;s=Bounce;
```

Click OK and enter Bounce for the display and alias names of the custom recipient. Then click OK to close the property sheet for the new custom recipient. But why have we created this custom recipient? We really don't need to actually, because the messaging link we want to monitor is within our own Exchange organization. If we wanted to monitor a messaging link to a foreign mail system, we would definitely need this nonexistent recipient so we could bounce email messages from the foreign mail system and receive NDRs in return. We'll create one just for fun and thus create two monitored links with our Exchange Server MICKEY.

Now select File, New Other, Link Monitor from the menu. If a message appears saying, `Monitors cannot be created in the select parent container. Do you want to switch to the 'Monitors' container of site 'Chicago'?`, then click OK. This opens up a blank property sheet for the new Link Monitor. Specify the following information:

- General tab
  - Directory name = Link Monitor on BUGS
  - Display name = Link Monitor on BUGS
  - Normal polling interval = Five minutes
  - Critical polling interval = Two minutes
- Notifications tab
  - Create only one new notification, namely an email message to Peter James in Atlanta that will be sent one minute after the monitored messaging link enters Alert condition. Test the notification.

- *Servers tab*
  - Specify MICKEY in Chicago as the Exchange Server that BUGS will be sending ping messages to in order to test messaging connectivity with the server.
  - Note that if we want to monitor a messaging link with an Exchange Server in our own organization MTIT, we configure the Servers tab but don't need to configure the Recipients tab. In other words, this tab is only for monitoring messaging links to servers in our own organization.
- *Recipients tab* (shown in Figure 19-12)
  - Add the custom recipient called Bounce to the left listbox on this tab.
  - Note that we really don't need to configure this tab, since we specified MICKEY's name on the Servers tab. The Recipients tab only needs to be configured when we are testing messaging connectivity with a foreign mail system (or a different Exchange organization for that

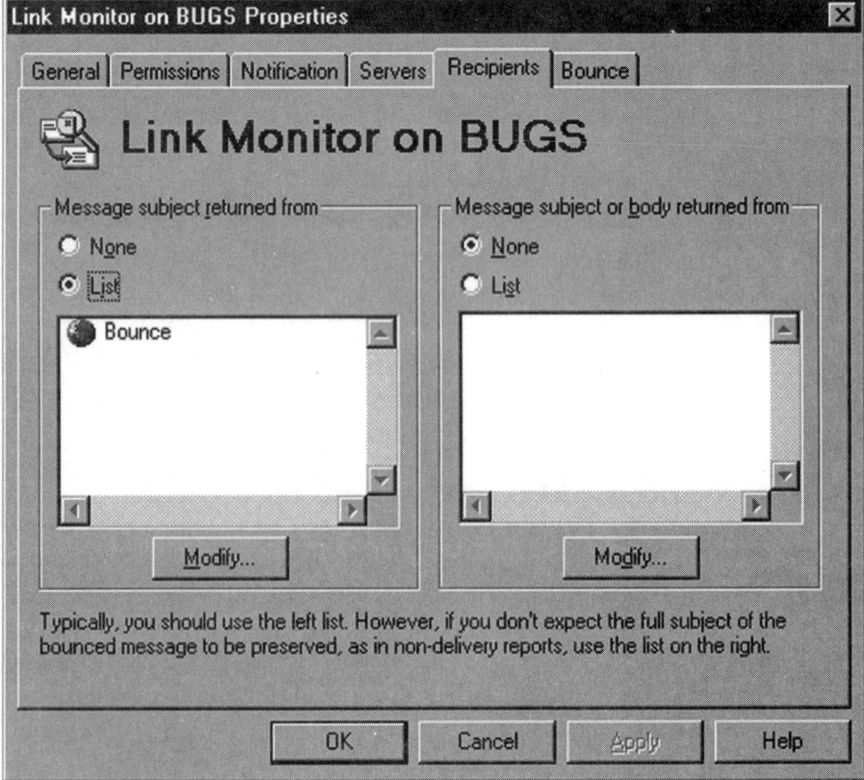

Figure 19-12 Specifying a custom recipient that will cause the message to bounce from the remote server.

matter). We'll configure this tab anyway and thus monitor two messaging links with MICKEY, instead of just one, which is more normal.

- *Bounce tab*
  - Specify that a Warning state is entered after one minute.
  - Specify that an Alert state is entered after two minutes.

  Click OK to close the property sheet for Link Monitor on BUGS.

Testing the Link Monitor

Start the monitor by selecting it in the contents pane of Exchange Administrator and choosing Start Monitor from the Tools menu. Specify BUGS as the server to connect to (the server on which the monitor is run) and click OK. A new child window is displayed in Exchange Administrator titled Monitor Link Monitor on BUGS (BUGS). The monitored server Atlanta\MICKEY should be displayed with an upwards-pointing green triangle beside it, indicating that the servers are running properly (it may remain a blue question mark for the first few minutes until the messaging links to MICKEY are verified). In addition, the nonexistent recipient in the remote site that is represented by the custom recipient called Bounce is also listed as a link being monitored.

In the Link Monitor window, double-click on server Atlanta\MICKEY to open the Atlanta\MICKEY Properties dialog box (see Figure 19-13). Here you can view the following status information about the messaging link to MICKEY:

- The *General tab* displays information about the last bounced mail.
- The *Notification tab* shows any notifications that have been sent by the monitor, when, how, and to whom. This listbox should be empty at this point, because there are no problems with the messaging link to MICKEY.
- The *Maintenance Status tab* shows the current maintenance status on the machine and the time of the last modification.

Now let's break the messaging connection between BUGS and MICKEY. Unplug the LAN cable from the network card on MICKEY so that BUGS no longer has a LAN connection to MICKEY. Wait a few minutes until the broken link is detected. Here's what should happen:

1. Both links should go into a Warning state, with a red exclamation point beside them (see Figure 19-14).

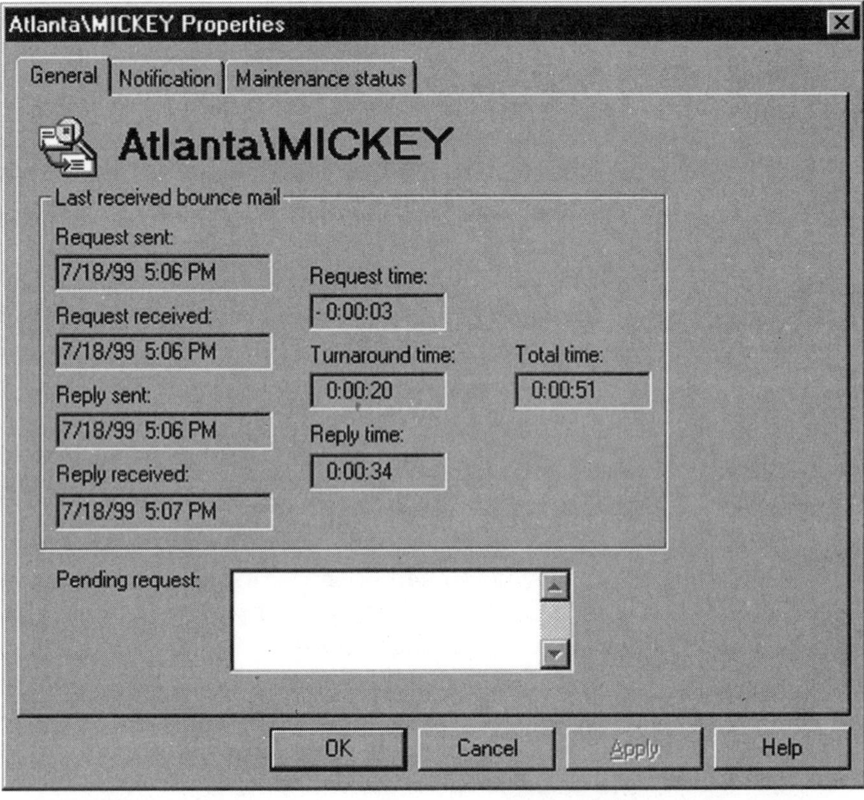

Figure 19-13 Displaying the status of the link to Atlanta\MICKEY.

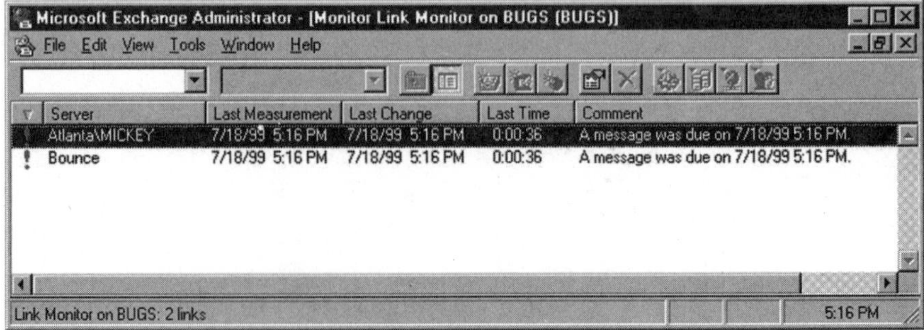

Figure 19-14 Messaging links in a Warning state.

2. Two minutes later the red exclamation points should change to downward-pointing red arrows, signifying that both links have gone into an Alert state.
3. One minute later a message should appear in Peter's inbox saying, `Bounce Alert since [date and time]. A message was due on [date and time].`

4. If you double-click on a link at this point, you will see on the General tab that several requests are pending.
5. Note that no more notifications are sent. Once a notification is triggered from the escalation path, the notification is deactivated so as not to inundate the receiver with too many messages.

Plug the LAN cable back into MICKEY and watch the links go back into operational (upwards-pointing green arrow) mode again in a few minutes. Will a message be sent to Peter when the link is operational again?

Performance Monitor

Finally, the Windows NT administrative tool Performance Monitor is useful for monitoring the health of your Exchange Servers and messaging connections. We won't go into detail here on how Performance Monitor works or which Performance Monitor counters should be used to monitor basic Windows NT Server system resources like those belonging to the memory, disk, network, and processor subsystems. Any good book on Windows NT can provide information about that sort of stuff. Instead, we'll briefly summarize a few of the more useful counters (out of the hundreds available!) that are specific to Exchange Server and can be used to monitor different Exchange components and services. More information on using Performance Monitor to monitor Exchange can be found in references listed in the section, "For More Information," at the end of this chapter. The counters listed here are displayed in the form *object:counter* for the Exchange service to which they relate:

- *Microsoft Exchange Directory service*
  - *MSExchangeDS:Pending Replication Synchronization*. This counter becomes zero when all servers in your organization have responded to a directory replication request. If this doesn't ever reach zero, you may have connectivity problems with some servers in your organization.
  - *MSExchangeDS:Remaining Replication Updates counter*. This counter becomes zero when your server has processed all directory replication updates it has received. If this never becomes zero, directory replication may not be completed before the next replication cycle is initiated.
- *Microsoft Exchange Information Store service*
  - *MSExchangeIS Private:Average Time for Local Delivery counter*. This counter shows how long messages sent to other recipients on the same

server wait in the Information Store queue before being delivered. If this is high, you may have problems with your Information Store.

- *MSExchangeIS Private:Average Time* for Delivery counter. This counter shows how long messages sent to recipients on other servers wait in the Information Store queue before being delivered. If this is high, you may have problems with your MTA.

- *Microsoft Exchange MTA service*

- *MSExchangeMTA:Messages / Sec counter*. This counter indicates messaging traffic (the number of messages your server's MTA sends and receives each second).
- *MSExchangeMTA:Work Queue Size counter*. This counter indicates how many messages are waiting in the MTA queues (inbound and outbound). If this is high, you may have a server performance problem—beef it up!
- *MSExchangeMTA Connections:Queue Length counter*. This counter enables you to examine the MTA queue for individual connections (instances) to see which connection, if any, is causing problems.

Event Viewer

A useful monitoring tool that we will not cover here is the Windows NT administrative tool Event Viewer. As we mentioned in previous chapters, Exchange logs its information, warning, and error events in the Application Log, which can be viewed using Event Viewer. The different kinds of events that can be logged are way too numerous to cover here. If you want to make use of Event Viewer to monitor Exchange, note that

- *Some of the objects in the Exchange directory hierarchy have a Diagnostic Logging tab on their property sheet that can be used to configure the "verbosity" of logging related to that object (that is, to the Exchange service related to that object). Keep logging set to None or Minimum unless you are troubleshooting problems associated with that particular object / service. Otherwise, numerous messages will be generated in the Application Log, and server performance might be degraded somewhat.*
- *Make sure that you have allocated sufficient disk space for the Application Log on your servers.*

Where Do We Go from Here?

In the next chapter, we will look at how we can maintain an Exchange organization by using command-line database maintenance utilities and performing backups.

For More Information

You can find out more about Link and Server Monitors in Chapter 3 and 4 of the *Maintenance and Troubleshooting* manual for Exchange, which is included as part of Exchange Books Online and can be separately ordered in hard copy format from Microsoft. These two chapters also include some useful information on monitoring Exchange Servers using the Performance Monitor tool for Windows NT. Diagnostic Logging is also covered in Chapter 4 of that manual.

Exchange Server 5.5 Resource Guide

This resource guide, which is also included on TechNet, has some useful information on monitoring Exchange in Chapter 8.

TechNet

The Technical Note, "Managing and Monitoring MS Exchange Server," within the MS Exchange section is also a useful source of information.

CHAPTER 20

Maintaining Exchange

In the previous chapter, we looked at how to monitor an Exchange organization using Server and Link Monitors and using the Windows NT administrative tool Performance Monitor. In this chapter, we will look at how to maintain an Exchange organization, in particular focusing on how to maintain the various Exchange database files through regular backups and using various command-line utilities. After reading this chapter, you will have an understanding of the following topics:

- Backing up Exchange
- Command-line maintenance utilities
- Disaster recovery tips

The walkthroughs in this chapter cover the use of some of the command-line utilities included with Exchange for maintaining and troubleshooting Exchange databases.

Backing up Exchange

Performing regular backups is an essential part of administering an Exchange organization. Backup and restore procedures are part of a larger issue called *disaster recovery*. Creating, documenting, implementing, maintaining, testing, and periodically reviewing a disaster recovery plan is one of the most important things that an Exchange administrator needs to do. Why? Because disasters are inevitable, whether hard drives failing on a machine leading to data loss, power outages bringing down servers and leaving critical database files in an inconsistent state, or fires and earthquakes causing physical damage to machines and networking infrastructure. This section deals with issues related to disaster recovery of Exchange Servers.

Windows NT Backup

Microsoft Windows NT includes an administrative tool called Windows NT Backup, whose command-line executable name is ntbackup.exe. Although this tool is primarily designed for offline backups of files, directories, and the Windows NT registry, installing Exchange Server on a Windows NT Server installs an additional DLL that enhances the Windows NT Backup tool to enable administrators to perform online backups of critical Exchange database files, including the information store and directory databases (see Figure 20-1). Performing online backups of Exchange Servers using Windows NT Backup enables you to back up the information store and directory databases without causing any interruption to messaging for users. Online backups take place while Exchange Services are still running and have no effect on Exchange's messaging capabilities while they are being performed. In today's 24/7 business paradigm, online backups are your main procedure for preparing for disaster.

Different types of online backups can be performed on Exchange Servers using the enhanced Windows NT Backup tool. Which types you use depend largely on whether or not you have circular logging enabled on your machines. Circular logging was discussed in Chapter 4, and is a way of saving on disk space used by Exchange databases by reusing transaction log files, instead of allowing them to continue to multiply. Unfortunately, circular logging, which is enabled by default, increases the probability that critical database data might be lost in a disaster. Most Exchange administrators recommend that circular logging be disabled and that Exchange Servers have the necessary disk space to enable the transaction logs to multiply between backups. To disable circular logging on an Exchange Server, open the property sheet for the Server object representing that server in the Exchange directory hierarchy and select the Advanced tab.

The common types of backups that can be performed on Exchange Servers using Windows NT Backup include the following:

- *Normal.* Also known as a Full backup, this type causes the entire directory and information store databases to be backed up. Transaction log files that are present are also backed up, after which the original

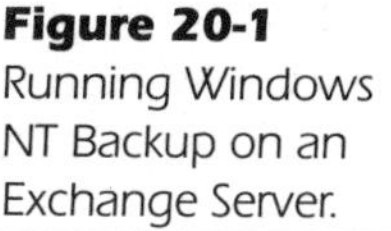

Figure 20-1 Running Windows NT Backup on an Exchange Server.

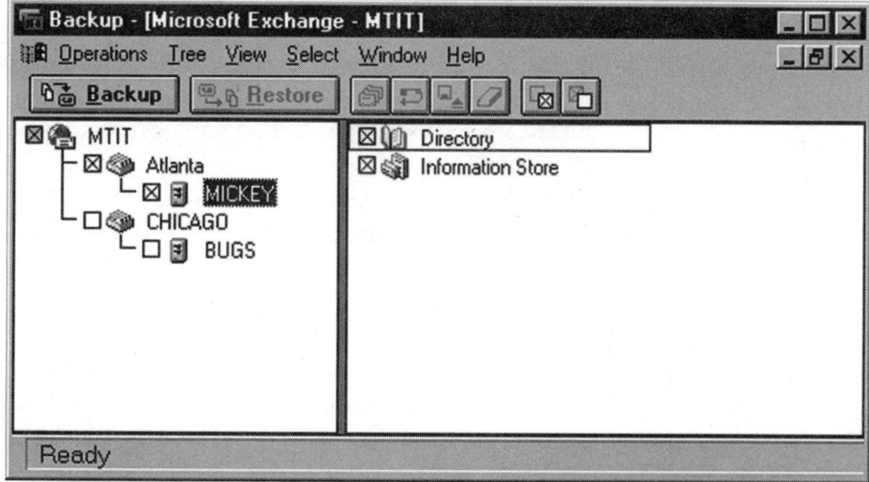

copies of the log files on the Exchange Server's hard drives are purged and deleted to make room for new ones. Normal backups keep disk space usage to a minimum for Exchange database files and are ultimately the safest form of backup to perform since a restore requires only the original normal backup tape (a single point of failure) and not multiple tapes, as in the types of backups described later. However, performing only normal backups is costly with regard to backup tape media and also with respect to the time needed to perform backups.

- *Incremental.* This type backs up only those portions of the databases that have changed since the last normal or incremental backup took place. These changes are backed up by copying the transaction log files to tape, after which the original log files are purged from the Exchange Server's hard drives. Incremental backups are typically used together with normal backups in a backup plan, as described later in this section. When you want to restore Exchange databases that are backed up using a combination of normal and incremental backups, you need the last normal backup and every incremental backup between the last normal backup and the present. If one of the incremental backups is lost, data is lost (a multiple point of failure). However, incremental backups use much less tape than normal backups and can be done much more quickly as well.
- *Differential.* This type backs up only those portions of the database that have changed since the last normal backup. Whereas each incremental backup includes only changes for that particular day, differential backups are cumulative with respect to changes in the databases. These changes are backed up by copying the transaction log files to tape, but the original log files are *not* purged from the hard disk afterwards. Instead, the transaction logs are allowed to accumulate until the next normal backup is performed. Differential backups are typically used together with normal backups in a backup plan as described later in this section. When you want to restore Exchange databases that were backed up using a combination of normal and differential backups, you need the last normal backup and yesterday's differential backup to accomplish this. Differential backups use less tape than normal ones, but more tape than incremental ones.

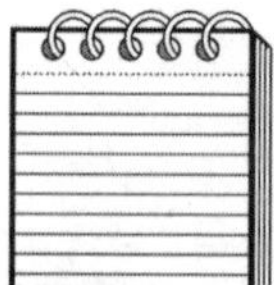

Circular Logging and Backup Types

When circular logging is enabled, you cannot perform incremental or differential backups; you can only perform normal backups.

How Online Backups Work

To perform backups while Exchange services are still running, Exchange makes use of additional files called Patch files. These files have the extension `*.pat` and are created in the Exchange database directories `\mdbdata` and `\dsadata` at the beginning of each online backup process They are deleted when the backup is completed. It works something like this:

1. Exchange starts by first backing up the database files (`*.edb` files) and then backing up the transaction log files (`*.log` files) for each database.
2. If a change is made to the directory or information store databases during the online backup process but the change is made to a portion of the database that has *not* yet been backed up, the change is processed and is backed up later in the backup process.
3. If a change is made to a database during online backup and is made to a portion of the database that has *already* been backed up, the change is recorded in a patch file for that database.
4. Once the transaction logs have been written to the backup tape, the patch files are then written to tape as well.
5. The old transaction log files on disk are then purged (deleted), except for any that are newer than the checkpoint at the start of the online backup. The patch files are deleted from disk as well.
6. The patch files on tape are then used together with the database and transaction files on tape when a restore needs to be performed.

Backup Plan

A backup plan is essentially a schedule for performing backups. There is no perfect backup plan that suits every situation. The plan you adopt will depend upon

- Your hardware configuration, such as the number and type of tape backup equipment you use and the way it is implemented on your network. Do you have a single centralized tape library unit or many small tape drive units?
- The size of your Exchange database files: the larger the files, the longer it takes to back them up. Windows NT Backup can back up Exchange database files at speeds up to 30 GB/hour. Remember that Exchange

Server 5.5 Enterprise Edition can have databases that are larger than the 16-GB limit of earlier versions, all the way up to the terabyte range. If you have a number of smaller Exchange Servers, you can back them up more quickly, but they require a tape drive for each server. If you have a humongous Exchange Server, you will need an expensive tape library unit to back it up and it may take many hours to do a normal (full) backup. And always remember: *The longer it takes to back up your Exchange Servers, the longer it will take to restore them after a disaster!*

- Your degree of concern for the integrity of the information you want to back up. Do you feel safe using a combination of normal and incremental backups, or do you feel you need to use only normal backups? Do you want to keep an extra copy offsite for each backup?

Some examples of typical backup plans are as follows:

- *Plan 1: Daily Normal*

  Monday: Normal

  Tuesday: Normal

  Wednesday: Normal

  Thursday: Normal

  Friday: Normal

  Saturday: Normal

  Sunday: Normal
- *Plan 2: Alternating Normal / Incremental*

  Monday: Normal

  Tuesday: Incremental

  Wednesday: Normal

  Thursday: Incremental

  Friday: Normal

  Saturday: Incremental

  Sunday: Normal
- *Plan 3: Single Normal, Then Incremental*

  Monday: Normal

  Tuesday: Incremental

  Wednesday: Incremental

  Thursday: Incremental

  Friday: Incremental

Saturday: Incremental

Sunday: Normal

In any of the plans above, you could replace all the Incrementals with Differential backups (usually it's not a good idea to mix Incremental and Differential backups in a single plan). Additionally, you'll probably want to archive the Sunday Normal backup tape offsite for extra protection.

The advantages of Plan 1 are that a restore only requires one tape, transaction logs are cleared out each day, and circular logging can be left enabled, if desired. The disadvantages are that this method requires the most tape and usually requires that tapes be swapped each day. It also affects the performance of the server for the longest interval of time.

Scheduling Backups

To schedule online backups using `ntbackup.exe` (Windows NT Backup), you can use either

- The command-line scheduler utility called `at.exe`, which is included with Windows NT
- The GUI version of the above utility called `winat.exe`, which is found in the Windows NT Server 4.0 Resource Kit

Both of these utilities make use of the Schedule service on Windows NT. For the syntax of the `at.exe` command, type `at /?` at the command prompt. For the syntax of `winat.exe`, see the Resource Kit documentation. The general procedure for scheduling online backups is as follows:

- Use Services in the Control Panel to open the Startup properties for the Schedule service. Assign the service a user account that belongs to the Backup Operators local group on the server (see Figure 20-2). (When you create this account, give it a secure password and make sure that this account is assigned the Admin role for the Organization, Site, and Configuration containers that contain the Exchange Servers you want to back up.) Configure the Schedule service for Automatic startup, close the Service box, and start the service by clicking on the Start button.
- Create a batch file to perform the online backup. A sample batch file that could back up the Directory Service (DS) and Information Store (IS) databases on Exchange Server MICKEY might be as follows for performing a normal backup:

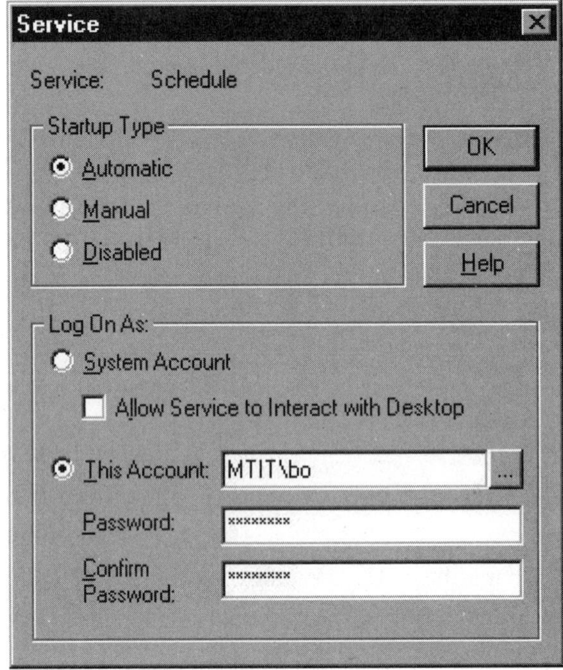

Figure 20-2 Assigning a backup account to the Schedule service.

```
rem BACKUP.BAT backs up the DS and IS on MICKEY

ntbackup DS \\MICKEY IS \\MICKEY /v /d "MICKEY IS-DS"

/b /t Normal /l c:\winnt\backup.log /e

exit
```

Information on the command-line parameters for Windows NT backup is included in the next section below. Make sure that the lines of your batch file do not exceed 256 characters in length.

Use `at.exe` or `winat.exe` to schedule the backup as desired.

Task Scheduler Service

If you have installed Internet Explorer 4.0 or higher on your Windows NT Server before installing Exchange, it replaces the Schedule service with the Task Scheduler service. Unfortunately, this can cause problems when attempting to perform backups using the methods shown in this chapter. To remove the Task Scheduler service from a machine and replace it with the original Scheduler service, see the article Q196731 entitled "Application That Requires Schedule Service Fails" in the Microsoft Knowledge Base.

Windows NT Backup Command-Line Switches

This section provides a brief summary of the switches and options that can be used with `ntbackup.exe` when running Windows NT Backup from the command line or from batch files (see above). For more information on using this utility, see any good book on Windows NT Server. Here is the general syntax for the utility:

```
ntbackup operation path [/a][/v][/r][/d text][/b][/hc:{on | off}]
[/t{option}][/l filename][/e][/tape:{n}]
```

Here's a description of the parameters:

- `operation` specifies the operation, which can be `backup` or `eject`.
- `path` specifies the paths of directories you want to back up. To back up Exchange Server database files, specify the files and the name of the server using the format

  ```
  DS \\SERVER IS \\SERVER
  ```

  where `SERVER` is the name of the Exchange Server where you want to back up the database files. Here `DS` indicates the directory service, while `IS` indicates the information store.
- `/a` indicates that backup sets are to be appended after the last backup set on the tape. If `/a` is not used, Windows NT Backup overwrites previous data on the tape.
- `/v` verifies the backup operation.
- `/r` restricts access.
- `/d` *text* provides a text label of the backup contents.
- `/b` indicates that the local Windows NT registry should be backed up.
- `/hc:on` or `/hc:off` turns hardware compression on or off.
- `/t {option}` indicates the type of backup to perform, which can include any of the following:

  ```
  Normal
  Copy
  Incremental
  Differential
  ```

  Note that the daily option is not available for backing up Exchange Server database files.

- `/l` *filename* indicates the name of the backup log file created during backup.
- `/e` indicates that only exceptions are included in the backup log file.
- `/tape:{n}` indicates the tape drive where the the files should be backed up (`n` ranges from 0 to 9).

Offline Backups

The key information in an online backup using Windows NT includes the directory database file (`dir.edb`), the IS database files (`pub.edb` and `priv.edb`), and their associated transaction logs and patch files. In addition, the Windows NT registry on the machine is backed up. However, you may want to periodically back up other areas that may require offline backups to be performed. This includes

- The Exchange executable and configuration files located in the `\exchsrvr` directory and its subdirectories
- User mail files like `*.pst`, `*.ost`, and `*.pab` files, which can be stored either on client machines (bad) or centrally located file servers (good)

Although your regular Exchange backups should be online ones, you should also perform offline backups from time to time to cover these key directories and files. To perform an offline backup, you must first stop Exchange services on the machine, do the backup, and finally restart the services. These steps must be included in any batch file you want to run for performing offline backups as well. Note that stopping and starting Exchange services needs to be done in a certain order because of dependencies between the services. The following batch file can be used as a model for creating a batch file for offline backups:

```
rem BACKUP.BAT for performing offline backups
rem
rem stopping Exchange services...
net stop MSExchangeMSMI
net stop MSExchangePCMTA
net stop MSExchangeFB
net stop MSExchangeDX
net stop MSExchangeIMC
net stop MSExchangeMTA
net stop MSExchangeIS
net stop MSExchangeDS
net stop MSExchangeSA
rem
rem insert ntbackup statements here
```

```
rem
rem starting Exchange services...
net start MSExchangeSA
net start MSExchangeDS
net start MSExchangeIS
net start MSExchangeMTA
net start MSExchangeIMC
net start MSExchangeDX
net start MSExchangeFB
net start MSExchangePCMTA
net start MSExchangeMSMI
```

Command-Line Maintenance Utilities

Exchange includes several command-line utilities that can be used for the maintenance and repair of the various Exchange database files and other components. These utilities should be used with care and in some circumstances should be run only in consultation with the Microsoft technical support staff, as they can cause irreparable damage to your Exchange database files, resulting in loss of data or even worse. What we're going to do in this chapter is summarize the use of these utilities and provide some examples and tips for their proper use.

eseutil

The `eseutil` utility enables you to check the integrity, to defragment, and to repair the IS and directory databases. The utility is found in the `\system32` system directory on an Exchange Server. Note that you must stop the Exchange services on a machine before running this utility; in other words, `eseutil` is an *offline* database maintenance utility. The `eseutil` utility is only included with Exchange 5.5. and replaces the earlier `edbutil` utility, which was used with Exchange Server 5.0 and earlier.

The `eseutil` utility can be dangerous to use and is therefore generally intended to be used in consultation with Microsoft technical support. Before using this utility, you should *always* back up your Exchange databases in case the utility causes corruption of Exchange database files.

Full syntax for `eseutil` can be found by typing `eseutil /?` at the command prompt. We'll only look at a few specific uses here:

- `Eseutil /g`
  This form is used when you check the integrity of an Exchange database by searching for records that are damaged or unreadable. This is safe to run, as it does not attempt to fix any problems that it finds. Exchange databases can be checked at a rate of about 10 GB/hour, so make sure you plan sufficient downtime for your server when running this utility.
- `Eseutil /r`
  This form performs a recovery of an Exchange database, a process also known as a *soft repair* (in contrast to the hard repair done using `eseutil /p`). A recovery brings all the files that are associated with the database to a consistent state. If the DS/IS Consistency Adjuster tool from Exchange Administrator is run and returns an error (see the Advanced tab of your Server container property sheet), try running `eseutil /r` to recover the database and then run the Consistency Adjuster again.
- `Eseutil /d`
  This form is used to compact database files to reduce the size of the files and thereby free up disk space. Running the `eseutil /d` command automatically causes a recovery (`eseutil /r`) to be performed first before compaction is done. Exchange automatically performs its own maintenance of its database files between 1 A.M. and 6 A.M., checking them, defragmenting them, and so on. However, you may want to run `eseutil /d` every few months or so to make your database more efficient. Exchange database files can be compacted at a rate of about five GB/hour.
- `Eseutil /p`
  This form is used to repair a damaged database. This is called a *hard repair* and should only be performed as a last resort in consultation with Microsoft support staff, as it can result in loss of data. `Eseutil /p` is generally only used when a backup of your Exchange database files is unavailable. *Make sure you have backed up your database files before running this utility!* After running `eseutil /p` you also need to run `isinteg -fix` as well (see below). The `eseutil /p` command works in three steps: first, it does an integrity check (like `eseutil /g`) of the database, then it scans the database for tables that contain corrupt pages, and finally it tries to repair those tables, usually by deleting the bad pages (which is where data can get lost). Make sure you have enough free disk space equal to 25 percent or more of the database files before you attempt to use `eseutil /p` to repair them. The first two steps are performed at about 10 GB/hour, while the third step may take more time, depending upon the extent of damage encountered.

Walkthrough: Using eseutil

Let's see what happens when we run the `eseutil` utility on an Exchange Server. We'll work with the Exchange private information store database on MICKEY (`priv.edb`) in this example, which is signified by the switches `/ispriv` and `/is` in our `eseutil` commands. Go to server MICKEY and log on as Administrator. Start by deleting some mailboxes on MICKEY so that unused space is created within the private information store database. We'll get rid of this space as part of this walkthrough by compacting the database.

Now open the Services utility in the Control Panel and stop the Microsoft Exchange System Attendant service. You are informed that stopping this service will cause all other Exchange services to stop as well (see Figure 20-3). Click OK to stop all Exchange services on MICKEY.

Then open a command prompt and type the following four commands. Wait for each to finish and observe the screen output before going on to the next command:

- `eseutil /g /ispriv`

  This checks the integrity of the private IS database. The `/v` switch can provide verbose output, while the `/x` switch can be give detailed error

Figure 20-3
Stopping Exchange services.

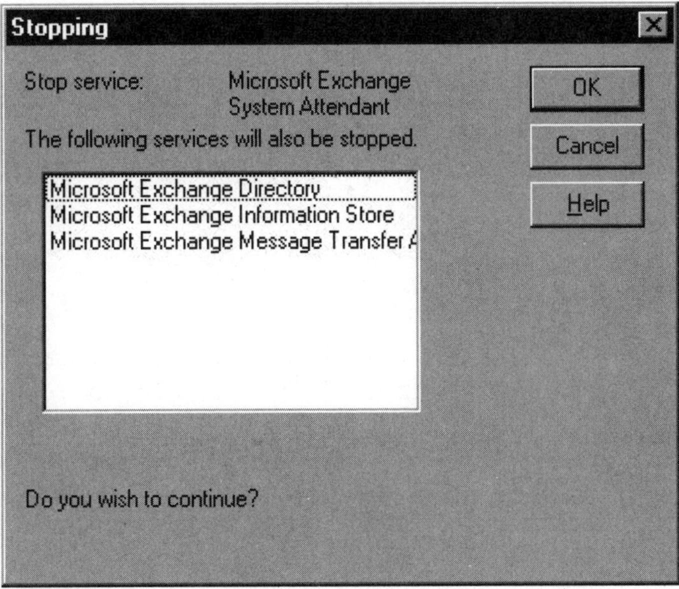

messages, should any errors occur. Here's the output we get when we run this on MICKEY:

```
C:\>cd winnt\system32

C:\WINNT\system32>eseutil /g /ispriv

Microsoft(R) Windows NT(TM) Server Database Utilities
Version 5.5
Copyright (C) Microsoft Corporation 1991-1998.  All Rights
Reserved.

Initiating INTEGRITY mode...
        Database: C:\exchsrvr\MDBDATA\PRIV.EDB
  Temp. Database: INTEG.EDB

checking database integrity

                    Scanning Status  ( % complete )

          0    10   20   30   40   50   60   70   80   90
100
          |—|—|—|—|—|—|—|—|—|—|

...................................................

integrity check completed.
Operation completed successfully in 13.369 seconds.
```

- `eseutil /r /is`

  This performs a soft repair (recovery) on the IS databases. Here is the screen output we get when we run this command on MICKEY:

```
C:\WINNT\system32>eseutil /r /is

Microsoft(R) Windows NT(TM) Server Database Utilities
Version 5.5
Copyright (C) Microsoft Corporation 1991-1998.  All Rights
Reserved.

Initiating RECOVERY mode...
       Log files: C:\exchsrvr\MDBDATA
    System files: C:\exchsrvr\MDBDATA

Performing soft recovery...

Operation completed successfully in 5.17 seconds.
```

- `eseutil /d /ispriv`

  This first performs a soft repair on the private IS database and then defragments the database. Here is the output from MICKEY:

```
C:\WINNT\system32>eseutil /d /ispriv
```

```
Microsoft(R) Windows NT(TM) Server Database Utilities
Version 5.5
Copyright (C) Microsoft Corporation 1991-1998.  All Rights
Reserved.

Initiating DEFRAGMENTATION mode...
        Database: C:\exchsrvr\MDBDATA\PRIV.EDB
       Log files: C:\exchsrvr\MDBDATA
    System files: C:\exchsrvr\MDBDATA
  Temp. Database: TEMPDFRG.EDB

                Defragmentation Status  ( % complete )

        0    10   20   30   40   50   60   70   80   90  100
          |—|—|—|—|—|—|—|—|—|—|

...................................................

Note:
  It is recommended that you immediately perform a full
backup
  of this database. If you restore a backup made before the
  defragmentation, the database will be rolled back to the
state
  it was in at the time of that backup.

Operation completed successfully in 23.664 seconds.
```

- `eseutil /p /ispriv /v /x`

  This performs a hard repair on the private IS database on MICKEY. Just for fun, we'll run it in verbose mode. The dialog box in Figure 20-4 is displayed at this point.

  Here is the results of running `eseutil /p /ispriv /v /x` on MICKEY:

```
C:\WINNT\system32>eseutil /p /ispriv /v /x

Microsoft(R) Windows NT(TM) Server Database Utilities
Version 5.5
Copyright (C) Microsoft Corporation 1991-1998.  All Rights
Reserved.
```

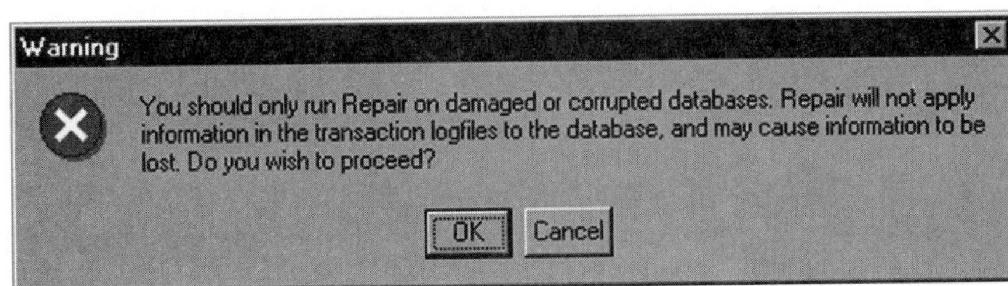
Warning
You should only run Repair on damaged or corrupted databases. Repair will not apply information in the transaction logfiles to the database, and may cause information to be lost. Do you wish to proceed?
OK
Cancel

Figure 20-4
Running `eseutil /p`.

```
Initiating REPAIR mode...
        Database: C:\exchsrvr\MDBDATA\PRIV.EDB
  Temp. Database: REPAIR.EDB
got 1331 buffers
checking database header
forcing database to consistent state

checking database integrity

                    Scanning Status  ( % complete )

     0    10   20   30   40   50   60   70   80   90  100
     |----|----|----|----|----|----|----|----|----|----|
           checking SystemRoot
           SystemRoot (OE)
          SystemRoot (AE)
    checking system table
           MSysObjectsShadow
...        MSysObjects
...        Name
..         RootObjects
           rebuilding and comparing indexes
    checking table "1-126" (54)
           checking data
           checking index "MsgFolderIndex7" (58)
           checking index "RuleMsgFolderIndex" (57)
           checking index "MsgFolderIndexPtagDeletedOn" (56)
           checking index "?T668f+B67aa-Te06+Q674a" (55)
           rebuilding and comparing indexes
    checking table "1-127" (59)
           checking data
           checking index "MsgFolderIndex7" (62)
           checking index "RuleMsgFolderIndex" (61)
           checking index "MsgFolderIndexPtagDeletedOn" (60)
           rebuilding and comparing indexes
    checking table "1-175E" (63)
           checking data
           checking index "MsgFolderIndex7" (68)
           checking index "RuleMsgFolderIndex" (67)
           checking index "MsgFolderIndexPtagDeletedOn" (66)
           checking index "?T668f+B67aa-Te06+Q674a" (65)
           checking index "?T668f+B67aa+Te06+Q674a" (64)
           rebuilding and comparing indexes
    checking table "1-175F" (69)
           checking data
           checking index "MsgFolderIndex7" (72)
           checking index "RuleMsgFolderIndex" (71)
           checking index "MsgFolderIndexPtagDeletedOn" (70)
           rebuilding and comparing indexes
    checking table "1-1760" (73)
           checking data
           checking index "MsgFolderIndex7" (76)
           checking index "RuleMsgFolderIndex" (75)
           checking index "MsgFolderIndexPtagDeletedOn" (74)
           rebuilding and comparing indexes
    checking table "1-1761" (77)
           checking data
           checking index "MsgFolderIndex7" (80)
           checking index "RuleMsgFolderIndex" (79)
```

```
            checking index "MsgFolderIndexPtagDeletedOn" (78)
            rebuilding and comparing indexes
    checking table "1-24" (81)
            checking data
            rebuilding and comparing indexes
    checking table "1-25" (82)
            checking data
            checking index "MsgFolderIndex7" (85)
            checking index "RuleMsgFolderIndex" (84)
            checking index "MsgFolderIndexPtagDeletedOn" (83)
            rebuilding and comparing indexes
    checking table "1-26" (86)
            checking data
            checking index "MsgFolderIndex7" (89)
            checking index "RuleMsgFolderIndex" (88)
            checking index "MsgFolderIndexPtagDeletedOn" (87)
            rebuilding and comparing indexes
    checking table "1-276C" (90)
            checking data
            checking index "MsgFolderIndex7" (95)
            checking index "RuleMsgFolderIndex" (94)
            checking index "MsgFolderIndexPtagDeletedOn" (93)
            checking index "?T668f+B67aa+T39+Q674a" (92)
            checking index "?T668f+B67aa-Te06+Q674a" (91)
            rebuilding and comparing indexes
    checking table "1-276D" (96)
            checking data
            checking index "MsgFolderIndex7" (99)
            checking index "RuleMsgFolderIndex" (98)
            checking index "MsgFolderIndexPtagDeletedOn" (97)
            rebuilding and comparing indexes
    checking table "1-3F5" (100)
            checking data
            checking index "MsgFolderIndex7" (106)
            checking index "RuleMsgFolderIndex" (105)
            checking index "MsgFolderIndexPtagDeletedOn" (104)
            checking index "?T668f+B67aa-Te06+Q674a" (103)
               checking index "?T668f+B67aa+Te06+Q674a" (102)
            checking index "?T668f+B67aa-S6800+Q674a 409" (101)
            rebuilding and comparing indexes
    checking table "1-3F6" (107)
            checking data
            checking index "MsgFolderIndex7" (111)
            checking index "RuleMsgFolderIndex" (110)
            checking index "MsgFolderIndexPtagDeletedOn" (109)
            checking index "?T668f+B67aa-Te06+Q674a" (108)
            rebuilding and comparing indexes
    checking table "1-3F7" (112)
            checking data
.......     checking index "MsgFolderIndex7" (118)
            checking index "RuleMsgFolderIndex" (117)
            checking index "MsgFolderIndexPtagDeletedOn" (116)
           checking index "?T668f+B67aa-Te06+Q674a" (115)
           checking index "?T668f+B67aa-T39-Te06+Q674a" (114)
           checking index "?T668f+B67aa+T39+Q674a" (113)
            rebuilding and comparing indexes
    checking table "1-3F8" (119)
            checking data
.           checking index "MsgFolderIndex7" (124)
```

```
        checking index "RuleMsgFolderIndex" (123)
        checking index "MsgFolderIndexPtagDeletedOn" (122)
        checking index "?T668f+B67aa-Te06+Q674a" (121)
        checking index "*T668f+B67aa-Te06+Q674a" (120)
        rebuilding and comparing indexes
checking table "1-3FA" (125)
        checking data
        checking index "MsgFolderIndex7" (129)
        checking index "RuleMsgFolderIndex" (128)
        checking index "MsgFolderIndexPtagDeletedOn" (127)
        checking index "?T668f+B67aa-Te06+Q674a" (126)
        rebuilding and comparing indexes
checking table "1-40F" (130)
        checking data
        checking index "MsgFolderIndex7" (134)
        checking index "RuleMsgFolderIndex" (133)
        checking index "MsgFolderIndexPtagDeletedOn" (132)
        checking index "?T668f+MQ67a6" (131)
        rebuilding and comparing indexes
checking table "1-410" (135)
        checking data
        checking index "MsgFolderIndex7" (139)
        checking index "RuleMsgFolderIndex" (138)
        checking index "MsgFolderIndexPtagDeletedOn" (137)
        checking index "?T668f+B67aa-Te06+Q674a" (136)
        rebuilding and comparing indexes
checking table "1-411" (140)
        checking data
        checking index "MsgFolderIndex7" (144)
        checking index "RuleMsgFolderIndex" (143)
        checking index "MsgFolderIndexPtagDeletedOn" (142)
        checking index "?T668f+B67aa-Te06+Q674a" (141)
        rebuilding and comparing indexes
checking table "1-412" (145)
        checking data
        checking index "MsgFolderIndex7" (149)
        checking index "RuleMsgFolderIndex" (148)
        checking index "MsgFolderIndexPtagDeletedOn" (147)
        checking index "?T668f+B67aa-Te06+Q674a" (146)
        rebuilding and comparing indexes
checking table "1-413" (150)
        checking data
        checking index "MsgFolderIndex7" (154)
        checking index "RuleMsgFolderIndex" (153)
        checking index "MsgFolderIndexPtagDeletedOn" (152)
        checking index "?T668f+B67aa-Te06+Q674a" (151)
        rebuilding and comparing indexes
checking table "1-415" (155)
        checking data
        checking index "MsgFolderIndex7" (158)
        checking index "RuleMsgFolderIndex" (157)
        checking index "MsgFolderIndexPtagDeletedOn" (156)
        rebuilding and comparing indexes
checking table "1-416" (159)
        checking data
        checking index "MsgFolderIndex7" (162)
        checking index "RuleMsgFolderIndex" (161)
        checking index "MsgFolderIndexPtagDeletedOn" (160)
        rebuilding and comparing indexes
```

```
checking table "1-424" (163)
       checking data
       checking index "MsgFolderIndex7" (166)
       checking index "RuleMsgFolderIndex" (165)
       checking index "MsgFolderIndexPtagDeletedOn" (164)
       rebuilding and comparing indexes
checking table "ACLList" (6)
       checking data
       checking index "ACLList2" (7)
       rebuilding and comparing indexes
checking table "ACLMember" (8)
       checking data
       checking index "ACLMember2" (9)
       rebuilding and comparing indexes
checking table "DeletedAttachments" (10)
       checking data
       rebuilding and comparing indexes
checking table "DeletedFolders" (11)
       checking data
       rebuilding and comparing indexes
checking table "DeletedMessages" (12)
       checking data
       rebuilding and comparing indexes
checking table "DeliveredTo" (13)
       checking data
       checking index "DeliveredTo2" (14)
       rebuilding and comparing indexes
checking table "Folder Tombstone" (15)
       checking data
       checking index "FolderTombstoneIndex2" (17)
       checking index "FolderTombstoneIndex3" (16)
       rebuilding and comparing indexes
checking table "Folders" (18)
       checking data
........       checking long value tree (27)
       checking index "FoldersIndex5" (26)
       checking index "FoldersIndex6" (25)
       checking index "FoldersIndex7" (24)
       checking index "FoldersIndex8" (23)
       checking index "FoldersIndex10" (22)
       checking index "FoldersIndex13" (21)
       checking index "?T668f+Q6749+S3001+Q6748 409" (20)
       checking index "*T668f+Q6749+S3001+Q6748 409" (19)
       rebuilding and comparing indexes
checking table "Global" (28)
       checking data
       rebuilding and comparing indexes
checking table "IndexAge" (29)
       checking data
       rebuilding and comparing indexes
checking table "Mailbox" (30)
       checking data
       checking index "MailboxIndex2" (31)
       rebuilding and comparing indexes
checking table "Message Tombstone" (32)
       checking data
       rebuilding and comparing indexes
checking table "Msg" (33)
       checking data
```

```
....        rebuilding and comparing indexes
    checking table "MsgFolderTemplate" (34)
            checking data
            rebuilding and comparing indexes
    checking table "NamedProps" (35)
            checking data
.           checking index "NamedPropsIndex2" (38)
            checking index "NamedPropsIndex3" (37)
.           checking index "NamedPropsIndex4" (36)
            rebuilding and comparing indexes
    checking table "NeedRN" (39)
            checking data
            rebuilding and comparing indexes
    checking table "OofHistory" (40)
            checking data
            checking index "OofHistoryIndex" (41)
            rebuilding and comparing indexes
    checking table "PerfMonRowsInTables" (42)
            checking data
            rebuilding and comparing indexes
    checking table "PerUserRead" (43)
            checking data
            checking index "PerUserReadIndex2" (44)
            rebuilding and comparing indexes
    checking table "ReceiveFolder" (45)
            checking data
            rebuilding and comparing indexes
    checking table "ReplidMap" (46)
            checking data
            checking index "ReplidMap2" (47)
            rebuilding and comparing indexes
    checking table "Search Queue" (48)
            checking data
            checking index "SearchQueueIndex1" (49)
            rebuilding and comparing indexes
    checking table "Synchronization table" (50)
            checking data
            checking index "SyncTableIndex1" (51)
            rebuilding and comparing indexes
    checking table "TimedEvents" (52)
            checking data
            checking index "TimedEvents2" (53)
            rebuilding and comparing indexes
....................


integrity check completed.
Warning:
  You MUST delete the logfiles for this database

Note:
  It is recommended that you immediately perform a full
backup
  of this database. If you restore a backup made before the
  repair, the database will be rolled back to the state
  it was in at the time of that backup.

Operation completed successfully in 13.329 seconds.
```

Leave the Exchange services stopped on MICKEY, as we need to run `isinteg -fix` after running `eseutil /p`. We'll cover this in the walkthrough in the next section. Note also the message at the end of the output of running `eseutil /p` that `You MUST delete the logfiles for this database`. We'll do that in the next walkthrough as well.

isinteg

This `isinteg` utility is the Microsoft Exchange IS Integrity Checker and can be used to locate and fix problems with the private and public IS databases. What's the difference between fixing the information using `isinteg -fix` described below versus fixing it with `eseutil /p` described above? The difference is that `eseutil /p` works at a low level, fixing bad pages in database tables, while `isinteg` works at a higher level, fixing things like unreferenced objects, incorrect reference counts, and errors in database tables. If you ever have to run `eseutil /p` for some reason, make sure you run `isinteg -fix` afterwards as well. Make sure, however, that you have backed up the Exchange databases prior to running either of these utilities.

The `isinteg` utility is found in the `\exchsrvr\bin` directory on an Exchange Server. Note that you must stop the Exchange services on a machine before running this utility. In other words, `isinteg` is an *offline* database maintenance utility.

The full syntax for `isinteg` can be found by typing `isinteg /?` at the command prompt (provided the current directory is `\exchsrvr\bin`). We'll only look at a few specific uses here. For these examples, the option `-pri` signifies that the utility will be run on the private information store, while the option `-pub` signifies the public information store:

- `Isinteg -test` ***testname*, *testname*, . . .**

  This form is used to run various database integrity tests on the IS databases. The possible tests that you can perform are listed in Table 20-1. Note that the test named `alltests` runs all `isinteg` tests. This is the usual test to run, and if you add the `-fix` option to it, then repairs will be attempted on any errors that are found as a result of running the tests. These repairs that are done will be written to a log file called `isinteg.pri` when the private IS is tested and `isinteg.pub` if the public IS is tested. Additional options you can use with this command are `-detailed`, which performs additional detailed tests; `-verbose`, which provides verbose output of the results for each test; and others that you can display by running `isinteg /?` from the command line. Microsoft does not recommend running `isinteg -test` with the `-fix` option for regular database maintenance but instead should be used in consultation with Microsoft technical support.

- `Isinteg -dump`

  This form enables you to dump the properties of the folder table for the specified database. The output is verbose and cryptic and is usually used in collaboration with Microsoft technical support to troubleshoot IS problems.

- `Isinteg -patch`

  This form is necessary to restart the Exchange IS service after an offline restore has been performed on the IS databases. Be sure to run `isinteg -patch` after the offline restore and prior to attempting to start the IS service (unless you only have one Exchange Server in your entire organization, in which case running `isinteg -patch` is unnecessary). Note that the Exchange Directory service must be running in order to run `isinteg -patch`.

Table 20-1

Description of Isinteg Tests.

Testname	Explanation
`aclitemref`	Verifies all reference counts for access control list items.
`acllist`	Examines all folders and validates their access control lists.
`acllistref`	Verifies all access control list reference counts.
`allacltests`	Runs a combination of the `acllist`, `acllistref`, and `aclitemref` tests.
`allfoldertests`	Runs a combination of the `folder`, `fldsub`, and `search` tests.
`alltests`	Runs all `isinteg` tests. Use this test when running the `-fix` option.
`artidx`	Checks the consistency of the NNTP article index. This test can only be run on the public IS.
`attach`	Validates the properties of all message attachments.
`attachref`	Validates all attachment reference counts.
`deleteextracolumns`	Deletes cached indexes and some extra columns.
`delfld`	Checks deleted folders, validates properties, and accumulates reference counts.
`dumpsterref`	Runs a combination of the `msgref` and `msgsoftref` tests. Checks the item count and size of the recoverable items available for Deleted Item Recovery.

Testname	Explanation
dumpsterprops	Runs the dumpsterref test and also validates the presence of required columns in the folder table.
fldrcv (priv.edb only)	Validates the counts of system folders such as Restrictions, Categorization, Inbox, Outbox, SentMail, Deleted Items, Finder, Views, Common Views, Schedule, and ShortCuts.
fldsub	Validates the counts of child folders and the number of child folders available for Deleted Item Recovery.
folder	Checks folder tables and validates properties. Checks message tables, validates properties, and accumulates reference counts.
mailbox	Checks folders, deleted folders, and tables for each mailbox. Validates properties, system folders (Inbox, Outbox, Sent Items, Deleted Items, and so on) in the folder table and checks their respective sizes. This test can only be run on the private IS.
message	Checks message tables and validates message table properties.
morefld	Tests all search links. When running the -fix option, deletes all cached categorization and restriction tables.
msgref	Validates message reference counts in all messages.
msgsoftref	Validates message reference counts in messages marked for Deleted Item Recovery.
namedprop	Checks the folder, message, and attachment tables and validates the named properties.
newsfeed	Validates all newsfeed table properties, including permissions. This test can only be run on the public IS.
newsfeedref	Validates all newsfeed reference counts. This test can only be run on the public IS.
oofhist	Validates out-of-office history information for all users. This test can only be run on the private IS.
peruser	Validates per user read/unread information.
rcvfld	Cross-checks receive folders against the folder table. This test can only be run on the private IS.
rowcounts	Validates the number of rows for all database tables.
search	Validates all search links.
timedev	Counts all timed events (maintenance, periodic tasks, and so on).

Walkthrough: Using isinteg

We're picking up where we left off with the previous walkthrough. We've stopped our Exchange services on MICKEY and have run `eseutil /p` from a command prompt. Now let's run the following command:

```
isinteg -pri -fix -test alltests
```

The following is the output of this command:

```
C:\>cd exchsrvr\bin

C:\exchsrvr\bin>isinteg -pri -fix -test alltests
Microsoft Exchange Information Store Integrity Checker
v5.5.2448.0
Copyright (c) 1986-1997 Microsoft Corp.   All rights
reserved.

WARNING!!! You have chosen to run all of the tests. This may
take a long time.

It is highly recommended that you select individual tests to
save time.
Please see the ISINTEG.DOC located on the Exchange Server
5.5 CD in the
\SERVER\SUPPORT\UTILS directory for additional information.

ISINTEG /? will display the list of individual tests.

<<<Press "y" to continue to do all tests, any other key to
quit>>> =>y

Started:    07/19/99 15:48:32
Server name: MICKEY
Store path: C:\exchsrvr\MDBDATA\PRIV.EDB
Store size: 2105344 bytes
Output log: isinteg.pri
Check mode: check and fix
Options: -pri -fix -test alltests

The Information Store has not been shut down clean.
Hence enabling the Row Count/Dumpster Count test.
You may also specify -test rowcounts (or) -test dumpsterref
to run these
tests
Starting test 1 of 22, 'Categorization Tables'
Finished Categorization Tables. Time: 0h:0m:0s
Starting test 2 of 22, 'Restriction Tables'
Finished Restriction Tables. Time: 0h:0m:0s
Starting test 3 of 22, 'Search Folder Links'
Finished Search Folder Links. Time: 0h:0m:0s
Starting test 4 of 22, 'Global'
Finished Global, number of rows = 1. Time: 0h:0m:0s
Starting test 5 of 22, 'Delivered To'
Finished Delivered To, number of rows = 16. Time: 0h:0m:0s
```

```
Starting test 6 of 22, 'Search Queue'
Finished Search Queue. Time: 0h:0m:0s
Starting test 7 of 22, 'Timed Events'
Finished Timed Events. Time: 0h:0m:0s
Starting test 8 of 22, 'reference table construction'
Finished reference table construction. Time: 0h:0m:0s
Starting test 9 of 22, 'Folder'
Finished Folder, number of rows = 86. Time: 0h:0m:5s
Starting test 10 of 22, 'Deleted Folders'
Finished Deleted Folders. Time: 0h:0m:0s
Starting test 11 of 22, 'Message'
Finished Message, number of rows = 71. Time: 0h:0m:0s
Starting test 12 of 22, 'Attachment'
Finished Attachment. Time: 0h:0m:0s
Starting test 13 of 22, 'Mailbox'
Finished Mailbox, number of rows = 5. Time: 0h:0m:0s
Starting test 14 of 22, 'Receive Folder'
Finished Receive Folder, number of rows = 20. Time: 0h:0m:0s
Starting test 15 of 22, 'ACL List'
Finished ACL List. Time: 0h:0m:0s
Starting test 16 of 22, 'ACL Member'
Finished ACL Member, number of rows = 2. Time: 0h:0m:0s
Starting test 17 of 22, 'Oof History'
Finished Oof History. Time: 0h:0m:0s
Starting test 18 of 22, 'Per-User Read'
Finished Per-User Read, number of rows = 4. Time: 0h:0m:0s
Starting test 19 of 22, 'special folders'
Finished special folders. Time: 0h:0m:0s
Starting test 20 of 22, 'Message Tombstone'
Finished Message Tombstone, number of rows = 2. Time:
0h:0m:0s
Starting test 21 of 22, 'Folder Tombstone'
Finished Folder Tombstone. Time: 0h:0m:0s
Starting test 22 of 22, 'reference count verification'
Finished reference count verification. Time: 0h:0m:1s
Starting test 23 of 22, 'Row Count/Dumpster Count'
Finished Row Count/Dumpster Count. Time: 0h:0m:0s, number of
warnings = 2, number of fixes = 1

. . . . . SUMMARY . . . . .
Total number of tests : 22
Total number of warnings : 2
Total number of errors : 0
Total number of fixes : 1
Total time : 0h:0m:8s
C:\exchsrvr\bin>
```

The screen output is also written to the log file `isinteg.pri`, which is located in the `\exchsrvr\bin` directory.

Just for fun, let's also run the following command:

```
Isinteg -dump -pri -l dumpfile.txt
```

Here the `-l` option specifies the name of the log file that the dump is performed on as having the name `dumpfile.txt`. Here is a small portion of the output of this command:

```
C:\exchsrvr\bin>isinteg -dump -pri -l logg.txt
Microsoft Exchange Information Store Integrity Checker
v5.5.2448.0
Copyright (c) 1986-1997 Microsoft Corp.    All rights
reserved.
Started:     07/19/99 16:03:55
Server name: MICKEY
Store path: C:\exchsrvr\MDBDATA\PRIV.EDB
Store size: 2105344 bytes
Output log: logg.txt
Check mode: check only
Options: -dump -pri -l logg.txt

Dump of the Index Age table

[1] Index Name=?T668f+B67aa+T39+Q674a
       FID=0001-0000000003F7
       Index Age= 7/13/1999 08:59:29
[2] Index Name=?T668f+B67aa+T39+Q674a
       FID=0001-00000000276C
       Index Age= 7/19/1999 17:58:06
[3] Index Name=?T668f+B67aa+T800d+Q674a
       FID=0001-000000000427
       Index Age= 7/18/1999 18:09:13
[4] Index Name=?T668f+B67aa+T800d+Q674a
       FID=0001-000000000428
       Index Age= 7/11/1999 20:24:26
[5] Index Name=?T668f+B67aa+Te06+Q674a
       FID=0001-0000000003F5
       Index Age= 7/18/1999 19:01:27
[6] Index Name=?T668f+B67aa+Te06+Q674a
       FID=0001-00000000175E
       Index Age= 7/11/1999 20:26:19
[7] Index Name=?T668f+B67aa-S6800+Q674a 409
       FID=0001-0000000003F5
       Index Age= 7/18/1999 19:01:45
[8] Index Name=?T668f+B67aa-S6800+Q674a 409
       FID=0001-0000000003FB
       Index Age= 7/18/1999 19:01:45
[9] Index Name=?T668f+B67aa-T3007+Q674a
       FID=0001-000000004C74
       Index Age= 7/11/1999 19:16:37
[10] Index Name=?T668f+B67aa-T39-Te06+Q674a
       FID=0001-0000000003F7
       Index Age= 7/16/1999 16:32:39
[11] Index Name=?T668f+B67aa-Te06+Q674a
       FID=0001-0000000003F5
       Index Age= 7/18/1999 18:09:05
[12] Index Name=?T668f+B67aa-Te06+Q674a
       FID=0001-0000000003F8
       Index Age= 7/11/1999 13:42:27
[13] Index Name=?T668f+B67aa-Te06+Q674a
       FID=0001-00000000175E
       Index Age= 7/11/1999 20:24:19
[14] Index Name=?T668f+MQ67a6
       FID=0001-00000000040F
       Index Age= 7/18/1999 18:09:12
[15] Index Name=?T668f+N67fe
       FID=0001-00000000040F
```

```
        Index Age= 7/18/1999 18:09:12

Table Index Age contained 15 rows

Dump of the Folder table

[1] Folder FID=0001-000000000009
        Parent FID=0000-000000000000
        Root FID=0001-000000000009
        ACL ID=0000-000000000000
        Folder Type=0
        Msg Count=0
        Msgs Unread=0
        Msgs Submitted=0
        Rcv Count=2
        Subfolders=13
        Name=
        Comment=
        Restriction=
        Search FIDs=
        Recursive FIDs=
        Search Backlinks=
        Categ FIDs=
[2] Folder FID=0001-00000000000A
        Parent FID=0001-000000000009
        Root FID=0001-000000000009
        ACL ID=0000-000000000000
        Folder Type=1
        Msg Count=0
        Msgs Unread=0
        Msgs Submitted=0
        Rcv Count=1
        Subfolders=4
        Name=Top of Information Store
        Comment=
        Restriction=
        Search FIDs=
        Recursive FIDs=
        Search Backlinks=
        Categ FIDs=

etc etc etc …

 [85] Folder FID=0001-000000002773
        Parent FID=0001-000000002768
        Root FID=0001-000000002768
        ACL ID=0000-000000000000
        Folder Type=1
        Msg Count=0
        Msgs Unread=0
        Msgs Submitted=0
        Rcv Count=1
        Subfolders=0
        Name=Schedule
        Comment=
        Restriction=
        Search FIDs=
        Recursive FIDs=
        Search Backlinks=
```

```
        Categ FIDs=
[86] Folder FID=0001-000000002774
        Parent FID=0001-000000002768
        Root FID=0001-000000002768
        ACL ID=0000-000000000000
        Folder Type=1
        Msg Count=0
        Msgs Unread=0
        Msgs Submitted=0
        Rcv Count=1
        Subfolders=0
        Name=Shortcuts
        Comment=
        Restriction=
        Search FIDs=
        Recursive FIDs=
        Search Backlinks=
        Categ FIDs=

Table Folder contained 86 rows
```

This same screen output is written to the log file `dumpfile.txt`, which is located in the `\exchsrvr\bin` directory. You can imagine how large this file could be with a really big information store.

Finally, go to the `\mdbdata` directory and delete the transaction log files (`edb`*nnnnn*`.log`) prior to restarting the Exchange services on MICKEY. Now would be a good time to perform another backup as well.

Mtacheck

This third command-line Exchange utility has to do with fixing problems with the Message Transfer Agent (MTA). The MTA uses a different type of database technology than the DS and IS databases. Instead of database files (`*.edb`), transaction logs (`edb.log`), and so on, the MTA uses a series of `*.dat` files and various other types of files located in the `\mtadata` directory (see Figure 20-5).

A problem that typically occurs with the MTA is a corrupt message blocking an MTA queue. This can result in the inability to send or receive messages, or it might even cause the Exchange MTA service to stop and refuse to be restarted using Services in the Control Panel. Running `mtacheck` removes any corrupt messages in the queues, rebuilds the queues if necessary, and tests the MTA database files for integrity. Any corrupt messages that are found are consigned to a file called `db*.dat` that is located in `\mtadata\mtacheck.out` and can be opened with a text editor like Notepad to examine the corrupt messages. Before you run `mtacheck`, stop the Exchange MTA service using Services in the Control Panel and delete the contents of `\mtadata\mtacheck.out` so you will have a clean output from the command.

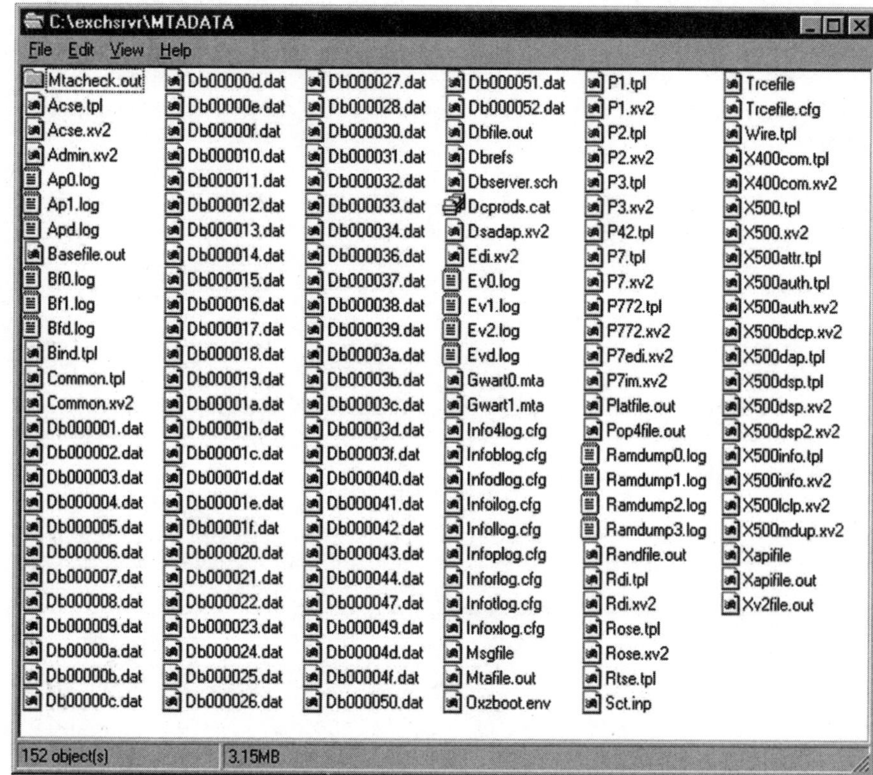

Figure 20-5
MTA database files.

Walkthrough: Using mtacheck

Begin by stopping the Exchange MTA service on MICKEY using Services in the Control Panel. Then find the `\mtadata\mtacheck.out` directory in Windows Explorer and delete any files contained within the directory. Now open a command prompt window, change the current directory to the `\exchsrvr\bin` directory, and type the following command:

```
Mtacheck /v
```

Here is the output of the command as shown within the command prompt window on MICKEY (the `/v` switch provides verbose output for the command and other switches can be displayed using `mtacheck /?`):

```
C:\>cd exchsrvr\bin

C:\exchsrvr\bin>mtacheck /v

Checking queue XAPIWRKQ (id 01000020)
```

```
Checking queue OOFINFOQ (id 01000025)

Checking queue REFDATQ (id 01000026)

Checking queue MTAWORKQ (id 01000027)

Checking queue
/O=MTIT/OU=ATLANTA/CN=CONFIGURATION/CN=CONNECTIONS/CN=MS
MAIL CON
NECTOR (MICKEY) (id 01000030)

Starting object integrity checks
  Checking object 03000002 - OK, on queue 01000026
  Checking object 0A000003 - OK, on queue 01000020
  Checking object 0B000004 - OK, on queue 01000020
  Checking object 0B000005 - OK, on queue 01000020
  Checking object 0C000006 - OK, on queue 01000020
  Checking object 0C000007 - OK, on queue 01000020
  Checking object 06000008 - OK, on queue 01000020
  Checking object 06000009 - OK, on queue 01000020
  Checking object 0600000A - OK, on queue 01000020
  Checking object 0600000B - OK, on queue 01000020
  Checking object 0600000C - OK, on queue 01000020
  Checking object 0600000D - OK, on queue 01000020
  Checking object 0600000E - OK, on queue 01000020
  Checking object 0600000F - OK, on queue 01000020
  Checking object 06000010 - OK, on queue 01000020
  Checking object 06000011 - OK, on queue 01000020
  Checking object 06000012 - OK, on queue 01000020
  Checking object 06000013 - OK, on queue 01000020
  Checking object 06000014 - OK, on queue 01000020
  Checking object 06000015 - OK, on queue 01000020
  Checking object 09000016 - OK, on queue 01000020
  Checking object 09000017 - OK, on queue 01000020
  Checking object 09000018 - OK, on queue 01000020
  Checking object 09000019 - OK, on queue 01000020
  Checking object 0900001A - OK, on queue 01000020
  Checking object 0900001B - OK, on queue 01000020
  Checking object 0600001C - OK, on queue 01000020
  Checking object 0600001D - OK, on queue 01000020
  Checking object 0600001E - OK, on queue 01000020
  Checking object 0600001F - OK, on queue 01000020
  Checking object 06000021 - OK, on queue 01000020
  Checking object 06000022 - OK, on queue 01000020
  Checking object 06000023 - OK, on queue 01000025
  Checking object 09000024 - OK, on queue 01000025

Database clean, no errors detected.
```

By the way, another way of clearing out corrupted messages from the MTA queues is to stop and then restart the Exchange MTA service. This often works, making it unnecessary to run `mtacheck` from the command line.

Disaster Recovery Tips

Let's end this chapter with a quick list of some tips to help you prepare for disaster recovery:

- Document the hardware and software configuration of each server thoroughly. This will save you a lot of time during a disaster.
- Check your Application Logs in Event Viewer each morning for any signs of present or impending problems. Use Crystal Reports or some other reporting tool to generate reports that are easier to read if you like.
- Schedule maintenance windows every month in which you can perform an offline backup for all Exchange-related files, install service packs and fixes, compact the Exchange databases using `eseutil /d`, and do other maintenance tasks on your servers.
- Tell users in advance when these scheduled maintenance times will occur, as your servers will be unavailable during these periods.
- Verify a normal backup from time to time. I mean *really* verify it by restoring your backed-up Exchange database files to a dedicated recovery server and then running `eseutil /g` on the server to check the databases.
- Keep an occasional normal backup tape offsite. What if your building burnt down?
- Check your UPS from time to time to make sure it still works!
- Use Performance Monitor to keep tabs on the size of the IS databases. Watch your disk space!
- Try running a fire drill and see what happens. Better talk to management before pulling the alarm, though!

Where Do We Go from Here?

In the next chapter, we will consider the topic of migrating users and their mail information from legacy and third-party mail systems to Exchange using the Migration Wizard.

For More Information

Some good information is contained in the *Maintenance and Troubleshooting* manual for Exchange, which is included in Exchange Books Online and can be obtained from Microsoft in print form as well.

Exchange Server 5.5 Resource Guide

Of special interest here are Chapters 4 and 12. The Resource Guide is currently included in your TechNet subscription.

TechNet

Many good articles in TechNet deal with maintenance and repair issues. Of special interest are the following articles in the Technical Notes section of the MS Exchange section:

- "Disaster and Recovery Planning"
- "MS Exchange 5.5 Backup and Restore Basics"
- "The Best practices for Exchange Database Management"
- "MS Exchange Disaster Recovery Part 1"
- "MS Exchange Disaster Recovery Part 2"

Also, many articles in the Knowledge Base cover specific maintenance issues, but these are too numerous to list here. Search the Knowledge Base using an appropriate keyword to find help on a particular issue.

CHAPTER 21

Migrating to Exchange

In an earlier chapter, we looked at how to establish messaging connectivity between Exchange and legacy Microsoft (MS) Mail 3.x systems. In this chapter, we will take this a step further and look at how to migrate users on legacy and third-party mail systems to Exchange Server using the Exchange Migration Wizard. After reading this chapter, you will have an understanding of the following topics:

- Exchange Migration Wizard
- Migrating from MS Mail to Exchange

The walkthrough in this chapter takes you through the process of migrating the contents of a MS Mail 3.5 postoffice to Exchange.

The Exchange Migration Wizard

The term migration essentially means moving users from one kind of system to another. Microsoft Exchange includes tools that make it easy for administrators to move users from other mail systems to Exchange. These tools enable administrators to copy mailboxes, Distribution Lists, address books, Public Folders, and other items from various legacy and third-party mail systems to Exchange. Some of the mail systems that can be migrated include specific versions of

- MS Mail for PC Networks
- Lotus cc:Mail
- Lotus Notes
- Novell GroupWise 4.x
- Novell GroupWise 5.x
- Collabra Share
- IBM PROFS
- Vermation MEMO MVS
- Digital ALL-IN-1

and so on. Migrating from some of these mail systems requires special tools, but most of them can be migrated using a single utility called the Exchange Migration Wizard. Most migrations require that you have a good understanding of the mail system being migrated. We will confine our walkthrough to a detailed look of only one scenario, that of migrating from legacy MS Mail 3.5 systems to Exchange.

The Exchange Migration Wizard

The Microsoft Exchange Migration Wizard is a tool included with Exchange that can assist network administrators in migrating from various legacy and third-party mail systems to Exchange (see Figure 21-1). Looking at the opening screen of the Migration Wizard, we can see that this tool can be used for a number of purposes:

- *Import from Migration Files*. This option takes the migration files generated by a source extractor and imports this information into Microsoft Exchange. Any mail system whose contents can be obtained using a third-party or home-grown source extractor can use this option to migrate their mail system to Exchange.
- *Migrate from MS Mail for PC Networks*. This gives the option of either migrating information directly from a MS Mail postoffice into Exchange or first extracting a User List from the MS Mail postoffice in the form of a comma-delimited (`*.csv`) text file. The extracted User List can then be edited if desired and then imported into Exchange by running the Migration Wizard a second time and selecting the same option, Migrate from MS Mail for PC Networks.
- *Migrate from Lotus cc:Mail*. This provides the option of either migrating information directly from a Lotus cc:Mail system into Exchange or using a source extractor to generate a series of migration files. These migration files can then be edited if desired and then imported into Exchange by running the Migration Wizard a second time and selecting the first option, Import from Migration Files.
- *Migrate from Lotus Notes*. This is essentially the same as the previous option, except for Lotus Notes systems instead of Lotus cc:Mail ones.
- *Migrate from Novell GroupWise 4.x/5.x*. These provide the option of either migrating information directly from a Novell GroupWise mail system into Exchange or using a source extractor to generate a series of migration files. These migration files can then be edited if desired and be imported into Exchange by running the Migration Wizard a second time and selecting the first option, Import from Migration Files.
- *Migrate from Collabra Share*. This has the option of either migrating information directly from a Collabra Share mail system into Exchange or of using a source extractor to generate a series of migration files. These migration files can then be edited if desired and be imported into Exchange by running the Migration Wizard a second time and selecting the first option, Import from Migration Files.

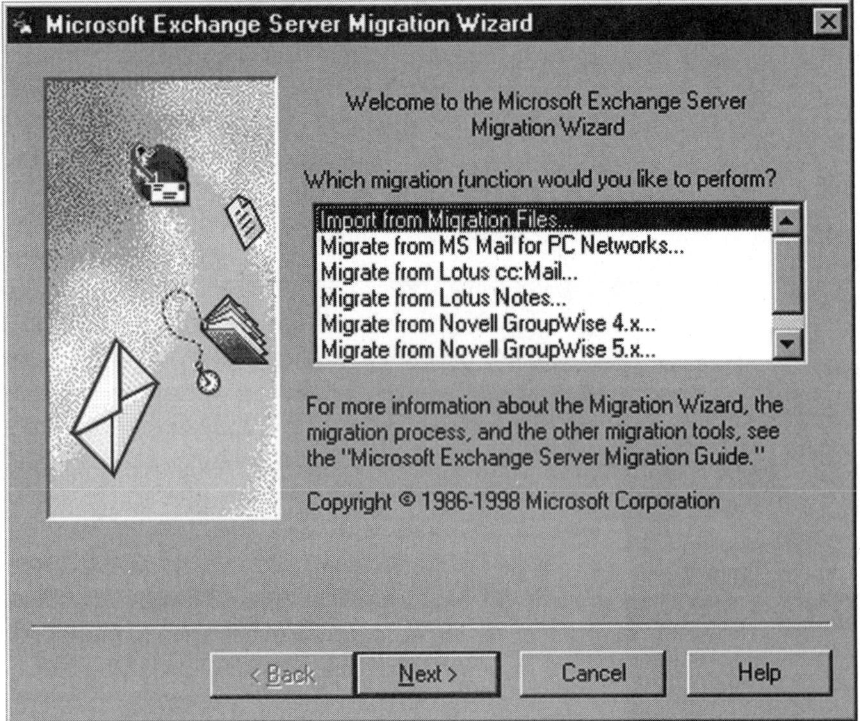

Figure 21-1 The Exchange Migration Wizard.

Migrating from Non-MS Mail Systems

The source extractors mentioned above for the cc:Mail, Notes, GroupWise, and Collabra migrations are different tools that extract directory and recipient information from a particular mail system and then output this information as a series of migration files. These migration files can be manually edited if desired and then imported into Exchange using the Migration Wizard's first option, Import from Migration Files. The migration files generated by a source extractor typically include the following:

- *Packing List file*. This file lists the primary and secondary migration files and specifies the code page for the files (for international use). The packing list file is a text file with a `*.pkl` extension but stores information in a comma-delimited `*.csv` format.
- *Primary files*. These contain directory information (recipient attributes like addresses and phone numbers), message headers, personal address book and Distribution Lists entries, and pointers to the secondary files.

The primary files have a `*.pri` extension but store the information in a comma-delimited `*.csv` format.

- *Secondary files*. These contain actual data such as message bodies, attachments, and schedule information. The secondary files have a `*.sec` extension and store information in both comma-delimited and raw binary format.

If a source extractor has been used to generate a series of migration files, the Migration Wizard can then be used to import these files into Exchange using the option, Import from Migration Files. Migration files are then imported the same way, regardless of the kind of mail system they came from. The steps involved in importing migration files are as follows:

1. Select the option Import from Migration Files in the Migration Wizard.
2. Specify the path to the Packing List File (`*.pkl`).
3. Specify the destination Exchange Server.
4. Select the destination Recipients container.
5. Specify a template recipient (optional).
6. Indicate rules for generating new Windows NT accounts.
7. Start the migration process.

The Migration Wizard should generally be run on the Exchange Server where you want to import the files, and the migration files themselves should be moved to the hard drive on your target Exchange Server prior to running the Wizard. These steps will ensure the best performance during migration.

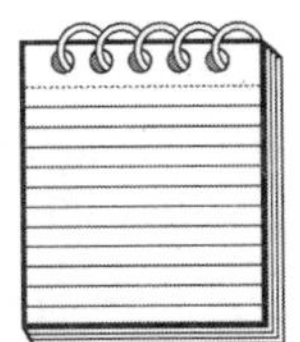

Performing Migrations

Real-life migrations of mail systems are generally performed in a series of steps that are often weeks or months apart. As each step is completed, tests must be performed to ensure users still have all the messaging capability they are used to and that the new capabilities they should have actually work. During migration, it is not unusual to have two or more mail systems coexisting together on your network, the new Exchange system and the legacy or third-party systems. You generally need to install the appropriate connectors on Exchange to enable coexistence and provide messaging connectivity between your Exchange organization and the other mail system during the migration period.

Migrating from MS Mail

Migrating from legacy MS Mail 3.x systems to Exchange can be done in three different ways:

- *The One-Step Method.* In this approach, the Migration Wizard is run only once, making the migration smooth and simple. We will follow this approach in the walkthrough later in this chapter.
- *The Two-Step Method.* In this approach, the Migration Wizard is run twice. The first time it is run, a User List file is extracted from the legacy system. This file can be edited to make changes, such as specifying the particular Windows NT account that will be mapped to each user once it is migrated to the new system. Once the User List has been edited appropriately, the Migration Wizard is run a second time to actually perform the migration.
- *The Batch Method.* In this approach, the Migration Wizard is run from the command line or using a batch file to automate the process. The command-line executable for the Migration Wizard is called `mailmig.exe` and is located in the `\exchsrvr\bin` directory on the Exchange Server. You can obtain help on how to use this utility by typing `mailmig /?` from the command line.

Note that connectivity with the MS Mail system using the MS Mail Connector is not a prerequisite for doing migrations from MS Mail to Exchange.

Walkthrough: Migrating an MS Mail 3.5 Postoffice

Now let's walk through the steps of migrating an MS Mail postoffice to Exchange Server. We'll be using the same postoffice that we connected to earlier in Chapter 15, "Administering MS Mail Connectors," using the MS Mail Connector. This postoffice is located on the Windows NT server LEONARDO in the directory `\PODATA` that is shared on the server. The postoffice is named `MYPOST` and the MS Mail network is named `MYWORLD`. The MS Mail administrator account is `SUPERUSER` and the password is `PASSWORD`. We're going to run the Migration Wizard from the Exchange Server BUGS in the Chicago site, and we'll use the one-step migration method.

Start by using Windows Explorer on BUGS to map the drive letter `M:` to the share `PODATA` on LEONARDO, specifying the UNC path to this share as `\\LEONARDO\PODATA`.

Now start the Exchange Migration Wizard and select Migrate from MS Mail for PC Networks on the opening screen. Click Next twice and enter the following information (see Figure 21-2):

Path to MS Mail Postoffice = M:\ (use the Browse button)

Account Name = SUPERUSER

Password = PASSWORD

Click Next and select the One-Step Migration method, which will enable the Wizard to extract all mailbox, message, address, and schedule information from the postoffice and import it directly into Exchange (see Figure 21-3). The Two-Step Migration method works differently, extracting a User List file first that you can edit before running the second stage of the Wizard. You might edit the User List, for example, to change the naming convention used on the accounts prior to importing them into Exchange so they agree with the naming convention used by your Exchange organization.

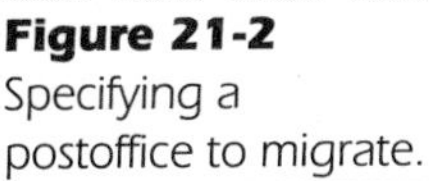

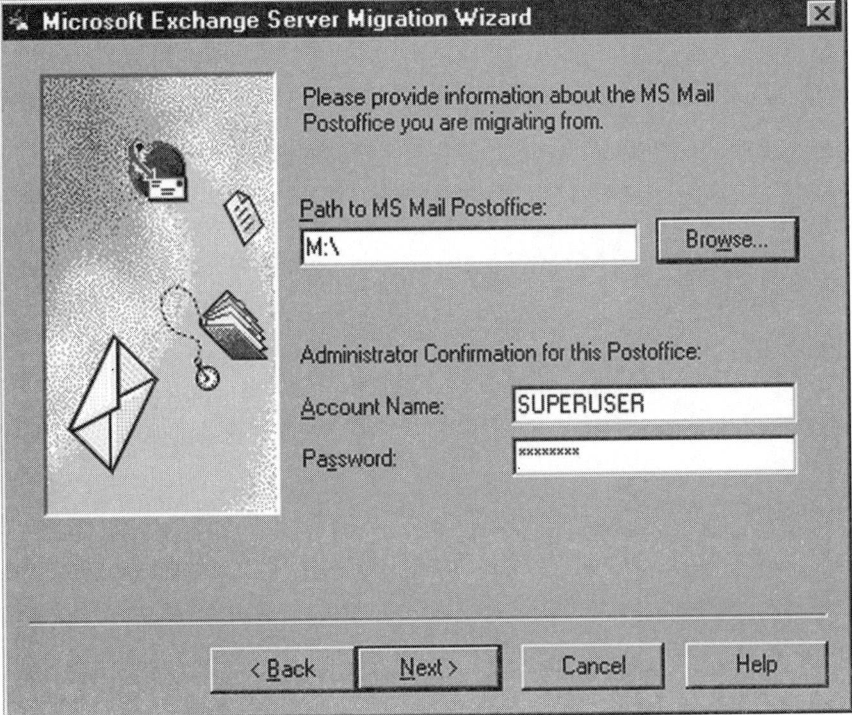

Figure 21-2 Specifying a postoffice to migrate.

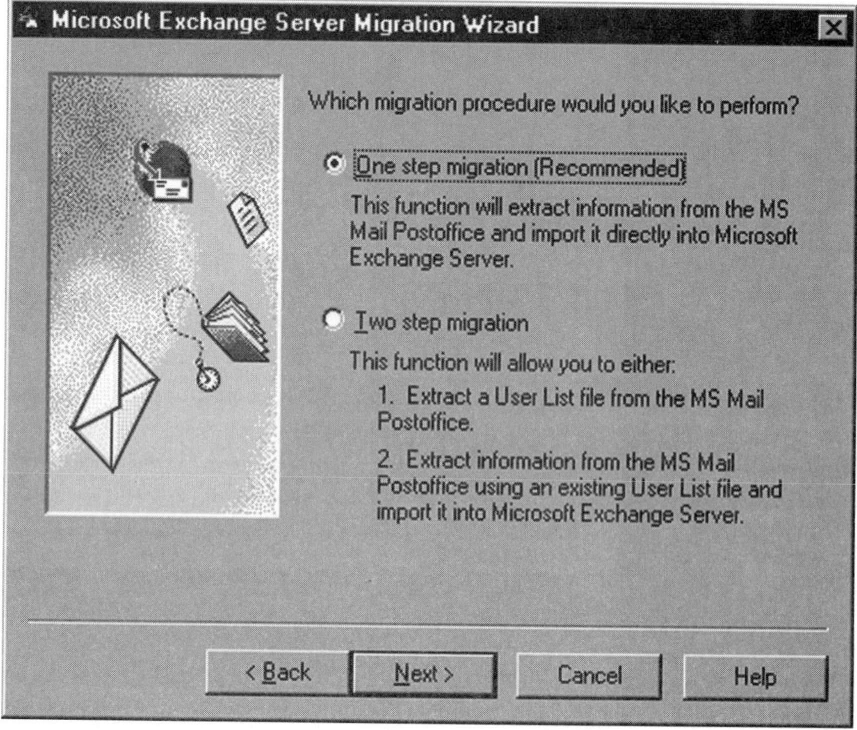

Figure 21-3 Specifying the One-Step Migration method.

Click Next and select Migrate to a Microsoft Exchange Server Computer (see Figure 21-4). The other option, migrating the postoffice information to `*.pst` files, might be used if you didn't have the Exchange Server to which you wanted to migrate the MS Mail users ready yet.

Click Next and specify which types of information you want to migrate to Exchange (see Figure 21-5). You can select any or all of the following:

- Mailboxes
- Email messages (mailbox contents)
- Shard folders
- Personal address books
- Schedule information

For migrating messages, you can specify a range of dates or simply migrate everything (the default).

Click Next and a list of user accounts (the User List) on the MS Mail postoffice is displayed, allowing you to specify which accounts you want to

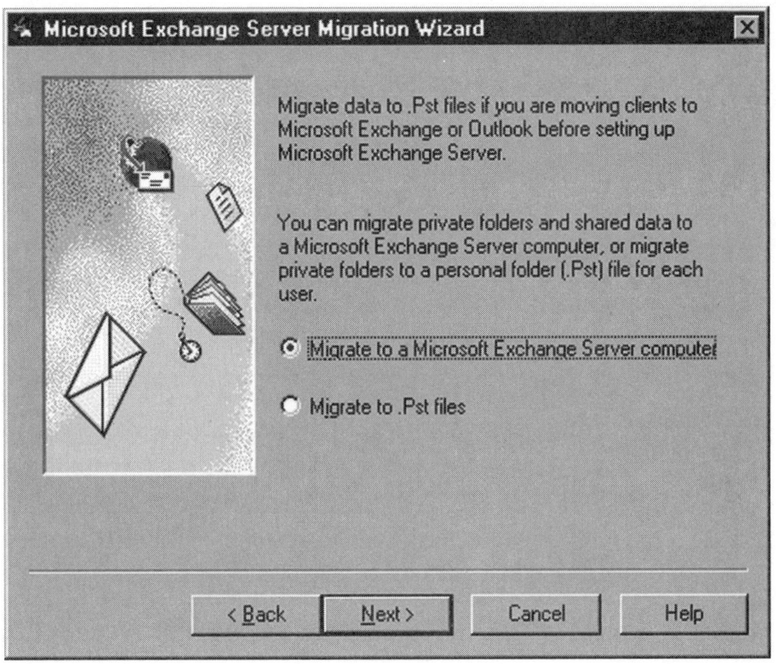

Figure 21-4
Specifying migration to an Exchange machine.

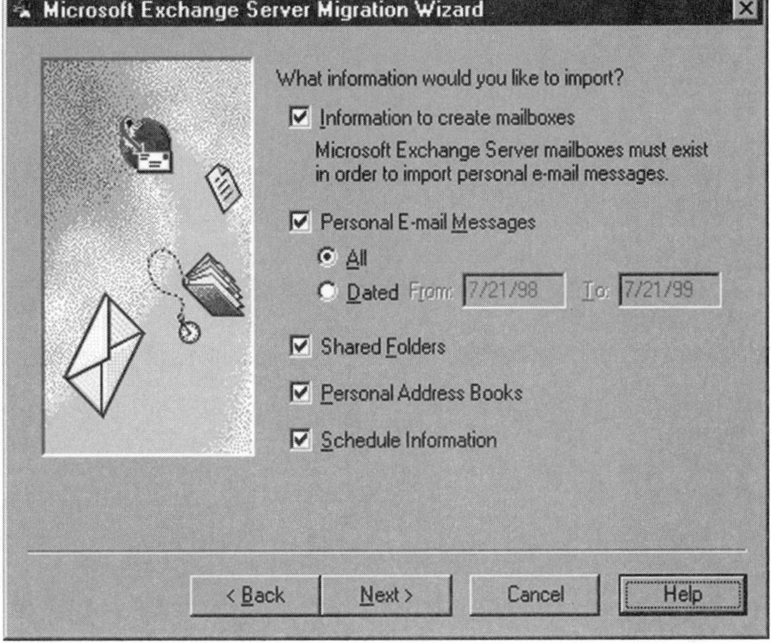

Figure 21-5
Specifying which types of information to migrate.

migrate (see Figure 21-6). We'll choose the Select All button here to migrate all the MS Mail users to Exchange.

Click Next and specify the name of the Exchange Server to which the MS Mail postoffice information is to be migrated (see Figure 21-7). You should normally specify the name of the Exchange Server that you are running the Migration Wizard on, which in this case is BUGS.

Click Next and specify the default permissions that you want to apply for any information that is migrated to Public Folders on your Exchange Server (see Figure 21-8). If you leave this set to its default setting, No Access, then no client permissions will be assigned to the migrated folders, but the administrator can later use Exchange Administrator to specify other permissions on the folders.

Click Next and specify which recipient will be the default owner for any Public Folders that are created during the migration process (see Figure 21-9). We choose Peter James, network administrator in Chicago, for this role.

Click Next and specify which recipients container on your Exchange Server will contain the migrated mailboxes and Distribution Lists from the

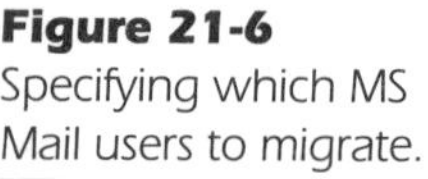

Figure 21-6 Specifying which MS Mail users to migrate.

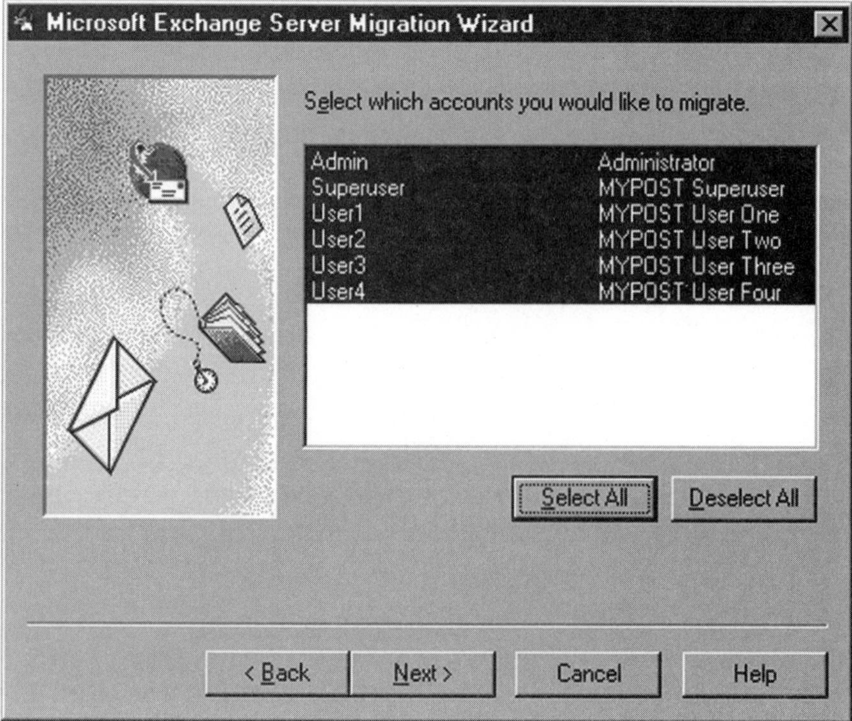

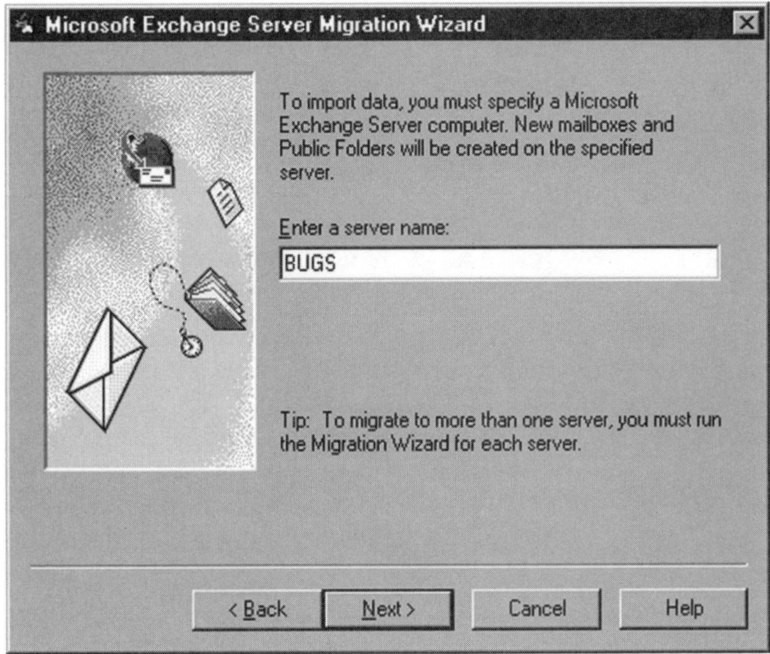

Figure 21-7 Specifying the Exchange Server to migrate to.

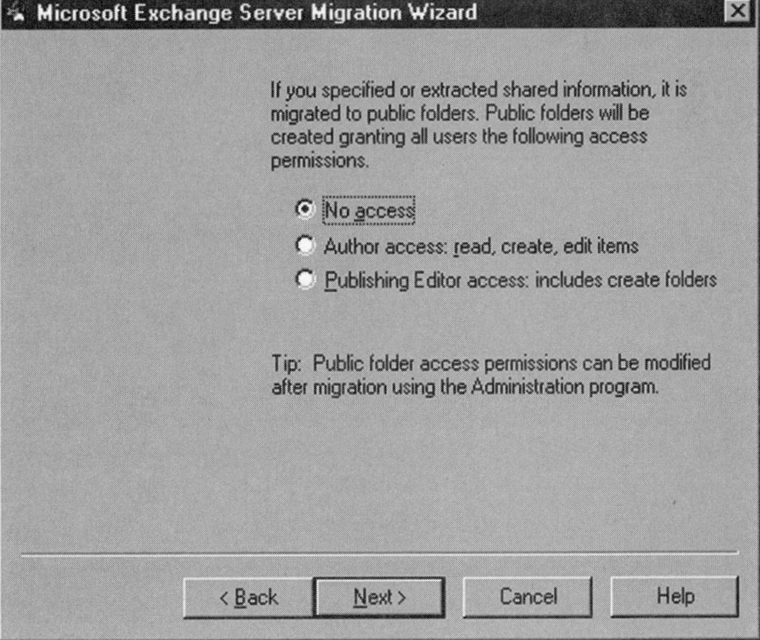

Figure 21-8 Specifying permissions for information migrated to Public Folders on Exchange.

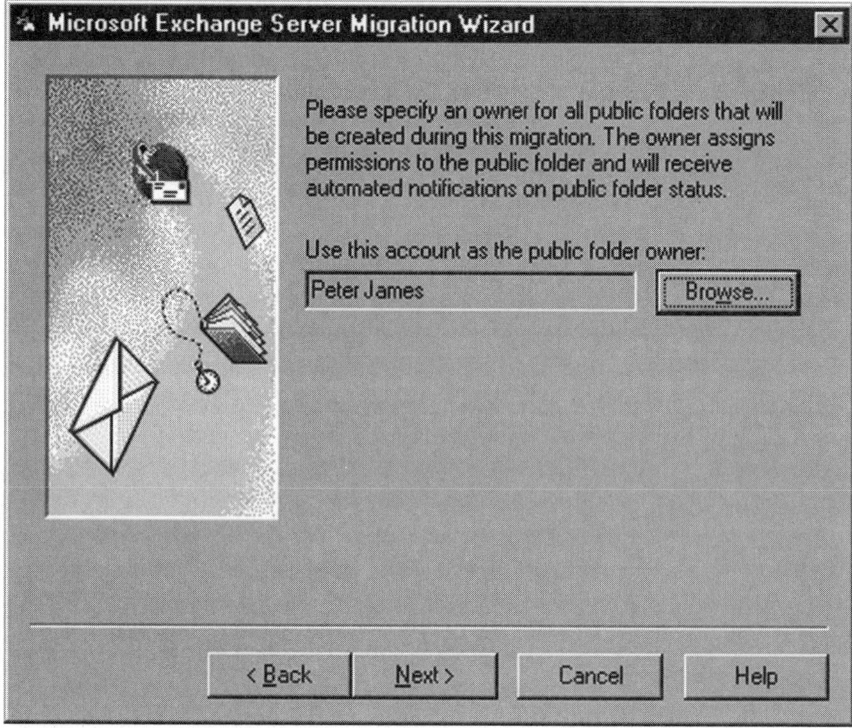

Figure 21-9 Specifying an owner for Public Folders created during the migration process.

postoffice (see Figure 21-10). The default here is the Recipients container for the Exchange Server where you are migrating. You can also specify an existing Exchange mailbox as a template for generating mailboxes for migrated users. This can help speed up the process of configuring the new mailboxes generated by the migration process. Note that any restrictions you place on the template mailbox, like limiting the Information Store (IS) storage limit to a certain number of MB, will be applied during the migration process. This could cause a problem if the MS Mail users being migrated have mailbox contents that exceed the limit of their Exchange mailboxes.

Click Next and specify how Windows NT user accounts should be assigned to the mailboxes being created by the migration process (see Figure 21-11). If the MS Mail users already have Windows NT accounts on the network, simply select the name of the domain where these accounts are located using the drop-down box on this screen. If the MS Mail users do not currently have Windows NT accounts on your network, you have three options to choose from:

- *Create accounts and generate random passwords*. This option creates new Windows NT accounts for the migrated MS Mail users. These new accounts have names that match the alias name of the migrated users. Random passwords are generated for the new accounts, and these are

Figure 21-10 Specifying the Recipients container where mailboxes are migrated.

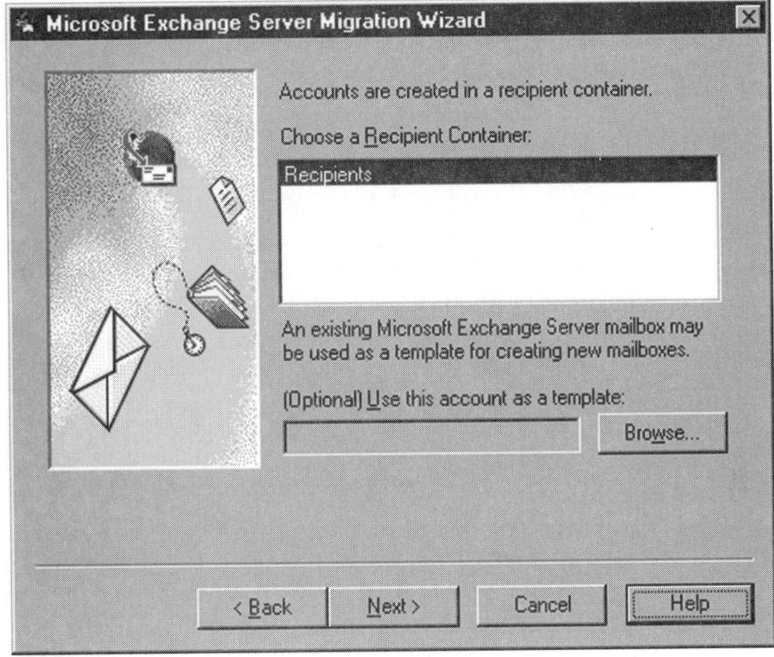

Figure 21-11 Specifying the assignment of Windows NT accounts to the migrated mailboxes.

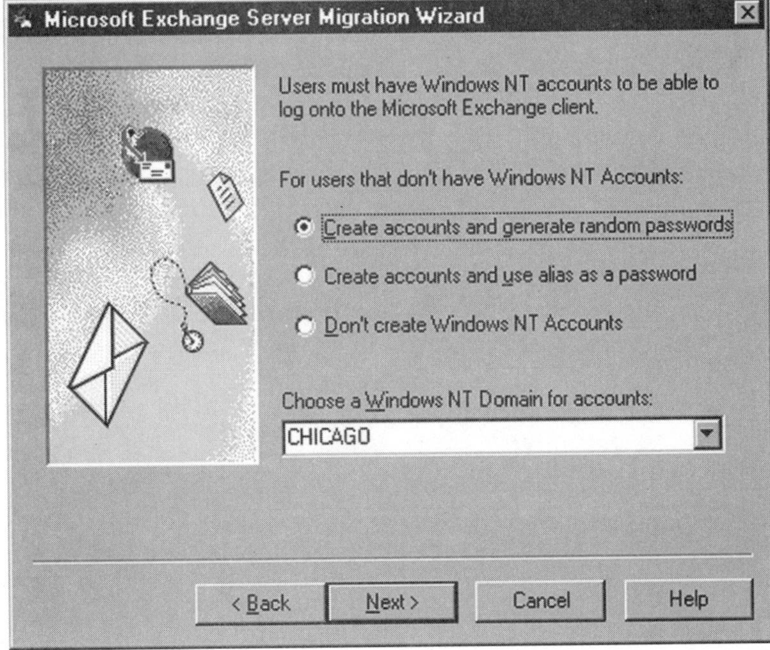

written in the ACCOUNT.PASSWORD file, which is found in the working directory of the Migration Wizard (\exchsrvr\bin). These passwords can then be distributed to users by the administrator in some fashion.

- *Create accounts and use alias as a password*. Same as the above, except the password for a user matches their alias name. You simply tell the users their alias name and they can log on to the network and access their Exchange mailboxes.
- *Don't create Windows NT accounts*. Mailboxes are created for migrated users without an associated Windows NT account. Administrators must afterwards create accounts for users and specify the user's account on the General tab of the property sheet for the mailbox. This method is good if you haven't made up your mind yet how you want to map accounts to users, but remember users can't access their mailboxes until accounts have been created and specified for them.

Now click Next to start the migration process. A dialog box displays the progress of the migration (see Figure 21-12). When the migration is complete, click Finish to close the dialog box (check the Errors and Warnings counts before you do this to see if everything worked). A message will appear, suggesting you check the Application Log in Event Viewer for any messages related to the migration process (do this especially if errors or warnings appear during migration).

The new mailboxes created for the migrated users are found in the Recipients container on the Exchange Server (see Figure 21-13). The six migrated MS Mail users, their associated Exchange mailbox alias, and their associated Windows NT accounts are listed in Table 21-1. All Windows NT accounts have been created in the CHICAGO domain in which the Exchange Server BUGS resides. Note that the display names and aliases of the new mailboxes are the same as those in the migrated MS Mail system (refer to Figure 21-6), except for the original MS Mail administrator account ADMIN that now has the alias MYPOST.

Here are the contents of the ACCOUNT.PASSWORD file that were generated when the new Windows NT accounts were created:

```
NT Account, Password
"CHICAGO\MYPOST", "6ESs"
"CHICAGO\Superuser", "iYSB"
"CHICAGO\User1", "UgyZ"
"CHICAGO\User2", "9EYA"
"CHICAGO\User3", "STZH"
"CHICAGO\User4", "Aw7Q"
```

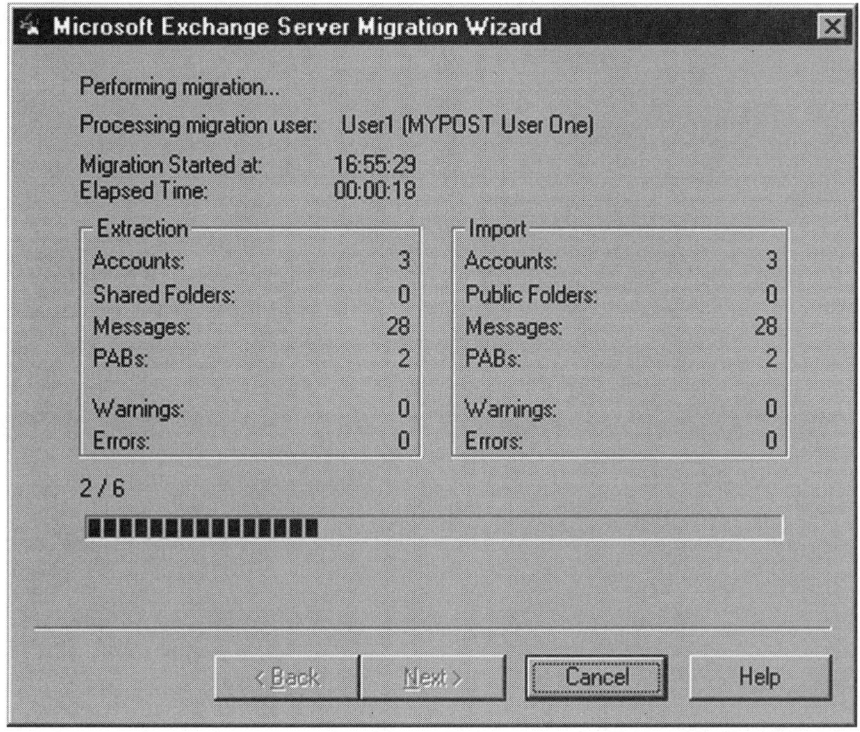

Figure 21-12 The progress of the migration is displayed.

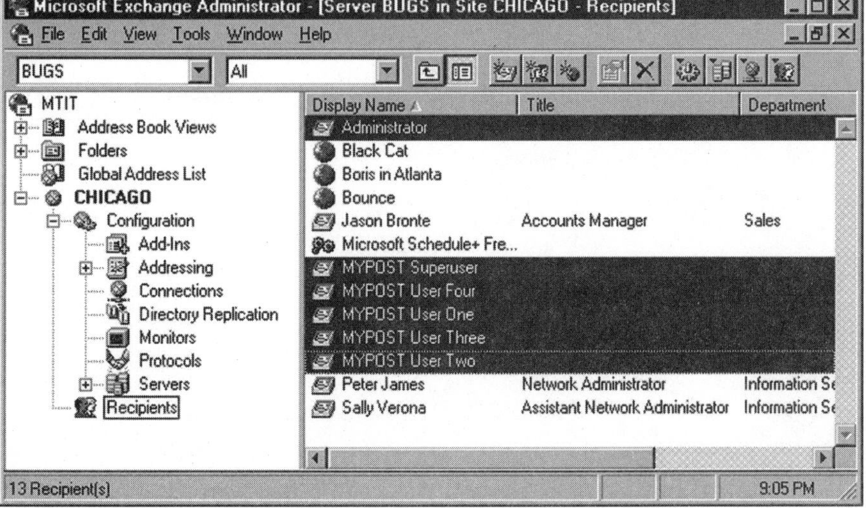

Figure 21-13 Migrated mailboxes in the Recipients container.

Table 21-1

Migrated Mailbox and Account Information.

MS Mail Alias	Exchange Mailbox Alias	Windows NT Account
ADMIN	MYPOST	MYPOST
SUPERUSER	Superuser	Superuser
USER1	User1	User1
USER2	User2	User2
USER3	User3	User3
USER4	User4	User4

Where Do We Go from Here?

In the next chapter, we will look at the optional Outlook Web Access component of Exchange Server that can be used in conjunction with Microsoft Internet Information Server (IIS) to provide users with access to their mailboxes and to Public Folders using a standard Web browser like Internet Explorer or Netscape Navigator.

For More Information

For useful information on performing migrations to Exchange, see the *Migrations* manual, which is part of Books Online. Unfortunately, this volume cannot be obtained from Microsoft in hard copy form (at time of this writing).

TechNet

Microsoft TechNet contains a number of useful articles on migration to Exchange in the Technical Notes of the MS Exchange section. These include the following:

- "MS Exchange Server: Coexistence and Migration from MSMail—Best Practices"
- "MS Exchange 5.x and Lotus cc:Mail Coexistence and Migration"
- "MS Exchange and Mail Coexistence and Migration with LAN and Host Mail Systems"
- "MS Exchange Server Migration and Coexistence: Planning Considerations and Components"
- "MS Exchange Server Host-Based Migration and Coexistence"

CHAPTER 22

Administering Outlook Web Access

In this chapter, we will look at the optional Outlook Web Access component of Exchange Server that enables users to access their mailbox and Public Folders using a standard Web browser like Internet Explorer or Netscape Communicator. After reading this chapter, you will have an understanding of

- What is Outlook Web Access
- Configuring Outlook Web Access
- Installing and testing Outlook Web Access

The walkthrough in this chapter takes you through the process of installing and testing Outlook Web Access.

What Is Outlook Web Access?

Outlook Web Access (or OWA for short) is an *Active Server Pages* (ASP) application written to run on Microsoft *Internet Information Server* (IIS) version 3.0 or higher. In conjunction with Exchange Server, OWA enables Exchange users to access their mailbox and Public Folders using only a standard Web browser like Microsoft Internet Explorer or Netscape Communicator without the need of dedicated mail client software like Microsoft Outlook. This makes Exchange a truly cross-platform product, because Web browsers can run on virtually any computing platform: PC, Mac, or UNIX. This also enables users to access their mail from any machine anywhere in the world that is connected to the Internet, provided the IIS Web server that is hosting the OWA application is registered with the *Domain Name System* (DNS) and is available on the Internet. And the amazing thing is that the OWA application provides much the same look and feel as Microsoft Outlook does, but within a Web browser window.

A user accesses OWA by entering the appropriate URL for the ASP application. The user then either enters the name of their mailbox alias in order to access their Exchange mailbox, or they just click on a hyperlink to access Public Folders hosted on Exchange Servers. If they try to access their mailbox, they are presented with an authentication dialog box that requires their user credentials, which must be authenticated by a Windows NT domain controller on the network. Once authenticated, users have full access to their personal mail folders, calendar, contacts, and many other resources accessible through their traditional Outlook mail client. Different forms of authentication can be configured for Outlook Web Access, including SSL for advanced security using digital certificates, making OWA secure for use over the Internet.

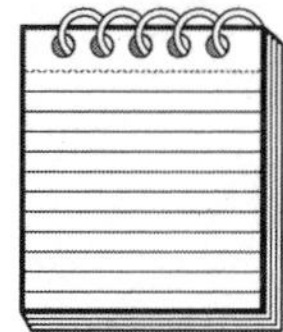

Internet Information Server (IIS)

Because OWA requires Microsoft IIS version 3.0 or higher to be running on a server on the network, you need to be proficient in your understanding of how to configure IIS settings. A good source of information on how to manage IIS can be found in my book, Administering IIS4 *(McGraw-Hill Professional Publishing, 1998).*

Configuring Outlook Web Access

OWA will work using the default settings for your Exchange directory objects, but a few things can be configured using Exchange Administrator. These settings all refer to accessing Public Folders and the Global Address List (GAL) by anonymous (non-Exchange) users, such as anonymous users who are using a Web browser to access your Exchange server.

The configurable settings for OWA are all found on the HTTP (Web) Site Settings object, which is located in the Protocols container within your site's Configuration container. We previously looked briefly at this directory object in Chapter 16. HTTP stands for *Hypertext Transfer Protocol*, the Internet protocol that is used by the *World Wide Web* (WWW), and OWA is based upon the WWW service of IIS, Microsoft's Web server platform. Let's look at the various tabs of the property sheet for the HTTP (Web) Site Settings object.

The General tab includes the following important settings (see Figure 22-1):

- *Enable protocol*. The HTTP protocol must be enabled for users to be able to use OWA for connecting to their mailboxes on Exchange Server using a Web browser.
- *Allow anonymous users to access the anonymous public folders*. Selecting the checkbox allows non-Exchange users on the Internet to access the contents of public folders on Exchange, provided the appropriate client permissions are assigned to the folders. This checkbox is selected by default.
- *Allow anonymous users to browse the global address list*. If you want non-Exchange users on the Internet to be able to access information published in the GAL on Exchange, you must enable this setting here. By default, this setting is disabled.

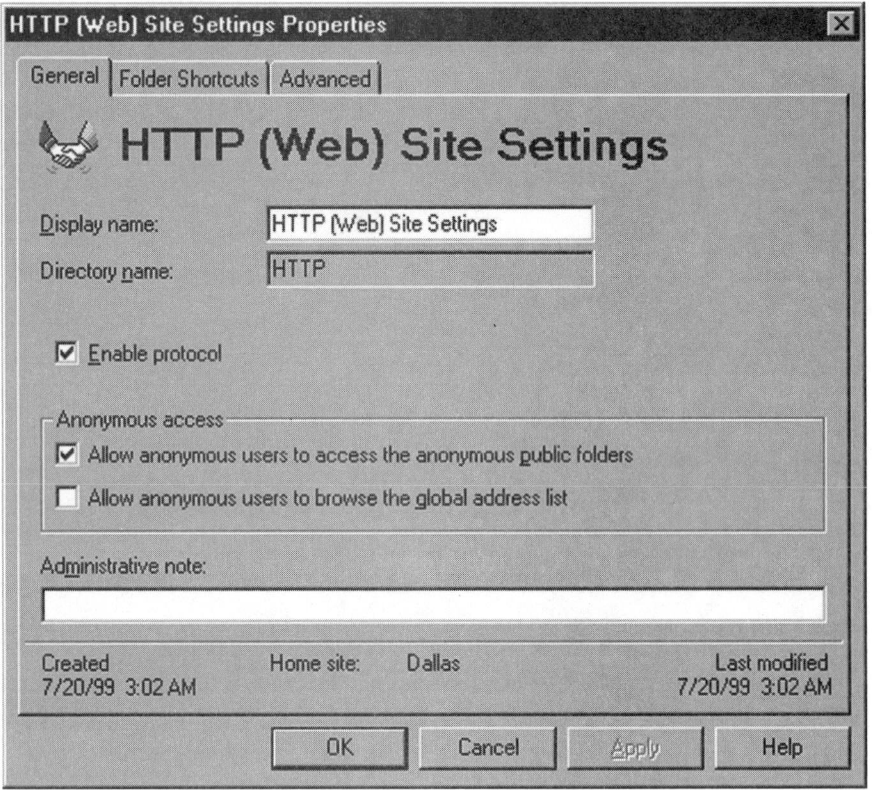

Figure 22-1 The General tab of the HTTP (Web) Site Settings property sheet.

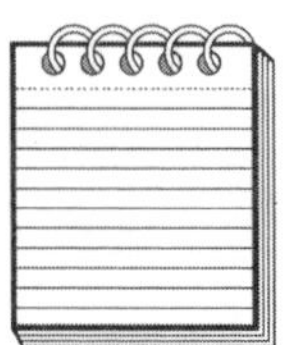

Enabling/Disabling HTTP

The setting "Enable protocol" on the HTTP (Web) Site Settings object enables or disables access to Exchange by Web browsers for all users indiscriminately. If you want to deny a particular user in your company from using OWA, open the property sheet for their mailbox object, select the Protocols tab, double-click on the HTTP (Web) entry in the listbox, and clear the checkbox labeled Enable HTTP for the Recipient.

The Folder Shortcuts tab displays Public Folder shortcuts that have been created and enables new ones to be created as well (see Figure 22-2). You must create a Public Folder shortcut for each Public Folder you want anonymous (non-Exchange) users on the Internet to be able to access using Outlook Web Access. These shortcuts are displayed to anonymous users when they connect to the Exchange Server from the Internet using their Web browser.

Figure 22-2 The Folder Shortcuts tab of the HTTP (Web) Site Settings property sheet.

To create a new Public Folder shortcut, click the New button to open the Public Folders dialog box. If the only entry listed here is the All Public Folders entry, double-click on this entry to display the Public Folder hierarchy for your organization (see Figure 22-3).

Click OK to return to the Folder Shortcuts tab on the HTTP (Web) Site Settings property sheet. Now we need to configure client permissions for anonymous users so they can access the Public Folder over the Internet. Select the Public Folder shortcut in the listbox and click the Properties button to open the property sheet for the Public Folder (see Figure 22-4).

The General tab should already be selected on the property sheet for the Public Folder. Click the Client Permissions button to open the Client Permissions dialog box for the selected Public Folder. The client permissions currently assigned to Anonymous is None (see Figure 22-5).

Change the permissions for Anonymous to whatever role you want anonymous Internet users to have, and click OK twice to close the Client Permissions box and the property sheet for the Public Folder.

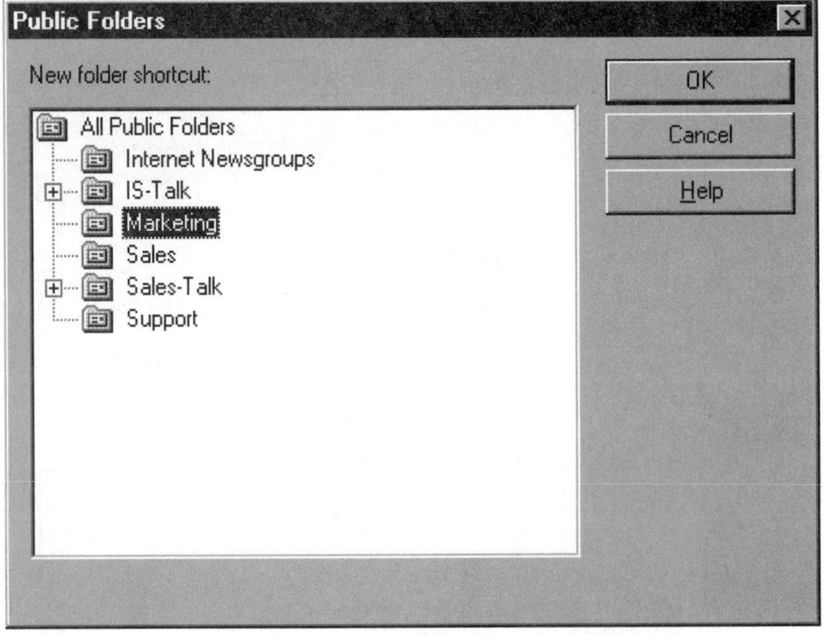

Figure 22-3
Selecting a Public Folder to create a shortcut to it.

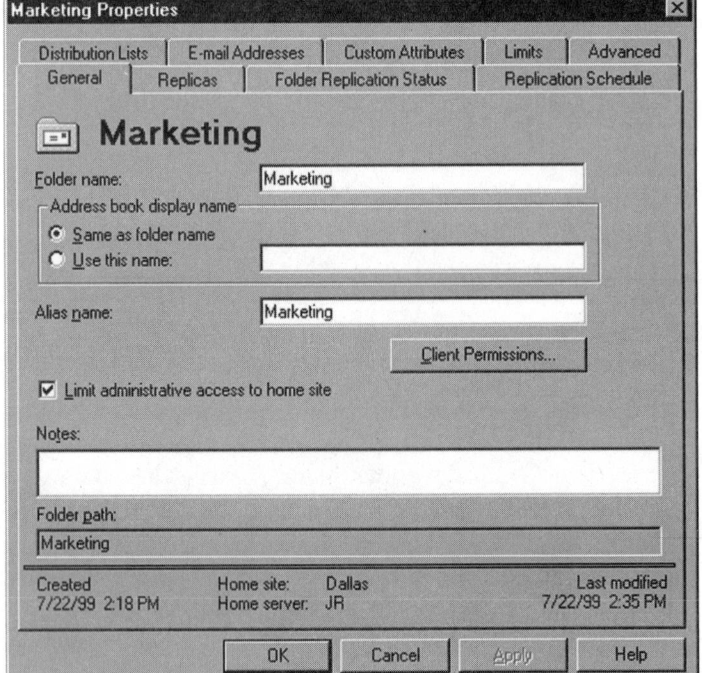

Figure 22-4
Property sheet for the Public Folder.

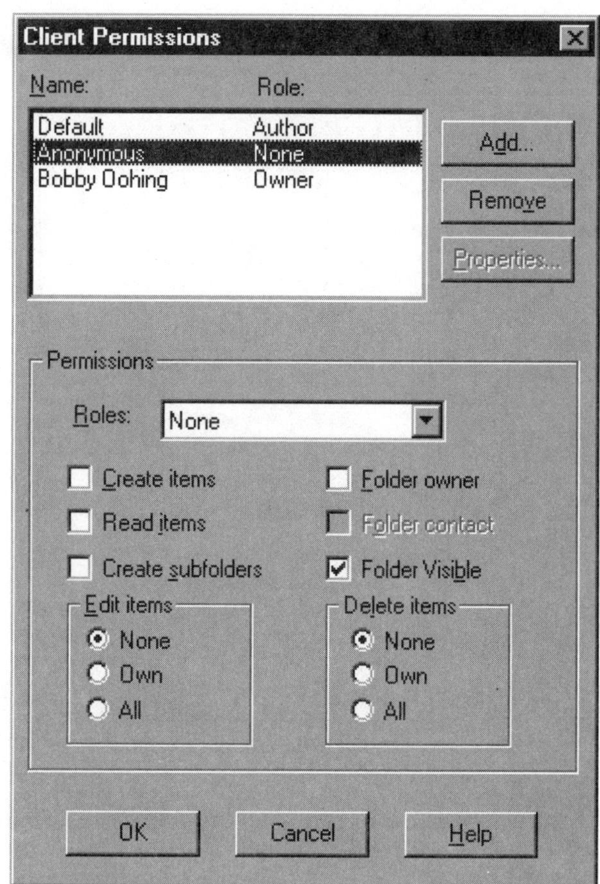

Figure 22-5 Client Permissions box.

Use the Advanced tab to specify the number of entries in the Global Address Book that are returned to users when they access the Exchange Server using a Web browser (see Figure 22-6). This setting applies to both anonymous and validated users. By default, this is set to 50 users. You can change this to No Limit if you like, but this is probably not wise if your GAL contains thousands of users.

Walkthrough: Installing and Testing Outlook Web Access

Now let's walk through the steps of installing and testing the OWA component of Exchange Server. To keep things simple, we'll assume we've

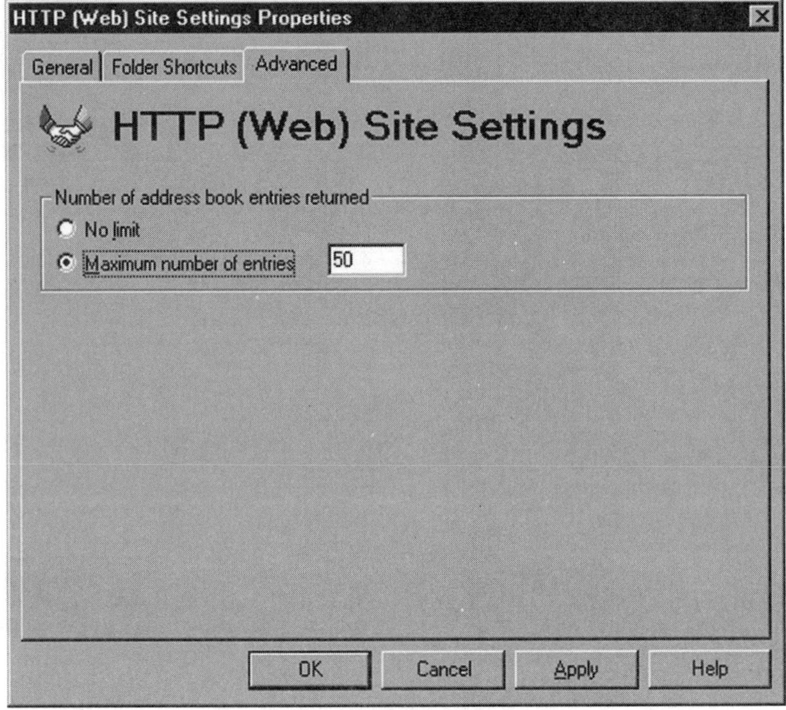

Figure 22-6 The Advanced tab of the HTTP (Web) Site Settings property sheet.

installed both Exchange Server 5.5 and Internet Information Server 4.0 on the machine (install IIS first). We won't go through the steps of installing IIS4; you can refer to my book on that subject which I mentioned above for information on installing and configuring IIS4. Note that in a real-world setup, the machine that OWA is installed on needs a lot of extra processing power to run the OWA ASP application. This is because all the processing work is done server-side when you are using OWA, as opposed to sharing the load between the client and server when you are using MAPI clients like Microsoft Outlook with Exchange.

Installing OWA is a no-brainer. Just rerun Exchange Setup, select the Add/Remove option to add or remove components of Exchange, and select to install the OWA component when the list of components you can install is displayed (see Figure 22-7). Then finish Setup.

That's it! Now let's test it. First, let's determine the URL to which our OWA ASP application on IIS is mapped. Start *Internet Service Manager* (ISM), which is part of the Windows NT 4.0 Option Pack program group, and the *Microsoft Management Console* (MMC) opens up with the ISM snap-in installed in it. Expand the console tree until you can select the Exchange virtual directory (see Figure 22-8).

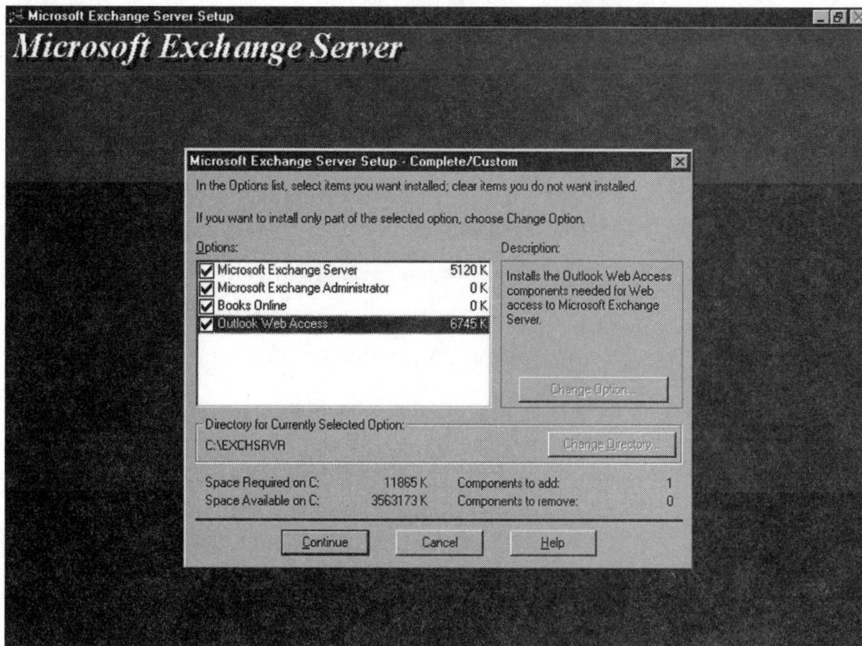

Figure 22-7
Installing OWA.

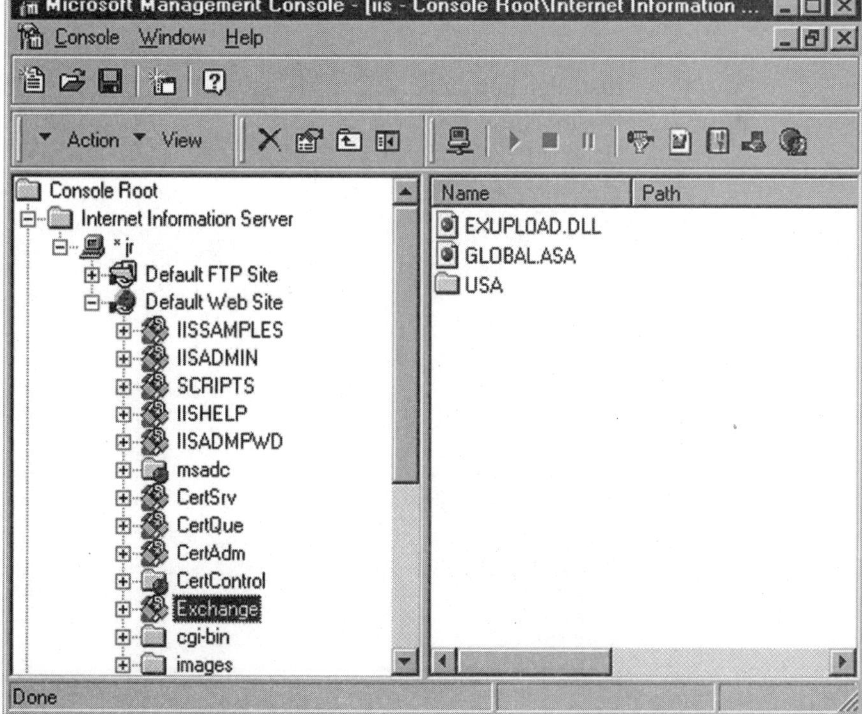

Figure 22-8
The Internet Service Manager MMC console for IIS.

Now click the Properties button on the toolbar to open the property sheet for the Exchange virtual directory (see Figure 22-9). Note that the starting point for this Web application is specified as the virtual directory:

```
<Default Web Site>/Exchange
```

where `<Default Web Site>` represents any valid means of representing the default Web site in a URL. Default possibilities could include

- The IP address of the IIS machine
- The NetBIOS name of the IIS machine
- The fully qualified DNS name of the IIS machine

Which naming method you use for the default Web site depends on whether the IIS machine is on a local or a remote network, whether there is a name server configured to resolve DNS names, and so on.

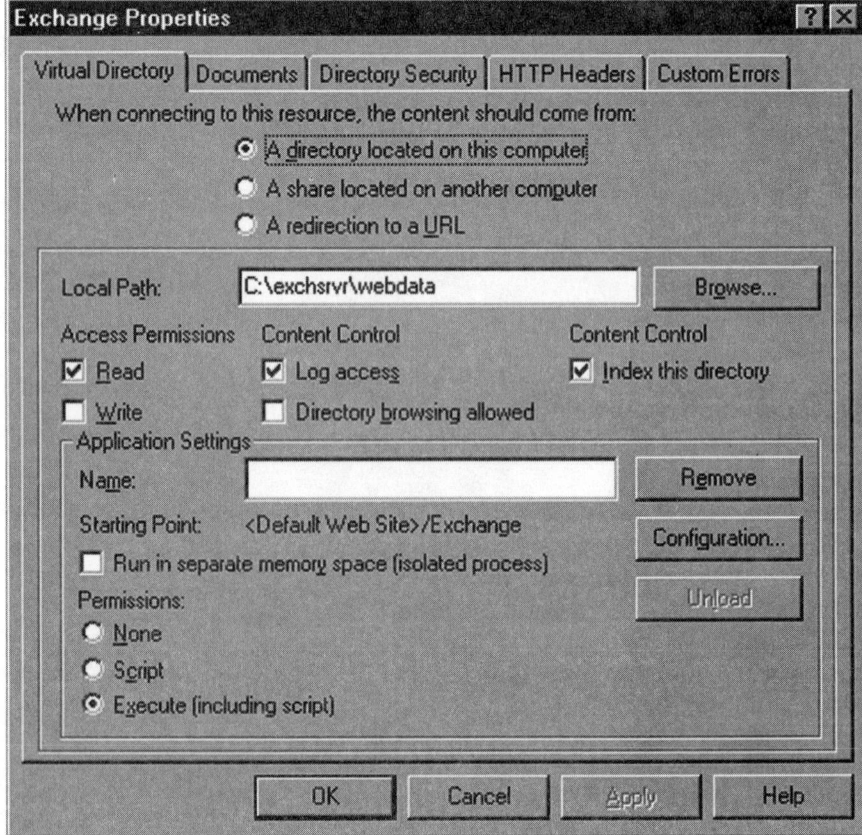

Figure 22-9
The Property sheet for the Exchange virtual directory.

We'll use the NetBIOS name of our machine, namely JR, as our naming method for the default Web site on our IIS machine. Let's try it: start Internet Explorer on another machine (we'll use SNOOPY) and open the following URL:

```
http://jr/exchange
```

The opening page for OWA now appears in the browser window (see Figure 22-10).

Enter the mailbox alias "Bobby" in the Log On textbox to log on to OWA as Bobby Oohing, the network administrator in Dallas. This opens the Enter Network Password dialog box (see Figure 22-11). The user name entered into the box must be a valid Windows NT account and must be in the form:

```
<domain_name>\<user_name>
```

Note that the entries here are not case-sensitive.

Click OK and the OWA application grants Bobby access to his mailbox using the Web browser (see Figure 22-12). Notice the Outlook interface displayed in this Web browser window, which includes an Outlook bar on the left, a folder list, a toolbar, and a main window showing the contents of Bobby's Inbox.

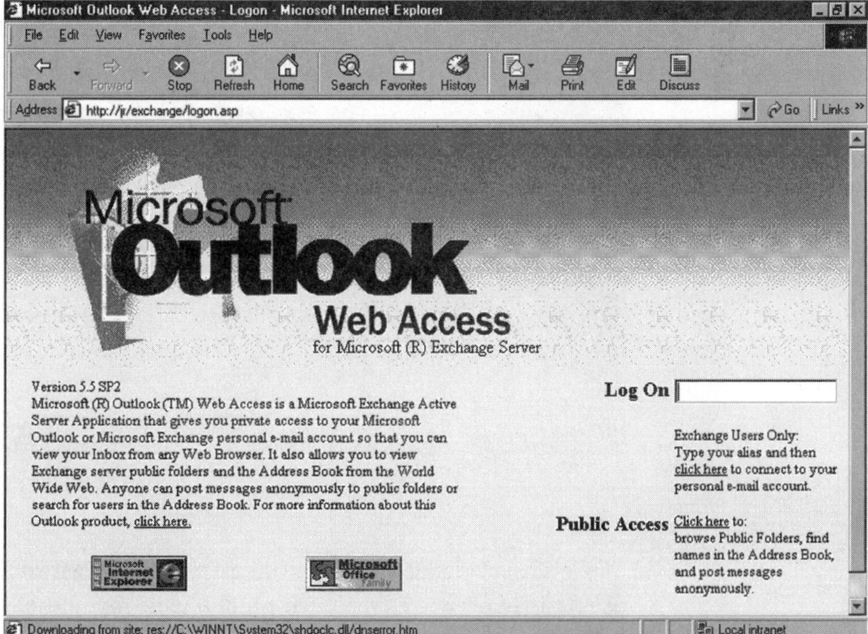

Figure 22-10 The OWA opening page.

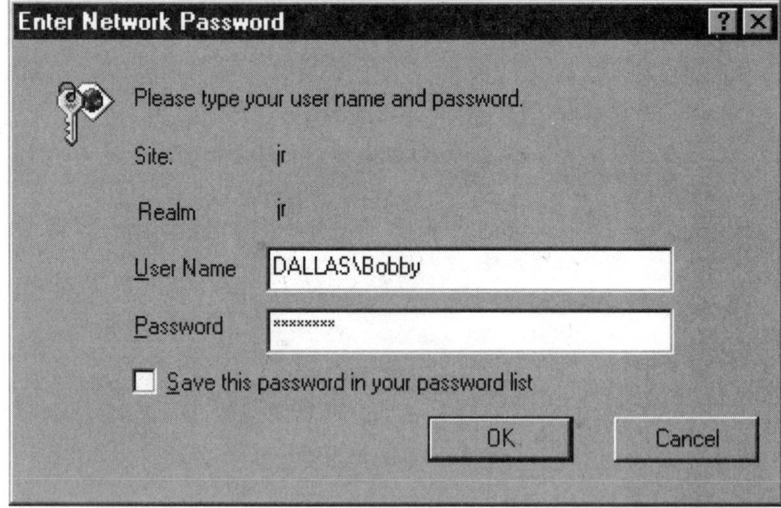

Figure 22-11 Prompt for user credentials.

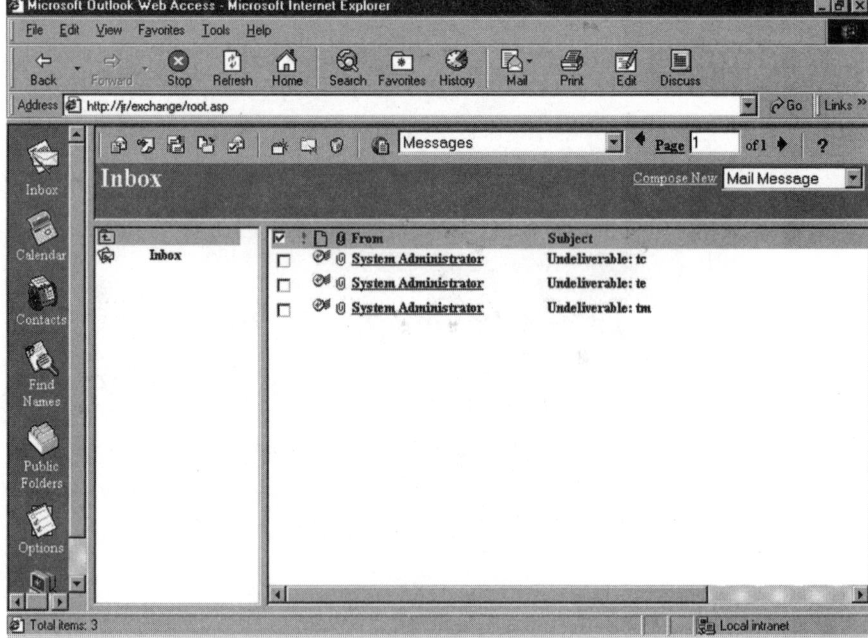

Figure 22-12 Bobby's Inbox in OWA.

We observe that several system messages are in Bobby's Inbox from a previous exercise. If we click on the link for one of the messages, a new browser window opens up displaying the message (see Figure 22-13).

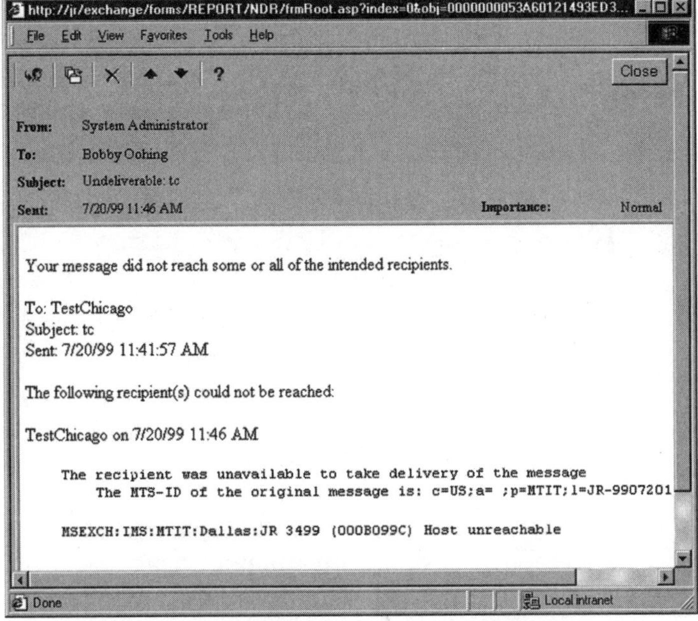

Figure 22-13
A message in Bobby's inbox.

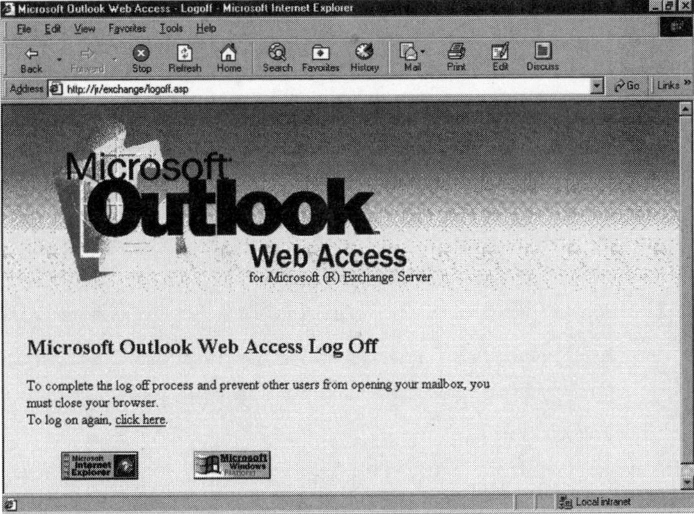

Figure 22-14
Logging off OWA

We could go on testing various aspects of OWA, but it's more fun if you just try it yourself. We'll just mention one more thing that's important: When you're finished using OWA, clock the Log Off icon at the bottom of the Outlook bar (the vertical scrolling window on the left of Figure 22-12 that has Inbox at the top). When you do this, the Microsoft Outlook Web Access Log Off page appears (see Figure 22-14).

Notice that it says you should close your Web browser after you finish accessing your mailbox. This is because if you leave the browser window open, another user could come by and click the Back button on the browser a few times until they access your mailbox page. That wouldn't be nice!

For More Information

Chapter 18 of the *Operations* manual, which is included in Exchange Books Online, contains a brief overview of OWA.

TechNet

Here are a few articles to check out from the Knowledge Base. Make sure you read the first one especially, as it provides a detailed overview of the permissions required for OWA to work properly:

- Q175892. XWEB: "Permissions Required for Outlook Web Access"
- Q175891. XADM: "OWA Needs Anonymous and Clear Text Authentication on IIS"
- Q125329. XWEB: "Deployment and Troubleshooting Outlook Web Access"
- Q196016. XWEB: "Outlook Web Access Fails Intermittently"
- Q192775. XCLN: "Outlook Web Access Cannot Use Contacts in Public Folder"
- Q175573. XWEB: "Outlook Web Access Gives Bus Error"
- Q175125. XWEB: "Outlook Web Access May Not See Outlook Schedule"
- Q175122. XWEB: "Error Msg: Failed to Get Inbox in Outlook Web Access"
- Q174745. XWEB: "Saved Appointments Do Not Show in Outlook Web Access"
- Q174030. XWEB: "Outlook Web Access Client Fails if JavaScript Disabled"
- Q173509. XADM: "Setup Fails when Installing Outlook Web Access"
- Q173497. XADM: "Session Timeout Settings for Outlook Web Access"

Where Do We Go from Here?

That's it! We've finished the book and covered most of the main features of Exchange Server 5.5, so where you go from here is entirely up to you. Good luck!

Mitch Tulloch, MCT, MCSE
http://www.mtit.com
info@mtit.com
Winnipeg, Canada 1999

INDEX

Note: Boldface numbers indicate illustrations.

ABOUT THE AUTHOR

Mitch Tulloch is an independent trainer, consultant, and author living in Winnipeg, Canada. He is a Microsoft Certified Trainer (MCT) and Microsoft Certified Systems Engineer (MCSE) with almost 20 years experience in teaching scientific and technical subjects. His previous books with McGraw-Hill include the popular *Administering IIS4* and two volumes of the *Accelerated MCSE Study Guide* series.

Mitch previously worked as a trainer and LAN administrator for Productivity Point International (`http://www.propoint.com`), one of the largest computer training companies in North America. He also worked as a Webmaster for an Internet startup company, and as a Physics teacher. His home page can be found at `http://www.mtit.com`.